T0189992

# IFIP Advances in Information and Communication Technology 577

## Editor-in-Chief

Kai Rannenberg, Goethe University Frankfurt, Germany

## Editorial Board Members

# IFIP – The International Federation for Information Processing

IFIP was founded in 1960 under the auspices of UNESCO, following the first World Computer Congress held in Paris the previous year. A federation for societies working in information processing, IFIP's aim is two-fold: to support information processing in the countries of its members and to encourage technology transfer to developing nations. As its mission statement clearly states:

*IFIP is the global non-profit federation of societies of ICT professionals that aims at achieving a worldwide professional and socially responsible development and application of information and communication technologies.*

IFIP is a non-profit-making organization, run almost solely by 2500 volunteers. It operates through a number of technical committees and working groups, which organize events and publications. IFIP's events range from large international open conferences to working conferences and local seminars.

The flagship event is the IFIP World Computer Congress, at which both invited and contributed papers are presented. Contributed papers are rigorously refereed and the rejection rate is high.

As with the Congress, participation in the open conferences is open to all and papers may be invited or submitted. Again, submitted papers are stringently refereed.

The working conferences are structured differently. They are usually run by a working group and attendance is generally smaller and occasionally by invitation only. Their purpose is to create an atmosphere conducive to innovation and development. Refereeing is also rigorous and papers are subjected to extensive group discussion.

Publications arising from IFIP events vary. The papers presented at the IFIP World Computer Congress and at open conferences are published as conference proceedings, while the results of the working conferences are often published as collections of selected and edited papers.

IFIP distinguishes three types of institutional membership: Country Representative Members, Members at Large, and Associate Members. The type of organization that can apply for membership is a wide variety and includes national or international societies of individual computer scientists/ICT professionals, associations or federations of such societies, government institutions/government related organizations, national or international research institutes or consortia, universities, academies of sciences, companies, national or international associations or federations of companies.

More information about this series at http://www.springer.com/series/6102

Luis M. Camarinha-Matos · Nastaran Farhadi ·
Fábio Lopes · Helena Pereira (Eds.)

# Technological Innovation for Life Improvement

11th IFIP WG 5.5/SOCOLNET
Advanced Doctoral Conference on Computing,
Electrical and Industrial Systems, DoCEIS 2020
Costa de Caparica, Portugal, July 1–3, 2020
Proceedings

 Springer

*Editors*
Luis M. Camarinha-Matos ⓘ
NOVA University of Lisbon
Monte Caparica, Portugal

Nastaran Farhadi ⓘ
NOVA University of Lisbon
Monte Caparica, Portugal

Fábio Lopes ⓘ
NOVA University of Lisbon
Monte Caparica, Portugal

Helena Pereira ⓘ
NOVA University of Lisbon
Monte Caparica, Portugal

ISSN 1868-4238             ISSN 1868-422X   (electronic)
IFIP Advances in Information and Communication Technology
ISBN 978-3-030-45126-4         ISBN 978-3-030-45124-0   (eBook)
https://doi.org/10.1007/978-3-030-45124-0

This Springer imprint is published by the registered company Springer Nature Switzerland AG
The registered company address is: Gewerbestrasse 11, 6330 Cham, Switzerland

# Preface

This proceeding, which collects selected results produced in engineering doctoral programs, focuses on research and development in technological innovation for life improvement. Nowadays, life improvement has become a trending topic across different areas due to technological advancements that focus on human wellbeing. Different scientific areas, such as electronics, telecommunications, computing, and energy, are innovating and changing their paradigms to promote a digital-oriented world. Concepts and tools coming from the areas of artificial intelligence, collaborative networks, virtual and augmented reality, machine learning, big data, cyber-physical systems, and the internet of things (IoT), can be adopted to provide a better and sustainable future with high quality of life. The impacts of these technological developments can result in enhancement of health care, environment, manufacturing, transportation, and communication systems across the globe, namely through new products and services. This ongoing digital transformation has a huge potential to face existing societal challenges, while increasing knowledge, wellbeing, quality of life, and collaboration among companies, organizations, people, and systems.

The 11th Advanced Doctoral Conference on Computing, Electrical and Industrial Systems (DoCEIS 2020) aims at providing a venue for sharing and discussing ideas and results from doctoral research in various interrelated areas of engineering, while promoting a strong multidisciplinary dialog. Furthermore, the conference aims at creating collaborative opportunities for young researchers as well as an effective way of collecting valuable feedback from colleagues in a welcoming environment. As such, participants were challenged to look beyond the specific technical aspects of their research question and relate their work to the selected theme of the conference, namely, to identify in which ways their research topics can contribute to life improvement. Furthermore, current trends in strategic research programs point to the fundamental role of multidisciplinary and interdisciplinary approaches in innovation. More and more funding agencies are including this element as a key requirement in their research agendas. In this context, the challenge proposed by DoCEIS is a contribution to the process of acquiring such skills, which are mandatory in the profession of a PhD.

DoCEIS 2020, which was sponsored by SOCOLNET, IFIP, and IEEE IES, attracted a good number of paper submissions from a large number of PhD students and their supervisors from 18 countries. This book comprises the works selected by the International Program Committee for inclusion in the main program and covers a wide spectrum of application domains. As such, research results and ongoing work are presented, illustrated, and discussed in areas such as:

- Collaborative systems
- Decision and optimization systems
- Communications systems

- Digital twins and smart manufacturing
- Energy systems
- Biomedical systems
- Instrumentation and health

We hope that this collection of papers will provide readers with an inspiring set of new ideas and challenges, presented in a multidisciplinary context, and that by their diversity these results can trigger and motivate richer research and development directions.

We would like to thank all the authors for their contributions. We also appreciate the efforts and dedication of the DoCEIS International Program Committee members, who both helped with the selection of articles and contributed valuable comments to improve the quality of papers.

July 2020

Luis M. Camarinha-Matos
Nastaran Farhadi
Fábio Lopes
Helena Pereira

# Organization

## Conference and Program Chair

Luis M. Camarinha-Matos    NOVA University of Lisbon, Portugal

## Organizing Committee Co-chairs

Luis Gomes    NOVA University of Lisbon, Portugal
João Goes    NOVA University of Lisbon, Portugal
João Martins    NOVA University of Lisbon, Portugal

## International Program Committee

Antonio Abreu, Portugal
Andrew Adamatzky, Poland
Vanja Ambrozic, Slovenia
Amir Assadi, USA
Olga Battaia, France
Luis Bernardo, Portugal
Erik Bruun, Denmark
Barbora Buhnova, Czech Republic
Giuseppe Buja, Italy
Luis M. Camarinha-Matos, Portugal
Roberto Canonico, Italy
Laura Carnevali, Italy
Wojciech Cellary, Poland
Noelia Correia, Portugal
Jose de la Rosa, Spain
Stefano Di Carlo, Italy
Matteo Faschini, Italy
Filipa Ferrada, Portugal
Florin G. Filip, Romania
Maria Helena Fino, Portugal
José M. Fonseca, Portugal
Paulo Gil, Portugal

João Goes, Portugal
Luis Gomes, Portugal
Paul Grefen, The Netherlands
Michael Huebner, Germany
Ricardo Jardim-Gonçalves, Portugal
Vladimir Katic, Serbia
Asal Kiazadeh, Portugal
Paula Louro, Portugal
Marin Lujak, France
João Martins, Portugal
Rui Melicio, Portugal
Paulo Miyagi, Brazil
Renato Moraes, Brazil
Filipe Moutinho, Portugal
Horacio Neto, Portugal
Rodolfo Oliveira, Portugal
Luis Oliveira, Portugal
Joaquin Ordieres, Spain
Angel Ortiz, Spain
Peter Palensky, Austria
Luis Palma, Portugal
Nuno Paulino, Portugal

Pedro Pereira, Portugal
Duc Pham, UK
João Pimentão, Portugal
Paulo Pinto, Portugal
Armando Pires, Portugal
Ricardo J. Rabelo, Brazil
Luis Ribeiro, Sweden
Juan Rodriguez-Andina, Spain
Enrique Romero-Cadaval, Spain
Carlos Roncero, Spain

Thilo Sauter, Austria
Eduard Shevtshenko, Estonia
Thomas Strasser, Austria
Kleanthis Thramboulidis, Greece
Damien Trentesaux, France
Manuela Vieira, Portugal
Ramon Vilanova, Spain
Soufi Youcef, France
Tamus Zoltán Ádám, Hungary

## Local Organizing Committee (PhD Students)

Fábio Lopes, Portugal
Helena Pereira, Portugal
Nastaran Farhadi, Portugal/Iran
Akashkumar Rajaran, Portugal/India
Guilherme Guerreiro, Portugal
Hugo Antunes, Portugal

Amineh Mazandarani, Portugal/Iran
Humberto Queiroz, Portugal/Brazil
Sonia Hosseinpour, Portugal/Iran
Carolina Lagartinho-Oliveira, Portugal
Dário Pedro, Portugal
Luis Mateus, Portugal

## Organizers of Special Session on Instrumentation for Health

Ricardo Vigário, Portugal
Sofia Pessanha, Portugal
Valentina Vassilenko, Portugal
Carla Pereira, Portugal

Hugo Gamboa, Portugal
Cláudia Quaresma, Portugal
Mauro Guerra, Portugal
José Paulo Santos, Portugal

## Technical Sponsors

 Society of Collaborative Networks

 Project

 IFIP WG 5.5 COVE
Co-Operation Infrastructure for Virtual Enterprises
and Electronic Business

        IEEE—Industrial Electronics Society

## Organizational Sponsors

## Organized by

The PhD Program in Electrical and Computer Engineering,
in collaboration with the PhD Program in Biomedical Engineering,
Faculty of Sciences and Technology at the NOVA University of Lisbon.

# Contents

## Communication Systems

## Optimization Systems

## Digital Twins and Smart Manufacturing

## Power Systems

## Energy Control

## Power Transportation

## Biomedical Analysis and Diagnosis

## Instrumentation in Health

# Collaborative Networks

# Performance Indicators of a Collaborative Business Ecosystem – A Simulation Study

Paula Graça[1,2(✉)] and Luís M. Camarinha-Matos[1]

[1] Faculty of Sciences and Technology, Uninova CTS and Socolnet,
NOVA University of Lisbon, Campus de Caparica, 2829-516 Caparica, Portugal
cam@uninova.pt
[2] Instituto Superior de Engenharia de Lisboa, Instituto Politécnico de Lisboa,
Rua Conselheiro Emídio Navarro 1, 1959-007 Lisbon, Portugal
paula.graca@isel.pt

**Abstract.** Collaborative Business Ecosystems have been benefiting from the technological advancements, allowing better collaboration among organisations to provide more innovative products and services in an increasingly demanding world. This collaboration can be assessed through a set of performance indicators, which also induce a self-adjustment of the organisations' behaviour, improving their profile and that of the ecosystem as a whole. In fact, their behaviour is expected to evolve (like individuals) according to the way they are evaluated. As such, this study presents a simulation model, which, together with the performance assessment and influence mechanism, is an essential contribution to measuring and influencing collaboration, enabling better management decisions. The model is based on agents and system dynamics, featuring a business ecosystem populated by organisations categorised according to a different profile, and configured and calibrated according to actual collaboration data. The samples were collected from two established companies operating in the same business ecosystem in the information technologies industry. Preliminary results of this approach, based on some simulation scenarios, are presented and discussed.

**Keywords:** Collaborative Networks · Collaborative Business Ecosystem · Performance indicators · Agent-based modelling · System dynamics

## 1 Introduction

Technological advances that promote a digital world have boosted business ecosystems, where organisations collaborate in the search for innovative solutions for an increasingly demanding society. Moore [1] first introduced the concept of Business Ecosystem as a metaphor inspired by ecological ecosystems. On the other hand, the scientific area of Collaborative Networks (CN) [2], encompassing a broader scope, also considers business ecosystems as a particular case of Virtual organisations Breeding Environments. As such, and to emphasise the collaborative aspect, the term Collaborative Business Ecosystem (CBE) has been adopted [3]. In order to study the dynamics of such systems, a simulation model was proposed in [4].

© IFIP International Federation for Information Processing 2020
Published by Springer Nature Switzerland AG 2020
L. M. Camarinha-Matos et al. (Eds.): DoCEIS 2020, IFIP AICT 577, pp. 3–17, 2020.
https://doi.org/10.1007/978-3-030-45124-0_1

The purpose of the current simulation study is to assess the influence of the performance indicators adopted in a CBE, which are likely to induce a self-adjustment of organisations, improving their profile and that of the ecosystem as a whole. A number of mechanisms to evaluate the performance of individual organisations are already established, of which the balanced scorecard (BSC) [5] is the best well-known. However, to assess collaboration and the associated benefits, only limited contributions can be found in the literature. As an example, [6] proposes a set of performance indicators for CNs based on collaboration benefits and a model to measure social capital in CNs providing indicators for assets and relationship analysis [7] inspired on Social Network Analysis (SNA) [8]. Another example, [9], suggests a conceptual model for value systems in CNs and proposes a method for assessing the alignment of the value systems of their members [10]. The research area of Supply Chain Collaboration (SCC) highlights the importance of collaboration in traditional supply chains and propose several metrics and methods [11, 12] and [13]. Nevertheless, the study of adequate performance indicators to be used in a business ecosystem remains a challenge. In this context, this work aims to contribute to the identification of suitable performance indicators to assess collaboration in a CBE, and more specifically to analyse the influence of such indicators in the ecosystem and its individual members.

The remaining sections of this paper are organised as follows: Sect. 2 briefly positions this study in the context of innovation for life improvement; Sect. 3 describes the proposed simulation model of the CBE, fundaments the choice and presents the performance indicators to assess the model, and explains the influence mechanism; Sect. 4 presents the experimental evaluation of the simulation model using collected data from two organisations in the information technologies (IT) industry and discusses the results achieved; the last section summarises the contributions and identifies ongoing research and future work.

## 2   Relationship to Innovation in Life Improvement

Today's demanding and competitive market is very challenging for organisations in all sectors, including the field of information technologies. Participation in business ecosystems can help organisations to face such challenges. Companies must take advantage of the knowledge and shared assets owned by the business ecosystem where they operate, collaborating to make use of all available tools and concepts to provide innovative solutions in response to rapid market changes. The notion of a CBE re-enforces the idea of "community", contributing to the survival and improvement of all its members. When properly managed to promote sustainability, a CBE can in fact, contribute to life improvement of local societies.

The simulation model proposed in this work uses data collected from two organisations operating in the same business ecosystem. They produce solutions that help in the digital transformation of the internal processes of the companies, significantly reducing the need for paper, as well as solutions that contribute to data privacy and security, avoiding vulnerabilities that are easy targets for hackers. As such, the simulation model, together with the performance assessment and influence mechanism, is an essential contribution to measuring and influencing collaboration, which could lead to better management decisions and thus an improvement of the involved organisations and the CBE as a whole.

## 3  A Model of a CBE for Performance Measure and Influence

Assessing the performance of a CBE is not an easy task due to the difficulty of gathering collaborative data from the organisations of the ecosystem. Simulation appears in this context as a way to overcome such difficulty. As such, for this research, a case study based simulation model which is tuned using information from two case companies. An analogous research methodology was also applied to supply chain collaboration [14]. As such, the performance indicators, the PAAM (Performance Assessment and Adjustment Model) and the influence mechanism proposed in [4] and [15], briefly described in the following sub-sections, are used to set up and assess the simulation model of the CBE presented in this simulation study.

### 3.1  Performance Indicators

The adopted performance indicators used to assess the collaboration of the organisations in a CBE are mainly based on measures borrowed from the area of social network analysis. The application of that area of research to inter-organisational contexts has seen an explosion of interest in the past recent years [16]. The network perspective, which is related to the structure of ties among organisations and the tie strength, has a significant influence on its behaviour and performance [16]. Coleman [17] identifies social capital in the relations among persons, which, as in physical and human capital, facilitates productive activity. In particular, the author highlights the importance of what he calls closure of social networks, a form of social capital, *"the trustworthiness of social structures that allows the proliferation of obligations and expectations"*, facilitating collective sanctions and promoting reputation [17]. On the other hand, Burt [18] states that network density is a form of network closure since contacts in a dense network (i.e., more connections) are in close communication, increasing the readiness to enforce sanctions if norms are violated. Burt [18] also describes social capital as network structures, a metaphor in which social structure is a kind of capital that can create for certain individuals or groups a competitive advantage. However, the argument is that *"social capital is a function of brokerage structural holes"*. The holes in the social structure of the market are weaker connections between groups, which create a competitive advantage for people whose relationships span the holes, giving them access to more information and control of communication because they reach more people indirectly [18]. Network betweenness proposed by Freeman in [19] and [20] measures the extent to which a node brokers indirect connections between all other nodes in a network.

Despite the existence of a large number of theories on inter-organisational networks in literature, most views argue that networks provide resources and capabilities from outside the organisations [16]. Based on a comprehensive study of the existing theories, an organising framework for inter-organisational research is presented in [16], identifying four mechanisms that underlie and distinguish networks: "as resource access", "as a source of trust", "as a tool for power and control", and "as a signalling mechanism". The framework also organises the mechanisms by three levels of analysis: the "dyadic" (nature of the ties between two organisations), "ego" (the organisation) and the "whole network". In short, findings at the dyadic level suggests: strong ties between two organisations increase trust between them and generate future ties, hight trust lowers transaction costs and increases benefits, and the most requested partner is argued to be the one with the most power [16]. At the ego level, different groups of findings can be found: hight degree centrality of organisations is positively related to their performance, structural holes and closure generate social capital, and network status explains organisational performance [16]. Finally, at the whole network level, the predominant research is focused on the characteristics of the entire inter-organisational network, such as density, centrality, clicks (clusters of connected organisations) [21] and small-worlds (clusters of locally dense clicks connected by a few bridging ties) [22]. Findings at the network level are extensive to discuss here, despite there is very little work about business networks [21]. However, there is evidence of the enhancement of the organisations' innovativeness in small-worlds networks [16].

Following the main lines of research and findings described above, the proposed performance indicators were designed to assess a CBE considering a business ecosystem as a network of organisations (the nodes), connected by relationships (the ties) that mean the market opportunities they share collaborating, called collaboration opportunities. The metrics consider the weight (tie strength) of the connections, due to their evidence in terms of performance and trust between organisations [16, 17] and [18].

The referred performance indicators are based on measures of density and weighted centrality in social networks analysis [19, 20, 23] and [24], and are calculated for the organisations as individuals and for the CBE as a whole. Tables 1, 2 and 3 describe these indicators, respectively, the Contribution Indicator (CI), the Prestige Indicator (PI), and the Innovation Indicator (II). CI measures the value created by collaboration in the CBE, PI the influence/prominence of the organisations in the CBE, and II the innovation potential of the CBE. These indicators are based on measures of weighted centrality in social networks analysis [19, 20, 23] and [24], are calculated both for the organisations as individuals and for the CBE as a whole.

**Table 1.** Description of the Contribution Indicator.

| Contribution Indicator (CI) | |
|---|---|
| **Metric** | **Description** |
| $O_1,\ldots,O_n$ | Organisations in the CBE |
| #O | Number of organisations in the CBE |
| #CoOp$_i$ in | No. of collaboration opportunities the organisation $O_i$ gained from the CBE |
| #CoOp$_i$ out | No. of collaboration opportunities the organisation $O_i$ brought in the CBE |
| $\sum_i$#CoOp$_i$ | Total no. of collaboration opportunities created in the CBE |
| $C_D(O_i)$ in/out | Weighted indegree/outdegree centrality ($C_D$) of the organisation $O_i$ in the CBE, which stands for the sum of direct connections in/out of $O_i$ to the n organisations $O_j$, with weight #CoOp$_{ij}$ |
| $C_D(O^*)$ in/out | Maximum indegree/outdegree centrality of $O_i$ |

| Contribution Indicator of an Organisation (CI$_i$) | |
|---|---|
| $$CI_i in = \frac{C_D(O_i)in}{C_D(O^*)in} = \frac{\sum_j O_{ij}\#CoOp_{ij}\,in}{\max \sum_j O_{ij}\#CoOp_{ij}\,in}$$ | Assesses the contribution of organisation Oi in terms of accepted collaboration opportunities (more related to the popularity of organisations) |
| $$CI_i out = \frac{C_D(O_i)out}{C_D(O^*)out} = \frac{\sum_j O_{ij}\#CoOp_{ij}\,out}{\max \sum_j O_{ij}\#CoOp_{ij}\,out}$$ | Assesses the contribution of organisation $O_i$ in terms of created collaboration opportunities (more related to the activity of |

Note: The values of CI$_i$ are normalised between [0..1] in relation to the maximum degree centrality for the current network.

| Contribution Indicator of the CBE (CI$_{CBE}$) | |
|---|---|
| $$CI_{CBE} t = \frac{\sum_i \#CoOp_i}{\#O}$$ | Ratio of the total number of collaboration opportunities created/accepted in the CBE by the total number of organisations |
| $$CI_{CBE} in = \frac{C_D(CBE)in}{\max C_D(CBE)in} = \frac{\sum_i [C_D(O^*)in - C_D(O_i)in]}{C_D(O^*)in * (\#O - 1)}$$ | Assesses the degree to which the most popular organisation (in terms of accepted collaboration opportunities) exceeds the contribution of the others |
| $$CI_{CBE} out = \frac{C_D(CBE)out}{\max C_D(CBE)out} = \frac{\sum_i [C_D(O^*)out - C_D(O_i)out]}{C_D(O^*)out * (\#O - 1)}$$ | Assesses the degree to which the most active organisation (in terms of created collaboration opportunities) exceeds the contribution of the others |

Note: The values of CI$_{CBE}$ are normalised [0..1] in relation to the maximum sum of differences of degree centralities for the current network.

**Table 2.** Description of the Prestige Indicator.

| Prestige Indicator (PI) | |
|---|---|
| **Metric** | **Description** |
| $O_1,...,O_n$ | Organisations in the CBE |
| #O | Number of organisations in the CBE |
| #CoOp$_i$ | No. of collaboration opportunities the organisation $O_i$ participated in the CBE |
| #CoOp$_{kj}$ | No. of collaboration opportunities between the organisation $O_k$ and $O_j$ in the CBE |
| $C_B(O_i)$ | Weighted betweenness centrality ($C_B$) of the organisation $O_i$ in the CBE, which stands for the sum of overall partial betweenness of $O_i$ relative to all pairs $O_{kj}$, assuming that connections between $O_k$ and $O_j$ have weight of #CoOp$_{kj}$ |
| $C_B(O^*)$ | Maximum betweenness centrality of $O_i$ |

Prestige Indicator of an organization (PI$_i$)

$$PI_i = \frac{C_B(O_i)}{C_B(O^*)} = \frac{\sum_k \sum_j O_{kj}(O_i)}{\max \sum_k \sum_j O_{kj}(O_i)}$$

Assesses the prominence/influence of organisation $O_i$ in terms of collaboration opportunities

Note: The value of PIi is normalised between [0..1] in relation to the maximum betweenness centrality for the current network.

Prestige Indicator of the CBE (PI$_{CBE}$)

$$PI_{CBE} = \frac{C_B(CBE)}{maxC_B(CBE)} = \frac{\sum_i [C_B(O^*) - C_B(O_i)]}{C_B(O^*) * (\#O - 1)}$$

Assesses the degree to which the most prominent/influent organisation exceeds the contribution of the others

Note: The value of PI$_{CBE}$ is normalised between [0..1] in relation to the maximum possible sum of differences of betweenness centralities for the current network.

**Table 3.** Description of the Innovation Indicator.

| Innovation Indicator (II) | |
|---|---|
| **Metric** | **Description** |
| $O_1,...,O_n$ | Organizations in the CBE |
| #VO | Number of virtual organizations created in the CBE |
| #VO$_i$ | Number of VOs in which $O_i$ participated |
| #PortPd | Total portfolio of products/services/patents of the CBE |
| #PortPd$_i$ | Portfolio of products/services/patents of the $O_i$ |
| #NewPd | Total of new products/services/patents generated in the CBE |
| #NewPd$_i$ | Number of new products/services/patents generated by $O_i$ |

Innovation Indicator of an Organisation (II$_i$)

$$II_i = \frac{\#NewPd_i}{\#PortPd_i}$$

Measures the ratio of the number of new products/services/patentes of the organisation $O_i$ by the total portfolio created

Note: The values of II$_i$ are normalised between [0..1] in relation to the sum of the values of the indicators of all

Innovation Indicator of the CBE (II$_{CBE}$)

$$II_{CBE} = \frac{\sum \#NewPd_i}{\sum \#PortPd_i} * r(\#VO, \#NewPd)$$

Calculates the ratio of the innovation of all the organisations in the CBE, weighted by the correlation between the collaboration (participation in VOs) and the new products/services/patents created

Note: The value of II$_{CBE}$ is normalised between [0..1].

## 3.2 Simulation Model

The simulation model PAAM, illustrated in Fig. 1 is built using AnyLogic tools [25]. The CBE is represented by an environment of agents, the organisations, whose behaviour is modelled using agent-based modelling (ABM), system dynamics (SD) and statecharts. The organisations collaborate by creating or accepting collaboration opportunities (CoOps) expressed by directed connections of weight $w_{ij}$, meaning the number of times the organisation i collaborated with the organisation j.

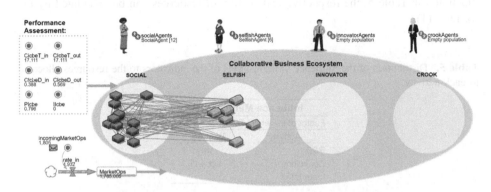

**Fig. 1.** PAAM simulation of a CBE using 12 social and 6 selfish agents.

The model supports a variety of organisations with different profiles, categorised into classes (Social, Selfish, Innovation and Crook), to better characterise the diversity of an actual business ecosystem. Each class, designated by Class of Responsiveness, is typified by the parameters described in Table 4, defining how organisations behave regarding collaboration in response to market opportunities.

**Table 4.** Parameters to characterise the classes of responsiveness in terms of collaboration.

| Classes of Responsiveness | |
| --- | --- |
| Contact rate | Willingness to invite other organisations to collaborate |
| Accept rate | Readiness to accept invitations |
| New products rate | Tendency to accept opportunities related to innovation |

It is expected that the performance evaluation method/indicators can influence the behaviour of organisations by causing them to self-adjust by enhancing their behaviour as a result of the metrics used. As such, if the indicators are properly chosen, this can result in an improvement of the ecosystem as a whole.

### 3.3 Influence Mechanism

The approach regarding the influence mechanism considered in this simulation study [15] is based on the importance (weight) given to each performance indicator. As such, the variation of the respective weights causes a redistribution of the percentage of resources allocated to each activity, by the organisations, trying to improve their performance according to the way they are evaluated. Thus, considering the resources allocated to three main activities: R&D, Consulting, and Inner tasks, the corresponding influence of the indicators, and a given factor of influence (% of improvement), as illustrated in Table 5, the respective reallocation of resources can be calculated by the formula (1).

**Table 5.** Distribution of the influence of the weights of the indicators to the resources allocated to each activity.

| Influence Mechanism | |
| --- | --- |
| Factor of Influence: FI (%) | |
| **Activity** | **Weights** |
| R&D | wII |
| Consulting | wCI, wPI |
| Inner tasks | - |

$$Resources_{forActivity} = Resources_{forActivity_{base}} - \frac{FI}{3} + \frac{(wCI + wPI + wII) * FI}{wII + wCI + wPI} \qquad (1)$$

## 4 Experimental Results of the Simulation Study

For the experimental results of this simulation study, several organisations operating in the same business ecosystem, in the IT industry, were contacted. From two of them who collaborate with some common partners, we were able to collect business and collaboration data regarding the year of 2019. Both organisations are established companies in the high-tech industry, having as technology vendors IBM and Outsystems, and operate in a business ecosystem that can be characterised in terms of entrepreneurship and strategic thinking as a mix of the "Orchestra" and "MOD Station" models [26].

Organisation1 is a system integrator with solutions focused on the management of non-structured contents like contracts, invoices, emails, forms among many others. The organisation integrates technologies from various vendors to build solutions for the corporate and government markets, has partnerships with Universities for R&D processes, and also has its own software products that in many projects act as the orchestrators of several technologies of its partners.

Organisation2 is a system integrator with solutions focused on cybersecurity and networking. The organisation integrates technologies from various vendors to build solutions for the corporate and government markets. Due to its high technical specialisation, it is often subcontracted by local big IT companies to provide consultancy and engineering services to their customers, or new suppliers suggest innovative solutions and areas of supply. Because the cybersecurity sector is evolving rapidly, the organisation has significant activity in managing the supplier ecosystem, being very dynamic in responding and inducing new ideas to market needs.

For each organisation, the collected data described in Tables 6 and 7 were: (1) Number of persons working in research and development, consulting or inner tasks; (2) Number of market opportunities received and accepted indicating the minimal, maximal and typical duration expressed in days/person; (3) Number of collaboration opportunities created by inviting partners, the percentage of business invites sent and the percentage of acceptance by the recipients; (4) Number of collaboration opportunities received from the partners and percentage of acceptance; (5) Total number of products/services produced and in how many of these there were innovation and collaboration.

**Table 6.** Sample data from organisation1 collected in the year 2019.

| Organisation1 | | | | | | |
|---|---|---|---|---|---|---|
| **Resources (persons)** | R&D | | Consulting | | Inner tasks | |
| | 2 | | 28 | | 3 | |
| **Market Opportunities** | Received | Accepted | Duration (days/person) | | | |
| | # | # | min | mode | max | |
| | 27 | 15 | 30 | 60 | 2000 | |
| **Collaboration Opport.** | Invites sent | | Business units sent | | Acceptance | |
| **Sent** | min | max | min | max | min | max |
| Partner1 | 1 | 2 | 0,8% | 1,7% | 50% | 100% |
| Partner2 | 2 | 3 | 3,0% | 4,5% | 80% | 100% |
| Partner3 | 1 | 2 | 0,4% | 0,8% | 50% | 75% |
| Partner4 | 3 | 4 | 1,2% | 1,7% | 50% | 75% |
| | Invites received | | Acceptance | | | |
| **Received** | min | max | min | | max | |
| Partner1 | 3 | 4 | 70% | | 80% | |
| Partner2 | 2 | 3 | 50% | | 60% | |
| Partner3 | 3 | 4 | 80% | | 90% | |
| Partner4 | 6 | 7 | 90% | | 100% | |
| Partner5 | 8 | 10 | 30% | | 50% | |
| Partner6 | 2 | 3 | 50% | | 70% | |
| Partner7 | 1 | 2 | 100% | | 100% | |
| Partner8 | 2 | 3 | 50% | | 50% | |
| Partner9 | 1 | 2 | 70% | | 100% | |
| Partner10 | 4 | 5 | 30% | | 50% | |
| Partner11 | 1 | 2 | 100% | | 100% | |
| **Products/Services** | Total portfolio | | Innovative | | In collaboration | |
| | 16 | | 10 | | 6 | |

**Table 7.** Sample data from Organisation2 collected in the year 2019.

| Resources (persons) | Organisation2 | | | | | |
|---|---|---|---|---|---|---|
| | R&D | | Consulting | | Inner tasks | |
| | 0 | | 14 | | 2 | |
| **Market Opportunities** | Received # | Accepted # | Duration (days/person) | | | |
| | | | min | mode | max | |
| | 98 | 88 | 0 | 10 | 30 | |
| **Collaboration Opport. Sent** | Invites sent | | Business units sent | | Acceptance | |
| | min | max | min | max | min | max |
| Partner4 | 0 | 1 | 0,0% | 4,7% | 0% | 100% |
| Partner12 | 1 | 1 | 5,5% | 5,5% | 100% | 100% |
| Partner13 | 1 | 3 | 5,5% | 16,7% | 100% | 100% |
| Partner14 | 1 | 2 | 1,7% | 3,4% | 100% | 100% |
| **Received** | Invites received | | Acceptance | | | |
| | min | max | min | | max | |
| Partner2 | 1 | 1 | 100% | | 100% | |
| Partner15 | 1 | 2 | 100% | | 100% | |
| Partner16 | 1 | 1 | 100% | | 100% | |
| **Products/Services** | Total portfolio | | Innovative | | In collaboration | |
| | 80 | | 10 | | 3 | |

After analysing the collected data, a consolidated summary is displayed in Table 8. The contact rate is the ratio between the number of collaboration opportunities sent by

**Table 8.** Consolidated samples of data from Organisation1 and Organisation2.

| | Organization1 (Social) | | | Organization2 (Selfish) | | |
|---|---|---|---|---|---|---|
| **Resources** | value | | | value | | |
| Total (persons) | 33 | | | 16 | | |
| Total (days/person) | 7260 | | | 3520 | | |
| R&D | 6% | | | 0% | | |
| Consulting | 85% | | | 87% | | |
| Inner Tasks | 9% | | | 13% | | |
| **Market Opportunities** | value | | | value | | |
| Accepted | 15 | | | 88 | | |
| | min | mode | max | min | mode | max |
| Duration regular (days/person) | 30 | 60 | 100 | 0 | 10 | 30 |
| Duration sparse (days/person) | 100 | | 2000 | 60 | | 200 |
| **Collaboration Opportunities** | min | mode | max | min | mode | max |
| Invites sent | 7 | | 11 | 3 | | 7 |
| Contact rate | 47% | | 73% | 3% | | 8% |
| Business units sent | 0,4% | 0,8% | 4,5% | 0,0% | 5,5% | 16,7% |
| Invites received | 33 | | 45 | 3 | | 4 |
| Accept rate | 30% | 50% | 100% | 100% | 100% | 100% |

the number of market opportunities accepted. The accept rate is the percentage of accepted collaboration opportunities concerning the number of invites received. It is also considered that the first organisation has a "social" profile because of the high contact and accept rate, and the second one a "selfish" profile because it accepts almost all invitations but has a low contact rate.

The PAAM system was configured using the data of Table 8 to simulate the behaviour of the agents, as shown in Fig. 1, populated with 12 social organisations and 6 selfish ones, to simulate a scenario that totals a similar number of agents as the actual CBE of the Organization1 and the Organization2. A different number of combinations can be set to simulate different scenarios. To simulate the contact rate, accept rate, and percentage of business sent, we used Bernoulli and triangular distributions [27], the last one parametrised with the corresponding min, mode and max values.

The simulation model represents a scenario of one year, bringing to the CBE 1500 market opportunities plus 20% of innovative opportunities using the Poisson distribution [28]. To the same scenario, we applied the influence mechanism considering Table 5 parametrised as shown in Table 9.

**Table 9.** The factor of influence and weights of the indicators considered for the scenario of simulation.

| Influence Mechanism | |
| --- | --- |
| Factor of Influence: FI=10 % | |
| **Activity** | **Weights** |
| R&D | wII=1 |
| Consulting | wCI=4, wPI=2 |
| Inner tasks | - |

The achieved results of the performance assessment before and after the influence mechanism are displayed in Table 10.

For a better perception of the results of Table 10, Figs. 2 and 3. Figures 4 and 5 show a visual graph representation of the models of the CBE using the graphic tool Gephi [29], highlighted by colour and size (darker colours and larger sizes), the organisations with a higher contribution and more prestige.

Analysing the results of the Contribution Indicator, the values of $CI_i$out show that the organisations tried to increase collaboration by sending more invitations, although some have accepted fewer opportunities ($CI_i$in), perhaps because they did not have enough resources. As a result, the ratio of collaboration opportunities in the CBE ($CI_{CBE}t$) has improved somewhat. On the other hand, $CI_{CBE}$out shows a more uniform collaboration in the CBE, but $CI_{CBE}$in has worsened.

Finally, analysing the results of the Prestige Indicator, it can be seen that almost all the organisations increased their influence/prominence ($PI_i$), also improved $PI_{CBE}$, resulting in a more uniform ecosystem in terms of the prestige of its organisations.

**Table 10.** Calculated values of the CI and PI for each organisation and for the CBE as a whole, before and after the influence mechanism.

| Performance Assessement of the CBE | | | | Performance Assessement of the CBE | | | |
|---|---|---|---|---|---|---|---|
| Class Resp. | $O_i$ | $CI_i$ in | $CI_i$ out | $PI_i$ | Class Resp. | $O_i$ | $CI_i$ in | $CI_i$ out | $PI_i$ |
| Social | 0 | 0,59 | 0,54 | 0,18 | Social | 0 | 0,38 | 0,56 | 0,02 |
|  | 1 | 0,48 | 0,70 | 0,06 |  | 1 | 0,41 | 0,71 | 0,19 |
|  | 2 | 0,44 | 0,76 | 0,26 |  | 2 | 0,53 | 0,88 | 1,00 |
|  | 3 | 0,37 | 0,76 | 0,11 |  | 3 | 0,41 | 0,74 | 0,64 |
|  | 4 | 0,63 | 0,62 | 0,34 |  | 4 | 0,41 | 0,79 | 0,09 |
|  | 5 | 0,63 | 1,00 | 1,00 |  | 5 | 0,53 | 1,00 | 0,87 |
|  | 6 | 0,81 | 0,62 | 0,48 |  | 6 | 0,38 | 0,74 | 0,72 |
|  | 7 | 0,48 | 0,57 | 0,42 |  | 7 | 0,38 | 0,76 | 0,17 |
|  | 8 | 0,52 | 0,57 | 0,22 |  | 8 | 0,32 | 0,91 | 0,67 |
|  | 9 | 0,30 | 0,65 | 0,00 |  | 9 | 0,18 | 0,59 | 0,09 |
|  | 10 | 0,59 | 0,59 | 0,31 |  | 10 | 0,38 | 0,56 | 0,39 |
|  | 11 | 0,59 | 0,70 | 0,29 |  | 11 | 0,26 | 0,71 | 0,02 |
| Selfish | 12 | 1,00 | 0,00 | 0,00 | Selfish | 12 | 0,85 | 0,00 | 0,00 |
|  | 13 | 0,78 | 0,03 | 0,00 |  | 13 | 0,68 | 0,09 | 0,00 |
|  | 14 | 0,96 | 0,08 | 0,00 |  | 14 | 0,62 | 0,03 | 0,00 |
|  | 15 | 0,74 | 0,03 | 0,00 |  | 15 | 1,00 | 0,09 | 0,19 |
|  | 16 | 0,85 | 0,08 | 0,00 |  | 16 | 0,85 | 0,09 | 0,01 |
|  | 17 | 0,63 | 0,03 | 0,00 |  | 17 | 0,68 | 0,03 | 0,01 |
|  | | $CI_{CBE}$ t = 17,1 | | | | | $CI_{CBE}$ t = 17,5 | | |
|  | | $CI_{CBE}$ in = 0,39 | | $PI_{CBE}$ = 0,80 | | | $CI_{CBE}$ in = 0,51 | | $PI_{CBE}$ = 0,72 |
|  | | $CI_{CBE}$ out = 0,57 | | | | | $CI_{CBE}$ out = 0,51 | | |

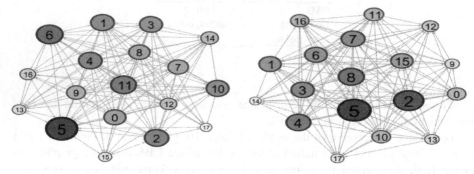

**Fig. 2.** Ranking of CI. (Color figure online)　　**Fig. 3.** Ranking of CI after influenced. (Color figure online)

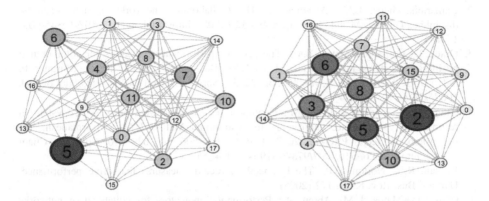

**Fig. 4.** Ranking of PI. (Color figure online)      **Fig. 5.** Ranking of PI after influenced. (Color figure online)

## 5 Conclusions and Further Work

The results of the experimental simulation study show that it is possible to populate and calibrate the PAAM system using actual data of organisations operating in the same business ecosystem. Then, it can be assessed by the adopted performance indicators and influenced by varying their significance (weights). Several scenarios can be set using a variable number or organisations of different profiles. As such, choosing the appropriate indicators, it can result in an improvement of the organisations and of the ecosystem as a whole. Such results can be used by managers to decide on the CBE governance.

The ongoing work aims to collect more collaboration data from organisations to improve the simulation model taken into account more characteristics of the business model, and also to enhance the influence mechanism by introducing more variables related to the motivation of organisations to evolve their collaboration behaviour.

The future work includes the calculation of the Innovation Indicator (II) and its correlation with collaboration.

**Acknowledgements.** This work benefited from the ongoing research within the CoDIS (Collaborative Networks and Distributed Industrial Systems Group) which is part of both the Nova University of Lisbon - Faculty of Sciences and Technology and the UNINOVA - CTS (Center of Technology and Systems). Partial support also comes from Fundação para a Ciência e Tecnologia through the program UID/EEA/00066/2019 and UIDB/00066/2020 and European Commission (project DiGiFoF (Project Nr. 601089-EPP-1-2018-1-RO-EPPKA2-KA).

## References

1. Moore, J.F.: Predators and prey: a new ecology of competition. Harvard Bus. Rev. **71**(3), 75–86 (1993)

2. Camarinha-Matos, L.M., Afsarmanesh, H.: Collaborative networks: a new scientific discipline. J. Intell. Manuf. **16**(4–5), 439–452 (2005). https://doi.org/10.1007/s10845-005-1656-3

3. Graça, P., Camarinha-Matos, L.M.: The need of performance indicators for collaborative business ecosystems. In: Camarinha-Matos, L.M., Baldissera, T.A., Di Orio, G., Marques, F. (eds.) DoCEIS 2015. IAICT, vol. 450, pp. 22–30. Springer, Cham (2015). https://doi.org/10.1007/978-3-319-16766-4_3

4. Graça, P., Camarinha-Matos, L.M.: Evolution of a collaborative business ecosystem in response to performance indicators. In: Camarinha-Matos, L.M., Afsarmanesh, H., Fornasiero, R. (eds.) PRO-VE 2017. IAICT, vol. 506, pp. 629–640. Springer, Cham (2017). https://doi.org/10.1007/978-3-319-65151-4_55

5. Kaplan, R.S., Norton, D.P.: The balanced scorecard: measures that drive performance. Harvard Bus. Rev. **83**(7), 172 (2005)

6. Camarinha-Matos, L.M., Abreu, A.: Performance indicators for collaborative networks based on collaboration benefits. Prod. Plan. Control **18**(7), 592–609 (2007)

7. Abreu, A., Camarinha-Matos, Luis M.: An approach to measure social capital in collaborative networks. In: Camarinha-Matos, Luis M., Pereira-Klen, A., Afsarmanesh, H. (eds.) PRO-VE 2011. IAICT, vol. 362, pp. 29–40. Springer, Heidelberg (2011). https://doi.org/10.1007/978-3-642-23330-2_4

8. Jackson, M.O.: Social and Economic Networks, vol. 3. Princeton University Press, Princeton (2008)

9. Camarinha-Matos, L.M., Macedo, P.: A conceptual model of value systems in collaborative networks. J. Intell. Manuf. **21**(3), 287–299 (2010). https://doi.org/10.1007/s10845-008-0180-7

10. Macedo, P., Camarinha-Matos, L.M.: A qualitative approach to assess the alignment of value systems in collaborative enterprises networks. Comput. Ind. Eng. **64**(1), 412–424 (2013)

11. Vereecke, A., Muylle, S.: Performance improvement through supply chain collaboration in Europe. Int. J. Oper. Prod. Manag. **26**(11), 1176–1198 (2006)

12. Ramanathan, U., Gunasekaran, A., Subramanian, N.: Supply chain collaboration performance metrics: a conceptual framework. Benchmarking Int. J. **18**(6), 856–872 (2011)

13. Ramanathan, U., Gunasekaran, A.: Supply chain collaboration: impact of success in long-term partnerships. Int. J. Prod. Econ. **147**, 252–259 (2014)

14. Ramanathan, U.: Performance of supply chain collaboration - a simulation study. Expert Syst. Appl. **41**(1), 210–220 (2014). 21st Century Logistics and Supply Chain Management

15. Graça, P., Camarinha-Matos, Luis M.: A model of evolution of a collaborative business ecosystem influenced by performance indicators. In: Camarinha-Matos, Luis M., Afsarmanesh, H., Antonelli, D. (eds.) PRO-VE 2019. IAICT, vol. 568, pp. 245–258. Springer, Cham (2019). https://doi.org/10.1007/978-3-030-28464-0_22

16. Zaheer, A., Gözübüyük, R., Milanov, H.: It's the connections: The network perspective in interorganizational research. Acad. Manag. Perspect. **24**(1), 62–77 (2010)

17. Coleman, J.S.: Social capital in the creation of human capital. Am. J. Sociol. **94**, S95–S120 (1988)

18. Burt, R.S.: The network structure of social capital. Res. Organ. Behav. **22**, 345–423 (2000)

19. Freeman, L.C.: A set of measures of centrality based on betweenness. Sociometry **40**(1), 35–41 (1977)

20. Freeman, L.C.: Centrality in social networks conceptual clarification. Soc. Netw. **1**(3), 215–239 (1978)

21. Provan, K.G., Fish, A., Sydow, J.: Interorganizational networks at the network level: a review of the empirical literature on whole networks. J. Manag. **33**(3), 479–516 (2007)

22. BarabÁ¡si, A.L.: Linked: the new science of networks. Am. J. Phys. **71**(4), 409–410 (2003)

23. Opsahl, T., Agneessens, F., Skvoretz, J.: Node centrality in weighted networks: Generalizing degree and shortest paths. Soc. Netw. **32**(3), 245–251 (2010)
24. Brandes, U.: A faster algorithm for betweenness centrality. J. Math. Sociol. **25**(2), 163–177 (2001)
25. Borshchev, A.: The Big Book of Simulation Modeling: Multimethod Modeling with AnyLogic 6. AnyLogic North America, Chicago (2013)
26. Zahra, S.A., Nambisan, S.: Entrepreneurship and strategic thinking in business ecosystems. Bus. Horiz. **55**(3), 219–229 (2012). Special Issue: Strategic Marketing in a Changing World
27. Uspensky, J. V.: Introduction to mathematical probability. Sci. Prog. (1933-) **33**(130), 350 (1938)
28. Haiqht, F.A., Fraxk, A.: Handbook of the Poisson Distribution. (Publications in Operation Research no. 11. Wiley, New york (1967). xi + 168 s. Biometrische Zeitschrift, 12(1),66–67 (1970)
29. Bastian, M., Heymann, Jacomy, G.: An open source software for exploring and manipulating networks (2009)

# Towards a Reference Model for Mass Collaborative Learning

Majid Zamiri[(⊠)] and Luis M. Camarinha-Matos

Faculty of Sciences and Technology and UNINOVA - CTS,
NOVA University of Lisbon, 2829-516 Lisbon, Portugal
zamiri_majid@yahoo.com, cam@uninova.pt

**Abstract.** The rapid development of collaborative activities (particularly beyond geographical boundaries) and the increasing demand for lifelong learning have opened immense opportunities for learners worldwide. Mass Collaborative Learning, as an emerging approach, shifts away from traditional teacher-centered milieu to self-driven learning practices where a large number of learners at various performance levels collectively work toward reaching a common goal. The implementation and development of mass collaborative learning communities however requires both further progress in understanding the involved processes and addressing the key affecting factors. Therefore, as a contribution in this context, a reference model for mass collaborative learning is pursued, aiming to facilitate the understanding of related concepts and highlighting the main internal and external components. Preliminary results of this research work are discussed.

**Keywords:** Mass collaborative learning · Collaborative Networks · Reference model · ARCON modeling framework

## 1 Introduction

The progress in Collaborative Networks (CNs) and the increasing demand for pervasive networked communities have given rise to an emerging new trend and powerful models of collaboration involving large numbers of participants. Away from hierarchy and control, this new method of collective action shifts towards self-organizing and autonomy that, per se, shapes mass collaboration. We are now entering an age of collaboration explosion towards massive contribution where reaping the benefits of diverse minds in solving complex problems becomes a major goal. When this fascinating phenomenon is applied to social learning contexts, standing for limitless public contribution, and benefiting from collective knowledge building and sharing, the notion of Mass Collaborative Learning (MCL) evolves. Under the umbrella of CNs [1], MCL occurs *"when a large number of scattered and self-directed contributors share their partial knowledge, information, data, and experiences with each other (typically by means of ICT platforms) in order to learn something new. In this collective action, knowledge is jointly and continually created, shared, and developed"* [2].

This evolving phenomenon is altering the boundaries and basic mechanisms of both collaboration and learning at an unprecedented rate. MCL moves for example, from

© IFIP International Federation for Information Processing 2020
Published by Springer Nature Switzerland AG 2020
L. M. Camarinha-Matos et al. (Eds.): DoCEIS 2020, IFIP AICT 577, pp. 18–30, 2020.
https://doi.org/10.1007/978-3-030-45124-0_2

funneling all learning programs through instructors (consumer culture) towards proactive public engagement (culture of participation), from confrontation in traditional learning to collaboration in online environment, from a formalized and centralized form to an informal and decentralized form of learning, from a passive role of knowledge acquisition (at individual level) to an active participation in knowledge creation (at community level) [3]. On this basis, a learning ecosystem can and should take the advantages of the unique opportunity that mass collaboration has brought today where plenty of contributors collectively, proactively, and positively engage in the process of knowledge acquisition, building, sharing, and developing.

However, despite notable progresses in understanding the MCL and achievements gained in this context, not all its aspects, characteristics, and components have explicitly defined yet. For instance, different researchers have different viewpoints about this approach, so there is not yet an integrative view about the concept and we are still far from having a common understanding and unified definition of MCL. The boundaries of MCL have not been precisely determined, the processes of formation, organization, and development of MCL communities are still vague [4]. All these points show that this field of study is still evolving and requires further investigation and contribution to provide better clarification.

To fill part of this gap, we believe that MCL requires a proper reference model for some reasons: to provide an abstract representation of the system, to address the environment characteristics, to guide the process of foundation and operation, and last but not least, to elucidate its inherited complexity. Given that, by inspiration from the ARCON (A Reference model for Collaborative Networks) [5], this study proposes a contribution to reference model in order to comprehensively and systematically cover different aspects of MCL. The overarching goal of developing this reference model for MCL communities is to enhance the understanding of the related concepts, environments, entities, relationships, and interactions. Therefore, the main contribution of this study is proposing a preliminary reference model for MCL (based on ARCON reference model framework) aiming to facilitate the understanding of related concepts and underlying the main internal components and external interactions with the surrounding environment.

The remainder of this paper is structured as follows: the relationship between the topic of this work with technological innovation for life improvement is explained in Sect. 2, the research directions and plans are addressed in Sect. 3, our proposed reference model for MCL is presented in Sect. 4, a discussion around the main findings of this study is developed in Sect. 5, and the paper ends with some concluding remarks and a brief look into possible future work.

## 2   Relationship to Technological Innovation for Life Improvement

Learning is one of the world's largest and fastest-growing fields of study (or even industry), and a major contributor to societies' growth. Traditionally learning was driven by instructors, contained planned curriculum, followed by strict timetable of the academic year, occurred in a physical location, and stand on face-to-face interactions. Despite, traditional learning is still a predominant method for training, innovative methods in meaningful ways are now reshaping the learning process and creating radical or incremental changes in learning ecosystems. Innovative methods of learning mainly focus on benefiting of new technologies, pedagogies/methods, and environments in alignment with learners' expectations. These methods are trying to move beyond existing routines. That is, they are not necessarily led by an instructor, nor do they follow a structured curriculum, or result in formal certification (particularly in informal method of direction) [6].

MCL as a holistic concept and an innovative learning approach introduces a social climate that stimulates interested learners who might be dispersed through time and space to work and learn together, and to grow up as an individual and community in the shadow of autonomy and flexibility. From the MCL point of view, learning is ubiquitous, it can take place over the lifetime, anywhere and anytime and in different formats (specifically informal). MCL provides concrete cases of innovative learning environments that "people acquire the intellectual heritage of their community" [7] where they can also create a bridge between educational contents and the issues that matter to their lives.

In order to support promoting the innovative methods of learning in MCL, it is essential to build and develop networks or Communities of Learning (CoL). Such type of virtual community creates a learning-centered environment in various shapes and sizes that in which group of interested learners actively and intentionally attempt to construct knowledge together. A CoL is, indeed, a dynamic and democratic learning society that shifts toward lifelong learning, rather than formal educational institution such as universities, schools, and colleges. It is predominantly generated by self-motivated voluntaries who individually and collectively not only share a range of values, beliefs, experiences, and knowledge, but also assist others in this process through developing heated discussions.

From the MCL perspective, a CoL embraces three major centered elements: (a) learners: the main asset of the community and contributor in learning process, (b) collaboration: the core process of performing activities, and (c) knowledge: the key concerning object. Even though communities of learning vary in form and context, an MCL community basically serves several significant purposes, from encouraging engagement in open collaboration to nurturing the culture of knowledge sharing, advancing the general knowledge of the domain, improving the shared body of knowledge developed in the community, sparking meaningful discussions, triggering self-reflection, reinforcing the links between participated entities, etc. [8].

A CoL can potentially benefit everyone involved in through diverse ways. It is also advocated that a strong CoL can "set the ambience for life-giving and uplifting experiences necessary to advance an individual and a whole society" [9]. Evidences show that CoL can positively influence the capacity, growth, and life of not only the participants, but also the community and society, directly or indirectly [10, 11]. Some of these benefits are separately listed below:

*Participants*

- Participants will find the chance to actively learn even outside the conventional educational frameworks.
- Participants can acquire useful information (that is generated and developed within the community), skills, talents, and potential (e.g., basic life management) that are applicable in any walk of life.

- Participants can contribute to the process of collective knowledge building, sharing, and development.
- Participants can choose and utilize the potential source(s) of information in the community that best suits their personal goals and aspirations.
- It can help participants to become active and informed citizens.
- It amplifies collaborative abilities and interpersonal relationships.
- It can help participants to put learning at the center of everything.
- It can help participants to enrich their education in unexpected ways.
- It can assist participants to advance their careers.
- It can assist participants to build relationships with new faces and minds.

*Community*

- It gives chances to the community for long-term, deeper, and problem-driven learning.
- It escalates the productivity of community with widespread availability of the various range of knowledge, information, and data.
- It increases the capacities of community for openness, diversity, and difference.
- It can address the learning needs of its locality.
- It opens the opportunities for productive collaboration with others (e.g., similar communities, public, private, and non-profit organizations, partners, competitors).
- It enables communities to create added value and social capital.
- It may enable communities to evaluate the validity and reliability of the knowledge (both, received and created) by means of collective intelligence and wisdom.

*Society*

- It creates in societies rare opportunities for inclusion in global and social learning.
- It offers societies a free, accessible, and reliable source for casual learning.
- It can promote the level of general knowledge and awareness of the societies.
- It can help societies to find better solutions for their issues (e.g., social, economic, health, safety).
- It helps societies to promote systematic societal change.
- It opens some doors and breaks down walls to honoring diversity and embracing novelty.
- It can promote social cohesion, culture, and economic.

In addition to these benefits, there are also risks if proper organizational structures and support mechanisms to guarantee quality of knowledge are not put in place.

## 3   Research Approach

This research work is part of a PhD thesis research about mass collaboration and learning. For the thesis, a systematic literature review was initially conducted to get an overview of the area, basic concepts, affecting factors, required organizational structure for MCL, and to identify the relations, contradictions, and gaps in related literature. In order properly guide the survey, a number of research questions were formulated.

Inclusion and exclusion criteria were then identified. Next, relevant works were picked out and required data extracted from. Then the collected data were qualitatively and quantitatively assessed. Subsequently, all collected evidences were synthesized and summarized. Finally, after interpreting the findings of the study, they were published in the form of one survey [2] and two articles [3, 12] in recognized journals and conferences. In this process, the received comments and feedbacks from the reviewers have greatly helped improving the understanding of the area.

As an extension of this study, at this stage, it is essential to identify an appropriate reference model for foundation and designing of the proposed MCL. It is believed that such reference model should provide an abstract representation with a high-level view of the MCL environment and related components. This model should also form the conceptual basis to derive more concrete models from which implementations could be developed. Prior to definition of such reference model, it is significant to consider the previous contributions from related works in the context of CNs. Although the current literature still lacks a well-developed and validated reference model for CNs, the investigation of relevant studies shows that the ARCON (A Reference model for Collaborative Networks) modeling framework is a promising proposal for this purpose. According to [13], ARCON can provide a generic abstract framework and representation for understanding of base concepts, involved entities, significant relationships, interfaces and data flow among the entities of CNs. As such, it can be used for the development of specifications supporting CN environments. The positive features that can be attributed mostly to the ARCON include:

- *Simplicity*: it is a simple, easy to understand and explicit model.
- *Comprehensiveness*: it tries to cover and involve the main relevant components of the environment characteristics of CNs.
- *Neutrality*: it tries to address different aspects of CNs from a neutral point of view.

In addition to these specific characteristics of ARCON, in comparison with other relevant previous approaches (e.g. Zachman, VERAM, CIMOSA, GERAM, IFIP-IFA TFAEI, GERAM, FEA, EGA, and SCOR) that contributed to related areas, it has less limitation when a holistic modeling is pursued, being focused on networked organizations [14]. The literature shows that ARCON has potential applications in variety of domains. It has, for example, been applied to the PROVE initiative (a Portuguese network in the agri-food sector that enables small farmers to sell their goods directly to consumers) [15]. ARCON has also been applied for different purposes including but not limited to, e-government and e-services [16], trust management [17], decomposing value for the customer [18], and learning in on-line and local University of the Third Age (U3A) in Australia [19].

It is note taking that defining a reference model for a new system like MCL is not an easy task. Since, from one side, the MCL is an emerging paradigm and not all its aspects are well understood and developed yet, and from another side, very few inputs are available in the literature regarding to reference models for CNs. In this context, our findings from reviewing previous studies along with our understanding from ARCON modeling framework are complementarily used in the current study as a basis to propose a reference model for MCL. This development, as a contribution to the area, is presented in Fig. 1. In addition to literature review, an analysis of emerging cases of mass collaboration was done in order to identify their relevant characteristics [12]. Since, identifying the positive and negative factors in existing and emerging successful examples of mass collaboration is one possible way of supporting community learning through mass collaboration. The 14 reviewed case studies of mass collaboration along with a short explanation are presented in Table 1.

**Table 1.** 14 reviewed case studies.

| 14 reviewed case studies |
|---|
| *Wikipedia* – a web-based, free-content encyclopedia used as an open collaboration project developed by a very large (open) community of volunteer editors. |
| *Digg* – a social networking and news aggregating website. Contributors submit their stories for consideration and promotion, and they are either voted to be digged, or buried. |
| *Yahoo! Answers* – a question-and-answer website driven by a community in which participants can ask and/or answer questions about anything. |
| *SETI@home* – an Internet-based public volunteer computing project which intends to evaluate radio signals, searching for signs of extra-terrestrial intelligence. |
| *Scratch* – a block-based visual programming language and online community which enables participants to build and share their stories, games, animations, and music on the web. |
| *Galaxyzoo* – a crowdsourced astronomy project that classifies the morphology of large numbers of galaxies through co-operation of interested participants. |
| *Foldit* – an online puzzle video game about protein folding. It invites people to fold the structures of selected proteins (cancer) by using tools provided in the game. |
| *Applications of the Delphi method* – a structured communication method that evaluates the results of multiple rounds of questionnaires sent to a panel of experts to gain group consensus. |
| *Climate Colab* – an online crowdsourcing platform that invites people to address the global climate changes. |
| *Assignment Zero* – an experiment in crowd-sourced journalism in which participants collectively produce a piece of work. |
| *DonationCoder* – a website hosting a community of programmers and software fans that collectively organize and finance software development. |
| *Experts Exchange* – a trusted global online community that tries to solve the world's technology problems. |
| *Waze* – a community driven GPS and navigational app that provides navigation information, route details, and travel times. |
| *Makerspaces* – a collaborative workspace where people can come together to use tools for exploring, making, sharing, learning, and and/or completing a project. |

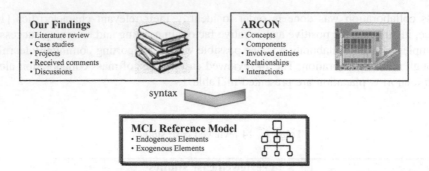

**Fig. 1.** Approach towards building a MCL reference model.

In our previous research study [12] the organizational structures of the above-mentioned 14 case studies were evaluated aiming to derive a general organizational structure for MCL through the analysis of their most significant features. The developed general organizational structure provides us helpful guidelines and directions in this work to help proposing a reference model for MCL.

## 4    Mass Collaborative Learning Reference Model

The ARCON modeling framework for CNs represents the involved environment features and specifications namely, internal aspects and external interactions. Internal aspects mainly concentrate on controllable entities, properties, function, and features of the network and thus address network's *Endogenous elements*, whereas external aspects focus on external interactions between the network and its surrounding area and thus address network's *Exogenous interactions* [14].

Endogenous elements comprise four dimensions, including:

- Structural dimension – refers to participants in the network, and their relationships and roles. This dimension also deals with compositional characteristics of the network (e.g. typology).
- Componential dimension – refers to all tangible resources (e.g. technologies) and intangible resources (e.g. knowledge) of the network.
- Functional dimension – refers to all those functions, operations, processes, procedures, and methods that are related to the network.
- Behavioral dimension – refers to the principles, policies, and governance rules that drive the behavior of the network.

Exogenous interactions also include four dimensions, as follows:

- Market dimension – refers to issues that are related to interactions between the network and its customers, competitors, and potential partners. Part of this dimension embraces the mission of the network, its value proposition, joint identity, etc.

- Support dimension – refers to interactions with those support services (e.g. financial, technical) that are provided by third-party entities outside the network.
- Societal dimension – refers to general interactions between the network and the society (e.g. public and private organizations).
- Constituency dimension – refers to interactions between the network and its potential new members (e.g. attracting and recruiting).

Given the above-mentioned environment characteristics of the ARCON and considering the basic requirements of mass learning communities, we accordingly adapt a general reference model for MCL (MCL-RM). See Tables 2 and 3.

**Table 2.** Endogenous elements for MCL.

| Endogenous Elements for MCL | | | |
|---|---|---|---|
| **Structural Dimension**<br>Network structure (e.g., participants, relationships, roles, and network typology) | **Componential Dimension**<br>Individual tangible/intangible elements (e.g., different resources) of the community | **Functional Dimension**<br>Base functions, operations, running, and procedures in the community | **Behavioral Dimension**<br>Principles, policies, and governance rules that drive the behavior of the community |
| *Participants*<br>• Participants are volunteer<br>• Participants are from diverse background<br>• Participants are autonomous<br>• Participants are distributed<br><br>*Roles*<br>• Based on participants' skills and interests<br>➢ Managerial roles:<br>  • Identity controllers<br>  • Content controllers<br>  • Administrators<br>  • Technical operators<br>➢ Participatory roles:<br>  • Experts<br>  • Ordinary members<br><br>*Roles Relationship*<br>• Based on collaboration, conversation, inquiry, discussion, friendship<br>• Mutual trust<br>• Internal and external of the community<br><br>*Network Typology*<br>• Community is open for everyone and for all interests, but may have access criteria<br>➢ Type:<br>  • Strategic alliances<br>➢ Size:<br>  • Unlimited | *Resources*<br>➢ Technological Resources:<br>  • CSCL tools<br>  • Internet<br>  • Social software<br>  • Web-based<br>➢ Human Resources:<br>  • Two types of groups:<br>   - User group<br>   - Managerial group<br>  • Two types of participants<br>   - Ordinary participants<br>   - Experts participants<br>  • Two types of members:<br>   - Active<br>   - Inactive<br>➢ Knowledge Resources:<br>  • Knowledge<br>  • Information<br>  • Data<br>➢ Community outcomes:<br>  • Developed knowledge<br>  • Findings<br>  • Gained successes | *Processes*<br>➢ Fundamental processes:<br>  • Managing, decision making, executing are done by managerial group and participants<br>➢ Background processes:<br>  • Network forming, setting up, operating, developing, creation of repository, ontology evolution and management, rewarding system are supported by managerial group<br>➢ Knowledge management processes:<br>  • Knowledge building, sharing, developing, evaluating, sorting, storing, and voting are carried out by participants<br><br>*Procedures*<br>➢ Community building:<br>  • Goals establishment<br>  • Rules setting<br>  • Foundation building<br>  • Facility provision<br>  • Member attracting<br>  • Contribution managing<br>➢ Knowledge evolution:<br>  • Knowledge creation is emphasized not knowledge acquisition<br>  • knowledge turns from tacit into explicit form<br>  • Knowledge quality assurance<br>  • Continual knowledge assessment<br>  • Learning from successful communities<br>➢ Community operation handling:<br>  • Community uses common sense<br>  • Community uses voting system<br>  • Experts' opinions are given special attention | *Governance Model*<br>• Self-governed community<br><br>*Power within the Community*<br>• Distributed<br>• Equally divided (not create influential effect)<br>• Hierarchy of permission is considered<br><br>*Rules and Policies*<br>• Freely publish the findings<br>• Participants provide reliable materials<br>• Contents are written from neutral viewpoint<br>• Participants take full responsibility of their contributions<br>• Participants keep the community safe and respectful<br><br>*Culture*<br>• Following the rules<br>• Supporting others<br>• Criticizing ideas, not people<br>• Flagging bad behaviors |

**Table 3.**  Exogenous interactions for MCL.

| | Market Dimension<br>Interaction with customers and competitors, and also the mission of community | Support Dimension<br>Support services provided by the third-party entities (outside of the community) | Societal Dimension<br>Interactions between the community and the society in general | Constituency Dimension<br>Interaction with the universe of potential new members of community |
|---|---|---|---|---|
| **Network Identity** | *Mission*<br>• Boundary extension (new/wider markets)<br>• Comprehensive lifelong learning<br><br>*Network Profile*<br>• Virtual community of practice<br>• Connection building by online platforms (e.g., website, social media, ICT)<br><br>*Market Strategy*<br>• Market development<br>• Being served as an innovative library<br>• Being served as an open knowledge lab | *Network's Social Nature*<br>• MCL is inherently a not for profit community<br>• MCL can also provide monetary services | *Status*<br>• MCL is informal community of learning<br>• MCL cultivates decentralized and deregulated learning | *Attracting and Recruiting Strategies*<br>• Community visibility (e.g., in social media)<br>• Word-of-mouth recommendations<br>• Partnerships<br>• Up to date online platform<br>• Easy approaches to inclusion and exclusion |
| **Interaction Parties** | *Customers*<br>• Public/Private organizations<br>• Individuals<br>• Problem-solving markets<br>• Knowledge intensive business services<br><br>*Competitors*<br>• Similar MCL projects (e.g., Wikipedia)<br><br>*Potential Suppliers*<br>• Massive Open Online Courses (MOOC) | *Financial Entities*<br>• Investors<br>• Sponsors<br><br>*Technical Entities*<br>• IT companies/experts<br>• Network service provider<br>• Storage service provider<br><br>*Informational Entities*<br>• Universities<br>• Libraries<br>• Research institutes<br>• Experts<br><br>*Social Entities*<br>• Public/Private organizations<br>• Charities<br>• Individuals | *Governmental Organizations*<br>• Educational and scientific organizations<br>• Intellectual property organizations<br>• Telecommunication organizations<br><br>*Private Sectors*<br>• Knowledge intensive business services<br>• Laboratories<br><br>*NGOs*<br>• Education charities<br>• Advocacy NGOs<br><br>*Interested Entities*<br>• Businesses<br>• Learning services<br>• Consulting services<br>• Training institutes<br>• Supporters | *Potential Participants*<br>➢ Public entities:<br>• Education centers<br>• Social services<br>• Libraries<br>• Laboratories<br><br>➢ Business entities:<br>• Companies<br>• Enterprises<br>• Corporations<br>• Partners<br><br>➢ Private entities:<br>• Individuals<br>• Developers<br>• Innovators<br>• Designers |
| **Interactions** | *Customer Interactions*<br>• Collaborating<br>• Consulting<br><br>*Competitor Interactions*<br>• Knowledge exchanging<br>• Partnering<br>• Supporting<br><br>*Supplier Interactions*<br>• Joining | *Support/Service Acquisition*<br>• Financial support<br>• Technological support<br>• Information service<br>• Consulting service<br>• Training service<br>• Donation service<br><br>*Agreement Establishment*<br>• Dealing<br>• Community affiliation | *Political Relations*<br>• New/Wider relationships between people and organizations<br><br>*Social Relations*<br>• Public engagement<br>• Participants practice how regard one another<br><br>*Learning*<br>• Public awareness<br>• Democratized learning<br>• New patterns of learning between organizations and social units<br><br>*Seeking Support*<br>• Knowledge sharing | *Member Searching*<br>• Advertising<br>• Participation is encouraged and supported<br>• Invitation can be sent<br>• Participants can bring in new faces<br>• Current participants should be maintained<br><br>*Joining Mechanism*<br>➢ Applicant: sends application for joining<br>➢ Community: evaluates the application, and:<br>• Accepts the application, or<br>• Rejects the application, or<br>• Requests correction |

As addressed in Table 3, three main groups of elements are considered for Exogenous Elements:

- *Network identity* – that defines the environment in which a MCL is positioned in, shows the position of MCL in the environment, and addresses the way in which a MCL presents itself in the environment.
- *Interaction parties* – identify the potential entities that MCL interacts with.
- *Interactions* – list the type of transactions that a MCL can develop with its interlocutors.

A MCL network and community needs to deal, among the others, with the issue of how to prove the value and quality of created and shared knowledge. The fact is that the key success factor for effective evaluation of collaboratively generated content is the trustworthiness and reliability of the involved participants [3]. "*As user-generated content is no more regarded as a second-class source of information, but rather a complex mine of valuable insights, it is critical to develop techniques to effectively filter and discern good and reliable content*" [20]. In order for the community participants to efficiently evaluate the reliability and quality of the created and shared contents/ knowledge, there are several proposed strategies. In this regards we believe that the integration of human and computer support can help reaching an optimal balance between simplicity and speed on one hand, and validity of result on the other. In this suggested method, the human part consists of two phases namely, individual phase and community phase. In the individual phase, a participant initially checks the created and shared content/knowledge based on a proposed check list, considering some criteria such as authority, accuracy, currency, accessibility, relevancy, purpose, and bias. Once a certain percentage of assurance upon the reliability of content or knowledge and its source is achieved, the content will be next evaluated by the community and benefit of collective intelligence through again completing the same checklist (but this time through collaboration), evidence-based reasoning, formal argumentation, and collective decision making. By means of a computer part, detecting tools (e.g. fact check extension, fake news detector, and other novel tools) can be envisaged to help the human part [3].

# 5   Discussion

In this study, the proposed MCL-RM aims to provide a generic representation and conceptual model which can enhance the knowledge and understanding of the main contributing elements and practices around the environments of a MCL community. It attempts adding some inputs to this field of study for the purpose of discussion among those dealing with this issue (e.g. researchers, educators, decision makers, developers, innovators, and the community stakeholders). It is expected that once a reference model is established, it could drive the process of developing, organizing, implementing, simulating and evaluating real cases of such type of community.

However, it is important to note that MCL not only involves a multidisciplinary nature, but also it is a highly complex system. Thus, it should be considered, described, and modeled from multiple perspectives in order to truly cover and reflect its different aspects and conditions. Thus, the findings of this study have to be seen in the light of some limitations. For example, there are lack of prior research studies on this topic, and neither CNs, nor learning areas have yet offered a suitable reference model for, or even developed considerable background around this particular topic. The complexity of MCL and the required reference model is another limiting factor that originally comes from, e.g. its nature, environment, multiple functions, stakeholders and applications.

Apart from these constraints, this study which relies on existing related models and also findings from reviewed literature, tries to propose a reference model for MCL to capture its complexity through identifying the core components that can directly or indirectly influence the internal environment and external interactions of MCL. It is our belief that this proposal can facilitate understanding the paradigm and provide the starting basis for future developments. However, we must take this fact into account that the proposed MCL-RM can only be considered as a first step towards defining a reference model for MCL, since this model is introduced for the first time. So that, it is quite clear that a complete model cannot be developed at this stage in time. On the other hand, this model, at the current stage, is proposed theoretically (although taking inputs from real cases) and undoubtedly it requires to be applied to a wider range of real cases (to determine its possible limits and weaknesses). Therefore, there is a need for further investigation, elaboration, development, dissemination actions, and feedback collection. In the next stage of development, this model should also be validated by some experts in this area.

## 6   Conclusion

Advances in knowledge discovery and management in the era of rapid expansion of collective activities has led to new emerging approaches for learning. MCL, as an example, is looking to solve a variety of complex problems by means of collective efforts and knowledge sharing. The developed communities from MCL will stand for collaborative knowledge construction and sharing through unlimited number of distributed but interested learners from around the world. Such communities, however, are still lacking a comprehensive refence model that can broadly and clearly elaborate the involved environment characteristics. This study, therefore, getting inspiration in the ARCON modeling framework, attempts to propose a general and appropriate reference model for MCL in order to develop a better understanding of related concepts, elements, and interactions. The preliminary findings of this work can be used for further investigation and development among interested and/or involved entities. Having reached this MCL-RM, we are then, as future work, going to apply it in furthers real case of learning communities.

**Acknowledgements.** This work has been funded in part by the Center of Technology and Systems and the Portuguese FCT program UID/EEA/00066/2019 and UIDB/00066/2020.

# References

1. Camarinha-Matos, L.M., Afsarmanesh, H.: Collaborative networks: a new scientific descipline. J. Intell. Manuf. **16**(4–5), 439–452 (2005). https://doi.org/10.1007/s10845-005-1656-3
2. Zamiri, M., Camarinha-Matos, L.M.: Mass collaboration and learning: opportunities, challenges, and influential factors. Appl. Sci. **9**, 2620 (2019). https://doi.org/10.3390/app9132620
3. Zamiri, M., Camarinha-Matos, L.M.: Learning through mass collaboration - issues and challenges. In: Camarinha-Matos, L.M., Adu-Kankam, K.O., Julashokri, M. (eds.) DoCEIS 2018. IAICT, vol. 521, pp. 3–17. Springer, Cham (2018). https://doi.org/10.1007/978-3-319-78574-5_1
4. Cress, U., Moskaliuk, J., Jeong, H. (eds.): Mass collaboration and education. CCLS, vol. 16. Springer, Cham (2016). https://doi.org/10.1007/978-3-319-13536-6
5. Camarinha-Matos, L.M., Afsarmanesh, H. (eds.): Collaborative Networks: Reference Modeling. Springer, Cham (2016). https://doi.org/10.1007/978-0-387-79426-6
6. Eilks, I., Byers, B.: Innovative Methods of Teaching and Learning Chemistry in Higher Education, 1st edn, p. 258. Royal Society of Chemistry, London (2015)
7. Scardamalia, M., Bereiter, C.: Knowledge building: theory, pedagogy, and technology. In: Sawyer, K. (ed.) Cambridge Handbook of the Learning Sciences, pp. 97–118. Cambridge University Press, New York (2006). http://ikit.org/fulltext/2006_KBTheory.pdf
8. Lima, M., Zorrilla, M.: Social networks and the building of learning communities an experimental study of a social MOOC. J. Int. Rev. Res. Open Distrib. Learn. **18**(1), 40–64 (2017)
9. Lenning, O.T., Ebbers, L.H.: The powerful potential of learning communities. J. Improv. Educ. Future **26**(6) (1999)
10. Mitchell, C., Sackney, L.: Profound Improvement: Building Learning-Community Capacity on Living System Principles, 2nd edn. Routledge, London (2011). https://doi.org/10.4324/9780203826027
11. Kilpatrick, S., Barrett, M., Jones, T.: Defining learning communities. CRLRA Discussion Paper (2003). Series ISSN 1440-480X
12. Zamiri, M., Camarinha-Matos, L.M.: Organizational structure for mass collaboration and learning. In: Camarinha-Matos, L.M., Almeida, R., Oliveira, J. (eds.) DoCEIS 2019. IAICT, vol. 553, pp. 14–23. Springer, Cham (2019). https://doi.org/10.1007/978-3-030-17771-3_2
13. Camarinha-Matos, L.M., Afsarmanesh, H.: A comprehensive modeling framework for collaborative networked organizations. J. Intell. Manuf. **18**(5), 527–615 (2007). https://doi.org/10.1007/s10845-007-0063-3
14. Camarinha-Matos, L.M., Afsarmanesh, H.: ARCON reference models for collaborative networks. In: Camarinha-Matos, L.M., Afsarmanesh, H. (eds.) Collaborative Networks: Reference Modeling, pp. 83–112. Springer, Boston (2008). https://doi.org/10.1007/978-0-387-79426-6_8
15. Macedo, P., Abreu, A., Camarinha-Matos, L.M.: Modelling a collaborative network in the agri-food sector using ARCON framework: the PROVE case study. In: Camarinha-Matos, L. M., Xu, L., Afsarmanesh, H. (eds.) PRO-VE 2012. IAICT, vol. 380, pp. 329–339. Springer, Heidelberg (2012). https://doi.org/10.1007/978-3-642-32775-9_34
16. Farooq, M.K.: Capability maturity model for ARCON implementation for e-government services. In: Proceedings of the 4th International Conference on Theory and Practice of Electronic Governance (ICEGOV), 25–28 October, Beijing, China (2010)

17. Beckett, R.C., Jone, M.: Collaborative network success and the variable nature of trust. Prod. Plan. Control **23**(4), 240–251 (2012). https://doi.org/10.1080/09537287.2011.62765
18. Nicola, S., Ferreira, E.P.: A novel framework for modeling value for the customer, an essay on negotiation. Int. J. Inf. Technol. Decis. Making **11**(3), 661–703 (2012). https://doi.org/10.1142/S0219622012500162
19. Beckett, R.C., Jones, M.: Active ageing: using an ARCON framework to study U3A (university of the third age) in Australia. In: Camarinha-Matos, L.M., Pereira-Klen, A., Afsarmanesh, H. (eds.) PRO-VE 2011. IAICT, vol. 362, pp. 189–196. Springer, Heidelberg (2011). https://doi.org/10.1007/978-3-642-23330-2_21
20. Dondio, P., Longo, L.: Trust-based techniques for collective intelligence in social search systems. In: Bessis, N., Xhafa, F. (eds.) Next Generation Data Technologies for Collective Computational Intelligence. Studies in Computational Intelligence, vol. 352, pp. 113–135. Springer, Berlin (2011). https://doi.org/10.1007/978-3-642-20344-2_5

# A Framework for Behavioural Change Through Incentivization in a Collaborative Virtual Power Plant Ecosystem

Kankam O. Adu-Kankam[1,2(✉)] and Luis M. Camarinha-Matos[1]

[1] Faculty of Sciences and Technology and UNINOVA - CTS, Nova University of Lisbon, Campus de Caparica, Monte Caparica, 2829-516 Caparica, Portugal
kankamadu@gmail.com, cam@uninova.pt
[2] School of Engineering, University of Energy and Natural Resources (UENR), P. O. Box 214, Sunyani, Ghana

**Abstract.** The penetration and growing diversity of Distributed Energy Resources in Renewable Energy Communities (RECs) are currently on the rise. The challenge with these emerging ecosystems is that their effective integration and management are becoming increasingly complex. The Collaborative Virtual Power Plant Ecosystem (CVPP-E) concept was proposed as a contribution to their effective management using a collaborative approach. Here, the CVPP manager promotes collaborative behaviour such as collaborative consumption by influencing the consumption behaviour of members through incentives. The objective is to influence community members to "delegate" their "deferrable loads" for effective management by the manager. In this work, a framework for modelling and simulation of incentivization and related behavioural intervention, adapting the CVPP-E as a digital twin model of a REC is described. The architectural structure, context of incentivization, behavioural change techniques, modelling methodology and expected outcomes of the model are outlined. Some key definitions for the model and future works are also introduced.

**Keywords:** Collaborative Networks · Collaborative Virtual Power Plants · Incentives · Behavioural change · Demand Response

## 1 Introduction

Incentives have been used in diverse sectors of society as a means to influence behavioural change. Many successful cases have been recorded in areas such as health [1], agriculture [2], natural resource conservation [3] waste management and recycling [4], as well as transportation [5]. Transposing this idea into the domain of energy is rare [6] and relatively contemporary, although tariff-based approaches have always been the dominant norm in the past [6]. Influencing behavioural change through incentives is nevertheless promising for the energy industry, particularly at the consumer end of the grid. This is because consumers' behaviour has been found to impact energy consumption in a very significant way, therefore, it is anticipated that, by altering the way consumers use energy at the household level, significant gains could be made in terms of energy conservation [7–9]. For instance, works such as [10–12] confirm the strong

© IFIP International Federation for Information Processing 2020
Published by Springer Nature Switzerland AG 2020
L. M. Camarinha-Matos et al. (Eds.): DoCEIS 2020, IFIP AICT 577, pp. 31–40, 2020.
https://doi.org/10.1007/978-3-030-45124-0_3

synergy between consumer behaviour and energy consumption. Further, works such as [13] revealed that there is a gap between people's desire/intentions towards energy-saving behaviours and their actual behaviours, therefore various forms of interventions including incentives are being considered to help fill this gap. For instance, works such as [6, 14, 15], describe cases where incentives have successfully been utilized to effect behavioural change in domestic energy use. Other works have also demonstrated diverse approaches and campaigns to behavioural change using various incentive models with the ultimate aim of inducing energy saving behaviour among users at the household's levels.

In this work we borrow and utilize three theories/models from the behavioural science/economics to help model behavioural change induced by incentives in a Renewable Energy Community (REC). A digital twin of a REC, called *Collaborative Virtual Power Plant Ecosystem (CVPP-E)* [16, 17], is modelled, using the combination of System Dynamics, Discrete Event and Multi-agent System (MAS) technology, thus a multi-modelling method approach. In the model, we test the effectiveness of "one-size-fits-all" and "customized incentives" (different incentives for different categories of community members, in this case households) in a REC. In order for our model to mimic the real world, we introduced other primary influences that are likely to come to play in real life scenarios. The model is also linked tightly to agents' behavioural change, resulting from incentives, to their decision to delegate. Therefore, at the global/community level, it is possible to analyse the aggregated effect and dynamics of incentives on the community as a whole (community behaviour), and also determine which kind of incentive has the prospect of being used as a more effective Incentive-based Demand Response Management technique. In this particular work, the general conceptual framework for the model and related definitions are described and defined respectively.

## 2    Contribution to Life Improvement

The need to provide a sustainable future with the highest level of quality life begins with the environment [18]. The ongoing discourse on climate change within the research, political, social and economic echelons of society are all intended to advance the livelihood and quality of life of earth's inhabitants. In the case of energy, the generation, transmission and consumption, are major contributors to environmental degradation in diverse forms and shades. In [19] the authors confirmed that energy consumption is inherent to quality of life and population growth. They further described some indices such as human development index of the United Nations (UNDP, the human welfare index of Meadows and Randers) etc. to measure quality of life in relation to energy consumption. In this context, the introduction of sustainability in the domain of energy was aimed at ensuring universal access to modern energy without compromising the environment. As it has already been established, energy is required to sustain and improve quality of life globally, therefore it is in the right direction to ensure it is generated, transported and consumed in a sustainable manner.

This work makes a direct contribution to the provision of sustainable energy in communities and subsequently contributes to environmental sustainability and related quality of life in the context of a community. By influencing community member to delegate their deferrable loads, two significant implication could be derived. (1) In instances where there are excess generation of solar energy in the community, the manager could shift the use of these appliances to utilize the excess energy so that the energy is not wasted or sold to the grid as feed-in-tariffs for less returns. Furthermore, in instances where there is less generation of solar energy the use of these appliances could be shifted into the night where energy tariffs are much lower. (2) In the case of large communities, curtailing the use of these appliance or shafting the time of use could enable the community aggregate unused energy and strategically sell to the grid at peak times for higher gains. These dynamics could enhance the financial gains of community members, hence, a significant contribution towards the improvement of quality of life.

## 3 Related Works

In recent years, as mentioned in the introduction, various publications have analysed the determinants of incentives on behaviour change in relation to domestic energy use. In a comprehensive literature review conducted in [7], the authors reviewed different intervention methods and practices affecting energy use behaviour change in the built environment. The review covered key intervention techniques such as labels, energy performance certificates, energy auditing, prompts, norm appeals, commitments, economic incentives and disincentives, feedbacks, community-based initiatives, benchmarking, goal setting and gamification. In a similar work described in [12], the authors applied the Comprehensive Action Determination Model to investigate the relative influence of intentional, normative, situational and habitual processes on energy-saving behaviour. Another work described in [20] tested the influence of a private commitment strategy in which people pledge to change their behaviour towards energy-saving practices. The authors concluded that effortful commitment strengthens one's personal norm to engage in the behaviour change. Other works like [21] and [22] considered various policy interventions in the form of tax incentives such as: private housing sector subsidies, grants, subventions, loans and moral suasion respectively, to influence consumers' behaviour. Financial incentives have also been found to feature prominently in this area. An investigative work conducted in [23] tried to find the motivation for participating in community energy initiatives that promoted sustainable energy use in communities. The authors' motivation was to enquire if peoples' motives for participating in such initiatives was due to money (financial component), environment, or community involvement. In the United Kingdom, a similar work [6], based on financial incentives, explored, through study trials, how financial payment and feedbacks facilitated load-shifting of residential energy consumption.

Complementarily, various forms of smart technologies are also being explored in this emerging area. For instance, a smartphone application called "Social Power App" which is a gamified digital app-based community challenge, designed to trigger electricity savings, is discussed in [21]. The concept of gamification is clearly demonstrated in this work. Another technological approach is seen in [10], where the authors adopted energy efficiency technologies described as "interactive" and "fixed" technologies, to influence residential energy consumption and householders' energy-related behaviours. An incentive-based optimization compensation scheme for demand management scheduling of appliances in a residential community is also proposed in [7]. The scheme is based on the level of inconvenience for participating in shifting of task-based appliances.

## 4   Modelling Framework

### 4.1   Categorization of Households in CVPP Ecosystem

In the considered CVPP-E, households are categorized into five distinct groups. The categorization is inspired by the Household Electricity Survey: A study of domestic electrical appliance usage that was conducted in the United Kingdom in 2012 [24], and considers: (a) Single pensioner household (b) Single non-pensioner household (c) Multiple pensioner household (d) Households with child/children (e) Multiple person households with no children living at home.

**Categorization of Household Appliances.** Household appliances in the model are aggregated and classified as shown in Table 1.

Table 1.   Classification of household appliances.

|   | Appliance type | Aggregated classification |
|---|---|---|
| 1 | Washing machine, dish washer, washer dryer clothes dryer | Deferrable loads |
| 2 | Refrigerator, fridge-freeze Upright freezer, chest freezer | Cold appliance |
| 3 | Oven, cooker hob, microwave oven, kettle | Cooking appliances |
| 4 | CRT television, LCD television Plasma television, computer | Audio-visuals |

**Modelling Households in the CVPP-E.** Each household in the ecosystem is modelled as an agent, using the AnyLogic platform [25]. Each agent goes through different states (stages) of behavioural change as they come under the effect of different kinds of state-specific influences. These influences could have negative or positive polarity. Negative and positive influences affect agents negatively and positively respectively. The polarity and intensity of influences are further explained in Sect. 4.5. Agents can also receive influences in the form of messages as well. These influences will cause agent to transition from one sate to another state. The more positive an influence the more it affects an agent's transition towards a positive behavioural change and vice versa. Table 2 shows the various sources on influence and their relative polarity in the model. The theories and models guiding this aspect of the work are discussed below, in Sect. 4.4.

**Table 2.** Sources and polarity of influences

| Source of influence | Polarity of influence |
|---|---|
| CVPP manager | Positive |
| Incentives | Positive |
| Community members | Positive or negative |
| Community/Social | Positive or negative |

## 4.2   Configuration of CVPP-E (Configuring Community Size)

In order to be able to create different communities with diverse composition (varying number of each category of households) and also model different scenarios in the communities, the model is designed to provide dynamic community creation capabilities. For instance, in one instance, one could create a community with a tentative configuration of 20- Single pensioner household, 140- Single non-pensioner household, 10- Multiple pensioner household etc. In another instance, one could create another community with a tentative configuration of 5- Single pensioner household, 300- Single non-pensioner household, 150- Multiple pensioner household etc. These configurations can be done on the fly while the model runs. The Graphical User Interface (GUI) designed to achieve these configurations is shown in Fig. 1.

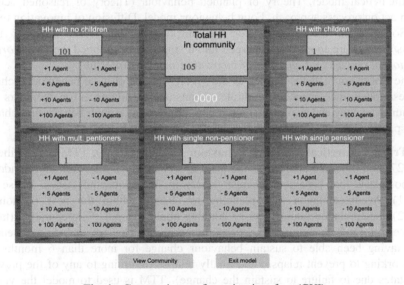

**Fig. 1.** Community configuration interface (GUI)

## 4.3   Incentivization

As mentioned in the introduction, incentives are introduced into the model as a means of influencing community members to delegate control of their deferrable loads to the CVPP manager. We consider two situations: one-size-fits-all and customized incentives. Table 3 illustrates the modes of incentives considered in this model and the respective target groups.

Table 3. Mode of incentive and target group in the model.

| | Mode of incentive | Category of incentive | Target group |
|---|---|---|---|
| 1 | One size fit all | Monitory | All households |
| 2 | Customized incentives | Gamification | i. Multiple person households with no children<br>ii. Single non-pensioner household |
| | | Environmental | i. Single pensioner household<br>ii. Multiple pensioner household |
| | | Monitory | i. Households with child/children |

## 4.4   Theoretical Framework of the Model

Behavioural science is addressed by various disciplines dealing with the subject of human actions [26]. Empirical evidence reveals several theories, concepts and models under this domain of science. These include: Social learning cognitive theory, Transtheoretical model, Theory of planned behaviour (Theory of reasoned action), Health action process approach, Fogg behaviour model, Diffusion of innovation theory and Social norm theory [26]. For the purpose of this work, three of these models/theories are adopted and merged into a single model dubbed the *Collaborative behavioural change and diffusion of innovation model (CoBeDim)*.

The CoBeDim model is defined as the synergy of one or more behavioural change theories/models that integrates multiple dimensions of influences on members in a community as they endeavour to adopt a new innovation through behavioural change.

Aspects of the adopted models are briefly introduced below.

i. **Trans-Theoretical Model of Behaviour Change (TTM).** TTM is described in [27] and [28], and adopted as the main theory in which this work is grounded. It postulates that behaviour change occurs in five sequential stages. These are: (1) Precontemplation (not planning to change within the next 6 months), (2) contemplation (ambivalent or thinking about change), (3) preparation (taking steps towards changing), (4) action (attempting the change), and (5) maintenance (having been able to sustain behaviour change for more than 6 months and working to prevent relapse) and finally relapse (returning to any of the previous states due to failure to sustain the change). TTM is used to model the various transition of behavioural change of agents as they are influenced to incentives and other forms of influences.

ii. **Diffusion and Innovation Theory (DIT).** DIT is described in [29] and seeks to explain how, why, and at what rate new ideas and technology spread. The theory claims that diffusion is the process by which an innovation is communicated over time among the participants in a social system. With this theory, adoption (acceptance) means a decision to use an innovation and rejection is a decision not to adopt an innovation. The theory described five stages of the adoption process, and five adopter categories. The DIT would be applied as a guide to the rate at which "delegation" thorough incentives spread within the ecosystem. The model will adopt the various stages of the adoption process as well as the adopter category to facilitate the dissemination of the idea of "delegation".

iii. **Social Norm Theory (SNT).** A theory expounded in [30, 31], that describes situations in which individuals incorrectly perceive the attitudes and/or behaviours of peers and other community members. Social norm theory adds a social dimension to our model.

## 4.5 Demonstration of the Modelling Technique

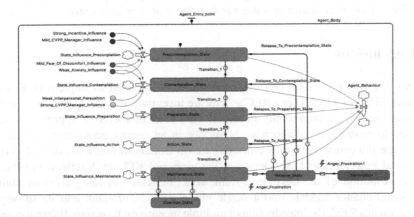

**Fig. 2.** A sample model of influences and rated effect on agent behaviour

The "agent body" represents the embodiment of the agent, and within the agent body lies the various states of transitions conforming to the various stages of behavioural change as borrowed from the TTL model. These states start from the precontemplation state and end at the maintenance state, with relapse and termination as possible options. At each state, an agent experiences an inflow of secondary influence called "State + Influence + Sate name", e.g. State Influence Precontemplation, which constitute an aggregation of primary influences such as Strong Incentive Influence, Mild CVPP Manager Influence, Mild Fear of Discomfort Influence, and Weak Anxiety Influence that affect the agent in the precontemplation state as shown in Fig. 2. These primary influences can carry a negative polarity as shown in red or positive polarity, shown in blue. Besides the polarity, an influence can also have intensity, which can be described as either strong, mild or weak. The intensity and polarity of influences are modelled using stochastic numbers generated within a predefined range. For instance, the model generates stochastic numbers between 10....14, which is the defined scale for positively strong influence. For weak and mild influences, the model generates stochastic numbers between 5....9 and 0....4 respectively. On the other hand, influences like

Anger/Frustration or Fear of discomfort are modelled as negative influences. A strong negative influence is modelled by generating stochastic numbers between (−14) …. (−10). Again, the model generates stochastic numbers between (−9) …. (−5) and (−4) …. (0) for negatively mild and negatively weak influences respectively. The transition from one state to the other is also conditional and is usually triggered when the "state + influence + sate name" influence acting on the agent in that particular state generates its highest possible number, resulting from the sum of all the primary influence acting on the agent in that state. In the relapse state, an agent can relapse to any of the previous states. Relapse is triggered by a message such as Anger/frustration. Termination state is a state of failure and is also triggered by a message. The final agent behaviour is the aggregation of all the "state + influences + State name" influences. Override is a temporal state where agents can opt to temporarily control their deferrable loads for a short period and return control to the manager afterwards.

## 5   Conclusions

This work forms part of an ongoing research work intended to implement Key Performance Indicators (KPIs) in a REC as they are incentivised to delegate control of their deferrable loads to a community manager. This is a collaborative approach which is intended to promote a collaborative behaviour in an energy ecosystem. We adopted knowledge and concepts from two disciplines: (a) Collaborative Networks [32–34] and (b) Virtual Power Plants [18]. Details of the proposed KPI are described in [35]. The main contribution of the developed framework includes: (a) Integration of multiple behavioural change models into a single model called-*CoBeDim* and its subsequent application in a REC, (b) Introduction of multiple incentives, targeting different category of agents, (c) Multimethod approach to modelling multiple incentives in a REC. The expected outcomes are: (i) Identify the kind of incentive that is suitable in a community such as a REC. (ii) Influence consumption behaviour of prosumers using the appropriate kind of incentives. (iii) Influence prosumers to delegate the control of their deferrable loads to the community manager thorough incentives. (iv) Study the aggregated behaviour/dynamics of deferent kinds of incentives on a community at the global level.

Ongoing and next stages of the work will focus on the development and implementation of this CVPP-E framework using the Anylogic platform. The proposed analysis discussed in this framework will also be performed. The outcome is anticipated to be published as an extended version of this work in a peer reviewed journal. Currently, the one size fits all model has successfully been completed. Significant progress has also been made towards the development of the customized model.

**Acknowledgement.** The authors acknowledge the contributions of the PTDC/EEI-AUT/32410/2017 – Project CESME Collaborative & Evolvable Smart Manufacturing Ecosystem and the Portuguese FCT program UID/EEA/00066/2019 and UIDB/00066/2020 for providing financial support for this work. Furthermore, we extend our appreciations to Ghana Educational Trust Fund (GETFund), the University of Energy and Natural Resources and UNINOVA CTS for supporting this work with their research facilities and resources.

# References

1. Vlaev, I., King, D., Darzi, A., Dolan, P.: Changing health behaviors using financial incentives: a review from behavioral economics. BMC Public Health **19**, 1–9 (2019). https://doi.org/10.1186/s12889-019-7407-8
2. Bopp, C., Engler, A., Poortvliet, P.M., Jara-Rojas, R.: The role of farmers' intrinsic motivation in the effectiveness of policy incentives to promote sustainable agricultural practices. J. Environ. Manage. **244**, 320–327 (2019). https://doi.org/10.1016/j.jenvman.2019.04.107
3. Rajapaksa, D., et al.: Do monetary and non-monetary incentives influence environmental attitudes and behavior? Evidence from an experimental analysis. Resour. Conserv. Recycl. **149**, 168–176 (2019). https://doi.org/10.1016/j.resconrec.2019.05.034
4. Bor, Y.J., Chien, Y.L., Hsu, E.: The market-incentive recycling system for waste packaging containers in Taiwan. Environ. Sci. Policy **7**(6), 509–523 (2004). https://doi.org/10.1016/j.envsci.2004.07.002
5. Jakobsson, C., Fujii, S., Gärling, T.: Effects of economic disincentives on private car use. Transportation (Amst) **29**(4), 349–370 (2002). https://doi.org/10.1023/A:1016334411457
6. Bradley, P., Coke, A., Leach, M.: Financial incentive approaches for reducing peak electricity demand, experience from pilot trials with a UK energy provider. Energy Policy **98**, 108–120 (2016). https://doi.org/10.1016/j.enpol.2016.07.022
7. Paudyal, P., Ni, Z.: Smart home energy optimization with incentives compensation from inconvenience for shifting electric appliances. Electr. Power Energy Syst. **109**, 652–660 (2019). https://doi.org/10.1016/j.ijepes.2019.02.016
8. Abrahamse, W., Steg, L.: How do socio-demographic and psychological factors relate to households' direct and indirect energy use and savings? J. Econ. Psychol. **30**(5), 711–720 (2009). https://doi.org/10.1016/j.joep.2009.05.006
9. Charlier, D.: Energy efficiency investments in the context of split incentives among French households. Energy Policy **87**, 465–479 (2015). https://doi.org/10.1016/j.enpol.2015.09.005
10. Adua, L.: Reviewing the complexity of energy behavior: technologies, analytical traditions, and household energy consumption data in the United States. Energy Res. Soc. Sci. **59** (101289), 1–11 (2020). https://doi.org/10.1016/j.erss.2019.101289
11. Iweka, O., Liu, S., Shukla, A., Yan, D.: Energy and behaviour at home: a review of intervention methods and practices. Energy Res. Soc. Sci. **57**, 101238 (2019). https://doi.org/10.1016/j.erss.2019.101238
12. van den Broek, K.L., Walker, I., Klöckner, C.A.: Drivers of energy saving behaviour: the relative influence of intentional, normative, situational and habitual processes. Energy Policy **132**, 811–819 (2019). https://doi.org/10.1016/j.enpol.2019.06.048
13. Kollmuss, A., Agyeman, J.: Mind the gap: why do people act environmentally and what are the barriers to pro- environmental behavior? Environ. Educ. Res. **8**(3), 239–260 (2002). https://doi.org/10.1080/13504620220145401
14. Ghesla, C., Grieder, M, Schmitz, J., Stadelmann, M.: Pro-environmental incentives and loss aversion: a field experiment on electricity saving behavior. Energy Policy, 111131 (2019). https://doi.org/10.1016/j.enpol.2019.111131
15. Mahmoodi, J., Prasanna, A., Hille, S., Patel, M.K., Brosch, T.: Combining 'carrot and stick' to incentivize sustainability in households. Energy Policy **123**, 31–40 (2018). https://doi.org/10.1016/j.enpol.2018.08.037
16. Adu-Kankam, K.O., Camarinha-Matos, L.M.: Towards collaborative virtual power plants: trends and convergence. Sustain. Energy Grids Netw. **16**, 217–230 (2018). https://doi.org/10.1016/j.segan.2018.08.003

17. Adu-Kankam, K.O., Camarinha-Matos, L.M.: Towards collaborative virtual power plants. In: Camarinha-Matos, L.M., Adu-Kankam, K.O., Julashokri, M. (eds.) DoCEIS 2018. IAICT, vol. 521, pp. 28–39. Springer, Cham (2018). https://doi.org/10.1007/978-3-319-78574-5_3
18. UNCED: Measuring sustainable development, Geneva (2013)
19. Pasten, C., Santamarina, J.C.: Energy and quality of life. Energy Policy **49**, 468–476 (2012). https://doi.org/10.1016/j.enpol.2012.06.051
20. van der Werff, E., Taufik, D., Venhoeven, L.: Pull the plug: how private commitment strategies can strengthen personal norms and promote energy-saving in the Netherlands. Energy Res. Soc. Sci. **54**, 26–33 (2019). https://doi.org/10.1016/j.erss.2019.03.002
21. Villca-Pozo, M., Gonzales-Bustos, J.P.: Tax incentives to modernize the energy efficiency of the housing in Spain. Energy Policy **128**, 530–538 (2019). https://doi.org/10.1016/j.enpol.2019.01.031
22. Ito, K., Ida, T., Makoto, T.: Moral suasion and economic incentives: field experimental evidence from energy demand, Chicago, no. 2018-13 (2018)
23. Sloot, D., Jans, L., Steg, L.: In it for the money, the environment, or the community? Motives for being involved in community energy initiatives. Glob. Environ. Chang. **57** (101936), 1–10 (2019). https://doi.org/10.1016/j.gloenvcha.2019.101936
24. Zimmermann, J.-P., et al.: Household Electricity Survey: A Study of Domestic Electrical Product Usage, p. 600. Intertek, London (2012)
25. AnyLogic: AnyLogic: Simulation Modeling Software (2018). https://www.anylogic.com/. Accessed 13 Feb 2020
26. Editors of Encyclopaedia Britannica: Behavioral Science - Britannica. https://www.britannica.com. Accessed 14 Jan 2020
27. Prochaska, J.O., Di Clemente, C.C.: Transtheoretical therapy: toward a more integrative model of change. Psychother. Theory Res. Pract. **19**(3), 276–288 (1982). https://doi.org/10.1037/h0088437
28. Felicíssimo, F.B., de Barros, V.V., Pereira, S.M., Rocha, N.Q., Lourenço, L.M.: A systematic review of the transtheoretical model of behaviour change and alcohol use. Psychologica **57**(1), 7–22 (2014). https://doi.org/10.14195/1647-8606_57_1_1
29. Rogers, E.M.: Diffusion of Innovations - Innovation, Technology and New Economies, 5th edn. The Free Press, New York (2003)
30. Social norms approach (2005). http://socialnorms.org/social-norms-approach/. Accessed 14 Jan 2020
31. Berkowitz, A.D.: An overview of the social norms approach. In: Changing the Culture of College Drinking: A Socially Situated Health Communication Campaign, pp. 194–215. Hampton Press (2005)
32. Camarinha-Matos, L.M., Afsarmanesh, H.: Collaborative networks: a new scientific discipline. J. Intell. Manuf. **16**, 439–452 (2005). https://doi.org/10.1007/s10845-005-1656-3
33. Camarinha-Matos, L.M.: Collaborative smart grids–a survey on trends. Renew. Sustain. Energy Rev. **65**, 283–294 (2016). https://doi.org/10.1016/j.rser.2016.06.093
34. Camarinha-Matos, L.M., Fornasiero, R., Afsarmanesh, H.: Collaborative networks as a core enabler of Industry 4.0. In: Camarinha-Matos, L.M., Afsarmanesh, H., Fornasiero, R. (eds.) PRO-VE 2017. IAICT, vol. 506, pp. 3–17. Springer, Cham (2017). https://doi.org/10.1007/978-3-319-65151-4_1
35. Adu-Kankam, K.O., Camarinha-Matos, L.M.: Emerging community energy ecosystems: analysis of organizational and governance structures of selected representative cases. In: Camarinha-Matos, L.M., Almeida, R., Oliveira, J. (eds.) DoCEIS 2019. IAICT, vol. 553, pp. 24–40. Springer, Cham (2019). https://doi.org/10.1007/978-3-030-17771-3_3

# Decision Systems

# Selecting Normalization Techniques for the Analytical Hierarchy Process

Nazanin Vafaei[✉], Rita A. Ribeiro, and Luis M. Camarinha-Matos

CTS-UNINOVA and Faculty of Sciences and Technology,
Nova University of Lisbon, 2829-516 Caparica, Portugal
{Nazanin.vafaei, rar, cam}@uninova.pt

**Abstract.** One of the matters which has influence on Multi-Criteria Decision Making (MCDM) methods is the normalizing procedure. Most MCDM methods implement normalization techniques to produce dimensionless data in order to aggregate/rank alternatives. Using different normalization techniques may lead to different rankings. So, selecting a more suitable normalization technique is a requirement in the decision process. Specially, by the advent of big data and its role in developing life's quality, finding the best normalization technique in MCDM models are more challenging. Collecting data from sensors causes more complex decision problems, thus, providing accurate normalized values (in the same unit) is more critical in these types of contexts. In this research, we analyze and evaluate the effect of different normalization techniques on the ranking of alternatives in one of the Multi-Criteria Decision Making (MCDM) methods called Analytical Hierarchy Process (AHP) using our developed assessment framework. An illustrative example (smart car parking) is used to discuss the suitability of the framework and recommend more proper normalization technique for AHP. Furthermore, the developing of technological innovation is expected by using the evaluation framework which can raise the accuracy of the normalized values in decision problems.

**Keywords:** Normalization · MCDM · AHP · Decision Making · Data fusion · Aggregation · Big data

## 1 Introduction

During the last decades, Multi-Criteria Decision Making (MCDM) has received much attention from researchers due to its abilities to deals with complex decision problems that depend on several criteria. Each MCDM problem is defined by a decision matrix that includes a set of alternatives $A_i$ ($i = 1, ..., m$), criteria $C_j$ ($j = 1, ..., n$), the relative importance of the criteria (or weights) $W_j$, and $r_{ij}$, corresponding the rating of alternative $i$ with respect to criteria $j$ [1]. In most MCDM problems, criteria are measured in different units (e.g. velocity, fuel consumption, design, etc., in selecting a car problem) while they should be defined in the "same scale" to make an effective comparison. Therefore, the pre-processing for making dimensionless data from heterogeneous input data is called normalization. The normalization procedure is the first step in most MCDM methods and using different normalization techniques may lead to different

© IFIP International Federation for Information Processing 2020
Published by Springer Nature Switzerland AG 2020
L. M. Camarinha-Matos et al. (Eds.): DoCEIS 2020, IFIP AICT 577, pp. 43–52, 2020.
https://doi.org/10.1007/978-3-030-45124-0_4

ranking/ordering of alternatives and may cause deviation from optimal ranking/ordering. Thus, choosing the suitable normalization techniques plays an important role in the final results of decision problems.

From another point of view, the role of normalization techniques is extended by developing technological innovations that contribute to the growth of life's quality by exploring new ideas in different discipline like big data which is a target discipline for new and evolved normalization techniques. Big data are collected from heterogeneous sensors and multiple other sources which need a suitable normalization technique to make them applicable for data fusion/aggregation. These reasons and important roles of the normalization process motivated us to propose an assessment framework to evaluate different normalization techniques in the MCDM methods.

In this work, the main research question that we address is: *Which normalization technique is more suitable for usage with the AHP method?*

This paper is an extended version of a preliminary study [2] which assessed the suitability of four normalization techniques in AHP method using Pearson and Spearman correlation (a part of the on-going evaluation framework). In this work, we assess the chosen normalization techniques with the additional developed evaluation assessment that was introduced in the recent submitted work by the authors [29] and recommend the most proper normalization technique for AHP method. In order to ensure the robustness of results, the same illustrative example (smart car parking place) from the above paper [2] was borrowed.

## 2 Contribution to Life Improvement

Life quality is defined as the level of wellbeing in terms of health, comfort, happiness, etc. for humans. Some elements like technological innovations have the power to change and improve life quality in different ways [3]. Nowadays, new developments in Artificial Intelligence, Machine Learning, Big Data, and Internet of Things (IoT)/ Cyber-Physical Systems, are likely to change our daily lives with new ideas [4]. For instances, in smart car parking, input data is collected from sensors and then delivered to data centers and after analyzing and finding the best parking place, related data will be transferred to the driver with the help of IoT. In the data center, all received data should be normalized and then options ranked by implementing one of the MCDM methods. Then data related to the best parking place should be transferred to the driver, saving time in finding where to park, often a stressful situation. This decision problem shows the improvement of life quality by increasing comfort, especially in big cities. In this paper, we aim to select the best normalization technique for using in AHP when ranking alternatives in a smart car parking decision problem.

## 3 Normalization

Numerous normalization techniques have been proposed in the literature and most MCDM methods use one of these techniques. Jahan and Edwards [1, 5] pointed to some important features that have influencing effects on capability of normalization techniques and should be considered when developing and evaluating of techniques (Fig. 1).

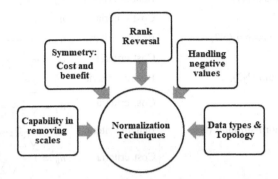

**Fig. 1.** Expected aspects for normalization techniques [1, 5]

As Fig. 1 shows, one of these aspects is the capability of removing scales, which is the basic role of normalization technique in converting the different measurement units of criteria (in MCDM models) into dimensionless units and making comparable decision matrices [1, 5]. Symmetry is another feature that belongs to some normalization techniques which can convert cost criteria into benefit one [1, 5]. This aspect would reduce the calculation process but is always not necessary for MCDM methods [1, 5]. The next property is rank reversal that causes ranking changes by adding or removing alternatives [1, 5]. Rank reversal could happen by selecting a unsuitable normalization technique [1, 5]. Handling negative values is an important capability for a normalization technique when dealing with negative values in MCDM methods [1, 5]. Figure 1 also depicts data types and topology as the last aspect which is added in the work of Jahan and Edwards [1].

Previous research done by the authors proved that the type of input data caused influencing effects on the normalized values and ranking alternatives as well in MCDM method [6]. For example, including zero or decimal numbers in the input data using Sum or Logarithmic normalization techniques are not recommended because of producing undefined and infinite normalized values with the mentioned techniques [6].

Several normalization techniques are proposed in literature. For instance, Jahan and Edwards [1] listed 31 normalization techniques and categorized them based on their applicability for material selection problems. They also, elaborated pros and cons of some techniques such as Max-Min which is affected by the number of alternatives because of changing maximum and minimum values by adding or removing alternatives [1]. Some other studies discussed the Max-Min normalization techniques which are very commonly used with MCDM methods [7, 8]. Another common normalization technique is Vector normalization which is implemented for TOPSIS method [1, 7].

Although there are many normalization techniques in the literature, since this paper is an extension of a previous study [2], we selected exactly the same normalization technique that were used in [2]. Therefore, we compare the suitability of the five more well-known normalization technique (Table 1) for using in AHP method.

**Table 1.** Well-known normalization techniques (adapted from [2]).

| Normalization technique | Condition of use | Formula |
|---|---|---|
| Linear: max (N1) | Benefit criteria | $n_{ij} = \frac{r_{ij}}{r_{max}}$ |
| | Cost criteria | $n_{ij} = 1 - \frac{r_{ij}}{r_{max}}$ |
| Linear: max-min (N2) | Benefit criteria | $n_{ij} = \frac{r_{ij}-r_{min}}{r_{max}-r_{min}}$ |
| | Cost criteria | $n_{ij} = \frac{r_{max}-r_{ij}}{r_{max}-r_{min}}$ |
| Linear: sum (N3) | Benefit criteria | $n_{ij} = \frac{r_{ij}}{\sum_{i=1}^{m} r_{ij}}$ |
| | Cost criteria | $n_{ij} = \frac{1/r_{ij}}{\sum_{i=1}^{m} 1/r_{ij}}$ |
| Vector normalization (N4) | Benefit criteria | $n_{ij} = \frac{r_{ij}}{\sqrt{\sum_{i=1}^{m} r_{ij}^2}}$ |
| | Cost criteria | $n_{ij} = 1 - \frac{r_{ij}}{\sqrt{\sum_{i=1}^{m} r_{ij}^2}}$ |
| Logarithmic normalization (N5) | Benefit criteria | $n_{ij} = \frac{\ln\left(r_{ij}\right)}{\ln\left(\prod_{i=1}^{m} r_{ij}\right)}$ |
| | Cost criteria | $n_{ij} = \frac{1-\frac{\ln\left(r_{ij}\right)}{\ln\left(\prod_{i=1}^{m} r_{ij}\right)}}{m-1}$ |

## 4 Assessment Framework for Evaluation of Normalization Techniques

As mentioned above, normalization is the unavoidable step in most MCDM problems to make dimensionless criteria from heterogonous data. Several studies focused on the effect of the normalization techniques and introduced some metrics that can help decision makers to select the more appropriate technique for using in aggregation/ranking process [1, 5, 8–25]. Among these articles some of them are more interesting due to the characteristic of the metric to be used for MCDM methods. For example, Celen [19] (Max-Min, Max and Sum) used consistency conditions to analyze the effects of three normalization techniques and recommended the more suitable one for the TOPSIS method. Furthermore, Charaborty and Yeh [18, 20] discussed the suitability of Vector, Max-Min, Max, and Sum normalization techniques and assessed the best technique using Ranking Consistency Index (RCI). In another study, Mathew et al. [24] presented Max-Min as the best normalization for the weighted aggregated sum product assessment (WASPAS) method using Spearman correlation. Moreover, Jahan [5] proposed the range target-based normalization technique and compared the efficiency of three types of normalization techniques (Non-monotonic, Comprehensive, and Target-based (point and range)) using ANOVA.

As mentioned, several research studies are done related to assessing normalization techniques while there is a need to define a general framework for the most well-known MCDM methods. The observed gaps motivated us to design and develop an assessment framework to recommend the most proper normalization techniques for more well-known MCDM decision models.

The preliminary framework was proposed in [2, 6, 26, 27, 29] and consists of a number of steps such as calculating RCI, correlation, Standard Deviation, Minkowski distances, and so on. The authors introduced the developed version of the framework that consists of three levels as shown in Fig. 2 to select the best normalization technique for MCDM decision models [29].

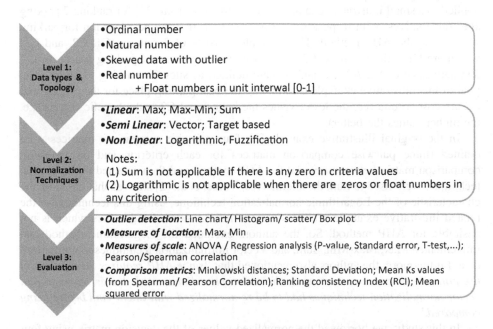

**Fig. 2.** Three level of the evaluation framework (adapted from [29])

As Fig. 2 shows, the first level of the developed framework identifies the topology of the input data set. The second level refers to the selection of the normalization techniques from different categories that are classified as linear (Max, Max-Min, and Sum), semi linear (Vector and Target-based) and non-linear (Logarithmic and Fuzzification) techniques. Also, considering the topology of the input data set (from first level) should be taken in this level in order to exclude the normalization techniques which are not fitted with the input data set. Vafaei et al. [6] showed that when the input data contains zero or decimal numbers, the elimination of the Logarithmic and Sum normalization technique is necessary because of producing infinite and undefined normalized values with these techniques (see [6]). Finally, in the third level of the assessment framework, we implement several metrics to analyze the effect of the selected normalization techniques on the MCDM problems and recommend the most appropriate technique. Further information about these levels are explained in the next section.

## 5　Comparison of Normalization Techniques with an Illustrative Example for Analytical Hierarchy Process (AHP) Method

We are going to compare the suitability of the selected normalization techniques when applied to a small illustrative example that is borrowed from [23] for ranking 7 parking sites (alternatives) with respect to a set of criteria to find the best location for parking place using the AHP method. This example consists of 3 criteria (C1, C2, and C3) which are C1 = time to park, C2 = distance, and C3 = size of parking space; also, 7 alternatives (A1, A2, A3, ..., and A7) are defined as sites for parking locations. The goal of this illustrative example is to finding the best parking place for the car, C1 and C2 are cost criteria (i.e. the lower values the better) and C3 is the benefic criteria (i.e. the higher values the better).

In the original illustrative example [2], four pairwise comparison matrices were defined (three pairwise comparison matrices for each criterion and one pairwise comparison matrix between criteria) for AHP method and then selected normalization techniques were used to rank the alternatives. Vafaei et al. [2] showed that based on the characteristic of the Logarithmic normalization technique, using this technique for the related illustrative example produces zero or infinite normalized values which is not desirable for AHP method. So, the authors excluded the Logarithmic method and implemented Max, Max-Min, Sum, and Vector normalization techniques to normalized data. Furthermore, the authors also mentioned that "*since AHP requires the columns of the pairwise matrices to sum up 1, the techniques: linear max, linear max-min and vector normalization techniques had to be re-normalized with linear sum before being compared.*"

In this study, we borrowed the normalized values of the decision matrix using four normalization techniques (Max, Max-Min, Sum, Vector) from [2] and implement the developed evaluation framework to assess the suitability of the chosen normalization techniques and recommend the most proper one for the AHP method. For more information about the AHP method and the normalizing process for this illustrative example please see [2]. Table 2 shows the global weights (re-normalized values) and ranking of alternatives for the smart car parking example that are borrowed from [2].

**Table 2.** Global weight (G) and Ranking (R) of alternatives for the smart parking example.

|    | Max | | Max-Min | | Sum | | Vector | |
|----|--------|---|--------|---|--------|---|--------|---|
|    | G | R | G | R | G | R | G | R |
| A1 | 0.1972 | 2 | 0.1925 | 2 | 0.1505 | 4 | 0.1693 | 2 |
| A2 | 0.0681 | 6 | 0.0634 | 6 | 0.0762 | 6 | 0.1165 | 6 |
| A3 | 0.1143 | 5 | 0.1161 | 5 | 0.0993 | 5 | 0.1297 | 5 |
| A4 | 0.2469 | 1 | 0.2658 | 1 | 0.2876 | 1 | 0.1755 | 1 |
| A5 | 0.0460 | 7 | 0.0291 | 7 | 0.0749 | 7 | 0.1101 | 7 |
| A6 | 0.1765 | 3 | 0.1869 | 3 | 0.1598 | 2 | 0.1450 | 4 |
| A7 | 0.1509 | 4 | 0.1462 | 4 | 0.1517 | 3 | 0.1538 | 3 |

Table 2 also shows that using different normalization techniques caused different global weights and different ranks for alternatives. It is not possible to select the best rank for the decision problem just by observing the results. So, we applied the evaluation framework (Fig. 2) to assess the normalization techniques and recommend the most proper one for AHP method.

The first level of the assessment framework (Fig. 2) indicates the topology of the input data sets. As mentioned in [2], input data in AHP are defined as pairwise comparison matrices using a [1–9] scale (corresponding to semantic interpretations; e.g. A1 is more important than A2 due to a criterion). So, considering the characteristic of input data sets in AHP, we skip this level and proceed to the next levels. In the second level, we should select normalization techniques from three categories (Linear, semi-linear, and non-linear). We initially selected Max, Max-Min, and Sum normalization techniques from the linear group the Vector technique from the semi-linear group, and the Logarithmic one from non-linear group. However, taking into account the reasons mentioned above, we excluded the Logarithmic technique from selected normalization techniques and continued the evaluation with four normalization techniques (Max, Max-Min, Sum, and Vector).

In the third level of the evaluation framework (Fig. 2), we deal with four types of metrics including outlier detection; measures of location; measures of scale; and comparison methods. Outlier detection and measure of location are applied to the input data set [29]. As mentioned above, the input data for the AHP method are defined as pairwise comparison matrices in the scale of [1–9] and detecting outliers and measuring location are meaningless for this method. So, we omitted all metrics which are applicable just by input data (such as Outlier detection, Measure of location, ANOVA, MSE, …) and proceed the evaluation with some other metrics that work with normalized values and rank of alternatives such as calculation Minkowski distances, Standard Deviation, Mean Ks values, and Ranking Consistency Index (RCI) from comparison metrics. We calculated Minkowski distances (Manhattan, Euclidean, and Chebyshev), as well as Standard deviation (STD) and Mean Ks values (the average of Pearson correlation) from Table 2 data. For more information about calculating Minkowski distances and Standard deviation please see [6] and for calculation of Pearson correlation and Mean ks value and Ranking Consistency Index (RCI) please see [27]. Table 3 shows the results of the above metrics using the smart park illustrative example with the AHP method.

**Table 3.** Results of applied metrics on illustrative example for AHP method

|         | Manhattan | Euclidean | Chebishev | STD    | Mean Ks | RCI     |
|---------|-----------|-----------|-----------|--------|---------|---------|
| Max     | 1.8468    | 0.4642    | 0.2010    | 0.0716 | 0.9606  | 18      |
| Max-Min | 2.0783    | 0.5258    | 0.2367    | 0.0811 | 0.9564  | 18      |
| Sum     | 1.7155    | 0.4758    | 0.2127    | 0.0734 | 0.9029  | 16.3333 |
| Vector  | 0.6520    | 0.1638    | 0.0655    | 0.0253 | 0.9263  | 17.6667 |

In order to sort the obtained results from different metrics, their interpretation regarding each metric is needed. So, based on the previous studies done by the authors [6, 27], and [29], their interpretations are as follow: for Minkowski distances (Manhattan, Euclidean, and Chebyshev), STD, Mean Ks, and RCI the higher values are better. For more information and the logics about this interpretation please see ([6, 27], and [29]). As shown in Tables 3 and 4 each metric ranked normalization techniques differently. So, still it is impossible to say that which normalization technique would be the best choice for the AHP method. Vafaei et al. [29] suggested to use plurality voting from social choice method [28] to find the best normalization technique. This method selects the alternative with the largest number of times that has the first rank/order in the decision problems. Therefore, we implemented the plurality voting method for each normalization technique with respect to the different metrics. The results are shown in Table 4.

**Table 4.** Ordering of normalization techniques with respect to the metrics and using plurality voting

|         | Manhattan | Euclidean | Chebishev | STD | Mean Ks | RCI | Plurality voting |
|---------|-----------|-----------|-----------|-----|---------|-----|------------------|
| Max     | 2         | 3         | 3         | 3   | 1       | 1   | 2                |
| Max-Min | 1         | 1         | 1         | 1   | 2       | 1   | 5                |
| Sum     | 3         | 2         | 2         | 2   | 4       | 4   | 0                |
| Vector  | 4         | 4         | 4         | 4   | 3       | 3   | 0                |

Summing up, using the plurality voting method showed that the best normalization technique for the AHP method is the Max-Min and the second best is the Max normalization technique. Comparing these results with the preliminary study conducted in [2] proves the robustness of the evaluation assessment and implemented metrics in order to help decision makers and recommend the best normalization technique for different MCDM methods.

# 6   Conclusions

The objective of this article was to recommend the most suitable normalization technique for the AHP method. The behaviour of four normalization techniques (Max, Max-Min, Sum, Vector) were analysed and an assessment framework was applied for selecting the normalization technique. To clarify the approaches, a smart car parking example was used. The evaluation results showed that the Max-Min is the best technique for the AHP method and that the Max normalization technique is the second best for the mentioned illustrative example. We propose the use of the suggested assessment framework and mentioned metrics to select adequate normalization techniques for the case studies (decision problems) involving ranking of alternatives as results may change for other case studies.

In order to generalize our results for selecting the most suitable normalization technique, a simulation with multiple representative scenarios will be performed.

Moreover, we plan to continue developing the assessment framework by adding more metrics to ensure the robustness of the results. Testing and validating this framework with several real-world case studies and adding more normalization techniques are also ongoing and future work.

**Acknowledgements.** This work was funded in part by the Center of Technology and Systems (CTS) and the Portuguese Foundation for Science and Technology (FCT) through the Strategic Program UID/EEA/00066/2019 and UIDB/00066/2020.

# References

1. Jahan, A., Edwards, K.L.: A state-of-the-art survey on the influence of normalization techniques in ranking: improving the materials selection process in engineering design. Mater. Des. **65**, 335–342 (2015). https://doi.org/10.1016/j.matdes.2014.09.022
2. Vafaei, N., Ribeiro, R.A., Camarinha-Matos, L.M.: Normalization techniques for multi-criteria decision making: analytical hierarchy process case study. In: Camarinha-Matos, L. M., Falcão, António J., Vafaei, N., Najdi, S. (eds.) DoCEIS 2016. IAICT, vol. 470, pp. 261–269. Springer, Cham (2016). https://doi.org/10.1007/978-3-319-31165-4_26
3. Branscomb, L.M.: Technological innovation. Int. Encycl. Soc. Behav. Sci., pp. 15498–15502 (2001). https://doi.org/10.1016/b0-08-043076-7/03208-3
4. Camarinha-Matos, L.M., Tomic, S., Graça, P. (eds.): DoCEIS 2013. IAICT, vol. 394. Springer, Heidelberg (2013). https://doi.org/10.1007/978-3-642-37291-9
5. Jahan, A.: Developing WASPAS-RTB method for range target-based criteria: toward selection for robust design. Technol. Econ. Dev. Econ. **24**(4), 1362–1387 (2018). https://doi.org/10.3846/20294913.2017.1295288
6. Vafaei, N., Ribeiro, R.A., Camarinha-Matos, L.M., Valera, L.R.: Normalization techniques for collaborative networks. Kybernetes, p. K-09-2018-0476 (2019). https://doi.org/10.1108/k-09-2018-0476
7. Opricovic, S., Tzeng, G.-H.: Compromise solution by MCDM methods: a comparative analysis of VIKOR and TOPSIS. Eur. J. Oper. Res. **156**(2), 445–455 (2004). https://doi.org/10.1016/s0377-2217(03)00020-1
8. Milani, A.S., Shanian, A., Madoliat, R., Nemes, J.A.: The effect of normalization norms in multiple attribute decision making models: a case study in gear material selection. Struct. Multidiscip. Optim. **29**(4), 312–318 (2005). https://doi.org/10.1007/s00158-004-0473-1
9. Chawade, A., Alexandersson, E., Levander, F.: Normalyzer: a tool for rapid evaluation of normalization methods for omics data sets. J. Proteome Res. **13**(6), 3114–3120 (2014). https://doi.org/10.1021/pr401264n
10. Eftekhary, M., Gholami, P., Safari, S., Shojaee, M.: Ranking normalization methods for improving the accuracy of SVM algorithm by DEA method. Mod. Appl. Sci. **6**(10), 26 (2012)
11. Jahan, A., Edwards, K.L., Bahraminasab, M.: Multi-Criteria Decision Analysis For Supporting the Selection of Engineering Materials in Product Design, 2nd edn. Butterworth-Heinemann, Oxford (2016)
12. Krylovas, A., Kosareva, N., Zavadskas, E.: Scheme for statistical analysis of some parametric normalization classes. Int. J. Comput. Commun. Control **13**(6), 972–987 (2018)
13. Migilinskas, D., Ustinovichius, L.: Normalisation in the selection of construction alternatives. Int. J. Manag. Decis. Mak. **8**(5/6), 623 (2007). https://doi.org/10.1504/ijmdm.2007.013422
14. Nayak, S.C., Misra, B.B., Behera, H.S.: Impact of data normalization on stock index forecasting. Int. J. Comput. Inf. Syst. Ind. Manag. Appl. **6**, 257–269 (2014)

15. Pavlicic, D.M.: Normalization affects the results of MADM methods. Yugosl. J. Oper. Res. **11**(2), 251–265 (2001)
16. Yazdani, M., Jahan, A., Zavadskas, E.K.: Analysis in material selection: influence of normalization tools on COPRAS-G. Econ. Comput. Econ. Cybern. Stud. Res., **51**(1) (2017)
17. Zavadskas, E.K., et al.: Evaluation of ranking accuracy in multi-criteria decisions. Informatica **17**(4), 601–618 (2006)
18. Chakraborty, S., Yeh, C.-H.: A simulation comparison of normalization procedures for TOPSIS. In: 2009 International Conference on Computers & Industrial Engineering, pp. 1815–1820. IEEE, Troyes (2009). https://doi.org/10.1109/iccie.2009.5223811
19. Celen, A.: Comparative analysis of normalization procedures in TOPSIS method: with an application to Turkish deposit banking market. Informatica **25**(2), 185–208 (2014)
20. Chakraborty, S., Yeh, C.-H.: A simulation based comparative study of normalization procedures in multiattribute decision making. In: Proceedings of the 6th Conference on 6th WSEAS International Conf. on Artificial Intelligence, Knowledge Engineering and Data Bases (AIKED 2007), vol. 6, pp. 102–109. World Scientific and Engineering Academy and Society (WSEAS) Stevens Point, Wisconsin, USA (2007)
21. Chatterjee, P., Chakraborty, S.: Investigating the effect of normalization norms in flexible manufacturing sytem selection using multi-criteria decision-making methods. J. Eng. Sci. Technol. **7**(3), 141–150 (2014)
22. Jahan, A., Zavadskas, E.K.: ELECTRE-IDAT for design decision-making problems with interval data and target-based criteria. Soft. Comput. **23**(1), 129–143 (2019). https://doi.org/10.1007/s00500-018-3501-6
23. Papathanasiou, J., Ploskas, N., Bournaris, T., Manos, B.: A decision support system for multiple criteria alternative ranking using TOPSIS and VIKOR: a case study on social sustainability in agriculture. In: Liu, S., Delibašić, B., Oderanti, F. (eds.) ICDSST 2016. LNBIP, vol. 250, pp. 3–15. Springer, Cham (2016). https://doi.org/10.1007/978-3-319-32877-5_1
24. Mathew, M., Sahu, S., Upadhyay, A.K.: Effect of normalization techniques in robot selection using weighted aggregated sum product assessment. Int. J. Innov. Res. Adv. Stud. **4**(2), 59–63 (2017)
25. Baghla, S., Bansal, S.: Effect of normalization techniques in VIKOR method for network selection in heterogeneous networks. In: 2014 IEEE International Conference on Computational Intelligence and Computing Research, pp. 1–6. IEEE (2014). https://doi.org/10.1109/iccic.2014.7238357
26. Vafaei, N., Ribeiro, R.A., Camarinha-Matos, L.M.: Selection of normalization technique for weighted average multi-criteria decision making. In: Camarinha-Matos, L.M., Adu-Kankam, K.O., Julashokri, M. (eds.) DoCEIS 2018. IAICT, vol. 521, pp. 43–52. Springer, Cham (2018). https://doi.org/10.1007/978-3-319-78574-5_4
27. Vafaei, N., Ribeiro, R.A., Camarinha-Matos, L.M.: Data normalisation techniques in decision making: case study with TOPSIS method. Int. J. Inf. Decis. Sci. **10**(1), 19 (2018). https://doi.org/10.1504/ijids.2018.090667
28. d'Angelo, A., Eskandari, A., Szidarovszky, F.: Social choice procedures in water-resource management. J. Environ. Manag. **52**(3), 203–210 (1998). https://doi.org/10.1006/jema.1997.0156
29. Vafaei, N., Ribeiro, R.A., Camarinha-Matos, L.M.: Comparison of normalization techniques on data sets with outliers. Computer Science and Information Systems (2020, to appear)

# ColANet: A UAV Collision Avoidance Dataset

Dário Pedro[1,3(✉)], André Mora[3], João Carvalho[2,3], Fábio Azevedo[2],
and José Fonseca[3]

[1] PDMFC Research Group, Lisbon, Portugal
dario.pedro@pdmfc.com
[2] Beyond Vision Research Group, Ílhavo, Portugal
{joao.m.carvalho,fabio.azevedo}@beyond-vision.pt
[3] CTS/Uninova, FCT, NOVA University of Lisbon, Caparica, Portugal
{atm,jmf}@uninova.pt

**Abstract.** Artificial Intelligence is evolving at an accelerating pace alongside the increasing number of large datasets due to vast number of image data on the Internet. Unnamed Aircraft Vehicles (UAVs) are also a new trend that will have a huge impact over the next years. The use of UAVs arises some safety issues, such as collisions with dynamic obstacles like birds, other planes, or random thrown objects. Those are complex and sometimes impossible to avoid with state-of-the-art algorithms, representing a threat to the applications. In this article, a new video dataset of collisions, entitled ColANet, aims to provide a base for training new Machine Learning algorithms for handling the problem of avoiding collisions with high efficiency and robustness. It is also shown that using this dataset is easy to build new neural network models and test them.

**Keywords:** UAS · UAV · Safety · Artificial Intelligence · Machine Learning · Neural network · Dataset · Collision avoidance

## 1 Introduction

Images contain a high amount of information in a relatively concise way [1]. However, their processing is hard and resource-consuming due to the infinite type of variations that might appear to represent the same structure. Adding a time reference and sequencing the images we can build videos. Due to the fast development of cameras, CPUs, and image and video processing algorithms [2], this kind of data source is becoming widely used. For example, on YouTube [3], are uploaded approximately 72 h of videos in every minute, being expected that, by the end of 2020, online video will be responsible for four-fifths of global internet traffic.

Unnamed Aircraft Vehicles (UAVs) have as main objective aiding or making possible the execution of difficult or impossible tasks by the human being [4, 5]. Nowadays, UAVs are not a strange but instead a trendy tool used in the industry market. Despite the advantages, UAVs' operation might be challenging when operating in complex or confined environments [6, 7]. The presence of obstacles is dangerous and requires the use of obstacle detection and collision avoidance algorithms. For the static obstacles, there are already algorithms that deal relatively well with them, being capable of generating safe paths to the desired positions [8]. However, in real applications,

© IFIP International Federation for Information Processing 2020
Published by Springer Nature Switzerland AG 2020
L. M. Camarinha-Matos et al. (Eds.): DoCEIS 2020, IFIP AICT 577, pp. 53–62, 2020.
https://doi.org/10.1007/978-3-030-45124-0_5

it is very frequent to find dynamic moving obstacles. The latter can be detected by using the video stream provided by the onboard cameras. Video processing is computationally heavy [9] and collision avoidance algorithms need to be fast enough to retrieve solutions without colliding. Therefore, a neural network trained for this kind of situations is useful. The problem of the convolutional neural networks is that they are generally data-hungry, turning them extremely hard to train with small datasets, which leads to a very likely memorization of the dataset [10].

Given this, the objective of this article is to present and make available a new open source dataset to accelerate and facilitate the development of new collision avoidance algorithms, increasing safety and performance of UAVs. This dataset, will also be one module of a bigger framework for designing safer UAVs.

The remaining of this article is structured in the following sections: Sect. 2 links the article with the PhD student work and technology for life improvement, Sect. 3 provides an overview of the existing datasets and their usage to build Machine Learning (ML) models. Section 4 introduces the ColANet dataset. In Sect. 5 it's presented the results of an experimental deep neural network model that was trained using the ColANet dataset. The article is then concluded, and the future work is discussed in Sect. 6.

## 2   Contribution to Life Improvement

The growth of the commercial UAV industry emphasises the need of a conceptual framework for UAV design and arrises the following research question:

> *What could be an adequate conceptual framework for designing generic autonomous vehicles that characterizes individual aircrafts behavior and aggregates them in a network, ensuring reliability and safety in the flight, regardless of the world conditions and unexpected events?*

A possible hypothesis for this question would be that the desired framework can be build utilizing different nodes, that are based on SoA architectures, handling atomic tasks separately but performing complex tasks in collaboration. Furthermore, new complex blocks that don't exist can be developed utilizing ML technology and then integrated into the developed framework.

A good implementation of this framework with all the relevant components working in symbiosis would increase commercial UAV safety by decreasing the number of UAV accidents in urban areas. UAVs are tackling everything in from disease control to vacuuming up ocean waste or even delivering pizza [11], which are all areas that safety is important, and such framework would improve their feasibility, ultimately improving daily lives. This article is a step towards the construction of such framework and the novel collision avoidance ML based blocks.

# 3   Related Datasets

In the last decade, there has been an increasing number of publications of datasets that are enabling the development of new ML models and solutions [12, 13]. In this section it's presented a review of existing datasets, highlighting their relevance and impact in the field. These datasets were selected using both a criteria of usefulness for the community (novel data or utility scenarios) and relevance (amount of citations reports, usage on benchmarks zoos, scientific quality extrapolated by top-tier conferences and journals). As can be found in other works [14], this paper related work review will be split according to their data representation, 2D or RGB datasets, 2.5D or RGB-Depth datasets and 3D or video (volumetric) datasets.

## 3.1   2D Datasets

Most of vision ML algorithms were developed using 2D datasets that tried to understand the correlation between pixels for image classification. In this section we describe 2D image datasets, whether they are RGB or grayscale.

Probably the most revolutionary that waken CNNs (Convolutional Neural Networks) is MNIST [15], which is a database of handwritten digits, has a training set of 60,000 examples, and a test set of 10,000 examples. As it is being used as an example in several papers and courses in this area, it is one of the most used worldwide.

Other popular 2D dataset are ImageNet [16, 17], LabelMe [18], Microsoft Common Objects in Context (COCO) [19] and Pascal Visual Object Classes (VOC) [20].

## 3.2   RGB-Depth Datasets

Recently, cameras with multiple sensors that capture both RGB and depth are becoming more popular due to their decrease in price and increase of applications. SUNRGBD [21] dataset is a good example within this category. It was captured with multiple RGB-D sensors, containing more than 10.000 images. It merges data from multiple other datasets such as NYU depth v2 [22], Berkeley B3DO [23] and SUN3D [24]. It is highly annotated with polygons, bounding boxes, layout info and categories, being excellent for scene understanding tasks.

Another similar datasets in content type are Objectnet3D [25], ScanNet [26] and others [24, 27–29].

## 3.3   Video Datasets

Three-dimensional databases are more unusual but are the ones that can be easily compared with the dataset introduced by our article. They are either point-clouds or videos, which are costly to store and difficult to segment and annotate.

From the point-cloud type, we have parts of databases such as Objectnet3D [25] used for 3D object recognition with 100 categories, 90,127 images, 201,888 objects in these images and 44,147 3D shapes. The objects in the 2D images are aligned with the 3D shapes, and the alignment provides both 3D pose annotation and the closest 3D shape annotation for each 2D object.

From the video type, a good example is ScanNet [26] which consists of a video dataset that contains 2.5 M views in 1513 scenes annotated with 3D camera poses, surface reconstructions, and semantic segmentations. The data was collected using a scalable RGB-D capture system that includes automated surface reconstruction and crowdsourced semantic annotation.

Other datasets can be found in [28–30] and cover more complex use cases, like occlusions or unstructured point clouds.

# 4   ColANet Dataset

The ColANet can be summarized as a Collision Avoidance Video Dataset. This dataset is an open repository of UAV collisions and intends to be an initial step towards safer UAV's operations without collisions.

The ColANet dataset has the particularity to let the user to upload a video, allowing an easier annotation of a video, frame by frame with an escape vector, like it's presented in Fig. 1.

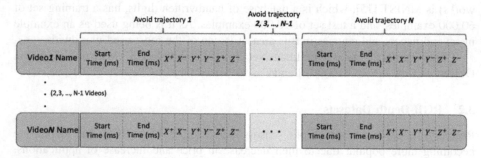

**Fig. 1.** File structure used on dataset annotated frames generation.

As Fig. 1 illustrates, each row consists of four elements:

- Video name.
- Start Time (in milliseconds).
- End Time (in milliseconds).
- Escape Vector $(X^+, X^-, Y^+, Y^+, Z^+, Z^-)$.

The start time, end time and escape vector can have multiple occurrences per row, representing multiple potential collision situations where the escape vectors might differ.

With this information, the server iterates over all videos (one per row) and generates a labeled set of images that are extracted from the video frames. For this purpose, the algorithm opens the video, retrieve the frames per second information, and then generates one image per frame, and a text file containing the annotations. The directions of the escape vector are illustrated in Fig. 2, where is possible to see a UAV with the directions vector overlaid.

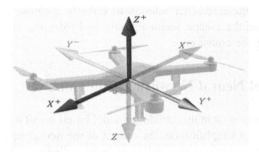

**Fig. 2.** UAV with escape vector.

The software written in python is open source and can be found alongside the dataset[1]. Note that this also gives the freedom to fine-tune the working dataset, since the user can run normalization and regularization when passing the data from a video to a temporal labeled set of images.

The provided version of the dataset already contains 100 videos of drone collisions that were recorded during flights of different models, with different environment conditions (sunny days, cloudy days and during the night), and some examples are represented in Fig. 3. In most videos, the drones are flying freely until the moment of collision. This videos are already labeled with escape vectors, and represent a total of over 2000 collision frames and 6000 free flying frames.

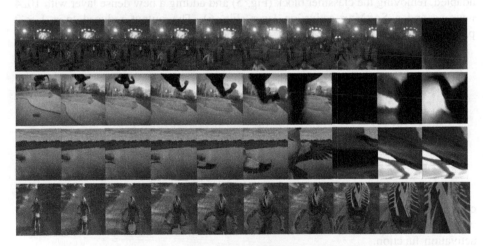

**Fig. 3.** Visualization of 10 frames from 4 different collision videos on ColANet.

To train an algorithm that classifies the current instant (frame) as collision or no collision, all it has to do is check if all the numbers on the row are 0, and he can label it

---

[1] The dataset can be downloaded at https://colanet.qa.pdmfc.com/.

as 'no collision'. If the researcher intends to directly estimate the escape route or trajectory, he can use the escape vector directly and from the algorithm output, take actions for avoiding the collision.

## 5    Experimental Neural Network Using ColANet

To test the dataset presented in this article, a model based on VGG16 [31] (Fig. 4) was trained. For the sake of simplification, the output of the neural network was translated from an escape vector to two labels (collision or no collision). The escape vector file was iterated and the frames whose all 6 escape values equaled 0, were labelled as 'no collision'; all the others received the label 'collision'.

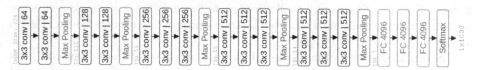

**Fig. 4.** VGG16 architecture.

As stated in Fig. 4, the output has the form of a $1 \times 1000$ probability vector, which is not what is pretended (only 2 classes). To overcome that, the VGG16 model was adapted, removing the classifier block (Fig. 5) and adding a new dense layer with 1024 neurons and a SoftMax activation layer (Fig. 6). The output reduced to a $1 \times 2$ probability vector.

**Fig. 5.** VGG16 without the classifier block.

The newly added layers are composed of a Flatten layer (because the input is from a convolutional layer), a Dense layer with a ReLU activation function, a Dropout layer with a dropout of 0.5 to prevent overfitting and, finally, a Dense layer with a SoftMax activation function.

**Fig. 6.** Our model based on the VGG16 architecture.

An epoch usually corresponds to a complete processing of the training-set. However, the data-generator used from TensorFlow produces batches of training-data for eternity. Therefore, it's required to define the number of steps we want to run for each *epoch*, that will be multiplied by the *batch-size* defined. In the illustrated mode, it's used 100 steps per *epoch* and a *batch-size* of 20. So a *pseudo-epoch* consists of 2000 random images from the training-set. It was run those *pseudo-epochs* 20 times.

These values were chosen empirically, because they were enough to complete the training with this model and dataset, taking around 12 h on an Intel i7 8700 with a Nvidia RTX 2070. The results also contain 20 data-points (one for each *pseudo-epoch*) which can be plotted afterwards. It is also worth noting that the input frames are all normalized in order to have values that range from 0 to 1.

Using Transfer Learning techniques [32], it is possible to check the compatibility and interoperability of the presented dataset. For that, it was used the network weights obtained in the ImageNet [16, 17]. For getting most of this pre-trained network without compromising the results of the classifier block (last layers of the model), the training was split into two phases. In the first phase, the layers of the default VGG16 model were freeze, having only the newly added layers released for training. After 20 *pseudo-epochs*, all the network model is released and the training proceeds, but now adjusting the weights of all the layers. This technique takes advantage of the pre-trained weights of the model with another dataset to calculate the initial weights of the new layers. Releasing all the layers for training in the last step can be considered as a fine-tuning of the weights calculated initially.

## 5.1 Training Results

The ColANet dataset was used to train the presented model. The training and test accuracies were measured during all the training procedure. In order to prove that the network must be trained, the test set was evaluated before any training. Then the results were evaluated both after training the classifier (keeping the default ImageNet weights) and after the fine-tuning. The results are shown in Table 1.

**Table 1.** Training classifier results.

| VGG – Pre train | VGG – Trained classifier | | VGG – Fully trained | |
|---|---|---|---|---|
| Test | Train | Test | Train | Test |
| 58,18% | 93,89% | 92,73% | 96,53% | 94,55% |

During the model training, on the first phase, it's able to reach an accuracy of 92,73% with the test data when training. After the fine-tuning, the final calculated weights allowed to get an accuracy of 94,55%. Due to the similarity with the training accuracies, we can assume that the model wasn't memorizing nor overfitting the training data. In Figs. 7 and 8 is depicted the evolution of the accuracy and loss values over all the *pseudo-epochs*.

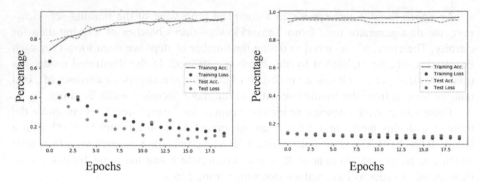

**Fig. 7.** Training classifier.          **Fig. 8.** Full training.

## 6  Conclusions

This article introduces a new video dataset with the purpose of training safer and reliable UAV models. On this paper was proposed both a module that consumes a meta-data file to generate per frame annotations with escape vectors, indicating how to avoid collisions, and also a new dataset of 100 UAV collision videos.

In addition, it was presented a prototype of a collision detector model based on VGG-16. The experimental results showed that is possible to train such a deep neural network, and reuse other datasets using Transfer Learning techniques. This work intends to be a starting point for new UAV architectures and new ML algorithms that leverage the dataset annotations.

Future work will consist of enlarging the dataset with more variety and different videos of UAV collisions, and also the development of new neural networks that leverage not only the spatial frame information (like the one presented on this article), but also the temporal information of the video (like Long Short-Term Memories); to produce better results on real case scenarios. New spatio-temporal algorithms are also envisioned, which combine CNNs and RNNs approaches.

**Acknowledgments.** This work was partially funded by FCT Strategic Program UIDB/00066/2020 of the Center of Technologies and System (CTS) of UNINOVA - Institute for the Development of new Technologies.

This work was supported by the European Regional Development Fund (FEDER), through the Regional Operational Programme of Lisbon (POR LISBOA 2020) and the Competitiveness and Internationalization Operational Programme (COMPETE 2020) of the Portugal 2020 framework [Project 5G with Nr. 024539 (POCI-01-0247-FEDER-024539)], and also SECREDAS, which received funding from the Electronic Component Systems for European Leadership Joint Undertaking under grant agreement nr.783119.

The authors would like to thank the PDMFC Research Group, in particularly Luis Miguel Campos.

# References

1. Berg, A.C., et al.: Understanding and predicting importance in images. In: Proceedings of the IEEE Computer Society Conference on Computer Vision and Pattern Recognition (2012)
2. Akyildiz, I.F., Melodia, T., Chowdury, K.R.: Wireless multimedia sensor networks: a survey. IEEE Wirel. Commun. **14**, 32–39 (2007)
3. Stewart, P.: YouTube. In: The Live-Streaming Handbook (2019)
4. Amazon.com Inc.: Determining safe access with a best-equipped, best-served model for small unmanned aircraft systems. In: NASA UTM 2015: The Next Era of Aviation (2015)
5. Hartmann, K., Giles, K.: UAV exploitation: a new domain for cyber power. In: International Conference on Cyber Conflict (CYCON) (2016)
6. Ryan, A., Zennaro, M., Howell, A., Sengupta, R., Hedrick, J.K.: An overview of emerging results in cooperative UAV control (2008)
7. Pedro, D., et al.: Localization of static remote devices using smartphones. In: IEEE Vehicular Technology Conference (2018)
8. Matos-Carvalho, J.P., Pedro, D., Campos, L.M., Fonseca, J.M., Mora, A.: Terrain classification using W-K filter and 3D navigation with static collision avoidance. In: Bi, Y., Bhatia, R., Kapoor, S. (eds.) IntelliSys 2019. AISC, vol. 1038, pp. 1122–1137. Springer, Cham (2020). https://doi.org/10.1007/978-3-030-29513-4_81
9. Waizenegger, W., Feldmann, I., Schreer, O.: Real-time patch sweeping for high-quality depth estimation in 3D video conferencing applications. In: Real-Time Image and Video Processing 2011 (2011)
10. Zhao, B., Wu, B., Wu, T., Wang, Y.: Zero-shot learning posed as a missing data problem. In: Proceedings of the 2017 IEEE International Conference on Computer Vision Workshops (ICCVW 2017) (2018)
11. PwC: How Drones Will Impact Society: From Fighting War to Forecasting Weather, UAVs Change Everything. CB Insights Research (2020). https://www.cbinsights.com/research/drone-impact-society-uav/. Accessed 05 Jan 2020
12. Hutter, F.: Automated Machine Learning (2019)
13. Wu, C.J., et al.: Machine learning at Facebook: understanding inference at the edge. In: Proceedings of the 25th IEEE International Symposium on High Performance Computer Architecture (HPCA 2019) (2019)
14. Garcia-Garcia, A., Orts-Escolano, S., Oprea, S., Villena-Martinez, V., Martinez-Gonzalez, P., Garcia-Rodriguez, J.: A survey on deep learning techniques for image and video semantic segmentation. Appl. Soft Comput. J. **70**, 41–65 (2018)
15. LeCun, Y., Bottou, L., Bengio, Y., Haffner, P.: Gradient-based learning applied to document recognition. Proc. IEEE **86**, 2278–2324 (1998)
16. Deng, J., Dong, W., Socher, R., Li, L.-J., Li, K., Fei-Fei, L.: ImageNet: a large-scale hierarchical image database. In: 2009 IEEE Conference on Computer Vision and Pattern Recognition (2009)
17. Russakovsky, O., et al.: ImageNet large scale visual recognition challenge. Int. J. Comput. Vis. **115**(3), 211–252 (2015). https://doi.org/10.1007/s11263-015-0816-y
18. Russell, B.C., Torralba, A., Murphy, K.P., Freeman, W.T.: LabelMe: a database and web based tool for image annotation. Int. J. Comput. Vis. **77**, 157–173 (2008)
19. Lin, T.-Y., et al.: Microsoft COCO: common objects in context. In: Fleet, D., Pajdla, T., Schiele, B., Tuytelaars, T. (eds.) ECCV 2014. LNCS, vol. 8693, pp. 740–755. Springer, Cham (2014). https://doi.org/10.1007/978-3-319-10602-1_48

20. Everingham, M., Eslami, S.M.A., Van Gool, L., Williams, C.K.I., Winn, J., Zisserman, A.: The pascal visual object classes challenge: a retrospective. Int. J. Comput. Vis. **111**, 98–136 (2014). 10.1007/s11263-014-0733-5

21. Song, S., Lichtenberg, S.P., Xiao, J.: SUN RGB-D: a RGB-D scene understanding benchmark suite. In: Proceedings of the IEEE Computer Society Conference on Computer Vision and Pattern Recognition (2015)

22. Silberman, N., Hoiem, D., Kohli, P., Fergus, R.: Indoor segmentation and support inference from RGBD images. In: Fitzgibbon, A., Lazebnik, S., Perona, P., Sato, Y., Schmid, C. (eds.) ECCV 2012. LNCS, vol. 7576, pp. 746–760. Springer, Heidelberg (2012). https://doi.org/10.1007/978-3-642-33715-4_54

23. Janoch, A., et al.: A category-level 3-D object dataset: putting the Kinect to work. In: Proceedings of the IEEE International Conference on Computer Vision (2011)

24. Xiao, J., Owens, A., Torralba, A.: SUN3D: a database of big spaces reconstructed using SfM and object labels. In: Proceedings of the IEEE International Conference on Computer Vision (2013)

25. Xiang, Y., et al.: ObjectNet3D: a large scale database for 3D object recognition. In: Leibe, B., Matas, J., Sebe, N., Welling, M. (eds.) ECCV 2016. LNCS, vol. 9912, pp. 160–176. Springer, Cham (2016). https://doi.org/10.1007/978-3-319-46484-8_10

26. Dai, A., Chang, A.X., Savva, M., Halber, M., Funkhouser, T., Nießner, M.: ScanNet: richly-annotated 3D reconstructions of indoor scenes. In: Proceedings of the 30th IEEE Conference on Computer Vision and Pattern Recognition (CVPR 2017) (2017)

27. Lai, K., Bo, L., Ren, X., Fox, D.: A large-scale hierarchical multi-view RGB-D object dataset. In: Proceedings of the IEEE International Conference on Robotics and Automation (2011)

28. Hackel, T., Wegner, J.D., Schindler, K.: Contour detection in unstructured 3D point clouds. In: Proceedings of the IEEE Computer Society Conference on Computer Vision and Pattern Recognition (2016)

29. Quadros, A., Underwood, J.P., Douillard, B.: An occlusion-aware feature for range images. In: Proceedings of the IEEE International Conference on Robotics and Automation (2012)

30. Chen, X., Golovinskiy, A., Funkhouser, T.: A benchmark for 3D mesh segmentation. In: ACM SIGGRAPH 2009 papers on - SIGGRAPH 2009 (2009)

31. Simonyan, K., Zisserman, A.: Very deep convolutional networks for large-scale image recognition, September 2014

32. Pan, S.J., Yang, Q.: A survey on transfer learning. IEEE Trans. Knowl. Data Eng. **22**, 1345–1359 (2009)

# A Decision-Making Tool to Provide Sustainable Solutions to a Consumer

Ricardo Santos[1,2(✉)], J. C. O. Matias[2,3,4], and Antonio Abreu[5]

[1] University of Aveiro, Aveiro, Portugal
ricardosimoessantos84@ua.pt
[2] GOVCOPP, University of Aveiro, Aveiro, Portugal
jmatias@ua.pt
[3] Department of Economics, Management, Industrial Engineering and Tourism (DEGEIT), University of Aveiro, Aveiro, Portugal
[4] C-MAST, University of Beira Interior, Covilhã, Portugal
[5] ISEL - Instituto Superior de Engenharia de Lisboa, Instituto Politécnico de Lisboa CTS Uninova, Faculdade de Ciências e Tecnologia, Universidade Nova de Lisboa, Lisbon, Portugal
ajfa@dem.isel.ipl.pt

**Abstract.** According to some existed studies, one of the economic sectors to achieve sustainability, is the household appliance sector. However, given the different issues (e.g. energy and water consumption, reliability, initial cost, design, noise, illuminance, etc.) to be considered, together with the existence of several brands and models from the market, brings some difficulties to a consumer, who wants to reach a good compromise between them, given its concerns, regarding each dimension of sustainability, namely; economic, social and environmental. By using multi-attribute value theory, combined with Evolutionary Algorithms (EA), it's possible to achieve sustainable solutions from the market. In this work, it's presented an approach to support a consumer, by achieving a set of sustainable household appliances from the market, based on its preferences and needs. A case study shall be used, to give an example of a global solution, where several benefits are achieved, including environment and economic ones.

**Keywords:** Decision support systems · Consumer preferences · Sustainability · Multi-objective optimization · Multi-Attribute Value Theory (MAVT) · Evolutionary Algorithms · Life Cycle Cost Analysis (LCCA)

## 1 Introduction

According to [1], sustainability measures are needed, with buildings representing about 39% of the global energy consumption.

From that percentage, approximately 16% of the world's final electrical energy, is due to the residential sector [2], thus representing an important sector to be improved, through the use of sustainable actions or measures.

© IFIP International Federation for Information Processing 2020
Published by Springer Nature Switzerland AG 2020
L. M. Camarinha-Matos et al. (Eds.): DoCEIS 2020, IFIP AICT 577, pp. 63–78, 2020.
https://doi.org/10.1007/978-3-030-45124-0_6

One way to do it, is through the electrical household appliances, where there has been made some improvements regarding energy efficiency and sustainability in general [3–6]. Such incentives, includes measures like the mandatory labeling [4], provides information to the consumer, regarding each electric household appliance (e.g. capacity (refrigerator), water and energy consumption (washing machine), initial investment (air-conditioner), etc.), with the goal of adjusting each available solution to the consumer's needs [4, 5].

Although the benefits achieved with this kind of measures, it's somehow hard for a typical consumer, to obtain the best solution, adjusted to its needs and preferences.

This happens due to the existence of different options/solutions, available on market, whether in terms of brands and models, or even related to its features [5–7].

The introduction of multicriteria methods, such as multi-attribute value theory (MAVT), can support the consumer to preform sustainable choices, that attends, not only its preferences, but its concerns and needs as well, according to three sustainability's dimensions, namely, environment, economic and social.

Through previous work, evolutionary algorithms (EA), based on NSGA II algorithm, have been applied with success, when solving the type of problems presented in this work [8–11], by even solving with more efficiency than other methods [10], providing different and feasible solutions.

Therefore, and by following the research line, presented on previous works ([9, 10] and [12, 13]), this work presents an approach, supported by MAVT and NSGAII methods, to assist the consumer, by providing from the market, a set of sustainable appliances, adjusted to its different needs and priorities.

The approach presented here, will be demonstrated through a case study, from which, it is achieved a set of sustainable equipment's, that not only maximizes the consumer's economic, social and environment wellbeing, but also attends its preferences and needs.

*Research Question*

How to support a consumer, by choosing energy services (equipment for the residential sector) to achieve sustainable solutions to promote their economic, social and environmental well-being?

*Hypothesis*

**H1:** If by using Multi-Attribute Value Theory (MAVT), to include criteria on behalf of economic, social and environmental dimensions, combined with Multi-objective Evolutionary Algorithms (EA), it's possible to achieve sustainable solutions from the market of household appliances.

## 2  Relationship Between the PhD Work and Technological Innovation for Life Improvement

This work is part of an approach, which was developed for a PhD work, applied on behalf of Technological Innovation for Life Improvement, with focus on human wellbeing.

By acting through different scientific areas, such as energy efficiency, decision support systems, ecological footprint, evolutionary algorithms, product life cycle assessment, among others, and promoting a digital world by suing tools and concepts such as evolutionary algorithms from artificial intelligence and multicriteria decision making, it's possible to provide a better and sustainable future with high quality of life.

The impacts of such approach allow to enhance health and environment across the globe, by achieving at the same time, suitable and sustainable products to each individual, and improving its quality of life.

Therefore, this work can make some contributions specially at a sustainable level, maximizing therefore, the environmental, social and economic wellbeing, of everyone. The main goal is to support the decision-agent decisions, with an approach, implemented through an app, that allows the provision of sustainable solutions, regarding a set of criteria pre-established.

## 3  Literature Review

From several approaches, available on literature, the use of simulation methods, based on "what if" scenarios, is one of them (e.g. [13, 14]), being normally used to explore a restricted number of an alternative solutions.

Other approaches, although, are mainly based on economic analysis, allowing to maximize energy savings, for a given initial investment (e.g. [15]), while other methods, explores retrofitting measures, based on benefit-cost analysis, $CO_2$ consumption, thermal comfort, investment savings, among others (e.g. [13, 16]), with some of them, being combined with other systems too (e.g. [15–17]).

However, many of these approaches, presents some limitations, since it doesn't consider other relevant issues (e.g. energy labelling, environmental, legal, social issues, among others) to achieve solutions, adjusted to the needs of each person/occupant. Furthermore, they don't account the different attributes regarding each appliance available on market and suitable to the number of building occupants.

Recently, there are some works where it was developed multicriteria decision making (MCDM) based methods, to support consumers, or even professionals, in order to solve problems regarding building's retrofitting, by considering issues, like energy efficiency, the internal environment comfort and the depreciation of building elements (e.g. [14, 15, 17, 18]). Others are based on the ranking of alternative options (e.g. [15, 18, 19]).

While MCDM methods, allows to choose the best set of feasible solutions, the adopted criteria are normally conflicted between each other, allowing thus, to obtain a solution that it is impossible to be optimal, considering all criteria.

Other MCDM models, found on literature, and based on Multiple-attribute value theory (MAVT), have been combined with optimization techniques to obtain feasible solutions (e.g. [11, 15, 17–20]).

However, these approaches don't account the different criteria regarding each electrical appliance available on market, regarding each dwelling and occupants.

Approaches, based on metaheuristics, have been also deployed into energy problems, as an efficient tool to achieve a set of feasible solutions, such as Particle Swarm

Optimization (PSO) methods (e.g. [8]) and methods based on Genetic Algorithms (GA) (e.g. [13]), among others.

Although, none of these approaches have been integrated into a combined approach to choose sustainable appliances to a consumer, based on a set of attributes.

## 4   Research Contribution and Innovation

The method presented in this paper, intends to support a consumer, who wants to buy a set of energy services (household appliances), existed in the market (Fig. 1).

Each set of equipment's, are related to a given household appliance (energy service), considered to be bought by the consumer, and it corresponds to a set of candidate solutions, from which, it will be selected one solution at a time, to be proposed by the approach (Fig. 1) as a sustainable individual solution, chosen based on the consumer's preferences, together with its concerns, regarding each sustainability's dimension.

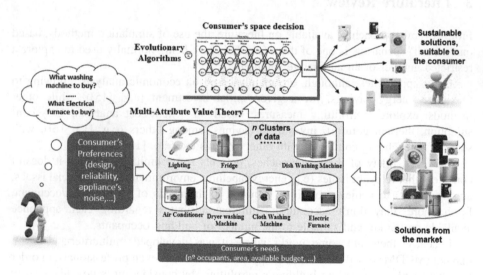

**Fig. 1.** Proposed approach (rough view).

The approach, presented on Fig. 1, can be better explained through a detailed view, presented on Fig. 2, where the 1st stage starts with the pre-selection of a set of candidate solutions $(x_{ij})$ from the market, and based on specific criteria.

Although the correspondent attributes/criteria, remains the same, the correspondent values, varies according to the number of occupants.

The adopted criteria used here, allows the pre-selection of the household appliances, available on market, so the decision space, can be reduced, considering only the options, adjusted to the consumer needs, as well as to increase the efficiency of NSGAII, by obtaining optimal and feasible solutions with less time.

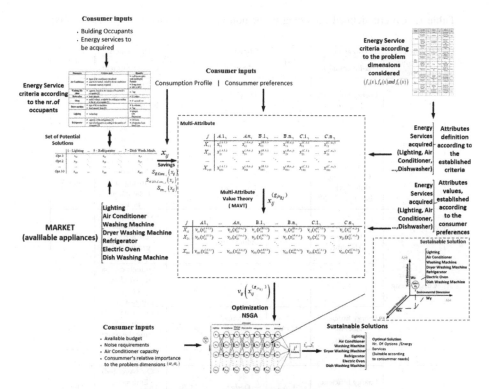

**Fig. 2.** Proposed approach (detailed view).

Therefore, and based on Fig. 2, the pre-selection gives us a set of candidate solutions $(x_{ij})$, where each one, can be formulated as an option $i$, associated to an energy service/household type $j$, to be bought by the consumer on market.

A consumer's consumption profile, was also considered, to preform Life Cycle Cost Assessment (LCCA) for each appliance, to achieve the corresponding savings, regarding energy consumption $(S_{E.Cons_{i,j}}(x_{ij}))$, initial investment $(S_{inv_{i,j}}(x_{ij}))$ and water consumption $(S_{H_2O.Cons_{i,j}}(x_{ij}))$. Such savings were obtained through the comparison between the sustainable solution and the correspondent "less sustainable" (i.e. standard) one.

Considering the several issues, associated to each solution, as well as the consumer's social, economic and environment concerns, a set of criteria was established, for each energy service, and regarding the three dimensions considered, i.e.: A-Economics, B-Social and C-Environment. These criteria are shown on Table 1.

**Table 1.** Criteria defined according to the household appliance (energy service) type.

| Household Appliance type | Dimension A-Economics | Ref. | Dimension B-Social | Ref. | Dimension C-Environment | Ref. |
|---|---|---|---|---|---|---|
| Ilu — light | Energy Efficiency Labeling | Ilu.A1 | Durability [h] | Ilu.B1 | CO₂e (Avoided) Emissions during the usage phase | Ilu.C1 |
| | ⋮ | ⋮ | ⋮ | ⋮ | Percentage of recycling material [%] | Ilu.C2 |
| | Energy Cons.Savings (Life Cycle— Usage phase) [€] | Ilu.A5 | Color Rendering Index (CRI) [%] | Ilu.B5 | CO₂e (Avoided) Emissions during the production phase | Ilu.C3 |
| AC — Air Conditioning | Energy Efficiency Labeling (Heating) | AC.A1 | Noise (Indoor) [dB] | AC.B1 | CO₂e (Avoided) Emissions during the production phase | AC.C1 |
| | ⋮ | ⋮ | ⋮ | ⋮ | Products can be repaired by other professionals | AC.C2 |
| | Energy Efficiency labelling (Cooling) | AC.A6 | Customer Service (warrant) | AC.B9 | CO₂e (Avoided) Emissions during the usage phase | AC.C3 |
| ⋮ | ⋮ | ⋮ | ⋮ | ⋮ | ⋮ | ⋮ |
| FE. — Oven (Electric) | Energy Efficiency Labelling | FE.A.1 | Design | FE.B1 | CO₂e (Avoided) Emissions during the usage phase | FE.C.1 |
| | ⋮ | ⋮ | ⋮ | ⋮ | Accessibility (Product repaired by other people) | FEC2 |
| | Investment cost[€] | FE.A.5 | Perceived Satisfaction (by other clients) | FE.B.5 | CO₂e (Avoided) Emissions during the end use phase | FE.C.3 |
| MLL — Dishwasher | Energy Efficiency Labelling | MLL.A.1 | Design | MLL.B.1 | CO₂e (Avoided) Emissions during the usage phase | MLL.C.1 |
| | ⋮ | ⋮ | ⋮ | ⋮ | CO₂e (Avoided) Emissions during the end use phase | MLL.C2 |
| | ⋮ | ⋮ | ⋮ | ⋮ | Durability | MLL.C3 |
| | Water Cons. Savings (Life Cycle—Usage phase) [€] | MLL.A.6 | Perceived Satisfaction (by other clients) | MLL.B.6 | Water Consumption (Life Cycle— Usage phase) | MLL.C.4 |

Therefore, MAVT was used to assist the consumer, by assessing a set of sustainable appliances, based on the attributes presented on Table 1.

Through these attributes, it was defined a decision variable $\left(x_{ij}^{(g_{jt})}\right)$, related to each candidate solution/household appliance $i$, and belonging to a given appliance type/energy service $j$. This variable is defined based on criteria $t$, associated to an appliance type $j$ and problem dimension $g$ (i.e. A-Economical; B-Social and C-Environmental), namely:

$$\begin{aligned} g &= \{A, B, C\} \wedge j = \{1, 2, .., 7\} \wedge t \\ &= \left\{\left\{1, 2, ..n_{A_j}\right\} \cup \left\{1, 2, ..n_{B_j}\right\} \cup \left\{1, 2, ..n_{C_j}\right\}\right\} \wedge n_{A_j}, n_{B_j}, n_{C_j}, t, j \in \mathbb{N} \end{aligned} \quad (1)$$

By following these notation and according to the criteria defined before, on Table 1, together with the assumptions made, the correspondent decision-variable, regarding each attribute considered $\left(x_{ij}^{(g_{jt})}\right)$, can be aggregated and framed into a set of pay-off/behavior tables, regarding each energy service $j$. On Fig. 3(a), it's shown an example of this table, considering the energy service/household appliance type "Air Conditioner". The correspondent table, regarding the respective $\left(v_{ij}^{(g_{jt})}\left(x_{ij}^{(g_{jt})}\right)\right)$ values, were achieved by using MAVT and the following relation:

$$x_{ij}^{(g_{jt})} \rightarrow \left(\frac{\left|x_{ij}^{(g_{jt})} - x_{ij(worst)}^{(g_{jt})}\right|}{\left|x_{ij(best)}^{(g_{jt})} - x_{ij(worst)}^{(g_{jt})}\right|}\right) \rightarrow v_{ij}^{(g_{jt})}\left(x_{ij}^{(g_{jt})}\right) \quad (2)$$

Since that each decision value $\left(v_{ij}^{(g_{jt})}\left(x_{ij}^{(g_{jt})}\right)\right)$, works with different scales and units, an equation was adopted to define the relation between the new and the previous value of $x_{ij}^{(g_{jt})}$, respectively $\left(v_{ij}^{(1)}\left(x_{ij}^{(g_{jt})}\right)\right)$ and $\left(v_{ij}^{(2)}\left(x_{ij}^{(g_{jt})}\right)\right)$, by also using the worst and better results, and by considering a given criteria $g_{jt}$, i.e.:

$$v_{ij}^{(1)}\left(x_{ij}^{(g_{jt})}\right) \rightarrow \left(\frac{\left|v_{ij}^{(1)}\left(x_{ij}^{(g_{jt})}\right) - v_{worst_{ij}}\left(x_{ij}^{(g_{jt})}\right)\right|}{\left|v_{better_{ij}}\left(x_{ij}^{(g_{jt})}\right) - v_{worst_{ij}}\left(x_{ij}^{(g_{jt})}\right)\right|}\right) \rightarrow v_{ij}^{(2)}\left(x_{ij}^{(g_{jt})}\right) \quad (3)$$

On Fig. 3, it's given an example for an evaluation table ("Air Conditioning").

| A.C. | $A_{21}$ | $A_{22}$ | ... | $A_{2n_{A_2}}$ | $B_{21}$ | $B_{22}$ | ... | $B_{2n_{B_2}}$ | $C_{21}$ | $C_{22}$ | ... | $C_{2n_{C_2}}$ |
|---|---|---|---|---|---|---|---|---|---|---|---|---|
| $X_{12}$ | $x_{12}^{(A_{21})}$ | $x_{12}^{(A_{22})}$ | ... | $x_{12}^{(A_{2n_{A_2}})}$ | $x_{12}^{(B_{21})}$ | $x_{12}^{(B_{22})}$ | ... | $x_{12}^{(B_{2n_{B_2}})}$ | $x_{12}^{(C_{21})}$ | $x_{12}^{(C_{22})}$ | ... | $x_{12}^{(C_{2n_{C_2}})}$ |
| $X_{22}$ | $x_{22}^{(A_{21})}$ | $x_{22}^{(A_{22})}$ | ... | $x_{22}^{(A_{2n_{A_2}})}$ | $x_{22}^{(B_{21})}$ | $x_{22}^{(B_{22})}$ | ... | $x_{22}^{(B_{2n_{B_2}})}$ | $x_{22}^{(C_{21})}$ | $x_{22}^{(C_{22})}$ | ... | $x_{22}^{(C_{2n_{C_2}})}$ |
| ... | ... | ... | $\ddots$ | ... | ... | ... | ... | ... | ... | ... | ... | ... |
| $X_{102}$ | $x_{102}^{(A_{21})}$ | $x_{102}^{(A_{22})}$ | ... | $x_{102}^{(A_{2n_{A_2}})}$ | $x_{102}^{(B_{21})}$ | $x_{102}^{(B_{22})}$ | ... | $x_{102}^{(B_{2n_{B_2}})}$ | $x_{102}^{(C_{21})}$ | $x_{102}^{(C_{22})}$ | ... | $x_{102}^{(C_{2n_{C_2}})}$ |

a)

| A.C. | $A_{21}$ | $A_{22}$ | ... | $A_{2n_{A_2}}$ | $B_{21}$ | $B_{22}$ | ... | $B_{2n_{B_2}}$ | $C_{21}$ | $C_{22}$ | ... | $C_{2n_{C_2}}$ |
|---|---|---|---|---|---|---|---|---|---|---|---|---|
| $X_{12}$ | $v_{12}(x_{12}^{(A_{21})})$ | $v_{12}(x_{12}^{(A_{22})})$ | ... | $v_{12}(x_{12}^{(A_{2n_{A_2}})})$ | $v_{12}(x_{12}^{(B_{21})})$ | $v_{12}(x_{12}^{(B_{22})})$ | ... | $v_{12}(x_{12}^{(B_{2n_{B_2}})})$ | $v_{12}(x_{12}^{(C_{21})})$ | $v_{12}(x_{12}^{(C_{22})})$ | ... | $v_{12}(x_{12}^{(C_{2n_{C_2}})})$ |
| $X_{22}$ | $v_{22}(x_{22}^{(A_{21})})$ | $v_{22}(x_{22}^{(A_{22})})$ | ... | $v_{22}(x_{22}^{(A_{2n_{A_2}})})$ | $v_{22}(x_{22}^{(B_{21})})$ | $v_{22}(x_{22}^{(B_{22})})$ | ... | $v_{22}(x_{22}^{(B_{2n_{B_2}})})$ | $v_{22}(x_{22}^{(C_{21})})$ | $v_{22}(x_{22}^{(C_{22})})$ | ... | $v_{22}(x_{22}^{(C_{2n_{C_2}})})$ |
| ... | ... | ... | $\ddots$ | ... | ... | ... | ... | ... | ... | ... | ... | ... |
| $X_{102}$ | $v_{102}(x_{102}^{(A_{21})})$ | $v_{102}(x_{102}^{(A_{22})})$ | ... | $v_{102}(x_{102}^{(A_{2n_{A_2}})})$ | $v_{102}(x_{102}^{(B_{21})})$ | $v_{102}(x_{102}^{(B_{22})})$ | ... | $v_{102}(x_{102}^{(B_{2n_{B_2}})})$ | $v_{102}(x_{102}^{(B_{21})})$ | $v_{102}(x_{102}^{(C_{22})})$ | ... | $v_{102}(x_{102}^{(C_{2n_{C_2}})})$ |

b)

**Fig. 3.** Example of evaluation table (Air Conditioner): (a) $x_{ij}^{(g_{jt})}$; (b) $v_{ij}(x_{ij}^{(g_{jt})})$.

The final values were then calculated and stored in evaluation tables such as the one presented on Fig. 3(b), regarding each variable and energy service considered.

Then, an additive model, was used to aggregate such values, by considering each solution $i$ regarding each household appliance $j$. Such aggregation is formulated by using three different objective functions, each one regarding to a sustainability's dimension considered. These functions are further optimized, by employing an optimization technique, based on NSGAII algorithm.

In this work, it was considered 10 appliances (candidate solutions), for each type of appliance. On total, there was considered here, 7 type of appliances (Figs. 1 and 2).

Besides the budget constraint, other constraints were considered in this work (e.g. appliances noise, air conditioner capacity, water consumption, among others).

Thus, and considering the MAVT model, this problem can be defined as:

$$\max \quad V_m(x), \quad c/m = A, B, C$$
$$subject\ to\ x \in X \quad c/V_m(x) = [V_A(x), V_B(x), V_C(x)]^T \tag{4}$$

With x, being the decision variable, being defined as:

$$x \in X : x \in \left\{ x_{ij}^{(A_{jt})}, x_{ij}^{(B_{jt})}, x_{ij}^{(C_{jt})} \right\} \wedge t, i, j \in \mathbb{N} \tag{5}$$

where,

$$j = \{1, .., 10\} \wedge j = \{1, 2, .., 7\} \wedge t$$
$$= \{\{1, .., n_{A_j}\} \cup \{1, .., n_{B_j}\} \cup \{1, .., n_{C_j}\}\} \wedge n_{A_j}, n_{B_j}, n_{C_j} \in \mathbb{N} \tag{6}$$

Being $V_A(x), V_B(x)$ and $V_C(x)$, objective functions, referring each one, to a sustainability's dimension considered, namely; A-Economics, B-Social and C-Environment.

Therefore, each aggregate objective function, is achieved by:

$$V_g(x) = \sum_{j=1}^{n_j} \sum_{t=1}^{n_{g_j}} v_j(x_j^{(g_{jt})}) \quad w/g = \{A, B, C\} \wedge v_j(x_j^{(g_{jt})}) \wedge n_j, n_{g_j}, t, j \in \mathbb{N} \tag{7}$$

Thus, and through (7), the 3 objective functions, can be defined as:

$$Economic\ Well\text{-}being : \max V_A(x) = \sum_{j=1}^{n_j} \sum_{t=1}^{n_{A_j}} v_j(x_j^{(A_{jt})}) \tag{8}$$

$$Social\ Well\text{-}being : \max V_B(x) = \sum_{j=1}^{n_j} \sum_{t=1}^{n_{B_j}} v_j(x_j^{(B_{jt})}) \tag{9}$$

$$Environment\ Well\text{-}being : \max V_C(x) = \sum_{j=1}^{n_j} \sum_{t=1}^{n_{C_j}} \left(1 - v_j(x_j^{(C_{jt})})\right) \tag{10}$$

The second objective function (Social Well-being), is defined based on the attributes, established in this work together with the ones already defined on previous works, and regarding the remain objective functions ([10, 12] and [9, 13]).

Furthermore, the functions of value $V_A(x)$, $V_B(x)$ and $V_C(x)$, were combined into a unique aggregated cost function, to be further optimized, as the model's objective function. This objective function, will be pondered by a weigh factor $(\omega_g)$, expressing therefore, the relative importance given by the consumer to each sustainability's dimension, thus resulting into:

$$V_{Total}(x) = V(V_A(x), V_B(x), V_C(x)) = \omega_A \cdot V_A(x) + \omega_B \cdot V_B(x) + \omega_C \cdot V_C(x) \quad (11)$$

Thus, and based on (2), (7) and (11), the model's cost function, can be described as:

$$V_{Total}(x) = \sum_{j=1}^{n_j} \left\{ \omega_A \cdot \sum_{t=1}^{n_{A_j}} \left( \frac{\left( x_{efect.j}^{(A_{jt})} - x_{pior.j}^{(A_{jt})} \right)}{\left( x_{melhor.j}^{(A_{jt})} - x_{pior.j}^{(A_{jt})} \right)} \right) + \omega_B \cdot \sum_{t=1}^{n_{B_j}} \left( \frac{\left( x_{efect.j}^{(B_{jt})} - x_{pior.j}^{(B_{jt})} \right)}{\left( x_{melhor.j}^{(B_{jt})} - x_{pior.j}^{(B_{jt})} \right)} \right) \right.$$
$$\left. + \omega_C \cdot \sum_{t=1}^{n_{C_j}} \left( 1 - \left( \frac{\left( x_{efect.j}^{(C_{jt})} - x_{pior.j}^{(C_{jt})} \right)}{\left( x_{melhor.j}^{(C_{jt})} - x_{pior.j}^{(C_{jt})} \right)} \right) \right) \right\} \quad (12)$$

This objective function, is subject to a set of constraints, regarding the sustainability's dimension, such as:

Economic – Budget:

$$r_1 : \sum_{j=1}^{n_{dim}} I_j(x_j) \leq available\, budget\, (\eta_{disp.}) \Leftrightarrow \sum_{\substack{j=1 \\ j \neq 2}}^{n_j} x_{ij}^{(A_{j4})} + x_{i2}^{(A_{25})} \leq \eta_{disp.} \quad (13)$$

Social (Comfort) - Lighting (minimum Illuminance)

$$r_2 : \frac{x_1^{(B_{15})}}{A} K_1 \geq E_{min} \quad with \quad K_1 = \frac{F_u \cdot n}{F_d} \, (light\, properties) \quad (14)$$

Social (Comfort) - Heating/Cooling needs

$$r_3 : x_2^{(B_{23})} \geq Q_{th.\,Aquec.(proj.)} \quad (15)$$

$$r_4 : x_2^{(B_{24})} \geq Q_{th.\,Arref.(proj.)} \quad (16)$$

Environment – Noise:

$$\begin{cases} r_{51} : x_{i1}^{(B_{11})} \leq Noise_{def.1} \\ r_{52} : x_{i2}^{(B_{21})} \leq Noise_{def.2} \\ \quad \vdots \qquad\qquad\qquad\qquad c/i = 5 \; ej = \{2,3,4,5,7\} \\ r_{56} : x_{i6}^{(B_{61})} \leq Noise_{def.6} \\ r_{57} : x_{i7}^{(B_{71})} \leq Noise_{def.7} \end{cases} \qquad (17)$$

Environment – Water consumption

$$\begin{cases} r_{61} : x_{i3}^{(A.3.6.)} \times 1/\tau_{H_2O} \leq C_{MLR} \\ r_{62} : x_{i7}^{(A.7.5.)} \times 1/\tau_{H_2O} \leq C_{MLL} \end{cases} \qquad (18)$$

Since this work reflects a PhD research, and given the relevant results achieved, it was considered (at first approach) a model, that accounted only 2 of the 3 dimensions referred here. Then, it was developed a model with the tree approaches.

Therefore, the NSGAII's individual framework (Fig. 4) used here, regards the approach for the 2 and 3 dimensions of sustainability, since that for the approach with 2 dimensions, the structure is the same, although considering only 2 dimensions each.

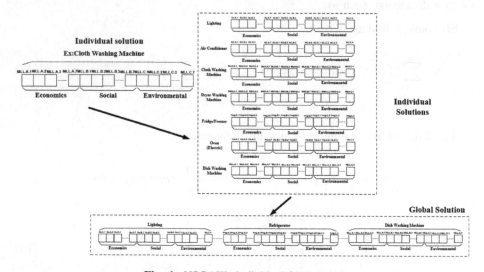

**Fig. 4.** NSGAII's individual framework.

Thus, on both approaches, it was used real codification for the NSGAII's individual framework (Fig. 5), given the nature of the decision variables, used in this work.

The case study, presented here, was used for both approaches, referred before and it was considered a consumer, who wants to buy a set of household appliances from the market to its home, namely; dryer machine, lighting, air conditioner, dish washing machine, washing machine, electric oven and refrigerator.

The same consumer has a budget of 2300 € to buy the appliances, and it's intended to obtain a set of sustainable options, that maximizes its social, economic and environment wellbeing, according to a set of tree relative importance weights, namely; $\omega_A$ (economic) and $\omega_B$ (social) and $\omega_C$ (environment).

The total number of the building's occupants is four. The area of the building, mainly the area of living room, was also considered, given the consumer's intention, by acquiring an air conditioner (heating and cooling needs), as well as to equip the building's living room with lighting.

The consumer's profile was also considered, through a set of assumptions based on the hours, weeks and years. However, the consumer can also define its usage profile, based on its needs, or by using the profile presented here, by default.

## 5 Results and Discussion

As it referred before, NSGAII (Non-Sorting Genetic Algorithm II) method was employed, by using Matlab, to optimize the aggregate function developed and presented on previous section.

Regarding the NSGAII's parameters, it was adopted the following techniques: roulette, as the selection method, double point, as the crossover method and normal random, as the mutation method.

The remaining parameters, regarding population size, crossover and mutation rate, were obtained and tested on previous works with only two dimensions [9, 13]. Such results were achieved after being performed several runs and experiments, regarding the change of such parameters.

The stop criteria were also tested, where it was achieved the maximum number of generations to be considered.

The behavior of NSGAII, in terms of combinations with crossover and mutation rates, was also tested on [9], by preforming several combinations of crossover and mutation rates, to achieve a suitable combination of both.

Thus, the NSGAII's parameters used, were; a population size of 120 individuals, a max number of generations of 80, a crossover rate of 0,75 and a mutation rate of 0,15.

The NSGA II, was then applied to preform several scenarios, given the consumer's possible concerns, which was expressed by the correspondent values in terms of "weights", and regarding each one to a sustainability's dimension, i.e.; $\omega_A$ (economics) and $\omega_B$ (social) and $\omega_C$ (environment).

Therefore, and for each scenario, it was considered a different set of weights $(\omega_A, \omega_B, \omega_C)$, in order to obtain different Pareto frontiers/surfaces, where each node represents a candidate solution, i.e., an aggregate sustainable solution, formed by the household appliances, regarding each energy service to be required.

The purpose, was to assess the model's behavior through the achieved results, namely by assessing the impact of changing $\omega_A$, $\omega_B$ and $\omega_C$.

On Fig. 5, it's presented different scenarios, regarding only two sustainability's dimensions.

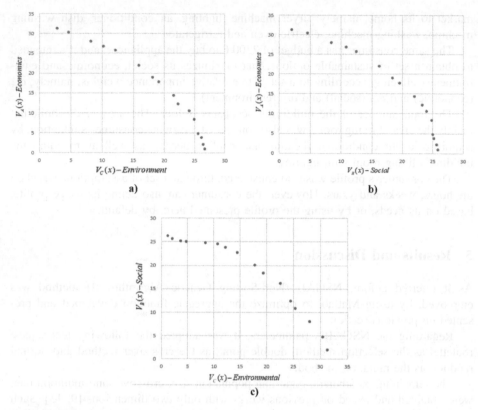

**Fig. 5.** A Pareto Frontier, considering different scenarios of $\omega_A$, $\omega_B$, $\omega_C$; (a) Economical vs Environmental ($\omega_A = 0,72$, $\omega_B = 0,00$, $\omega_C = 0,28$), (b) Economical vs Social ($\omega_A = 0,72$, $\omega_B = 0,28$, $\omega_C = 0,00$), (c) Social vs Environmental ($\omega_A = 0,00$, $\omega_B = 0,72$, $\omega_C = 0,28$).

Sixteen candidate solutions were chosen considering the last generation by the algorithm, achieving therefore, a Pareto frontier.

Each point (or node) shows a global sustainable solution, formed by a set of sustainable (and individual) solutions (electrical appliances) by considering each appliance type, to be acquired by the consumer.

By looking at Fig. 5, it's possible to see the different trade-offs existed between the different scenarios and the impact of the correspondent weights (relative importance) used. For instance, on Fig. 5(a), we can see the trade-off, existed between the Economic and the Environmental well-being, with other trade-offs being noticed on Figs. 5 (b) and (c).

The impacts of the weights ($\omega_A, \omega_B, \omega_C$), are also evident, where the predominance of each dimension is achieved with raising of the correspondent weight (e.g. Fig. 5(c)).

One of the nodes, it's presented on Table 2, regarding each scenario, by accounting a budget of 2300 € and 10 years of life cycle.

**Table 2.** A set of achieved solutions, regarding different scenarios ($\omega_A$, $\omega_B$, $\omega_C$).

| | Electrical Household Appliance | Standard Solution Total Invest. (€) | Efficient sol. Total Invest (€) | Investment Saving (€) | Energy Consumption Savings (€) | Water Consumption (avoided) (l) | CO2 emissions (avoided) (kg) | Manufacturer | Model type |
|---|---|---|---|---|---|---|---|---|---|
| **Scenario 1** Economics vs Social $\omega_A = 0,72, \omega_B = 0,00, \omega_C = 0,28$ | Light | 15.89 | 09.53 | 5.34 | 59.40 | - | 28.90 | GE | EFL23W |
| | Air Conditioning | 368.00 | 299.00 | 69.00 | 1320.60 | - | 1315.70 | Whirlpool | PACW9HP |
| | Refrigerator | 234.00 | 399.00 | −265.00 | 709.30 | - | 9.72 | BECKEN | Bc2016 lx |
| | Washing Machine | 310.00 | 349.00 | −39.00 | 3.20 | 423.00 | 6.90 | Bosch | SMS25AI00E |
| | Dishwasher Machine | 272.20 | 249.90 | −33.00 | 5.60 | 322.10 | 95.10 | INDESIT | EWE71252 W |
| | Oven | 170.00 | 199.00 | −29.00 | 1.70 | - | 2.20 | Zanussi | ZZB21601XV |
| | Clothes dryer | 349.00 | 419.00 | −70.0 | 12.30 | - | 1.70 | Electrolux | EDP2074PDW |
| | Total | 1719.09 | 1924.43 | −361.66 | 2111.15 | 745.10 | 1460.22 | - | - |
| **Scenario 2** Economics vs Environmental $\omega_A = 0,72, \omega_B = 0,00, \omega_C = 0,28$ | Light | 15.89 | 09.53 | 5.34 | 59.40 | - | 28.90 | GE | EFL23W |
| | Air Conditioning | 368.00 | 299.00 | 69.00 | 1320.60 | - | 1315.70 | Whirlpool | PACW9HP |
| | Refrigerator | 250.00 | 529.00 | −279.00 | 708.10 | - | 8.70 | Candy | CFET 6182W |
| | Washing Machine | 310.00 | 349.00 | −39.00 | 3.20 | 423.00 | 6.90 | Bosch | SMS25AI00E |
| | Dishwasher Machine | 262.00 | 294.00 | −32.00 | 6.90 | 317.00 | 94.80 | Siemens | WI12A222ES |
| | Oven | 170.00 | 199.00 | −29.00 | 1.70 | - | 2.20 | Zanussi | ZZB21601XV |
| | Clothes dryer | 349.00 | 419.00 | −70.0 | 12.30 | - | 1.70 | Electrolux | EDP2074PDW |
| | Total | 1727.89 | 2098.53 | −374.66 | 2112.20 | 740.00 | 1458.90 | - | - |
| **Scenario 3** Social vs Environmental $\omega_A = 0,00, \omega_B = 0,52, \omega_C = 0,48$ | Light | 15.89 | 69.65 | 5.34 | 59.40 | - | 28.90 | OSRAM | 3316242 |
| | Air Conditioning | 352.00 | 279.00 | 69.00 | 1319.50 | - | 1322.60 | SAMSUNG | AQV09PSBN |
| | Refrigerator | 250.00 | 529.00 | −279.00 | 708.10 | - | 8.70 | Candy | CFET 6182W |
| | Washing Machine | 320.10 | 351.99 | −38.10 | 2.20 | 432.05 | 7.80 | BALAY | 3VS303IP |
| | Dishwasher Machine | 262.00 | 294.00 | −32.00 | 6.90 | 317.00 | 94.80 | Siemens | WI12A222ES |
| | Oven | 171.00 | 701.00 | −28.30 | 2.82 | - | 2.33 | Electrolux | EZC2430AOX |
| | Clothes dryer | 368.00 | 449.00 | −68.00 | 10.20 | - | 1.82 | BOSCH | WTE84107EE |
| | Total | 1738.99 | 2673,64 | −371.06 | 2109.12 | 749.05 | 1466.95 | - | - |

According to Table 2, if the consumer, choses the solutions provided by this method, he can save for about 1727,89 €, avoid for about 1458,9 kg of $CO_2$ and saving approximately 740,06 L, regarding water consumption, based on the life cycle defined (10 years).

Based on Table 2, Scenario 3, if the consumer choses the solutions, provided by this method, he can save for about 1738,99 €, avoid for about 1466,95 kg of $CO_2$ and saving approximately 749,05 regarding water consumption.

Based on both trade-offs, presented above, it was considered a scenario with three dimensions and their correspondent consumer's relative importance, i.e., $\omega_A = 0,65$, $\omega_B = 0,25$ and $\omega_C = 0,10$. The correspondent Pareto surface is obtained on Fig. 6.

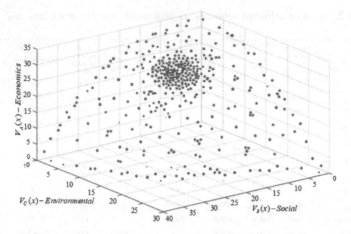

**Fig. 6.** Pareto Surface. Economical vs Social vs Environmental ($\omega_A$ = 0,65, $\omega_B$ = 0,25, $\omega_C$ = 0,10).

Based on Fig. 6, in the obtained Pareto surface, the crowding distance between the final solutions obtained, is higher in the region where the Economic dimension has more dominance, followed by Social, and at last, the Environmental one. This dominance order, between each dimension of sustainability, is somehow expected, given the relative importance's values (weight) considered ins this case for each dimension ($\omega_A$ = 0,65, $\omega_B$ = 0,25 and $\omega_C$ = 0,10).

One of the nodes from that region, are shown on Table 3, regarding a sustainable solution, achieved for a budget of 2300 € and a life cycle defined, of 10 years.

**Table 3.** One of sustainable solutions, achieved from the pareto surface ($\omega_A$ = 0,65, $\omega_B$ = 0,25 and $\omega_C$ = 0,10).

| Electrical Household Appliance | Standard Solution Total Invest. (€) | Efficient sol. Total Invest (€) | Investment Saving (€) | Energy Consumption Savings (€) | Water Consumption (avoided) (l) | CO2 emissions (avoided) (kg) | Manufacturer | Model type |
|---|---|---|---|---|---|---|---|---|
| Light | 16.88 | 49.04 | 5.35 | 62.20 | - | 27.60 | Phillips | LEDspotMV |
| Air Conditioning | 352.00 | 279.00 | 69.00 | 1319.50 | - | 1322.60 | SAMSUNG | AQV09PSBN |
| Refrigerator | 234.00 | 399.00 | −265.00 | 709.30 | - | 9.72 | BECKEN | Bc2016 Ix |
| Washing Machine | 310.00 | 349.00 | −39.00 | 3.20 | 423.00 | 6.90 | Bosch | SMS25AI00E |
| Dishwasher Machine | 272.20 | 249.90 | −33.00 | 5.60 | 322.10 | 95.10 | INDESIT | EWE71252 W |
| Oven | 171.00 | 701.00 | −28.30 | 2.82 | - | 2.33 | Electrolux | EZC2430AOX |
| Clothes dryer | 368.00 | 449.00 | −68.00 | 10.20 | - | 1.82 | BOSCH | WTE84107EE |
| Total | 1724. 80 | 2475.94 | −262.65 | 2112.30 | 745.10 | 1466.07 | - | - |

According to Table 3, if the consumer, choses the solutions from this method, he can save for about 2112,30 €, avoiding for about 1466,07 kg of $CO_2$ and saving (approx.) 745,10 L in terms of water consumption, according to the life cycle considered in this study.

## 6 Conclusions and Future Work

In this work, it was proposed a decision support method, to achieve sustainable electrical appliances, existed on market to a consumer, according to tree dimensions of sustainability, namely, Economic, Social and Environment.

The proposed approach has made use of a set of established criteria, in order to preselect a set of candidate solutions, existed on market, and by following the consumer requirements.

By using such criteria (adjustable to each consumer's requirements), it's possible to define the decision space, formed by a set of candidate solutions, according to each type of appliance considered to be bought by the consumer.

Additionally, it was used additional criteria, integrated with MAVT, in order to model the preferences of the consumer, based on the tree dimensions of the problem, presented in this study.

The main goal of these procedure was to improve the consumer well-being, by acting on tree problem dimensions referred above, and according to the importance, given by the decision-agent (consumer).

After modelling the preferences of the consumer, where it was also accounted the ecological impact in terms of savings (e.g. water and $CO_2$), together with economic issues (energy consumption and initial investment savings) based on the lifecycle cost assessment (LCCA) of each household appliance, NSGAII was then applied, by maximizing the tree objective functions referred before.

The method presented in this work, allows to maximize all the tree dimensions of sustainability, considered here, by getting a group of sustainable (and alternative) appliances, existed on market, and suitable to each consumer preferences and concerns.

This also allows the consumer, to achieve a set of savings regarding energy consumption, CO2 emissions, and water consumption.

As a future work, this approach could be extended into other energy services with a relevant impact in terms of sustainable development, like information technology's equipment's (e.g. computers, printers, among others).

According to what was mentioned before, all the defined attributes can be used into other world regions, although with some adjustments, given the differences on energy label classification frameworks.

**Acknowledgments.** This work was partially supported by the Fundação para a Ciência e Tecnologia, UIDB/00066/2020 (CTS – Center of Technology and Systems).

## References

1. IEA: Energy Efficiency 2017 – Market Reports Series, OECD/IEA (2017)
2. Gul, M., Patidar, S.: Understanding the energy consumption and occupancy of a multipurpose academic building. Energy Build. **87**, 155–165 (2015). ISSN 0378-7788

3. Manual da Etiqueta Energética, ADENE, Lisboa (2017). ISBN 978-972-8646-36-3
4. Wong, I.L., Krüger, E.: Comparing energy efficiency labelling systems in the EU and Brazil: implications, challenges, barriers and opportunities. Energy Policy **109**, 310–323 (2017)
5. Fell, M.: Energy services: a conceptual review. Energy Res. Soc. Sci. **27**, 129–140 (2017)
6. Hoxha, E., Jusselme, T.: On the necessity of improving the environmental impacts of furniture and appliances in net-zero energy buildings. Sci. Total Environ. **596–597**, 405–416 (2017). ISSN 0048-9697
7. Ting, T.O., Rao, M.V., Loo, K.C.: A novel approach for unit commitment problem via an effective hybrid particle swarm optimization. IEEE Trans. Power Syst. **21**, 411–418 (2006)
8. Ko, M.J., Kim, Y.S., Chung, M.H., Jeon, H.C.: Multi-objective design for a hybrid energy system using genetic algorithm. Energies **8**, 2924–2949 (2015)
9. Matias, J.C.O., Santos, R., Abreu, A.: A decision support approach to provide sustainable solutions to the consumer, by using electrical appliances. Sustainability **11**, 1143 (2019)
10. Santos, R., Matias, J.C.O., Abreu, A.: Energy efficiency in buildings by using evolutionary algorithms: an approach to provide efficiency choices to the consumer, considering the rebound effect. In: Camarinha-Matos, L.M., Adu-Kankam, K.O., Julashokri, M. (eds.) DoCEIS 2018. IAICT, vol. 521, pp. 120–129. Springer, Cham (2018). https://doi.org/10. 1007/978-3-319-78574-5_12
11. Randall, M., Rawlins, T., Lewis, A., Kipouros, T.: Performance comparison of evolutionary algorithms for airfoil design. Procedia Comput. Sci. **51**, 2267–2276 (2015)
12. Santos, R.S., Matias, J.C.O., Abreu, A., Reis, F.: Evolutionary algorithms on reducing energy consumption in buildings: an approach to provide smart and efficiency choices, considering the rebound effect. Comput. Ind. Eng. **126**, 729–755 (2018). https://doi.org/10. 1016/j.cie.2018.09.050. ISSN 0360 8352
13. Santos, R., Matias, J.C.O., Abreu, A.: A new approach to provide sustainable solutions for residential sector. In: Camarinha-Matos, L.M., Almeida, R., Oliveira, J. (eds.) DoCEIS 2019. IAICT, vol. 553, pp. 329–342. Springer, Cham (2019). https://doi.org/10.1007/978-3-030-17771-3_29
14. Chuah, J.W., Raghunathan, A., Jha, N.K.: ROBESim: a retrofit oriented building energy simulator based on EnergyPlus. Energy Build. **66**, 88–103 (2013)
15. Pombo, O., Allacker, K., Rivela, B., Neila, J.: Sustainability assessment of energy saving measures: a multi-criteria approach for residential buildings retrofitting—a case study of the Spanish housing stock. Energy Build. **116**, 384–394 (2016)
16. Asadi, E., da Silva, M.G., Antunes, C.H., Dias, L.: Multi-objective optimization for building retrofit strategies: a model and an application. Energy Build. **44**, 81–87 (2012)
17. Kaklauskas, A., Zavadskas, E.K., Raslanas, S.: Multivariant design and multiple criteria analysis of building refurbishments. Energy Build. **37**(4), 361–372 (2005)
18. Jafari, A., Valentin, V.: An optimization framework for building energy retrofits decision-making. Build. Environ. **115**, 118–129 (2017). ISSN 0360-1323
19. Mauro, G.M., Hamdy, M., Vanoli, G.P., Bianco, N., Hensen, J.L.M.: A new methodology for investigating the cost-optimality of energy retrofitting a building category. Energy Build. **107**, 456–478 (2015)
20. Heo, Y., Augenbroe, G., Graziano, D., Muehleisen, R.T., Guzowski, L.: Scalable methodology for large scale building energy improvement: relevance of calibration in model-based retrofit analysis. Build. Environ. **87**, 342–350 (2015)

# A Risk Assessment Model for Decision Making in Innovation Projects

Vitor Anes[1,3](✉), Luis Reis[3], Elsa Henriques[3], and António Abreu[1,2]

[1] Instituto Superior de Engenharia de Lisboa, Instituto Politécnico de Lisboa,
Rua Conselheiro Emídio Navarro, 1, 19559-007 Lisbon, Portugal
vitor.anes@isel.pt
[2] CTS - Uninova, Lisbon, Portugal
[3] IDMEC, Instituto Superior Técnico, Universidade de Lisboa,
Av. Rovisco Pais, 1, 1049-001 Lisbon, Portugal

**Abstract.** Recent studies on innovation show a marked trend towards an increasing complexity of innovation management. As a result, innovative project managers are normally confronted with ever-increasing complexities and ever-increasing degrees of uncertainty in decision making. In this paper, a new qualitative risk assessment model is proposed in order to overcome the limitations found in practice, providing new insights regarding the suitability of qualitative risk assessment models to support decision making activities in innovation projects.

**Keywords:** Innovation · Risk assessment · Qualitative risk · Aggregated risk · Decision making

## 1 Introduction

In many cases, innovation projects have been postponed or canceled due to incorrect risk evaluations, leading to financial and/or opportunity losses which creates negative impacts on organizations and societies. In this sense, it is important to select innovation projects using reliable risk analysis tools and techniques. Risk assessment is becoming critical to organizations especially in the innovation area; however, important risk factors are being systematically omitted because quantitative data is usually unavailable in innovation projects, which makes quantitative risk assessment tools inappropriate to deal with such risk scenarios. The alternative is to use qualitative risk assessment tools which are becoming important in risk related activities. Despite the importance of qualitative risk analysis in modern economic activities, there are very few qualitative risk models available in literature. A literature survey shows that further developments are needed to extend qualitative risk models to incorporate risk assessment and management in projects. In this approach developments are needed in several areas, such as risk integration in project development and implementation, risk modulation of needs and wants, risk of underperformance in project phases, risk of combined project phases, and risk in quality control. The risk evaluation in these areas is of utmost importance, especially in the selection of innovation projects which is a decision-making activity that has several challenges in practice. The objective is to choose the best alternative

© IFIP International Federation for Information Processing 2020
Published by Springer Nature Switzerland AG 2020
L. M. Camarinha-Matos et al. (Eds.): DoCEIS 2020, IFIP AICT 577, pp. 79–90, 2020.
https://doi.org/10.1007/978-3-030-45124-0_7

among possible alternatives to obtain maximum outcomes with lower resources allocation. This can be a hard task when available information is scarce and imprecise, therefore, uncertainty is a common factor in decision making that strongly challenges decision makers. In this sense, qualitative models to evaluate aggregated risk in innovative projects are important tools that need to be developed and improved for innovation activities. In this paper, a model to evaluate qualitative risk of projects is proposed. The model evaluates qualitative aggregated risk considering a generic framework easily applicable to a wide range of projects. It will allow to prioritize innovation projects according to their risk feature that supports decision making activities.

## 2 Contribution to Life Improvement

Risk evaluation is an important procedure that supports decision making activities. It allows to set risk scenarios with risk variables that model scenario behaviors (outputs) accordingly to resources and inputs. Consequently, decisions can be monitored regarding their influence on a given risk scenario, which can be useful to optimize results. For instance, in mechanical design, risk assessment can be used to improve reliability of new products and services during their design and development phases. In this case, risk can be evaluated based on a set of decisions steps that range from user's requirements identification to acceptance testing, each one of these decisions can increase or decrease the risk of obtaining unwanted results in design. This subject becomes extremely important in cases where human lives can be jeopardizing due to a poor design. There are many cases where human lives were lost due unreliable decisions in design activities. One example is the space shuttle Challenger disaster in 1986 where 7 crew members were killed due to an o-ring seal that was not designed to handle the low temperatures experienced in this launch. Later, in 2003 the space shuttle Columbia disintegrated upon reentering Earth's atmosphere killing 7 people. The risk-management scenario failed to recognize the implications of a debris impact on the Columbia left wing leading to the catastrophic accident. Other example is the Chinese bullet train crash in 2011 that killed 40 people due to a lightning strike. The accident report pointed out design flaws in control equipment that lead to an improper handling of the lightning strike. In literature one can find many other examples like the ones mentioned above that lead to conclude that risk management in association with design activities is of utmost importance to avoid catastrophic accidents with loss of human lives. The most used tools in risk assessment and management are strongly based on quantitative data, however, in many cases, like the aforementioned ones, information required to use these tools is scarce or none, i.e. the typical tools in risk assessment are data based which are useless in cases where information is scarce, because they are statistically based which in turn requires access to events log which is a condition difficult to fulfill in innovation projects. The alternative to overcome this issue is to use qualitative risk assessment tools making use of expert's experience to evaluate risk scenarios and respective failure modes. Therefore, qualitative risk assessment of innovative projects actively contributes to the life improvement of societies by promoting reliability in innovation.

# 3 State of the Art

The most common way to rank projects according to their risk is using Multi-Criteria Decision Making (MCDM) methods which in some cases are complex to implement due to their formulation or due to the limitations to get reliable quantitative data [1]. Very few of them can deal with uncertainty and human judgment; examples of these models are the Multi-Attribute Utility Theory (MAUT), Fuzzy Set Theory, ELECTRE, PROMETHEE, and DEMATEL [2]. Multi-Attribute Utility Theory [3] is an improvement of the Multi-Attribute Value Theory and considers risk and uncertainty to support multi criteria decision making of real-world problems. These methods need a large amount of data which can be a shortcoming for applications with scarce information available. Moreover, it requires an accurate identification of the decision makers' preferences which can be difficult to get since the decision makers weights may change during the project design and implementation. The strong feature of these models is the capability to account with uncertainty which is the reason of their popularity. Fuzzy Set Theory [4] also allows to consider imprecise and insufficient information, it is widely applied in a wide range of applications including MCDM. Fuzzy logic models comprise a set of input and output functions to model a given system. It is based on predefined if-then rules to define the relation between inputs and outputs. It depends on the user expertise and experience to adequately select or create membership functions which for a non-fuzzy logic user can be quite difficult to develop being a drawback. Fuzzy logic has been used in risk assessment in decision making activities and risk management in several areas of application ranging from engineering and economics to medical and management [5, 6]. ELECTRE is an outranking method developed in the 1960s by Bernard Roy to solve problems related to the weighted sum technique [7]. This method has several versions, at least 6 versions, and the main applications are on choosing, ranking and sorting. The main advantage is the ability to consider imprecise information; disadvantages are the high complexity of results interpretation, and the outranking procedure do not allow the comparison between alternatives [8]. PROMETHEE stands for Preference Ranking Organization METhod for Enrichment Evaluation and is also a MCDA outranking method. There are two versions of this method, the first one is the PROMETHEE I which performs partial rankings, and the second one is the PROMETHEE II which makes a complete ranking [9]. The method advantages are the ease of use, the capability to deal with quantitative and qualitative data and criteria. Disadvantages are the strong computational requirements, rank reversal [10], an unstructured decision problem which makes difficult decision makers to have a complete overview over the problem. The original method does not have a procedure to weight criteria; however, more recently pair-wise comparison procedures have been included into PROMETHEE analysis to overcome this issue [11, 12]. DEMATEL stands for DEcision MAking Trial and Evaluation Laboratory, it is a MCDM technique developed by the Battelle Geneva Research Centre to structure causal relationships [13]. This method considers the interdependence between factors and can be used to analyze complex problems being strongly used in decision making activities under imprecise and uncertain information [14]. The aforementioned models have been used to evaluate risk of projects, most of them requires quantitative data to deal with uncertainty and the ones that do not require quantitative data are complex to implement. These models were developed to generic MCDM applications and were not specific developed to risk evaluation, in this sense the development of specific models to evaluate qualitative risk is of utmost importance to support decision making activities in situation of scarce information.

## 4 Research Contribution

In this section, a fuzzy logic model is proposed based in the v-model framework to evaluate aggregated risk of projects under qualitative approaches. This framework is applicable to a wide range of projects which makes the developed model also applicable to an extensive number of risk scenarios, which is a feature very appreciated by the end user which normally pursuits a universal tool to deal with different scenarios. The v-model framework was initially developed to characterize the life cycle and management activities of projects and graphically summarizes the main phases usually found in any project, where the project phases activities and results are described and dynamically analyzed. The objective is to improve quality, reduce production and development costs, and improve communication between the project stakeholders and project developers.

The v-model was independently developed in the 1980s by the German government and by the Hughes Aircraft Company, an USA company. Nowadays, it is widely used in commercial and defense programs being the v-model the official project management methodology of these two countries.

There are three main versions, namely, the German v-model which is similar to PRINCE2, a UK government project management methodology, the General testing v-model framework commonly used in software development, and the US government standard which is more focused on narrower systems development.

The main advantage of this framework is the users' participation in the model implementation and maintenance. This feature brings a strong insight to the v-model users which promotes quality and flexibility when improvements or changes to meet requirements are needed. Moreover, each project phases, inherent activities and objectives are described in detail during the v-model implementation, which promotes focus and assistance during the project implementation and update.

The mind-set required to use the v-model framework is particularly suitable to perform risk analysis because it promotes an in-deep knowledge of each project phase, considering internal and external factors as well has the interconnection between the project phases, due to this reason the v-model was chosen among many others such as the waterfall or spiral model. The v-model framework is graphically represented by a v comprising seven phases sorted into two branches as depicted in Fig. 1. The left branch comprises three phases, namely, the user requirements, functional requirements, and design specifications at both high and low levels. The right branch comprises the testing project phases where verification and validation activities are performed together with the project phases. The v-model implementation starts at the v top-left (requirements identification) then proceeds down towards the implementation phase and then up reaching the top-right (system testing), highlighting different phases with different levels, including verification and testing.

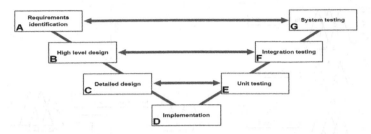

**Fig. 1.** The v-model 7 phases.

The v-model framework starts with the requirements identification activities (phase A) to identify the user's needs. Next, follows the high-level design (phase B) where conceptual design and integration tests are defined. Phase C, detailed design, is a low-level design activity that produces all technical components and specification documents needed to implement the project, in this phase the unit tests are also defined. Phase D, implementation, covers the project implementation activities based on the outcomes achieved in phases A, B and C. Next, in phase E, the tests defined in phase C are implemented. The results are correlated with the specifications established in phase C, if the specifications are not met then a redesign is needed. Phase F, integration testing, tests the conceptual design in order to verify the system function across all components. Phase G, system testing, correlates the product performance with the users' requirements, this phase also may include acceptance tests performed in live environment.

**Qualitative Risk Assessment Model**
Figure 2 shows the conceptual idea of the qualitative risk assessment model implemented to evaluate aggregated risk of projects using the seven v-model phases and fuzzy logic functions. In the most-left region, it is depicted the v-model seven phases, ranging from A to G. For each phase, it is identified the three most critical basic events that may lead to the phase hazard. For each one of these basic events it is evaluated the respective qualitative risk in respect to the phase hazard.

Next, the phase risk in respect to the phase hazard is computed using a fuzzy logic function (MISO), this function has as input the qualitative risk values of the phase basic events and has as output the phase risk. This approach will allow to enter with more than one basic event in phase risk assessment, which is a contribution, since the common practice is to consider only the basic event that has the highest qualitative risk, however, this approach underestimates the phase risk.

To illustrate this subject, Fig. 3 shows two different scenarios, (a) and (b), for a given project phase, where it is represented the risk of three basic events for each scenario. Both cases have the same maximum risk, i.e., 0.7, however in case 3 (Fig. 2b) the risk of basic events 2 and 3 is much higher than in case 1 (Fig. 3a), in this sense, and considering that a basic event occurrence has a probabilistic behavior, neglecting

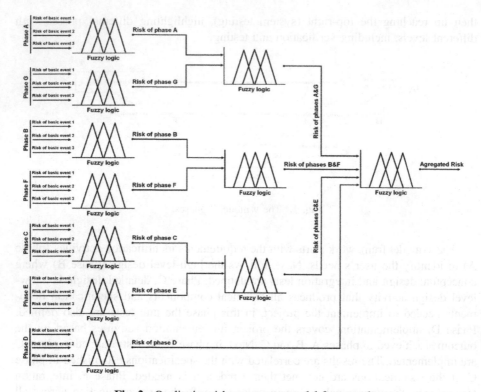

**Fig. 2.** Qualitative risk assessment model framework

the contribution of secondary basic events by considering only the maximum risk value found underestimates the overall risk. In this sense, the proposed approach overcomes this issue by entering with more than one basic event in risk assessment.

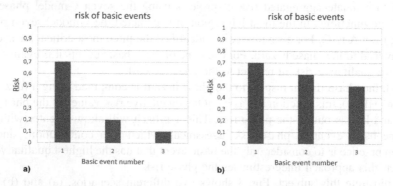

**Fig. 3.** Basic events risk (a) risk scenario 1, (b) risk scenario 2.

After evaluating the risk of single phases, the aggregated risk between the v-model phases is computed in two stages, first, the aggregated risk of phases within the same level (AG, BF, CE) is evaluated using a TISO type of fuzzy functions. The inputs are the risk obtained for single phases and the output is the risk of combined phases, namely, AG, BF and CE. Then, the project aggregated risk is computed considering the risk calculated for the aggregated phases AG, BF, CE, and phase D, using a four variable fuzzy logic function (MISO), where the inputs are the risk obtained for the three combined phases (AG, BF and CE) plus the risk of the single phase D.

**Input Membership Functions**
To evaluate the risk of single and combined phases described in previous subsection it was used triangular membership functions for input as presented in Fig. 4; vertical axis represents the degree of membership and the horizontal axis represents the risk. Triangular membership functions are an effective way to modulate fuzzy inputs in decision problems and are easy to implement [1].

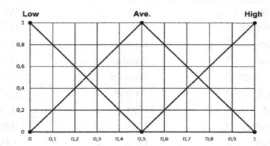

**Fig. 4.** Typical triangular membership functions.

**Output Membership Functions**
Trapezoidal membership functions for output were developed and modelled using the risk isosurface function (RI) [15] to evaluate the risk of single and combined phases where the order of importance of each input is considered.

The risk isosurface function is a FMEA based risk assessment function to evaluate qualitative risk and was developed to overcome the shortcomings found in the original risk priority number (RPN), namely, the non-injectivity and non-surjectivity which may lead to incoherent results. Equation (1) shows the RI function for n risk variables.

$$RI(x_1, x_2, \ldots, x_n)_{x_1 > x_2 > \ldots > x_n} = \sum_{i=1}^{n} (x_i - 1) \cdot \mu^{n-i} + 1 \tag{1}$$

where $x_1, x_2, \ldots, x_n$ are risk variables, $\mu$ is the scale rating maximum value, and $x_1 > x_2 > \ldots > x_n$ is the order of importance between risk variables. Equation (2) shows an example of Eq. (1) set for a four variables risk space.

$$RI(x_1, x_2, x_3, x_4)_{x_1 > x_2 > x_3 > x_4} = (x_1 - 1) \cdot \mu^3 + (x_2 - 1) \cdot \mu^2 + (x_3 - 1) \cdot \mu + (x_4 - 1) + 1 \quad (2)$$

To introduce the new method developed to create the output membership functions, the data described in Table 1 is used as an illustrative example. In this Table, two inputs A and B are considered; each one of them has three membership functions Low, Average, and High which can be represented in a fuzzy set score as 1, 2, and 3 respectively. These fuzzy set scores can also represent the weight of each membership function, therefore, Low weights 1, it has the lowest weight and High weights 3, which means that has the highest weight. The number of permutations with repetition is given by $n^k$, where $n$ is the number of elements in a set and $k$ is the number of elements in the subset. Therefore, in this case $3^2$ yields 9 permutations as shown in Table 1.

**Table 1.** Example of rules and output definition for two inputs – single output function.

| Rule number | Input A | Fuzzy set score | Input B | Fuzzy set score | RI | α | β |
|---|---|---|---|---|---|---|---|
| 1 | Low | 1 | Low | 1 | 0,11 | 0 | 0,11 |
| 2 | Average | 2 | Low | 1 | 0,22 | 0,11 | 0,22 |
| 3 | High | 3 | Low | 1 | 0,33 | 0,22 | 0,33 |
| 4 | Low | 1 | Average | 2 | 0,44 | 0,33 | 0,44 |
| 5 | Average | 2 | Average | 2 | 0,56 | 0,44 | 0,56 |
| 6 | High | 3 | Average | 2 | 0,67 | 0,56 | 0,67 |
| 7 | Low | 1 | High | 3 | 0,78 | 0,67 | 0,78 |
| 8 | Average | 2 | High | 3 | 0,89 | 0,78 | 0,89 |
| 9 | High | 3 | High | 3 | 1,00 | 0,89 | 1,00 |

In the first column we have the rule number from 1 to 9, at columns 2 to 5 we have the linguistic and fuzzy set scores for inputs A and B. The number of lines is equal to the number of permutations. In case of three inputs we have $3^3$ permutations and so on, also the number of rules is given by the number of unique permutations. These permutations are not repeated; therefore, they are unique combinations that can be related to their inherent risk. This can be made using the risk isosurface function set for the number of inputs of the fuzzy logic function considering their order of importance.

Therefore, firstly it is necessary identify the inputs order of importance which sets the position of each input value (fuzzy set score) in the risk isosurface function. For example, suppose that input B is more important than input A the risk isosurface function is set as follows in Eq. (3)

$$RI(A, B)_{B > A} = \frac{3 \cdot B + A - 3}{9} \quad (3)$$

where 3 is the number of possible scores in the fuzzy set, namely 1, 2 and 3, and 9 is the RI maximum value for the fuzzy set values considered.

Column 6 of Table 1 shows the RI results for each permutation obtained for this example. Considering that, inputs A and B represent inputs of risk therefore the output evaluated by the RI function represents also a measure of risk which is a aggregated risk between inputs A and B. Correlating the fuzzy sets scores and their permutations with the RI results it can be concluded that there is a conformity between the permutations and the risk level obtained with RI. For example, comparing rules 2 and 4 it can be concluded that the order of importance considered, B > A, allows to differentiate these two rules, also the highest measure of risk in input (rule 6) has as output the highest RI value, the opposite occurs for rule 1 which has the lowest input risk. In the last two columns of Table 1 it is shown the values to define the output membership functions for each rule.

Regarding this approach we use a trapezoidal membership function for each permutation in order to define the output of the fuzzy logic function. The implementation of these membership functions usually requires four points to create the trapezoidal shape as shown in Fig. 5 where the output membership function graph for the example of Table 1 is shown as well as the points $x_1$ to $x_4$ of membership function number 3. In this sense, the coordinates of these points are given for each permutation as $x_{1i}(\alpha_i, 0)$; $x_{2i}(\alpha_i, 1)$; $x_{3i}(\beta_i, 1)$; and $x_{4i}(\beta_i, 0)$, where $\alpha$ and $\beta$ are the values of columns 7 and 8 of Table 1, and $i$ represents the permutation number which ranges from 1 to $n^k$.

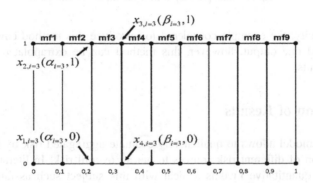

**Fig. 5.** Example of output membership functions.

The $\alpha$ values are obtained by shifting down 1 row the RI results and the $\beta$ values are equal to the respective RI values. In this way, there is no overlap between membership functions which allows to create an injective and surjective risk function, therefore each permutation has their unique measure of risk. Since each permutation has their own numbered membership function and since each rule definition is based on the fuzzy set scores permutation, thus the rule number is equal to the number of the membership function. In this approach there is no overlap between output membership functions which allows to differentiate the risk measure of each fuzzy set permutation. The methods described in this example can be applicable to define fuzzy logic output membership functions for functions with more than two inputs, to do that it is necessary define the order of importance of each input and them set the risk isosurface function to the number of inputs to obtain the RI results for each possible permutation. Figure 6 shows the output graph of the combined risk for inputs A and B of Table 1 example. The surface shape is in accordance with the risk inference performed based on the inputs and outputs considered showing a continuous range from 0 to 1.

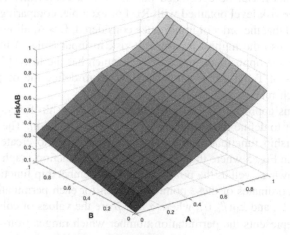

**Fig. 6.** Example output plot for inputs A and B.

For simplicity, the example considered to introduce this method covers only two risk inputs and one output, however, this method can be extrapolated for a higher number of inputs.

## 5  Discussion of Results

The proposed model allows to qualitatively evaluate aggregated risk by incorporating the contribution of different risk sources to get an overall risk. In literature it can be found several quantitative models to deal with this subject such as fault tree based models, event tree based models or even MCDM models as discussed in the state of the art section, but at the best authors' knowledge, qualitative models to evaluate aggregated risk are not available in literature. In this sense the proposed model contributes to the body of knowledge in qualitative risk assessment.

In fact, there are several qualitative models to evaluate risk, but none of them evaluates aggregated risk. Failure modes and effect analysis (FMEA) is the most known qualitative risk model and the most used in practice. This model is easy to learn and use but has several shortcomings related to the way in which the risk is evaluated, due to that FMEA only prioritizes the risk of basic events and do not evaluates the respective risk of each basic event which is a drawback. Despite that it is widely disseminated in industry due to its ease of use. On the other hand, the Risk Isosurface function overcomes the limitations found in FMEA allowing the evaluation of qualitative risk with a difficulty level very similar to the one found in FMEA.

Due to that, the RI function was used to develop the output membership functions and inference rules used in the aggregated risk model. The method proposed to implement the inference rules and output membership functions guarantees that the fuzzy logic model is totally defined in its domain which is a plus since the quality of the output results is strongly related to the uniformity of the inference rules. Moreover, the risk surface depicted in Fig. 6 shows that the risk variation is in accordance with the variation of inputs which indicates that an increase of inputs levels will increase the output level, this shows that the fuzzy logic model is injective and surjective which are properties that guarantee a unique relation between inputs and outputs.

The model limitations are related with the quality of the qualitative data. The better the qualitative data the better the model estimates. This limitation is shared by all qualitative models and is a drawback pointed out by quantitative models' developers. However, there is several strategies to overcome this limitation such as the selection of experienced experts or the use of Delphi surveys. The use of qualitative models is reserved for cases where quantitative data is not available therefore the comparison between quantitative and qualitative models must be avoided since they are applicable to different situations.

# 6 Conclusions and Further Work

In this work, a risk assessment model was proposed to evaluate aggregate risk of projects under a qualitative approach. The developed model is particularly suitable to evaluate the risk of innovative projects where the absence of probabilistic data does not allow the use of typical risk assessment tools which are typically based on quantitative data. The proposed model was developed using the v-model as a generic framework to evaluate the aggregated risk of projects. For each one of the seven v-model phases it is qualitatively identified three basic events that have the highest risk using qualitative risk models, such as FMEA or RPI. Then the phase risk is evaluated using a fuzzy logic model where the inputs are the risk of each basic event and the output is the respective risk phase. Next, the aggregated risk of project phases is evaluated using the same approach where the fuzzy logic inputs are the risk of each phase and the output is the aggregated risk of the respective phases. A new method to implement the output membership functions and respective inference rules was proposed considering the relative weights between input variables. The developed model contributes to the body of knowledge in qualitative risk assessment of projects considering the causal effect between project phases which allows to evaluate the aggregated risk of projects being suitable to assist in decision making. Further works are needed to implement and adapt the developed model to a real time aggregated risk evaluation approach which will allow to dynamically monitor the project risk during its implementation considering external and internal risk variables as well as their aggregation according to the project phases as suggested in [16]. This has numerous advantages such as the capability to forecast in real time the project cost, forecast the end date or even identify critical phases that need to be closely monitored allowing mitigation initiatives if needed.

**Acknowledgments.** The first author gratefully acknowledges financial support from FCT-Fundação para Ciência e Tecnologia (Portuguese Foundation for Science and Technology), for the Ph.D. Grant PD/BD/52344/2013, and UIDB/00066/2020 (CTS – Center of Technology and Systems). This work was also supported by FCT, through IDMEC, under LAETA, project UIDB/50022/2020.

# References

1. Grabisch, M.: The application of fuzzy integrals in multicriteria decision making. Eur. J. Oper. Res. **89**(3), 445–456 (1996)
2. Liu, H.-C., Liu, L., Liu, N.: Risk evaluation approaches in failure mode and effects analysis: a literature review. Expert Syst. Appl. **40**(2), 828–838 (2013)
3. Keeney, R.L.: The art of assessing multiattribute utility functions. Organ. Behav. Hum. Perform. **19**(2), 267–310 (1977)
4. Zadeh, L.A.: Fuzzy sets, information and control. Inf. Control **8**, 338–353 (1965)
5. Balmat, J.-F., Lafont, F., Maifret, R., Pessel, N.: A decision-making system to maritime risk assessment. Ocean Eng. **38**(1), 171–176 (2011)
6. Liu, H.-C., Zhao, H., You, X.-Y., Zhou, W.-Y.: Robot evaluation and selection using the hesitant fuzzy linguistic MULTIMOORA method. J. Test. Eval. **47**(2), 1405–1426 (2019)
7. Roy, B.: Classement et choix en présence de points de vue multiples. Revue française d'informatique et de recherche opérationnelle **2**(8), 57–75 (1968)
8. Konidari, P., Mavrakis, D.: A multi-criteria evaluation method for climate change mitigation policy instruments. Energy Policy **35**(12), 6235–6257 (2007)
9. Brans, J.-P., Vincke, P.: Note—a preference ranking organisation method: (the PROMETHEE method for multiple criteria decision-making). Manag. Sci. **31**(6), 647–656 (1985)
10. De Keyser, W., Peeters, P.: A note on the use of PROMETHEE multicriteria methods. Eur. J. Oper. Res. **89**(3), 457–461 (1996)
11. Liu, H.-C., Li, Z., Song, W., Su, Q.: Failure mode and effect analysis using cloud model theory and PROMETHEE method. IEEE Trans. Reliab. **66**(4), 1058–1072 (2017)
12. Macharis, C., Springael, J., De Brucker, K., Verbeke, A.: PROMETHEE and AHP: the design of operational synergies in multicriteria analysis: Strengthening PROMETHEE with ideas of AHP. Eur. J. Oper. Res. **153**(2), 307–317 (2004)
13. Gabus, A., Fontela, E.: World problems, an Invitation to Further Thought Within the Framework of DEMATEL, pp. 1–8. Battelle Geneva Research Center, Geneva (1972)
14. Si, S.-L., You, X.-Y., Liu, H.-C., Zhang, P.: DEMATEL technique: A systematic review of the state-of-the-art literature on methodologies and applications. Math. Probl. Eng. **2018** (2018)
15. Anes, V., Henriques, E., Freitas, M., Reis, L.: A new risk prioritization model for failure mode and effects analysis. Qual. Reliab. Eng. Int. **34**(4), 516–528 (2018)
16. Mahmood, K., Shevtshenko, E., Karaulova, T., Otto, T.: Risk assessment approach for a virtual enterprise of small and medium-sized enterprises. Proc. Estonian Acad. Sci. **67**(1), 17–27 (2018)

# Analysis and Synthesis Algorithms

# Reachability Graph of IOPT Petri Net Models Using CUDA C++ Parallel Application

Carolina Lagartinho-Oliveira[1]([⊠]), Filipe Moutinho[1,2], and Luís Gomes[1,2]

[1] Faculdade de Ciências e Tecnologia, Universidade Nova de Lisboa, Caparica, Portugal
ci.oliveira@campus.fct.unl.pt, {fcm,lugo}@fct.unl.pt
[2] UNINOVA – CTS, Caparica, Portugal

**Abstract.** The construction of reachability graphs is suited to verify the properties and behavior of Petri net models based on the structure of the net and the initial marking. It allows checking whether a model conforms to the intended specification of a system and to obtain information about it. This paper proposes an algorithm to compute the reachability graphs of IOPT (Input-Output Place-Transition) nets, which is a Petri net class, using NVIDIA's CUDA (Compute Unified Device Architecture), which supports the co-processing using GPU and CPU. While CPU is used to schedule threads on GPU, GPU is used to calculate all the child nodes of the reachability graph, including the management of a hash-table for efficiently storing the new states and retrieving the states stored in the database. The presented algorithm takes advantage of CUDA memory functions to allocate and access data that can be used by code running on CPU or GPU, supporting the share of data between the two processor units. Six IOPT net models were used to validate the proposed algorithm.

**Keywords:** Co-processing · CUDA · GPU · IOPT nets · Reachability graph

## 1 Introduction

The increasing complexity of distributed embedded systems have been a motivation for the use of Petri nets [1, 2]. This graphical modelling formalism enables the explicit specification of concurrent systems, their synchronization and conflicts, and the share of resources [3]. As a result, they ensure that systems behavior conforms to the intended specification so as not to endanger people.

IOPT-Tools, which are online available at http://gres.uninova.pt/IOPT-Tools/ supports the development of embedded systems controller using Petri nets [4, 5]. This framework offers a set of tools to support the creation of IOPT-net models [1], their verification, and the automatic code generation (C and VHDL) [6, 7]. To enable the verification, an automatic code generator is used to compute the models' reachability graphs [8]. As real world applications can present exponential reachability graphs with a huge number of states, their generation can take a long time to compute [2], requiring high computational performance [9]. Some tools generate the condensed reachability graph of a Petri net model, preventing the exponential growth of the graph [10–12].

© IFIP International Federation for Information Processing 2020
Published by Springer Nature Switzerland AG 2020
L. M. Camarinha-Matos et al. (Eds.): DoCEIS 2020, IFIP AICT 577, pp. 93–100, 2020.
https://doi.org/10.1007/978-3-030-45124-0_8

The work presented in this paper is focused on obtain the complete reachability graph of a model, based on a new model-checking algorithm to compute the reachability graphs of IOPT Petri net models using NVIDIA's CUDA. NVIDIA's CUDA supports CPU-GPU co-processing for parallel computing [13]. As a matter of fact, GPU calculates all the child nodes of the reachability graph and handles their storing with the support of a hash-table. In addition, the CPU schedules the threads to be launched on the GPU, which are needed to process a new set of unprocessed states of the graph.

Section 2 mentions how this paper contributes to life improvement. In Sect. 3 IOPT Petri nets and IOPT-Tools are briefly described, including the current reachability graph generation tool. In the following section, it is mentioned how CUDA Toolkit contributes to program and run parallel C++ applications on GPU. Section 5 presents the proposed algorithm, for the computation of reachability graphs, for IOPT Petri net models. In Sect. 6 are presented the results supported by an NVIDIA Titan V GPU, and finally in Sect. 7 the conclusions about the results and future work are presented.

## 2  Relationship to Life Improvement

Currently, technological advances enabled the creation of many types of distributed embedded systems that contribute to a significant improvement in people's quality of life across different areas, ranging from appliances and home products, medical and health solutions, surveillance and security equipment, to transportation and communication systems, among others.

Concerning to safety-critical systems, to make sure that they are safe and free of development errors, they must be formally verified, by checking all possible interactions and potential unwanted properties [14–16]. There are large number of Petri net tools [17], which support not only the models edition and simulation, but also their formal verification and analysis, to ensure that the system specification conforms to the desired properties or has no unwanted properties. This work, addressing the construction of reachability graph for IOPT nets, aims to contribute for the safety-critical systems properties verification.

## 3  IOPT Nets

The IOPT nets are a low-level and non-autonomous Petri net class proposed to develop automation and embedded systems, allowing the rapid prototyping of system controllers through IOPT-Tools framework [18–20]. The IOPT Petri net relies on signals and events to specify the interaction of the models with the environment: while input signals and events constraint the evolution of the net, directly associated with transition firing, outputs are updated according with the marking of the net and transition firing. In detail, a transition fires if it is enabled from the point of view of place marking, the associated events occur and if the associated guards are verified. When more than one transition is enabled, but not all of them are allowed to firing, transition priorities and test arcs can be used [8]. As a result, each system's state is composed of a vector of all places' marking; and an output event signal vector, with the values of all signals associated with output events [19].

### 3.1 Reachability Graph Generator

The IOPT-Tools offer a tool to compute the reachability graphs [19] of IOPT Petri net models. During graph generation, the tool gathers information about the model, namely the influence of input signals and events on the firing of transitions, as well as all combinations of all enabled transitions. The automatic C code generated by the reachability graph generator provides libraries to compute a model's reachability graph, managed with a hash-table that allows ordering multiple states for each key, to help search for repeated states. At the end of the computation, the resulting reachability graph is stored in a hierarchical XML file, in which the connections between the states are represented.

The reachability graph algorithm [21] initiates with the creation of the database and initial state, obtained from the initial marking $M_0$ and the values of all output event signals presented on the net at that moment. After that, the initial node is added into the database and hash-table, and the algorithm proceeds from there or any other state by modifying the value of net's initial marking. The algorithm will continue until all the unprocessed states are treated, or the graph reaches the maximum size, which is specified according to the computation platform available resources. Each evaluation of an unprocessed state is carried out with the calculation of its child states (the next unprocessed states), by executing a function that recursively analyzes all transitions that are enabled to firing. Then, all child nodes are stored in the database and sorted in the hash-table if they are not repeated states, whose marking and outputs refer to previously existing nodes. Finally, the new child nodes are added to the set of unprocessed states, waiting to be processed. The generated reachability graph includes the nodes, the arcs that connect them, and links that represent existing nodes.

## 4  CUDA Architecture

To increase the performance of the IOPT reachability graphs generation, the use of GPU is proposed in this paper. The GPU is used to improve the processing of each state, parallelizing the calculation and analysis of its child nodes. For that, it was used a NVIDIA GPU and the CUDA Toolkit, which enable the co-processing of C++ programs in platforms with CPU and GPU [22, 23]. The execution starts and ends in the CPU, which exchanges data with the GPU and launch the kernels to running on the GPU.

A kernel is a sequential program that runs in parallel as many times as the number of threads running on the GPU distributed by blocks in a grid. Although, there is a limit to the number of threads per block, a kernel can be executed by multiple blocks in parallel, so the total number of threads launched is equal to the number of threads per block times the number of blocks thar compose the grid. A set of functions, such as __threadfence, __syncthreads, and atomic operations, can be used to ensure the correct access to shared and global memory, avoiding hazards that can occur from simultaneous read and write operations at the same memory address [24].

## 5 Proposed Approach and Algorithm

The reachability graph generation at IOPT-Tools is mainly composed of two parts: for each state, it is calculated its child nodes; and for each child node it is inspected if it is a new independent state or if it is equal to a previously existing one. In the generator of the IOPT tool framework, this entire process is done sequentially in CPU, with each state being analyzed one at a time. An algorithm proposed in [25] reused part of IOPT-Tools generator code and adapted it to run on a GPU used to perform the calculation all the child nodes of unprocessed states in parallel, while the CPU schedules threads on the GPU, handles the hash-table and the categorization of states.

The algorithm proposed in this paper also uses co-processing, taking even more advantage of the GPU. For that, the initialization of the database and the creation of the initial state are handled by the CPU, and from that moment onwards the task of searching for new states it's responsibility of the GPU until all graph it's done. During the computation, the CPU receives feedback on the status of the graph through memory copies from the device to the host, receiving the update of the number of calculated states and the number of states to be processed. This allows the continuity of the algorithm that ends only when there are no more unprocessed states to process or the maximum number of states associated with the allocation of the database is reached. So, three kernels were implemented, each one responsible for a specific part of the algorithm, as described in Fig. 1.

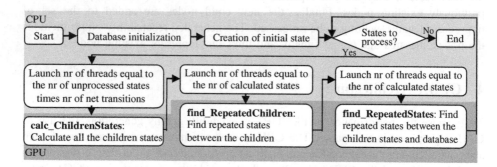

**Fig. 1.** Sequence of actions of the algorithm.

When the kernel calc_ChildrenStates, presented in Algorithm 1, is invoked, the values of the number of states to be processed and the current number of states stored in the database are passed. The first instruction performed is the assignment of an unprocessed state from the array states to the threads of a block. At this point, CPU has been launched as many blocks as the number of unprocessed states that need to be processed, and as many threads as the number of transitions of the Petri net. The way to provide each thread the state to process is using the unique index of the block, the size of the array states, that stores all the states, and the number of blocks launched.

**Algorithm 1.** Kernel calc_ChildrenStates

```
program calc_ChildrenStates(unp_states, n_states)
  __shared__ state s*
  netMarking init_m, m, avail_m
  eventOutputSignals init_out, out
  outputSignalEvents ev
  begin
    IF threadIdx.x == 0
      s = &states[blockIdx.x+n_states-gridDim.x]
    __syncthreads()
    calc_FiringBlends(threadIdx.x, init_m, m, avail_m, unp_states,
      n_states, s->id, ev, out, init_out)
end.
```

Using the __syncthreads() function all the threads in the current block will synchronize, waiting for thread 0 to share the state that needs to be processed. The kernel continues with a recursively analysis of all enabled transitions of a state, calculating all the combinations between them. The transition with the highest priority will analyze the remaining ones; the second most priority will analyze the other ones except the first one, and so on. The latter transition will only consider itself. As there is one thread per transition, each one of them will analyze the combinations in parallel for each state, saving the founded new states inside the array childs.

After that, the kernel returns the number of child nodes calculated to proceed with the search of repeated children. The CPU launches a number of threads equal to the number of founded states, one for each thread to compare with the others. The comparison of the states is made at find_RepeatedChildren kernel, presented in Algorithm 2, by comparing the marking and outputs of the Petri net. If there is a repeated sibling, the value of the link flag and the id of the state are changed, followed by the storage of the state in the array links.

**Algorithm 2.** Kernel find_RepeatedChildren

```
program find_RepeatedChildren(n_links)
  For i=0; i<threadIdx; i++:
    int cmp = memcmp(childs[threadIdx.x].m, childs[j].m)
    IF cmp == 0:
      cmp = memcmp(childs[threadIdx.x].o, childs[j].o)
      IF cmp == 0:
        childs[threadIdx.x].link = -1
        childs[threadIdx.x].id = dev_childs[j].id
        memcpy(links[atomicAdd(n_links,1)], childs[threadIdx.x])
end.
```

The last kernel, presented in Algorithm 3, compare the child nodes that have not been copied to the array links with all existing nodes. For that, it was implemented a multivalue hash-table where multiple values for the same key are represented by different key-state_id pairs. In the same way as the previous kernel, the CPU launches a number of threads equal to the number of founded states. Each thread will search on hash-table for repeated states starting by calculating the key based on the marking and outputs of the state, using it to limit the search to elements with the same key. Several threads could access the hash-table, including threads whose states have the same key. If there is no repeated state at the database, the value of the id of the child state is actualized, and the state is stored in the array states; if there is a repeated state it is stored in the array links.

**Algorithm 3.** Kernel find_RepeatedStates

```
program find_RepeatedStates(unp_states, n_states, n_links)
   IF childs[threadIdx.x].link != -1:
      key = calcHash(childs[threadIdx.x].m, childs[threadIdx.x].o)
      p = findHash(key, childs[threadIdx.x].m, childs[threadIdx.x].o)
      IF p < 0:
         state_id = atomicAdd(n_states,1)
         addHash(h, state_id, -p)
         childs[threadIdx.x].id = state_id
         memcpy(states[state_id], childs[threadIdx.x])
      Else:
         childs[threadIdx.x].id = p
         memcpy(links[atomicAdd(n_links,1)], childs[threadIdx.x])
   end.
```

## 6  Results of Experiments

The algorithm presented was applied to six IOPT-net models. These models were also used to document the results at [25], and are available online at http://gres.uninova.pt/IOPT-Tools/, in the user account "models". Using these models, we could compare the results between the two approaches. The results are presented in Table 1. Considered the amount of time that GPU took to calculate the entire reachability graph and the time spent on co-processing we have obtained much better results with this algorithm. The results are, in some cases, two or three orders of magnitude better than the ones presented at [25].

**Table 1.** Results obtained with an GPU TITAN V.

| Models | Trans. | Cycles | States | Links | Time CPU + GPU(ms) | Time on GPU(ms) |
|---|---|---|---|---|---|---|
| ICIT13_bldc_commut | 24 | 2 | 7 | 0 | 0.8 | 0.6 |
| PNSE-53b | 8 | 9 | 21 | 8 | 2.3 | 1.8 |
| ICIT13_denoise | 14 | 9 | 14 | 11 | 2.5 | 2.0 |
| concrete_mixer_6xA | 11 | 56 | 110 | 108 | 17.5 | 14.7 |
| ICIT13_quad_encoder | 12 | 103 | 1025 | 1020 | 67.3 | 59.7 |
| ICIT13_pwm_gen | 6 | 1025 | 4096 | 12287 | 655.5 | 561.7 |

The number of cycles and nodes presented express the graph with the respect to its size and format. This characteristic can affect the execution time depending on the number of states processed in parallel as well as the number of transitions of the net. The models PNSE−53b and ICIT13_denoise presented the same number of cycles processed; for the first was calculated 29 nodes and for the second 25. Although the number of transitions in the second is almost twice that of the first, the execution times obtained were approximately equal, such that parallel threads were launched and used at the same time to exploit the computing power of the GPU.

## 7    Conclusions and Future Work

The proposed algorithm presents an improvement in the computation of the reachability graph for IOPT Petri net models in GPU. Threads were used to analyze combinations of transitions in parallel, improving the calculation of child states; and the use of a hash-table implemented in GPU prevented the time spent with memory management. As future work we intend to analyze the impact of the proposed algorithm using GPU as a function of the number of global states obtained, namely as a function of the initial marking. Additionally, the impact of computation efforts necessary for evaluating transition enabling conditions and output expressions is intended to be analyzed.

**Acknowledgments.** The work presented in this paper was partially supported by Portuguese Agency FCT ("Fundação para a Ciência e a Tecnologia"), in the framework of the project with the reference UID/EEA/00066/2019 and UIDB/00066/2020 (CTS – Center of Technology and Systems). We would also like to thank NVIDIA Corporation for the donation of the GPU used in this work, a Titan V.

## References

1. Gomes, L., Barros, J., Costa, A., Nunes, R.: The Input-Output Place-Transition Petri net class and associated tools. In: Proceedings of the 5th IEEE International Conference on Industrial Informatics (INDIN 2007), Vienna, Austria, July 2007
2. Girault, C., Valk, R. (eds.): Petri Nets for Systems Engineering: A Guide to Modeling, Verification, and Applications. Springer, Heidelberg (2003). https://doi.org/10.1007/978-3-662-05324-9
3. David, R., Alla, H. (eds.): Discrete, Continuous, and Hybrid Petri Nets. Springer, Heidelberg (2010). https://doi.org/10.1007/978-3-642-10669-9
4. Pereira, F., Moutinho, F., Gomes, L.: IOPT-Tools—towards cloud design automation of digital controllers with Petri nets. In: Proceedings of the 2014 International Conference on Mechatronics and Control (ICMC 2014), Jinzhou, China, July 2014
5. Gomes, L., Moutinho, F., Pereira, F.: IOPT-Tools—a web based tool framework for embedded systems controller development using Petri nets. In: Proceedings of the 23rd International Conference on Field Programmable Logic and Applications, Portugal (2013)
6. Pereira, F., Gomes, L.: Automatic synthesis of VHDL hardware components from IOPT Petri net models. In: IECON 2013 – 39th Annual Conference of the IEEE Industrial Electronics Society (IECON 2013), Vienna, Austria, November 2013

7. Gomes, L., Rebelo, R., Barros, J., Costa, A., Pais, R.: From Petri net models to C implementation of digital controllers. In: Proceedings of the ISIE 2010 - IEEE International Symposium on Industrial Electronics, Bari, Italy, July 2010
8. Pereira, F., Moutinho, F., Gomes, L.: A state-space based model-checking framework for embedded system controllers specified using IOPT Petri nets. In: Camarinha-Matos, L.M., Shahamatnia, E., Nunes, G. (eds.) DoCEIS 2012. IAICT, vol. 372, pp. 123–132. Springer, Heidelberg (2012). https://doi.org/10.1007/978-3-642-28255-3_14
9. Pereira, F., Moutinho, F., Gomes, L., Rebelo, R.: IOPT Petri net state space generation algorithm with maximal-step execution semantics. In: Proceedings of the 2011 9th IEEE International Conference on Industrial Informatics, Caparica, Lisbon, July 2011
10. Jensen, K.: Condensed state spaces for symmetrical Coloured Petri Nets. J. Form. Method Syst. Des. 9(1), 4–40 (1996)
11. Christensen, S., Kristensen, L.M., Mailund, T.: Condensed state spaces for timed Petri Nets. In: Colom, J.-M., Koutny, M. (eds.) ICATPN 2001. LNCS, vol. 2075, pp. 101–120. Springer, Heidelberg (2001). https://doi.org/10.1007/3-540-45740-2_8
12. Valmari, A.: Stubborn sets for reduced state space generation. In: Rozenberg, G. (ed.) ICATPN 1989. LNCS, vol. 483, pp. 491–515. Springer, Heidelberg (1991). https://doi.org/10.1007/3-540-53863-1_36
13. Nickolls, J., Dally, W.J.: The GPU computing Era. IEEE Micro 30(2), 56–69 (2010)
14. Knight, J.C.: Safety critical systems: challenges and directions. In: Proceedings of the 24th International Conference on Software Engineering (ICSE 2002), Orlando, USA, May 2002
15. Hsiung, P., Chen, Y., Lin, Y.: Model checking safety-critical systems using safecharts. IEEE Trans. Comput. 56(5), 692–705 (2007)
16. Moutinho, F., Gomes, L.: Distributed Embedded Controller Development with Petri Nets. SECE, vol. 150. Springer, Cham (2016). https://doi.org/10.1007/978-3-319-20822-0
17. Petri Nets Tool Database. https://www.informatik.uni-hamburg.de/TGI/PetriNets/tools/db.html
18. Gomes, L., Costa, A., Barros, J.P., Lima, P.: From Petri net models to VHDL implementation of digital controllers. In: IECON 2007 - 33rd Annual Conference of the IEEE Industrial Electronics Society, Taipei, Taiwan, November 2007
19. Gomes, L., Lourenco, J.: Rapid prototyping of graphical user interfaces for Petri-net-based controllers. IEEE Trans. Industr. Electron. 57(5), 1806–1813 (2010)
20. Pereira, F., Moutinho, F., Ribeiro, R., Gomes, L.: Web based IOPT Petri net Editor with an extensible plugin architecture to support generic net operations. In: IECON 2012 - 38th Annual Conference on IEEE Industrial Electronics Society, Canada, December 2012
21. Moutinho, F., Gomes, L.: State space generation algorithm for GALS systems modeled by IOPT Petri nets. In: IECON 2011 - 37th Annual Conference of the IEEE Industrial Electronics Society, Melbourne, VIC, Australia, November 2011
22. Parande, J.G., Kulkarni, M., Bawaskar, A.: GPGPU processing in CUDA architecture. Adv. Comput. Int. J. 3(1), 105–120 (2012)
23. Jin, H., Li, B., Zheng, R., Zhang, Q., Ao, W.: memCUDA: map device memory to host memory on GPGPU platform. In: Ding, C., Shao, Z., Zheng, R. (eds.) NPC 2010. LNCS, vol. 6289, pp. 299–313. Springer, Heidelberg (2010). https://doi.org/10.1007/978-3-642-15672-4_26
24. Cuda Toolkit Documentation. https://docs.nvidia.com/cuda/cuda-c-programming-guide/
25. Lagartinho-Oliveira, C., Moutinho, F., Gomes, L.: GPGPU applied to support the construction of the state-space graphs of IOPT Petri net model. In: IECON 2019 - 45th Annual Conference on IEEE Industrial Electronics Society, Lisbon, Portugal, October 2019

# Automatic Flat-Level Circuit Generation with Genetic Algorithms

Miguel Campilho-Gomes[1,2(✉)], Rui Tavares[3,4], and João Goes[3,4]

[1] NOVA-FCT, Nova School of Science and Technology of Universidade Nova de Lisboa, Caparica, Portugal
[2] Instituto Superior de Engenharia de Lisboa, Lisbon, Portugal
mpcg@isel.ipl.pt
[3] CTS/UNINOVA, Centre of Technology and Systems of UNINOVA, Caparica, Portugal
[4] DEEC/NOVA-FCT, Computer and Electrical Engineering Department of Nova School of Science and Technology of Universidade NOVA de Lisboa, Caparica, Portugal
{rmt,goes}@fct.unl.pt

**Abstract.** This paper describes a novel methodology to generate analog and digital circuits, autonomously, using the transistor (or other elementary device, e.g. resistor) as the basic elementary block – flat-level. A genetic algorithm is employed as the generation engine and variable length chromosomes are used to describe the circuit topology that evolves during the search. The circuit devices type and sizing are described by each gene of genetic algorithm. The automatic process starts with the circuit input and output specifications, and proceeds with the circuit topology and sizing evolution to meet those specifications, eventually, ending up with a novel topology. During the evolution, each generated circuit is electrically evaluated by a spice-like circuit simulator, i.e. Ngspice, using full model specifications - like BSIM3 for transistors - in a highly parallelized architecture built over a multi-thread model.

**Keywords:** Automatic topology generation · Genetic algorithm · Variable Length Chromosome · Digital circuit · Analog circuit · Ngspice · Amplifier

## 1 Introduction

Digital and analog circuit design for Integrated Circuits (ICs) classically has three distinctive stages: topology choice, component sizing and layout generation. For some years now, digital synthesis is almost fully automated [1] but analog ICs, or the analog part of modern Mixed-Signal System on-a-Chip (MS-SoC), still take a lot of human intervention in the topology choice stage in spite of the research effort of the past few decades in the automated synthesis field.

The Electronic Design Automation (EDA) field, a trend in research effort for the past three decades, targeted in technology roadmaps like International Technology Roadmap for Semiconductors (ITRS) [2], focuses in reduction of designer effort, minimization of time-to-market and minimization of production costs. Included in

© IFIP International Federation for Information Processing 2020
Published by Springer Nature Switzerland AG 2020
L. M. Camarinha-Matos et al. (Eds.): DoCEIS 2020, IFIP AICT 577, pp. 101–108, 2020.
https://doi.org/10.1007/978-3-030-45124-0_9

EDA, the subfield of Analog Design Automation (ADA) deals specifically with analog circuits, and it also contains the three stages mentioned above: topology synthesis, component sizing and layout generation, though when the circuit is not to be integrated the layout stage is replaced by a Printed Circuit Board (PCB) generation stage.

The topology synthesis stage is the least developed stage. Automatic topology synthesis of analog circuits is far from being a straightforward task and, despite having received some research effort in recent decades, it has not yet matured enough to become available in software packages for the integrated circuit industry. Analog circuit design is still essentially based on expert designers and has often been considered an art [3]. This design work is generally geared toward the reuse of well-known topologies in new circuit functions or to improve existing circuit topologies and, less often, to create new circuit topologies. But these procedures not always achieve the best performance within the shortening design-to-market cycle time. Furthermore, as the technology is heading to deep sub-micrometer sizes, the present circuit topologies and design methods are often not good enough to completely fulfill the final circuit high-end specifications. It is imperative to develop a systematic and automatic method to generate novel circuit topologies that combine high efficiency with full specification compliance, accommodate submicron technology constraints, reduce the trial and error cycle of the circuit design lifecycle.

## 1.1   Research Question, Hypothesis and Motivations

Generation of circuit topologies can be seen as a search and optimization problem and, therefore, it can be performed with Genetic Algorithms (GAs). What is unclear is to what extent this can be accomplished by a GA, particularly when handled at flat circuit-level, and in concrete for the case of CMOS amplifiers. If some human designed topologies can be generated by GAs, perhaps GAs may also generate new topologies.

As a natural result of the development of amplifier design conducted to this day, and also boosted by the current submicron technologies used in today's Integrated Circuits (ICs), CMOS integrated amplifiers have high efficiencies and very optimized specifications compared to the not-so-distant past. The main research question adopted in this work is therefore:

- Is it possible to generate new circuit topologies for CMOS amplifiers, at flat circuit-level, in an automatic way (software generated), with optimized specifications and high efficiency at submicron technologies?

And the proposed hypothesis to address this problem and to guide the research effort is:

- It is possible to develop a methodology and a software tool based in genetic algorithms to, automatically, generate novel at circuit-level topologies for CMOS amplifiers with high efficiency at submicron technologies.

The research question and the proposed hypothesis enclose some other questions that will be addressed in the course of this work, such as:

- To what extent does the canonical genetic algorithm is suited to circuit synthesis? Since Holland's presentation of canonical (or conventional) Genetic Algorithm (GA − c) [4] there have been many developed variants for the algorithm, and some may be better suitable for circuit synthesis than others. It is unclear what are the actual limitations of GA-c when applied to analog circuit synthesis, particularly to amplifier synthesis, so it is relevant to try to get some sense of what can actually be accomplished by the GA-c before any of its variants are considered.
- What circuit codification is best suited for circuit synthesis, namely for the synthesis of analog topologies?

  It is well known that part of the difficulty of obtaining good results with GAs is to choose a good codification scheme of the problem. It should be evaluated whether the classical GA-c bit strings are suitable for circuit synthesis, such as analog synthesis, or whether it is necessary to experiment with other schemes that may prove more suitable.

## 1.2    Contribution to Life Improvement

Life improvement is expected to be the main outcome of technology advances across different areas for human well-being. In the area of circuit design and electronic systems, the advances are certainly in reducing energy consumption, improving performance and reducing the area used in integrated circuits. These technological developments have impacts on health, environment, transportation and communication systems worldwide.

More energy-efficient electronic circuits and systems contribute to extend the duration of the battery cycles. Extending battery life is expected to reduce the negative environmental impact of the batteries.

Integrated Pico and Nano-scale electronic circuits and systems are the primary vehicle for building data collectors, either for real-time monitoring or for building bigdata containers. Two possible examples are the freight sector and the healthcare domain. In the freight sector, during packaging, transport and storage, the goods are constantly tracked, and their conditions are supervised throughout the process. In the healthcare domain, technological evolution closely related to life improvement is being driven by monitoring the patient all the time and collecting data closer to the patient. To minimize the hassle to the patient, the circuits' size must be reduced, and efficiency maintained. The bigdata collected from the patient is real-time processed with local hardware processors.

Energy and performance improvements are prime indicators to consider in transducers in-between real-world analog domain and the digital domain of the cyber physical systems. These electronic circuits are the first system block in the analog front end and, again, must be energy efficient, with low area consumption.

To cope with the momentum of the IC industry to embrace all the real-world needs to increase knowledge, wellbeing, quality of life, and facilitate the collaboration among different entities, one must come up with more efficient hardware: electronic circuits and systems.

This paper pretends to contribute with a novel methodology to, automatically, generate electronic circuits, efficiently outcome the state-of-the-art circuit performance specifications and simultaneously deal with downsizing of the technology complexity and challenges.

## 2  Genetic Algorithms and Circuit Synthesis

Genetic Algorithms (GAs) are search and optimization algorithms based on the mechanics of natural selection and natural genetics. They were developed by Holland and colleagues [4] in the early seventies and today have broad application in the areas of business, engineering and science. GAs belong to the larger group of Evolutionary Algorithms (EAs), which constitute a class of stochastic search and optimization methods that simulate the process of natural evolution.

Problem representation, which translates to individual encoding in GAs, is a major component of GAs application to a concrete problem, and therefore encoding a circuit in a GA is a topic frequently discussed and object of significant research effort [5, 6]. In this work there was a first attempt to use a codification technique for circuits that applies the classic bit strings used by GA-c to represent a circuit. In this representation there is a fixed number of components available to the GA and the evolution takes place by changing the nodes to which each component terminal is connected to. The circuit of Fig. 1 was generated automatically by the GA using this codification technique.

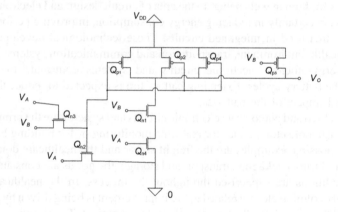

**Fig. 1.**  Circuit generated for a NAND gate.

Although it was possible to accomplish the generation of simple circuits, this codification scheme suffers from lack of scalability to higher complexity topologies. Therefore, it was necessary to try another codification technique, and Variable Length Chromosomes (VLCs) were tested. This concept is a model that has been around for quite some time [7, 8], and has been applied in several scientific fields [9, 10].

In this work we use VLCs and an encoding scheme in which a chromosome is a circuit descriptor and each gene is a component descriptor. Each chromosome has a variable number of genes, and this number may either increase or decrease during execution of the GA. In this encoding scheme each gene is comprised of three fields, as depicted in Fig. 2. The first field identifies the component type and is typically implemented as an integer variable. The second field is a set of parameters needed to describe the characteristics of the component, which are typically implemented as real variables. And the third field is a set of nodes indicating where the component terminals are connected (implemented as positive integer variables).

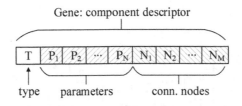

**Fig. 2.** Circuit component encoding using VLCs.

VLCs poses some questions to the crossover and mutation operators, so these operators are often adapted to work in populations with chromosomes that don't have a constant length. In this work we use a gene boundary crossover operator that implements equal crossover and inside crossover operations [11] and a mutation operator that can alter any allele of a gene, which means, for instance, that it can change the transistor channel type, its width or length, and the node connected to any of its terminals. This operator also implements *insertion*, *replication* and *deletion* operations [12]. Another feature of this mutation operator is the ability of refusing a mutation if it worsens the chromosome fitness. The probability $p_r$ of refusing a mutated chromosome is not constant, instead it is adapted during evolution of the population. The probability $p_a$ of acceptance ($p_a = 1 - p_r$) starts high and decreases over time, similarly to a simulated annealing process [13], allowing broader regions of space to be searched in early generations but later narrowing this search to small regions around the solution(s) already obtained (local exploitation). Instead of decreasing the probability of acceptance over time, in our work we use a heuristic that adapts it according to a function $f_Q$ which measures the quality of the solutions obtained so far (and converts it to a probability). This measure can be obtained in two ways: (1) by the average of all chromosome's fitness smoothed by $2^{nd}$ order discrete low pass filter; (2) by the fitness of the best chromosome in the population. Both ways were tested and both performed similarly well in the synthesized circuits, making this approach a robustness enhancer of the adaptative process by decreasing its sensitivity to the convergence speed of the GA (which is known to be highly irregular and dependent of numerous factors, such as initial solution and general GA parametrization).

Using VLCs with the proposed codification scheme, and using a SPICE-based circuit simulator like *Ngspice* [14] for fitness evaluation, the GA was able to generate circuits of higher complexity, like the half-adder depicted in Fig. 3 and the 20 dB DC amplifier depicted in Fig. 4. A common characteristic of the circuits shown in Figs. 1, 3 and 4 is that there are numerous superfluous (either because they are redundant or useless) components. To minimize the number of these components we propose a technique based in dynamically adapting the weight of a penalty constraint function. This weight must be quite low in early generations, or the GA will hardly converge at all, but it should be high enough in late stages of the GA, particularly after the main objectives of the circuit are fulfilled, so that the GA "cleans" the circuit by removing unnecessary components (but without loosing "sight" of those main objectives).

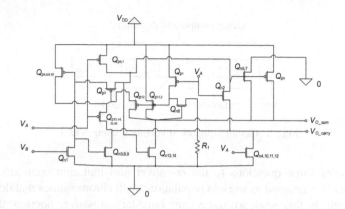

**Fig. 3.** An half-adder automatically generated by a GA using VLCs.

To adapt that weight we reuse function $f_Q$ described earlier which measures the quality of the solutions obtained so far, and use a heuristic that converts it to the penalty weight.

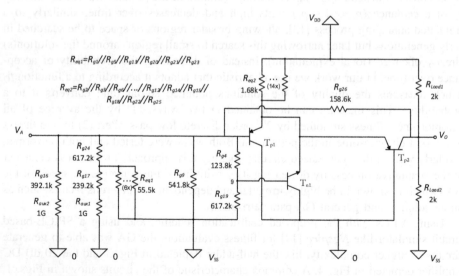

**Fig. 4.** A 20 dB DC amplifier automatically generated by a GA using VLCs.

This technique has proven to be effective and the circuits depicted in Fig. 5 illustrate its outcome when applied to the circuits previously introduced in Figs. 1 and 4.

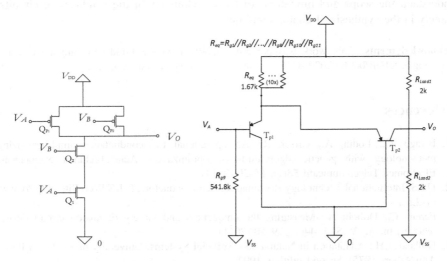

**Fig. 5.** Circuits generated by an GA using unnecessary component removal heuristics.

## 3  Conclusions

The main research topic of this work is to better understand how GAs can be used in circuit synthesis. As part of this study, we intended to understand the main constraints of GA-c for this task and to investigate possible improvements that make these algorithms more suitable for circuit synthesis.

With GA-c, and using a simple codification scheme for circuit representation based in GA-c bit strings, the algorithm was able to generate several simple digital and analog circuits, of which an example of a logic NAND gate was introduced. But scalability for more complex circuits has proved to be an impractical task, at least with the available computing power. The research effort was then focused on using VLCs and using a new circuit coding technique. This shift in the research effort implied several changes and improvements to the original algorithm, namely in the crossing and mutation operations. Another improvement is a "circuit cleaning" technique that eliminates redundant components in the circuit. In this technique we dynamically adapt some parameters of the GA in order to steer the algorithm towards the sub-objective of minimizing the number of components. One more improvement presented is a heuristic that implements an adaptive probability of acceptance of mutated chromosomes according to a measure of the quality of the solutions obtained. The combination of these changes and enhancements has enabled the generation of more complex digital and analog circuits without compromising the scalability of the entire synthesis procedure accomplished by the GA.

Some experimental results were presented to illustrate the results obtained with the methodology and techniques described here. Other experimental results already obtained sustains the scalability of these procedures. Current and future work aims to understand the scope and limitations of these techniques in the synthesis of circuits, namely in the synthesis of analog amplifiers.

**Acknowledgments.** This work was partially supported by the Fundação para a Ciência e Tecnologia, UIDB/00066/2020 (CTS – Center of Technology and Systems).

# References

1. Faragó, C., Lodin, A., Groza, R.: An operational transconductance amplifier sizing methodology with genetic algorithm-based optimization. Acta Technica Napocensis. Electronica-Telecomunicatii **55**(1), 15–20 (2014)
2. ITRS: International Technology Roadmap for Semiconductors, ITRS Web-Site. http://www.itrs2.net
3. Ferent, C., Doboli, A.: Measuring the uniqueness and variety of analog circuit design features. Integr. VLSI J. **44**(1), 39–50 (2011)
4. Holland, J.H.: Adaptation in Natural and Artificial Systems. University of Michigan Press, Ann Arbor (1975). Second Edition, 1992
5. Lohn, J.D., Colombano, S.P., Haith, G.L., Stassinopoulos, D., Norvig, P.: A parallel genetic algorithm for automated electronic circuit design. In: Proceedings Computational Aerosciences Workshop (2000)
6. Sapargaliyev, Y.A., Kalganova, T.G.: Challenging the evolutionary strategy for synthesis of analogue computational circuits. J. Softw. Eng. Appl. **3**(11), 1032–1039 (2010)
7. Zebulum, R.S., Pacheco, M.A., Vellasco, M.: Comparison of different evolutionary methodologies applied to electronic filter design. In: 1998 IEEE International Conference on Evolutionary Computation Proceedings. IEEE World Congress on Computational Intelligence, pp. 434–439. IEEE (1998)
8. Lohn, J.D., Colombano, S.P.: Automated analog circuit synthesis using a linear representation. In: Sipper, M., Mange, D., Pérez-Uribe, A. (eds.) ICES 1998. LNCS, vol. 1478, pp. 125–133. Springer, Heidelberg (1998). https://doi.org/10.1007/BFb0057614
9. Pawar, S.N., Bichkar, R.S.: Genetic algorithm with variable length chromosomes for network intrusion detection. Int. J. Autom. Comput. **12**(3), 337–342 (2015)
10. Ni, J., Wang, K., Huang, H., Wu, L., Luo, C.: Robot path planning based on an improved genetic algorithm with variable length chromosome. In: 2016 12th International Conference Natural Computation, Proceedings of the Fuzzy Systems and Knowledge Discovery (ICNC-FSKD), August 2016, pp. 145–149 (2016)
11. Deif, D.S., Gadallah, Y.: Wireless sensor network deployment using a variable-length genetic algorithm. In: Proceedings IEEE Wireless Communications and Networking Conference (WCNC), April 2014, pp. 2450–2455 (2014)
12. Hutt, B., Warwick, K.: Synapsing variable-length crossover: meaningful crossover for variable-length genomes. IEEE Trans. Evol. Comput. **11**(1), 118–131 (2007)
13. Barros, M., Guilherme, J., Horta, N.: Analog circuits optimization based on evolutionary computation techniques. Integr. VLSI J. **43**(1), 136–155 (2010)
14. SourceForge: Mixed Mode-Mixed Level Circuit Simulator based on Berkeley's SPICE 3F5. http://ngspice.sourceforge.net/

# Towards the Detection of Malicious URL and Domain Names Using Machine Learning

Nastaran Farhadi Ghalati[1(✉)], Nahid Farhady Ghalaty[2],
and José Barata[1]

[1] Universidade Nova de Lisboa (UNL), CTS-UNINOVA, Lisbon, Portugal
n.ghalati@campus.fct.unl.pt, jab@uninova.pt
[2] George Mason University, Fairfax, VA, USA
nfarhady@gmu.edu

**Abstract.** Malicious Uniform Resource Locator (URL) is an important problem in web search and mining. Malicious URLs host unsolicited content (spam, phishing, drive-by downloads, etc.) and try to lure uneducated users into clicking in such links or downloading malware which will result in critical data exfiltration. Traditional techniques in detecting such URLs have been to use blacklists and rule-based methods. The main disadvantage of such problems is that they are not resistant to 0-day attacks, meaning that there will be at least one victim for each URL before the blacklist is created. Other techniques include having sandbox and testing the URLs before clicking on them in the production or main environment. Such methods have two main drawbacks which are the cost of the sandboxing as well as the non-real-time response which is due to the approval process in the test environment. In this paper, we propose a method that exploits semantic features in both domains and URLs as well. The method is adaptive, meaning that the model can dynamically change based on the new feedback received on the 0-day attacks. We extract features from all sections of a URL separately. We then apply three methods of machine learning on three different sets of data. We provide an analysis of features on the most efficient value of N for applying the N-grams to the domain names. The result shows that Random Forest has the highest accuracy of over 96% and at the same time provides more interpretability as well as performance benefits.

**Keywords:** Cyber-security · URL classification · Machine learning

## 1 Introduction

With the advent of new communication technologies, a huge amount of growth has been observed in the sector of business applications such as e-commerce, healthcare, education, travel, and commute, etc. Many of these applications are critical since their database contains private information and critical information of the customers. Therefore, technique that can be misused to access this information violates the privacy of the customers and may lead to irreparable consequences for the business.

The World Wide Web (WWW) provides massive amounts of information for the users. This information could be benign or malicious. The information is transferred to people by clicking on the Universal Resource Locator (URL). Unfortunately, the

© IFIP International Federation for Information Processing 2020
Published by Springer Nature Switzerland AG 2020
L. M. Camarinha-Matos et al. (Eds.): DoCEIS 2020, IFIP AICT 577, pp. 109–117, 2020.
https://doi.org/10.1007/978-3-030-45124-0_10

advance of technology is also coupled with the advent of new cyber-attacks on such technologies. Such attacks include rogue websites that try to sell counterfeit goods, or intrigue people to share the sensitive information in exchange for subscriptions or gifts, as well as phishing attacks that install malicious software or malware on the user's device without him/her knowing. These attacks have resulted in billions of dollars lost every year. The techniques to launch such attacks is a long list starting with spam campaigns, pop-ups, spyware and malware [11].

A URL has three main components: (1) the protocol identifier and (2) the IP address or domain name for the resource of the page, (3) The path that specifies a resource in the host. The protocol and the identifier are separated by :// shown in Fig. 1.

It has been shown that 39% of URLs are malicious or compromised [12]. Popular types of attacks using malicious URLs include: Drive-by Download, Phishing and Social Engineering, and Spam [16]. Drive-by download [6] refers to the (unintentional) download of malware upon just visiting a URL. Such attacks are usually According to the RSA Online Fraud Report3 for 2018, "Phishing accounted for 48% of all cyber-attacks observed by RSA. Canada, the United States, India and Brazil were the countries most targeted by phishing" [1]. Such attacks are carried out by injecting vulnerabilities and malicious code using Javascript.

In this paper, we first go over our motivation on solving the problem of phishing attacks and malicious URLs and how it affects the industrial, electrical and computing community. Then, we go over the previous works and the advantages and disadvantages of several methods. In Sect. 4, we go over the proposed method, the details of the model and features. In Sect. 5, we provide the results of the prediction model and an overview of the dataset and compare our achievement with the previous works. Finally, we conclude the paper with proposals on how to continue this effort and future works.

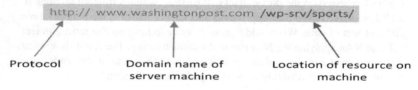

**Fig. 1.** Example of a URL

## 2   Contribution to Industrial and Service

DoCEIS has been focused on representation of innovative technologies such as Industry 4.0, manufacturing systems, and Internet of Things. Cyber-security is one of the main concerns around the new industrial technologies. With the rapid growth of the digital world and the expansion of the Internet, along with the improvement of technological advances in business and industrial systems, business users inevitably involve taking serious risks. Detection and prevention of such threats will improve the security of these technologies which results in life improvement.

Phishing attacks is the practice of sending fraudulent communications to business and personal services to look like they are coming from a reputable source. Symantec has reported that the average user receives 16 phishing attempt emails per month [2]. According to Wombat Security 76% of businesses experienced a phishing attack in 2018 [3]. Also, Verizon's 2018 Data Breach Investigation Report showed that 93% of security incidents are the result of phishing. Phishing attempts are only successful if they are clicked on by the user, otherwise they are harmless. Therefore, efforts on development of techniques to avoid exposing the users to these threats is valuable to industry. In this paper, we work on the development of a fast technique for phishing attack detection and prevention.

## 3  Related Work

Over the years, researchers have worked on several methods for detection of malicious URLs. One of the traditional methods that has been deployed by many anti-viruses is Blacklist method. In this method, a list of previously known URLs that have been confirmed is stored and maintained in a database. The database often becomes compiled by several toolbars such as PhishBook [8], and PhishTank [15]. The method is very fast since it is only querying against a database, however, because the new technology has made the attackers capable of only hosting malicious domains for only a couple of hours, this method is no longer as effective [19]. Also, there are techniques that can be used for obfuscation of the URLs so there are several equivalents even for one malicious URL. There are also methods that are being used to shorten the URL to make it look legit such as [5].

Since Blacklist methods cannot be trusted with the newly generated URLs, there are several techniques such as Heuristic methods that look at the signature generated by the behavior of specific attacks. In these methods, the tool looks for monitoring the behavior of the URL such as the number of redirects it makes, or the unusual process creation. These behaviors are the so-called signatures of the URL [17, 20]. The attackers launched several attacks that exploited obfuscation of the signature. As a result, the signatures are not detectable in such attacks.

To overcome the above methods for breaking the blacklist and signature-based methods, researchers have relied on machine learning techniques. Machine learning methods are based on extracting features from a set of training dataset and performing statistical analysis to be able to predict and classify the URLs into benign and malicious. There are two types of features that can be extracted from the URLs, the dynamic features and the static features. The static features include lexical attributes of the URL, the host and sometimes the JavaScript and other content of the host. The dynamic features require the execution and clicking on the URL in a sandboxing environment and monitoring the live behavior of the URLs. It is expected that the behavior of the URL is considered anomalous compared to the behavior of benign URLs [4, 21]. One of the drawbacks of the second category is that the decision-making process takes longer compared to the static feature detection methods.

## 4  Proposed Method

In this section, the problem formulation is explained. Our system architecture has three main parts as shown in the list below. In the following sections, we go over the details of the proposed architecture.

- The feature extraction
- The training module
- The prediction component

The framework for this model has been shown in Fig. 2. The approach schematically presents the procedure of detecting malicious URLs. As it is shown in Fig. 2, the URLs should be analyzed in terms of the available information and their corresponding websites. To achieve these, two different methods have been proposed naming static and dynamic. The static method only uses the information and executing of the analyzed URLs is not necessary. This advantage makes the static method safer compared to the dynamic model. Further extensions were performed by researchers to improve the static method. They employed machine learning techniques to increase the accuracy of the response of the static based features. Despite the advantages of the static procedure, in real world applications, they usually suffer from some major limitations. To overcome these limitations some online learning methods have been considered by researchers.

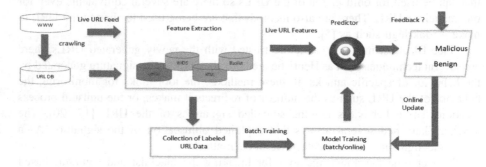

**Fig. 2.** Machine learning for URL detection framework

### 4.1  Problem Statement

The problem of this paper is explained as a binary classification problem. The classes for prediction are either malicious URL versus Benign URL. Consider a set of $N$ URLs as in

$$\{(u_0, y_0), (u_1, y_1), \ldots, (u_n, y_n)\} \tag{1}$$

Where $u_n$ is defined as the URL string number $n$ and $y_n$ is the corresponding label for $u_n$, in which $y_n = +1$ depicts malicious and $y_n = -1$ depicts benign. The first step in this framework is to extract feature $u_n \rightarrow x_n$ where $x_n \in R^d$ presents a numerical feature of the URL. The next step is to train prediction function $f : R^d \rightarrow R$ which is predicting the class for URL $x$ which is represented by $y'$. The subtraction of the predicted value from the actual value, $y - y'$, is defined as the mistake in the prediction and the goal of the machine learning algorithm is to minimize the amount of total mistake for all predictions. The first part of the algorithm, feature extraction, is mostly based on available knowledge of the URL, while the second part is mostly achieved by trying different models in training the machine learning model.

## 4.2    Feature Extraction

The first step in the feature extraction is to split a URL into three sections:

1. Protocol
2. Domain
3. Path

As a result, the first feature extracted is whether the string format of the domain is a URL or an IP address. The reason that we divided our database into three sections is that the features extracted from a domain will be different from a URL or from an IP address. The extracted features from URL such as bag of word or n-grams will show only 0 for domains or IP addresses and this will result in an unbalanced bias in training the model.

Here is the list of different features extracted:

**Blacklist Features:** As mentioned, blacklist features cannot be trusted with the new URLs generated by the attackers. But it has been shown that most of the attackers make very small changes to the URL string [9]. So, we applied a method of fuzzy matching using the *fuzzybuzzy* and *difflib* library of python and used the resulting number of similarity matches as a feature. This number could be any value from 0 to 100 as a percentage. The database used for comparison is PhishTank [15].

**Lexical Features:** These features are mostly extracted from the URL string. The features we extracted from the strings are the length of the string, number of dots, number of characters such as /, = , *, ?, .., , number of sub-domains, Shannon entropy of the URL string [13]. The list of features will be shown in detail below.

- N-grams: Previous research has shown that the obfuscation of the URLs will cause bias in the distribution of the characters. N-grams are extracted from the URL characters. The value of $N$ can be anything between 1 to 10. For example, the first three bigrams of *google.com* are go, oo, og. This is much stronger than the bag of words method used in [10], since it captures punctuation as well.

**Host-Based Features:** The host-based features are extracted from the URLs. They help with knowing the location, identity, management style and properties of the URL [14]. Phishers tend to use short-term services, WHOIS information [7], location and domain name properties. This information can be extracted using **PyWhois** library.

There are several other host-based features that could be extracted; however, the disadvantage of host-based features is that they need to be extracted based on a response by running the algorithm live (dynamic features) and we need a sandboxing environment for that.

### 4.3    Training Model

The unpredictable nature of this problem, and the fact that attackers can generate any type of string, only by changing a couple of characters in a legit URL has made us choose a classification algorithm that is more resistant against noise. Also, malicious URL and phishing detection are the main tasks of CSOC (Cyber Security Operations Center) in industrial firms and companies. Machine learning is a tool that can be used to assist CSOC analysts in their decision-making process. As a result, choosing an algorithm that makes interpretable results is key in helping CSOC make the final decision easier. These circumstances made us try out the results of Random Forest Classification because we can extract the importance of features from the output of this algorithm and present it as part of the results. Random Forest is a good choice in this problem because the training is on multiple clusters of the data and this will lead to reduction invariance.

## 5    Experimental Result

In this section, we explain what datasets we have used for our experiments and also go over the evaluation method and result of training the model.

### 5.1    Dataset

The experiment for this work has been collected using three different sources of data. The first source is the Ebbu2017 Phishing Dataset. Due to the lack of public malicious URL dataset, they have developed their own scripts to query for the Yandex Search engine to create a balanced dataset [18]. The dataset contains about 74k URLs, out of which 36k are legitimate and 37k are phishing. The second source of dataset is the DMOZ dataset and the Alexa.com dataset for providing benign data sources. We also used the prepared malicious URL dataset from [14].

### 5.2    Results

The results of the Random Forest have been compared against other machine learning algorithms will be discussed in this section.

The analysis of the results is first on the exploration of the percentage of overlapping and reusing in N-grams. The percentages of the N-gram overlaps and reuse is shown Fig. 3. According to the results, as the value of the $N$ increases, the number of overlapping decreases. Also, as the overlap decreases between the data sources, the accuracy increases because the features will be more useful for distinguishing the benign vs the malicious URL.

Next, we test the accuracy of our model against other models. For the sake of a fair comparison with previous works, we use our extracted features with other models. Table 1 shows the results. The ROC (Receiver Operating Characteristic) curve is shown in Fig. 4. As shown in this table, the results for the Random Forest outweighs the results of the two other approaches. On top of the simplicity and explain ability of the model. It also has higher accuracy.

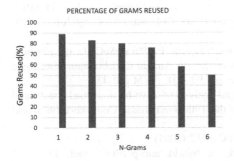

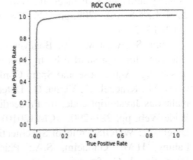

**Fig. 3.** Reused N-grams          **Fig. 4.** Roc curve

**Table 1.** Comparison of classifiers (%)

| Algorithm | Accuracy | F-Score | Recall | Precision |
|---|---|---|---|---|
| Random forest | 96.786 | 94.453 | 95.8 | 90.1 |
| Linear regression | 92.324 | 93.183 | 95.58 | 90.90 |
| Naive Bayes | 87.634 | 89.231 | 82.23 | 85.57 |

## 6    Conclusion and Future Work

This paper proposes a static lexical feature-based Random Forest Classification model to classify malicious vs benign URLs. The results extracted from this experiment show that lexical features can be used for a high-performance and light-weight method for fast generation of URL labels. Our study also shows the result of feature importance on the N-grams lexical feature. Based on our analysis, it will be more useful to use a higher number for $N$ as a feature because it has higher overlap and will result in better accuracy. The future steps for this work are to provide more analysis on the effects of separation of domain names and URLs and also observe the effects of speed vs the number of features extracted.

**Acknowledgments.** This work was supported in part by the FCT/MCTES (UNINOVA-CTS funding UID/EEA/00066/2019), UIDB/00066/2020 (CTS – Center of Technology and Systems), and the FCT/MCTES project CESME - collaborative and Evolvable Smart Manufacturing Ecosystem, funding PRDC/EEI-AUT/32410/2017.

# References

1. RSA Quarterly Fraud Report, vol. 1, no. 3Q3 (2018)
2. Nahorney, O.C.H.L.B., O'Gorman, D.O.B.B., Paul, J.P.P.S.W., Cleary, W.C.W.G., Corpin, M.: Internet security threat report. Technical report 23, Symantec Corporation (2018)
3. State of the Phish™ Report: Wombat security technologies (2018)
4. Canfora, G., Medvet, E., Mercaldo, F., Visaggio, C.A.: Detection of malicious web pages using system calls sequences. In: Teufel, S., Min, T.A., You, I., Weippl, E. (eds.) CD-ARES 2014. LNCS, vol. 8708, pp. 226–238. Springer, Cham (2014). https://doi.org/10.1007/978-3-319-10975-6_17
5. Chhabra, S., Aggarwal, A., Benevenuto, F., Kumaraguru, P.: Phi.sh/$oCiaL: the phishing landscape through short urls. In: Proceedings of the 8th Annual Collaboration, Electronic messaging, Anti-Abuse and Spam Conference, pp. 92–101. ACM (2011)
6. Cova, M., Kruegel, C., Vigna, G.: Detection and analysis of drive-by-download attacks and malicious JavaScript code. In: Proceedings of the 19th International Conference on World Wide Web, pp. 281–290. ACM (2010)
7. Daigle, L.: WHOIS Protocol Specification, RFC 3912 (2004)
8. Fahmy, H.M., Ghoneim, S.A.: PhishBlock: a hybrid anti-phishing tool. In: 2011 International Conference on Communications, Computing and Control Applications, pp. 1–5 (2011)
9. Felegyhazi, M., Kreibich, C., Paxson, V.: On the potential of proactive domain blacklisting. LEET 10, 6-6 (2010)
10. Gyawali, B., Solorio, T., Montes-y Gómez, M., Wardman, B., Warner, G.: Evaluating a semisupervised approach to phishing URL identification in a realistic scenario. In: Proceedings of the 8th Annual Collaboration, Electronic Messaging, Anti-Abuse and Spam Conference, pp. 176–183. ACM (2011)
11. Hong, J.: The state of phishing attacks. Commun. ACM 55(1), 74–81 (2012)
12. Liang, B., Huang, J., Liu, F., Wang, D., Dong, D., Liang, Z.: Malicious web pages detection based on abnormal visibility recognition. In: 2009 International Conference on e-Business and Information System Security, pp. 1–5. IEEE (2009)
13. Lin, J.: Divergence measures based on the shannon entropy. IEEE Trans. Inf. Theor. 37(1), 145–151 (1991)
14. Ma, J., Saul, L.K., Savage, S., Voelker, G.M.: Identifying suspicious urls: an application of large-scale online learning. In: Proceedings of the 26th Annual International Conference on Machine Learning, pp. 681–688. ACM (2009)
15. LLC OpenDNS: PhishTank: an anti-phishing site (2016). https://www.phishtank.com
16. Patil, D.R., Patil, J.: Survey on malicious web pages detection techniques. Int. J. u-and e-Serv. Sci. Technol. 8(5), 195–206 (2015)
17. Rieck, K., Krueger, T., Dewald, A.: Cujo: efficient detection and prevention of drive-by-download attacks. In: Proceedings of the 26th Annual Computer Security Applications Conference, pp. 31–39. ACM (2010)
18. Sahingoz, O.K., Buber, E., Demir, O., Diri, B.: Machine learning-based phishing detection from URLs. Exp. Syst. Appl. 117, 345–357 (2019)

19. Sheng, S., Wardman, B., Warner, G., Cranor, L.F., Hong, J., Zhang, C.: An empirical analysis of phishing blacklists. In: 6th Conference on Email and Anti-Spam (CEAS), California, USA (2009)
20. Shibahara, T., et al.: Malicious url sequence detection using event denoising convolutional neural network. In: 2017 IEEE International Conference on Communications, pp. 1–7 (2017)
21. Tao, Y.: Suspicious URL and device detection by log mining. Ph.D. thesis, Applied Sciences: School of Computing Science (2014)

# Communication Systems

# Cooperative Communication Mechanisms Applied to Wireless Sensor Network

Suelen Laurindo[1]([✉]), Ricardo Moraes[2], and Carlos Montez[1]

[1] Department of Automation and Systems, Federal University of Santa Catarina,
Florianópolis, Brazil
suelen.m.l@posgrad.ufsc.br, carlos.montez@ufsc.br
[2] Department of Computing, Federal University of Santa Catarina,
Araranguá, Brazil
ricardo.moraes@ufsc.br

**Abstract.** The purpose of this paper is to present ongoing PhD work that investigates both the cooperative diversity and techniques of network coding needed to improve communication reliability in wireless sensor networks. In this context, we propose a relay selection technique. It aims to select the smallest number of relay nodes under certain constraints. One of the main innovations is that this approach is formulated as an optimisation problem. In addition, we analyse the best approach for solving the proposed optimisation problem. The assessment results highlight that the proposed technique significantly improves the communication reliability of the network in comparison with the state-of-the-art techniques for selection of relay nodes. Network coding techniques will be tackled in the second stage of development of this research.

**Keywords:** Wireless sensor network · Industry 4.0 · Relay selection

## 1 Introduction

Industry 4.0 is a recent concept that is transforming physical objects into intelligent virtual objects and can promote better control in all industries. One of the technologies that supports the Industry 4.0 paradigm involves wireless sensor networks (WSNs). WSN nodes link the physical world with the digital, thus integrating machines, humans and/or environments with the cyber-physical world [1].

However, WSNs are subject to restrictions on their reliability when exchanging messages between network nodes. The quality of communication provided by the link layer depends on the channel condition and inter-node distance, which vary with the environment in which the WSNs are deployed [2]. In this context, this ongoing PhD work investigates new solutions for improving the reliability of WSNs using cooperative diversity and network coding techniques.

This work has been partially funded by CAPES, The Brazilian Agency for Higher Education, under the project Print CAPES-UFSC "Automation 4.0" and CNPq/Brasil (Project 870048/2007-4).

L. M. Camarinha-Matos et al. (Eds.): DoCEIS 2020, IFIP AICT 577, pp. 121–128, 2020.
https://doi.org/10.1007/978-3-030-45124-0_11

When cooperative diversity techniques are used, the relay nodes transmit both their own data and the data previously stored from other nodes. Relay selection is a critical step that may affect the quality of transmission, and it is important to find the most appropriate relay selection criteria for the operation of the network [3].

In addition, network coding techniques can be used to allow relay nodes to perform retransmissions. In this technique, intermediary nodes acting as relays retransmit stored messages according to specific mathematical coding techniques. The use of these techniques can increase the effective transmission rate of the network and the overall communication reliability [3].

This study aims to address the communication limitations of WSNs by treating the selection of relay nodes in a holistic way, combining both cooperative diversity techniques and the use of network coding algorithms to enhance the communication reliability of WSN networks. The fundamental issue addressed here can be summarised in the form of the following research question:

"Is it possible to increase the reliability of WSN communication by proposing a relay selection technique that considers a set of relevant criteria for the operation of the network, combined with a network coding technique for message retransmissions?"

For this question, the research hypothesis is that, considering the appropriate criteria for the selection, only nodes with optimal characteristics will be relays. This will increase the reliability of the network without generating excessive energy consumption. In addition, the use of a network coding technique in the retransmissions will allow encoding several messages in a single packet, with a size t, which is equal to the size of a single message before encoding.

This paper is organised as follows. In Sect. 2, we present the contributions to life improvement; Sect. 3 discusses some relevant research works on the selection of relay nodes in WSNs; Sect. 4 describes the primary contributions of this ongoing PhD research and explains the proposed relay selection technique. Section 5 contains a discussion of the simulation results, and finally, conclusions and future work are presented in Sect. 6.

## 2    Contribution to Life Improvement

This work aims to improve the reliability of communications in WSNs, one of the technologies enabling the dissemination of the Internet of Things (IoT) and Industry 4.0 paradigms. This research positively impacts several applications, and consequently makes a contribution to improving daily life in several areas, for example healthcare, smart cities, smart agriculture, Industry 4.0 and the sustainable use of terrestrial ecosystems.

In the healthcare domain, IoT devices can be used to monitor a patient's health status, regardless of his or her location. A monitoring system is often used to oversee a patient's vital parameters, such as blood pressure, heart rate and body temperature. This monitoring system permits the patient greater mobility due to the fact that it is a wireless technology [4].

In smart cities, WSNs can be used in several applications that combine advanced sensors with information and communication technologies to help in efficiently managing the assets of the city and to promote sustainable development. These applications include home automation, city security services, parking optimisation, road traffic management, environmental monitoring, and energy management [5].

The use of IoT applications in agriculture helps to minimise challenges such as extreme weather conditions and climatic changes. These applications have helped farmers to monitor temperature, humidity and water levels in real-time, making the irrigation process more efficient, increasing food's production.

Industry 4.0 impacts the way in which products are manufactured, and allows a higher level of operational effectiveness, productivity and better working conditions to be achieved. To improve productivity, many products may have an electronic identification throughout the product life cycle, thus enabling the collection of data on the use of this product. This makes it possible to understand the patterns of consumption and to improve products to meet the requirements of users [6].

Finally, IoT sensors can be used to monitor terrestrial ecosystems in many applications, for example monitoring animal behaviour and the movements of animal species in a natural environment with minimal human interference. Analysis of monitored data allows us, for example, to find new ways of managing the populations under study, to determine the impact of human development on them, or to understand whether there are enough individuals of a species in a given area to ensure survival. Another application is the forest monitoring, which permits the efficient detection of forest fires and the avoidance of major catastrophes [7].

WSNs are increasingly present in people's everyday lives, facilitating the development of daily activities and improving the quality of life.

## 3  Related Work

In the literature, there are many works about relay selection techniques. However, most of them do not give importance to the criteria used to select the relay nodes. We can classify the state-of-the-art relay selection techniques into five categories, considering the criteria used for relay selection, i.e. those based on quality of link [8–12], quality of link and energy [13–16], quality of link and neighbourhood [17, 18], quality of link and data rate [19, 20], and random relay selection [21].

Table 1 summarises the works cited here, and compares them to each other with respect to the following set of classifiers: the category used to select the relays, whether or not the reason for choosing the parameters used to select the relay nodes is specified, and whether or not the use of additional message is required.

From Table 1, we can observe several similarities between these works. For instance, most of these studies consider only the quality of link criterion, which may generate an incorrect relay selection [22]. The main reason for this is that hardware metrics are based on a sample of only the first eight symbols of a successfully received message, and do not consider lost messages. Therefore, this can provide an inaccurate estimate of the quality of the link.

Another characteristic is that additional message exchanges are necessary to make the selection in most state-of-the-art techniques. However, when WSNs are used, these messages may generate a significant overhead in the network.

**Table 1.** Characteristics of the state-of-the-art relay selection techniques.

| State-of-the-Art | Classification Categories | Analysis of the Used Criterion | Additional Messages |
|---|---|:---:|:---:|
| Liu et al. [8] | Quality of Link | | |
| Senanayake et al. [10] | Quality of Link | | |
| Zhu et al. [12] | Quality of Link | | ✓ |
| Marchenko et al. [9] | Quality of Link | | ✓ |
| Valle et al. [11] | Quality of Link | | |
| Etezadi et al. [18] | Quality of Link and Neighborhood | | ✓ |
| Alkhayyat, Gazi and Sadkhan [17] | Quality of Link and Neighborhood | | ✓ |
| Brante et al. [14] | Quality of Link and Energy | | |
| Ahmed, Razzaque and Hong [13] | Quality of Link and Energy | | ✓ |
| Pham and Kim [16] | Quality of Link and Energy | | ✓ |
| Cheikh, Simpson and Sun [15] | Quality of Link and Energy | | ✓ |
| Gokturk and Gurbuz [19] | Quality of Link and Data Rate | | |
| Ouyang et al. [20] | Quality of Link and Data Rate | | |
| Willing and Uhlemann [21] | Random Relay Selection | | ✓ |
| **Proposed Technique** | Multi Parameters | ✓ | |

Source: Adapted from [23].

Finally, all of these works mention only the criteria used to select the relay nodes, without performing any analysis of their real impact. It is worth mentioning that factors such as the different combinations of relay selection criteria, the way in which they are modelled and the parameters they use directly impact on the relay selection performance.

To minimize some of the disadvantages observed in this analysis, the relay selection technique proposed in this paper considers the parameters that are relevant for network operation as criteria for the relay selection. In addition, it does not require the exchange of any additional messages.

## 4    Research Contributions

This work aims to investigate new solutions for improving the reliability of WSNs using cooperative diversity and network coding techniques. In the initial phase of this PhD research, it was proposed a relay selection technique (PRST) [23]. This formed the first step of the present research and is almost finished. The second stage of the research, relating to network coding, is currently in progress, together with the development of the proposed technique using a real WSN prototype.

### 4.1    Proposed Relay Selection Technique

The proposed relay selection was formulated as an optimisation problem, considering a benefit function with the following selection criteria: (a) the number of neighbours of the candidate node; (b) the remaining battery energy; (c) the quality of the link between the candidate node and its neighbour nodes; and (d) the historical success rate of recent node transmissions. The mentioned criteria were selected because they have a great impact on the adequate operation of the network. In addition, this paper considers an adaptive relay selection in which the interval between each relay selection occurs dynamically based on the success rate of the network.

The system model considers a network organised in a star topology. It is also assumed that relay nodes will be used as intermediate nodes to establish communication between the nodes without a direct communication with the coordinator node. A slotted communication approach is used in which the medium access is based on a TDMA (Time Division Multiple Access) scheme. The IEEE 802.15.4 communication standard is used for the PHY (physical) and MAC (medium access control) layers of the network. It operates in time-slot mode and with beacon-enabled. The PRST assumes that specific configuration information is exchanged between the coordinator and the nodes in each beacon interval, i.e. the coordinator sends configuration commands piggybacked with the beacon frame, and the nodes send configuration information along with the sensed data. When the relay nodes have been selected, communication takes place through two stages: transmission and retransmission. In the transmission stage, each node makes one transmission; the relay nodes will stand by, listening to and storing all messages received together with the identification (ID) of the sending node. If the node is not a relay, after its transmission step, it will enter sleep mode.

In the retransmission stage, each relay node will retransmit one message to the coordinator node, containing all the IDs of the received messages. In a table, the coordinator stores all messages received. Whenever the coordinator receives a retransmission message, it verifies if all the messages in this retransmission are in the table. If they are, it counts this retransmission as a duplicate; otherwise, it adds the messages to the table. After retransmission, the relay enters sleep mode.

In order to find the minimum number of relay nodes, while ensuring that each node has a reachable relay, an optimisation problem was formulated. Due to space limitations, the details are omitted in this paper. For further details, the reader is referred to [23].

## 5    Discussion and Results

The relay selection technique proposed in this work was evaluated by simulation experiments. The network simulation tool called OMNeT++ was used along with the Castalia framework. A total of 5 simulation scenarios were defined, varying the number of nodes. The scenarios were defined to have 20, 40, 60, 80 and 100 nodes. In each scenario, an extra node was configured as a coordinating node. Nodes were randomly deployed over a $50 \times 50$ m$^2$ area, with the PAN coordinator placed in the center of the area. Castalia supports some propagation channel models to be used in the simulation, and the free space was used to be simple and efficient. Each simulation was executed for 450 s, which corresponds to the time needed for the coordinator to send up to 50 beacons. In each simulation experiment, the topology was dynamically generated, as proposed in [23].

In the first assessment, the proposed relay selection technique (PRST) was analysed and contrasted with other techniques. This paper describes the comparison with three techniques considered as the state-of-the-art: opportunistic [11], random around the coordinator (RAC) [18], and completely random (CR) relay selection [21].

Figure 1(a) illustrates the correlation between the total of cooperation messages sent by each node. This correlation allows us, for example, to verify how many cooperation sent by each node are necessary to obtain a minimum success rate. PRST achieved the best results. In all situations, their success rate reached values above 95%, and it also showed the smallest number of cooperation messages. This behavior was obtained thanks to the proposed optimization technique, which selects a smaller number of relay nodes. Of the state-of-the-art techniques, the opportunistic scheme achieved the best results for the success rate. However, it was one of the worst techniques analysed when considering the metric that assesses the number of cooperation messages sent by each node. The CR scheme achieved the worst results for both metrics.

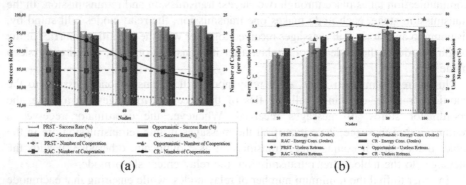

(a)                                    (b)

**Fig. 1.** Correlation between (a) success rate and number of cooperation messages per node; and (b) energy consumption and percentage of useless retransmission messages.

Figure 1(b) shows the correlation between the energy consumption and the percentage of redundant retransmitted messages. This correlation illustrates that when the network contained numerous redundant retransmitted messages, some unnecessary relay nodes were selected and, consequently, more energy was expended by these nodes. The PRST technique achieved the best results, with the lowest energy consumption and the smallest number of unnecessary retransmitted messages, showing that an adequate number of relay nodes was selected. The other analysed techniques performed a large number of unnecessary retransmission messages, meaning that they required a higher energy consumption.

In the second assessment, we evaluated the performance and solution quality of three different algorithms, a greedy algorithm [24], a genetic algorithm [25] and branch and bound algorithm (B&B) [26], which are suitable for solving the optimisation problem of the PRST technique. The B&B algorithm was used in the first stage of this assessment (Fig. 1(a) and (b)).

These three algorithms were coded in the C++ language, and were tested on the same computer using a Ubuntu 18.04 operating system, with an Intel® Xeon® E3-1240 v2 (3.40 GHz) CPU and 16 GB memory. The execution time for each algorithm represents the simulation time required to perform the relay selection. This metric allows us to evaluate whether the algorithm is a viable solution for use in a real-time WSN. In the system model used by the proposed relay selection technique [23], the coordinator node must use only a 15.36 ms time slot to select the relay nodes and to send the beacon.

The genetic algorithm needs a longer time (63 ms) than the greedy algorithm (0.7 ms) in order to achieve a similar success rate (98,54% for the genetic algorithm and 98,74% for the greedy algorithm). The B&B algorithm performs the relay selection in 12 ms and achieves a success rate of 98.9%. The greedy and genetic algorithms showed many redundant retransmissions (14% for the greedy algorithm and 15% for the genetic algorithm). The B&B presented 9% of the redundant retransmissions. In this way, the greedy algorithm can be considered a viable solution to this problem, based on characteristics such as extremely low execution time and a success rate that was very similar to that of the B&B algorithm. The B&B algorithm was the approach that showed the best results for all metrics, and this can be considered the best solution.

## 6 Conclusion and Future Work

Relay selection is an essential step in guaranteeing adequate cooperative communication. The primary research of this doctoral work is on techniques for the best selection of retransmission nodes. These techniques are being designed to have low overhead and without consuming energy from the nodes unnecessarily.

In future work, we intend to merge cooperative diversity techniques with a network coding technique. The basis of this idea is an improvement in the communication success rate of the WSN nodes. We also expect to implement the proposed technique in a real WSN prototype, running some real-world applications in a variety of scenarios.

## References

1. Dargie, W., Poellabauer, C.: Fundamentals of Wireless Sensor Networks. Wiley, Hoboken (2010)
2. Ez-Zazi, I., Arioua, M., El Oualkadi, A., Lorenz, P.: A hybrid adaptive coding and decoding scheme for multi-hop wireless sensor networks. Wirel. Pers. Commun. **94**, 3017–3033 (2017)
3. Guo, Q., Li, X.: A safety relay selection method based on network coding. Int. J. Commun. Netw. Syst. Sci. **10**, 167–175 (2017)
4. Sadiku, M., Eze, K., Musa, S.: Wireless sensor networks for healthcare. J. Sci. Eng. Res. **5**, 210–213 (2018)
5. Bukhari, S.H.R., Siraj, S., Rehmani, M.H.: Wireless sensor networks in smart cities: applications of channel bonding to meet data communication requirements. In: Mouftah, H. T., Erol-Kantarci, M., Hussain Rehmani, M. (eds.) Transportation and Power Grid in Smart Cities: Communication Networks and Services, pp. 247–268. Wiley, Hoboken (2018)

6. Ślusarczyk, B.: Industry 4.0: are we ready? Polish J. Manag. Stud. **17**, 232–248 (2018)
7. Bouabdellah, K., Noureddine, H., Larbi, S.: Using wireless sensor networks for reliable forest fires detection. Procedia Comput. Sci. **19**, 794–801 (2013)
8. Liu, L., Hua, C., Chen, C., Guan, X.: Relay selection for three-stage relaying scheme in clustered wireless networks. IEEE Trans. Veh. Technol. **64**, 2398–2408 (2015)
9. Marchenko, N., Andre, T., Brandner, G., Masood, W., Bettstetter, C.: An experimental study of selective cooperative relaying in industrial wireless sensor networks. IEEE Trans. Ind. Inf. **10**, 1806–1816 (2014)
10. Senanayake, R., Atapattu, S., Evans, J.S., Smith, P.J.: Decentralized relay selection in multi-user multihop decode-and-forward relay networks. IEEE Trans. Wirel. Commun. **17**, 3313–3326 (2018)
11. Valle, O., Montez, C., Medeiros de Araujo, G., Vasques, F., Moraes, R.: NetCoDer: a retransmission mechanism for WSNs based on cooperative relays and network coding. Sensors **16**, 799 (2016)
12. Zhu, K., Wang, F., Li, S., Jiang, F., Cao, L.: Relay selection for cooperative relaying in wireless energy harvesting networks. IOP Conf. Ser. Earth Environ. Sci. **108**, 52059 (2018)
13. Ahmed, M.H.U., Razzaque, M.A., Hong, C.S.: DEC-MAC: delay- and energy-aware cooperative medium access control protocol for wireless sensor networks. Ann. Telecommun. Ann. Des Télécommunications **68**, 485–501 (2013)
14. Brante, G., Peron, G.D.S., Souza, R.D., Abrão, T.: Distributed fuzzy logic-based relay selection algorithm for cooperative. Sensors **13**, 4375–4386 (2013)
15. Cheikh, M., Simpson, O., Sun, Y.: Energy efficient relay selection method for clustered wireless sensor network. In: 23rd European Wireless Conference, European Wireless 2017, pp. 92–97. Offenbach, Berlin (2017)
16. Pham, T.L., Kim, D.S.: Efficient forwarding protocol for dual-hop relaying wireless networks. Wirel. Pers. Commun. **89**, 165–180 (2016)
17. Alkhayyat, A., Gazi, O., Sadkhan, S.B.: The role of delay and connectivity in throughput reduction of cooperative decentralized wireless networks. Math. Probl. Eng. **2015**, 10 (2015)
18. Etezadi, F., Zarifi, K., Ghrayeb, A., Affes, S.: Decentralized relay selection schemes in uniformly distributed wireless sensor networks. IEEE Trans. Wirel. Commun. **11**, 938–951 (2012)
19. Gokturk, M.S., Gurbuz, O.: Cooperation with multiple relays in wireless sensor networks: optimal cooperator selection and power assignment. Wirel. Netw. **20**, 209–225 (2014)
20. Ouyang, F., Ge, J., Gong, F., Hou, J.: Random access based blind relay selection in large-scale relay networks. IEEE Commun. Lett. **19**, 255–258 (2015)
21. Willig, A., Uhlemann, E.: On relaying for wireless industrial communications: is careful placement of relayers strictly necessary? In: 9th IEEE International Workshop on Factory Communication Systems (WFCS), pp. 191–200 (2012)
22. Baccour, N., et al.: F-LQE: a fuzzy link quality estimator for wireless sensor networks. In: Marrón, P.J., Whitehouse, K. (eds.) Wireless Sensor Networks: 8th European Conference, pp. 240–255 (2010)
23. Laurindo, S., Moraes, R., Nassiffe, R., Montez, C., Vasques, F.: An optimized relay selection technique to improve the communication reliability in wireless sensor networks. Sensors **18**, 1–25 (2018)
24. Chandu, D.P.: Improved greedy algorithm for set covering problem. SSRG Int. J. Comput. Sci. Eng. **10**, 1–4 (2015)
25. Srinivas, M., Patnaik, L.M.: Genetic algorithms: a survey. Computer **27**, 17–26 (1994)
26. Morrison, D.R., Jacobson, S.H., Sauppe, J.J., Sewell, E.C.: Branch-and-bound algorithms: a survey of recent advances in searching, branching, and pruning. Discret. Optim. **19**, 79–102 (2016)

# Probabilistic Network Coding for Reliable Wireless Sensor Networks

Eman AL-Hawri[(⊠)], Faroq AL-Tam, Noelia Correia,
and Alvaro Barradas

CEOT, University of Algarve, 8005-139 Faro, Portugal
{esalhawri,ftam,ncorreia,abarra}@ualg.pt

**Abstract.** Energy consumption and packet loss are common concerns in wireless sensor networks. However, designing protocols to minimize both metrics becomes very challenging because these are competing goals. In this paper, a data dissemination approach is proposed that uses probabilistic network coding to achieve a balance between energy consumption and packet loss. A subset of the network nodes, forming a directed acyclic graph, is selected to perform the encoding process under a certain probability. These nodes are the ones responsible for data delivery towards the gateways. The encoding probability is based on the kind of packet received: the more innovative the packet is, the higher the probability of going through the encoding process. The results show that random linear network coding, under such conditions, is able to adequately minimize energy consumption and packet drops, while being a very practical solution.

**Keywords:** Wireless sensor network · Network coding · Reliability · Energy saving

## 1 Introduction

Wireless sensor networks (WSNs) are used in many applications and are now a key element in the increasingly growing Internet of Things. A WSN is a network of spatially distributed sensing devices, usually of low cost, that may have self-organizing ability, or not, and may vary in their features and capabilities. These are able to sense their surrounding, communicate with their neighbors, and send their observations to a sink/gateway where the observed data is analyzed, processed and sent to the end user.

WSNs are usually considered constrained networks because nodes are equipped with restricted processing, memory, and energy capabilities [1]. Such resource limitations make the design of high Quality of Service (QoS) and energy-efficient applications a very challenging task. In fact, most methods and routing protocols try to solve this tradeoff between achieving QoS while using as little energy as possible. To develop applications with reasonable long lifetime, energy-saving policies should be followed [2]. Here in this article a data dissemination protocol is proposed that improves reliability, through packet loss minimization, while having energy-saving concerns for long application lifetimes.

The reminder of this article is organized as follows: Sect. 2 provides the related work while Sect. 3 presents the contribution of this article to life improvement. Section 4 addresses the network coding principle. Section 5 details the proposed method

© IFIP International Federation for Information Processing 2020
Published by Springer Nature Switzerland AG 2020
L. M. Camarinha-Matos et al. (Eds.): DoCEIS 2020, IFIP AICT 577, pp. 129–136, 2020.
https://doi.org/10.1007/978-3-030-45124-0_12

while Sect. 6 discusses the results analysis. Finally, Sect. 7 provides the conclusions and future work.

## 2 Related Work

Network coding (NC) has been explored for different types of networks, including wired, wireless, sensor, and mobile. Each type of network applies NC to achieve a certain goal, which may relate to throughput increase, security improvement, reliability (decrease of packet drops), and energy saving.

In [3], dynamic network coding is used in multi-source systems that organize nodes as peers to form a P2P network. In these systems, a coordinator server is used to assign the roles for peers, ensuring that the NC process is accomplished successfully. The paper employs dynamic NC, where all peers in the P2P distributed system participate in the encoding/decoding process. The NetCoder in [4] mixes transmit diversity and random linear network coding techniques for WSN reliability purposes. Inter-flow Network Coding based Opportunistic Routing (INCOR) in [5] incorporates both opportunistic routing and inter-flow network coding to increase the performance of WSNs.

CodeDrip, proposed in [6], is a data dissemination protocol that utilizes network coding to achieve reliability, energy saving, and to increase the data dissemination speed in WSNs. CodeDrip uses a probability to decide whether to send the packet or to combine it with other messages for sending. To combine packets, binary coding with finite field $\mathbb{F}_2$ (XOR) is used to reduce the overhead induced by the random linear coding. In [7], the adequate number and location of encoding nodes is planned, considering predefined failure scenarios. This means that the number and location of critical links must be previously identified, which may not be possible in dynamic environments.

The method proposed here can achieve reliability while reducing the energy consumed, and can be applied in dynamic networks.

## 3 Contribution to Life Improvement

Sensor nodes can now be deployed anywhere and in any number to cover any intended area, and WSNs have now many different applications [8, 9]. Sensor networks have mainly been used in:

- *Military applications*: This was one of the first applications of WSNs. Nowadays sensor networks play a significant role in military commands, communication, monitoring of either friend or enemy force, intelligence, and surveillance.
- *Health applications*: Sensor networks became an essential part of health care systems. Hospitals are equipped with numerous sensor networks that monitor patients and return their state and location. This can be critical for patients requiring constant monitoring. Additionally, life expectancy will increase in the coming years, and healthcare systems can be equipped with technology distributed in the surrounding area of aged people, for monitoring of their state without affecting their daily activities [10].

- *Industrial applications*: One of the fields getting most benefits from WSNs is the industry. There are applications in buildings, constructions, and bridge condition monitoring, and other. Furthermore, sensor nodes can monitor the condition of machines, providing in some cases automatic maintenance, very important in production processes. Another vital role of sensor networks is to monitor production performance [11].

In this paper we aim to achieve two goals: (*i*) help constrained networks to have longer life; (*ii*) provide reliable information to the interested users. Achieving these goals will contribute to improve the lives of those who depend on these networks.

## 4  Network Coding

Network coding allows network nodes to perform linear combinations on received packets, and route one or more combined packets. In linear network coding, packets are represented as symbols over finite field $\mathbb{F}(2^m)$ of size $m$ and an encoding node performs a linear combination per symbol position as follows:

$$Y_k = \sum_{i=1}^{n} \alpha_i \times X_k^i \qquad (1)$$

where the $\alpha_1, \alpha_2, \ldots, \alpha_n$ is a set of random coefficients, called encoding vector, and $n$ is the number of packets to be encoded. For decoding, the receiver needs to wait until it has enough independent coded packets to be able to perform the decoding and retrieve the original packets. Technically speaking, if a receiver node has received sufficient coded symbols and encoding vectors $(\alpha_m, Y_m)$, it can solve the linear system of equations $X = \beta^{-1} \times Y$ to retrieve the original symbols, where $\beta^{-1}$ is the encoding matrix that contains the coefficients used in the encoding process, [12].

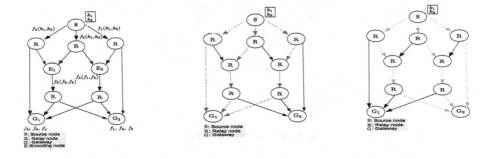

a. Flows towards G1.          b. Flows towards G2.          c. Transmission with NC.

**Fig. 1.** Network coding robustness in multicast network

Network coding can achieve robustness against packet drops resulting from link failures, with no need for retransmission or rerouting. Figure 1 shows an example of a multicast network with one source and two gateways. As shown in Fig. 1a and b, the maximum flow from source s to any gateway is 3, assuming the link capacity is one unit. Regardless of the output port through which packets $k_1$ and $k_2$ go out, in a link failure scenario one of the gateways may not receive both packets. In case of network coding, illustrated in Fig. 1c, the source and nodes $E_1$ and $E_2$ can linearly combine the received data. Consequently, when a link fails, regardless of its location, both gateways can decode and recover the lost data. This is so because each gateway will receive at least two out of three independent coded data units [13]. Thus, with network coding, a multicast rate of 2 is always achieved no matter which link fails. In this work, random linear network coding is used with finite field $\mathbb{F}_{2^8}$.

## 5   Proposed Method

The idea behind the proposed method is to: (*i*) reduce the number of transmissions by giving each packet an encoding probability; (*ii*) reduce the number of encoding nodes by dividing network nodes into three sets, each with a different role, as illustrated in Fig. 2:

- *Source nodes*: These nodes can send their data, and what they hear from their neighbors, to the collector nodes to which they are associated.
- *Collector nodes* (CN): Smallest possible set of nodes chosen to serve the other source nodes. Collectors receive data from their sources, encode them, and forward the coded packets to another CN or to the nearest gateway.
- *Gateways*: These nodes participate in the P2P overlay and their responsibility is to store the packets, coming from the wireless sensor network section, in the P2P where the decoding process can take place to retrieve the original data.

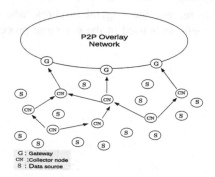

**Fig. 2.** Proposed architecture

This way, the problem can formally be described as follows: *given a network topology represented as a graph* $\mathcal{G} = \{N, L\}$, *where N and L are the set of nodes and links, respectively, and given a set of gateways* $G \subset N$, *the objective is to select the set of collectors C, sources S, and subsets of sources* $Z_c \subset S, \forall c \in C$ *(each subset connected to a* $c \in C$*) such that* $|C|$ *is minimized and reliability is ensured when one or more links fail.*

The proposed solution for this problem is detailed in Algorithm 1. The idea is to create a directed acyclic graph (DAG), from C and connections between its elements, to ensure the flow of packets towards the gateways. This requires the definition of a topological order for $C$. A topological order of $C$ is any $\tau$ such that if $(c_i, c_j) \in L$, then $c_i$ precedes $c_j$ in $\tau$. That is, $\tau_{c_i} \leq \tau_{c_j}$. This DAG is used to forward coded packets toward gateways. More specifically, and as shown in Algorithm 1, the tuple $\{N, L, G\}$ is received and failing links, denoted by $F$, are selected according to a predefined failure probability. Then the following steps are followed:

- *Initialization*: Choose the smallest possible set $C$ taking into account the connectivity of nodes. This criteria reduces the overhead caused by network coding. Build the DAG, towards the multiple gateways, using the nodes in $C$.
- *Dissemination*: Each source sends its packets, and what it hears from neighbors, to the CN to which it is associated. A CN calculates the occurrence of each packet in order to define its encoding probability, and accordingly applies the encoding process. Thus, the probability of encoding depends on the number of occurrences of each packet received by a CN. The rarest packets are more likely to experience an encoding process. The coded packets, generated from the encoding, are then sent through the DAG.
- *Regeneration*: Gateways store the received coded packets in the P2P overlay network, where the decoding can be performed to retrieve the original packets.

**DAG Based Probabilistic network coding (DAG-PNC)**
```
1.  INPUT: N, L, G, F
2.  Begin

        // Initialization
3.      select C
4.      build the DAG by defining a topology order τ for C
5.
        // Dissemination
6.      ∀s ∈ S:
7.          collect its own packet and packets heard from
                neighbors
8.      ∀s ∈ S, ∀l: source(l) = s ∧ l ∉ F:
9.          send collected packets to c ∈ C to which s is
        associated to
10.     ∀c ∈ C:
11.         receive packets from Z_c, k = |Z_c|
12.         calculate the occurrence of each packet
13.         define the probability of encoding
14.         generate k coded packets
15.         send coded packets to neighbors of c ∈ C
                (considering the DAG) or g ∈ G

        // Regeneration
16. ∀g ∈ G: store received coded packets in P2P
```
**Algorithm 1:** The proposed method

## 6    Experimental Results

A set of random dense and sparse physical topologies of 30 nodes were generated and used to compare the performance of the proposed method with CodeDrip [6]. The proposed algorithm and network coding methods were all implemented in Matlab[1]. The parameters adopted in the tests are: (*i*) 4 gateways; (*ii*) link failure probability ranges from 0.05 to 0.3; (*iii*) network connectivity degree of 0.2 for sparse and 0.3 for dense network topologies.

To evaluate both methods, random failure scenarios are generated. In each scenario a link failure probability is assumed, such that one or more links become inoperable. For a specific link failure probability, 20 folds are performed (failing links change randomly at each fold) and the average is used for reporting the results.

### 6.1    Analysis of Results

We consider two performance metrics to evaluate the performance of the methods: **reliability**, which is measured through the number of recovered packets, and the **number of transmissions**, which has impact on energy consumption.

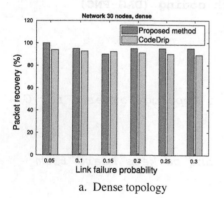
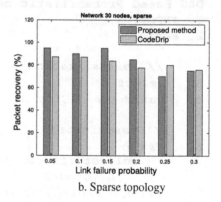

a. Dense topology                    b. Sparse topology

**Fig. 3.**  Reliability

Figure 3 shows the results of packet recovery for both CodeDrip and the proposed method. Figure 3a shows the results for 30-node dense topologies while Fig. 3b shows the results for 30-node sparse topologies. For dense topologies we can see that the proposed method outperforms the CodeDrip and can retrieve more original packets using the decoding process. In sparse topologies, the proposed method also shows better performance, except for two cases of failure rates. This is because CodeDrip also sends original packets towards the gateways. On the other hand, in the proposed method if the decoding process is not accomplished, because enough linearly independent packets cannot reach the P2P successfully, there will be no recovered packet.

---

[1] MathWorks, Inc.

In general, the superior performance of the proposed method over CodeDrip can be related with: (*i*) better design of encoding nodes' location; (*ii*) overhearing performed by sources allows collector nodes to receive packets not only from their sources but also from sources associated with the neighbor collectors; (*iii*) performing the decoding process at the P2P overlay network and not at each gateway.

Even though CodeDrip nodes broadcast their original or coded packets through all paths, this does not ensure better results. The reason is that CodeDrip uses a probability to decide whether to send the packet or to combine it with other packet for sending. Also, XOR is used to combine packets, which means that some packets may not go through the coding process and some lost packets will not be recovered.

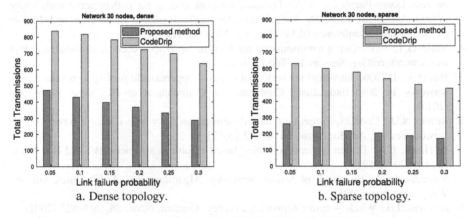

**Fig. 4.** Total transmissions.

Figure 4 shows the total number of transmissions generated by each method. This can help to decide which method consumes more energy. Both Fig. 4a and b show the large number of transmissions generated by CodeDrip. This is because all nodes in CodeDrip broadcast packets through all outgoing links, which results in a huge number of transmissions. In the proposed method, on the other hand, hearing is performed only by sources while collector nodes send a small number of coded packets. More specifically, the number of coded packets generated by a CN is the number of the sources associated with this CN.

## 7   Conclusions and Future Work

In this paper, a probabilistic network coding based WSN is proposed. This includes selecting which packets will be encoded and which nodes will be encoding nodes. The proposed method could recover the packet drops by applying decoding at the P2P overlay network. This means that using network coding in certain nodes and applying the encoding process on the more innovative packets can help in recovering lost packets with no need of a massive number of transmissions. This balancing between reliability and energy consumption can be achieved by sending the adequate number of coded packets to overlay networks. Results show the effectiveness of the proposed approach when compared with the state of art. In the future, we will try to implement binary coding due to the low overhead resulted from such technique when compared to random linear coding.

# References

1. Yick, J.A.: Wireless sensor network survey. Comput. Netw. **52**, 2292–2330 (2008)
2. Matin, M.A.: Overview of wireless sensor network. In: Wireless Sensor Networks-Technology and Protocols (2012)
3. de Asis Lopez-Fuentes, F.A.-A.: Dynamic network coding for collaborative multisource system. In: 2018 IEEE 9th Annual Information Technology, Electronics and Mobile Communication Conference (IEMCON), pp. 378–382. IEEE (2018)
4. Valle, O.T.: NetCoDer: a retransmission mechanism for WSNs based on cooperative relays and network coding. Sensors **16**, 766 (2016)
5. Hu, D.A.: INCOR: inter-flow network coding based opportunistic routing in wireless mesh networks. In: 2015 International Conference on Communications (ICC), pp. 3666–3671 (2015)
6. Junior, N.D.: CodeDrip: improving data dissemination for wireless sensor networks with network coding. Ad Hoc Netw. **54**, 42–52 (2017)
7. Al-Hawri, E.A.: Design of network coding based reliable sensor networks. Ad Hoc Netw. **91**, 101870 (2019)
8. Stojmenovic, I.: Handbook of Sensor Networks: Algorithms and Architectures, vol. 49. Wiley, Hoboken (2005)
9. Akyildiz, I.F.: Wireless sensor networks: a survey. Comput. Netw. **38**, 393–422 (2002)
10. Tennina, S.A.-V.: WSN4QoL: Wireless Sensor Networks for quality of life. In: 2013 IEEE 15th International Conference on e-Health Networking, pp. 277–279 (2013)
11. Erdelj, M.A.: Applications of industrial wireless sensor networks. In: Industrial Wireless Sensor Networks: Applications, Protocols, and Standards, pp. 1–22 (2013)
12. Goncalves, D.A.: Random linear network coding on programmable switches. In: 2019 ACM/IEEE Symposium on Architectures for Networking and Communications Systems (ANCS), pp. 1–6 (2019)
13. Kamal, A.E.: Network coding-based protection. Opt. Switching Netw. **11**, 189–201 (2014)

# Joint Channel and Information Estimation on Symbol Decomposition-Based Secure Point-to-Point Communications

Akashkumar Rajaram[1,3,4], David Borges[1,2], Paulo Montezuma[1,2],
Rui Dinis[1,4(✉)], Dushnatha Nalin K. Jayakody[3], and Marko Beko[4,5]

[1] DEE, FCT, Universidade Nova de Lisboa, Lisbon, Portugal
rdinis@fct.unl.pt
[2] IT, Instituto de Telecomunicações, Lisbon, Portugal
[3] School of Computer Science and Robotics,
National Research Tomsk Polytechnic University, Tomsk, Russia
[4] Copelabs, Universidade Lusófona, Lisbon, Portugal
[5] UNINOVA, Monte de Caparica, Portugal

**Abstract.** Energy efficiency and physical layer security are important features in future wireless communication networks. A secure point to point communication is established by using a symbol decomposition method where higher order modulation symbols are decomposed into bits or smaller symbols as separate components and then transmitted to the receiver through multiple amplifiers on the same channel. One of the main challenges in symbol decomposition is accurate channel knowledge for the case of non-static transmitter and receiver position, which necessitates employing a robust and accurate channel estimation with this technique. To improve the accuracy of the channel estimate, an iterative block decision feedback equalizer (IB-DFE) is used at the receiver for joint channel and information estimation. In this paper, we study the symbol decomposition method along with the channel estimation technique and analyze the performance of the system model by using bit error rate parameter and results showcase the effectiveness of IB-DFE receiver.

**Keywords:** Channel estimation · Efficient power amplification · Low complexity detection

## 1 Introduction

In this work, the massive multiple-input multiple-output (mMIMO) system model is adopted with secure point to point communication based on symbol decomposition. Massive MIMO has several advantages over the single input single output model due to its high spectral efficiency [1]. The idea of maximizing the spectral efficiency of mMIMO by using higher order modulation symbols can lead to high peak-to-average power ratio (PAPR), which can lead to distortion and reduce amplification efficiency [2]. Naturally, higher order modulation signals have amplitude difference in the multilevel constellation points to high envelope fluctuations. Alternatively, higher order modulation symbols can be decomposed into low order modulation symbols to

L. M. Camarinha-Matos et al. (Eds.): DoCEIS 2020, IFIP AICT 577, pp. 137–146, 2020.
https://doi.org/10.1007/978-3-030-45124-0_13

experience low envelope fluctuations which results in improved amplification efficiency over signal with high envelope fluctuations. In this method, we decompose sixty four Quadrature Amplitude Modulation (64-QAM) symbol into six Binary Phase Shift Keying (BPSK) symbols and amplify all the six components in six transmitting antenna and eventually beamforms all the components simultaneously through a single channel. The receiver receives all the components as a single 16-QAM symbol [3]. In this paper, we decompose 64-QAM symbol into six BPSK symbols instead of three QPSK symbols, since using BPSK will have low envelop as compared to using QPSK. Also, based on the results from [3] in terms of security aspects, we use BPSK.

This method involves multi-layer system: a multi-branch amplification circuit forms the first layer; each branch is connected in parallel to an antenna array forming the second layer; the third layer is composed of a spatial multiplexing circuit. This multi-layer approach can create complex channel matrix and self-interference in the received signal. Therefore, this requires Iterative Block Decision Feedback Equalization (IB-DFE) to reduce the self-interference in the signal detection block [4]. IB-DFE is a low complexity receiving technique because it does not require matrix inversion unlike mMIMO conventional receivers, improving estimation and the information estimate with each iteration [5, 6].

We consider that both the transmitter and receiver positions are dynamic and, in this condition, the communication channel will also be dynamic, thus it is imperative to estimate channel information at the receiver. If receiver does not know accurate channel knowledge, then the symbol components will for distorted higher order modulation symbols. A robust channel estimation technique is employed in his system model, in which, we superimpose pilot symbol for every single data symbol and estimate at the receiver [7, 8]. This technique is robust and gives accurate estimates but consumes higher energy as compared to other techniques and this excess energy can be harvested from the superimposed signal at the receiver by using power splitting based simultaneous wireless power and information transmission technique (PS-SWIPT) with an power splitting circuit [9, 10]. The physical layer security aspects of the decomposition-based transmitter were already explained in [3]. Thus, in this paper we focus on energy efficiency and channel estimation technique with IB-DFE receiver.

The paper is organized as follows: Sect. 2 describes the system model. Section 3 describes joint information and channel estimation technique. The performance analysis is illustrated with simulation results in Sect. 4. Conclusion and future works are given in Sect. 5.

## 1.1   Technological Innovation and Contribution for Life Improvement

From autonomous cars to health monitoring systems, many real time mobile applications depend on the resilience of the communication system. The presented system combines energy efficiency, information security and improved channel estimation for non-static channels. It means that the overall communication will be more robust compared with classic schemes, thus providing a solid based for the development of more and better products for life improvement. This paper also adopts green communication technology SWIPT to improve energy efficiency and opportunistically use the available excess energy from RF signals and thereby this system model is suitable for sustainable wireless communication system.

## 2  System Model

In this system model, a 64-QAM signal is decomposed to six BPSK polar components and transmitted over Rayleigh frequency selective fading channel, which is denoted as $H_k$. Single-carrier frequency-division multiple access (SC-FDMA) transmission scheme is used for transmitting all the symbol components over $H_k$. The 64-QAM symbols are converted to its corresponding bits [5]. The modulated symbol set is given as $S = \{s_0, s_1, \ldots, s_{N-1}\}$, where $N$ is the total number of symbols, where $s_n \in \mathbb{C}$ and $\mathbb{C}$ denotes constellation. To each constellation point i.e. $s_n$ is associated to a set of bits, the total number bits in constellation points is denoted as $\mu$, $\mu = \log_2(M)$. The bits in polar form for each symbol is given as $B = \{b_n^0, b_n^1, \ldots, b_n^{(\mu-1)}\}$, with $b_n^{(i)} = \pm 1 = 2\beta_n^{(i)} - 1$, $\beta_n^{(i)} = 0 \text{ or } 1$. The set of six bits can be decomposed from each 64-QAM constellation points and the bit subsets of the transmitted signal is given as $B_m$, $m = 0, 1, \ldots, M - 1$, where $M$ is the total number of constellation points. The bits of 64-QAM signal can be written as

$$s_n = \sum_{m=0}^{M-1} g_m \prod_{b_n^{(i)} \in B_m} b_n^{(i)}; \ n = 0, 1, \ldots, M - 1; \tag{1}$$

and this forms a system of $M$ equations for each constellation points in $S$ and $g_m$ is the unknown variable. Without loss of generality, $m$ is associated with its corresponding $\mu$ bits and then $m$ is given as, $m = \left( \gamma_{(\mu-1,m)}, \gamma_{(\mu-2,m)}, \ldots, \gamma_{(1,m)}, \gamma_{(0,m)} \right)$, This defines $B_m$ as the set of bits, where $b_n^{(i)}$ is included if $\gamma_{(i,m)}$ is 1.

Then, $s_n$ can be written as

$$s_n = \sum_{m=0}^{M-1} g_m \prod_{i=0}^{\mu-1} \left( b_n^{(i)} \right)^{\gamma_{(i,m)}}. \tag{2}$$

The transmitter has 3 layers, in the $1^{st}$ layer, the symbols is decomposed into 6 BPSK polar components. In the $2^{nd}$ layer, all the 6 polar components amplified by 6 parallel non-linear amplifiers and these amplifiers are connected to 6 parallel antennas. These 6 parallel antennas denoted as $N_m$, where $m = 1, 2, 3, 4, 5, 6$. In the $3^{rd}$ layer, to reduce the complexity in channel estimation, $N_m$ is combined and connected to only 1 transmitting antenna as in [11] and therefore this system model is similar to single input and multiple output antenna model. Due to amplification of low envelop BPSK components, the power efficiency improves with the decrease in amplifier distortion and lower PAPR of smaller components, it is possible to use non-linear amplifier in transmitter with negligible distortion [12]. All the six components are beamformed by using an angle $\Theta$ to a desired direction towards the receiver like conventional beamforming mMIMO and here all the components are transmitted in a single communication channel. The total number of receiving antennas are denoted as $R$.

Similar to [3, Fig. 1] here, six antennas with the BPSK components have a uniform distance $d$ between them, this $d$ can create time delay of the transmitted components at the receiver. The difference between each component at the receiver due to $d$ and angle $\theta$ can be compensated by using phase shift in the transmitter. The antennas $R$ receives this signal at a time delay $\Delta t$ between each antenna due to the angle $\theta$ and this time delay is assumed to be uniform, which is due to multiple receiving antennas. $\theta$ is originally meant for transmitting all the components in a uni-direction, however due to multiple receiving antenna, there is space $d$ between each antenna is similar to transmitting antenna. In practice, $\Delta t$ is common in all beamforming mMIMO systems and it can be compensated.

## 3   Joint Channel and Information Estimation

The joint channel estimation and signal detection method by using IB-DFE receiver as shown in Fig. 1, which is presented in this section. The received signal at $R$ is given as

$$Y_{k,l,i} = (1 - \alpha)\big(H_{k,l}\big(\sqrt{P_x}X_{k,l} + \sqrt{P_q}Q_{k,l}\big) + N_l\big) + N_{e,l}, \tag{3}$$

where $X_{k,l}$ and $Q_{k,l}$ are the data and pilot symbols and $k$ is the frequency of block $l$, then $k = 0, 1, \ldots, K - 1$   and   $l = 0, 1, \ldots, L - 1$.   $X_{k,l} = DFT\{X_{n,l}\}$   and   $Q_{k,l} = DFT\{q_{n,l}\}$ are the information and pilot signals converted from time to frequency domain, respectively. $N_l$ is additive Gaussian white noise (AWGN) due to signal transmission and $N_{e,l}$ is due to power allocation at power splitting circuit. $(1 - \alpha)$ is power allocated for information and $\alpha$ is the power allocated for energy harvesting.

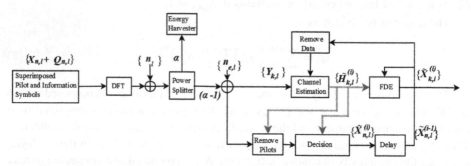

**Fig. 1.** Block diagram of IB-DFE receiver with joint channel and information estimate.

To perform joint channel and information estimation; the average channel estimate $\tilde{H}_{k,l}^{avg}$ without using IB-DFE receiver is estimated over a set of signal block. By using received $\tilde{H}_{k,l}^{avg}$ in IB-DFE, the information estimate $X_{k,l}^{(i)}$ and new channel estimates $\tilde{H}_{k,l}^{(i)}$ are estimated, where $i$ is the number of IB-DFE iterations. In each iteration, the accuracy of estimate improves, and the final information estimate is denoted as $X_{k,l,F}^{(i)}$.

The channel can be estimated by using the received signal and pilot signal, which is given as

$$\tilde{H}_{k,l} = \frac{Y_{k,l,i}}{P_q Q_{k,l}}$$

$$= (1 - \alpha)\left(\frac{H_{k,l}\sqrt{P_X}X_{k,l} + N_l}{\sqrt{P_q}Q_{k,l}}\right) + (1 - \alpha)H_{k,l} + \frac{N_{e,l}}{P_q Q_{k,l}} = (1 - \alpha)H_{k,l} + eH_{k,l};$$

$$(4)$$

$$eH_{k,l} = (1 - \alpha)\left(\frac{H_{k,l}\sqrt{P_X}X_{k,l} + N_l}{\sqrt{P_q}Q_{k,l}}\right) + \frac{N_{e,l}}{P_q Q_{k,l}}, \tag{5}$$

where $eH_{k,l}$ is the channel estimation error. $eH_{k,l}$ depends on the power of the information, noise and pilot signal. The frame structure has $N$ sub carriers per block and it is modelled as in [7]. The expected value of $H_{k,l}$, $N_l$, $N_e$, $X_{k,l}$ and $Q_{k,l}$, respectively is given as

$$\mathbb{E}\left[H_{k,l}\right] = 2\sigma_{h,k,l}^2; \ \mathbb{E}[N_l] = 2\sigma_{n,l}^2; \ \mathbb{E}[N_{e,l}] = 2\sigma_{n,e}^2;$$
$$\mathbb{E}\left[X_{k,l}\right] = N\mathbb{E}\left[X_{n,l}^2\right] = 2\sigma_{X,k,l}^2; \tag{6}$$
$$\mathbb{E}\left[Q_{k,l}\right] = N\mathbb{E}\left[q_{n,l}^2\right] = 2\sigma_{Q,k,l}^2,$$

then applying (6) in (5) gives

$$\mathbb{E}\left[eH_{k,l}\right] = (1 - \alpha)\left(\frac{\sigma_{X,k,l}^2 + \sigma_{n,l}^2}{\sigma_{Q,k,l}^2}\right) + \frac{\sigma_{n,e}^2}{\sigma_{Q,k,l}^2}. \tag{7}$$

Even though channel fades with the change in frequency but remains constant for the respective frequency of a set of transmitted signals. Therefore, (7) can be is written as

$$eH_{k,l}^{avg} = \frac{1}{l}\sum_0^{L-1}\left(\mathbb{E}\left[eH_{k,l}\right]\right), \ l = 0, 1, \ldots, L - 1; \tag{8}$$

$$\tilde{H}_{k,l}^{avg} = (1 - \alpha)\left(H_{k,l} + eH_{k,l}^{avg}\right), \tag{9}$$

Where $eH_{k,l}^{avg}$ and $\tilde{H}_{k,l}^{avg}$ are the average of channel estimation error and channel estimate over $l$ blocks, respectively. The information estimated from the received signal by using channel estimate $\tilde{H}_{k,l}^{avg}$ and $Q_{k,l}$ is given as

$$X_{k,l}^{hd} = \frac{Y_{k,l,i}}{\tilde{H}_{k,l}^{avg}} - (1-\alpha)\sqrt{P_q}Q_{k,l}$$

$$= \frac{(1-\alpha)\left(H_{k,l}\left(\sqrt{P_X}X_{k,l} + \sqrt{P_q}Q_{k,l}\right) + N_l\right) + N_{e,l}}{(1-\alpha)\left(H_{k,l} + eH_{k,l}^{avg}\right)} - (1-\alpha)\sqrt{P_q}Q_{k,l}. \tag{10}$$

The information estimate by using IB-DFE is written as

$$X_{k,l}^{(i)} = \left(Y_{k,l,i} - (1-\alpha)\sqrt{P_q}Q_{k,l}\tilde{H}_{k,l}^{(i)}\right)F_{k,l}^{(i)} - X_{k,l}^{(i-1)}B_{k,l}^{(i)}, \tag{11}$$

where $i$ is the number of iterations with $i = 0, 1, \ldots, n$. In the first iteration, $\tilde{H}_{k,l}^{(0)} = \tilde{H}_{k,l}^{avg}$, then, the feed forward coefficient $F_{k,l}^{(i)}$ is given as

$$F_{k,l}^{(i)} = \frac{F_{k,l}^{(i)}}{\frac{1}{N}\sum_{k=0}^{N-1}\left(F_{k,l}^{(i)}\tilde{H}_{k,l}^{(i)}\right)}, \tag{12}$$

where $F_{k,l}^{(i)}$ is given as

$$F_{k,l}^{(i)} = \frac{\tilde{H}_{k,l}^{(i)}}{\left(\frac{\sigma_{n,k,l}^2}{\sigma_{x,k,l}^2}\right) + |\tilde{H}_{k,l}^{(i)}|^2\left(1 - \left(Cr^{(i-1)}\right)^2\right)} \tag{13}$$

and the correlation factor $Cr^{(i-1)} = \frac{\mathbb{E}\left[X_{n,l}^{(i)}X_{n,l}^*\right]}{\mathbb{E}\left[|X_{n,l}^2|\right]}$. The feedback co-efficient $B_{k,l}^{(i)}$ is given as

$$B_{k,l}^{(i)} = F_{k,l}^{(i)}\tilde{H}_{k,l}^{(i)} - 1. \tag{14}$$

By using $X_{k,l}^{(i)}$ and $Q_{k,l}$ in (4), the improved channel estimates is given as

$$\tilde{H}_{k,l}^{(i)} = (1-\alpha)\left(\frac{H_{k,l}\left(\sqrt{P_X}\left(X_{k,l}^{(i)}\right) + \sqrt{P_q}Q_{k,l}\right) + N_l}{\sqrt{P_X}X_{k,l}^{(i)} + \sqrt{P_q}Q_{k,l}}\right) + \frac{N_{e,l}}{\sqrt{P_X}X_{k,l}^{(i)} + \sqrt{P_q}Q_{k,l}}. \tag{15}$$

Here, two channel estimate obtained from this receiver, they are:

- The channel estimate i.e. (9), obtained without by using IB-DFE.
- The channel estimate i.e. (15), obtained by using IB-DFE block. Here, estimate accuracy improves with each IB-DFE iteration until a saturation point.

Applying (15) instead of (9) in (11) gives information estimates than the previous estimates, which is denoted as $X_{k,l,F}^{(i)}$. Here, three information estimates obtained from this receiver, they are:

- The information estimate obtained by using $\tilde{H}_{k,l}^{avg}$.
- The information estimate i.e. (11), obtained by using $\tilde{H}_{k,l}^{avg}$ and by using IB-DFE.
- The information estimate i.e. $X_{k,l,F}^{(i)}$, obtained by using improved channel estimate obtained with the help of IB-DFE i.e. (15) and by using IB-DFE.

## 4 Results

The performance of the system model is analyzed by using Monte Carlo simulations. Bit error rate (BER) analysis is considered as the performance metric for this model. For all the simulation results $R = 32$ and $K = 256$, while $l = 2; 3$. The power ratio between pilot signal and the data symbols at the transmitter is denoted as $\beta$. To analyze the impact of channel estimation, energy harvesting power allocation $\alpha$ is considered zero except Fig. 4.

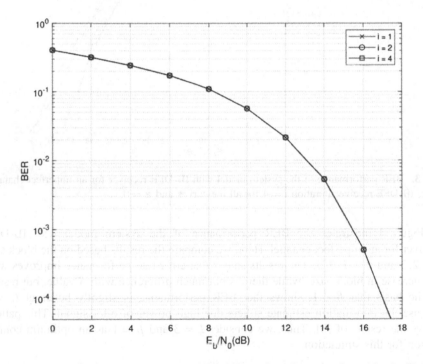

**Fig. 2.** BER performance of the system model with perfect channel, where $i$ is the IB-DFE receiver iteration and $\alpha = 0$.

Figure 2 illustrates the BER performance of the system model with IB-DFE, where irrespective of number of iterations, the BER does not improves with iteration due to high diversity provided by $R$. The results demonstrate that, under high order diversity,

BER reaches its saturation point and there is no scope of improvement. Therefore, this simulation model is can be used in imperfect channel model condition, to understand the impact of IB-DFE receiver on the channel estimation technique.

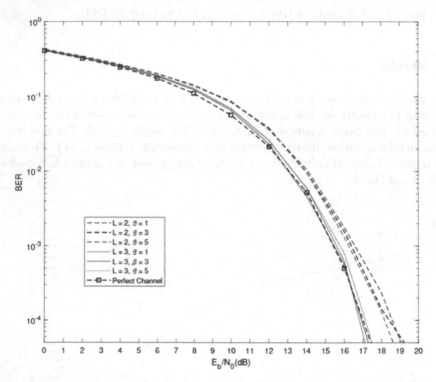

**Fig. 3.** BER performance of the system model with IB-DFE receiver for an imperfect channel. Here, IB-DFE receiver iteration $i = 4$ for all the curves and $\alpha = 0$.

Figure 3 illustrates the BER performance of the system model with IB-DFE receiver for an imperfect channel. Here, we compare the results based on the block size $L = 2, 3$ and $\beta = 1, 3, 5$. The results shows that error rate performance improves with the increase in block size, while there is not much difference with $\beta$ value, but results on the basis that $\beta = 1$, shows that BER performance is slightly better at $L = 3$, because the information estimate suffers due high power of pilot signal. This pattern shows the results of [8]. Thus, we consider $L = 3$ and $\beta = 1$ as an optimum configuration for this simulation.

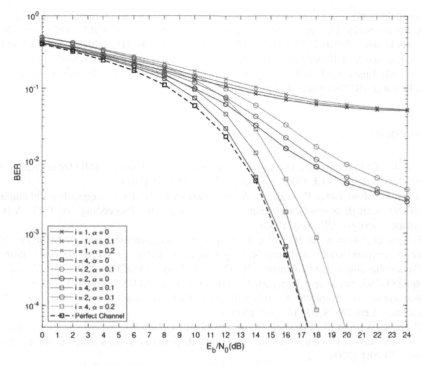

**Fig. 4.** BER performance the system model with imperfect channel condition, where $\alpha = \{0, 0.1, 0.2\}$, $L = 3$ and $\beta = 1$.

Figure 4 illustrates BER performance under imperfect channel condition and, the BER performance improves with increase IB-DFE iterations. The impact of power loss due to energy harvesting increases with increase in $\alpha$ value. Thereby, IB-DFE incorporation with this channel estimate technique helps to achieve better performance as similar to system with perfect channel condition and helps in improving BER performance under energy harvesting condition. This simulation analysis explicitly demonstrates the advantage of using IB-DFE receiver for allowing rectenna to harvest 10% of the total energy of the received signal with the loss of 1 dBm SNR.

## 5 Conclusions

In this paper, we have analyzed the efficiency of IB-DFE receiver for joint channel and information estimation. The results show the improvement of error rate performance under the imperfect channel condition proves that IB-DFE receiver is perfect choice for employing SWIPT, which results in less one dBm SNR loss for using up to 10% of power for energy harvesting. Also employing efficient power amplifier with less distortion due to signal low envelop makes this system model energy efficient at both transmitter and receiver. For the future, this work can be extended to multiple channel estimation for multi-user scenarios.

**Acknowledgments.** Work is supported by FCT/MCTES through national funds and when applicable co-funded EU funds under the project MASSIVE5G (PTDC/EEI-TEL/30588/2017), PhD scholarship (SFRH/BD/131093/2017), Copelabs (UIDB/04111/2020) and Instituto de Telecomunicações (UIDB/EEA/50008/2020). The research work is developed in part with Universidade Lusòfona/ILIND funding and supported, in part, by the Russian Foundation for Basic Research (RFBR) grant No 19-37-50083\19.

# References

1. Larsson, E.G., Edfors, O., Tufvesson, F., Marzetta, T.L.: Massive MIMO for next generation wireless systems. IEEE Commun. Mag. **52**(2), 186–195 (2014)
2. Dinis, R., Montezuma, P., Gusmao, A.: Performance trade-offs with quasi-linearly amplified OFDM through a two-branch combining technique. In: Proceedings of IEEE VTC96, Atlanta, Georgia, US (May 1996)
3. Borges, D., Montezuma, P., Dinis, R., Viegas, P.: Energy efficient massive MIMO point-to-point communications with physical layer security: BPSK vs QPSK decomposition. In: Camarinha-Matos, L.M., Almeida, R., Oliveira, J. (eds.) DoCEIS 2019. IAICT, vol. 553, pp. 283–295. Springer, Cham (2019). https://doi.org/10.1007/978-3-030-17771-3_25
4. Benvenuto, N., Tomasin, S.: Block iterative DFE for single carrier modulation. IEEE Electron. Lett. **39**(19), 1144–1145 (2002)
5. Dinis, R., Kalbasi, R., Falconer, D., Banihashemi, A.: Iterative layered space-time receivers for single-carrier transmission over severe time-dispersive channels. IEEE Commun. Lett. **8**(9), 579–581 (2004)
6. Borges, D., Montezuma, P., Dinis, R.: Low complexity MRC and EGC based receivers for SC-FDE modulations with massive MIMO schemes. In: 2016 IEEE GlobalSip, Washington, DC, USA (December 2016)
7. Dinis, R., Lam, C.T., Falconer, D.: Joint frequency-domain equalization and channel estimation using superimposed pilots. In: Wireless Communications and Networking Conference, pp. 447–452 (2008)
8. Rajaram, A., Jayakody, D.N.K., Dinis, R., Kumar, N.: Receiver design to employ simultaneous wireless information and power transmission with joint CFO and channel estimation. IEEE Access **7**, 9678–9687 (2019)
9. Perera, T.D.P., Jayakody, D.N.K., Sharma, S.K., Chatzinotas, S., Li, J.: Simultaneous wireless information and power transfer (SWIPT): recent advances and future challenges. IEEE Commun. Surv. Tutor. **20**(1), 264–302 (2018)
10. Rajaram, A., Khan, R., Tharranetharan, S., Jayakody, D., Dinis, R., Panic, S.: Novel SWIPT schemes for 5G wireless networks. Sensors **19**(5), 1169 (2019)
11. Astucia, V., Montezuma, P., Dinis, R., Beko, M.: On the use of multiple grossly nonlinear amplifiers for higly efficient linear amplification of multilevel constellations. In: Proceedings of IEEE VTC2013-Fall, Las Vegas, NV, US (September 2013)
12. Montezuma, P., Gusmão, A.: Design of TC-OQAM schemes using a generalised nonlinear OQPSK-type format. IEEE Electron. Lett. **35**(11), 860–861 (1999)

# Self-interference in Multi-tap Channels for Full-Duplex Wireless Systems

Ayman T. Abusabah[1,2], Rodolfo Oliveira[1,2(✉)], and Luis Irio[1,2]

[1] Departamento de Engenharia Electrótecnica e de Computadores,
Faculdade de Ciências e Tecnologia, Universidade Nova de Lisboa,
Lisbon, Portugal
rado@fct.unl.pt
[2] Instituto de Telecomunicações, Aveiro, Portugal

**Abstract.** Residual self-interference (SI) is primarily a key challenge when designing In-Band Full-duplex (IBFDX) wireless systems. Channel estimation errors are one of the major causes of residual SI. Consequently, a deeper understanding of the impact of the channel effects on the residual SI becomes indispensable. In this paper, we investigate the influence of multiple taps on the residual SI power of IBFDX systems. We first formulate the effect of having independent taps on the residual SI power mathematically. The derivations take into account the amount of interference cancellation on each tap by considering phase and amplitude estimation coefficients. We conclude that the increase in the number of taps always leads to an additive effect of the residual power. Such findings are shown mathematically and also reported in different results obtained by simulation. Finally, we compare the distribution of the residual SI power with different known distributions, concluding that Weibull and Gamma distributions are the closest ones in terms of accuracy. In-Band Full-Duplex communication Residual self-interference Independent fading taps channel.

**Keywords:** In-Band Full-Duplex communication · Residual self-interference · Independent fading taps channel

## 1 Introduction

In In-Band Full-Duplex (IBFDX) communications, the nodes can transmit and receive the signals simultaneously on the same frequency [1]. Compared with half-duplex communication systems, where the resources are divided between transmission and reception, the capacity of the communication link can be double in IBFDX systems [2].

The key challenge, when designing IBFDX systems, is the self-interference (SI), which is the transmitted signal being interfered with the received signal at the receiver of the same node. The SI can be mitigated by a combination of passive and active methods [3]. Passive methods use the antenna design to achieve the maximum delay spread for the SI signal. On the other hand, active methods exploit the knowledge of the SI, i.e., transmitted signal, to remove it and obtain the desired signal. Active methods are unable to eliminate the SI signal totally. This is due to the fact that the transmitted signal is being affected by channel and hardware impairments before reaching the

Published by Springer Nature Switzerland AG 2020
L. M. Camarinha-Matos et al. (Eds.): DoCEIS 2020, IFIP AICT 577, pp. 147–155, 2020.
https://doi.org/10.1007/978-3-030-45124-0_14

receiver. Therefore, subtracting the SI signal is insufficient to suppress the residual power perfectly.

We define the residual SI as the amount of remaining signal after the cancellation of the SI signal. In order to reduce the amount of residual SI, the effects of the propagation channel have to be estimated and injected in the cancellation process before the subtraction. Therefore, it is significant to explore the effect of the propagation channel on the residual SI power. In this work, we study the behavior of the residual SI power in multiple taps channel for IBFDX systems. We characterize the power distribution for a different number of taps and cancellation errors through analytical formulation and simulation results.

## 1.1 Research Question and Motivation

The key challenge when designing the IBFDX system is to reduce the amount of residual SI. Apart from hardware impairment, the amount the residual SI power is mainly related to the accuracy of the estimated channels. Most of times, the transmitted signal is propagated over multiple paths, so, multiple copies, with different gains and phases, are combined at the receiver. The motivation of this work is to explore the effect of multiple taps channel on the residual SI power. Our focus is to understand the bottlenecks that limit the SI power from being totally eliminated when multiple taps are considered, by answering the following research questions:

- Question 1: What is the effect of having multiple taps channel on the residual SI power and how to characterize the residual SI power in such scenario?
- Question 2: What is the relationship between the number of propagation taps and the residual SI power?
- Question 3: What is the distribution of the residual SI power when considering a multiple taps channel?
- Question 4: What is the effect of gain, phase, and estimation error on the residual SI power?

## 1.2 Related Work

Despite of its importance, the characterization of the stochastic properties of the residual SI has received limited attention due to the difficulty of the mathematical modeling process [4–6]. In [4], the amount of cancellation and the strength of residual SI are computed considering a single-tap delay channel. The authors adopted a narrow-band signal model to characterize the residual SI power, i.e., it is assumed that the signal time is less than the coherence time of the channel. The similarity of the residual SI distribution with known distributions was analyzed in [5] for a single-tap delay channel. In [6], the distribution of the residual SI power is also characterized for a single-tap delay channel. In particular, the proposed modeling methodology assumes that the signal takes the same value for a consecutive number of samples, since the carrier frequency (and consequently the sampling frequency) is higher than any frequency component of the input signal. To the best of our knowledge, our work is the first to consider a multi-tap channel scenario in IBFDX communication systems.

## 1.3   Contributions

In this work, the effect of multiple taps channel on the residual SI power in IBFDX systems is studied. First, the residual SI power considering multiple taps channel is mathematically formulated. We show that the residual SI power increases with the number of channel taps. We demonstrate that the amount of the cumulative power is a function of gain and phase estimation errors of each tap. Finally, we evaluate the similarity of the residual SI distribution with other known distributions. Such findings are supported through the mathematical analysis and simulation results.

# 2   Technological Innovation for Life Improvement

Over the last two decades wireless communications have changed our lives not only in terms of the way we live, but also on the way we interact socially and work. Two decades ago wireless communications already supported multiple mobile voice services, being a very important asset for a wide range of people, enabling permanent communication and the support of new and more active business schemes. While voice services were and still being a crucially important service, the need to support mobile information systems through wireless communications was also an important challenge. Consequently, the need of high-speed and low-latency mobile data communications services was quickly identified. These requirements are still under development and motivate the entire scientific and technological community in this field. This is the main reason why in the last two decades we witnessed the development of one of the fastest growing industries in the world.

Wireless connectivity has a huge impact in our lives by making certain tasks simpler than ever. Innovative services supported by wireless communications can be found in a plethora of fields: in public safety and security, where unexpected events (e.g. natural calamities) can be quickly communicated to people and machines, no matter where they are; in health care, where the fast dissemination of information can be helpful to improve treatments of remote rural areas; in the automation of traditional processes (e.g. autonomous driving, precision agriculture, industrial networks), where the mobility and/or lack of wired connectivity requires the existence of robust wireless communication services. Additionally to life improvement, the wireless communications drive and support important economic sectors, ranging from the commercial and industrial to agricultural, impacting the world in many important ways.

Although the importance of wireless communications is well recognized, the challenges related with their efficiency and latency are still under development. Traditionally, wireless communications were supported by half-duplex communication schemes, where uplink and downlink data flows were transmitted over different frequency bands. One of the multiple topics of research and innovation in wireless communications is the adoption of the so-called IBFDX communications, where both downlink and uplink flows are transmitted and received over the same frequency band. However, the shared nature of wireless channel demands for an efficient cancellation of the transmitted signal received in the antenna of the full-duplex device, which is particularly difficult to achieve because of the hardware impairments and the time-varying nature of the wireless communication channels. The work presented in this paper presents a contribution to better understand stochastic aspects of the residual SI due to cancellation errors in tapped-delay line wireless channels, which represent the inefficiency of the full-duplex cancellation schemes. We believe that the current study will effectively contribute to the design of more efficient full-duplex cancellation schemes, by handling the complexity of multi-tap channels in a more efficient way.

## 3   System Model

### 3.1   In-Band Full-Duplex Canceller

In this model, we consider a full-duplex scheme adopting an active analog canceler [4] that reduces the SI at the angular carrier frequency $\omega_c = 2\pi f_c$. The system model is depicted in Fig. 1. The channel is assumed to be a multiple taps channel with $I$ taps, thus, multiple shifted versions of the self-interfered signal $x_s(t)$ with different amplitudes are observed at the receiver side. Each tap, i.e., $i^{th}$ tap, is characterized by a delay $\tau_i$ and gain $h_i$. To obtain the residual SI signal $y_{res}(t)$, the estimated delay $\hat{\tau}_i$ and estimated gain $\hat{h}_i$ of each tap has to be injected to perform the cancellation [4].

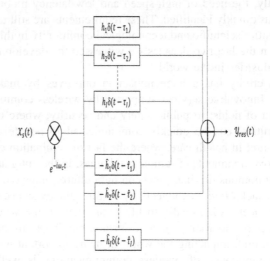

**Fig. 1.**  Block diagram of multi-tap IBDFDX system.

### 3.2   Residual Self-interference Power

Generally, for $I$-taps channel and according to Fig. 1, the $y_{res}(t)$ can be written as follows

$$y_{res}(t) = \sum_{i=1}^{I} h_i x_s(t - \tau_i) e^{j\omega_c(t-\tau_i)} - \sum_{i=1}^{I} \hat{h}_i x_s(t - \hat{\tau}_i) e^{j\omega_c(t-\hat{\tau}_i)}, \tag{1}$$

where channel gains are complex, i.e., $h_i = h_{r_i} + jh_{j_i}$, and uncorrelated, i.e., $E[h_m h_n] = E[h_m]E[h_n]$. The estimated gain is given by $\hat{h}_i = \epsilon_i h_i$, where $(1 - \epsilon_i)$ is the gain estimation error of the $i^{th}$ tap, i.e., $\epsilon = 1$ when the channel is perfectly estimated and $\epsilon = 0$ when estimation is totally corrupted. We also assume that $x_s(t)$ is a circularly-symmetric complex random signal and given by $x_s = x_r + jx_j$.

Assuming a narrow band channel, i.e., $x_s(t - \tau_i) = x_s(t - \hat{\tau}_i) = x_s(t)$, then (1) can be represented as follows

$$y_{res}(t) = x_s(t) \sum_{i=1}^{I} h_i c_i, \tag{2}$$

where $c_i = \left( e^{j\omega_c(t-\tau_i)} - \epsilon_i \, e^{j\omega_c(t-\hat{\tau}_i)} \right)$ is a constant. Since the terms $x_s(t)$, $h_i$, and $c_i$ are complex, and considering that the gains of the taps are uncorrelated, then, the residual SI power can be expressed as

$$P_{y_{res}} = \left( X_r^2 + X_j^2 \right) \sum_{i=1}^{I} \left( H_{r_i}^2 + H_{j_i}^2 \right) C_i, \tag{3}$$

where $C_i = \left( 1 + \epsilon_i^2 - 2\epsilon_i \cos(\phi_i) \right) = \left( (\Re(c_i))^2 + (\Im(c_i))^2 \right)$ is also a constant which represents the power of $c_i$. $\phi_i = \omega_c(\tau_i - \hat{\tau}_i)$ is the phase estimation error of the $i^{th}$ tap.

According to (3), the residual SI power is the product of the power of the transmitted signal with the summation of scaled power gains. By definition, the power of the signal and channel gains are positive, and the constant $C_i$ is a non-negative constant. Thus, the residual SI power increases with the number of taps when the cancellation of each tap is not perfect. When $\phi_i = 0$ and $\epsilon_i = 1$, then, $C_i = 0$ and therefore the additive power of the $i^{th}$ tap is null because it is completely cancelled. On the other hand, when $\phi_i = \pi$ and $\epsilon_i = 1$, then, $C_i = 4$ and therefore the additive power is maximum. Clearly, the amount of the additive power of each single tap is a function of the gain and phase errors and the minimum value it can achieve is 0. Consequently, each single-tap produces an additive effect on the residual SI power when it is not totally canceled.

## 4  Performance Analysis

### 4.1  Evaluation Methodology

The evaluation is based on simulation. The system design in Fig. 1 is adopted. The IBFDX communication system is operating at a carrier frequency of 1 GHz. The residual SI power given in (3) is generated using empirical data. The values of $X_r$ and $X_j$ are sampled from Normal distributions, i.e., $X_r \sim \mathcal{N}(0, \sigma_x^2)$ and $X_j \sim \mathcal{N}(0, \sigma_x^2)$, with

152     A. T. Abusabah et al.

$\sigma_x^2 = \frac{1}{2}$. $H_{r_i}$ and $H_{j_i}$ are sampled from independent Rayleigh distributions, i.e., $H_{r_i} \sim \mathcal{N}\left(0, \sigma_{h_i}^2\right)$ and $H_{j_i} \sim \mathcal{N}\left(0, \sigma_{h_i}^2\right)$.

To support the conclusions presented in Sect. 3, we find the cumulative density function (CDF) of the residual SI power for a different number of independent taps, $I = 1, \ldots, 6$. We consider different gain and phase estimation parameters to figure out the amount of interference cancellation on each tap. Finally, we seek to find the best distribution describing the residual SI power by comparing its probability density function (PDF) with well-known distributions.

### 4.2 Accuracy Assessment

First, we evaluate the fact that the increase in the number of taps always leads to an additive effect of the residual power. To achieve that, we simulate (3) for $I = 2, 3, 4, 5$ and 6 independent Rayleigh fading taps, with $\sigma_{h_i}^2 = \frac{1}{2}$ for all $i$. Figure 2 plots the CDF of each $P_{y_{res}}$ for different number of taps, $I$, and adopting different channel's gain estimation values ($\epsilon = 1$ and $\epsilon = 0.9$). The phase estimation errors adopted in this simulations are given by $\phi_1 = \frac{\pi}{6}, \phi_2 = \frac{\pi}{3}, \phi_3 = \frac{2\pi}{3}, \phi_4 = \frac{7\pi}{6}, \phi_5 = \frac{5\pi}{3}$ and $\phi_6 = \frac{8\pi}{9}$. As shown in Fig. 2, the increase in the number of taps produces an additive effect on the residual power. The amount of the additive power varies according to the gain and phase estimation error.

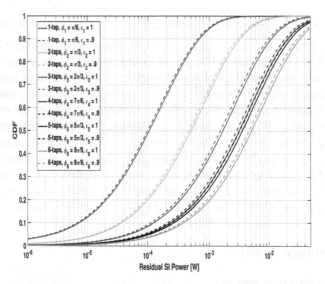

**Fig. 2.** CDF of residual SI power for I = 2, 3, 4, 5 and 6 independent Rayleigh fading channels.

According to (3), the amount of the accumulative power depends on $C_i$, which is a function of gain and phase estimation errors. To support this conclusion, we simulate the residual SI power trying to achieve the minimum additive power, i.e., $C_i = 0$ when

$\epsilon_i = 1$ and $\phi_i = 0$. Figure 3 depicts the CDFs of the residual SI power for $I = 2, 3, 4, 5$ and 6. Perfect gain estimation error, i.e., $\epsilon_i = 1$, is utilized for all taps and the following phase estimation errors are adopted, $\phi_1 = \frac{\pi}{6}, \phi_2 = 0, \phi_3 = \frac{2\pi}{3}, \phi_4 = 0, \phi_5 = \frac{5\pi}{3}$ and $\phi_6 = 0$. As seen in Fig. 3, the amount of the residual SI power for 2 taps is identical to the residual SI power of 1 tap. Also, the amount of the residual SI power for 4 and 6 taps is identical to the residual SI power of 3 and 5 taps, respectively. This is due to the fact that for $I = 2, 4$, and 6, the additive power is almost null, mainly because of the predefined values of gain and phase estimation errors.

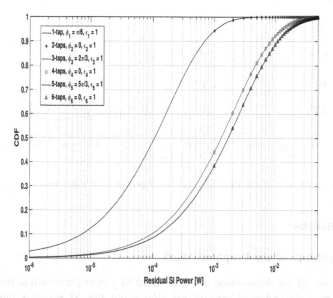

**Fig. 3.** CDF of residual SI power for I = 2, 3, 4, 5 and 6 independent Rayleigh fading channels.

Finally, we evaluate the similarity of the residual SI power with other known distributions. The comparison was done adopting the empirical simulated data obtained from the distributions plotted in Fig. 2 for 2 and 6 taps ($\epsilon_i = 1$ for all $i$). The empirical data was used in a maximum log likelihood estimation process to determine the parameters of the known distributions. The following known distributions were compared: Gamma, Exponential, Nakagami, Rayleigh, Weibull, and Lognormal. Figure 4 plots the PDF of the two distributions that exhibited the best accuracy (Weibull and Gamma) against the PDF of the empirical data. As can be seen, Gamma and Weibull distributions exhibit almost the same level of accuracy. However, they fail to represent the probability density values at particular regions of the domain, which is even more significant as the number of taps increases. The similarity comparison clearly shows that the chosen distributions are not capable of fitting the empirical data in an accurate way over all the domain.

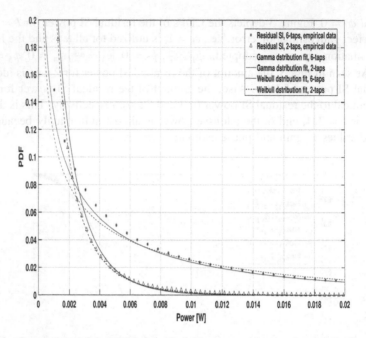

**Fig. 4.** Comparison of the PDF of residual SI power with other known distributions.

# 5   Conclusions

## 5.1   Applicability of the Proposed Work

The conclusions of the distribution of the residual SI power presented in this paper may be used to provide technical criteria for alleviating the SI residual interference in practical IBFDX communication systems. One of the practical applications is the compensation of the cancelation errors, i.e., the gain cancelation error $(1 - \epsilon)$ and the phase cancellation error $(\phi)$. Moreover, the obtained results can also be helpful for the academic community in general, to determine different aspects related to the performance analysis of IBFDX communications. For example, by using the residual SI power to derive the outage probability of a specific FDX system, the capacity of IBFDX communication systems can be achieved.

## 5.2   Final Comments

In this paper, we have investigated the influence of multiple taps on the residual SI power of IBFDX systems. We have shown that the increase of the number of taps always leads to an additive effect of the residual power. Finally, we compared the distribution of the residual SI power with different known distributions, concluding that Gamma and Weibull only exhibit high accuracy at specific regions of the domain and a more accurate solution is desirable. Finally, we highlight that our work can be an initial step for exploring the theoretical distribution of residual SI power in multiple tap channel. The current work compared the residual SI power distribution with know distributions. Deriving the exact distribution may be considered as a future work.

**Acknowledgments.** This work has received funding from the European Union's Horizon 2020 research and innovation programme under the Marie Sklodowska-Curie ETN TeamUp5G, grant agreement No. 813391.

# References

1. Heino, M., et al.: Recent advances in antenna design and interference cancellation algorithms for in-band full duplex relays. IEEE Commun. Mag. **53**(5), 91–101 (2015)
2. Xie, X., Zhang, X.: Does full-duplex double the capacity of wireless networks? In: Proceedings of IEEE INFOCOM, Toronto, ON, Canada, pp. 253–261, April 2014
3. Masmoudi, A., Le-Ngoc, T.: A maximum-likelihood channel estimator for self-interference cancelation in full-duplex systems. IEEE Trans. Veh. Technol. **65**(7), 5122–5132 (2016)
4. Sahai, A., Patel, G., Dick, C., Sabharwal, A.: On the impact of phase noise on active cancelation in wireless full-duplex. IEEE Trans. Veh. Technol. **62**(9), 4494–4510 (2013)
5. Irio, L., Oliveira, R.: On the impact of fading on residual self-interference power of in-band full-duplex wireless systems. In: 2018 14th International Wireless Communications Mobile Computing Conference (IWCMC), pp. 142–146, June 2018
6. Irio, L., Oliveira, R.: Distribution of the residual self-interference power in in-band full-duplex wireless systems. IEEE Access **7**, 57516–57526 (2019)

# Optimization Systems

# Distributed Approach to Traffic Management Automation Implemented According to IEC 61499

Dmitry Elkin[1(✉)] and Valeriy Vyatkin[2,3]

[1] Institute of Computer Technologies and Information Security,
Southern Federal University, Chekhova. 2, 347900 Taganrog, Russia
delkin@sfedu.ru
[2] Department of Electrical Engineering and Automation, Aalto University,
Otakaari 1B, 00076 Aalto, Finland
[3] Department of Computer Science, Electrical and Space Engineering,
Luleå University of Technology, Luleå 97187, Sweden
vyatkin@ieee.org

**Abstract.** The number of vehicles on public roads is increasing while the road infrastructure is not keeping up to this. It is necessary to apply advanced algorithms and approaches to transport management to maximize the use of the existing road network and increase the capacity of roads. In this article, we propose a way to control traffic flows and automate road infrastructure using a multi-agent approach. The proposed approach involves the distributed management of various elements on the road network and their direct relationship with each other in a peer to peer manner. To implement this concept, we used the open standard of distributed control and automation systems IEC 61499, and to validate the approach we used the SUMO - microscopic and continuous road traffic simulation package.

**Keywords:** Multi-agent system · IEC 61499 · Traffic management · Intelligent transportation system · ITS · Traffic · Traffic jam

## 1 Introduction

Today, there are several different automation approaches to cope with traffic management in high traffic conditions and to improve road safety. Usually, to control traffic at intersections, traffic lights with hard-wired non-programmable control are used [1]. To increase the effectiveness of such control, the period of traffic signals varies depending on the time of day [2]. Also, to increase the traffic capacity of the road, the Green Wave approach is used. In this approach, transport engineers calculate the phase shift in the work of traffic lights for various intersections located nearby [3]. The considered approaches are useful when traffic flows are predictable and lose their effectiveness when traffic changes dramatically [4]. In sections of the road network with high traffic intensity and variability, adaptive approaches to traffic control are most effective [5–7]. Approaches to adaptive control are based on the analysis of traffic congestion and changes in the phases of the traffic light, depending on it. Adaptive

© IFIP International Federation for Information Processing 2020
Published by Springer Nature Switzerland AG 2020
L. M. Camarinha-Matos et al. (Eds.): DoCEIS 2020, IFIP AICT 577, pp. 159–167, 2020.
https://doi.org/10.1007/978-3-030-45124-0_15

traffic management shows much better results compared to tight control, significantly reduces traffic delays, travel time, and emissions of harmful substances into the atmosphere [8]. Therefore, modern researchers are developing new and improving existing approaches and algorithms for adaptive traffic management. For example, approaches to adaptive traffic management are actively developing, based on the concept of IoT [9–11] and the use of cloud computing [12]. The concepts of applying the agent approach to adaptive management are also being developed [13–15]. According to the review of the developed solutions for adaptive transport management, the main problems are the complexity of developing and implementing new approaches for the existing road infrastructure. These factors increase the cost of introducing new approaches, as well as the period from the publication of the proposed approach to testing and direct application.

To solve these problems, we propose an approach to adaptive traffic management by intellectualizing the existing road infrastructure. The proposed approach involves the management of intelligent devices at intersections and sections of the road network (traffic lights, sensors, detectors, signs). All these devices are elements of the road infrastructure and are combined by communication channels, forming a single distributed system for managing traffic flows.

To develop and implement the proposed approach of distributed optimization, we used the open standard of distributed control and automation systems IEC 61499 [16]. The IEC 61499 standard does naturally support distributed application development and allows for quick creation of a prototype system to test the operability of the proposed approach, as well as deploy the resulting logic to the industrial grade PLCs, embedded into each traffic light. Combination of these features makes IEC 61499 the technology of choice for our application.

In the next section, we will consider the contribution of this research to improving people's lives. Then in the second part of the work, we describe the essence of the proposed approach to adaptive traffic management. In the third part, we will consider the implementation of the developed approach in a modeling environment and verify its operation on a simulation model of a road network section. In the fourth part of the work, we will present comparative results of traffic flow management using various approaches to the organization of traffic.

## 2    Contribution to Life Improvement

The uninterrupted functioning of the road transport complex is a necessary condition for the sustainable development of the country's economy and the social well-being of the population. Motorization plays a decisive role in the development of the economy and society. However, without the appropriate infrastructural reinforcement, it raises many severe problems in the field of traffic, which have far-reaching consequences for the social and economic sphere. The most serious of these problems is the limited capacity of the road network; the growth of transport infrastructure is not keeping pace with the growth in the number of vehicles. Also, due to the constant growth of the urban population, this problem will sooner or later become relevant in most settlements. High costs for the construction of new road network infrastructure facilities, travel restrictions, as well as environmental factors push companies to study specialized solutions for managing traffic flows to mitigate the negative consequences of traffic jams and optimize the use of limited public funds.

# 3  Approach to Adaptive Traffic Management Based on Interconnected Intelligent Agents

Similarly, to many other areas of industrial automation, system flexibility increases with use of smart IoT devices with embedded intelligence. This implies transition to decentralised control architecture.

In the present control architectures, control actions on traffic flows are formed in the traffic control center, and data on the situation on the road network are also processed centrally. As a result, the system loses its flexibility, and control solutions are slow. However, flexibility and speed of decision making are essential properties for managing dynamic environments.

A popular architecture for distributed decision making is agent-based approach. Its application to traffic management makes the system flexible and intelligent. For example, in [17], a new architecture of a multi-agent approach for traffic control in a section of a road network is proposed. But a significant drawback of the proposed solutions is that it is necessary to create a new infrastructure for implementation and develop specialized equipment. This process is often expensive and lengthy.

At the same time, the use of IoT devices based on modern microcontrollers [18, 19] allows one to partially solve the problem with equipment for the new road infrastructure. However, the questions of reliability of such equipment and integration with existing traffic control systems remain acute.

We offer the concept of traffic management using interconnected intelligent agents. Each of the agents has the authority to apply control actions on vehicles inside the intersection by changing the traffic light cycles or turning it off. Agents also transmit data on traffic congestion in their area of responsibility to agents managing neighboring intersections to provide more efficient traffic control.

At this stage, the following principle of the agent's work at the crossroads is considered:

(1) Receiving data from sensors and sensors located on the road network;
(2) Analysis of traffic congestion according to the logic embedded in the agent;
(3) Transfer of information about workload to neighboring agents;
(4) Obtaining information from neighboring agents;
(5) Decision-making on the control impact on the road network section;
(6) Application of control action (color change of traffic lights).

To verify the presented concept, we used the environment for working with the open standard for the design of distributed systems "NxtStudio" [20] and the traffic flows simulation environment SUMO [21].

# 4  The Implementation of the Concept of Multi-agent Management

At the moment, at the beginning of the development of our concept, we consider implementation of intelligent control of one intersection on the road network with the help of an intelligent agent - traffic controller whose logic is as follows:

The traffic controller determines the number of cars moving in each direction using information from sensors installed on the road network. If the number of cars on the road does not exceed the acceptable value for an uncontrolled intersection, the agent is inactive. As soon as the number of vehicles has exceeded the allowable limit, the traffic controller checks in which direction more cars are moving and analyzes each lane to adjust the intensity of passing cars in each lane individually. After determination, on the selected lanes, the enable signal of the traffic light is turned on. The traffic controller regularly updates the number of vehicles to be passed in each lane: as soon as the number of cars in the moving direction exceeds the half of the number of cars waiting to be driven, the traffic light changes to the enable signal for the waiting cars. The traffic controller works until the number of vehicles at the intersection is reduced to the allowable level for disabling traffic signals.

The proposed simple traffic controller logic when the traffic light is turned on for various directions at the intersection can be represented in the form of formula $\frac{100 \sum_{l=1}^{n} l}{\sum_{r=1}^{k} r} > 50$, where:

n - is the total number of lanes for movement in a moving direction,

l - the number of strips in the moving direction,

k - is the total number of lanes for movement in the waiting direction,

r - is the number of lanes in the waiting direction.

The agent traffic controller was implemented as a function block made according to IEC 61499 as illustrated in Fig. 1.

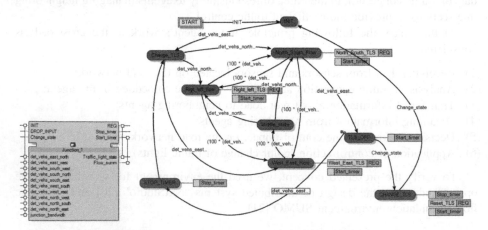

**Fig. 1.** Function block - traffic controller with the adaptive traffic control algorithm implemented as ECC.

Input event INIT initializes the operation of the function block and allows reading data about the current traffic intersection from transport detectors that transmit data to input variables: «det_vehs_east_north» … «det_vehs_north_east». The input variable «junction_bandwidth» determines the maximum congestion for the intersection without traffic lights. Input event «Change_state» - initiates a change by resetting traffic lights when the number of cars at the intersection has decreased to an acceptable level.

Output event REQ - initializes the output variable «Traffic_light_state» in which the traffic light cycle formed by the traffic controller is located.

Output events «Start_timer» and «Stop_timer» are used to control the on and off traffic control mode at the intersection.

The logic of the traffic controller at the intersection is implemented in the function block using the ECC chart with algorithms in the state actions programmed in the Structured Text language.

To verify the concept, we created two models of x-shaped crossroads (Fig. 2). The Crossroad B was created without taking into account the real transport and geometric characteristics of the road network. The intersection has one lane in each direction and a random volume of traffic flows and a standard traffic light cycle.

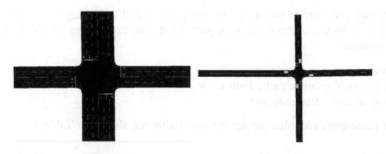

**Fig. 2.** Crossroads – A and Crossroads – B.

Crossroad A is created based on data on transport and geometric characteristics from a specialized manual for transport engineers [22]. It has 3 lanes for movement in each direction from north to south and 2 from west to east. Also, the traffic light cycle based on traffic congestion was specially designed for it. Next, we developed a means for the traffic controller to communicate with a simulation model of a road network section.

The IEC 61499 standard for the design of distributed systems provides for the possibility of communication between devices and the environment using the TCP protocol. This feature was implemented as a NETIO function block. NETIO was used to let the developed traffic controller communicate with the SUMO simulation environment using the Python programming language and the standard SUMO tool - TraCi. In Python, an asynchronous server was implemented for receiving and processing data from the function block of the traffic controller to the simulation model of the inter-section implemented in SUMO (Fig. 3).

After combining the components into a testing environment, we conducted a series of experiments to control traffic at intersections A and B in various ways.

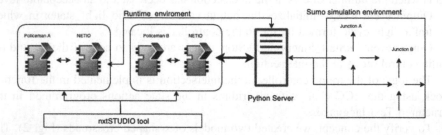

**Fig. 3.** Architecture for testing the distributed automation logic of the road intersection.

## 5 Experimental Validation

Experiments were carried out at two intersections A and B. During the experiments, a simulation of 3600 s of the traffic was performed with three types of traffic control at the intersection:

(1)  Management of a regulatory agent;
(2)  Hard control using a traffic light cycle;
(3)  No regulation (free passage).

The parameters recorded during the simulation are shown in Table 1.

**Table 1.** Simulation parameters.

| Parameter | Unit of measurement | Description |
| --- | --- | --- |
| departDelay | (simulation) seconds | The time the vehicle had to wait before it could start his journey |
| arrivalSpeed | m/s | The speed the vehicle had when reaching the destination |
| waitingTime | s | The time in which the vehicle speed was below 0.1 m/s (scheduled stops do not count) |
| timeLoss | seconds | The time lost due to driving below the ideal speed. (ideal speed includes the individual speedFactor; slowdowns due to intersections, etc., incur timeLoss, scheduled stops not counted) |
| number_cars | pieces | The number of cars that drove the intersection during the simulation period |

**Table 2.** Results for intersection B.

|  | Without traffic control | Agent traffic controller | With standard traffic light |
|---|---|---|---|
| DepartDelay | 349,8 | **259,6** | 1368,1 |
| arrivalSpeed | 8,4 | **8,4** | 9,3 |
| waiting time | **4,9** | 18,8 | 22 |
| timeLoss | 41,3 | **39,3** | 57 |
| number_cars | 1782 | **1950** | 1558 |

As a result of the simulation, the following results were obtained. «departDelay», when using a traffic controller, is about 25% lower without traffic control at the intersection and 80% lower than when using a tight traffic light cycle (Table 2).

The "arrivalSpeed" parameter for control by a traffic controller and without any control is almost the same. When using standard traffic lights, the speed is higher.

The shortest waiting time for vehicles is typical for an intersection without control, but this is relevant only in ideal modeling conditions where no accidents occur. At a controlled intersection, a driving agent reduces latency by 14% compared to a regular traffic light.

The "timeLoss" parameter also takes the smallest value when controlling the traffic controller with an advantage of 31%. With agent control, intersection throughput is increased by 25% compared to standard traffic control. In this case, departDelay without traffic lights is significantly lower than at a regulated intersection, but the agent approach also has an advantage of 19%.

The final speed of vehicles, as well as at the previous intersection, remains approximately the same (Table 3).

**Table 3.** Results for intersection A.

|  | Without traffic control | Agent traffic controller | With standard traffic light |
|---|---|---|---|
| DepartDelay | **42,5** | 410,2 | 506,5 |
| arrivalSpeed | 8,4 | **8,3** | 8,3 |
| waiting time | 34,3 | **26,6** | 30,6 |
| timeLoss | 42,4 | **40,1** | 43,2 |
| number_cars | 1844 | **2220** | 2016 |

As one can see, at a more complex intersection, the traffic controller provides the least time loss for vehicles, up to 7% compared to standard traffic lights. The waiting time for the crossing, which is controlled by the traffic controller, is 22% lower than at the intersection without regulation, and 13% lower than at the intersection with a hard traffic light. And as a result, the traffic capacity of the intersection managed by the traffic controller is 10% higher than with a regular traffic light and 20% higher than without a traffic light, since without a traffic light at this type of intersection there was a big traffic jam on the side of the secondary road.

# 6 Conclusion and Future Work

The work described a novel adaptive agent approach to traffic control at intersections, which switches traffic signals depending on traffic directions.

As a result of the simulations, we have identified advantages in the adaptive intersection control by an intelligent traffic controller, compared to the classic traffic light control, as well as to an unregulated intersection. In most of the studied parameters, control by the adaptive agent is superior to the reference cases, in some cases by several times. At the same time, to implement the agent, the open standard IEC 61499 and the NxtStudio environment were used, which allowed us to quickly create a prototype of the developed solution for the supported controller and implement it on the experimental section of the road network. This approach allows one to quickly move from the development and prototyping stage to the stage of implementation on real equipment. This increases the economic and practical effectiveness of the research.

In future work, we plan to apply this adaptive algorithm to traffic control at several intersections simultaneously. Agents at the intersections will influence the decision on the impact on the traffic flow of each other, exchanging data on the workload of the controlled road network.

Future work will also consider an approach to traffic control, where at each intersection, many agents collectively make decisions when forming the next phase of the movement of vehicles. The decision of such agents would be based on the workload of the controlled strip. First of all, the agent assesses the impact of the decision on the transport situation as a whole. Also, in the process of work, the opinions of neighboring agents on the necessary phases of vehicle movement are taken into account.

**Acknowledgments.** The reported study was funded by RFBR, project number 19-37-90102.

# References

1. Roess, R.P., Prassas, E.S., McShane, W.R.: Traffic Engineering. Pearson/Prentice Hall, Upper Saddle River (2004)
2. Heung, T.H., Ho, T.K., Fung, Y.F.: Coordinated road-junction traffic control by dynamic programming. IEEE Trans. Intell. Transp. Syst. **6**(3), 341–350 (2005)
3. Nagatani, T.: Vehicular traffic through a sequence of green-wave lights. Physica A **380**, 503–511 (2007)
4. Gershenson, C., Rosenblueth, D.A.: Self-organizing traffic lights at multiple-street intersections. Complexity **17**(4), 23–39 (2012)
5. Smith, S.F., et al.: Smart urban signal networks: initial application of the surtrac adaptive traffic signal control system. In: Twenty-Third International Conference on Automated Planning and Scheduling (2013)
6. Hunter, M.P., et al.: A probe-vehicle-based evaluation of adaptive traffic signal control. IEEE Trans. Intell. Transp. Syst. **13**(2), 704–713 (2012)
7. Pandit, K., et al.: Adaptive traffic signal control with vehicular ad hoc networks. IEEE Trans. Veh. Technol. **62**(4), 1459–1471 (2013)
8. Tielert, T., et al.: The impact of traffic-light-to-vehicle communication on fuel consumption and emissions. In: 2010 Internet of Things (IOT). IEEE (2010)

9. Khanna, A., Anand, R.: IoT based smart parking system. In: 2016 International Conference on Internet of Things and Applications (IOTA). IEEE (2016)
10. Bui, K.-H.N., Jung, J.E., Camacho, D.: Game theoretic approach on real-time decision making for IoT-based traffic light control. Concurr. Comput.: Pract. Exp. **29**(11), e4077 (2017)
11. Phan, C.T., et al.: Applying the IoT platform and green wave theory to control intelligent traffic lights system for urban areas in Vietnam. TIIS **13**(1), 34–51 (2019)
12. He, W., Yan, G., Da Xu, L.: Developing vehicular data cloud services in the IoT environment. IEEE Trans. Ind. Inf. **10**(2), 1587–1595 (2014)
13. Mzahm, A.M., Ahmad, M.S., Tang, A.Y.C.: Agents of Things (AoT): an intelligent operational concept of the Internet of Things (IoT). In: 2013 13th International Conference on Intellient Systems Design and Applications. IEEE (2013)
14. Liu, Y., Liu, L., Chen, W.-P.: Intelligent traffic light control using distributed multi-agent Q learning. In: 2017 IEEE 20th International Conference on Intelligent Transportation Systems (ITSC). IEEE (2017)
15. Bui, K.-H.N., Jung, J.J.: Internet of agents framework for connected vehicles: a case study on distributed traffic control system. J. Parallel Distrib. Comput. **116**, 89–95 (2018)
16. IEC61499-1: Function Blocks - Part 1 Architecture. International Electrotechnical Commission, Geneva, International Standard (2005)
17. Kaminski, N.J., Murphy, M., Marchetti, N.: Agent-based modeling of an IoT network. In: 2016 IEEE International Symposium on Systems Engineering (ISSE). IEEE (2016)
18. Misbahuddin, S., et al.: IoT based dynamic road traffic management for smart cities. In: 2015 12th International Conference on High-Capacity Optical Networks and Enabling/Emerging Technologies (HONET). IEEE (2015)
19. Chong, H.F., Ng, D.W.K.: Development of IoT device for traffic management system. In: 2016 IEEE Student Conf on Research and Development (SCOReD). IEEE (2016)
20. The tool for engineering of distributed systems. https://www.nxtcontrol.com/en/engineering/
21. The vehicular traffic simulator. http://sumo.sourceforge.net/
22. Stolyarov, V., et al.: Guidelines to practical work and diploma design for students of the specialty 190700 "Substantiation of duration of the lighting cycle" (2012)

# Formal Verification of IEC 61499 Enhanced with Timed Events

Viktor Shatrov[1]($\boxtimes$) and Valeriy Vyatkin[1,2,3]($\boxtimes$)

[1] ITMO University, Saint Petersburg, Russia
vvshatrov@yandex.ru
[2] Aalto University, Helsinki, Finland
[3] Lulea University of Technology, Lulea, Sweden
vyatkin@ieee.org

**Abstract.** Many applications of Cyber-Physical Systems (CPS) play a crucial role in shaping the quality of life. The malfunction of such systems can lead to dangerous consequences, hence safety takes an important role. One of the common issues of CPS is the variability of event delays. This paper addresses formal verification of system ability to withstand event delays. To achieve such property, we use the concept of event timestamps. The paper proposes changes in IEC 61499 syntax to introduce timestamps into the programming language. The application of new syntax introduces better opportunities for formal verification. We enhanced FB2SMV tool to generate SMV models automatically from the initial system. The paper presents a case study of an elevator system that illustrates the proposed approach. Results of verification show that the system can perform time-aware computations. The proposed approach has shown better verification performance compared to timestamps manually added through the data connections between function blocks.

**Keywords:** Cyber-physical systems · Formal verification · IEC 61499 · Time-aware computations

## 1 Introduction

The application of the distributed Internet of Things (IoT) architecture in industrial control systems raises questions about the robustness of the system and guarantees of invariance of physical system behavior when the same software is executed on different IoT configurations. CPS software based on the IoT architecture is executed on distributed devices that communicate via network and changes in the physical environment such as wireless communication distortions, battery discharge, physical location change, and many other environmental parameters change may affect the behavior of the system. The cyber-physical agnosticism (CPA) is a property of automation software that was proposed in [1] and it is defined as the system's ability to maintain the programmed behavior of the physical process despite interference from the physical environment. Event timestamps for IEC 61499 were proposed in [1] to achieve the CPA property. We elaborate the proposal of [1] by introducing the extension of the language of function blocks (FBs), which is described by the standard IEC 61499, with event timestamps. A formal verification approach can be applied to verify that CPA

© IFIP International Federation for Information Processing 2020
Published by Springer Nature Switzerland AG 2020
L. M. Camarinha-Matos et al. (Eds.): DoCEIS 2020, IFIP AICT 577, pp. 168–178, 2020.
https://doi.org/10.1007/978-3-030-45124-0_16

property holds. Formal verification of programs in the language of function blocks usually is carried out by translating the source program into a model in the input language of model-checkers. The review of early works on formal modeling of IEC 61499 was conducted in [11]. Work [13] presented a method of FB modelling with timed-automata. However, the actual execution of the algorithms has not been modelled, only the time of their execution, which allowed to verify the properties based only on the structure of the system, but not dependent on data. Works [7, 12] proposed rules for formal modelling of IEC 61499 FB's for popular model checking environment of SMV using Abstract State Machines as an intermediate model. This allowed an automatic generation of models for the verifier. To support verification of function block systems there exists an open source tool called FB2SMV [4], which allows generating models of basic and composite function blocks in the language of the NuSMV[1] model-checker. However, this system does not support event timestamps so it cannot be used as is. A timestamp simulation approach was used in works [2, 3] to check the CPA property. The following points can be made as a drawbacks of the simulation approach:

- The verifiable model does not correspond to the semantics of programs with timestamped events;
- The method requires numerous changes in the original system;
- It is not possible to utilize all the advantages of timestamps. For example, it is not possible to order events based on timestamps;
- The method uses *service interface function blocks* (SIFB), which depend on particular hardware, which makes automatic generation of models for verification impossible;
- Verification time increases dramatically because of the addition of numerous function blocks to simulate timestamps.

Taking this into consideration another approach to verify CPA property is required.

The rest of the paper is organized as follows. In Sect. 2 it is shown how verifying the CPA property relates to life improvement. In Sect. 3 we describe event timestamps semantics and propose special syntax for them. Section 4 describes the necessary formal models. Section 5 presents a case study of the elevator system. The paper is concluded with a summary, acknowledgments and references.

## 2   Relationship to Life Improvement

The technological advances of cyber-physical systems have enabled us to develop systems and applications that have changed our daily life. The impact of CPS on people's well-being has increased, but at the same time the possible harmful consequences of the malfunctioning of these systems have also increased. Application areas of CPS that contribute to life-improvement is very diverse. These areas include *personalized healthcare* with examples such as health monitoring systems and cardiac

---

[1] NuSMV: a new symbolic model checker. http://nusmv.fbk.eu/.

pacemakers; *transportation systems* with examples of adaptive cruise control and self-braking cars; *building automation* systems with examples of lift control, escape systems and many others.

All the provided examples have a great impact on shaping the quality of life and at the same time malfunction of these systems can lead to dangerous consequences. Taking into account the points made, the safety and reliability of such systems become very important.

One of the possible causes of systems malfunctioning could be event delays. Event delays can occur because of the distributed nature of CPS. Wireless transmission interference, hardware reconfiguration, changes in network topology and many other reasons can cause event delays. Event delays can cause a violation of deadlines in systems that need to provide an immediate reaction if some condition occurs. Design of such systems must be robust against event delays, which is a feature of the cyber-physical agnosticism property. In this regard, methods for verifying the CPA property contribute to the safety of cyber-physical systems which is an essential part to improve human well-being.

## 3   Event Timestamps

### 3.1   Timestamps Semantic

The work [1] proposes to use event timestamps in IEC 61499 to achieve cyber-physical agnosticism. Events are considered as data structures containing timestamps.

Adding timestamps to events can help to solve several problems:

- Non-determinism of the system. One of the features of IEC 61499 is an event-triggered execution. If several events occur simultaneously at the event inputs of the function block, there is an uncertainty in which of the events should be processed. Adding timestamps directly to the events enables the events to be ordered and thus make the system execution deterministic;
- Robustness of the system to the event delays. Timestamps can be used directly by the control program to determine the occurrence of delays and to make the necessary adjustments related to changes in the physical process that have occurred during the delay of the event.

There are different approaches to defining the semantics of timestamps. The work [5] proposes to determine the deadline for each service FB by which the event initiated by the block should be processed. The time limit is determined according to the hardware specification. For example, it can depend on the polling rate at which the sensor updates the readings. By the time new data becomes available, the data from the previous poll is not relevant and should, therefore, be ignored by the system. However, it is worth noting that this approach makes the system dependent on the hardware configuration. If a sensor needs to be replaced with a sensor with a different polling rate, the control program is required to be changed, as the timestamps are directly related to the polling frequency of the sensor.

In [1] it was proposed to supplement the events with two timestamps not related to the hardware configuration: a stamp reflecting the time of event creation (*TB*) and a stamp reflecting the time of the last processing of the event in the system (*TL*). The paper [8] describes the formal semantics of composite FBs with timestamps on the basis of the theory of abstract state machines. At the same time, a formal model for basic FBs and timers has not been defined.

During the propagation of an event signal through the system, the TB stamp keeps the time of the creation of the first event in the event chain. The first event in the chain is created by the service interface blocks and the value of the TB stamp is set. The TL stamp is set each time the event is processed in the chain. The process diagram is shown in Fig. 1 (EI/EO – names of event input/output; DI/DO – names of data input/output).

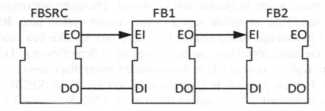

**Fig. 1.** Distribution of events [1].

At source functional block (FBSRC), timestamps are initialized with the value of the current system time:

```
FBSRC.EO.TL := System time in FBSRC;
FBSRC.EO.TB := System time in FBSRC;
```

When FB1 is invoked by the event produced by FBSRC, timestamp is copied from FBSRC.EO:

```
FB1.EI1 := FBSRC.EO;
FB1.INVOKEDBY := FB1.EI1;
```

When FB1 emits event EO, birth timestamp is copied from event that invoked execution and last execution timestamp is assigned to current system time:

```
FB1.EO.TB := FB1.INVOKEDBY.TB;
FB1.EO.TL := System time in FB1;
```

### 3.2  Timestamps Syntax

To determine the necessary syntax changes to the IEC 61499 function blocks language, it is necessary to identify contexts in which access to information about event timestamps values can be required. These contexts are:

- Event dispatcher;
- Function block algorithms;
- Guard conditions of EC transitions.

In the first case, timestamps can be used by event dispatcher to order events. The event dispatcher is a system's internal component, and there is no explicit use of timestamps by the programmer.

In the second case, to enable usage of event timestamps values in algorithms, the syntax of the Structured Text (ST) language which is used in algorithms must be extended.

Considering the third case, IEC 61499 allows ST expressions as well as events to be used in guard conditions. Hence, the syntax from the second case may be applied.

To access event timestamps values, two new identifiers are needed. *'ts_born'* to access event creation time and *'ts_last'* to access event last processing time. In addition to these identifiers, two more are needed. To compute event delay in guard conditions and ST algorithms, access to system time is needed. Therefore, we suggest adding an identifier 'Systemclock' to enable access to the current system time. Regarding the application of timestamps in algorithms, it is necessary to take into account that the execution of the same algorithm can be caused by different events. Therefore, it is necessary to provide an opportunity to determine the event that caused the execution of the algorithm. For this purpose, it is proposed to add the 'INVOKEDBY' identifier.

ST syntax is defined in the standard IEC 61131-3 [6]. Section B.3.1 defines production rules for expressions. To introduce the proposed identifiers, these production rules should be changed as follows:

B.3.1 Expressions PRODUCTION RULES

...

```
primary_expression ::= constant
            | enumerated_value
            | variable
            | '(' expression ')'
            | function_name
                '(' param_assignment {',' param_assignment} ')'
```
Proposed changes:

```
primary_expression ::= constant
            | enumerated_value
            | variable
            | '(' expression ')'
            | function_name
              '(' param_assignment {',' param_assignment } ')'
            | structured_event
            | time_reference
time_reference ::= 'Systemclock'
structured_event ::= event_reference ['.' time_attribute]
event_reference ::= 'INVOKEDBY' | identifier
time_attribute ::= 'ts_last' | 'ts_born'
```

# 4  Formal Modelling and Verification

## 4.1  Function Blocks

Formal model of the IEC 61499 in abstract state machines was described in [7]. The most important parts and changes related to the introduction of event timestamps are given below. The notation used for the formal model is the same as in [7].

First of all, events defined as a tuple:

```
E = (V, TB, TL)
V - event variable, Dom(V) = {true, false}
TB - event creation time, Dom(TB) = Time
TL - event last processing time, Dom(TL) = Time
Time = {undef, 0, 1, ...} - set of discrete time values
                    in the system.
```

The event inputs are reset before the Execution Control Chart (ECC) Operation State Machine (OSM) is started. Therefore, the basic FB needs a buffer to save the timestamps of the event that activated the execution of the block. When event inputs are reset, timestamps are stored in the IB (InvokedBy) buffer. Buffer values are used to access timestamps from algorithms, guard conditions of EC transitions, as well as to create new events.

Transition rules for the function of resetting the event inputs (Rule Set 1 [7]) is redefined by the following rules:

$$p_{EI}^{B,1}[k] : S = s_1 \wedge selectEI_k \rightarrow IB = (Z_{TB}(ei_k), Z_{TL}(ei_k))$$
$$\wedge Z_V(ei_k) = false | ei_k \in EI$$
$$p_{EI}^{B,2}[m] : \alpha \wedge S = s_0 \wedge \overline{selectEI_m} \rightarrow Z_V(ei_m) = false | ei_m \in EI$$

where $selectEI_k$ is a predicate which indicates k-th event input activation. The first sub-rule states that once the current OSM state is $s_1$ and the input signal is selected, then we need to save timestamp values to buffer $IB$ and reset $ei_k \in EI$. Second sub-rule resets all non-selected input signals.

Transition rules for the function of triggering of event outputs (Rule Set 8 [7]) is redefined by the following rules:

$$p_{EO}^{B,1}[k] : putoutEO_k \rightarrow Z_V(eo_k) = true \wedge Z_{TB}(eo_k) = Z_{TB}(IB)$$
$$\wedge Z_{TL}(eo_k) = \tau | eo_k \in EO,$$

where $putoutEO_k$ is a predicate which indicates k-th event output activation and $\tau$ represents the value of current systems time. The rule states that once k-th event output is activated, its value is set to *true* and birth timestamp value is copied from buffer $IB$ and last execution timestamp value is taken from $\tau$.

For composite function blocks with event timestamps, the formal model described in [8] is used.

## 4.2    Timers Models

The concept of time, timers' formal model and the system of time schedulers were described in [3, 9]. These models need to be adjusted to operate properly in the systems with timestamped events. IEC 61499 defines two types of timers: E_DELAY and E_CYCLE.

At first, we will consider E_DELAY function block. When creating an EO event, E_DELAY must record current system time in the TL timestamp. The EO event is a continuation of the event chain after the START event, therefore the event chain creation time must be copied from the START event TB timestamp. Therefore, the E_DELAY block needs additional buffer TB to store the timestamp. Semantical rules from [9] are changed as follows (the rules are listed in descending order of priority):

$$p_s^{D,1} : (\alpha \wedge D = 0) \rightarrow (Z_V(EO) = true \wedge Z_{TL}(EO) = \tau \wedge Z_{TB}(EO) = TB \wedge D = -1)$$
$$p_s^{D,2} : (\alpha \wedge Z_V(STOP)) \rightarrow D = -1$$
$$p_s^{D,3} : (\alpha \wedge Z_V(START) \wedge D = -1) \rightarrow (D = DT \wedge TB = Z_{TB}(START))$$

Considering E_CYCLE function block, each EO event creates a new event chain and at this point, both timestamps must record the current system time. Hence, E_CYCLE does not need any additional buffers for timestamps. The only difference is that it needs to record current system time in timestamps when EO event is triggered.

## 4.3    Modelling Event Delays

The standard assumes that there are no delays when events are transmitted between function blocks within a single resource. However, when an application is deployed, function blocks can be mapped to different resources. At the same time, the IEC 61499 standard specifies that data and event connections between function blocks distributed to different resources are redirected through the communication SIFBs and messages are transmitted through the communication network [10]. Message delays may occur while messages are being sent over the communication network. To verify the robustness of the system against event delays, it is necessary to simulate the delays of events. To this end, when generating SMV models, the selected event inputs and outputs are supplemented by the communication SIFBs models and the network communication model represented by the FIFO event queue. Thus, no changes to the original system are required to simulate delays and resulting model conforms to formal specification. The system's robustness against delays is checked by adding non-determinism on selection of the event delay time in the queue.

## 4.4    Automatic Models Generation

The presence of the formal specification makes it possible to generate models for verification automatically. For generation of models of programs with timestamps, FB2SMV tool was modified. We added support for generation of SMV models based on the formal model defined previously. These changes have been implemented in the FB2SMV project.[2]

# 5  Case Study

As a case study we continue an elevator example from [2]. The system model in IEC 61499 consists of three components: a controller, a plant simulation model and sensors (Fig. 2(b)). The experimental model differs from the previous one in that the sensors are moved into a separate component. Previously, they were incorporated into the plant model. However, the plant simulation model is usually modelled separately, which requires separation of components. In addition, the controller configuration has been modified to support an arbitrary number of floors. Sensors and the controller are located on different devices and transmit signals wirelessly. Random delays may occur during wireless transmission. Due to these delays, the controller can stop the motors when the elevator cabin has already passed the floor, which can lead to the opening of the doors when the elevator is between the floors (Fig. 2(a)).

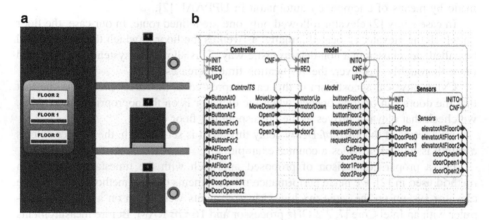

**Fig. 2.** (a) Elevator error; (b) Closed-loop elevator model

The controller must take into account the delay time of the event in order to be able to withstand delays. When receiving an event from the *AtFloor* variable event sensor, the controller does not immediately enter the floor EC-state (Fig. 3). The first step is to check that the event delay does not exceed the *MaxSafeDelay* threshold. If the delay is greater than the allowable one, the controller switches to the state of correction of the elevator cabin position and issues a command to move in the opposite direction for the duration equal to the delay of the event.

---

[2] https://github.com/dmitrydrozdov/fb2smv/tree/timestamps.

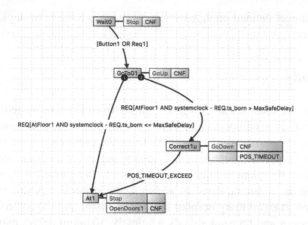

**Fig. 3.** ECC for correction of the elevator cabin position

The SMV models of the controller and sensors are generated automatically by enhanced FB2SMV, and then combined with the SMV model of the plant, which is made by means of a temporary automaton in UPPAAL [2].

In case study [2] elevator followed only one predefined route. In our case, the floor on which the elevator is located initially, as well as the floor to which the elevator will be called, are chosen in a non-deterministic way. This allows the system to be checked more thoroughly, however, the verification time increases.

Cyber-physical agnosticism in this case expressed as the safety property—the fact that the doors can only be opened when the elevator is on the appropriate floor. Also, we check that elevator arrives at the corresponding floor on call.

As a result, if the *MaxSafeDelay* delay threshold is set too high, the verifier detects a safety issue and provides a counter example.

For a proper comparison of proposed approach with the timestamp simulation method used in [2], we made performance measurements of both methods on the same elevator system on the same machine. Measurements were taken on a personal computer with an Intel Core i7, 2.2 GHz processor and 16 GB RAM. Before measurements were made, a variable ordering file was created with the option of NuSMV verifier '*dynamic_var_ordering -e sift_converge*'.

Table 1 shows the results of comparison of verification time and memory consumption for non-deterministically selected delay times. As can be seen from the table, the proposed approach shows better performance, consuming less memory and requiring less time for verification. The improvement is achieved due to the fact that the final SMV models are simpler than the models resulting from the simulation method.

**Table 1.** Verification performance comparison

| Property | Proposed approach | | Simulation | |
|---|---|---|---|---|
| | Time, *min* | Memory, *Mb* | Time, *min* | Memory, *Mb* |
| $G(DoorOpen0 \rightarrow AtFloor0)$ | 31.5 | 191 | 871 | 704 |
| $G(DoorOpen1 \rightarrow AtFloor1)$ | 31.2 | 201 | 866 | 703 |
| $G(DoorOpen2 \rightarrow AtFloor2)$ | 31.3 | 192 | 879 | 704 |
| $G(Button0 \rightarrow FAtFloor0)$ | 41.3 | 222 | 1280 | 739 |
| $G(Button1 \rightarrow FAtFloor1)$ | 35.1 | 208 | 1246 | 734 |
| G(Button2 → FAtFloor2) | 41.7 | 213 | 1293 | 744 |

## 6  Conclusion

As the result of this work, special syntax and formal models for event timestamps were defined. The FB2SMV tool was modified and based on this automatic generation of models was implemented. The elevator case study has shown the usage of timestamps to achieve systems safety. The results of the comparison with the method of timestamps simulation have shown an improvement in verification performance.

**Acknowledgments.** This work was partially supported by the JetBrains Research initiative.

## References

1. Vyatkin, V., Pang, C., Tripakis, S.: Towards cyber-physical agnosticism by enhancing IEC 61499 with PTIDES model of computations. In: IECON 2015-41st Annual Conference of the IEEE Industrial Electronics Society, pp. 001970–001975. IEEE (2015)
2. Drozdov, D., Patil, S., Dubinin, V., Vyatkin, V.: Towards formal verification for cyber-physically agnostic software: a case study. In: IECON 2017-43rd Annual Conference of the IEEE Industrial Electronics Society, pp. 5509–5514. IEEE (2017)
3. Drozdov, D., Patil, S., Vyatkin, V.: Formal modelling of distributed automation CPS with CP-agnostic software. In: Borangiu, T., Trentesaux, D., Thomas, A., Leitão, P., Barata Oliveira, J. (eds.) Service Orientation in Holonic and Multi-Agent Manufacturing. SCI, vol. 694, pp. 35–46. Springer, Cham (2017). https://doi.org/10.1007/978-3-319-51100-9_4
4. Drozdov, D.: FB2SMV Tool. https://github.com/dmitrydrozdov/fb2smv
5. Dai, W., Pang, C., Vyatkin, V., Christensen, J.H., Guan, X.: Discrete-event-based deterministic execution semantics with timestamps for industrial cyber-physical systems. IEEE Trans. Syst. Man Cybern. Syst. **50**, 851–862 (2017)
6. International Standard IEC 61131-3: Programmable controllers – Part 3: Programming languages/International Electrotechnical Commission (2013)
7. Patil, S., Dubinin, V., Vyatkin, V.: Formal verification of IEC61499 function blocks with abstract state machines and SMV–modelling. In: 2015 IEEE Trustcom/BigDataSE/ISPA, vol. 3, pp. 313–320. IEEE (2015)
8. Drozdov, D., Dubinin, V., Vyatkin, V.: Formal semantics of IEC 61499 functional blocks with temporary tags. In: University Proceedings. Volga Region. Engineering Sciences, no. 1 (49) (2019). (in Russian)

9. Drozdov, D., Patil, S., Dubinin, V., Vyatkin, V.: Formal verification of cyber-physical automation systems modelled with timed block diagrams. In: 2016 IEEE 25th International Symposium on Industrial Electronics (ISIE), pp. 316–321 (2016)
10. International Standard IEC 61499. Function blocks for industrial-process measurement and control systems. Part 1: Architecture/International Electrotechnical Commission (2005)
11. Hanisch, H.M., Hirsch, M., Missal, D., Preuße, S., Gerber, C.: One decade of IEC 61499 modeling and verification-results and open issues. In: Preprints of the 13th IFAC Symposium on Information Control Problems in Manufacturing (2009)
12. Patil, S., Dubinin, V., Vyatkin, V.: Formal modelling and verification of IEC61499 function blocks with abstract state machines and SMV - execution semantics. In: Li, X., Liu, Z., Yi, W. (eds.) SETTA 2015. LNCS, vol. 9409, pp. 300–315. Springer, Cham (2015). https://doi.org/10.1007/978-3-319-25942-0_20
13. Stanica, M., Guéguen, H.: Using timed automata for the verification of IEC 61499 applications. In: Discrete Event Systems 2004 (WODES 2004): A Proceedings Volume from the 7th IFAC Workshop, Reims, France, 22–24 September 2004, p. 375. Elsevier (2005)

# Thin Film Refractive Index and Thickness

Paulo Lourenço[2,3(✉)], Manuela Vieira[1,2,3], and Alessandro Fantoni[1,3]

[1] ISEL - Instituto Superior de Engenharia de Lisboa, Instituto Politécnico de Lisboa, Rua Conselheiro Emídio Navarro, 1, 1959-007 Lisbon, Portugal
[2] Faculdade de Ciências e Tecnologia, FCT, Departamento de Engenharia Eletrotécnica, Universidade Nova de Lisboa, Campus da Caparica, 2829-516 Caparica, Portugal
pj.lourenco@campus.fct.unl.pt
[3] CTS-UNINOVA, Departamento de Engenharia Eletrotécnica, Faculdade de Ciências e Tecnologia, FCT, Universidade Nova de Lisboa, Campus da Caparica, 2829-516 Caparica, Portugal

**Abstract.** Integrated optics are a contemporaneous reality in which thin-film technology and methods utilized in the development of integrated circuitry, are applied to both optical circuits and devices. This provides systems that show improved characteristics when compared to their electronic counterparts. Optical systems enable wider bandwidth operation, less power consumption, more immunity to interference and higher cost-efficiency. These features definitely represent a huge improvement in our daily lives when completely embedded in Information and Communications Technologies, replacing a large percentage of contemporaneous electronic based systems. The building blocks of these optical systems consist on waveguides and structures formed by deposited thin films. Two characteristics of utmost importance for these structures are the height and refractive index of the deposited film. In this work and by using a prism coupler, we will be presenting an optical setup and the experimental method that is used to determine both refractive index and thickness of the wave guiding structure.

**Keywords:** Thin film · Refractive index and thickness determination method · Optical setup · Prism coupling

## 1 Introduction

Electromagnetic (EM) radiation is present anywhere and propagates through open space linearly spreading its initial beam's cross section, when unperturbed by any other physical phenomenon or obstacle. Nevertheless, EM energy may be confined within a structure and guided propagation may take place if proper circumstances are given. Confinement and propagation of EM radiation within a structure is governed by a phenomenon known as Total Internal Reflection (TIR), which consists on consecutive reflections of the EM wave on the structure's internal boundaries.

Contemporaneous need for integrated photonics is a reality. Laser beams can be guided into thin film structures, where manipulating processes such as modulation, switching, frequency conversion and more, may be accomplished entirely within these structures. Assembling all components of a system within the same structure will

L. M. Camarinha-Matos et al. (Eds.): DoCEIS 2020, IFIP AICT 577, pp. 179–188, 2020.
https://doi.org/10.1007/978-3-030-45124-0_17

contribute to the reduction of ambient conditions effects, an increase of reliability, lower systems' footprint and increase their cost-effectiveness. Moreover, the thickness of these structures is in the order of hundreds of nanometres. This enables the propagation of EM waves with very high power densities by unit area, which is beneficial for both electro-optic conversion and non-linear effects. These features may then be exploited to further promote photonics integration.

Photonic Integrated Circuits (PIC) are assembled through the deposition of consecutive material layers. These are thin layers, few hundreds of nanometres thick, of a given material and their optical properties are different from bulk material properties. In order to fabricate these photonic systems, one must know the optical properties of each deposited layer. This brings us to this paper main driving research purpose:

- Is it possible to devise an optical setup based on an off-the-shelf laser diode, which is able to determine the optical properties of a given material thin layer?

This document describes the work developed to experimentally quantify, in a non-intrusive way, the refractive index and thickness of deposited thin films. Towards that end, an optical setup has been designed and assembled. The obtained results were verified against simulations executed in a software package [1] implementing the Finite Differences Time Domain (FDTD) numerical method.

The remaining of this paper is organized as follows:

- Next section presents how this document relates to the context of Technological Innovation for Life Improvement, which is the main focus of DoCEIS2020 Doctoral Conference;
- Then follows the Experimental Setup section, where the developed optical setup is presented and correspondent obtained results were post-processed by a developed Matlab application, to provide the refractive index and thickness of the material under analysis;
- Next, it follows the Simulations section, where an FDTD simulation is carried out, considering previously obtained thin film refractive index and thickness to design the workspace. This way, we were able to verify the results obtained both experimental and numerically;
- Finally, there is the Conclusions section where obtained results are gathered, analysed and conclusions are drawn, and reported. Here, future areas of related research will also be discussed.

## 2    Technological Innovation for Life Improvement Association

Information and Communications Technology (ICT) systems have had an increasing and remarkable relevance in our daily lives for the past few decades and in many sectors of contemporaneous society. Even in traditional sectors of our economy, namely the agricultural sector, technological proliferation is now evident and the overall trend points at an increasing dissemination throughout every aspect of our lives.

Together with this technological proliferation, there has been tremendous achievements focused on the individual's wellbeing and life improvement, and associated to innovative changes resulting from technology related research. In many ICT research fields, namely optoelectronics/electronics, telecommunications and software development, the specifications for a digital world demand a paradigm change. This will be a fertile ground provider for innovation, with newly developed tools and concepts, and aiming at providing a better and sustainable future, with high quality of life for all mankind.

There has been a number of initiatives concerning the evaluation of the impact and effectiveness of technological development on society, namely literature that addresses ICT applications which were designed to help individuals monitor self-health. From dealing with chronic diseases, to prevent unhealthy behaviour or to facilitate doctor-patient communication. Concurrently, considering design constraints regarding easily understandable information, wearable devices comfort issues, user's motivation and interest over time. Examples of such applications are not difficult to find.

On the other hand, the constant growth of senior population worldwide and its incompatibility with contemporaneous available home and community services, is a reality. Moreover, older citizens with health conditions prefer to remain in familiar living surroundings, instead of moving into health institutions, being them private or public. Lattanzio et al. [2] present a set of research initiatives throughout Europe that intend to deal with the increasing demand for e-health care services and smart technologies. This demand has been generated by a growing elder population with chronic diseases and also for those involved in active aging. The adoption of smart wearable devices is illustrated in an article by Uem et al. [3], where smart wearable devices are used to monitor/collect data and to quantify wellbeing, and health-related quality of life associated to Parkinson's disease condition. This article [3], is substantiated by the real life testimonials of three of its co-authors who, in their turn, have extensive experience dealing with smart wearable devices and that have been enduring with this condition for a long time.

Our work is part of a broader project that consists on the development and characterization of a disposable optoelectronic sensor for point of care detection of Acute Kidney Injury (AKI) biomarkers. This sensing device will be implemented by assembling in one monolithic PIC several individual components. Each of these components will be formed by one or more deposited thin film layers of material on a substrate [4, 5]. For development reasons, it is required to know, as precisely as possible, the refractive index and thickness of each individual deposited thin film layer. Hence, the need to develop a non-intrusive method to determine both refractive index and thickness of the deposited layer. With this purpose in mind, an optical setup has been created and the employed light source is an off-the-shelf semiconductor based lasing device (i.e. a laser diode). The articles in the literature considering this subject mentioned the utilization of hardly inexpensive gas lasers, namely the Argon (Ar) and Helium-Neon (He-Ne) lasers [6–11], while our approach considers a common laser diode. This implementation is, to the best of our knowledge, a novel approach to determine thin films refractive indices and their thicknesses.

## 3  Experimental Setup

Our approach considered the top surface of a Corning glass substrate, where a thin layer of a known semiconductor has been deposited and for which its refractive index and thickness are to be determined; for the remaining of this paper, this assembly will be referred to as the *sample*. Next, a laser beam is focused on the face of an adequately chosen prism (Thorlabs ADT-6 - Rutile Coupling Prism), which has been placed over the sample as depicted in Fig. 1. If all possible waveguide modes of the thin film are to be excited, the prism refractive index ($n_p$) must be higher than the refractive indices of the semiconductor film, gap or substrate ($n_f$, $n_g$ or $n_s$, respectively).

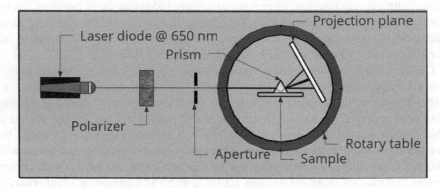

**Fig. 1.** Optical setup schematic.

On the above figure, one is able to identify the laser diode (Thorlabs L650P007 operating at the 650 nm wavelength) providing the incident plane wave, the polarizer that enables the selection of transversal magnetic (TM) or transversal electric (TE) polarization and an aperture that has been used to minimize the diffraction effects associated to the laser beam. Next follows the rotary table (Thorlabs RBB300A/M), where the sample, prism and projection plane have been securely placed and fastened. This allows their angular motion with the rotary table, while maintaining the prism centred in the rotary table. Prism refractive index is polarization and wavelength dependent, being established through Sellmeier's Eqs. (1) and (2) for TM and TE polarizations, respectively [12]:

$$n^2 = 3.2089 + \frac{3.4000 \times 10^{-5}}{1.2270 \times 10^{-5} - \lambda^{-2}} - 3.2545 \times 10^{-8} \lambda^2 \tag{1}$$

$$n^2 = 2.9713 + \frac{5.1891 \times 10^{-5}}{1.2280 \times 10^{-5} - \lambda^{-2}} - 4.2950 \times 10^{-8} \lambda^2 \tag{2}$$

which, at the 650 nm operating wavelength, yielded the refractive indices 2.5746 and 2.8614 for TM and TE polarizations, respectively.

According to the literature [8], the coupling principles for the excitation of prism-semiconductor film modes may be explained in simple terms:

- Incoming laser beam goes through the prism face and is totally reflected at the base of the prism;
- Total reflection of the laser beam generates a standing wave inside the prism and, consequently, an evanescent field extending from its base into the air gap below;
- Boundary conditions of EM fields at the prism base require that fields below and above the prism base propagate with the same wave motion, thus the evanescent field varies in the z-axis as $e^{(ikn_3 z \sin \theta_3)}$;
- If the air gap spacing is thin enough ($< \lambda_0/2$), the evanescent field penetrates into the semiconductor film and may excite a propagating mode (phenomenon described as optical tunnelling);
- If the x-axis component of the wave vector mode in the film, which varies in the z-axis as $e^{(ikn_1 z \sin \theta_1)}$, coincides with the correspondent component of the evanescent field below the prism base, the EM wave inside the prism is exclusively coupled to the waveguide mode and the laser beam is considered to be in a synchronous direction;
- Hence, it is possible to couple the EM standing wave developed within the prism to any semiconductor film mode by selecting the correct synchronous direction for the incoming laser beam.

Figure 2 shows in (a) the propagation of the EM field within the a-SiNx:H thin film. The streak of light observed reveals some brighter points which might indicate surface roughness on the deposited thin film. Figure 2(b) shows the first generated line on the projection plane as the prism is rotated counter-clockwise. Figure 2(c) presents the projection plane at a later stage of the prism rotation. The bright light point indicated as "angular position" moves horizontally on the projection plane as "mode line 1" vanishes and "mode line 2" appears. The two marked lines correspond to the fundamental and first modes that are being guided by the a-SiNx:H thin film. The obtained angular synchronous directions, relative to the prism base normal, for the excitation of these modes were:

- 39.8°;
- 48.3°.

According to Tien et al. [6], the incident beam on the prism base must have the right angle of incidence for its associated evanescent field phase velocity matches the phase velocity of the propagating mode in the semiconductor. The component of the propagating vector, parallel to the thin film, inside the prism is $kn_p \sin \theta_p$, where $k = \omega/c$ is the wave number, $\omega$ is the angular frequency and $c$ is the speed of light in free space. Considering $\beta_m$ as the propagation constant of the mode in the wave guiding film, a synchronous direction $\theta_p$ of the standing wave generated inside the prism is verified when:

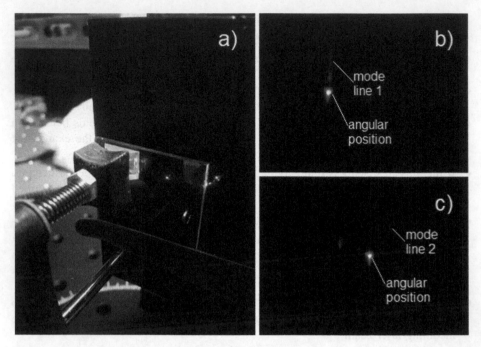

**Fig. 2.** Experimental results: (a) Propagation of light on the thin film; (b) Projected line when the fundamental mode is excited on the thin film; (c) Projection plane when another mode is excited on the thin film.

$$\beta_m = kn_p \sin \theta_p \tag{3}$$

After calculating the modal indices of the excited modes, these parameters were fed into a developed Matlab application which returning outcome are the refractive index and thickness of the semiconductor wave guiding structure. The obtained results for this sample were:

$$a = 6.016695e - 01\mu m, n = 2.365337e + 00,$$

where $a$ and $n$ represent thin film thickness and refractive index, respectively.

## 4    Simulations

The experimental setup provided the angle readings for the encountered synchronous directions. This data has been processed by a developed Matlab routine which computed the refractive index and thickness of our sample. Nevertheless, to confirm the obtained results, a simulation workspace has been designed on a known and well established software [1]. This software includes a package [13] to perform FDTD numerical method simulations and which has been utilized to conduct the verification of the obtained experimental results.

Simulations considered a plane wave at the operating wavelength of 650 nm, propagating within a dielectric medium, which refractive index matches the rutile prism refractive index that has been used in the experimental setup. This plane wave direction is aimed at the separation interface between this dielectric medium and an air gap, representing the rutile prism base and its separation gap from the sample, respectively. The sample is represented in the simulation by two adjacent media. First, a medium which refractive index and thickness correspond to the outcome obtained by previously executed Matlab computation of experimental data. Then, a second medium that emulates the Corning glass on which the semiconductor film has been deposited.

The working principle of the simulation consisted on iterating the plane wave incidence angle, at the separating interface between the first dielectric medium (rutile prism) and the air gap, while monitoring the correspondent reflection. According to Ulrich et al. [14], a laser beam coupling through a prism into a planar dielectric film is governed by the angle of incidence $\theta$ of the beam onto the prism base. This angle corresponds to the phase velocity $v_p = c/n_p \sin\theta$ in the propagation direction of the wave in the prism (refractive index $n_p$) and in the air gap. Exclusive coupling of EM energy into the semiconductor film occurs only when $v_p$ matches one of the phase velocities of the modes allowed within the film $v_m$ (where $m = 0, 1, 2, \ldots$). Hence, by determining the synchronous angles $\theta_m$ that correspond to the strongest coupling, one is able to infer the propagation constant, relatively to the propagation constant of vacuum ($k_0 = \omega_0/c$), of each allowed mode of a given semiconductor film,

$$n_{rel}^m = c/v_m = n_p \sin\theta_m \tag{4}$$

Figure 3 represents the simulation workspace where it is possible to identify, from left to right, the dielectric medium associated to the rutile prism (light blue area), the first thick line representing the reflected energy monitor (dark green area) and the plane wave which incidence angle is to be iterated (orange line). Follows the air gap (white area), the thin semiconductor film (red area), the dielectric medium associated to the Corning glass on which the film has been deposited (blue rectangle) and the second thick line representing the transmission monitor (dark green area). The purple rectangular line sets the simulation domain limits.

FDTD simulations have been carried out considering an iterated incidence angle initiating at 30° and ending at 80°, while monitoring the reflected energy amplitude by the separation interface between the dielectric and the air gap. Boundary conditions were set to Perfectly Matched Layer (PML) and grid and step sizes were set to obtain convergence of the FDTD algorithm and realistic results. The air gap width has been set to 100 nm for it should be within a quarter to an eighth of the operating wavelength [8].

Results obtained in simulations for monitored reflected beam power show three dips as presented in Fig. 4. These three features correspond to the three allowed modes, considering the operating wavelength and the thin film characteristics. These modes have been excited within the semiconductor film while the plane wave incidence angle has been iterated and correspond to the synchronous directions of 47.5°, 51.5° and 55°.

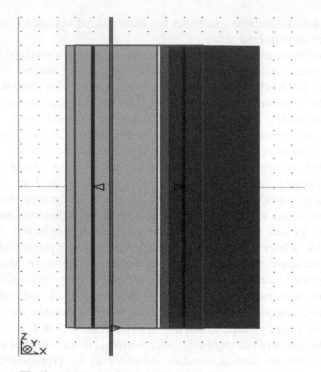

**Fig. 3.** FDTD simulation workspace. (Color figure online)

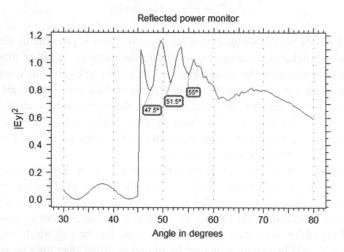

**Fig. 4.** Synchronous directions obtained in simulations.

Considering that, the presented synchronous directions in Fig. 4 have as zero angle reference the x-axis and that the positive angle direction is anti-clockwise, the angles obtained experimentally (39.8° and 48.3°) are their $\pi/2$ complement for they are measured against the normal at the plane of incidence. Also, the experimental synchronous directions were visually acquired and annotated, which is definitely prone to errors. Plus, thin film surface roughness plays a decisive role when it comes to efficient coupling of the evanescent field, at the base of the prism, into the thin film waveguide. Moreover, both simulations and experimental readings revealed a range of several degrees that are able to excite the mode under observation, instead of being a selective and precise direction.

## 5 Conclusions

The refractive index and thickness determination of a semiconductor thin film has been accomplished experimentally through the development and implementation of an optical setup and the prism coupling method. The synchronous directions obtained by observing the prism projected reflections on a screen were, subsequently, used as input parameters of a developed Matlab implementation. The outcome result of the processing software were the thin film sample refractive index and thickness. To confirm these results, an FDTD simulation workspace has been developed and executed, considering previously obtained sample refractive index and thickness.

Some discrepancies were noted between the results obtained experimentally and the ones acquired through simulation, but it may be explained by the lack of precision of experimental visual readings, by an excessive surface roughness and by existing a range of synchronous directions which are able to excite a particular mode.

Future work will consist on the evaluation of different samples, improvement of synchronous directions experimental readout, verification/improvement of Matlab application and attempt to verify/quantify the correlation between thin film surface roughness and the verified results' discrepancies.

**Acknowledgements.** This research has been supported by EU funds through the FEDER European Regional Development Fund and by Portuguese national funds provided by FCT – Fundação para a Ciência e a Tecnologia through grant SFRH/BD/144833/2019 and projects PTDC/NAN-OPT/31311/2017 and UID/EEA/00066/2019, and by projects IPL/2019/BioPlas_ISEL and IPL/2019/MO-TFT_ISEL, and also UIDB/00066/2020 (CTS – Center of Technology and Systems).

## References

1. Synopsys RSoft Solutions. https://www.synopsys.com/optical-solutions/rsoft.html. Accessed 02 Nov 2019
2. Lattanzio, F., et al.: Advanced technology care innovation for older people in Italy: necessity and opportunity to promote health and wellbeing. J. Am. Med. Dir. Assoc. **15**(7), 457–466 (2014)
3. Van Uem, J.M.T., et al.: A viewpoint on wearable technology-enabled measurement of wellbeing and health-related quality of life in Parkinson's disease. J. Parkinsons. Dis. **6**(2), 279–287 (2016)

4. Lourenço, P., Fantoni, A., Costa, J., Vieira, M.: Lithographic mask defects analysis on an MMI 3 dB splitter. Photonics **6**(4), 1–8 (2019)
5. Fantoni, A., Costa, J., Fernandes, M., Vygranenko, Y., Vieira, M.: A simulation analysis for dimensioning of an amorphous silicon planar waveguide structure suitable to be used as a surface plasmon resonance biosensor. In: Fourth International Conference on Applications of Optics and Photonics, p. 28 (2019)
6. Tien, P.K., Ulrich, R., Martin, R.J.: Modes of propagating light waves in thin deposited semiconductor films. Appl. Phys. Lett. **14**(9), 291–294 (1969)
7. Tien, P.K., Ulrich, R.: Theory of prism-film coupler and thin-film light guides. J. Opt. Soc. Am. **60**(10), 1325–1337 (1970)
8. Tien, P.K.: Light waves in thin films and integrated optics. Appl. Opt. **10**(11), 2395–2413 (1971)
9. Tien, P.K., Smolinsky, G., Martin, R.J.: Thin organosilicon films for integrated optics. Appl. Opt. **11**(3), 637–642 (1972)
10. Kersten, R.T.: A new method for measuring refractive index and thickness of liquid and deposited solid thin films. Opt. Commun. **13**(3), 327–329 (1975)
11. Adams, A.C., Schinke, D.P., Capio, C.D.: An evaluation of the prism coupler for measuring the thickness and refractive index of dielectric films on silicon substrates. J. Electrochem. Soc. **126**(9), 1539–1543 (1979)
12. Coupling prisms - Thorlabs. https://www.thorlabs.com/newgrouppage9.cfm?objectgroup_id=3243. Accessed 28 Dec 2019
13. FullWAVE - FDTD method. https://www.synopsys.com/photonic-solutions/rsoft-photonic-device-tools/passive-device-fullwave.html. Accessed 29 Dec 2019
14. Ulrich, R., Torge, R.: Measurement of thin film parameters with a prism coupler. Appl. Opt. **12**(12), 2901 (1973)

# Digital Twins and Smart Manufacturing

# The Role of Digital Twins in Collaborative Cyber-Physical Systems

Artem A. Nazarenko[✉] and Luis M. Camarinha-Matos

Faculty of Sciences and Technology, UNINOVA-CTS,
Nova University of Lisbon, 2829-516 Monte Caparica, Portugal
a.nazarenko@campus.fct.unl.pt, cam@uninova.pt

**Abstract.** The growing smartification of devices and systems, combining physical and virtual parts, offers a great potential to improve the daily life of people through the establishment of context-rich environments. Cyber-Physical Systems (CPS), embedding collaborative features, can be considered as one of the key enablers of such environments, providing support for life quality improvement. Besides the general aim of the conventional CPS, further aspects related to co-existence and collaboration among different heterogeneous and autonomous components within a system, are in the scope of Collaborative CPS. These systems allow looking at the technical and organisational challenges from the perspective of interconnected and jointly acting entities. Such entities can be the physical devices or their virtual representations, which are called Digital Twins (DT), understood as digital replicas of physical assets. However, a DT provides more than just a digital simulation of the physical device or process, including reasoning and prediction mechanisms. This work is devoted to the discussion of how Digital Twins can be used in the design, development, and functioning of Collaborative CPS. As such, a design approach is suggested and illustrated with a smart home scenario.

**Keywords:** Collaborative cyber-physical systems · Digital Twins · Smart Home

## 1 Introduction

Smart interconnected systems, which can easily adapt to changing conditions, are playing an important role in modern manufacturing as well as in other domains, such as smart buildings, healthcare, etc. This led to emergence of the ongoing digital transformation processes, encompassing various concepts such as Cyber-Physical Systems, Internet of Things, Data Mining, Cloud Computing and Digital Twins. Some of these concepts are tightly interrelated, as for instance Cyber-Physical Systems and Digital Twins. Both concepts are bridging physical entities and processes, and virtual artefacts. More specifically, the Digital Twin is a term that, in a simplified way, can be described as digital replica or an avatar of the physical entity/system, being one of the key enabling technologies for Cyber-Physical systems, as well as for Collaborative CPS (CCPS) [1].

L. M. Camarinha-Matos et al. (Eds.): DoCEIS 2020, IFIP AICT 577, pp. 191–205, 2020.
https://doi.org/10.1007/978-3-030-45124-0_18

Further smartification of modern digital systems and to higher extent the Collaborative CPS, combining virtual and physical elements, has created the need for adequate design approaches, which have to provide a reliable methodology for developers, whereas integrating several relevant approaches in the clear way. A framework that can, on one hand, integrate available achievements in the form of generic models and on the other hand bridge those models with the real case scenarios is a promising research direction. However, to be able to provide proper methods and an associated framework several difficulties have to be addressed, namely: (i) models, used during the design process, need to be generic enough to be applied to various use-cases, (ii) clear definitions of the concepts used in the approach need to be given and explained, (iii) design steps also need to be generic in order to cover various application areas and use cases, and (iv) the order of design steps need to be clearly identified.

Besides the technological and design challenges, the goal of improving life quality has a significant impact on the aimed systems. Although there is a lack of a proper definition and metrics for the "life quality", in [40] several approaches for assessing the impact on life quality improvement are given. For instance, one of the approaches is the "theory of needs" taking into consideration how the users' needs are satisfied by the system. This approach should be reflected in design frameworks through the users' requirements or desirable functionality to satisfy formulated needs.

Often existing research works directed towards the design of complex CPS are focused on some partial aspects of the design methodology, as for instance the models for some concrete use cases as smart home and social services [2], or focused on particular issues related to information model building [3], without giving a general picture and indentifying the steps for designing a complex Collaborative CPS. In order to offer some guidance for CCPS design, a proposal for a Design Framework for CCPS covering various aspects including the role of DTs is presented and illustrated.

The remaining of the paper is structured as follows:

- Relation of the presented topic and in particular the CCPS and DTs for the life improvement with the focus on smart home;
- Related literature mostly focused on the concept of DT itself, as well as its significance for the CCPS;
- Introduction of a Design Framework aimed at giving the general understanding and guidance for design of CCPS;
- Example scenario representing the application of the proposed Design Framework;
- Conclusions and direction of further work.

## 2    Relation to Life Improvement

Smart Home and Smart City are two important application areas, where CPS and DT can have significant contributions to life quality improvement. One example can be the road traffic and parking issues, informing the drivers about available parking opportunities or providing information on-fly about the traffic in various city parts to avoid traffic jams or even consider the usage of public transport instead of a personal vehicle. In the case of the Smart Home, the spectrum of issues that can be supported by the CPS is large. For instance, improving the energy and resources consumption, if the inhabitants of the house forget to turn off the light or water tape, this can be done automatically, heating can be reduced if no one is in the room, etc. By acting collaboratively Smart Homes can improve the energy efficiency even more. For instance, if solar panels are installed and during the day the load drops, the excess of energy can be distributed among other participants of a collaborative community or for the public purpose considering local needs. Moreover, resorting to DT provides the necessary basis for simulating and predicting various aspects from resources usage and needs to human behaviour, detecting the patterns of human habits. Another example is the use of systems to monitor and assist people with special needs to help them living independently [4].

In summary, the integration of physical and virtual spaces can significantly support people in daily activities, from business routine to health care and elderly care. This implies integration of different data flows coming from different sources and building predictive models. In its turn DT can significantly contribute to service evolution, when a service can be updated based on historical data and current status of the physical device or system.

## 3 Related Literature

Modern Cyber-Physical Systems can be considered as complex systems of systems, incorporating heterogeneous, distributed and collaborating components [1]. These components have a physical part and a cyber part that can be modelled as a digital twin. In this section the evolution path of the DTs is presented along with possible benefits they have for the CPS and in particular for CCPS. An earlier reference to a DT-similar concept goes back to 2003, when the concept of "Digital Thread" was proposed [5]. A Digital Thread at that time was a set of 3D models to represent a physical product for facilitating collaborative engineering. In 2005 the term "Digital Representation" for Product Lifecycle Management was introduced [6]. This concept was closer to the current understanding of DT. However, the term "Digital Twin" started to have a widespread use later in 2010 [7, 8]. A more comprehensive definition of DT, including some intelligent functionality for product life prediction analysis or decision making, was stated in [9]. In a next development stage, DT is also considered to represent the human being within a manufacturing process, whereas emulating the human employee's behaviour [10]. This aspect was also extended with the creation of DT to represent human organs [11]. In [8] the DT concept was refined to include integration levels and further concepts of Digital Model and Digital Shadow were introduced. To visualise the evolution of DT notion, Fig. 1 presents a brief timeline perspective.

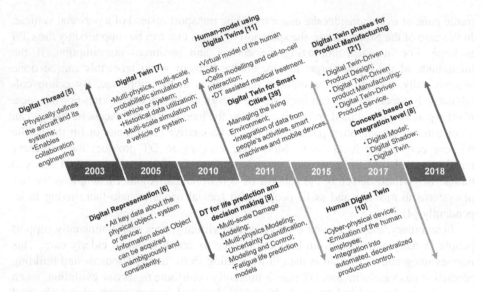

**Fig. 1.** Some important stages of the DT notion development.

Therefore, there is a need for a definition which, on one hand, is generic enough to be used in various application areas and at the same time extending the various existing partial views of the DT concept. In order to refine the notion of DT and include its different dimensions, [12] introduces 4 levels of virtual representation of an artefact in a virtual space, namely: (i) Pre-Digital Twin – virtual prototype created before its physical twin, (ii) Digital Twin – which is a virtual model of a physical artefact used for exploring the system behaviour in a controlled system environment, (iii) Adaptive Digital Twin – according to which the DT is able to extract the priorities and preferences of the users in various contexts, and (iv) Intelligent Digital Twin – providing not only internal adaptive capabilities, but also considering other entities and subsystems coexisting in the environment, as well as the environmental factors. Moreover, a DT can be considered in terms of scale, thus it can represent a single unit/component/ artefact or a complex system or even a system of systems. In [13] authors consider the DT as based on a five-dimensional, three-layered model. Where layers identify the scale of the DT: (i) Unit level (single DT), (ii) System Level (integration of several single DT), and (iii) System of Systems level (cross system interconnection and collaboration). And the dimensions reflect the nature of the DT in conjunction with a service-oriented approach, namely: (i) physical entities, (ii) virtual models, (iii) connections, (iv) fusion data (combination of data from entities, models, etc.), and (v) services (functions encapsulation).

An important purpose of a Digital Twin is to capture the behaviour of the physical component or system that it represents [14]. One example is described in [15], where the behaviour of a system is simulated through different modules. These modules follow the Functional Mock-Up Units (FMI) standard that allows building a single model of a system through adding and combining the models of system components. The modular way of adding new simulation modules is particularly important when considering complex Digital Twins. A Digital Twin includes, according to [16], a "comprehensive physical and functional description of a component, product or system", possessing the relevant information used during the whole lifecycle of the product/system/component. However, it is very difficult to include all the relevant aspects about the product, as they largely depend on a lot of factors involving interaction with other systems and characteristics of the environment. Thus, the modular approach might enable adding the missing models in consideration with the current status of the system, product or component. Another challenge regarding the simulation process of complex systems is to generate models at the level of components and integrate them for simulation at the system level [17]. This might be even more challenging if the modelled system collaborates with other complex systems or components, as it will require some additional methods to deal with collaborative factors.

The digital twin concept can be considered from different perspectives: (i) digital replica of a device, system or system component, (ii) support for the products during their lifecycles, and (iii) digital representation of human or human organs. Considering the first perspective, a DT can be established based on the information retrieved from the Cyber-Physical System [18], as it possesses data about itself and its components. This information is used to build models of the system and its components or even the buildings where the system is deployed [3]. According to [19], a Digital Twin is, first of all, a "real-time reflection of a physical device being permanently synchronised with a real-world asset"; secondly a "complete integration with physical device assuming the access to real-time data flows", as well as historical data, and finally allowing verification and analysis of measured and predicted values. Moreover, according to [20], a DT is responsible for condition monitoring, control and real-time simulation. Thus, the notion of the DT evolved from just a digital replica of a physical artefact to a more sophisticated definition including simulation, data analysis, and prediction techniques, interaction with the artefact, user experience consideration, etc.

Another perspective of DT refers to the lifecycle of smart products, from the design and manufacturing to the recycling phases. In this regard the concept of Digital Twin Driven Product Design (DTPD) has appeared [21]. DTPD can be seen as an intelligent support tool for designers, delivering the "information, recommendations and assessments throughout a product design process" [21]. In [22] the authors propose to divide the whole product design process assisted by the DT into several steps:

- Conceptual design – a stage, when the concept and functionalities of the product are defined. It also includes the analysis of users' feedback and data about product utilization which are delivered by the DT.
- Detailed design – a stage during which the development of the product prototype is accomplished, which also includes the simulation tests. Data can be gathered during the lifecycle of the previous product's version through the DT, whereas DT can evolve together with the product.
- Virtual verification that is the process of predictive analysis of the product utilization (environment influence, faults, etc.) and manufacturing, before the product is physically produced.

Another paper devoted to Twin-driven Manufacturing states three levels or scales for the manufacturing data aggregation [23], namely: (i) Physical, (ii) Cyber and

(iii) Social. Physical data are gathered directly from devices; on the cyber level they are analysed and knowledge is extracted; and on Social level the human-factor is considered. The topic of improving the process of recycling the manufactured products using DT is raised in [24], where four main actors (physical layer) with appropriate product lifecycle stages (cyber layer) are identified as follows: (i) Producer/Distributor – Product Design, (ii) End User – Product Status, (iii) Collector – Logistic and Exam Results, and (iv) Recycler – Recovered Material or Component.

Digital Twins can be also used for human behaviour modelling or modelling of functioning of human organs in order to detect diseases or deviations from the normal behaviour. An example can be the Digital Twin of the human heart. Some research activities are directed towards analysis of cardio diagrams with further classification to detect disorders [25]. This type of Digital Twins can be described as passive, as they only monitor the heart conditions and reason over the gathered data, helping the diagnostics process by doctors. However, there is another type of Digital Twins which can act actively, for instance, being able to regulate the heart rate through the pacemaker, combining both sensing and reasoning parts with actuation [26]. The vision of the future development of Digital Twin in the area of healthcare expressed by Siemens Healthineers is that the whole human body can be represented into a Digital Twin. This might allow early detection of diseases and application of preventive measures. Moreover, this can be used for athletes in order to optimise their training processes. Another example of the application of the DT for human behaviour modelling can be found in industry considering anthropometric data for calculation if the task can be performed by the human-worker or needs to be performed by a robot [27].

Most of the mentioned works are focusing on technical issues of building the DT and mostly ignoring the question if the DTs can be considered as smart entities, which are interconnected and collaborate. Let's assume that fully operable DTs can be applied to all technical systems, buildings or even humans. Then there is a need to define new architectural and methodological principles for developing such environment where they are able to operate. Thus, as every DT is assigned to a real-world object which can change the environment, the possibility of simulating or modelling the outcome is a crucial advantage of the DT. For instance, if the DT can discover other DTs which can provide the necessary functionality to fulfil some need and assess how efficient could be the process of collaboration, it can turn the DT into a more complex entity going far beyond the controlling capabilities. In this regard, some major collaborative challenges are mentioned in [28], namely: (i) Information sharing (internal and external data), (ii) Data ownership, and (iii) Over-dependency (one component or entity is too dependent on another). In this work we aim at contributing to representing the DT from a collaborative point of view with respect to different aggregation and hierarchical layers.

## 4    Design Approach

As Collaborative CPS are complex systems containing smart/intelligent and autonomous components, thereby their design is a non-trivial task. This requires new approaches for the design process to give developers a clear understanding of the whole workflow. Some research works in the area even go further while combining systems' design with product's design, following the V-model approach [29]. The issues of modular CCPS design appear in the scope of some research groups such as in [30]. However, most of the authors agree, to some extent, on similar design steps [29–31], namely: (i) requirements clarification, (ii) selection of technical tools and approaches, (iii) structuring the developed system, and (iv) technical implementation.

For our research, the design science research methodology presented in [32] was chosen. This approach combines the behaviour-science and design-science paradigms and comprises three pillars: Environment, Information System Research, and Knowledge Base, with appropriate relations among these pillars. In our work the Application domain is equivalent to the Environment, as it defines the problem space, the CCPS Design pillar corresponds to the IS Research, containing the Development and Evaluation phases, and finally the Knowledge Base accumulates foundations and methodologies along with reference models, methods, frameworks, instruments, etc. One of the advantages of the adopted design method compared to some others [29–31] is, that it considers the Knowledge Base for accumulating the knowledge generated during the design process, but also allows importing and reusing some key technical models and approaches to support the workflow in the CCPS Design. Another work [33] considers reusing knowledge generated during the design process, dividing generated knowledge in two key categories – system models and verification methods, but the presented design framework does not reflect in detail input parameters from the application area. A second advantage of adopted method is that it supports iterative design, which is also the case of some other methods [31, 29] in which, however, iterative design is only considered between System Design and Expert Design blocks.

Digital Twin can be considered as a key component of the CCPS. On the stage of Pre-Digital Twin the concept is used in order to test various aspects of the designed system. During the development stage, physical artefacts which are implemented within the system are having the digital replicas which allow controlling the physical assets. Adaptive and intelligent DTs can supply the necessary data on how to improve digital models in the knowledge base, as well as better adjust the entities developed within the CCPS design pillar to user requirements identified in the Application Domain, as well as ensure the evolution of the developed system.

The framework based on the adopted design method described above is represented in Fig. 2.

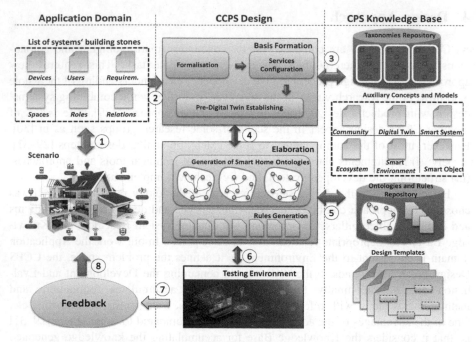

**Fig. 2.** CCPS design framework inspired by the design science research method.

The proposed framework includes three pillars:

- Application Domain;
- CCPS Design;
- Knowledge Base.

The Application Domain contains some basic building blocks for the CCPS Design workflow, among which are lists of: roles, devices, spaces, users, requirements and relations. These are extracted from the problem stated within the scenario (1). The Application Domain is also receiving feedback from CCPS Design workflow (8) to adjust deliverables with the defined requirements and problem stated within scenario (7). It is important to mention that there are no clearly defined services or detailed descriptions of devices, but only a set input parameters and components at this stage/in this pillar.

The next stage – CCPS Design, is the core part of the framework. It contains three blocks:

- Basis Formation, which is intended to formalise the building blocks retrieved from the Application Domain (2), whereas loading the models and taxonomies from the Knowledge Base (3), as well as keeping the models and taxonomies up-to-date. A taxonomy, in this case, serves the goal of classification of items or components exported or loaded from the Application Domain. Subsequently the capillary services to satisfy the needs and requirements received from the Application Domain, are configured The final step is formation of DT prototypes or Pre-Digital Twins

frames – virtual prototypes to be launched in the *Testing Environment* to validate the design process outcome;
– Elaboration, which aims to generate ontologies based on taxonomies delivered by Basis Formation block (4) and generate the rules for appropriate functioning of the system. Rules specify the conditions of how the components collaborate with each other. CCPS Rules and ontologies might be exported to the Knowledge Base to be reused in the future (5). An example of rule can be, for instance, a rule regulating the order of tasks executed in regard to daily electricity consumption. At this stage new collaborative forms and complex collaborative services can be formed. Testing Environment is, in fact, a test bench for the system models, generated during the CCPS Design workflow. Thus, Testing Environment is launched at the run-time, whereas previous stages CCPS Design pillar are implemented at design-time. The entities, which are executed inside the Testing Environment, are the Pre-Digital Twins aimed at testing and validating designed system in a virtual environment to fix the problems and adjust all components and services (6), before building the system's physical part.

The Knowledge Base pillar accumulates the base knowledge that can be used during the design process and provides technical tools and models. Examples of the Knowledge Base can be found in the literature [34], where it is used to support digital twins and containing domain ontology and its associated rules. In the current work this pillar is used to support the design of the whole Collaborative CPS including the DTs. The main idea is to provide to the designer some ready-to-use building blocks, which can be used to build the system's core elements. Moreover, its content can evolve as a result of the processes happening within the CCPS design pillar. Key constituents of the Knowledge Base include:

– Rules and ontologies: The rules can be considered from several viewpoints: as internal rules for the Smart Components and global rules which are applied to the environment where the entities are deployed [35].
– Design Templates repository: which encapsulates the Model of a Problem and Solution Model. The Model of a Problem [36] is composed of some templates allowing determining the basic elements of the Design Space as input for the Solution Model. For instance, when the designer plans to develop a system in some application area, by choosing a template in the Problem Model she/he will get access to the templates of core components. In its turn the Solution Model provides information about topologies, relations, successful examples of smart objects coalitions, hierarchical interrelations of components, etc.
– Concepts' Models Repository contains important formalized models of key concepts related to CCPS, such as Smart Environment, Cyber-Physical Ecosystem, Smart Object, Digital Twin, Users' Community, etc. It also contains Templates, which are used to provide information about the virtual and physical entities, such as: state, quality of service, etc, allowing high-level abstractions.

## 5 Example Scenario and Implementation

In this section we present a model of a DT in the context of other concepts that were previously identified and discussed in [1] (Fig. 3), and a small illustrative scenario implementing the proposed model. This model is divided into three layers: Ecosystem, Organisational, and Entities layers. The Ecosystem Layer is the highest abstraction layer which integrates the cyber-physical and social aspects. The Ecosystem itself can be composed of, or in other words, possess other Ecosystems. The Organisational Layer groups technical components as well as humans into the organisational units, namely through the concepts of Smart Environment and Smart Community. At the same time, Smart Environment and Smart Community can be composed, including subordinate constituents. The Entities Layer contains the single entities represented through DTs and/or Human DTs.

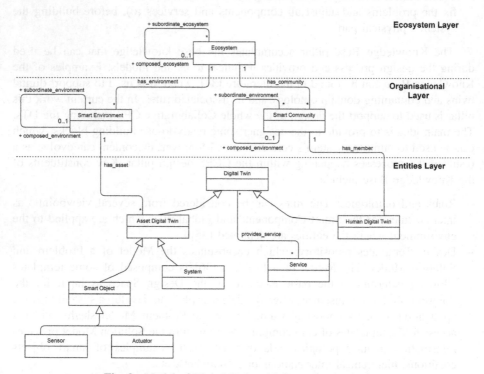

**Fig. 3.** Model of Digital Twin with interrelated concepts

Besides the core concepts identified in [1], as for instance Ecosystem, Smart Environment and Smart Community, or the concept of Digital Twin which was discussed in Sect. 3, some other elements require specification. As a DT has a dual nature, i.e. representing the physical and virtual entities, it includes the model of the represented asset. The model should reflect the attributes of the physical entity, as for instance a sensor (e.g. identifying the measurement units, data type and other relevant data) in order to reproduce the physical asset as a virtual replica. An asset can, on its turn, be a Smart Object, e.g. sensors and actuators, or a (complex) System. On the other hand, the Human DT is representing the Human members of the Smart Community. Separation of DTs into Asset DT and Human DT is needed to consider the dual nature of Human DT. From one side, the Human DT can be considered as part of the system or system asset, but from the other side the human-user is involved in social, administrative and organisational tasks. For instance, a user can own various physical artefacts possessing corresponding role and regulate (introduce new, change existing) the access policy for the other users. The social part is also of big importance, an illustrative example could be the emotional state of the human [38] and how this specific topic can be addressed by digital twins. Thus, the Human DT is the combination of both: (i) being virtual replica of all smart things deployed in or used by the human (e.g. smart bracelets, wearables, pacemaker, etc), and (ii) covering other tasks, such as administrative or social, which are not directly related to replication of physical assets.

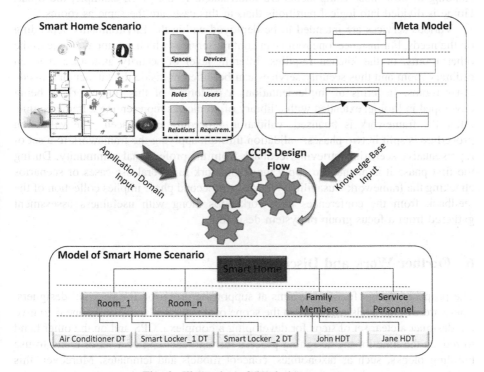

**Fig. 4.** Illustration of the design process.

For a test case scenario, the Smart Home domain was chosen. A Smart Home can be represented as an Ecosystem (Fig. 4), whereas each room inside a home is an environment encapsulating various devices providing services within this unit. Some services can be provided by several collaboratively acting systems. Thus, a temporary coalition of digital twins can be formed, similar to the one described in [37], thus reflecting the notion of collaborative CPS. Moreover, combining various Asset DTs and Human DTs into the temporary coalitions can improve the variety of tasks that can be solved, whereas improving the context awareness of the system.

Smart Communities are organised based on belonging to a certain group as for instance, "Family Members" and "Service Personnel". In the proposed illustrative scenario, there are 2 family members, John and Jane belonging to the "Family Members" community. Both are represented through their Human DTs, which can also provide some services, such as "Personal Health Condition Service". The process of generating the Scenario Model based on the input from the Knowledge Base (Meta Model) and Smart Home Scenario requirements is illustrated in Fig. 4.

The Smart Home Scenario part of the design process identifies the number of users, their demands, requirements, responsibilities and groups they belong to with corresponding roles, which in conjunction with Access Policies determine the access to the services of the Smart Home. The Meta Model coming from the Knowledge Base supports the formalisation of the systems' components, whereas giving the understanding of how those components are interrelated. In the given example, the Smart Home is divided into logical partitions that, in this case, are the same as rooms.

Various services are intended to be deployed within the Environments depending on the needs. For instance, one room can contain services which are not available in the other rooms, or the kitchen requires different level of security assurance than an ordinary room and thus security services can be different inside the kitchen and inside other rooms. In terms of implementation, a prototype of this framework is being developed in Prolog, extended with a library of predicates representing a frame engine. After the framework is finalised, validation procedure is foreseen. The validation procedure is split in two phases: validation through applying the framework to a set of representative scenarios retrieving feedback from the professional community. During the first phase it is planned to apply the framework to several use-cases or scenarios checking the framework's usability. Whereas the second phase implies collection of the feedback from the conferences and workshops along with usefulness assessment gathered from a focus group of system designers.

# 6　Further Work and Discussion

The proposed design framework aims at supporting provision for systems' designers. There are various goals which are in the scope of this particular research: one is to give the designer a clear set of steps for developing a complex CCPS and on the other hand to reduce the time for the designing process through enabling of a set of ready-to-use building blocks, such as taxonomies, concept models and templates. Moreover, this article discusses various types of the DTs depending on the abstraction level or the systems' design phase and their application in CCPS. The application area is defined in the Smart Home domain targeting the life improvement aspects. As the life improvement is a very broad term including a lot of notions and ideas, the "theory of needs" is considered in the design framework.

For the next stages we will progress towards completing the implementation of the framework that follows the methodology described in this work. As such, the next stages include the development of: (i) the templates of the models used in the knowledge base to support the development, (ii) developing the set of functions guiding the designing process, and finally (iii) elaborating a set of scenarios (some are already partially mentioned in the current work) for validating the framework. One of the aspects which are only slightly covered within this work is the issue of DT utilization for the system's evolution, along with DTs being used during all stages of the system's lifecycle. However, it is partially covered, as the framework assumes the constant update of the Knowledge Base with knowledge acquired during all design phases. Another challenge is the transition from the Pre-DT, being used during the design phase for the testing purposes, and DT that will be assigned to the real-world item or artefact.

**Acknowledgements.** This work has been funded in part by the Center of Technology and Systems and the Portuguese FCT program UID/EEA/00066/2019 and UIDB/00066/2020 and European Commission (project DiGiFoF (Project Nr. 601089-EPP-1-2018-1-RO-EPPKA2-KA).

# References

1. Nazarenko, A.A., Camarinha-Matos, L.M.: Basis for an approach to design collaborative cyber-physical systems. In: Camarinha-Matos, L.M., Almeida, R., Oliveira, J. (eds.) DoCEIS 2019. IAICT, vol. 553, pp. 193–205. Springer, Cham (2019). https://doi.org/10.1007/978-3-030-17771-3_16
2. Evchina, Y., Dvoryanchikova, A., Martinez Lastra, J.L.: Semantic information management for user and context aware smart home with social services. In: IEEE International Multi-Disciplinary Conference on Cognitive Methods in Situation Awareness and Decision Support (CogSIMA), San Diego, USA, 25–28 February 2013, pp. 262–268 (2013)
3. Delbrugger, T., Lenz, L.T., Losch, D., Rosmann, J.: A navigation framework for Digital Twins of factories based on building information modeling. In: 22nd IEEE International Conference on Emerging Technologies and Factory Automation (ETFA), Limassol, Cyprus, 12–15 September 2017 (2017)
4. Baldissera, T.A., Camarinha-Matos, L.M., De Faveri, C.: An elderly care ecosystem application. In: 45th Annual Conference of the IEEE Industrial Electronics Society, Lisbon, Portugal, 14–17 October 2019, pp. 2773–2778 (2019)
5. Linhart, Ed.: Production Operations in F-35 2003 Year In Review (2003). https://www.nist.gov/system/files/documents/2018/04/09/2p_kinard_digitalthreadi4pt0.pdf
6. Grieves, M.W.: Product lifecycle management: the new paradigm for enterprises. Int. J. Prod. Dev. **2**(1/2), 71–84 (2005)
7. Shafto, M., Conroy, M., Doyle, R.: NASA Modeling, Simulation, Information Technology & Processing. https://www.nasa.gov/pdf/501321main_TA11-MSITP-DRAFT-Nov2010-A1.pdf
8. Kritzinger, W., Karner, M., Traar, G., Henjes, J., Sihn, W.: Digital Twin in manufacturing: a categorical literature review and classification. IFAC-PapersOnLine **51**(11), 1016–1022 (2018)
9. Tuegel, E.J., Ingraffea, A.R., Eason, T.G., Spottswood, S.M.: Reengineering aircraft structural life prediction using a Digital Twin. Int. J. Aerosp. Eng. **11**, 14 (2011). Article No. 154798
10. Graessler, I., Poehler, A.: Integration of a Digital Twin as human representation in a scheduling procedure of a cyber-physical production system. In: IEEE International Conference on Industrial Engineering and Engineering Management (IEEM), Singapore, Singapore, 10–13 December, pp. 289–293 (2017)

11. Matlis, D.R.: Medical experiments on your Digital Twin. In: 2015 Dassault Analyst Conference. http://axendia.com/blog/wp-content/uploads/2015/07/Dassault-2015-Analyst-Conference-report-Final.pdf

12. Madni, A., Madni, C., Lucero, S.: Leveraging Digital Twin technology in model-based systems engineering. Systems **7**(1), 9 (2019)

13. Qi, Q., Tao, F., Zuo, Y., Zhao, D.: Digital Twin service towards smart manufacturing. Procedia CIRP **72**, 237–242 (2018)

14. Eckhart, M., Ekelhart, A., Weippl, E.: Enhancing cyber situational awareness for cyber-physical systems through Digital Twins. In: 24th IEEE International Conference on Emerging Technologies and Factory Automation (ETFA), Zaragoza, Spain, 10–13 September 2019, pp. 1222–1225 (2019)

15. Negri, E., Fumagalli, L., Cimino, C., Macchi, M.: FMU-supported simulation for CPS Digital Twin. Procedia Manuf. **28**, 201–206 (2019)

16. Boschert, S., Rosen, R.: Digital Twin–the simulation aspect. In: Hehenberger, P., Bradley, D. (eds.) Mechatronic Futures, pp. 59–74. Springer, Cham (2016). https://doi.org/10.1007/978-3-319-32156-1_5

17. Schluse, M., Priggemeyer, M., Atorf, L., Rossmann, J.: Experimentable Digital Twins—streamlining simulation-based systems engineering for Industry 4.0. IEEE Trans. Ind. Inform. **14**(4), 1722–1731 (2018)

18. Biesinger, F., Meike, D., Kraß, B., Weyrich, M.: A Digital Twin for production planning based on cyber-physical systems: a case study for a cyber-physical system-based creation of a Digital Twin. Procedia CIRP **79**, 355–360 (2019)

19. Martínez, G.S., Sierla, S., Karhela, T., Vyatkin, V.: Automatic generation of a simulation-based Digital Twin of an industrial process plant. In: 44th Annual Conference of the IEEE Industrial Electronics Society (IECON), Washington, USA, 21–23 October 2018, pp. 3084–3089 (2018)

20. Stark, R., Fresemann, C., Lindow, K.: Development and operation of Digital Twins for technical systems and services. CIRP Ann. **68**(1), 129–132 (2019)

21. Tao, F., Sui, F., Liu, A., Qi, Q., Zhang, M., Song, B., Nee, A.Y.C.: Digital twin-driven product design framework. International Journal of Production Research, pp. 3935–3953 (2018)

22. Tao, F., Cheng, J., Qi, Q., Zhang, M., Zhang, H., Sui, F.: Digital Twin-driven product design, manufacturing and service with big data. Int. J. Adv. Manuf. Technol. **94**, 3563–3576 (2017)

23. Leng, J., Zhang, H., Yan, D., Liu, Q., Chen, X., Zhang, D.: Digital Twin-driven manufacturing cyber-physical system for parallel controlling of smart workshop. J. Ambient Intell. Hum. Comput. **10**(2), 1155–1166 (2018)

24. Wang, X.V., Wang, L.: Digital Twin-based WEEE recycling, recovery and remanufacturing in the background of Industry 4.0. Int. J. Prod. Res. **57**, 3892–3902 (2018)

25. Martinez-Velazquez, R., Gamez, R., El Saddik, A.: Cardio Twin: a Digital Twin of the human heart running on the edge. In: IEEE International Symposium on Medical Measurements and Applications (MeMeA), Istanbul, Turkey, 26–28 June 2019

26. Exploring the possibilities offered by Digital Twins in medical technology. White paper. https://www.siemens-healthineers.com/press-room/press-videos/im-20181204001shs.html

27. Baskaran, S., et al.: Digital human and robot simulation in automotive assembly using siemens process simulate: a feasibility study. Procedia Manuf. **34**, 986–994 (2019)

28. Andersson, E., Eckerwall, K.: Enabling successful collaboration on digital platforms in the manufacturing industry. A study of Digital Twins. http://www.diva-portal.org/smash/record.jsf?pid=diva2%3A1324680&dswid=1279

29. Sinnwell, C., Krenkel, N., Aurich, J.C.: Conceptual manufacturing system design based on early product information. CIRP Ann. **68**(1), 121–124 (2019)
30. Francalanza, E., Mercieca, M., Fenech, A.: Modular system design approach for cyber physical production systems. Procedia CIRP **72**, 486–491 (2018)
31. Cuckov, F., Rudd, G., Daly, L.: Framework for model-based design and verification of human-in-the-loop cyber-physical systems. In: IEEE International Conference on Software Testing, Verification and Validation Workshops (ICSTW), Tokyo, Japan, 13–17 March 2017, pp. 401–402 (2017)
32. Hevner, A.R., March, S.T., Park, J., Ram, S.: Design science in information systems research. MIS Q. **28**(1), 75–105 (2004)
33. Sztipanovits, J., Bapty, T., Koutsoukos, X., Lattmann, Z., Neema, S., Jackson, E.: Model and tool integration platforms for cyber-physical system design. Proc. IEEE **106**(9), 1501–1526 (2018)
34. David, J., Lobov, A., Lanz, M.: Attaining learning objectives by ontological reasoning using Digital Twins. Procedia Manuf. **31**, 349–355 (2019)
35. Terroso-Saenz, F., Hernandez-Ramos, J.L., Bernal Bernabe, J., Skarmeta, A.F.: Opportunistic smart object aggregation based on clustering and event processing. In: IEEE International Conference on Communications (ICC), Kuala Lumpur, Malaysia, 22–27 May 2016 (2016)
36. Wang, R., Nellippallil, A.B., Wang, G., Yan, Y., Allen, J.K., Mistree, F.: Systematic design space exploration using a template-based ontological method. Adv. Eng. Inform. **36**, 163–177 (2018). https://doi.org/10.1016/j.aei.2018.03.006
37. Barata, J., Camarinha-Matos, L.M.: Coalitions of manufacturing components for shop floor agility - the CoBaSA architecture. Int. J. Netw. Virtual Organ. **2**, 50–77 (2003)
38. Ferrada, F., Camarinha-Matos, L.M.: A modelling framework for collaborative network emotions. Enterp. Inf. Syst. **13**(7–8), 1164–1194 (2019)
39. Virtual Singapore and the Economy of the Digital Twin. https://blogs.3ds.com/perspectives/virtual-singapore-and-the-economy-of-the-digital-twin/
40. Nevado-Peña, D., López-Ruiz, V.-R., Alfaro-Navarro, J.-L.: Improving quality of life perception with ICT use and technological capacity in Europe. Technol. Forecast. Soc. Chang. **148**, 119734 (2019)

# Production Process Modelling Architecture to Support Improved Cyber-Physical Production Systems

Fabio Seixas-Lopes[1,2]([✉]), Jose Ferreira[2], Carlos Agostinho[2], and Ricardo Jardim-Goncalves[2]

[1] Department of Electrical Engineering, FCT, NOVA University of Lisbon, 2829-516 Caparica, Portugal
fas.lopes@campus.fct.unl.pt
[2] Centre of Technology and Systems, UNINOVA, 2829-516 Caparica, Portugal
{japf, ca, rg}@uninova.pt

**Abstract.** With the proliferation of intelligent networks in industrial environments, manufacturing SME's have been in a continuous search for integrating and retrofitting existing assets with modern technologies that could provide low-cost solutions for optimizations in their production processes. Their willingness to support a technological evolution is firmly based on the perception that, in the future, better tools will guarantee process control, surveillance and maintenance. For this to happen, the digitalization of valuable and extractable information must be held in a cost-effective manner, through contemporary approaches such as IoT, creating the required fluidity between hardware and software, for implementing Cyber-Physical modules in the manufacturing process. The goal of this work is to develop an architecture that will support companies to digitize their machines and processes through an MDA approach, by modeling their production processes and physical resources, and transforming into an implementation model, using contemporary CPS and IoT concepts, to be continuously improved using forecasting/predictive algorithms and analytics.

**Keywords:** Cyber-physical systems · Internet of Things · Model driven architecture · Interoperability · Process modelling · Artificial Intelligence

## 1 Introduction

The term cyber-physical systems (CPS) refers to intelligent systems with integrated computational, networking and physical capabilities [1]. In industrial production, the advantage of applying this paradigm to existing systems is to fill the gap between the cyber world, where data is exchanged and transformed, and the physical world in which we live [2]. By creating means to utilize data from pre-existing physical machinery and devices, every extractable information becomes a mean of observing the current processes, feeding different improvement possibilities and production mechanisms such as energy efficiency, waste management, resource planning, scheduling and process monitoring. These mechanisms have a meaningful impact to achieve financial,

L. M. Camarinha-Matos et al. (Eds.): DoCEIS 2020, IFIP AICT 577, pp. 206–213, 2020.
https://doi.org/10.1007/978-3-030-45124-0_19

social and environmental benefits, especially in thriving SME's that wish to compete for larger economy markets while keeping a sustainable production [3].

Contemporarily, the CPS represent many opportunities and research challenges that include the design and development of next-generation airplanes and space vehicles, high-end factories of the future, fully autonomous urban driving and prostheses that allow brain signals to control physical objects [4]. The focus of the concept is to expand the capabilities of the physical world through computation, communication and control, as key enablers for future technological developments.

In the physical world, unlike most of the software processes which are procedural, many things happen at once and are compositions of many parallel processes. In CPS, measuring and controlling the dynamics of such processes and using them in feedback loops that affect the computations is very important to orchestrate beneficial actions that influence their effectiveness. Consequently, concurrency is intrinsic in CPS. Many of the technical challenges in designing and analyzing embedded software stem from the need to bridge an inherently sequential semantics with an intrinsically concurrent physical world [5].

Considering that, this work tries to correspond to the following question: how can cyber-physical systems be improved using a model driven architecture such it is able to provide modular solutions/suggestions based on real-time data from the production processes?

In this work, the aim is to develop a simplified model driven architecture that allows the integration of modular optimization tools, that support the overall efficiency in the implementation of sustainable CPS in the manufacturing industry. The idea is to support existing SME's with a cheap but scalable solution for technological improvement. For this to be sustainable, the whole process must be analyzed, from the input of raw materials to the output of finished products.

With business notation (e.g. Business Process Model Notation (BPMN)) and the creation of data-driven models that represent the current production processes, a digital twin of the factory can be created and fed using real-time data. This data can be acquired using current cost-effective methodologies such as presented in [6] to retrofit any machinery and devices. The use of wearables on factory workers can also be regarded in a way that supports security and safety methodologies (e.g. insoles that measure weight and textiles to measure posture). The conception of such models allows for the creation of a decision support system that considers existing KPIs (Key Performance Indicators) to suggest possible improvements. These suggestions are based on AI (Artificial Intelligence) and machine-learning techniques, with forecasting/predictive analytics that dynamically adapt to the real-time acquired data (big data algorithms and complex event processing (CEP) methodologies will be used).

Thus, this work proposes an architecture that is able to consider the manufacturing ecosystem and create a decision support system that not only displays valuable information to management personnel but also actively thrives to propose improvements that, ideally, were proven to be successful in other implementations, or during validation. The idea is for the architecture to be translated into a secure platform, where the main blocks are the manufacturing resources and their specifications (machinery, materials, devices and people), the process models (it also includes the devices configurations), the enterprise system (factory production orders, the legacy ERP and other existing software that outputs valuable information), the data management system (real-time data acquisition and handling, CEP, DB's for resources, production orders and process models), the decision support block (with KPI's, AI, validated optimization tools and other testing community tools) and the process orchestrator (with a process engine, a process interface for monitorization and for the user to handle the production decision points and an optimization interface to manage the implemented optimization tools). These blocks must be fully interoperable to allow the introduction of any information source to be valuable to this architecture. In this way, any information source is also modular, not strictly necessary, but valuable for the performance, even if they are redundant (in case of malfunctioning, see [7]). The implementation of information sources and their location/specifications (what types of sensors, where they are placed considering the type of industry, etc.) is also something that could be suggested by the decision support system when it may result in optimization.

From the factory's management perspective, the *modus operandi* is the initial specification of the production processes and resources in the platform, to enable the creation of a digital model. After that, the data management block is populated with information, that can be complemented with the connection of the enterprise system block (to use legacy software and existing production orders), and the process orchestrator is able to provide a monitorization and data visualization, regarding the actual production processes. With this, the main blocks of the architecture are in place and the tools for process improvement are ready to be of value. By matching KPI's and AI technology, the decision support block is able to suggest and pre-configure tools based on real-time data from the processes. The tools can be modular and added during time, considering cost and other constraints.

The direction of this work is to have a simplified solution for companies to digitize their assets, build an implementation model, have production process monitorization and quickly act on acquired information, resulting in performance improvements.

## 2 Relationship to Tech Innovation for Life Improvement

Digital innovation is a requisition for industrial improvement but to be sustainable, on a business but also on an environmental level, solutions must be planned and considered within a scalable and responsible paradigm. Considering the contemporary industry and the respective environmental impacts, it is very important to define sustainable mechanisms along with the optimization of manufacturing processes. Usually, the implementation of such mechanisms can disrupt the existing functioning of factories, which imposes the necessity of not repeatedly trying to implement new solutions. Considering that, an architecture that dynamically envisions environmental sustainability, from the start, as a mean to pursuit economic growth by reducing costs, can be very appealing and beneficial by not defining specific procedures that may need to be replaced in the future. This impacts the environmental footprint but also the stability of companies, specially SME's which then are more at easy to provide better working conditions and stable jobs for their workers. Also, people are regarded in this architecture from the start, which enables the application of security and safety methodologies (e.g. acquiring wearables) as optimization tools.

## 3 Background

To specify and better understand the methodology proposed in this paper, some key concepts will be mentioned and explained. The objective is to provide a brief insight on the concepts that generate the modules proposed in the next section.

**IoT and Data Acquisition.** The Internet of Things (IoT) is an emerging topic that aims to combine consumer products, sensors and industrial components and other everyday objects with Internet connectivity and powerful data analytic capabilities that have the ability to transform the way we work and live [8]. With this, objects can become optimized, as every extractable information becomes a mean of analyzing and computing the functioning processes. The results of such analysis are oriented to provide better performance, enhanced context functioning and new purposes that come into play when connecting objects to an intelligent network [7].

For the purpose of this work, IoT represents the ideal conception of data acquisition within the SME's industrial environment, where data sources tend to provide heterogenous data, if there are any in place. It can be a cost-effective solution of implementing intelligent network nodes that pre-filter data, considering context, and pass on valuable information for decision-making processes on higher levels of the architecture [9]. Depending on how this concept is envisioned, the data acquisition process can also consider existing knowledge bases, data/event handlers and other mechanisms that contribute to a better understanding of data and how it can be handled, considering objectives, context, incorrect input and fault detection.

**Cyber-Physical Systems.** This concept was briefly defined in the introduction section of this work as a mean to connect the digital world to the physical world. Its importance stems from the necessity to have a digital form of acquirable physical information that can be quickly displayed and analyzed, i.e. a digital twin [10].

This methodology allows to monitor production as a whole and to plan and model optimization based on the acquired information. In other words, by designing models that represent the manufacturing process and connect them to the acquisition modules, there is space for designing a runtime solution that implements mechanisms such as scheduling, waste and energy consumption/efficiency, that result in direct optimization of processes and also contribute for more complex decision-making processes that need a global overview of data and resources in order to be effective.

In this work, CPS conceptually represents the environment for the purposed architecture, since the idea is to have real-time information, fed by gradually implementable information sources, to develop sustainable optimization mechanisms and contribute to an intelligent and dynamic decision-making system.

**Process Modelling and Model-Driven Architectures.** The process modelling process can be described as a design procedure to reinforce or create methodologies for enabling mechanisms such as simulation and production monitorization, and in this case the implementation or improvement of a CPS and production processes, by creating a digital twin [11]. This is where the user's knowledge gains shape to result in a representation of the factories resources and production processes.

A Model-Driven Architecture puts the process models in the center of the software development process and it is driven by the activity of these models [12]. The models typically derive from requirements, which are subject to analysis, followed by low-level design, the design itself, testing and deployment.

The proposed architecture of this work is heavily model-driven and for making sense of the proposed modules, the specification of the assets is crucial to have a real understanding of the optimization possibilities. The flow of the production is as essential too, because it delineates how the process occurs, which steps can provide feedback, when do materials are needed and transformed, when mechanisms of maintenance, scheduling and other strategic planning situations may occur, etc.

## 4   Production Process Modelling Architecture

In this section, an overview of the general architecture for this work is proposed. It is important to mention that this architecture is currently based on a process modelling architecture that envisions the application of possible complex technological processes (AI, machine-learning, big data, etc.) that may induce alterations along its design and the continuity of this work. Also, guidelines from area standard architectures/models/ontologies/frameworks such as ARROWHEAD, IoT-A, W3C SSN Ontology and IoT Lite, were considered to develop this work, with the objective of developing a real-world integrable and interoperable solution.

This work also considers previous work and early results obtain, within the scope of IoT and CPS, by the authors of this paper in ongoing and finished European research projects, for the purpose of designing this architecture's modules and how they are envisioned to be interoperable.

### 4.1   Architecture's Overview

A high-level view of the architecture proposed in this work is presented in Fig. 1.

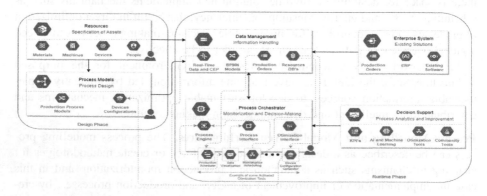

**Fig. 1.** General overview of the proposed architecture with examples of an implementation of some optimization modules.

The main idea for this architecture, in addition to each module functionalities, is the interoperability that is aimed to be achieved during the runtime phase by combining the functionalities of a process orchestrator engine with incoming real-time data to provide production monitorization, decision points, user input and data visualization, and the decision support system which is fed with the information handled in the process orchestrator and compares it with previously obtained knowledge (from assets, models, type of industry and materials, and other implementations) stored in specific databases to suggest valuable improvements that can be the implementation of optimizing modules (e.g. capacity planner, scheduler engine, process simulation), alterations in specific points of the production process, addition of sensors or data sources, re-configuration of resources, analyzing the cost-benefit ratio for upgrading machinery or suggesting to hire more workers, etc.

## 4.2   Architecture's Blocks

In this sub-section, a brief description of the main blocks of this architecture is given, to explain the main functionalities and support their interaction and interoperability.

**Resources and Process Models.** For enabling the architecture with real-time data, the production assets must be specified. This specification is very important not only to establish data sources, through IoT nodes and hubs, but also to empower the decision support system with possibilities regarding the characteristics of machinery, sensors, actuators, and other production assets.

After the assets are digitalized, the overall production flow is created and connected to the data sources, so it can enable the monitorization of the production processes in real-time with live input of collected data.

For this to be optimized, the methodologies implied by following an MDA approach are applied to implement the designing of models (e.g. using BPMN) based on the process requirements and subsequent analysis. For this, a low-code programming tool, such as Node-RED, can be used wire together the IoT implementation. Within the models, the sensors and their characteristics are very important because it allows to combine them with the mentioned requirements to transformed them in actual code to be used in the devices. With this, the IoT nodes and hubs implementation is faster and it can always be re-configured by higher-level blocks, since these models and configurations are stored in the data management block, that is accessible by the process orchestrator.

Once these processes are finished, the data management and decision support blocks are engaged, and the user interacts with an interface. Further inclusion of additional data sources can or not require the adaptation of the process models, depending on how it can change the production flow (e.g. if creates a decision point).

**Enterprise System.** Already implemented mechanisms for the factory functioning must be used to not totally disrupt operations. Production orders and the output from the ERP (Enterprise Resource Planning) and other existing software are fed into the data management block to be stored and used by the process orchestrator.

**Data Management.** Acquired information, from the various data sources defined in the production resources, moves from phase to phase and needs to be managed in order to provide important contextual value. This includes mechanisms such as data filtering, fault detection, event processing and other data management processes, that ensure the real-time monitorization carried out by the process orchestrator.

Within properly structured databases, information about the production models, resources and the production orders are kept during reasonable durations of time.

**Decision Support System.** This block considers the company's existing knowledge bases (for the assets, type of industry, etc.), correlates them with the production assets and process models using forecasting/predictive analytics and algorithms, to create suggestions for improving the current production processes. These improvements may be based on the data source configuration, implementation of modules such as a raw material planner, creation/deletion of decision points in the production flow, etc.

The idea that motivates this system is to provide a dynamic approach for improvement and adaptation of production processes, creating an additional layer within the conventional CPS architectures.

**Process Orchestrator.** The purpose of this block is to provide an interface for the monitorization of the production processes and to enable a platform for decision-making. Here, is where the user gets process improvement suggestions (originated by the decision support block) through an optimization interface.

The Process Orchestrator runs on process engine and enables the inclusion of already developed and pre-configured modular tools such as scheduling, resource planning, device configuration generator. These modules, once activated, can be fine-tuned with more advanced configurations, and run inside the process orchestrator, serving specific functions and providing feedback for the user.

## 5 Conclusions and Future Work

This work provides an architecture for enhancing CPS with process modelling that considers all the production processes that transform the raw materials into the final products. Architectural structures to support optimizations were defined, on the data acquisition (combining them with models), data management, process monitorization and decision-making, to create an environment that allows step by step optimization, that will use predictive and forecasting algorithms that suggest the suitability for each production case. This approach follows current tendencies for technological development, using potentially complex concepts such as AI to dynamically adapt to real-time data and allocate the data analysis to processors and away from the user, which interacts with graphical interfaces that allow the drag-and-drop of features.

In the future, the proposed architecture is going to be validated using real-time data from industry to determine how the decision support block reacts and improves during time. The inherent technological concepts to achieve this are going to be included step by step, to ensure functionality and proper validation of their usefulness. Other industry standard methodologies and frameworks will serve as guidelines to ensure proper real-world integration and interoperability.

The specifications of production resources and the resulting process models are major tasks for ensuring the functionalities of this architecture which the degree of specification is something that is being currently validated, so it can reach a sustainable ratio of effort-benefit to the user.

The process orchestrator validation relies on previous work from this paper authors that pursued the implementation of an orchestrator based on BPMN process modeling and engine. Future work on this will be to develop this orchestrator as a cloud-enabled solution to include modular optimization tools. An interface for the user for decision-making, a graphical visualization of data and process monitorization, are also important achievements to validate this architecture for future use-case scenarios.

**Acknowledgments.** This work was partially supported by the Fundação para a Ciência e Tecnologia, UIDB/00066/2020 (CTS – Center of Technology and Systems).

# References

1. Baheti, R., Gill, H.: Cyber-physical systems: the impact of control technology. IEEE Control Syst. Soc. **12**(1), 161–166 (2011)
2. Ferreira, J., Lopes, F., Ghimire, S., Doumeingts, G., Agostinho, C., Jardim-Goncalves, R.: Cyber-physical production systems to monitor the polishing process of cutlery production. In: 9th International Conference on Intelligent Systems (IS) Theory (2018)
3. Moeuf, A., Pellerin, R., Lamouri, S., Tamayo-Giraldo, S., Barbaray, R.: The industrial management of SMEs in the era of Industry 40. Int. J. Prod. Res. **56**(3), 1118–1136 (2018)
4. Baheti, R., Gill, H.: Cyber-Physical Systems: From Theory to Practice (2011)
5. Lee, E.A., Seshia, S.A.: Introduction to Embedded Systems. A Cyber-Physical Systems Approach, Second edn. Mit Press, Cambridge (2017)
6. Agostinho, C., Lopes, F., Ferreira, J., Ghimire, S., Marques, M.: A lightweight IoT hub for SME manufacturing industries. In: Popplewell, K., Thoben, K.-D., Knothe, T., Poler, R. (eds.) Enterprise Interoperability VIII. PIC, vol. 9, pp. 371–383. Springer, Cham (2019). https://doi.org/10.1007/978-3-030-13693-2_31
7. Lopes, F., Ferreira, J., Jardim-Goncalves, R., Agostinho, C.: Semantic maps for IoT network reorganization in face of sensor malfunctioning. In: 2017 IEEE International Conference on Systems, Man, and Cybernetics (SMC), SMC 2017, Janua, vol. 2017, pp. 1914–1919 (2017)
8. Rose, K., Eldridge, S., Chapin, L.: The Internet of Things: An Overview. Understanding the Issues and Challenges of a More Connected World. Internet Society, Reston (2015)
9. Huang, Y., Li, G.: Descriptive models for Internet of Things. In: Proceedings of 2010 International Conference on Intelligent Control and Information Processing, ICICIP (2010)
10. Uhlemann, T.H.J., Lehmann, C., Steinhilper, R.: The digital twin: realizing the cyber-physical production system for industry 4.0. Proc. CIRP **61**, 335–340 (2017)
11. Rodič, B.: Industry 4.0 and the new simulation modelling paradigm. Organizacija **50**(3), 193–207 (2017)
12. Kleppe, A., et al.: The Model Driven Architecture: Practice and Promise. Addison-Wesley, Boston (2003)

# The Impact of Additive Manufacturing on Supply Chain Resilience

Bardia Naghshineh[✉] and Helena Carvalho

UNIDEMI, Department of Mechanical and Industrial Engineering,
NOVA School of Science and Technology, Universidade NOVA de Lisboa,
2829-516 Caparica, Portugal
b.naghshineh@fct.unl.pt

**Abstract.** Additive Manufacturing is changing the structure and dynamics of supply chains, influencing their ability to cope with disturbances, i.e. supply chain resilience. To date, no empirical research has investigated how using this technology influences resilience in a supply chain. Hence, the focus of this research is to investigate this knowledge gap in an industry context using survey method. The results of this research will help managers and decision-makers to determine which resilience practices to capitalize on, when using Additive Manufacturing technology, in order to better provide services and products in their supply chains.

**Keywords:** Additive Manufacturing · Supply chain · Resilience · Impact

## 1 Introduction

Additive Manufacturing (AM), also known as 3D-printing, rapid-prototyping, rapid-manufacturing, or rapid-tooling is a digital manufacturing technology that digitizes supply chains (SCs) [1]. There has been significant progress in the adoption of AM technologies over the recent years, and today it enables the possibility to revolutionize production, operations and SCs [2]. Using data from 3D computer models, AM technology can directly create objects by the incremental addition of material layers without the penalties inherent in conventional manufacturing, e.g. tooling, and thereby offering considerable opportunities for manufacturing practices. AM has the potential to cause significant changes in SCs [3, 4]. However, there is a considerable lack of empirical evidence on what are the implications of AM adoption for SCs, and most of the academic research is conceptual and limited to predictions.

Some of the expected AM impacts on SCs are related to the customer-centricity in the manufacturing process in addition to changes in the SC structure and SC capabilities, e.g., agility, flexibility, resilience [5]. AM allows for fast product and process reconfiguration in both volume and design to address the ever-changing consumer demands [6]. Moreover, decentralized production networks enabled by AM make SCs more flexible as production facilities will be located closer to the customers. One important implication of AM for SCs that has not received attention in the extant literature is supply chain resilience (SCR). A concise definition of SCR is the ability of an SC to cope with unexpected disruptions [7]. SCs are often vulnerable to numerous

L. M. Camarinha-Matos et al. (Eds.): DoCEIS 2020, IFIP AICT 577, pp. 214–221, 2020.
https://doi.org/10.1007/978-3-030-45124-0_20

disruptions, and their effects are quite detrimental if compounded and not dealt with promptly [8]. The frequent occurrence of such disruptive events has created a notable interest in SCR [8], as endeavors to deal with them via traditional risk management techniques are inadequate [9].

The SCR construct has been analyzed and presented in the form of different frameworks throughout the extant literature. One comprehensive framework, which is also used in this research, is proposed by [10] that conceptualizes SCR as a multidimensional and hierarchical construct. The theoretical foundation for this research is based on the dynamic capability view (DCV). The DCV focuses on the competitiveness of a firm in dynamic and unpredictable markets [11]. The underlying constituents of the DCV relate to identifying strategic organizational processes, reconfiguring resources, and identifying the path to gain a competitive advantage [11]. In this light, SC management is a major strategic organizational process [12] for which SCR should be assessed; making it possible to take corrective actions by identifying and reconfiguring resources. In this research, the DCV is a relevant theoretical foundation due to the fact that AM adoption affects the strategic organizational processes [13], which consequently calls for the reconfiguration of a firm's resources to achieve competitive advantage. In view of the foregoing, the main research question is:

What are the impacts of AM adoption on the primary dimensions of SCR in an industrial context?

The rest of this paper is structured as follows: in Sect. 2, the contribution of AM technology adoption and SCR in terms of life improvement are discussed. In Sect. 3, the extant literature is reviewed, and research hypotheses are developed. In Sect. 4, the methodology that will be used in this research is described. Section 5 presents the conclusions and further work.

## 2 Contribution to Life Improvement

One important challenge in SCs is to efficiently deliver the right products and services to customers [3]. Being able to produce innovative, customized products via a responsive and efficient SC can bring about increased customer satisfaction [6]. At the same time, with globalization, there is a need for increasing SC efficiency. Hence, it can be stated that the implementation of SCR practices can be considered as an important strategy for businesses to increase their efficiency and to create competitive advantage [14]. Also, SCR allows companies to sustain their normal operations even when disruptive events happen [7].

In the meanwhile, the emergence of AM technology avails the opportunity of manufacturing products on demand. AM reduces the number of stages in the traditional SC, and it offers the opportunity to redesign products with fewer components (component consolidation), which leads to SC complexity reduction [15], and manufacture products closer to the final consumer (i.e. distributed manufacturing). These instances translate into less need for packaging, transportation, and warehousing [16] that lead to fewer environmental impacts and more SC efficiency. AM also enables changes in business model innovation [17] such as production by consumers, i.e. "prosumer". AM is also capable of causing fundamental changes to different aspects of SCs, e.g. SCR, as the inherent qualities of SCR such as flexibility, responsiveness, integration, and efficiency [8, 18] are influenced by this technology. Due to its additive nature, AM technology also supports sustainable production. Evaluating AM technology adoption through a life cycle perspective, sustainability improvements across the "product and process redesign", "material input processing", "make-to-order component and product manufacturing" and "closing the loop" stages have been identified [19].

# 3  Literature Review and Hypothesis Development

Using a critical literature review, we have mainly focused on the papers addressing the implications of AM technology for SCR. We used different combinations of the keywords: "Additive Manufacturing", "3D printing", "supply chain", and "resilience" to search Scopus and Web of Science. The search was focused on the title, abstract and keywords field. Our search results showed that to date, no empirical research addressed the theme of the current study.

In this research, a comprehensive SCR framework proposed by [10] is used. They conceptualized SCR by using three main dimensions: proactive capability, SC design, and reactive capability. The following sections establish the connection between AM adoption and the afore-mentioned dimensions.

## 3.1  Additive Manufacturing and Proactive Capability

Proactive capabilities are necessary for SCs to be resilient against disruptions [9, 20, 21]. Based on the similarities in the extant literature, flexibility, integration, efficiency, redundancy, financial strength, market strength, and disaster readiness of SCs are considered as proactive capabilities of SCR [8–10, 18, 20, 22].

[1] proposes that volume and product manufacturing flexibility increase by using AM. In contrast to conventional manufacturing technologies, once AM machines are in place and running, the manufacturing of new products does not require expensive and complicated setups. This enables setting up AM machines at almost all points across the SC, including manufacturing plants at various tiers and warehouses [23].

AM adoption has a significant positive influence on SC integration [24]. This was implied through the pre-requisites of integration that firms had established within their SCs, e.g., integrated inventory management systems, integrated logistics support systems, inter-functional data sharing, etc.

[25] suggest that AM can enhance the efficiency of a SC as a result of availing postponement and waste elimination that will decrease the overall inventory level and material movement. It is also proposed that AM enables the production of light-weight products. This can result in potential considerable fuel consumption and energy savings during transport and the use phase [23].

AM enables the customization of service parts in a very short time period and eliminates significant amounts of redundancy that are accumulated in SCs to allow for parts and products to be dispatched quickly [26]. Utilizing AM can result in fewer production steps and reduce redundancy investments in production equipment [1].

The financial strength of the firms is another sub-dimension that is influenced by AM. AM drastically reduces the benefits of economies of scale attributed to conventional manufacturing. Consequently, local manufacturing firms can become more profitable [27]. Also, it is predicted that AM will have a global economic impact of approximately 550 billion US dollars per year by 2025 [27].

Regarding market strength, AM lowers barriers to market entry and provides the possibility of serving multiple markets at once. By taking advantage of the fewest possible number of assembly steps, AM fabricates products with functionally enhanced designs that can be dispatched with short lead time and makes it possible to increase the overall market strength and market responsiveness [23].

AM improvers readiness of an SC by manufacturing parts for hard to reach locations, e.g., disaster areas, and also improving the equipment uptime [28]. Based on these observations, we hypothesize that:

H1. AM adoption has a positive impact on the proactive capability of SCR.

### 3.2 Additive Manufacturing and Reactive Capability

The reactive aspect of SCR can be attributed to the response and recovery capabilities of firms [18, 22]. Response in SCs concerns the mitigation of disruptions in the shortest time with the least possible impacts [8]. Being able to promptly respond to market needs during critical situations is an important SCR determinant [18, 29]. AM is capable of improving SC responsiveness by manufacturing products faster. This can be due to faster time-to-market or faster production of complex products enabled by AM [1].

On the other hand, timely recovery from disruptions is also an important and distinct capability of resilient firms within their SCs [18]. In this context, for instance, if a natural disaster occurs, a deployable AM system can be installed on-site to permit addressing emergency needs with notable decreased turn-around times [28]. Based on these observations, we hypothesize that:

H2. AM adoption has a positive impact on the reactive capability of SCR.

### 3.3 Additive Manufacturing and Supply Chain Design

Several studies indicate the relevance between SC design and SCR. For instance, [30] identify SCR as an SC's ability to proactively design its network to predict impending disruptions and to plan effective responses accordingly. SC design can be conceptualized in terms of complexity, node density, and node criticality.

Complexity is assessed based on the number of nodes (i.e. SC members or actors) and their interconnections in an SC. Increased complexity normally causes more vulnerabilities in SC and reduces SCR [31]. AM technology enables the consolidation of many components into a single product, which reduces the number of parts in the manufacturing flow and stock-keeping units in a production system. It also allows the replacement of many assembly steps and consequently decreases complexity [15] by reducing the number of nodes and the interconnections between them in an SC.

In an SC, node density is higher when in a limited geographical area many nodes exist, which decreases SCR [31, 32]. This problem can be tackled by the decentralization of manufacturing enabled by AM technology, which can bring about significant benefits such as on-location production and prompt responses to demand [15].

Node criticality can be assessed by the importance of a node in an SC [31]. A crucial node (e.g., an important supplier whom other SC members depend on) makes the SC more vulnerable. AM can alleviate node criticality by decreasing the dependency on suppliers of complex components [1]. Based on these observations, we hypothesize that:

H3. AM adoption has a positive impact on the SC design.

## 4    Research Methodology

A conceptual model (Fig. 1) is proposed to measure the impact of AM adoption on the primary dimensions of SCR. In the conceptual model, the relationship between SCR and its representative sub-constructs is operationalized as reflective. This is because these sub-constructs are interconnected and interdependent [33]. For instance, to increase flexibility, integration and redundancy are essential and should be increased [18].

A questionnaire was prepared by adopting items from [10] and [24], which is based on a 5-point Likert scale. The questionnaire was then sent to an academic who specializes in the field of SCR and AM technology for revision and correction. Table 1 provides an example of the survey items. Later, the questionnaire will be sent to an expert engaged in producing spare parts using AM in a Portuguese company for review and comments. In the next step, the modified questionnaire is meant to be sent to experts in the field as a pilot survey for testing. After validation, in order to collect the necessary data, the questionnaire will be sent to experts engaged in using AM in companies across Europe.

**Table 1.** An example of the survey items

| Construct/subconstruct | Item description |
| --- | --- |
| AM adoption | *Please rate the extent to which AM technology is used in your firm (1-very low; 5-very high)* |
| | AM in direct part manufacturing |
| | AM in maintenance and repair |
| | *Please rate to what extent you believe AM technology adoption has impacted the following qualities/conditions within your firm or its supply chain: (1-very low; 5-very high)* |
| Proactive capability | Producing different types of products to meet customer requirements |
| Reactive capability | Recovery in a short time |
| Supply chain design | Being critically dependent on a specific supplier |

In order to estimate the research model, this study will apply PLS-based SEM [34] for analyzing the collected data due to the following reasons. The conceptual model developed in this research is hierarchical. PLS-based SEM is able to easily find solutions to such complex hierarchical models due to its component-based approach [34, 35]. PLS also generates less complexity when assessing hierarchical models and can present parsimonious theoretical results [36].

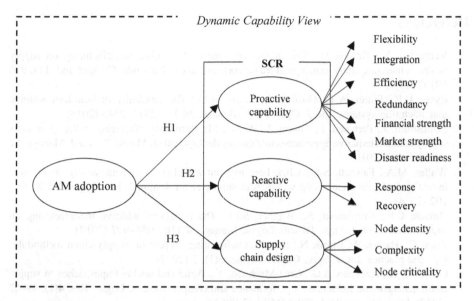

**Fig. 1.** Research model

# 5 Conclusions and Further Work

The adoption of AM technology by various industries is changing the structure and dynamics of SCs. Throughout the past few years, some attention has been given to studying such changes in the SC research. However, the studies addressing AM implications for SCs are mostly conceptual and lack empirical evidence. This gap is even more pronounced when considering the concept of resiliency in SCs. To date, no empirical research has explored the possible impacts of AM technology adoption on SCR. The results of an empirical research can help determine whether AM adoption can help to enhance SCR and consequently improve SC service levels for greater customer satisfaction and life improvement.

In this study, with the help of a comprehensive SCR framework, we managed to propose a research model that examines the impact of AM adoption on the main three dimensions of SCR, namely, proactive capability, reactive capability, and SC design. The next step would be to take the necessary actions and implement this research model in an industry setting using a deductive research approach.

Future work can extend the research model by including further variables. One suggested variable is SC performance. In this fashion, researchers can examine the direct and indirect impacts of AM adoption on SC performance via SCR.

**Acknowledgements.** The authors acknowledge Fundação para a Ciência e a Tecnologia (FCT - MCTES) for its financial support via the project UIDB/00667/2020 (UNIDEMI) and project KM3D (PTDC/EME-SIS/32232/2017).

# References

1. Verboeket, V., Krikke, H.: The disruptive impact of additive manufacturing on supply chains: a literature study, conceptual framework and research agenda. Comput. Ind. **111**, 91–107 (2019)
2. Eyers, D.R., Potter, A.T., Gosling, J., Naim, M.M.: The flexibility of industrial additive manufacturing systems. Int. J. Oper. Prod. Manage. **38**(12), 2313–2343 (2018)
3. Holmström, J., Partanen, J., Tuomi, J., Walter, M.: Rapid manufacturing in the spare parts supply chain: alternative approaches to capacity deployment. J. Manuf. Technol. Manage. **21**(6), 687–697 (2010)
4. Waller, M.A., Fawcett, S.E.: Click here to print a maker movement supply chain: how invention and entrepreneurship will disrupt supply chain design. J. Bus. Logist. **35**(2), 99–102 (2014)
5. Durach, C.F., Kurpjuweit, S., Wagner, S.M.: The impact of additive manufacturing on supply chains. Int. J. Phys. Distrib. Logist. Manage. **47**(10), 954–997 (2017)
6. Tuck, C., Hague, R., Burns, N.: Rapid manufacturing: impact on supply chain methodologies and practice. Int. J. Serv. Oper. Manage. **3**(1), 1 (2007)
7. Carvalho, H., Azevedo, S.G., Cruz-Machado, V.: Agile and resilient approaches to supply chain management: influence on performance and competitiveness. Logist. Res. **4**(1), 49–62 (2012). https://doi.org/10.1007/s12159-012-0064-2
8. Pettit, T.J., Croxton, K.L., Fiksel, J.: Ensuring supply chain resilience: development and implementation of an assessment tool. J. Bus. Logist. **34**(1), 46–76 (2013)
9. Jüttner, U., Maklan, S.: Supply chain resilience in the global financial crisis: an empirical study. Supply Chain Manage. **16**(4), 246–259 (2011)
10. Chowdhury, M.M.H., Quaddus, M.: Supply chain resilience: conceptualization and scale development using dynamic capability theory. Int. J. Prod. Econ. **188**, 185–204 (2017)
11. Eisenhardt, K.M., Martin, J.A.: Dynamic capabilities: what are they? Strateg. Manage. J. **21**(10–11), 1105–1121 (2000)
12. Tan, K.C., Lyman, S.B., Wisner, J.D.: Supply chain management: a strategic perspective. Int. J. Oper. Prod. Manage. **22**(6), 614–631 (2002)
13. Oettmeier, K., Hofmann, E.: Impact of additive manufacturing technology adoption on supply chain management processes and components. J. Manuf. Technol. Manage. **27**(7), 944–968 (2016)
14. Pires Ribeiro, J., Barbosa-Povoa, A.: Supply chain resilience: definitions and quantitative modelling approaches – a literature review. Comput. Ind. Eng. **115**, 109–122 (2018)
15. Mohr, S., Khan, O.: 3D printing and its disruptive impacts on supply chains of the future. Technol. Innov. Manage. Rev. **5**(11), 20 (2015)
16. Liu, P., Huang, S.H., Mokasdar, A., Zhou, H., Hou, L.: The impact of additive manufacturing in the aircraft spare parts supply chain: supply chain operation reference (scor) model based analysis. Prod. Plan. Control **25**(13–14), 1169–1181 (2014)

17. Rayna, T., Striukova, L.: From rapid prototyping to home fabrication: how 3D printing is changing business model innovation. Technol. Forecast. Soc. Change **102**, 214–224 (2016)
18. Sheffi, Y., Rice, J.B.: A supply chain view of the resilient enterprise. MIT Sloan Manage. Rev. **47**(1), 41 (2005)
19. Ford, S., Despeisse, M.: Additive manufacturing and sustainability: an exploratory study of the advantages and challenges. J. Clean. Prod. **137**, 1573–1587 (2016)
20. Pettit, T.J., Fiksel, J., Croxton, K.L.: Ensuring supply chain resilience: development of a conceptual framework. J. Bus. Logist. **31**(1), 1–21 (2010)
21. Christopher, M., Peck, H.: Building the resilient supply chain. Int. J. Logist. Manage. **15**(2), 1–13 (2004)
22. Ponomarov, S.Y., Holcomb, M.C.: Understanding the concept of supply chain resilience. Int. J. Logist. Manage. **20**(1), 124–143 (2009)
23. Zanoni, S., Ashourpour, M., Bacchetti, A., Zanardini, M., Perona, M.: Supply chain implications of additive manufacturing: a holistic synopsis through a collection of case studies. Int. J. Adv. Manuf. Technol. **102**(9–12), 3325–3340 (2019)
24. Delic, M., Eyers, D.R., Mikulic, J.: Additive manufacturing: empirical evidence for supply chain integration and performance from the automotive industry. Supply Chain Manage. **24**(5), 604–621 (2019)
25. Huang, S.H., Liu, P., Mokasdar, A., Hou, L.: Additive manufacturing and its societal impact: a literature review. Int. J. Adv. Manuf. Technol. **67**(5–8), 1191–1203 (2013)
26. Attaran, M.: Additive manufacturing: the most promising technology to alter the supply chain and logistics. J. Serv. Sci. Manage. **10**(03), 189–206 (2017)
27. Thiesse, F., et al.: Economic implications of additive manufacturing and the contribution of MIS. Bus. Inf. Syst. Eng. **57**(2), 139–148 (2015)
28. Meisel, N.A., Williams, C.B., Ellis, K.P., Taylor, D.: Decision support for additive manufacturing deployment in remote or austere environments. J. Manuf. Technol. Manage **27**(7), 898–914 (2016)
29. Durach, C.F., Wieland, A., Machuca, J.A.D.: Antecedents and dimensions of supply chain robustness: a systematic literature review. Int. J. Phys. Distrib. Logist. Manage. **45**(1/2), 118–137 (2015)
30. Ponis, S.T., Koronis, E.: Supply chain resilience: definition of concept and its formative elements. J. Appl. Bus. Res. **28**(5), 921–930 (2012)
31. Hult, G.T.M., Craighead, C.W., Ketchen Jr., D.J.: Risk uncertainty and supply chain decisions: a real options perspective. Decis. Sci. **41**(3), 435–458 (2010)
32. Falasca, M., Zobel, C.W., Cook, D.: A DS framework to assess SC resilience a decision support framework to assess supply chain resilience. In: Proceedings of the 5th International ISCRAM Conference, pp. 596–605 (2008)
33. Jarvis, C.B., MacKenzie, S.B., Podsakoff, P.M.: A critical review of construct indicators and measurement model misspecification in marketing and consumer research. J. Consum. Res. **30**(2), 199–218 (2003)
34. Chin, W.W.: The partial least squares approach for structural equation modeling. Mod. Methods Bus. Res. **295**(2), 295–336 (1998)
35. Ketchen, D.J.: A primer on partial least squares structural equation modeling. Long Range Plann. (2013)
36. Akter, S., D'Ambra, J., Ray, P.: Development and validation of an instrument to measure user perceived service quality of mHealth. Inf. Manage. **50**(4), 181–195 (2013)

# Big Data Acquisition Architecture: An Industry 4.0 Approach

Felipe A. Coda<sup></sup>(⌧), Diolino J. Santos Filho(⌧), Fabrício Junqueira(⌧),
and Paulo E. Miyagi(⌧)

Escola Politécnica da Universidade de São Paulo, Cidade Universitária,
Av. Prof. Mello Moraes, São Paulo, SP 2231, Brazil
{coda.felipe, diolinos, fabri, pemiyagi}@usp.br

**Abstract.** In an Industry 4.0 (I4.0) context there is significant increase in information exchange and storage through the interaction among assets (machines, systems, and people). These data are important because it can lead to the autonomy of assets in decision making. However, the entire organization of I4.0 assets in terms of the quantity and the quality of information to be managed makes the system very complex. Thus, a systematic is needed to deal with this complexity where reference architectures can be used to identify the functionality required to handle this large amount and diversity of data, and how they can be organized. Therefore, the aim here is the specification of a big data acquisition process for its implementation within I4.0 context to ensure quality data for analysis and decision making. The proposed solution is based on reference architectures NBDRA and RAMI 4.0.

**Keywords:** Industry 4.0 · Big data · Reference architecture · RAMI 4.0 · NBDRA

## 1 Introduction

Rüßmann et al. [1] recognize that I4.0 is a revolution sustained by nine technological pillars. Among them, several researchers such as [2] confirm big data and its analysis as a fundamental aspect.

Regarding the concepts of data acquisition systems (DAQ), manuals like [3] present the main fundamentals. However, in I4.0 the features involved in DAQ require a review, not only on the magnitude of the data involved but mainly of the activities necessary for productive and service processes improvement. An example of said magnitude generated by the connectivity between modern industry, cloud-based solutions and business management is the report [4], which forecasts an increase from 130 to 40,000 exabytes of data generated between 2005 and 2020, and that it doubles every two years onwards [5].

In this context, aiming to implement big data in I4.0, past works [6, 7] centered initially on requirements elicitation. The present work focuses on the development and specification of a system architecture for data acquisition in I4.0, thus, answering the research question of how the big data acquisition relates and is organized within he

L. M. Camarinha-Matos et al. (Eds.): DoCEIS 2020, IFIP AICT 577, pp. 222–229, 2020.
https://doi.org/10.1007/978-3-030-45124-0_21

I4.0. The architecture proposed here derived from reference architectures for big data systems and the I4.0.

## 2   Relationship to Technological Innovation for Life Improvement

Brown *et al.* [8] claim that big data will become an asset responsible for optimizing business models, serving as a fundamental basis for competition, and [5] associate big data analysis to enhancements to the development of products and services. These works confirm the expected impact of big data for life improvements that can be extended to I4.0.

Rüßmann *et al.* [1] also evaluates the benefits that I4.0 will bring across four areas:

- **Productivity**: I4.0 is expected to bring improvements in the productivity. The gain in productivity percentage may vary across different industrial areas up to 30%;
- **Revenue growth**: I4.0 is expected to encourage revenue growth. Through the increasing demand for smart equipment and data applications by manufacturers, and the increasing demand for customized products by consumers, pushing an extra revenue growth;
- **Employment**: I4.0 is expected to lead an increase in the employment. As the productive and service systems get more and more complex, I4.0 is expected to further the demand for professionals in the engineering, software development and IT areas;
- **Investment**: I4.0 is expected to increase the amount of investments made in the industrial area. It is expected that in Germany, companies invest €250 billion from 2015 to 2025 to incorporate I4.0 to its production processes.

Within this context, it is recognized the opportunities that big data for I4.0 can bring to productive and service systems, and consequently, carrying technological innovations for life improvements along the value chain[1]. Improvements in analytical capabilities and the quantities and quality of data are also expected to bring about improvements in sustainability (economic, social and environmental) [9].

Consequently, this work has contributions toward said life improvements: fomenting the discussion of big data and specifying an architecture of the big data acquisition activities within the I4.0.

## 3   Background

In this section, the background related to this work is presented. A thorough review of the big data concepts was discussed in previous work [6].

---

[1] The value chain is a reference to the set of activities that a company operating in an industrial context performs to deliver a product or service to the consumer market [10].

## 3.1 System Architecture

An "architecture" is defined as an organizational structure of a system (i.e., an information system plus its devices), containing its parts, relationships, principles and guidelines that serve to its design, implementation and evolution over time [11].

A "reference architecture" is defined by [12] as a document or set of documents that represents the recommended product and service structures and integrations to form a solution (the system architecture), incorporating accepted practices and answering the questions that arise during its development. Adolphs *et al.* [13] argue that reference architectures play an important role in describing key aspects of system structure and are the starting point for developing the tools needed to effectively deploy a system architecture.

## 3.2 NBDRA

The National Institute of Standards and Technology (NIST) is one of the oldest scientific laboratories in the United States. Among the projects developed at NIST is the NIST Big Data Interoperability Framework, which has generated a 7-volume collection of studies to create a reference architecture that facilitates understanding of the operational complexities of dealing with big data, providing a tool for describing, discussing and developing specific architectures from a common framework [14].

The architecture was developed considering reputable data science companies and ICT (Information and Communication Technologies) solutions.

The NIST Big Data Reference Architecture (NBDRA) considers a big data system with five logical functional components ("**System Orchestrator**", "**Data Provider**", "**Big Data Application Provider**", "**Data Consumer**" and "**Big Data Framework Provider**") connected by interoperability interfaces (i.e., services) and surrounded by two frameworks ("**Security and Privacy**" and "**Management**") that represent the intertwined nature of management and security and privacy in all components.

In this context, the NBDRA provides the structure and necessary functionalities, that is, the background for the big data acquisition enabling its relationship within I4.0.

## 3.3 RAMI 4.0

The RAMI 4.0 (Reference Architectural Model for Industry 4.0) was developed as reference architecture conceived as a model for systems in I4.0 [15].

Within its three axes, all aspects of I4.0 can be mapped allowing elements to be classified according to this three-dimensional view. The concepts involved in I4.0 can be explored and implemented using RAMI 4.0, enabling a stepwise migration from the present to the I4.0 [15].

According to [16], each axis can be summarized as:

- **Layers:** This axis describe every asset`s technical <u>functions</u> and special <u>properties</u> along its six layers. Through this, all of its characteristics can be virtually mapped;
- **Life Cycle and Value Stream:** This axis characterizes the state of the asset at a specific location at a specific time during its entire life cycle. Through this it is

possible to maintain a record for the life cycle, including the <u>time</u>, <u>location</u> and <u>state</u> parameters, and, at the minimum, the <u>type</u> and <u>instance</u> states;

- **Hierarchical Levels:** This axis is responsible for assigning the asset to the entity responsible for its <u>control</u>. Through this, the intelligence within a machine or system can also be taken in consideration for the decision making along with the control device [13].

A summary of each layer was discussed in previous work [7].

The NBDRA and related literature, is here used to structure the necessary functionalities for the big data acquisition process under the RAMI 4.0.

## 4 Big Data Acquisition Architecture

In this section, the architecture for big data acquisition with its components and the interactions among them is presented. Additionally, the data flow is detailed, determining the procedure for collecting, integrating, storing and analyzing data. The commands to be sent back to the devices based on the decision making made from the entities that analyzed data are also identified.

### 4.1 Architecture Components

The proposed architecture elucidates and organize the necessary functionalities in a productive system's context within I4.0. For this purpose, the architecture brings together the functionalities of the components necessary for the acquisition of data organized according to the RAMI 4.0 "layers" axis.

In the first layer, **Asset**, are the physical elements of the process (e.g. equipment, products, sensors, actuators, etc.). This layer references the "Data Provider" discussed in the NBDRA.

In the second layer, **Integration**, are the functionalities responsible for connecting the real and virtual worlds. Also, in this layer is the process of associating the communication technology to the data collected.

In the third layer, **Communication**, data collected from every source are integrated and filtered, removing irrelevant or redundant data. Also, in this layer the communication protocols are associated to the data.

In the fourth layer, **Information**, the data are stored in a solution compatible with its necessities. This layer references the functionalities addressed in the NBDRA as the "Big Data Framework Provider". Also, in this layer are performed the data analysis and visualization of the results, followed by the decision-making process, addressed in as the "Big Data Application Provider" in the NBDRA.

In the fifth layer, **Functional**, are the interfaces for the horizontal integration and the description of all functionalities. This layer is also responsible for generating the rules to be followed and the decision-making logic, addressing the "Data Consumer" in the NBDRA.

In the sixth and last layer, **Business**, are the rules to be followed to ensure that the functions performed maintaining the integrity of every asset. This layer is responsible for the orchestration of the services in the functional layer, addressing concepts from the "System Orchestrator" from the NBDRA.

Figure 1(a) illustrates the architecture components proposed for big data acquisition in the I4.0.

## 4.2  Interactivity Among Components

Figure 1(b) illustrates the proposed data acquisition process through the interaction of the architecture's components, starting with the occurrence of an event.

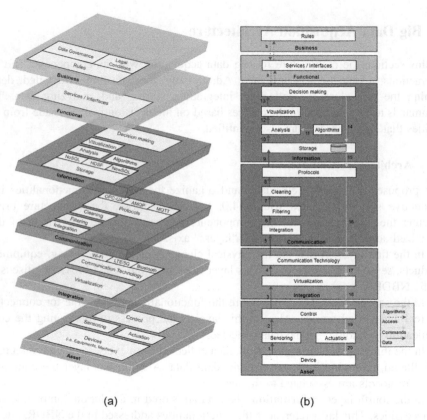

(a)                                            (b)

**Fig. 1.** (a) Architecture's components within the "**Layers**" axis of RAMI 4.0 (b) Detailing of the data flow among components

The data flow in the architecture establish from the sensing to the data preparation, the steps for its storage and analysis. The decision-making process can access these data and consult the available services and the rules to be followed. After the decision making, commands are sent back to act on devices.

## 4.3 Architecture Evaluation

Among the various techniques for modeling systems, the Petri net (PN) stands out in principle for its graphical form of representing processes, and systems and is recognized as useful and effective for a structural and functional analysis. In this context, the architecture was evaluated though the use of the PFS/PN (Production flow Schema/Petri net) technique [17].

The PFS model is an interpreted graph that originated from PN to describe processes and systems at different levels of abstraction. PFS allows for a progressive detailing of the activities and flows of relevant items (e.g. materials or data) and, because of their intuitive language, generated models can be effortlessly comprehended by many experts (e.g. engineers, designers or architects). Figure 2 illustrates the PFS model of the data acquisition process along the RAMI 4.0 layers.

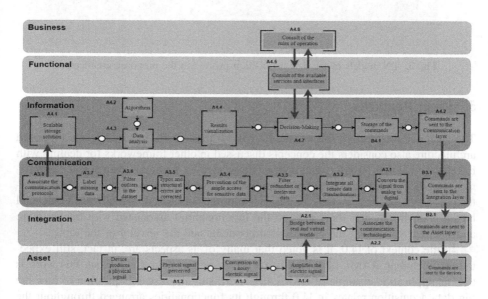

**Fig. 2.** PFS model of the data acquisition process in the proposed architecture

Through the PFS model it was possible to derive a PN model of the proposed architecture and the interactions among its components. The resulting PN models in turn were formally analyzed and/or simulated, allowing for the evaluation of the architecture structure (e.g. the dynamic of its functionalities such as the existence of deadlocks[2]).

As a sample of the developed models, Fig. 3 illustrates the basic (data) flow and activities (states) of the data acquisition process along the RAMI 4.0 layers. Model

---

[2] A deadlock occurs when a process goes into permanent standby (i.e. unable to change its state indefinitely) because the resources required by it are being used by another process also permanently waiting [18].

simulations are omitted here for space reasons, since the model has 204 achievable states with 403 situations/scenarios that describe the evolution between those states.

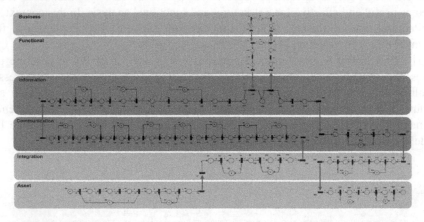

**Fig. 3.** PN models of the data acquisition process in the proposed architecture

## 5  Final Remarks

The proposed architecture follows the RAMI 4.0 framework. In addition, the proposed architecture also considers the concepts discussed in other frameworks for dealing with big data, including NBDRA and architectures used by reputable data science companies and ICT (Information and Communication Technologies) solutions. The architecture proposed here is thus based on solutions discussed in both academic and business environments where assured the functionalities associated with the structure and interactivity among the proposed components and the novelty of the topic.

In the context of I4.0, it is noted that many of its aspects are, in fact, still expectations, including RAMI 4.0 which is a work in progress. In this respect, this work is also an application example of RAMI 4.0, addressing the research question of how the big data acquisition relates in I4.0 through its functionalities arranged throughout the RAMI 4.0.

It is noteworthy that, with the proposed architecture, there are possibilities in considering existing data acquisition systems, mapping their functionalities. It is believed that this practice contributes to elucidate existing systems establishing a path for modernization and implementation, as well as its adaptation to the I4.0 paradigms.

**Acknowledgement.**  This study was financed in part by the Coordenação de Aperfeiçoamento de Pessoal no Nível Superior - Brazil (CAPES), Fundação de Amparo à Pesquisa do Estado de São Paulo - Brazil (FAPESP), Conselho Nacional de Desenvolvimento Científico e Tecnológico - Brazil (CNPq) and PETROBRAS.

# References

1. Rüßmann, M., et al.: Industry 4.0: the future of productivity and growth in manufacturing industries. Boston Consult. Group **9**(1), 54–89 (2015)
2. Sun, Y., Song, H., Jara, A.J., Bie, R.: Internet of Things and big data analytics for smart and connected communities. IEEE Access **4**, 766–773 (2016). https://doi.org/10.1109/access. 2016.2529723. [s.l.], v. 4, Institute of Electrical and Electronics Engineers (IEEE)
3. Omega Engineering, Inc.: The Omega Transactions and Master Index, vol. 2. Putman Publishing Company and OMEGA Press LLC (2000). www.omega.com/literature/ transactions/Transactions_Vol_II.pdf
4. Gantz, J., Reinsel, D.: The digital universe in 2020: Big data, bigger digital shadows, and biggest growth in the far east. IDC iView: IDC Analyze Fut. **2**, 1–16 (2012). https://www. speicherguide.de/download/dokus/IDC-Digital-Universe-Studie-iView-11.12.pdf
5. Yin, S., Kaynak, O.: Big data for modern industry: challenges and trends. Proc. IEEE **103**, 143–146 (2015)
6. Coda, F.A., et al.: Big data systems requirements for Industry 4.0. In: IEEE International Conference on Industry Applications (INDUSCON) (2018)
7. Coda, F.A., et al.: Big data on machine to machine integration's requirement analysis within Industry 4.0. In: Doctoral Conference on Computing, Electrical and Industrial Systems, pp. 247–254 (2019)
8. Brown, B., Chui, M., Manyika, J.: Are you ready for the era of 'big data'. McKinsey Q. **4**(1), 24–35 (2011)
9. Watanabe, E.H., da Silva, R.M., Blos, M.F., Junqueira, F., Santos Filho, D.J., Miyagi, P.E.: Framework to evaluate the performance and sustainability of a disperse productive system. J. Braz. Soc. Mech. Sci. Eng. **40**(6), 277 (2018)
10. Porter, M.E.: Competitive Advantage: Creating and Sustaining Superior Performance. Simon and Schuster, New York City (2008)
11. Geraci, A., et al.: IEEE Standard Computer Dictionary: Compilation of IEEE Standard Computer Glossaries. IEEE Press, Piscataway (1991)
12. Hewlett Packard Enterprise: What is a Reference Architecture. Hewlett Packard Enterprise Development LP (2018). https://www.hpe.com/us/en/what-is/reference-architecture.html
13. Adolphs, P., et al.: Reference architecture model Industrie 4.0 (RAMI 4.0). ZVEI and VDI, Status Report (2015)
14. NBD-PWG, Nist Big Data Public Working Group, Reference Architecture Subgroup: NIST Big Data Interoperability Framework: volume 6, reference architecture, version 2. Nist Special Publication 1500-6r1, [s.l.], pp. 1–52 (2017). http://dx.doi.org/10.6028/nist.sp.1500-6r1
15. Hankel, M., Rexroth, B.: The reference architectural model Industrie 4.0 (RAMI 4.0). ZVEI (2015)
16. DIN; DKE; VDE: German Standardization Roadmap Industrie 4.0 - DIN/DKE Roadmap (2016). https://www.din.de/blob/65354/57218767bd6da1927b181b9f2a0d5b39/roadmap-i4-0-e-data.pdf
17. Hasegawa, K., Takahashi, K., Miyagi, P.E.: Application of the mark flow graph to represent discrete event production systems and system control. Trans. Soc. Instrum. Control Eng. **24** (1), 69–75 (1988)
18. Silberschatz, A., Galvin, P.B., Gagne, G.: Operating system principles. John Wiley, Hoboken (2006)

# Power Systems

# Study of Electric Field Emissions in Wireless Energy Transfer

Elena N. Baikova[1,2], R. Melicio[3,4(✉)], and S. S. Valtchev[1]

[1] UNINOVA-CTS, FCT, Universidade Nova de Lisboa, Lisbon, Portugal
[2] EST Setúbal, Instituto Politécnico de Setúbal, Setúbal, Portugal
[3] Escola de Ciências e Tecnologia, Departamento de Física, ICT,
Universidade de Évora, Evora, Portugal
ruimelicio@gmail.com
[4] IDMEC, Instituto Superior Técnico, Universidade de Lisboa, Lisbon, Portugal

**Abstract.** The thesis focuses on the study of the electrical component of the electromagnetic field, radiated by the wireless energy transfer system into the adjacent environment. The wireless energy transfer and the wireless data transfer are studied simultaneously, focusing on the appropriate wireless communication channel between the transmitter and the receiver, so to make that channel improved. An implementation of a wireless energy transfer experimental prototype that operates simultaneously with a wireless data transmission is assembled. A computational application that allows tuning the operational frequency of the prototype to correspond to the resonant mode operation is developed.

**Keywords:** Wireless energy transfer · Wireless data transmission · Electromagnetic field · Electromagnetic interference

## 1 Introduction

The rational use of energy is associated with energy efficiency, which can be defined as the possibility of improving energy consumption, namely in the electricity and transport sectors, respectively. A mental and social shift towards energy consumption is urgently needed to mitigate the dependence on fossil fuels and to reduce greenhouse gas (GHG) emissions into the atmosphere. One way to mitigate the dependence on fossil fuels and GNG emissions in the transport sector is to promote further research into the development of electric vehicles (EV) and hybrids. EV/hybrids have advantages over internal combustion vehicles, namely, energy efficiency, mitigation of GHG emissions into the atmosphere, significantly lower maintenance costs. Thus, EV/hybrids can be considered as a measure of GHG emission mitigation and external dependence on primary energy [1–3].

However, there are still significant limitations on the use of EVs (land and air), particularly regarding batteries. The main disadvantages are the high price and reduced battery life. One way to overcome the disadvantage of battery life is to study new charging systems, namely using wireless energy transfer (WET) systems [1–3].

L. M. Camarinha-Matos et al. (Eds.): DoCEIS 2020, IFIP AICT 577, pp. 233–245, 2020.
https://doi.org/10.1007/978-3-030-45124-0_22

## 1.1   Wireless Energy Transfer

There are two different WET methods, defined by physical phenomena of the electromagnetic (EM) fields' propagation: near field and far field. Between the main methods of near field, the inductive coupling, the capacitive coupling and the magnetic resonance coupling can be identified [3–9]. Far field methods, namely microwave and laser energy transfer with directional antennas could be used over long distances in space, in military industry or industrial applications [3–9].

## 1.2   Research Questions

The magnetic resonant coupling method presented by MIT team is recognized as the most suitable to achieve highly efficient wireless energy transfer for EV battery charging [8–13]. An important step is to combine power transfer with data transmission. Data transmission, such as vehicle identification, frequency, power values, user data are some examples of the required information.

Communication between Tx and Rx is important, especially when high intensity EM fields produced be WET system may have undesirable influence on the data channel. The strong EM fields produced by the WET system can not only negatively influence other adjacent electrical and electronic equipment, but also interact with living beings in the immediate vicinity of the EV while charging the battery with potentially harmful effects. The World Health Organization recommends that electrical/electronic devices must comply with the safety limits of human exposure to EM radiation. Safety limits are set primarily by the ICNIRP [14, 15] and the IEEE [16].

Considering the described aspects, the main research question chosen for this work is as follows:

**Q1.** How can be evaluated the impact of the high intensity EM field produced by the WET system on living beings and the communication channel between Tx and Rx?

The hypothesis proposed to solve this research question is as follows:

**H1.** In order to answer Q1 it is important to evaluate the values of the EM fields produced by the WET systems and to make a comparison with the safety limits set by the recognized international organizations. It is important to use computational simulations for exploring of EM field distribution and for comparing with the experimental results.

The proposed additional research questions are:

**Q1a.** Does the EM field produced by the WET system comply with established safety standards and secure?

**Q1b.** Can EM fields from the WET system influence or disturb the communication channel?

In order to find answers to research questions Q1a and Q1b the following steps should be taken into consideration:

– Measuring the intensity of the EM field produced by the WET system and comparing the results with the safety levels established by international organizations;
– Conducting Tx-Rx communications performance testing on the WET system to assess the impact of EM field emissions on the wireless data transfer channel.

The second research question chosen for this thesis is as follows:

**Q2.** How can the mode of operation of the WET system for the resonance regime be tuned?

**H2.** In order to respond to Q2, it is necessary to implement the communication channel between Tx and Rx and to develop a computational application that allows coordinating the WET process and tuning the system operation mode to the resonance regime.

## 1.3 Approach

Since most studies are dedicated to the simulation and measurement of the magnetic field produced by the WET system, and there is a gap regarding the study of the electric field. Thus, it was decided in this thesis to investigate the electrical component of the EM field produced by the WET system.

In the simultaneous WET and wireless data transmission (WDT), to increase the efficiency of the WET process, it is necessary to quickly and securely exchange data between Tx and Rx. Thus, to increase the efficiency of the WET, a system is proposed not only for energy transfer, but also for WDT between Tx and Rx. The possibility of data transmission in a WET system provides interaction between Tx and Rx, facilitating the task of device detection and identification, and coordinating the battery charging process.

In the proposed WET system, a communication between Tx and Rx is implemented using microcontrollers (MCs). The use of MCs allows real time WDT and tuning the system operation mode to the resonance regime. The operation of the WET system in the resonance regime increases the system performance due to the communication capacity between Tx and Rx.

*Wireless Data Transmission*

Wireless communications have demonstrated potential in industrial and commercial applications, more precisely in the acquisition of data that can be collected and transferred for coordination and monitoring of technological processes.

The communication between Tx and Rx is indispensable for the coordination of energy transfer, so it is necessary to define a communication protocol between the MCs. In order to define proper Tx-Rx communication, it is necessary to analyze and compare the available wireless communication protocols, which can be linked to WET systems for battery charging and information exchange between Tx and Rx.

The EM field radiated by the Tx and Rx coils is the fundamental property of the WET system based on magnetic resonant coupling [17].

Studies show that EM fields are harmful and can have adverse effects on the human body [18, 19]. Although some works in the literature state that WET is safe for living beings [8], it is impossible to predict the impact of such exposure on human health over time. Electromagnetic compatibility (EMC) issues of WET systems are related to research and analysis of EM processes in the human body exposed to EM energy from them. Thus, measuring the intensity of the EM field produced by the WET system and comparing the results with the safety levels established by international organizations is important for assessing the impact of the field.

Data transmission between Tx and Rx via a communication channel is intended to coordinate the energy transfer process in the WET system. However, the high intensity EM field of the order of a few kW to the tens of kW of a WET system may have an undesirable influence on the communication channel that operates at tens of mW. In this case the transferred data may be influenced by transmitting erroneous information.

Thus, the performance of the communication channel between Tx and Rx exposed to the EM field produced by the WET system should be properly evaluated.

## 2 Technological Innovation for Life Improvement (TILI)

The TILI is a fundamental driver of economic and human progress [20]. The modern level of society development, success in the study and modeling of various technologies, processes and systems, allow developing revolutionary technologies in all areas of human activity, including medicine, education, agricultural industry, environment, transportation and communication systems. Technological innovation not only generates significant economic, environmental and social benefits, which contributes to the improvement of life, but also aids social advancement in all areas of human activity [21].

This WET technology could improve design and make products smarter, smaller and more effective, functionally and economically, improving human life. The WET systems with simultaneous data transmission are an example of the technological innovation as intelligent structure capable to optimize and integrate corresponding systems, to improve performance and service and to reduce resource consumption. The "smart" WET systems have a great potential and capability to completely transform the way devices and equipment are powered, what remarkably improves quality of life.

## 3 State of the Art

### 3.1 Magnetic Resonant Coupling

In the last decade, progress has been made in the area of WET using magnetic resonant coupling to increase system performance [8–10, 22]. Technological advances make magnetic resonant coupling WET very attractive for EV battery charging applications in either stationary or dynamic charging scenarios.

In the available literature research directions, approaches, and techniques are proposed including system architectures [10, 22–24], frequency splitting [10, 22, 25], adaptation impedance matching [10, 13, 26], frequency tuning models for the resonance regime [11, 25, 27], practical applications [9, 26].

### 3.2 Wireless Energy Transfer - Frequency Tuning

A key issue in WET systems is to maximize energy transfer efficiency [11, 25, 28]. The system configuration of the WET prototype studied in [11] is presented in Fig. 1.

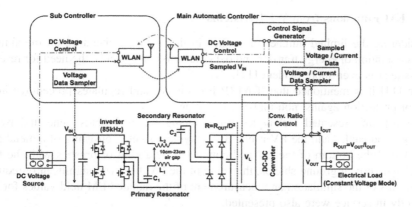

**Fig. 1.** System configuration of the WET prototype [11].

In [29] is proposed a frequency automatic tuning of the system in response to misalignments of Tx and Rx coils without using communication channel.

### 3.3 Wireless Energy Transfer and WDT

Different methods have been proposed in the literature for the simultaneous transfer of energy and data transmission in the WET systems, in order to increase efficiency and reliability.

In WET systems simultaneously with data transmission, the tuned resonant circuits can be used in a single operating frequency. In order to transmit the data simultaneously with the transfer of energy in these systems, the modulation of the signal sent by the Tx can be used. Thus, the carrier frequency has one of its parameters, namely amplitude, phase or frequency, modified according to the information to be transmitted. In [30–33] the WET systems running simultaneously with data transmission systems are studied, using different techniques of modulation of the transmitted signal, with the use of a single pair of Tx and Rx coils. In [30] the WET system is described. In [33] the data signal is binary phase-shift keying modulated with a carrier frequency.

However, the application of the modulation method in the WET systems reduces the energy transfer efficiency since the modulation operation of the signal decreases the average power of the modulated signal.

The WET and WDT system using two sets of coils is shown in [34, 35]. The geometry of data coils reduces the mutual coupling. Thus, the voltage induced in the data coils by the electromagnetic field of WET system can be reduced. The data transmission rate and power transfer efficiency are limited. In addition, the interaction between the power and data coil is complicated and cannot be completely eliminated [35].

The use of higher frequencies allows a higher data rate [36] and reduces the noise introduced by the WET on the data channel. In [36, 37] are proposed WET systems with data channel operating at 2.4 GHz. Thus, the energy and data can be transferred independently without affecting each other. The drawback of such systems is the complex paring between the Tx and Rx sides.

### 3.4    EM Emissions from WET Systems

Considering the limited number of studies in the available literature on the simultaneous operation of energy transfer and data transmission systems, the need for research in this area is even more evident [17].

In [14] it is mentioned that ICNIRP investigates and regulates procedures in the area of protection against non-ionizing radiation.

In [6] are presented techniques for reducing the EM fields generated by the underground cables and the EV itself. By applying a shield consisting of a metal plate mounted at the bottom of the EV and connected by a kind of brushes with the horizontal and vertical ground shields, the value of the EM field was significantly reduced. The results of the simulation and measurement of the radiated EM field values for EVs currently in service were also presented.

The EMC issues of the WET system increase the need for a detailed analysis of EM processes in the human body and other living beings exposed to radiated electromagnetic energy.

In [38] is presented the FEM modeling methodology and the simulation used in WET system.

## 4    Radiation Safety Limits for WET Systems

It is important to underline that the standardization of WET systems, equipment, components is relatively new. In recent years in all international and regional organizations related to WET systems, the WET systems regulatory regime is under development. As regards recommendations for exposure to EM fields in general, as the standard the ICNIRP 1998 recommendations [14], updated in 2010 [15], are globally recognized. In this thesis to evaluate exposure to EM fields irradiated by the TESC system, the ICNIRP recommendations [14, 15] were adopted.

The electric field exposure limits by ICNIRP [4, 15, 39] is shown in Fig. 2.

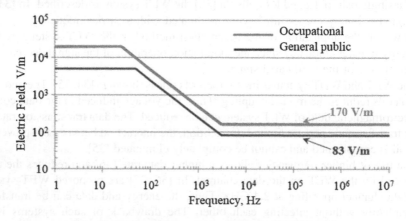

**Fig. 2.** Electric field exposure limits by ICNIRP [15]

## 5  Prototype Modeling and Implementation

The WET system with capacitor compensation in series with the coils is shown in
Fig. 3(a), (b) and is used in Case Study_1, Case Study_2 and in the developed
experimental prototype.

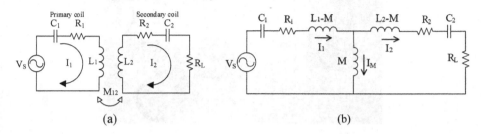

**Fig. 3.** (a) Configuration; (b) Circuit of the WET prototype

The WET equivalent circuit [12, 40] is shown in Fig. 3(b).

The topology of prototype and Tx and Rx circuit parameters was shown already by
the authors in [12, 40] and is shown in Fig. 4 and is in Fig. 5.

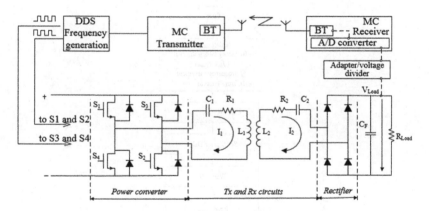

**Fig. 4.** Topology of the implemented prototype

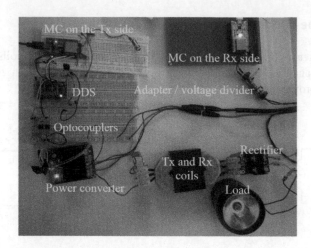

**Fig. 5.** WET prototype

The process of tuning operating frequency $f_{curr}$ to resonant frequency $f_{res}$ is organized according to flowchart shown in Fig. 6.

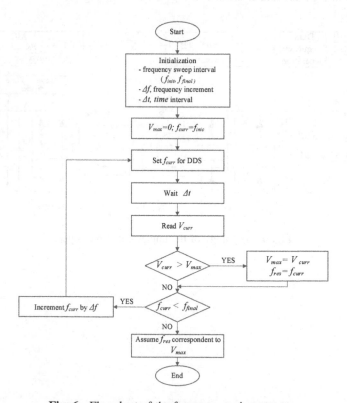

**Fig. 6.** Flowchart of the frequency tuning process.

A video showing the tuning to the resonant frequency reported in this paper can be found in https://www.youtube.com/watch?v=KAsASXtZrt0.

## 6   Experimental Results

This thesis deals with the topic of simulation and measurement of electric fields irradiated by WET systems [6, 29, 44].

Simulations and measurements of the electric field are exposed in two case studies.

### Case Study_1

The purpose of Case Study_1 is the simulation and measurement of electric field intensities produced by the prototype of the Technical University of Sofia.

The modelling, simulation and measurements of electric field (E-field) produced by the prototype of the Case Study_1 is presented in [4, 39, 41]. In Fig. 7 are shown the 3D Model and the result of E-field simulation for Case Study_1.

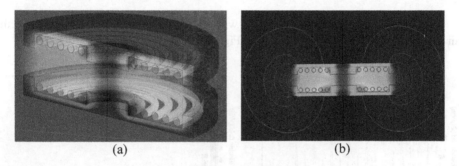

(a)                                    (b)

**Fig. 7.** (a) 3D model: Case Study_1; (b) Distribution of electric field lines.

The E-field harmonics generated by the WET system with Pout of 800 W (a) and 228 W (b) are shown in Fig. 8.

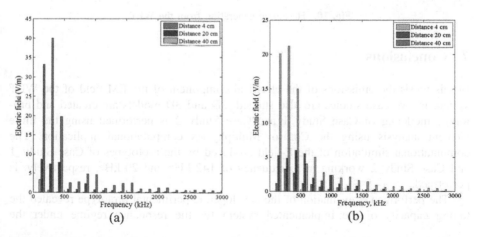

(a)                                    (b)

**Fig. 8.** E-field harmonics generated by the WET system with Pout of 800 W (a) and 228 W (b).

## Case Study_2

Simulation and measurement of E-field intensities produced by the prototype of Universidade Nova de Lisboa. The modelling, simulation and measurements of E-field produced by the prototype of the Case Study_2 is presented in [42, 43]. In Fig. 9 are shown the 3D Model and the result of E-field simulation (V/m) for Case Study_2.

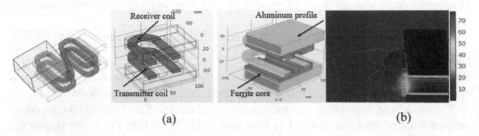

(a)                                                                          (b)

**Fig. 9.**  (a) 3D model: Case Study_2; (b) Distribution of electric field lines.

The harmonics generated by the WET with output power value of 262 W and with air gap of 20 mm [12, 45] are shown in Fig. 10.

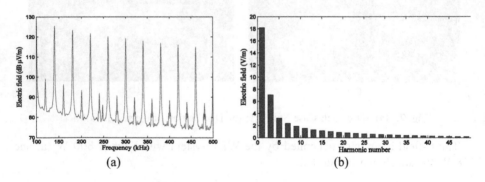

(a)                                                                          (b)

**Fig. 10.**  Harmonic generation from the WPT.

## 7   Conclusions

In this thesis the emissions of the electrical component of the EM field of the WET system in two case studies are also studied. 2D and 3D models are created and prototype modeling of Case Study_1 and Case Study_2 is performed using the finite element analysis using the Comsol Multiphysics computational application. The computational simulation of the E-field produced by the prototypes of Case Study_1 and Case Study_2 working at a frequency of 142 kHz and 20 kHz, respectively, is performed.

The performance evaluation of the developed experimental prototype revealed the tuning capacity of the implemented system for the resonance regime under the conditions of distance variation and misalignment between the coils Tx and Rx, increasing the system yield.

**Acknowledgments.** This work was supported by: European Union through the European Regional Development Fund, included in the COMPETE 2020 (Operational Program Competitiveness and Internationalization) through the ICT project (UID/GEO/04683/2019) with the reference POCI010145FEDER007690; FCT, through IDMEC, under LAETA, project UIDB/50022/2020 and UIDB/00066/2020 of the Center of Technologies and System (CTS).

# References

1. Zhu, C., Liu, K., Yu, C., Ma, R., Cheng, H.: Simulation and experimental analysis on wireless energy transfer based on magnetic resonances. In: Proceedings of the IEEE Vehicle Power and Propulsion Conference, Harbin, China, pp. 1–4 (2008)
2. Jang, Y.J., Ko, Y.D., Jeong, S.: Optimal design of the wireless charging electric vehicle. In: Proceedings of IEEE International Electric Vehicle Conference (IEVC), pp. 1–5 (2012)
3. Li, S., Mi, C.: Wireless power transfer for electric vehicle applications. IEEE J. Emerg. Sel. Top. Power Electron. **3**(1), 4–17 (2015)
4. Baikova, E.N., Valtchev, S.S., Melicio, R., Krusteva, A., Pires, V.F.: Study of the electromagnetic interference generated by wireless power transfer systems. Int. Rev. Electr. Eng. **11**(5), 526–534 (2016)
5. Boys, J.T., Covic, G., Green, A.: Stability and control of inductively coupled power transfer systems. IEE Proc. Electr. Power Appl. **147**(1), 37–43 (2002)
6. Ahn, S., et al.: Low frequency electromagnetic field reduction techniques for the on-line electric vehicle (OLEV). In: The IEEE International Symposium on Electromagnetic Compatibility, Fort Lauderdale, USA, pp. 625–630 (2010)
7. Kline, M., Izyumin, I., Boser, B., Sanders, S.: Capacitive power transfer for contactless charging. In: The IEEE 26th Annual Applied Power Electronics Conference and Exposition, Fort Worth, USA, pp. 1398–1404 (2011)
8. Kurs, A., Karalis, A., Moffatt, R., Joannopoulos, J.D., Fisher, P., Soljačić, M.: Wireless power transfer via strongly coupled magnetic resonances. Science **317**(5834), 83–86 (2007)
9. Imura, T., Okabe, H., Hori, Y.: Basic experimental study on helical antennas of wireless power transfer for electric vehicles by using magnetic resonant couplings. In: IEEE Vehicle Power and Propulsion Conference (2009)
10. Sample, A.P., Meyer, D.A., Smith, J.R.: Analysis, experimental results, and range adaptation of magnetically coupled resonators for wireless power transfer. IEEE Trans. Industr. Electron. **58**(2), 544–554 (2009)
11. Ishihara, H., et al.: A voltage ratio-based efficiency control method for 3 kW wireless power transmission. In: Proceedings of the 29th Annual IEEE Applied Power Electronics Conference and Exposition, pp. 1312–1316 (2014)
12. Baikova, E.N., Baikov, A.V., Valtchev, S.S., Melicio, R.: Frequency tuning of the resonant wireless energy transfer system. In: IECON 2019 – 45th Annual Conference of the IEEE Industrial Electronics Society (2019)
13. Beh, T.C., Kato, M., Imura, T., Oh, S., Hori, Y.: Automated impedance matching system for robust wireless power transfer via magnetic resonance coupling. IEEE Trans. Industr. Electron. **60**, 3689–3698 (2013)
14. ICNIRP: Guidelines for limiting exposure to time-varying electric, magnetic and electromagnetic fields (up to 300 GHz). Health Phys. **74**(4), 494–521 (1998)

15. ICNIRP: Guidelines for limiting exposure to time-varying electric and magnetic fields (1 Hz–100 kHz). Health Phys. **99**, 818–836 (2010)
16. IEEE Std C95.1-2005, Safety Levels with Respect to Human Exposure to Radio Frequency Electromagnetic Fields, 3 kHz to 300 GHz. International Committee on Electromagnetic Safety, The Institute of Electrical and Electronics Engineers, New York (2005)
17. Kong, S., Bae, B., Jung, D.H., Kim, J.J.: An investigation of electromagnetic radiated emission and interference from multi-coil wireless power transfer systems using resonant magnetic field coupling. IEEE Trans. Microw. Theory Tech. **63**(3), 833–846 (2015)
18. Redlarski, G., et al.: The influence of electromagnetic pollution on living organisms: historical trends and forecasting changes. Biomed. Res. Int. **2015**, 1–18 (2015)
19. International Agency for Research on Cancer (IARC): Non-ionizing Radiation, Part 2: Radiofrequency Electromagnetic Fields. IARC Monograph, Lyon, France, vol. 102 (2013)
20. Broughle, J., Thierer, A.: Technological innovation and economic growth: a brief report on the evidence. Mercatus Center, George Mason University (2019)
21. Diaconu, M.: Technological innovation: concept, process, typology and implications in the economy. Theor. Appl. Econ. **XVIII**(10(563)), 127–144 (2011)
22. Cannon, B.L., Hoburg, J.F., Stancil, D.D., Goldstein, S.C.: Magnetic resonant coupling as a potential means for wireless power transfer to multiple small receivers. IEEE Trans. Power Electron. **24**(7), 1819–1825 (2009)
23. Chen, C.-J., Chu, T.-H., Lin, C.-L., Jou, Z.-C.: A study of loosely coupled coils for wireless power transfer. IEEE Trans. Circuits Syst. II Express Briefs **57**, 536–540 (2010)
24. Kim, J.-W., Son, H.-C., Kim, K.-H., Park, Y.-J.: Efficiency analysis of magnetic resonance wireless power transfer with intermediate resonant coil. IEEE Antennas Wirel. Propag. Lett. **10**, 389–392 (2011)
25. Hoang, H., Bien, F.: Maximizing efficiency of electromagnetic resonance wireless power transmission systems with adaptive circuits. In: Kim, K.Y. (ed.) Wireless Power Transfer-Principles and Engineering Explorations. InTech Publisher, London (2012)
26. Yamakawa, M., Shimamura, K., Komurasaki, K., Koizumi, H.: Demonstration of automatic impedance-matching and constant power feeding to and electric helicopter via magnetic resonance coupling. Wirel. Eng. Technol. **5**, 45–53 (2014)
27. Brusamarello, V., Blauth, Y.B., Azambuja, R., Muller, I., Sousa, F.R.: Power transfer with an inductive link and wireless tuning. IEEE Trans. Instrum. Meas. **62**(5), 924–931 (2013)
28. Hu, W., Zhou, H., Deng, Q., Gao, X.: Optimization algorithm and practical implementation for 2-coil wireless power transfer systems. In: American Control Conference (ACC), Portland, Oregon, USA (2014)
29. Gao, Y., Farley, K., Tse, Z.: A uniform voltage gain control for alignment robustness in wireless EV charging. Energies **8**, 8355–8370 (2015)
30. Hmida, G.B., Ghairani, H., Samet, M.: Design of a wireless power and data transmission circuits for implantable biomicrosystem. Biotechnology **6**(2), 153–164 (2007)
31. Tibajia, G.V., Talampas, M.C.R.: Development and evaluation of simultaneous wireless transmission of power and data for oceanographic devices. In: IEEE SENSORS, Limerick, Ireland, pp. 254–257 (2011)
32. Wu, C.-T.M., Sun, J.S., Itoh, T.: A simple self-powered AM-demodulator for wireless power/data transmission. In: Proceedings of the 42nd European Microwave Conference, pp. 325–328 (2012)
33. Trautmann, M., et al.: Implementation of simultaneous energy and data transfer in a contactless connector. In: IEEE Topical Conference on Wireless Sensors and Sensor Networks (WiSNet), pp. 101–104 (2016)

34. Rathge, C., Kuschner, D.: High efficient inductive energy and data transmission system with special coil geometry. In: Proceedings of 13th European Conference – Power Electronics and Applications, pp. 1–8 (2009)
35. Wang, G., Wang, P., Tang, Y.: Analysis of dual band power and data telemetry for biomedical implants. IEEE Trans. Biomed. Circuits Syst. **6**, 208–215 (2012)
36. Yashchenko, V.N., Kozlov, D.S., Vendik, I.B.: Dual-mode resonator for the dual-band system of wireless energy transfer with simultaneous data transmission. Prog. Electromagn. Res. Lett. **50**, 61–66 (2014)
37. Yokoi, Y., Taniya, A., Horiuchi, M., Kobayashi, S.: Development of kW class wireless power transmission system for EV using magnetic resonant method. In: Proceedings of the 1st International Electric Vehicle Technology Conference, Yokohama, Japan, pp. 1–6 (2011)
38. Jorgetto, M.F.C., de A. e Melo, G., Canesin, C.A.: Wireless inductive power transfer, oriented modeling and design. In: 2015 IEEE 13th Brazilian Power Electronics Conference and 1st Southern Power Electronics Conference (COBEP/SPEC) (2015)
39. Baikova, E.N., et al.: Electromagnetic field generated by a wireless energy transfer system: comparison of simulation to measurement. J. Electromagn. Waves Appl. **32**(5), 554–571 (2017)
40. Baikova, E.N., Valtchev, S.S., Melicio, R., Pires, V.F.: Wireless power transfer impact on data channel. In: Proceedings of the IEEE SPEEDAM, pp. 582–587 (2016)
41. Baikova, E.N., Romba, L., Valtchev, S.S., Melicio, R., Krusteva, A., Gigov, G.: Study on electromagnetic emissions from wireless energy transfer. In: Proceedings of the 17th IEEE PEMC, pp. 492–497 (2016)
42. Baikova, E.N., Valtchev, S.S., Melício, R., Pires, V.M.: Electromagnetic interference impact of wireless power transfer system on data wireless channel. In: Camarinha-Matos, L.M., Falcão, A.J., Vafaei, N., Najdi, S. (eds.) DoCEIS 2016. IAICT, vol. 470, pp. 293–301. Springer, Cham (2016). https://doi.org/10.1007/978-3-319-31165-4_29
43. Baikova, E.N., Romba, L., Melicio, R., Valtchev, S.S.: Simulation and experiment on electric field emissions generated by wireless energy transfer. In: Camarinha-Matos, L.M., Adu-Kankam, K.O., Julashokri, M. (eds.) DoCEIS 2018. IAICT, vol. 521, pp. 243–251. Springer, Cham (2018). https://doi.org/10.1007/978-3-319-78574-5_23
44. Baikova, E.N., Romba, L., Valtchev, S.S., Melício, R., Pires, V.M.: Electromagnetic influence of WPT on human's health: modelling, simulation and measurement. In: Triviño-Cabrera, A., Aguado, J.A. (eds.) Emerging Capabilities and Applications of Wireless Power Transfer, pp. 141–161. IGI Global, Hershey (2019)
45. Baikova, E.N., Valtchev, S.S., Melicio, R., Pires, V.M.: Electromagnetic interference from a wireless power transfer system: experimental results. Renew. Energy Power Qual. J. (RE&PQJ) **1**(14), 1020–1024 (2016)

# Scenario Reduction for Stochastic Optimization Applied to Short-Term Trading of PV Power

Isaias L. R. Gomes[1,2], Rui Melicio[1,2(✉)], and Victor M. F. Mendes[1,3]

[1] Escola de Ciências e Tecnologia, Departamento de Física, ICT,
Universidade de Évora, Evora, Portugal
ruimelicio@gmail.com
[2] IDMEC, Instituto Superior Técnico, Universidade de Lisboa, Lisbon, Portugal
[3] CISE, Electromechatronic Systems Research Centre,
Universidade da Beira Interior, Covilha, Portugal

**Abstract.** This paper addresses the scenario reduction for stochastic optimization applied to short-term trading of photovoltaic (PV) power. Stochastic optimization becomes a useful technique when leading with problems involving uncertainty. Short-term trading of PV power in electricity markets is an example of a problem involving a high level of uncertainty, namely uncertain parameters as PV power and market prices. As the level of uncertainty raises and the optimization problem becomes more complex, the prerequisite of scenario reduction becomes crucial without losing the representativeness of the original scenarios. Thus, in this paper is proposed an effective scenario reduction algorithm based on backward method in order to obtain a profitable trading of PV power in electricity markets. The scenario reduction method is applied to a two-period scenario tree, i.e., a scenario fan including uncertainty on day-ahead market (DAM) prices, on imbalance prices and on PV power. Through a case study is analyzed the performance of the scenario reduction algorithm and the comparison with the original set of scenarios. The results show that the reduced set of scenarios still has a very high level of accuracy.

**Keywords:** Scenario reduction · Backward method · Stochastic optimization · PV power · Electricity markets

## 1   Introduction

Short-term trading of PV power in electricity markets is an example of a decision-making problem where a high level of uncertainty exists [1]. Therefore, becomes even more important the necessity for making optimum and consistent choices under scenarios of this level of uncertainty. Although uncertainty can be included easily in decision-making problems, the inclusion of the exact probability distribution usually implies nonlinearity and additional efforts for numerical integration in the model [2]. Therefore, some approaches include a limited quantity of scenarios representing the uncertainty distribution by discretizing the probability of those scenarios, namely stochastic optimization [3]. In approaches as stochastic optimization the solution

© IFIP International Federation for Information Processing 2020
Published by Springer Nature Switzerland AG 2020
L. M. Camarinha-Matos et al. (Eds.): DoCEIS 2020, IFIP AICT 577, pp. 246–255, 2020.
https://doi.org/10.1007/978-3-030-45124-0_23

obtained is reached considering all the possible scenarios. Generally, a large quantity of scenarios is needed to emulate the uncertainty of the high number of uncertain parameters present in a decision-making problem, resulting in large-scale problems that are hard to solve due to limitations of computational resources [2]. Thus, becomes essential to determine a set of representative scenarios that best represent the initial set of scenarios. The determination of these representative scenarios leads to an important branch in decision-making problems under uncertainty which is scenario reduction. The scenario reduction concept proposed by [4] and by [5] aims to define a subset of scenarios and define optimum rearrangement of probabilities of conserved scenarios. The idea in [4] and [5] arises from quantitative stability results in terms of a probability metric, resulting in two scenario reduction heuristics, the forward selection and backward reduction. Additionally, [5] outspreads the initial idea developed by [4], and refines the iterative method, resulting in two new versions: a new version of forward selection, the fast forward selection; and a new version of the backward reduction, the simultaneous backward reduction. While stochastic optimization has been widely applied in decision-making problems, the need to use representative scenarios through scenario reduction methods has received limited attention from researchers in the past [4–6]. Due to its importance, scenario reduction is applied in the most diverse areas of knowledge, namely in supply chain [7] and particularly in the scope of this research, in electricity markets [4]. In power systems, most applications of scenario reduction methods focus on unit commitment and short-term operation [8–10]. This paper addresses the scenario reduction in a two-stage stochastic optimization applied to the short-term trading of PV power in a DAM, reformulated as a mixed-integer linear programming approach. The paper has as contribution, in the scope of short-term trading of power in electricity markets, the analysis of scenario reduction based on backward method over a two-period scenario tree, i.e., a scenario fan including uncertainty on DAM prices, on imbalance prices and on PV power.

The rest of this paper is organized as follows: Relationship of this paper to Innovation for Life Improvement in Sect. 2. Theoretical basis of Scenario Reduction are described in Sect. 3. The proposed Backward Scenario Reduction Method is presented in Sect. 4. The Problem Formulation of Short-term Trading of PV power in electricity markets is presented in Sect. 5. The Case Studies and the results are discussed in Sect. 6. Conclusion is presented in Sect. 7.

## 2    Relationship to Innovation for Life Improvement

The paradigm shift to a clean, energy-efficient and climate-resilient economy will demand a more decentralized, open system with the participation of all sectors of society [11]. The power system, and the electricity industry in general, is under a huge change paradigm, changing from the dominance of large companies' incumbents of large-scale and centralized technological projects to a paradigm where the innovation of the consumers is from great importance. In the upcoming years consumer must be at the center of the energy system: demanding competitive low-carbon solutions; participating as producer and manager of decentralized energy networks; acting as an investor, through decentralized platforms; and driving change through user innovation

[11]. Europe Union claims that a more bottom-up, user-centered energy system is a driver for more innovation [11]. From our point of view the innovation is the key for the sustainable development. Apart of the innovation of the consumers, this innovation is based on other innovations, namely, the digitization of the core aspects of transportation and electricity markets and electricity industry in general. Achieving more and more this level of modernization, the local community and the small start-up can all participate and even lead in the development energy innovations. For instance, the aggregation of micro-power sources, and loads of end-users, while increasing size and dimension to take part in electricity markets as a single entity, can produce at the same time energy efficiency and even profits as result of an optimal management. The consideration of smart systems will probably increase the data to be processed by machines and humans. Thus, as in the scope of this paper, the scenario reduction, i.e., the reduction of cardinality of a set of data, is from great importance in the transition to the new paradigm in the context of smart cities and smart grids.

## 3  Scenario Reduction

Stochastic optimization is one of the most used methodologies in problems involving uncertainties, having the advantage of considering a set of possible realizations of a parameter, the so-called scenarios. A variable changing over time is said to be a stochastic process. Assume a probability distribution $P$ of a n-dimensional stochastic process $\xi$ with $n$ components as photovoltaic power, DAM prices and imbalance prices with finite possible realizations $\xi = \{\xi_s\} = \{\xi_1 \ldots \xi_S\}$, $s = 1, \ldots, S$. To each realization $\xi_s$ is associated a probability $\pi_s$, where $\sum_1^S \pi_s = 1$. Now assume another probability distribution $P'$ of another n-dimensional stochastic process $\xi_{s'}$ with $n$ components with finite possible realizations $\xi = \{\xi_{s'}\} = \{\xi_1 \ldots \xi_{S'}\}$, $s' = 1, \ldots, S'$. To each realization $\xi_{s'}$ is associated a probability $\pi_{s'}$, where $\sum_1^S \pi_{s'} = 1$. Assume that $\xi_s$ is the possible realizations of the n-dimensional stochastic process representing the stochasticity present in a problem formulation of a trading PV power in competitive electricity markets. Now consider that each uncertain parameter has $S_*$ scenarios each one. Considering that the number of uncertain parameters is 3, the number of the scenarios of the problem is $S = S_{PV} \times S_{DA} \times S_I$. Theoretically the number of possible scenarios is huge. This implies large-scale problems and eventually high computational requirements. In addition, the difficulty of the analysis of the simulation results of large-scale problems may increase. Here appears the necessity of reduction of the number of scenarios, i.e., reduce the cardinality of the initial set of scenarios. Hence, due to the computational requirements, the initial n-dimensional stochastic process $\xi_s$ is approximated by a new n-dimensional stochastic process $\xi_{s'}$, which represents a subset of the initial number of scenarios. Likewise, the initial probability distance $P$ is approximated by a new probability distribution $P'$ which represents a subset of the initial number of scenarios. A scenario reduction algorithm aims the reduction of the number of the initial data without losing the representativeness of the original scenarios. In other words, a scenario reduction algorithm aims to reduce a scenario set while keeping as intact as possible the stochastic information included in it [12]. The aim of the scenario reduction is the to find a new distribution that minimizes de Kantorovich distance from the probability distribution of the original scenario tree [4].

The scenario reduction algorithms developed in [4] and [5] determine a scenario subset and allocate new probabilities to the conserved scenarios such that the corresponding reduced probability $P'$ is the closest to the original measure $P$ in terms of a certain probability distance $Dist$ between $P$ and $P'$. The probability distance $Dist$ trades off scenario probabilities and distances of scenario values. One of the most used probability distances in stochastic programming is the Kantorovich distance $Dist_K$. For two-stage problems and the Kantorovich distance can be stated as follows [12]:

$$Dist_K(P, P') = \sum_{s \in S \setminus S'} \pi_s \min_{s' \in S'} c(\xi_s, \xi_{s'}) \tag{1}$$

In (1) $\pi_s$ is the scenario probability and $c(\xi_s, \xi_{s'})$ is often referred to as cost function based on the norm between two random vectors. $c(\xi_s, \xi_{s'})$ is stated as follows:

$$c(\xi_s, \xi_{s'}) = \|\xi_s - \xi_{s'}\| \tag{2}$$

The $Dist_K(P, P')$ expressed in (1) can be used to derive several heuristics in order to obtain a smaller quantity of scenarios without losing the representativeness of the initial set of scenarios. Next to the reduction is applied the so-called optimal redistribution rule, where the probability of a conserved scenario is equal to the sum of its previous probability and the probability of all removed scenarios that were close to it before the reduction with respect to the cost function $c(\xi_s, \xi_{s'})$. In this paper the scenario reduction method used is the backward reduction method.

## 4 Backward Scenario Reduction Method

The backward scenario reduction method is based on the recursive elimination of scenarios of the initial set of scenarios until the minimum value of $Dist_K$ is reached. An extensive description the backward scenario reduction method is available in [4]. The backward scenario reduction method works as follows:

Step 1: Compute the distances of each scenario pairs $(\xi_s, \xi_j)$

$$c_{sj} = c(\xi_s, \xi_j), s, j = 1, \ldots, S. \tag{3}$$

$$S^D = \emptyset. \tag{4}$$

Step i: Compute

$$c_{ss'}^i = \min_{j \neq s} c_{sj}, s \in S^{Ri-1} \text{ and select } s' \text{ that min } c_{sj} \text{ with respect to a } s \tag{5}$$

$$z_{ss'}^1 = \sum_{s' \in S^{Ri-1}} \pi_{s'} c_{ss'}^1. \tag{6}$$

$$\text{select } s_i \in \arg\min_{s \in S^{Ri-1}} z_{ss'}^i. \tag{7}$$

Add the deleted scenarios to the set $S^{Di} = S^{Di-1} \cup \{s_i\}$. (8)

Remove the deleted scenarios from the set $S^{Ri} = S^{Ri-1} \backslash s_i$. (9)

Final step: update the scenario probabilities

$$\pi_{s'} = \pi_{s'} + \pi_{s_i}. \tag{10}$$

The backward scenario reduction method defines a subset of scenarios that is the closest to the initial set of scenarios using the Kantorovich distance and calculate the new probabilities of the conserved scenarios. The Kantorovich distance weigh the scenario probabilities and the distances between scenario values. Discarded scenarios have probability zero. The method stops the process when the number of reduced scenarios defined by the user is reached or when a predefined distance is reached.

## 5  Problem Formulation – Short-Term Trading of PV Power

This section summarizes the mathematical formulation of short-term trading of PV Power in electricity markets. Despite this formulation is applied to short-term trading of PV power, can be applied as well for other variable-renewables, namely wind power. Complete formulation can be found in [13]. The stochastic linear programming to support the bidding strategies of a PV power producer is stated as follows:

$$\max Profit = \sum_{s'=1}^{S'} \sum_{t=1}^{T} \pi_{s'} \left( \lambda_{ts'}^{DM} P_t^{PV} + \lambda_{ts'}^{DM} pr_{ts'}^+ d_{ts'}^+ - \lambda_{ts'}^{DM} pr_{ts'}^- d_{ts'}^- \right) \tag{11}$$

Subject to:

$$0 \leq P_t^{PV} \leq P^{max}. \tag{12}$$

$$d_{ts'} = P_{ts'}^{PV} - P_t^{PV}. \tag{13}$$

$$d_{ts'} = d_{ts'}^+ - d_{ts'}^-. \tag{14}$$

$$0 \leq d_{ts'}^+ \leq P_{ts'}^{PV}. \tag{15}$$

$$0 \leq d_{ts'}^- \leq P^{max}. \tag{16}$$

In (11) the three terms are: the revenue associated with the bid in DAM at scenario $s$ and period $t$; the income associated with the excess of energy in the imbalance market at scenario $s$ and period $t$; and the cost associated with the deficit of energy in the balancing market at scenario $s$ and period $t$. In (12) the upper bound off the bid is set to be the rated power of the PV power plant. In (13) the energy deviation is defined as the difference between the PV power at scenario s and the bid in DAM. In (14) the energy deviation is divided in two nonnegative deviations. In (15) and (16) the upper bounds associated with the positive and the negative deviations are set.

## 6   Case Studies

Inputs: The effectiveness of the application of the scenario reduction based on the backward scenario reduction is evaluated using a PV system of rated power of 100 MW located in Iberian Peninsula. The day-ahead energy prices $\lambda_{ts'}^{DM}$ and the price ratios $pr_{ts'}^+$ e $pr_{ts'}^-$ are obtained from [14]. PV power scenarios are obtained from [15]. The simulation is carried out using GAMS/SCENRED performing the fast backward reduction method. The initial set of scenarios are 10 for PV power, 10 for DAM prices and 10 for positive and negative price ratios, a total of 1000 initial scenarios, correspondent to the all possible combinations between the 3 set of uncertain parameters. The DAM price scenarios and the price ratios scenarios are shown in Fig. 1.

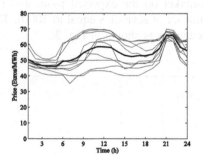 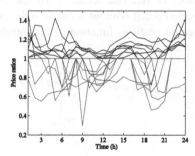

**Fig. 1.** Left, DAM scenarios (blue) and average – (black). Right, price ratios: positive (blue), negative (black). (Color figure online)

The PV power scenarios are shown in Fig. 2.

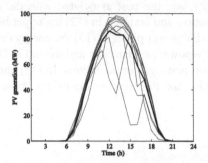

**Fig. 2.** PV power scenarios (blue) and average scenario (black). (Color figure online)

*Case Studies and Results:* The case studies are based on the analysis of stability of the application of the fast backward scenario reduction method applied to the short-term trading of PV power, namely the effect that the definition of a certain number of scenarios by the decision-maker can make on the optimal values of the decision variables of the problem formulated in Sect. 5.

*#Case1 – The Effect of the Number of Reduced Scenarios on the Expected Profit:* This case study makes the comparison between the effect of the definition of S different number of reduced scenarios by the decision-maker on the expected profit and the expected profit without scenario reduction (initial set of scenarios equal to 1000). The expected profit as function of the number of scenarios is shown in Fig. 3.

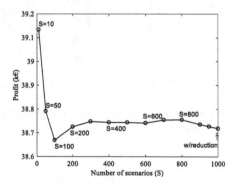

**Fig. 3.** Expected profit as function of the quantity of reduced scenarios.

In Fig. 3 it is possible to conclude that for the value of the quantity of reduced scenarios equal to s = 10, the profit reaches a high value. However, this result may not be optimal as the increase in the quantity of reduced scenarios stabilizes the expected profit value. Reducing the number of scenarios by half the value, i.e. s = 500, reduces profit by only 0.06%, a value considered insignificant. Further, reducing the number of scenarios even further s = 300 still ensures a good approximation of the actual value, i.e. without scenario reduction. Therefore, reducing scenarios for a reasonable set for this application does not guarantee a significant change in the expected profit value.

*#Case2 – The Effect of the Number of Reduced Scenarios on the Bid and on the Positive and Negative Deviations:* This case study makes the comparison between the effect of the definition of S different number of reduced scenarios by the decision-maker on the bid and on the positive and negative energy deviations and respective values without scenario reduction, i.e., considering the initial set of scenarios equal to 1000. The bid in the DAM and the energy deviations as function of the quantity of reduced scenarios are shown in Fig. 4.

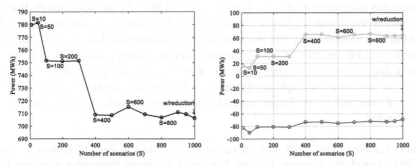

**Fig. 4.** Left, bid in the DAM as function of the quantity of reduced scenarios. Right, positive and negative energy deviations as function of the number of scenarios.

In Fig. 4 left it can be concluded that for a reduced number of scenarios s = 10, the total daily supply in the daily market is high. However, this value may not be ideal, since by increasing the supply value to higher values closer to s = 400 the market supply begins to stabilize by settling on a range of values [706, 715]. This range of values is considered a small value considering the volume of energy that is traded. In Fig. 4 right it can be concluded that as more scenarios are considered during the optimization problem, the negative energy deviations decrease, and the positive energy deviations increases as an expected profit of the short-term trading of PV power is calculated that hedges the system against more the non-profitable scenarios. Therefore, as the bid decreases the expected profit decreases considerably. Contrary, when the bid decreases the absolute value of the energy deviations increases. The main advantage of fast backward method over fast forward method and other backward methods is the computational performance for huge scenario trees. Thus, this paper takes advantage of the best expected performance with respect with running time of the fast backward method.

# 7  Conclusion

The application of a scenario reduction method for stochastic optimization applied to the short-term trading of PV power is proposed in this paper. The transaction of energy from renewable sources in the electricity market requires a convenient consideration of uncertainty, which tends to be increased. Thus, in this paper it is proposed the scenario reduction based on a backward reduction method. The case studies show that the consideration of an incorrect number of reduced scenarios can lead to undesirable results and losses in the producer's expected profit. Thus, whenever possible, such an analysis is advisable in formulating the decision-making problem in problems that include a considerable number of uncertainties in order to obtain a firm basis of the correct number of scenarios to consider. The case study analyzing the effect of considering a certain quantity of scenarios on the expected profit of the producer demonstrates that reducing the number of scenarios by 90% leads to a profit that does not consider the worst scenarios, so the energy transaction in market can be done erroneously. The case study that analyzes the effect of considering a certain number of scenarios on the amount of energy traded and the energy deviations shows that reducing the number of scenarios by up to 60% leads to high values of negative imbalances as a result of high energy offers in the market. Therefore, considering the results of deviations to lower scenario reduction values, this practice is not recommended.

**Acknowledgments.** This work was supported by: Bolsas Camões, I.P./Fundação Millennium BCP through the Programa Empresa Promotora da Língua Portuguesa; European Union through the European Regional Development Fund, included in the COMPETE 2020 (Operational Program Competitiveness and Internationalization) through the ICT project (UID/GEO/04683/2019) with the reference POCI010145FEDER007690; FCT, through IDMEC, under LAETA, project UIDB/50022/2020; Portuguese Foundation for Science and Technology (FCT) under Project UID/EEA/04131/2019.

# References

1. Gomes, I.L.R., Melicio, R., Mendes, V.M.F., Pousinho, H.M.I.: Decision making for sustainable aggregation of clean energy in DAM: uncertainty and risk. Renewable Energy **133**, 602–702 (2019)
2. Li, Z., Li, Z.: Linear programming-based scenario reduction using transportation distance. Comput. Chem. Eng. **88**, 50–58 (2016)
3. Silvente, J., Papageorgiou, L.G., Dua, V.: Scenario tree reduction for optimization under uncertainty using sensitivity analysis. Comput. Chem. Eng. **125**, 449–459 (2019)
4. Dupačová, J., Gröwe-Kuska, N., Römisch, W.: Scenario reduction in stochastic programming. Math. Program. **95**(3), 493–511 (2003). https://doi.org/10.1007/s10107-002-0331-0
5. Heitsch, H., Römisch, W.: Scenario reduction algorithms in stochastic programming. Comput. Optim. Appl. **24**(2–3), 187–206 (2003). https://doi.org/10.1023/A:1021805924152
6. Karuppiah, R., Martín, M., Grossmann, I.E.: A simple heuristic for reducing the number of scenarios in two-stage stochastic programming. Comput. Chem. Eng. **34**(8), 1246–1255 (2010)

7. Paulo, H., Cardoso-Grilo, T., Relvas, S., Barbosa-Póvoa, A.P.: Designing integrated biorefineries supply chain: combining stochastic programming models with scenario reduction methods. Comput. Aided Chem. Eng. **40**, 901–906 (2017)
8. Aravena, I., Gil, E.: Hydrological scenario reduction for stochastic optimization in hydrothermal power systems. Appl. Stoch. Models Bus. Ind. **31**(2), 231–240 (2015)
9. Xiong, G., Liu, X., Chen, D., Zhang, J., Hashiyama, T.: PSO algorithm-based scenario reduction method for stochastic unit commitment problem. IEEJ Trans. Electr. Electron. Eng. **12**, 206–213 (2016)
10. Yilidz, C., et al.: A day-ahead wind power scenario generation, reduction and quality test tool. Sustainability **9**(5), 1–15 (2017)
11. European Commission: Communication from the Commission to the European parliament, the council, the European economic and social committee, the committee of the regions, and the European investment bank – Accelerating clean energy Innovation (2019). https://ec. europa.eu/
12. Conejo, A.J., Carrión, M., Morales, J.M.: Decision making under uncertainty in electricity markets, vol. 153. Springer, New York (2010). https://doi.org/10.1007/978-1-4419-7421-1
13. Gomes, I.L.R., Pousinho, H.M.I., Melicio, R., Mendes, V.M.F.: Stochastic coordination of joint wind and photovoltaic systems with energy storage in DAM. Energy **124**, 310–320 (2017)
14. REE-Red Eléctrica de España. http://www.esios.ree.es/web-publica/
15. CGE-Centro de Geofísica de Évora. http://www.cge.uevora.pt

# Model Predictive Current Control of Switched Reluctance Motor Drive: An Initial Study

Manuel Pereira[1(✉)] and Rui Esteves Araújo[2(✉)]

[1] Faculty of Engineering, University of Porto, Rua Dr. Roberto Frias,
4200-465 Porto, Portugal
ee12314@fe.up.pt
[2] INESC TEC, Faculty of Engineering, University of Porto,
Rua Dr. Roberto Frias, 4200-465 Porto, Portugal
raraujo@fe.up.pt

**Abstract.** A considerable amount of research within the last few decades has been focusing on controllers for switched reluctance motor drives and how they affect the torque ripple. Despite all its potentials, there are still major concerns and obstacles to overcome concerning the dependency of the magnetic characteristic of the switched reluctance motor. This work targets these concerns by proposing an initial study of the fundamentals of a drive scheme using a finite set model predictive control for a switched reluctance motor through an asymmetric bridge converter. The implementation of this scheme is the main contribution of this paper. The method uses the dynamic model of the motor to estimate the future behavior of the current for each converter state. A cost function then evaluates which switching state minimizes the current error and applies it to the motor. Some simulation results illustrate the technique. Simulation results show the good performance of the method with fast and accurate transient response.

**Keywords:** Model predictive control · Switched reluctance motor · Electric drives

## 1 Introduction

During the last years, the interest in the switched reluctance motor (SRM) has increased due to their manufacturing simplicity, large speed range, fault-tolerant operation and essentially for the non-use of rare elements in both the rotor and the stator. Due to these advantages, in the future this motor may be preferable compared to the induction and synchronous motor. However, there are still some disadvantages to solve originated by the operating process of the motor, namely the produced torque ripple component and audible acoustic noise.

These disadvantages can be greatly reduced by an adequate control, which is the main topic of this PhD work. A scalable controller is proposed with three subparts, the *speed controller*, the *current reference generator* and the *current controller*. The *speed controller* is not addressed in this study. For systems where the electrical time constant is much smaller than the mechanical time constant, the current control loop must be

L. M. Camarinha-Matos et al. (Eds.): DoCEIS 2020, IFIP AICT 577, pp. 256–264, 2020.
https://doi.org/10.1007/978-3-030-45124-0_24

treated as an ideal current source, i.e. given a set-point current, it will be tracked immediately. With this assumption, any linear control design technique can be used for speed control. The *current reference generator* is the connection between torque and current reference, and due to the motor's highly non-linearity, this process may not be a straightforward issue. These two subparts will be a matter for future work.

For now, the *current controller* subpart is our main focus. As the traditional controllers, such as linear PI and hysteresis, cannot achieve the performance level we wish, an initial study of the model predictive control is carried out for this subpart of the controller. The research findings of this study are expected to build a solid foundation for better development in next research phase, which is generically supported by the following questions.

### 1.1 Research Questions

Why and how can the model predictive control (MPC) to the switched reluctance motor drive be implement? To successfully answer this question, the problem may be divide into some sub questions.

- **Why do we place the MPC at the heart of our research?**

In previous work, traditional controllers like PI and hysteresis control were used [1]. Although they are the most used in the literature, their performance may not be sufficient. For example, in the case of PI control, in order to achieve the best performance, it would be necessary to know exactly how the machine behaves at every operating point. For the hysteresis control, it would be necessary to increase the switching frequency. And neither the behavior of the machine is exactly known nor we want to increase the switching frequency. Further investigation is thus certainly warranted.

The major difference between these traditional controllers' whit the MPC is that they work by looking to the past to decide a converter state to get the system close to the reference, while the MPC looks forward to decide the best converter state that will approximate the system to the reference. In other words, the MPC knows in advance what is expected to happen.

- **Is this control suitable for high frequency operations?**

Looking to the past, from at least 20 years ago, the control systems started to have been completely based on digital controllers. It started with simple microprocessors, then the microcontrollers came about and then by the digital signal processors (DSP) [2]. Nowadays, even hybrid solutions using microprocessors and field programmable gate arrays are an option [3]. These innovations allow the use of heavy methods, not only for control but also for prediction, filtering and data saving. Neural controllers and Kalman filters are examples of heavy processing methods used in DSP's.

- **Which state should be predicted and which constraints are related?**

From the viewpoint of controllability of the SRM, the machine state variables that can be predicted are the torque, flux or current. In all of them have pros and cons in their implementation. The torque is the one we want to control in order to keep it constant, while the problem is in its estimation. As the SRM model is highly nonlinear, it makes the torque estimation a quite difficult task, and is only possible by using the machine characteristics in tables or approximated by functions. Also, the characteristic may change during the motor operation leading to loss of accuracy of the estimation. The same happens when the flux is used as state variable, as it is necessary to know the flux-current characteristic to convert current and rotor position into flux.

The use of the current as state variable has the advantage of directly controlling the state that is measured. However, the problem is similar because it is necessary to know the inductance characteristic of the machine for the prediction.

This paper is organized as it follows. In Sect. 2 the relationship to technological innovation for life improvement is addressed. A synthesis of the state of the art is then presented in Sect. 3 and the model of the SRM and power converter are the topics of discussion in Sect. 4. Section 5 proposes the current control solution based on predictive control technique, followed by simulation results in Sect. 6. Finally, Sect. 7 concludes the paper and indicates guidelines for future work.

## 2    Contribution to Life Improvement

According to the European Green Deal, Europe has to become climate-neutral by the year of 2050 in order to improve the well-being of people [4]. This objective aims to take effect not only in the energy sector but also in household appliances, in the industry and in public and private mobility. Electric motors play an important role in all of these sectors, so motor efficiency and reliability are always of great concern.

Transitioning to a low-carbon society is vital to improve the quality of life in different dimensions and realizing sustainable development. Improving products efficiency and creating reliable solutions are an important part of this process. In this line, the SRM may play an important role for different products due its advantages, such as reliability. Since the motor has no windings or rare rotor elements, it is free from electromagnetic rotor failures and no rotor cooling is required. As the stator phases are independent, a failure in one phase does not necessarily imply a system shutdown. Another advantage is being well suited for high-speed operation. Some applications like dry machines, machine tools and electric vehicles may need to work at high speeds, which is not a limitation for the SRM.

Considering the advantages of the SRM described, the main contribution of this PhD work for "Technological Innovation for Life Improvement" consists of the development of a high-performance, scalable-speed controller in order to reduce the torque ripple component and the acoustic noise. As a result, the proposed controller may contribute to mitigating some constraints and consequently the wider dissemination of SRM applications.

# 3 State of the Art

In the literature, the number of works using the model predictive control has been greatly increasing in the recent years. In [5], the basic principle of nonlinear MPC is reviewed, and advantages, disadvantages and implementation aspects are also discussed. Another good reference is the book [6], where the author approaches the method and describes the application of it to power converters and motor drives.

In general, the MPCs can be classified in current, flux and torque prediction. For example, in [7] and [8] a model predictive current control is implemented in order to reduce the torque ripple. In these works, the simulations are comparative and do not validate the method, preventing readers from evaluating the accuracy of the current prediction. In [9] and [10], the authors developed a scheme where the inductance profile in current prediction is updated throughout the operating process. For the flux prediction, in [11] the MPC is used together with the direct torque control method, and in [12] a virtual-flux MPC is created using the machine flux characteristic. Finally, for torque prediction, in [13] a nonlinear model is used to estimate and predict the instantaneous torque and in [14] the author uses an analytical model for torque estimation. Besides the controlled state is the torque itself, simulation results do not seem very effective. To sum up, only a few papers study the use of the MPC in the SRM, and provide few definitive answers, so further research is certainly warranted.

# 4 The Switched Reluctance Motor System

The SRM voltage and magnetic equations are expressed by:

$$V = R_s.i + \frac{d\Psi(\theta, i)}{dt} \tag{1}$$

$$\Psi(\theta, i) = L(\theta, i).i \tag{2}$$

where $V$ is the supply voltage, $R_s$ the stator resistance, $i$ the current, $\Psi$ the flux-linkage, $\theta$ the rotor position and $L$ the self-inductance.

The most used power converter for the SRM is the asymmetric bridge. Each converter phase is composed by two diodes and two transistors. It can feed the motor phase with the $V_{DC}$ state by activating both transistors, $-V_{DC}$ state while there is still current in the windings and by putting both transistors off, and the 0 V state by only activating one of the transistors, letting the current flow either in the top or bottom mesh. The advantages of this converter are the independent control by phase, unidirectional current and allowing current to the source voltage to regenerate.

# 5  Model Predictive Current Control of SRM

The proposed control scheme for the SRM drive is shown in Fig. 1. The control, the power converter and the motor are presented. This proposed solution is in a modular format, where the control can be separated into speed controller, current reference generator and current controller. In this study, our concern is to have an ideal solution for the current control so the speed controller and reference generator are not addressed. At first, it is assumed that there exists an outer control loop providing a desired current, $i_{ref}$.

This input, of the current controller, is expected to have both a slow and fast dynamic in its waveform. To follow this unpredictable reference, the current control has to be fast and accurate. These characteristics can be found in the Finite Set Model Predictive Control, where its application to the SRM is the main contribution of this work.

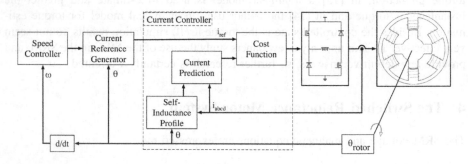

**Fig. 1.** Proposed block diagram.

## 5.1  Model Predictive Control for the SRM

For this system, the MPC is divided into a *current prediction* block, *a self-inductance profile* block and a *cost function* block. In the current prediction block a discretization of the model of the motor for the prediction of the future behavior of the current is required. This model is iteratively computed using each available inductance value with the measured mechanical position and stator phase current to estimate the future value of the stator current. With this information, the controller has the objective of determining which is the ideal voltage vector to apply in the next cycle in order to minimize the cost function. The one that has the minimum value is the converter state that is applied in the next cycle. The process is then repeated for each phase and for every cycle. In order to simplify the controller, the MPC time horizon is only designed for one sampling time.

## 5.2   Current Prediction

Using the Forward Euler method and rearranging the Eqs. (1) and (2) with some simplifications, the discrete equation is obtained

$$i(k+T) = \frac{T}{L(k)}.[V^*(j) - R_s.i(k)] + i(k) \tag{3}$$

where $T$ is the sampling period, $k$ is the actual sampling and $V^*(j)$ is the voltage value for the converter state $j$, as already seen $V^*(j)$ can be equal to $V_{DC}$, $-V_{DC}$ or 0. The value of $L(k)$ is from the self-inductance profile block, which is a table with the machine characteristic obtained by the finite element method.

## 5.3   Cost Function Minimization

Having estimated the current for all the converter states, the cost function is then calculated, which is simply the error module given by

$$Error(j) = |i_{ref} - i(k+T,j)| \tag{4}$$

where $i(k+T,j)$ is the current prediction at time $k+T$ for the converter state $j$. The state $j$ that has the lowest error value is the one applied in the next cycle.

# 6   Simulations

In order to validate the proposed diagram block, a Matlab/Simulink® simulation environment was created. A number of simulations have been performed in order to evaluate the performance of the developed control technique. Table 1 shows the parameters used in the simulation studies.

**Table 1.** Simulation parameters.

| Parameters | Values |
|---|---|
| Source voltage | 325 V |
| Maximum current | 7 A |
| N° of rotor poles | 6 |
| N° of stator poles | 8 |
| Minimum inductance | 0.021 H |
| Maximum inductance | 0.31 H |
| Sampling time | 0.00002 s |

As the work is around the current control, it is simulated a scenario for two-step levels of acceleration. Figure 2 summarize the simulations results. There is a start-up transient under no-load, with current reference set to 5.5 A from time 0 s to time 0.05 s and of 2.5 A from time 0.05 s to time 0.2 s. The current reference is also multiplied by a sinusoidal waveform of small magnitude to represent the fast changes that the current reference can have. The mechanical speed, stator current responses and applied voltage are shown.

Good tracking of the current reference can be observed for both current levels. Even for the high frequency sinusoid component there is no problem for the controller, where the absolute current error percentage always being less than 10%. Looking at the zoom of the predicted and the real current it can be seen that they are close but not too much. This is due to less satisfactory precision of the self-inductance profile. Because of this, the control is somewhat aggressive, commutating several times between the $V_{DC}$ and $-V_{DC}$ states in the middle of phase conduction.

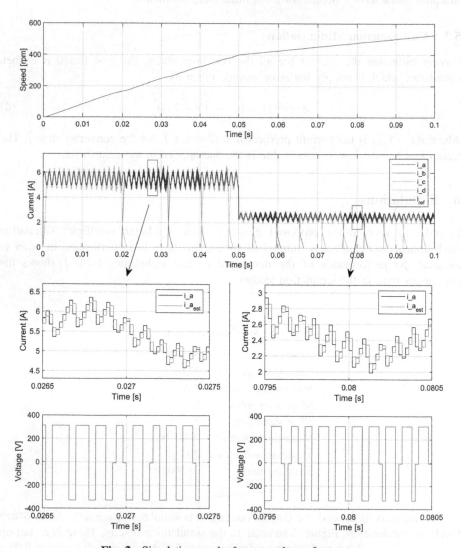

**Fig. 2.** Simulation results for two values of current.

# 7 Conclusions and Further Work

In this work, a method for the current control of a switched reluctance motor, based on predictive control technique, was introduced. The method avoids the use of a modulation to command the asymmetric bridge converter, providing an accurate current control on the basis of the cost function and the discrete model of the motor.

The control scheme was studied and analyzed using a Matlab/Simulink® environment. Simulation results show the good performance of predictive current controller for tracking the current reference.

Further work, currently under way, includes improving the current prediction, which although already good, should be improved with estimation techniques, for example. The connection between the output of the speed controller and the reference current will be the second major part of this PhD work. In this part, it will be possible to manipulate the input signal in order to minimize the torque ripple as much as possible.

# References

1. Pereira, M., Araújo, R.E.: Analysis and design of a speed controller for switched reluctance motor drive. UPorto J. Eng. **5**, 46–58 (2019). https://doi.org/10.24840/2183-6493_005.001_0004
2. Capolino, G.A.: Recent advances and applications of power electronics and motor drives-Advanced and intelligent control techniques. In: IECON Proceedings (Industrial Electronics Conference). IEEE Computer Society, pp. 37–39 (2008)
3. Zynq-7000 SoC. https://www.xilinx.com/products/silicon-devices/soc/zynq-7000.html. Accessed 18 Dec 2019
4. A European Green Deal| European Commission. https://ec.europa.eu/info/strategy/priorities-2019-2024/european-green-deal_en. Accessed 19 Dec 2019
5. Findeisen, R., Allgower, F.: An introduction to non-linear model predictive control. In: 21st Benelux Meet Systems and Control, Veidhoven, vol. 11, pp. 1–23 (2002)
6. Rodriguez, J., Cortes, P.: Predictive Control of Power Converters and Electrical Drives. John Wiley and Sons, Hoboken (2012)
7. Hui, C., Li, M., Hui, W., et al.: Torque ripple minimization for switched reluctance motor with predictive current control method. In: 2017 20th International Conference on Electrical Machines and Systems, ICEMS 2017. Institute of Electrical and Electronics Engineers Inc. (2017)
8. Abdel-Fadil, R., Szamel, L.: Enhancement of the switched reluctance motor performance for electric vehicles applications using predictive current control. In: CANDO-EPE 2018 - Proceedings IEEE International Conference and Workshop in Obuda on Electrical and Power Engineering. Institute of Electrical and Electronics Engineers Inc., pp. 195–199 (2019)
9. Li, X., Shamsi, P.: Inductance surface learning for model predictive current control of switched reluctance motors. IEEE Trans. Transp. Electrif. **1**, 287–297 (2015). https://doi.org/10.1109/TTE.2015.2468178
10. Li, X., Shamsi, P.: Model predictive current control of switched reluctance motors with inductance auto-calibration. IEEE Trans. Ind. Electron. **63**, 3934–3941 (2016). https://doi.org/10.1109/TIE.2015.2497301

11. Shang, C., Xu, A., Huang, L., Chen, J.: Flux linkage optimization for direct torque control of switched reluctance motor based on model predictive control. IEEJ Trans. Electr. Electron. Eng. **14**, 1105–1113 (2019). https://doi.org/10.1002/tee.22906
12. Valencia, D.F., Filho, S.R., Callegaro, A.D., et al.: Virtual-flux finite control set model predictive control of switched reluctance motor drives. In: IECON 2019-45th Annual Conference of the IEEE Industrial Electronics Society, pp. 1465–1470 (2019)
13. Peyrl, H., Papafotiou, G., Morari, M.: Model predictive torque control of a switched reluctance motor. In: Proceedings of the IEEE International Conference on Industrial Technology (2009)
14. Li, C., Wang, G., Li, Y., Xu, A.: An improved finite-state predictive torque control for switched reluctance motor drive. IET Electr. Power Appl. **12**, 144–151 (2018). https://doi.org/10.1049/iet-epa.2017.0268

# A Simple Analysis to Determine the Limits of a CMOS Technology to Implement SC DC-DC Converters

Ricardo Madeira[1,2(✉)] and Nuno Paulino[1,2]

[1] Department of Electrical Engineering (DEE),
Faculty of Sciences and Technology (FCT NOVA), Caparica, Portugal
r.madeira@campus.fct.unl.pt, nunop@uninova.pt
[2] Centre for Technologies and Systems (CTS) – UNINOVA, Caparica, Portugal

**Abstract.** This paper presents a simple analysis that allows to determine the maximum power density and efficiency of a SC DC-DC converter for a given CMOS technology. By determining the values of the ratio between the switches' gate capacitance and channel width, and between the ON resistance and the channel width, together with the parasitic capacitances from the flying capacitors, it is possible to plot the efficiency as a function of the power density for a given input and output voltage of the converter, allowing to quickly determine both the expected efficiency and clock frequency ranges of the converter, for a given CMOS technology.

**Keywords:** Power Management Unit · Switched-capacitor (SC) converter · Design techniques

## 1 Introduction

Nowadays, with the growing number of Internet-of-things (IoT) devices, the collection of real live raw data from innumerous processes has greatly increased, e.g., in industrial, health, transportation, communications processes and others [1]. This raw data can be analyzed inside of the IoT device thus distributing the data processing capabilities and decreasing the reaction time. This sensing and processing of information costs energy. Hence, it is extremely important to have efficient systems, in a macro scale it contributes for reducing the carbon footprint, and at a small scale, it allows improving the battery life of devices thus reducing maintenance costs.

There are several energy sources, like solar, piezoelectrical, thermal, and others [2]. This energy can be fed directly to the system, and/or be stored in an energy storing device, like a battery or supercapacitor. These energy sources produce a variable voltage, which requires the use of a Power Management Unit (PMU) to obtain a constant output voltage. The PMU provides a bridge between the energy sources and the system using, for example, DC-DC converters. These can be inductive or capacitive, where the latter has receiving a lot of attention in recent years since they are composed by switches and capacitors that are native in CMOS technology and thus, they can be easily integrated, resulting in a smaller footprint and cost, and still achieve high performance values [2–6].

© IFIP International Federation for Information Processing 2020
Published by Springer Nature Switzerland AG 2020
L. M. Camarinha-Matos et al. (Eds.): DoCEIS 2020, IFIP AICT 577, pp. 265–273, 2020.
https://doi.org/10.1007/978-3-030-45124-0_25

The Switched-Capacitor (SC) DC-DC converters transfer charge from the input to the output through a capacitor, where the frequency at which the charge is transferred will determine the output voltage value of the converter. This charge transferring is controlled by a clock signal, allowing for different circuit configurations on each clock phase. The quality of both the capacitors and switches will affect the converter's energy efficiency and power per area value [6–8]. The characteristics of the passive devices depend on the CMOS technology node for the system implementation, for example, the lower the CMOS node, the higher the capacitance per area of the capacitors. This is because smaller oxide thickness means higher capacitance values. However, small oxide thickness also means lower breakdown voltage values and larger current leakage. The same goes for switches, the lower the node, the higher switching frequency can be. This raises the question, what is the expected performance for each technological node? To answer this, this work shows an analysis that characterizes both the capacitors and switches of the 130 nm bulk CMOS technology into a set of coefficients that are used to determine the converter efficiency and power per area. This can be applied to any technology node.

## 2  Relationship to Technological Innovation for Life Improvement

The IoT devices can enhance our life quality in many ways, e.g., increasing the surgery span of patient with medical embedded devices, like pacemakers, by increase the battery life of the devices. Such devices can also be used to monitoring our health, which can give us a better control of our daily life needs. There are several number of other examples in different areas, where all these devices, which need energy to operate, will benefit from energy efficient PMUs. The energy improvement of such devices will consequently have a direct impact on the human's life quality.

## 3  SC DC-DC Converter Theoretical Analysis

Figure 1 shows the schematic of a Step-down Series-Parallel (SP) SC DC-DC converter with a Conversion Ratio (CR) of 1/2. It is composed by 1 flying capacitor $C_{FLY}$ and 4 switches, where $S_{1,3}$ are ON in the phase $\phi_1$ and $S_{2,4}$ are ON in phase $\phi_2$, where $\phi_{1,2}$ are two clock signals complementary to each other. Hence, on $\phi_1$, $C_{FLY}$ connects between the input voltage $V_{IN}$ and the output voltage $V_{OUT}$, and on $\phi_2$, $C_{FLY}$ connects between $V_{OUT}$ and ground. In the schematic it is also represented the $C_{FLY}$ parasitic capacitances by $\alpha$ and $\beta$, these refer to the top and bottom parasitic capacitance, respectively, as percentage of $C_{FLY}$. Assuming that $V_{OUT}$ is kept at a constant voltage, the charge equations can be drawn:

$$(V_{IN} - V_{OUT}) C_{FLY} + V_{IN} (\alpha C_{FLY}) = V_{OUT} (C_{FLY} + \alpha C_{FLY}) + \Delta q_o^{\phi_2}, \tag{1}$$

$$-V_{OUT} C_{FLY} = (V_{OUT} - V_{IN}) C_{FLY} + V_{OUT} (\beta C_{FLY}) + \Delta q_o^{\phi_1}, \tag{2}$$

$$V_{OUT}(C_{FLY} + \alpha C_{FLY}) = (V_{IN} - V_{OUT}) C_{FLY} + V_{IN}(\alpha C_{FLY}) - \Delta q_i^{\phi_1}. \tag{3}$$

where $\Delta q_o^{\phi_{1,2}}$ are the amount of charge absorbed by $V_{OUT}$, in the respective phase, and $\Delta q_i^{\phi_1}$ the amount of charge drawn by the circuit from $V_{IN}$, in this case only during $\phi_1$.

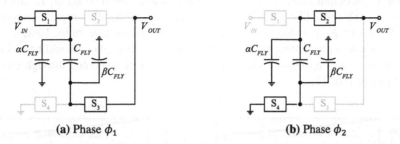

(a) Phase $\phi_1$                    (b) Phase $\phi_2$

**Fig. 1.** Simplified schematic of the SP 1/2 SC DC-DC converter in each clock phase [3, 4].

These equations can be solved in respect to $\Delta q_i^{\phi_1}$, $\Delta q_o^{\phi_1}$, and $\Delta q_o^{\phi_2}$, and used to determine the input and output current and power:

$$I_{IN} = \Delta q_i^{\phi_1} F_{CLK} = C_{FLY}(V_{IN}(1+\alpha) - V_{OUT}(2+\alpha)), \tag{4}$$

$$I_{OUT} = (\Delta q_o^{\phi_1} + \Delta q_o^{\phi_2}) F_{CLK} = C_{FLY} F_{CLK}(V_{IN}(2+\alpha) - V_{OUT}(4+\alpha+\beta)), \tag{5}$$

$$P_{IN} = V_{IN} I_{IN} = C_{FLY} F_{CLK} V_{IN}(V_{IN}(1+\alpha) - V_{OUT}(2+\alpha)), \tag{6}$$

$$P_{OUT} = V_{OUT} I_{OUT} = C_{FLY} F_{CLK} V_{OUT}(V_{IN}(2+\alpha) - V_{OUT}(4+\alpha+\beta)). \tag{7}$$

The converter efficiency $\eta$ can be obtained by (8) and its output impedance $R_{OUT}$ by (9). Both $V_{OUT}$ and $F_{CLK}$ can be determined by (10) and (11), where $R_L$ is the load resistor and $P_{OUT} = V_{OUT}^2/R_L$.

$$\eta = \frac{P_{OUT}}{P_{IN}} = \frac{V_{OUT}(V_{IN}(2+\alpha) - V_{OUT}(4+\alpha+\beta))}{V_{IN}(V_{IN}(1+\alpha) - V_{OUT}(2+\alpha))}, \tag{8}$$

$$R_{OUT} = \frac{CR V_{IN} - V_{OUT}}{I_{OUT}} = \frac{V_{IN} - 2 V_{OUT}}{2 C_{FLY} F_{CLK}(V_{in}(2+\alpha) - V_{OUT}(4+\alpha+\beta))} = |_{\alpha,\beta=0} \frac{1}{4 C_{FLY} F_{CLK}}, \tag{9}$$

$$V_{OUT} = I_{OUT} R_L \Rightarrow V_{OUT} = \frac{C_{FLY} F_{CLK} R_L V_{IN}(2+\alpha)}{1 + C_{FLY} F_{CLK} R_L (4+\alpha+\beta)}, \tag{10}$$

$$F_{CLK} = \frac{V_{OUT}}{C_{FLY} R_L (V_{IN}(2+\alpha) - V_{OUT}(4+\alpha+\beta))} = \frac{P_{OUT}}{C_{FLY} V_{OUT}(V_{IN}(2+\alpha) - V_{OUT}(4+\alpha+\beta))}. \tag{11}$$

Figure 2 shows the converter's $\eta$ and $F_{CLK}$ as a function of $V_{IN}$ for different values of $\alpha$ and $\beta$, with $C_{FLY} = 100$ pF, and $P_{out} = 1$ mW. The graphs show that while both parasitic capacitances have a negative impact on both $\eta$ and $F_{CLK}$, the top parasitic capacitance has a smaller impact when compared to the bottom parasitic capacitance. Moreover, it pushes the peak efficiency for lower $V_{IN}$ values while decreasing $F_{CLK}$ for the same input/output ratio. This is because the charge absorbed on $\phi_1$ is supplied to $V_{OUT}$ on $\phi_2$. This acts like a parallel 1/1 converter and thus allowing the converter to work at a lower $F_{CLK}$ value for the same input/output voltage ratio. Hence, in this topology, when implementing the $C_{FLY}$ the highest parasitic plate should be connected as the top parasitic capacitance [9]. These equations were validated through electrical simulations in [10, 11].

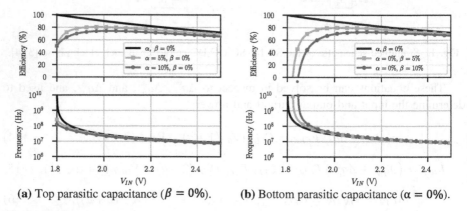

(a) Top parasitic capacitance ($\beta = 0\%$).     (b) Bottom parasitic capacitance ($\alpha = 0\%$).

**Fig. 2.** Efficiency as a function of $V_{IN}$, for $V_{OUT} = 0.9$ V, $C_{FLY} = 100$ pF, and $P_{out} = 1$ mW.

Expression (8) assumes that the clock phases are long enough to allow $C_{FLY}$ to completely charge (or discharge), however, the finite $R_{ON}$ value of the switches cause partial charging depending on $F_{CLK}$, hence it will have an impact on the converter efficiency [5]. According to [5], $R_{OUT}$ can be re-written to take in the effect of partial charging:

$$R_{OUT} = \frac{1}{\gamma} \frac{1}{4\,C_{FLY}\,F_{CLK}}, \tag{12}$$

this equation is identical to (9) except for a scaling factor, $\gamma$, which accounts for incomplete charging [5]. Let $\tau'$ be everything else that is in the exponential before $F_{CLK}$ ($\tau' = 2\,R_{ON_{tot}}\,C_{FLY}$), then the number of time constant in a period sets the value of $\gamma$. For 3 $\tau'$, the $\gamma$ value is 90.05%, for 4 $\tau'$, it is 96.40%, and for 5 $\tau'$ it is 98.66%. Thus, for values lower than $4\tau'$, the value of $\gamma$ drops significantly. Hence, $4\tau'$ offers a good compromise point for sizing the converter switches without having a significant impact on the converter's efficiency. The $4\tau'$ allows to size the switches $R_{ON}$ and thus determining the transistor's $W$. This allows to determine the power required to charge the gate switches' parasitic capacitance ($C_{GG}$), which will also impact the converter's efficiency.

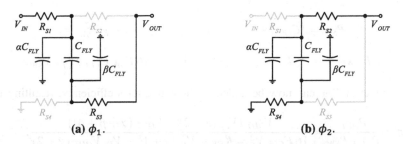

**Fig. 3.** Simplified schematic of the converter with the switches replaced by $R_{ON}$.

Figure 3 shows the converter's schematic with its ON switches replaced by the respective $R_{ON}$. Both $\phi_1$ and $\phi_2$ have the same time constant given by:

$$\tau = R_{ON_{tot}} C_{FLY} = \frac{1}{2F_{CLK}}, \tag{13}$$

where $R_{ON_{tot}} = R_{ON_{S1}} + R_{ON_{S2}}$ is the total resistance value of switches in series per phase. Assuming that $R_{ON_{S1}} = R_{ON_{S2}} = R_{ON}$ which means that $R_{ON} = R_{ON_{tot}}/2$, then, the $R_{ON}$ value for the $4\tau'$ operation point is given by

$$R_{ON_{total}} = \frac{1}{4\tau'} = \frac{1}{8\,C_{FLY}\,F_{CLK}} \Rightarrow R_{ON} = \frac{1}{16\,C_{FLY}\,F_{CLK}}. \tag{14}$$

For small drain-to-source voltages ($V_{DS} \ll V_{GS} - V_{TH}$), the switch $R_{ON}$ and $C_{GG}$ are given by:

$$R_{ON} \cong \frac{L}{C_{ox}\mu_n W(V_{GS} - V_{TH})} \approx \frac{k_R}{W}, \tag{15}$$

$$C_{GG} = C_{GD} + C_{GS} \cong WLC_{ox} + WC_{ov} \approx k_C W. \tag{16}$$

These equations show that $R_{ON}$ is inversely proportional to the transistor's width ($W$), and that $C_{GG}$ is directly proportional to $W$. Furthermore, if $V_{GS}$, $L$, $C_{ox}$ and $\mu_n$ are kept constant, and $V_{DS} \ll V_{GS} - V_{TH}$, then the previous equations can be approximated by a constant coefficient, $k_R$ and $k_C$, that relates both $R_{ON}$ and $C_{GG}$ with $W$ [10, 12]. Hence, $C_{GG}$ can be given by (17). The switches' power dissipation can be determined by summing all the switches' $C_{GG}$ and multiplying it by $F_{CLK}$ and the switches drive voltage $V_{SW}$ squared, as shown in Eq. (19). Notice that $P_{SW}$ is given by the sum of the

$k_R$ and $k_C$ coefficients of each switch, where $N$ is the total number of switches, where $K_{SW} = k_{C_1} k_{R_1} + k_{C_2} k_{R_2} + \ldots + k_{C_N} k_{R_N}$.

$$C_{GG} = \frac{K_R K_C}{R_{ON}} = 16 \, k_C \, k_R \, C_{FLY} \, F_{CLK}, \tag{17}$$

$$P_{SW} = (C_{GG_{S1}} + C_{GG_{S2}} + C_{GG_{S3}} + C_{GG_{S4}}) \, F_{CLK} \, V_{SW}^2 = \tag{18}$$

$$= 16 \, (k_{C_1} k_{R_1} + \ldots + k_{C_N} k_{R_N}) \, C_{FLY} \, F_{CLK}^2 \, V_{SW}^2 = 16 \, K_{SW} \, C_{FLY} \, F_{CLK}^2 \, V_{SW}^2. \tag{19}$$

The effect of $P_{SW}$ can now be added to the converter's efficiency, resulting in

$$\eta = \frac{P_{OUT}}{P_{IN} + P_{SW}} = \frac{V_{OUT} \, (V_{IN} \, (\alpha + 2) - V_{OUT} \, (\alpha + \beta + 4))}{16 \, F_{CLK} \, V_{OUT}^2 \, K_{SW} + V_{IN}^2 \, (\alpha + 1) - V_{IN} \, V_{OUT} \, (\alpha + 2)}. \tag{20}$$

Due to the $F_{CLK}^2$ in (19), $F_{CLK}$ does not cancel out in (20). Thus, replacing $F_{CLK}$ by (11) and considering that $C_{FLY}$ can be given by the capacitance area $A_c$ times $C_{den}$ of the device chosen to implement it, e.g. $10 \, \text{fF}/\mu\text{m}^2$ in the MOS capacitor. Then, $C_{FLY}$ can be re-written by $C_{FLY} = A_c \times C_{den}$. This gives $\eta$ as a function of $P_{OUT}$ per capacitance area, i.e. power density, as shown below.

$$\eta = \frac{V_{OUT} \, (V_{IN} \, (\alpha + 2) - V_{OUT} \, (\alpha + \beta + 4))}{V_{IN}^2 \, (\alpha + 1) - V_{IN} \, V_{OUT} \, (\alpha + 2) + \frac{16 \, K_{SW} \, P_{OUT} \, V_{OUT}}{A_c \, C_{den} \, (V_{IN} \, (2 + \alpha) - V_{OUT} \, (4 + \alpha + \beta))}}. \tag{21}$$

The equation above allows to determine the converter's efficiency as a function of the power density for a given $V_{IN}$ and $V_{OUT}$, and for a given $K_{SW}$, which depends on the type of transistors chosen to implement the switches. Considering four different cases, where the transistors are all implemented by 1.2 V ($k_R = 577.40 \, \Omega \cdot \mu\text{m}^2$ and $k_C = 1.34 \, \text{fF}/\mu\text{m}^2$) and 3.3 V ($k_R = 5337.56 \, \Omega \cdot \mu\text{m}^2$ and $k_C = 1.77 \, \text{fF}/\mu\text{m}^2$) NMOS transistors, 1.2 V ($k_R = 2709.51 \, \Omega \cdot \mu\text{m}^2$ and $k_C = 1.41 \, \text{fF}/\mu\text{m}^2$) and 3.3 V ($k_R = 20570.40 \, \Omega \cdot \mu\text{m}^2$ and $k_C = 1.95 \, \text{fF}/\mu\text{m}^2$) PMOS transistors, the $k_R$ and $k_C$ were taken for a $V_{GS} = 0.9$ V through electrical simulations. Figure 4 (a) and (b) show the efficiency (21) as a function of the power density for $V_{SW} = V_{OUT} = 0.9$ V and for $C_{FLY}$ implemented by a PMOS transistor ($C_{den} = 10\text{fF}/\mu\text{m}^2$, $\alpha = 4.5$ %, and $\beta \approx 0$ %). As expected, the graph clearly show that 1.2 V transistors are preferable in comparison with 3.3 V transistors. Furthermore, 1.2 V NMOS transistors allow maximizing the efficiency and power density. However, 1.2 V transistors may not be an option if their voltages exceed the transistor's breakdown voltage. Moreover, 1.2 V NMOS requires $V_{GS} > V_{th}$, which in the case switch $S_1$ it would require a gate voltage higher than $V_{IN}$. Hence, choosing to implement $S_1$ with a 1.2 V PMOS transistor can be a good compromise given the complexity of the NMOS driver would require.

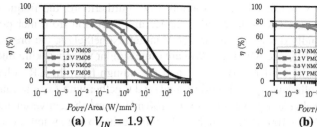

**Fig. 4.** Converter's $\eta$ as a function of $P_{OUT}/A_c$ for different switches' implementation with $V_{OUT} = 0.9$ V.

Figure 5 (a) and (b) show the efficiency (21) as a function of the power density with $S_{1,2,3}$ implemented with PMOS transistors and $S_4$ with an NMOS transistor, $C_{FLY}$ implemented with a PMOS transistor, and for $V_{OUT} = 0.9$ V. The graphs show that depending on the input voltage limit, the maximum power density, whilst keeping efficiency constant, is within the 10 to 100 mW/mm$^2$, depending if either 1.2 V or 3.3 V transistors are used.

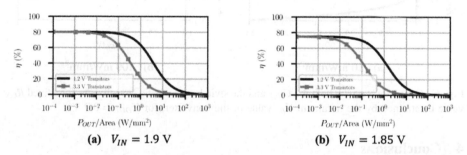

**Fig. 5.** Converter's $\eta$ as a function of $P_{OUT}/A_c$ with $S_{1,2,3}$ implemented with PMOS transistor and $S_4$ with NMOS transistor, for $V_{OUT} = 0.9$ V.

It is important to notice that once the switch is sized, the switches' $R_{ON}$ is fixed throughout the whole $V_{IN}$ range. In the previous graphs, the switch's $R_{ON}$ was modified according to the $V_{IN}$ value. In a real scenario, the converter's minimum $V_{IN}$ value must be fixed, which sets the minimum $R_{ON}$ value. Hence, the previous analysis is used to set $R_{ON_{Min}}$ and then $\eta$ is recalculated using the constant $R_{ON_{Min}}$ value throughout the whole $V_{IN}$ range.

Figure 6 (a) and (b) show $\eta$ recalculated using the $R_{ON}$ calculated for different $V_{IN}$, for 10 mW/mm$^2$ and 100 mW/mm$^2$. The efficiency values after $V_{IN_{limit}}$ are not drawn because $F_{CLK}$ increases beyond the $4\tau'$ limit resulting in incomplete settling, making the equation no longer valid. These graphs show that as $V_{IN_{limit}}$ gets closer to the voltage CR there is a significantly impact on $\eta$, especially at high power density values, such as 100 mW/mm$^2$. Hence, avoiding working close to the CR voltage value (1.8) is recommend because the value of $R_{ON}$ is extremely low. Furthermore, the frequency increases rapidly close to the CR voltage value, hence any deviation from that point would cause $V_{OUT}$ to rapidly deviate from the 0.9 V target. Nonetheless, the previous analysis with the variable $R_{ON}$ and with fixed $R_{ON}$ are quite similar when working under the maximum power density ($< 100\,\text{mW}/\text{mm}^2$) and far enough from the CR voltage value ($V_{IN} > 1.85$). The efficiency plot should be analyzed together with $F_{CLK}$ because, as Fig. 6 (b) shows, to achieve a power density of $100\,\text{mW}/\text{mm}^2$ the converter must work at frequencies of 10 to 100 MHz, which adds complexity to the system design, mainly the clock generator and the switch drivers. Hence lower power densities, such has the ones in Fig. 6 (a) may be preferable, due to the lower $F_{CLK}$ value.

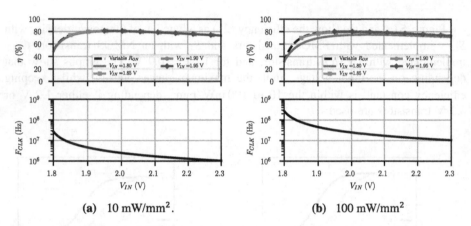

**(a)**   10 mW/mm$^2$.

**(b)**   100 mW/mm$^2$

**Fig. 6.** Converter's $\eta$ with both the $C_{FLY}$ and the switches' parasitic capacitances for a fixed $R_{ON}$ value determined by the minimum $V_{IN}$ value of the converter, for $V_{OUT} = 0.9$ V.

## 4   Conclusions

This paper describes a theorical analysis that allows characterizing the performance of an SC DC-DC converter for a given technological node. In this case, the 130 nm CMOS technology was chosen to implement a 1/2 SP SC DC-DC converter for converting an input voltage range of 2.3 to 1.8 V to an output voltage of 0.9 V. The results show that with this topology and technology the maximum efficiency would be around 80% and the power density per area in the range of 10 to 100 mW/mm$^2$, depending on the transistors chosen to implement the passive devices.

**Acknowledgments.** This work was supported by the Portuguese Foundation for Science and Technology under a Ph.D. Grant (SFRH/BD/115543/2016), and UIDB/00066/2020 (CTS – Center of Technology and Systems).

# References

1. Abdelwahab, S., Hamdaoui, B., Guizani, M., Rayes, A.: Enabling smart cloud services through remote sensing: an internet of everything enabler. IEEE Internet Things J. **1**(3), 276–288 (2014)
2. Liu, X., Ravichandran, K., Sanchez-Sinencio, E.: A switched capacitor energy harvester based on a single-cycle criterion for mppt to eliminate storage capacitor. IEEE Trans. Circ. Syst. I Regul. Pap. **65**(2), 1–11 (2017)
3. Bang, S., Wang, A., Giridhar, B., Blaauw, D., Sylvester, D.: A fully integrated successive-approximation switched-capacitor DC-DC converter with 31 mV output voltage resolution. In: Digest of Technical Papers - IEEE International Solid-State Circuits Conference, vol. 56, no. June 2009, pp. 370–371 (2013)
4. Bang, S., et al.: A Successive-approximation switched-capacitor DC–DC converter with resolution of for a wide range of input and output voltages. IEEE J. Solid-State Circ. **51**(2), 543–556 (2016)
5. Harjani, R., Chaubey, S.: A unified framework for capacitive series-parallel DC-DC converter design. In: Proceedings of the IEEE 2014 Custom Integrated Circuits Conference, pp. 1–8 (2014)
6. Le, H.P., Sanders, S.R., Alon, E.: Design techniques for fully integrated switched-capacitor DC-DC converters. IEEE J. Solid-State Circ. **46**(9), 2120–2131 (2011)
7. Sarafianos, A., Steyaert, M.: Fully integrated wide input voltage range capacitive DC-DC converters: the folding dickson converter. IEEE J. Solid-State Circ. **50**(7), 1560–1570 (2015)
8. Kudva, S.S., Harjani, R.: Fully integrated capacitive DC–DC converter with all-digital ripple mitigation technique. IEEE J. Solid-State Circ. **48**(8), 1910–1920 (2013)
9. Madeira, R., Paulino, N.: Improving the efficiency of a 2:1 SC DC-DC converter using the parasitic capacitances. In: 2015 Conference on Design of Circuits and Integrated Systems (DCIS), pp. 1–5 (2015)
10. Serra, H., Madeira, R., Paulino, N.: Analysis of a multi-ratio switched capacitor DC-DC converter for a supercapacitor power supply. In: Technological Innovation for Cloud-Based Engineering Systems, pp. 477–485 (2015)
11. Madeira, R., Paulino, N.: Analysis and implementation of a power management unit with a multiratio switched capacitor DC-DC converter for a supercapacitor power supply. Int. J. Circ. Theory Appl. **44**(11), 2018–2034 (2016)
12. Carvalho, C.: CMOS Indoor Light Energy Harvesting System for Wireless Sensing. Faculdade de Ciências e Tecnologia (2014)

# Energy Control

# Prospects for the Improvement of Energy Performance in Agroindustry Using Phase Change Materials

Carlos Simão[1,2], João Murta-Pina[2,3(✉)], Luís Coelho[4,5],
João Pássaro[4,5], Rui Amaral Lopes[3], Fernando Reboredo[2,6],
Tiago Jorge[7], and Diogo Lemos[8]

[1] CQS Unipessoal Lda., Largo São Sebastião 44, 1050-205 Lisbon, Portugal
csimao@cqs.pt
[2] NOVA School of Science and Technology, Campus da FCT NOVA,
2829-516 Caparica, Portugal
{jmmp, fhr}@fct.unl.pt
[3] Centre of Technology and Systems (CTS-UNINOVA),
Campus da FCT NOVA, 2829-516 Caparica, Portugal
rm.lopes@fct.unl.pt
[4] Polytechnic Institute of Setúbal, Campus do IPS, Estefanilha,
2910-761 Setúbal, Portugal
{luis.coelho, joao.passaro}@estsetubal.ips.pt
[5] Centre for Energy and Environment Research (CINEA), Campus do IPS,
Estefanilha, 2910-761 Setúbal, Portugal
[6] Geobiosciences, Geotechnologies, and Geoengineering (GeoBioTec),
Campus da FCT NOVA, 2829-516 Caparica, Portugal
[7] Metalogonde – Indústria Metalomecânica, Lda., Zona Industrial N.º 2,
3720-069 Loureiro, Portugal
tiago.jorge@metalogonde.com
[8] Novarroz – Produtos Alimentares, S.A., Rua da Moura N.º 43,
3720-581 Adães, Portugal
diogo.lemos@novarroz.pt

**Abstract.** The use of Phase Change Materials (PCMs), able to store latent heat, represents an opportunity to improve energy efficiency in the agroindustry by means of thermal energy storage. PCMs provide higher energy density then sensible heat storage mediums, thus paving the way to multiple applications, like supporting the integration of renewables or allowing for new storage architectures, decentralized and directly installed in the chain production equipment, creating e.g. the opportunity to recover and value low-grade operational heat sub-products. Such new and decentralized architecture, not currently applied in agroindustry, is proposed in this work. A chocolate tempering machine using an organic PCM is conceived and analyzed using ANSYS Fluent software for computational fluid dynamics simulations, comparing the main aspects in the storage capacity and discharging process with a conventional sensitive heat storage solution that uses water. PCMs allows improving the stored energy, keeping the chocolate in the working temperature after being tempered for more than four times longer than using only hot water. If the PCMs are charged by renewables, the self-consumption ratio can be improved while providing energy flexibility to the user.

© IFIP International Federation for Information Processing 2020
Published by Springer Nature Switzerland AG 2020
L. M. Camarinha-Matos et al. (Eds.): DoCEIS 2020, IFIP AICT 577, pp. 277–289, 2020.
https://doi.org/10.1007/978-3-030-45124-0_26

**Keywords:** Agroindustry · Latent heat storage · Phase Change Materials (PCM) · Thermal energy storage

# 1   Introduction

Agroindustry is a broad sector, that can be defined as the "post-harvest activities involved in the transformation, preservation, and preparation of agricultural products for intermediate or final consumption" [1]. It involves commercializing and adding value to agricultural products, and the links between enterprises and supply chains for developing, transforming and distributing those products [2]. A broader definition of agroindustry, although not worldwide accepted, involves forestry activities, leather products, and cotton textiles, i.e. non-food sectors [3], beyond fishery activities.

According to the Food and Agriculture Organization (FAO) of the United Nations, agriculture and agroindustry systems are characterized by a high dependency of energy, in particular, fossil fuels, accounting for around 30% of worldwide energy consumption and 22% of greenhouse gases emissions (GHG) [4]. Specifically, for the food sector, FAO envisages the transition to energy-smart food systems as a means to make them energy sustainable, with low GHG emissions, more robust to energy price variations, and able to contribute to food safety and sustainable development. This can be achieved by the simultaneous action in distinct but strongly interlinked vectors, namely energy efficiency, renewable energy integration, and circular economy.

Thermal energy storage (TES), and the management of stored energy, is an essential feature for the processing and transformation of food raw materials. It usually relies on sensible heat, where the storage medium increases its temperature while storing heat. Water is often used due to its low cost and availability, but its applicability is limited to temperatures ranging from the freezing to the boiling points i.e. 0 to 100 °C (at 1 atm), although this is still adequate for many agroindustry processes. Water is also inert (non-toxic, non-flammable, and non-corrosive through the addition of corrosion inhibitors), and has the highest volumetric thermal capacity (4.17 MJ/m$^3$ · K) when compared to other mediums typically used for sensible heat storage [5]. The volume of water required for an application is calculated straightforward, using the requisites on thermal energy/power, as well as the corresponding temperature change. In addition, water can be directly integrated with solar thermal systems, and its high thermal stratification ability has demonstrated to improve the efficiency of TES systems.

Unlike sensible heat, latent heat storage allows storing thermal energy at a constant temperature, through the phase change of a material. Materials used for this purpose are called Phase Change Materials (PCM) and water is itself a PCM, allowing storing thermal energy at 100 °C when changing to its gaseous phase, or at 0 °C when changing to its solid phase. PCMs with adequate temperature and enthalpy of phase change have the potential of being directly integrated into agroindustry equipment and operations. This is foreseen to allow for higher amounts of stored energy for the same volume and temperature range when comparing to sensible heat storage, while passively maintaining the operating temperature. Simultaneously, new solutions and approaches for energy efficiency are foreseen, like those based on distributed energy storage, directly integrated into the production chain equipment. This has not been applied in the agroindustry sector so far and is proposed in this work to improve the energy performance of that equipment. A chocolate tempering machine is used as a case study for the paradigm of distributed TES, demonstrating to be able to assist the integration of renewables while additionally providing energy flexibility.

This work aims at answering the following research question: *is it possible to improve the energy performance of the agroindustry sector by means of storing thermal energy in PCM materials, with a reduced impact on the production chain equipment?* The following hypothesis is defined: *if it is possible to find a PCM adequate for agroindustry critical stages temperatures, it should be possible to apply and operate it in chain production equipment, in a way that allows maximizing its energy performance.*

In the next section, the relation of the present work to the theme "Technological Innovation to Life Improvement" is described. PCM principles and characteristics are presented in Sect. 3, while the energy consumption in the agroindustry is characterized in Sect. 4. The potential applications of PCMs in that sector are summarized in Sect. 5, and the chocolate tempering machine case study is described in Sect. 6. Conclusions and future work are drawn in Sect. 7.

## 2 Relation with Technological Innovation for Life Improvement

The technological innovation proposed in this work, namely a distributed storage concept for the agroindustry production chain equipment, is related to life improvement by several means. It aims at assisting the integration of renewables and providing energy flexibility in that sector, which ultimately contributes to increasing the competitiveness of agroindustry companies by decreasing their energy bill. At the same time, it allows reducing the consumption of fossil fuels and associated GHG, which is a global concern.

## 3 Phase Change Materials

As mentioned, storing thermal energy as latent heat relies on the phase change of a material, often between solid and liquid phases, but also between distinct solid phases or between liquid and vapor phases. Throughout the phase change process, the temperature remains constant, see Fig. 1, while the energy at the molecular level is increased. In sensible heat storage (SHS), the amount of thermal energy stored, $Q$, is given by [6]

$$Q = m \cdot \overline{C}_p \cdot (T_f - T_i),\tag{1}$$

where $m$ is the mass of the storage medium, and $\overline{C}_p$ is the average specific heat between the initial and final temperatures of the medium, respectively $T_i$ and $T_f$.

In latent heat storage (LHS) a term corresponding to the heat exchanged during the phase change adds to the stored energy [6],

$$Q = m \cdot \left[ \overline{C}_{sp} \cdot (T_{pc} - T_i) + a_m \cdot \Delta H_m + \overline{C}_{lp} \cdot (T_f - T_{pc}) \right], \qquad (2)$$

where $T_{pc}$ is the phase change temperature, $\overline{C}_{sp}$ is the average specific heat between $T_i$ and $T_{pc}$ (corresponding to the solid phase, in the solid to liquid transition), $\overline{C}_{lp}$ is the average specific heat between $T_{pc}$ and $T_f$ (corresponding to the liquid phase), $a_m$ is the fraction of the total mass that is melted, and $\Delta H_m$ is the phase change enthalpy. Latent heat storage is thus a more efficient TES method.

There are no relevant sector or regulatory barriers to the application of PCMs, and its exploration is often dictated by their cost, besides technical characteristics that may limit the use of these materials. Some challenges that industry and researchers face are developing materials able to store higher amounts of energy in less mass, at different temperature levels, that are thus able to address multiple energy efficiency solutions, in distinct sectors. Besides agroindustry, PCMs have been used mostly in construction, automotive, storage and transportation of medication and food, telecommunications, solar energy, and space industry, among others [6, 7].

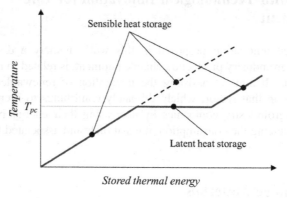

**Fig. 1.** Sensible and latent heat storage, where $T_{pc}$ is the temperature of the phase change (adapted from [8]).

PCMs are classified into three major groups [9]:

*Organic.* These can be divided into paraffin (saturated hydrocarbons) and non-paraffin (fatty acids, alcohols, and glycols) compounds. These materials crystallize with negligible or no supercooling [10], and they show a wide range of phase-change temperatures, which allows them to address a multitude of applications. Yet, they have a relatively low thermal conductivity and they are incompatible with some plastic materials. One major drawback is the fact that they are inflammable.

*Inorganic.* These are essentially salt hydrates and metallic alloys. The latter show a high phase change temperature, in the range of hundreds of Celsius degrees, that limits

its exploration often to solar energy applications [11], although several advances with low melting point metals and alloys are undergoing [7]. Hydrated salts are composed of inorganic salts and water. The phase change of these PCMs corresponds, in reality, to the hydration and dehydration of the salt [9]. They are cheaper to produce than organic PCMs and have higher latent heat per mass and volume unit, as well as higher thermal conductivity. Besides, they are not flammable and have a lower variation in the densities of the liquid and solid phase, when compared to the latter. Their main disadvantage is incongruent melting and supercooling [9], being in addition often corrosive to metals.

*Eutectic.* These are composed of two or more substances with similar phase-change temperatures, that melt and solidify congruently, making a mixture of the components crystals throughout crystallization [6]. A wide range of such PCMs is available, including combinations of organic, inorganic and organic-inorganic substances. Their main advantage is the possibility of adjusting their melting point to match the required operating point. Yet, their latent heat and specific heat are lower than the ones of paraffins and salt hydrates [12].

PCMs typically contact with other elements, requiring encapsulation to avoid leaking in their surroundings or corrosion issues [12].

## 4   Energy Consumption in the Agroindustry Sector

Agroindustry, as an aggregator of activities related to the processing of raw materials generated by agriculture (including livestock), fishery and forestry, integrates the value chain between production and consumption, for food and non-food purposes. Agroindustry itself is considered a non-intensive energy industry, yet, due to its size, it is a major global energy consumer [13].

Figure 2 illustrates the per capita energy consumption and GHG emissions of the EU-27 related to the food sector. Its value chain is divided into agriculture (including forestry and fishery), processing, logistics, packaging, use and end of life. Agroindustry, ranging from agriculture (processing) to packaging, is thus responsible for more than 80% of the energy consumption and for 90% of GHG emissions of the food sector. The industrial processing stage represents almost 30% of energy consumption in the food value chain, which corresponded in 2013 to burning around 655 L of diesel fuel per EU-27 inhabitant [14].

Agroindustry requires electrical and thermal energy for distinct purposes, besides the raw material production, namely its transportation, processing, preservation, packaging, and storage, as well as non-process uses, related to e.g. lighting or space heating and cooling [15]. Electrical energy may typically be used as the source of any process, namely those requiring thermal energy, while burning fuels to produce the latter has more restricted use.

The share of electrical and thermal (fuels) energy to supply each of the previous processes may change drastically within companies, depending on its positioning on the value chain, its size, its geographical location or the type of products produced, among many others [15]. According to the analysis in [14], cold supply and electric motors are responsible for more than half of the electrical energy consumption in the food sector chain. Nevertheless, while in some agroindustries electrical energy may constitute nearly all the energy sources, as wineries [16], others may depend more on fuels, like olive oil mills [17] (these examples concern representative companies in the EU). It is estimated that 85% of the fuels burnt by agroindustry aims producing steam and hot water for cooking, sterilizing, washing and sanitation [18].

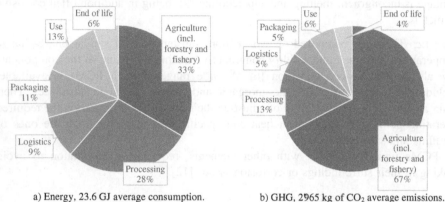

a) Energy, 23.6 GJ average consumption.     b) GHG, 2965 kg of $CO_2$ average emissions.

**Fig. 2.**  Per capita statistics of the energy consumption and GHG emissions of the food sector in the EU-27, in 2013 (adapted from [14]).

Despite the previous indicators, energy corresponds to a small fraction of the total cost of production in the food sector, namely 3%, which may often constitute an obstacle to adopting energy efficiency practices in this sector [13]. Nevertheless, considering the scale of the food sector, this 3% factor is relevant.

# 5   PCM Application and Improvement of Energy Performance

TES with PCMs has several potential applications, as previously mentioned. The main prospects for its use in the agroindustry sector are described below.

## 5.1   Industrial Waste Heat Recovery

Agroindustry is a major user of low-temperature process heat, i.e. below 120 °C. Several applications making use of storing and reusing industrial waste heat (IWH) have already been identified, such as for heating fresh water for the different food processes or heating a factory clean-up water. IWH could be collected e.g. from the refrigeration systems commonly used in agroindustrial plants. A review of these topics is described in [18].

## 5.2   Heating and Reduction of Peak Temperatures in Greenhouses

PCMs find applications in the building envelope, to provide extra thermal inertia [19]. In agroindustry, they have been applied to heat greenhouses, often with solar air collectors, keeping its temperature stable and reducing peak temperatures, such as the ones occurring in summer [20, 21].

## 5.3   Food Storage and Transportation

There are commercially available containers with PCMs to store and transport food (and beverage) products, allowing them to keep the latter either hot, either cold, for the time required for delivering after production [8].

## 5.4   Support to the Integration of Renewables

PCMs can assist in the integration of renewables, particularly solar-based technologies, like photovoltaics (PV) and solar thermal. PV produces electrical energy which can be used in resistors to generate heat, and this allows charging PCMs (although this is not technically reasonable, and PV plants in self-consumption are connected to a whole user, not to particular loads [22]). Solar thermal consists of using solar radiation to increase the temperature of a working fluid, like water, and this energy can later be transferred to a PCM through a heat exchanger, also charging it. These schemes are flexible in what concerns the temperature of the targeted PCM. Controlling the heat generated by Joule effect in a resistor is trivial, and distinct solar thermal collectors allow addressing distinct temperature ranges [23]. PCMs are thus foreseen to maximize the self-consumption ratio, i.e. the amount of renewable energy produced locally that is consumed in the premises of the user.

## 5.5   Provision of Energy Flexibility

As illustrated in Sect. 5, the thermal properties of PCMs can be used to decouple energy consumption from a device's heating needs. This is an instrumental property to provide energy flexibility [24], which can be used for different purposes. As an example, the energy flexibility provided by TES with PCMs can be used to improve the self-consumption of local PV generation or to shift electric energy consumption to periods with cheaper tariffs. The characterization and use of the energy flexibility provided by these devices can be supported by the work already developed under the context of IEA (International Energy Agency) EBC (Energy in Buildings and Communities program) Annex 67, which defined the energy flexibility of a building as *"the ability to manage its demand and generation according to local climate conditions, user needs, and energy network requirements"* [25]. A comprehensive review of methodologies used to characterize energy flexibility of buildings can be found in [26], while a generic methodology, which can also be applied to TES with PCMs, has been described in [27].

## 6    Application Example

The goal of this research is to assess the opportunity of using PCMs for multiple purposes, namely building a distributed TES paradigm, providing energy flexibility to agroindustry and supporting the integration of renewables. For such, a chocolate tempering process was selected as a case study. Chocolate must undergo a tempering pre-treatment process, which allows a controlled crystallization of the vegetable fat in its composition in one of six possible polymorphic states, named as form V [28]. This form is considered ideal for the manufacturing of chocolate products. Besides good color, texture, hardness, gloss and demolding properties, crystallization in the latter form leads to a melting point of around 28 to 32 °C (depending on the composition), which allows chocolate to be solid at ambient temperature and to melt in the mouth [29], thus making it ideal for consumption.

Simulations will demonstrate that PCMs allow improving the performance of the tempering machine, keeping the chocolate at the working temperature for a longer period.

### 6.1    Chocolate Tempering Process and Equipment

Tempering requires an industrial water bath-based equipment, where chocolate can be processed continuously or in batch. This work refers to the latter, and a tempering kettle is used for the batch process, see Fig. 3. In this equipment, water is heated up to a temperature set-point by an electric resistor located at the bottom of the kettle, where a simple on-off control system maintains the temperature inside an admissible range. The set-points are changed according to a predetermined temperature profile.

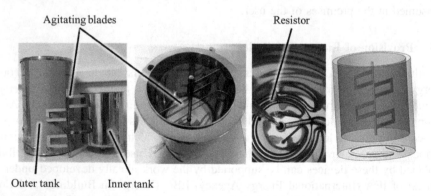

Agitating blades    Resistor

Outer tank    Inner tank

**Fig. 3.** Water bath-based chocolate tempering kettle considered in the work. The rightmost image is the computer representation of the equipment.

The parameters of the tempering kettle are given in Table 1. The equipment is built by two stainless steel (A316) coaxial cylindrical tanks. A water jacket is built between the tanks and, in the inner one, an agitator assures chocolate homogenization.

Water is used to provide a temperature profile required to temper the chocolate, but also for SHS. Water allows keeping an adequate working temperature during the several hours that may be required for the chocolate molding tasks, where it is transformed in products like candies or chocolate bars. Water temperature is controlled by an electric resistor at the base of the kettle. An example of a tempering cycle (and its description) is shown in Fig. 4. After the cycle, chocolate is ready for molding, being kept at a working temperature of 32 to 36 °C.

**Table 1.** Parameters of the tempering kettle used in this work.

| Parameter | Value |
|---|---|
| Water volume | 14 L |
| Maximum chocolate batch volume | 22 L |
| Power of the heating resistor | 3 kW |
| Typical maximum tempering duration (for commercial chocolate) | 40 min |

## 6.2 Simulations

Computational fluid dynamics (CFD) simulations were run to assess and compare the performance of the tempering machine, both with a PCM and water as heat storage mediums. The water jacket will be filled either with water (SHS), either with a PCM (LHS). Simulations concern stage 5 of Fig. 4.

**PCM Selection.** Paraffin was selected as a phase change material, with parameters described in Table 2. This choice, instead of a salt hydrate, is justified by the vertical configuration of the equipment, which may lead to segregation and total reversibility of the phase change cycles of the PCM.

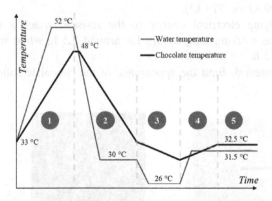

**Fig. 4.** Kreuter interval pre-crystallization procedure (adapted from [30]), which includes the following stages [28, 30]: 1 – chocolate is heated until all fat is melted; 2 – precooling, without crystal formation; 3 – slow cooling, for growth of stable type V crystals, where unstable are also formed; 4 – re-heating, for melting of unstable crystals; 5 – end of cycle, chocolate is kept at a working temperature, allow molding it into the desired form.

**CFD Simulations.** Simulations were performed in ANSYS Fluent software. The geometry and respective mesh are shown in Fig. 5.

A transient thermal analysis was performed, to study the change in thermal energy stored as sensible heat and as latent heat, using both materials, water and paraffin, as well as the process of cooling and solidification of the chocolate, its relevant thermal gradients and the evolution of its liquid mass fraction. The Boussinesq approach, the $\kappa - \varepsilon$ turbulence model and the Fluent's PCM model. As initial conditions, it was considered both for the chocolate, as well as for the PCM, that they were totally liquid at 36 °C. As boundary conditions, an air temperature of 20 °C was considered. Convection losses were set to $3 \text{ W} \cdot \text{m}^{-2} \cdot \text{K}^{-1}$. Figure 6 shows the results of the water-chocolate scenario and Fig. 7 the PCM-chocolate scenario.

**Table 2.** Properties of the selected PCM.

| Property | Value |
|---|---|
| Phase change temperature | 35 °C |
| Density, $\rho$ | 776 kg $\cdot$ m$^{-3}$ |
| Specific heat, $c_p$ | 2.37 kJ $\cdot$ kg$^{-1}$ $\cdot$ K$^{-1}$ |
| Thermal conductivity, $k$ | 0.18 W $\cdot$ m$^{-1}$ $\cdot$ K$^{-1}$ |
| Dynamic viscosity, $\mu$ | 5.9 kg $\cdot$ m$^{-1}$ $\cdot$ s$^{-1}$ |
| Phase change enthalpy, $\Delta H_m$ | 130 kJ $\cdot$ kg$^{-1}$ |

The comparison of temperatures' evolution in both scenarios is shown in Fig. 8(a), while the liquid fraction of chocolate also for both cases is represented in Fig. 8(b). From those figures, the following can be concluded:

- The amount of thermal energy stored in the PCM nearly doubles when compared to the water (1799 kJ vs. 879 kJ).
- Without supplying electrical energy to the resistor, water is able to keep the chocolate in the working temperature for around 2.5 h, while with the PCM this goes beyond 12 h.
- The previous intervals limit the appearance of the chocolate solid phase.

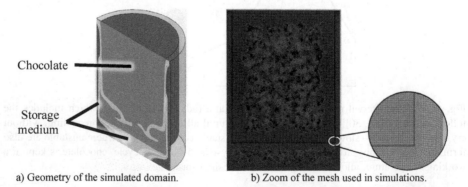

a) Geometry of the simulated domain.    b) Zoom of the mesh used in simulations.

**Fig. 5.** Geometry built in ANSYS Fluent CFD simulation software. A hexahedral hybrid mesh was used, with 150000 elements and 150000 nodes.

**Fig. 6.** Temperature evolution in the simulation of the scenario with water used for SHS. After 9000 s, water temperature decreased to 32 °C and the chocolate temperature is around 35.5 °C.

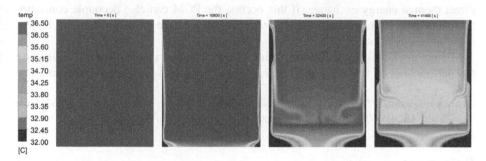

**Fig. 7.** Temperature evolution in the simulation of the scenario with the PCM used for LHS. After 41400 s the PCM is still all solid, and the chocolate is hotter than in the previous case.

To be able to obtain an amount of storage by sensible heat comparable to the one by latent heat (with the PCM at 36 °C), the water temperature would have to be raised above 50 °C, which could represent a risk to the conservation of organoleptic and functional properties for other food products and applications.

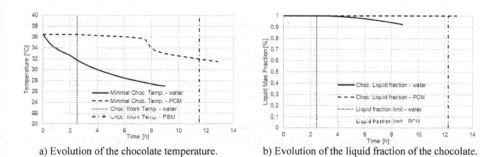

a) Evolution of the chocolate temperature.          b) Evolution of the liquid fraction of the chocolate.

**Fig. 8.** Comparison of the performance of the system either with water, either with PCM. The intersection of the vertical lines with the curves gives the moment where both the minimum chocolate temperature is reached, in (a), or the minimum liquid fraction, in (b).

# 7 Conclusion and Further Work

In this work it was demonstrated that the PCM, used as a storage medium, allowed improving the performance of an industrial tempering machine, keeping chocolate at the working temperature for longer. One key aspect, not mentioned in the case study description, is that to go above the 35 °C phase change temperature of the PCM, as required by the tempering process, additional energy needs to be supplied to the material. This is clear from (1) and Fig. 1, and that additional energy corresponds to the one that is stored in the PCM when its phase changes. Therefore, in this case, to gain the advantages of PCMs, improving the energy performance of the system, that surplus energy needs to be free of charge, i.e. should be provided by renewables. Solar energy is suited for this application, as it can charge the PCM either by photovoltaics or by direct thermal energy exchange. If this occurs, the PCM can also decouple consumption from generation, thus providing energy flexibility to the system and improving the self-consumption ratio.

Future work will consist of developing the encapsulation that will allow optimizing the performance of the PCM and running real experiments to validate simulations.

**Acknowledgments.** This work was partially supported by the Fundação para a Ciência e Tecnologia, UIDB/00066/2020 (CTS – Center of Technology and Systems).

# References

1. United Nations Industrial Development Organization (UNIDO): Industrial Development Report 2009: Breaking In and Moving Up: New Industrial Challenges for the Bottom Billion and the Middle-Income Countries (2009)
2. Konig, G., Silva, C.A., da Mhlanga, N.: Enabling environments for agribusiness and agro-industries development: Regional and country perspectives (2013)
3. The Food and Agriculture Organization of the United Nations, The United Nations Industrial Development Organization: Agro-industries for Development. CAB International (2009)
4. Food and Agriculture Organization: Policy Brief: The Case for Energy-Smart Food Systems (2014)
5. Cabeza, L.F. (ed.): Advances in Thermal Energy Storage Systems: Methods and Applications. Woodhead Publishing, Cambridge (2015)
6. Sharma, A., Tyagi, V.V., Chen, C.R., Buddhi, D.: Review on thermal energy storage with phase change materials and applications. Renew. Sustain. Energy Rev. **13**, 318–345 (2009)
7. Ge, H., Li, H., Mei, S., Liu, J.: Low melting point liquid metal as a new class of phase change material: an emerging frontier in energy area. Renew. Sustain. Energy Rev. **21**, 331–346 (2013)
8. Mehling, H., Cabeza, L.F.: Heat and Cold Storage with PCM - An up to date Introduction into Basics and Applications. Springer, Heidelberg (2008). https://doi.org/10.1007/978-3-540-68557-9
9. Sarbu, I., Sebarchievici, C.: A comprehensive review of thermal energy storage. Sustainability **10**, 191 (2018)
10. Oró, E., de Gracia, A., Castell, A., Farid, M.M., Cabeza, L.F.: Review on phase change materials (PCMs) for cold thermal energy storage applications. Appl. Energy **99**, 513–533 (2012)

11. Pielichowska, K., Pielichowski, K.: Phase change materials for thermal energy storage. Prog. Mater Sci. **65**, 67–123 (2014)
12. Su, W., Darkwa, J., Kokogiannakis, G.: Review of solid–liquid phase change materials and their encapsulation technologies. Renew. Sustain. Energy Rev. **48**, 373–391 (2015)
13. Muller, D.C.A., Marechal, F.M.A., Wolewinski, T., Roux, P.J.: An energy management method for the food industry. Appl. Therm. Eng. **27**, 2677–2686 (2007)
14. Monforti-Ferrario, F., et al.: Energy use in the EU food sector: State of play and opportunities for improvement. Publications Office (2015)
15. Latini, A., Viola, C., Scoccianti, M., Campiotti, C.A.: Efficient Fruit and Vegetables Processing Plants, Handbook (2014)
16. Fuentes-Pila, J., García, J.L.: Efficient Wineries, Handbook (2014)
17. Baptista, F., Murcho, D., Silva, L.L.: Efficient Olive Oil Mills, Handbook (2014)
18. Miró, L., Gasia, J., Cabeza, L.F.: Thermal energy storage (TES) for industrial waste heat (IWH) recovery: a review. Appl. Energy **179**, 284–301 (2016)
19. Kuznik, F., David, D., Johannes, K., Roux, J.J.: A review on phase change materials integrated in building walls. Renew. Sustain. Energy Rev. **15**, 379–391 (2011)
20. Hassanien, R.H.E., Li, M., Lin, W.D.: Advanced applications of solar energy in agricultural greenhouses. Renew. Sustain. Energy Rev. **54**, 989–1001 (2016)
21. Kürklü, A.: Energy storage applications in greenhouses by means of phase change materials (PCMs): a review. Renew. Energy **13**, 89–103 (1998)
22. Chiaroni, D., Chiesa, V., Colasanti, L., Cucchiella, F., D'Adamo, I., Frattini, F.: Evaluating solar energy profitability: a focus on the role of self-consumption. Energy Convers. Manag. **88**, 317–331 (2014)
23. Pérez-García, M., Silva, R., Cabrera Corral, F.J.: Solar heat for agro-industrial processes: an analysis of its potential use in Southern Spain. In: Proceedings of the EuroSun 2014 Conference, pp. 1–9. International Solar Energy Society, Freiburg (2015)
24. Pereira, T.C., Lopes, R.A., Martins, J.: Exploring the energy flexibility of electric water heaters. Energies **13**, 1–11 (2019)
25. Jensen, S.Ø., et al.: IEA EBC annex 67 energy flexible buildings. Energy Build. **155**, 25–34 (2017)
26. Reynders, G., Amaral Lopes, R., Marszal-Pomianowska, A., Aelenei, D., Martins, J., Saelens, D.: Energy flexible buildings: an evaluation of definitions and quantification methodologies applied to thermal storage. Energy Build. **166**, 372–390 (2018)
27. Junker, R.G., et al.: Characterizing the energy flexibility of buildings and districts. Appl. Energy **225**, 175–182 (2018)
28. Cohen, K.C., Luccas, V.: Review: tempering or precrystallization of chocolate. Brazilian J. Food Technol. **7**, 23–30 (2004)
29. Baichoo, N., MacNaughtan, W., Mitchell, J.R., Farhat, I.A.: A STEPSCAN differential scanning calorimetry study of the thermal behavior of chocolate. Food Biophys. **1**, 169–177 (2006)
30. Beckett, S.T., Fowler, M.S., Ziegler, G.R.: Beckett's Industrial Chocolate Manufacture and Use. Wiley Blackwell, Hoboken (2015)

# Modeling of Asymmetric Supercapacitor Cells Based on Electrode's Laboratorial Tests Data

Leonardo Malburg[1](✉) and Rita Pereira[1,2,3](✉)

[1] Instituto Superior de Engenharia de Lisboa (ISEL),
R. Conselheiro Emídio Navarro 1, 1959-007 Lisbon, Portugal
a44351@alunos.isel.pt, rpereira@deea.isel.ipl.pt
[2] LCEC, R. Conselheiro Emídio Navarro 1, 1959-007 Lisbon, Portugal
[3] ISRC, Rua Dr. António Bernardino de Almeida, 431, 4200-072 Porto, Portugal

**Abstract.** This paper concerns the modeling of asymmetric supercapacitor cells based on electrode's data obtained throughout laboratorial tests, such as hydrogen bubble evolution electrodeposition. The electrode's data type here implemented concerns three electrodes system tests, which are designed to provide a single electrode output. This procedure provides instructions on the extraction of electrodes tests parameters, the device's design throughout dimensional basis and comparison with commercially available products and the estimation of energetic output by forecasting the resulting capacitance, voltage, energy and mass of the theoretical supercapacitor.

**Keywords:** Supercapacitor · Energy storage systems · Hybrid supercapacitor

## 1 Introduction

Among the various known commercial energy storage devices, supercapacitors or electrochemical capacitors, are highly rated due to their interesting characteristics such as grater power density, cyclability and longer service life [1, 2], resulting in an overwhelming candidate as part of the global energy crisis solution. Such devices can be generically divided in four different types, high voltage ceramic capacitors, electric double-layer capacitors, pseudocapacitors and hybrid supercapacitors [1].

Although the mentioned characteristics, those devices lack energy density when compared to electrochemical batteries, which is fundamental when choosing a long-term device as main energy storage system for a specific implementation [1, 3]. Therefore, promising materials, as is the case of electrodes, have been constantly investigated with higher hopes of surpassing the abovementioned limitation. However, it is not always possible for experimental supercapacitor cells to be produced, which can cause unwanted research setbacks or obstacles. Therefore, this document is focused on modeling of asymmetric supercapacitors of hybrid nature, composed of two different electrode materials of both capacitive and faradaic characteristics, allowing theoretical devices based on experimental electrode materials to be analyzed and implemented in energy storage systems designs, calculations and computational

The original version of this chapter was revised: The numbers in Table 1 and subsequent errors were corrected. The correction to this chapter is available at https://doi.org/10.1007/978-3-030-45124-0_45

L. M. Camarinha-Matos et al. (Eds.): DoCEIS 2020, IFIP AICT 577, pp. 290–298, 2020.
https://doi.org/10.1007/978-3-030-45124-0_27

simulations. Furthermore, this manuscript presents the modeling procedure and calculations of an asymmetric hybrid supercapacitor cell for widespread implementation, accounting for variances in equations regarding the laboratorial data towards cell values.

## 2 Supercapacitors for Life Improvement

Supercapacitors as a mean of energy storage are a key factor for more efficient and reliable electrical systems [1]. SC's applications encompass mobile and stationary implementations, from transportation to industrial and renewable energy requirements [4]. Macro and micro-scale applications of supercapacitors can be found in the power grid, providing support to power quality improvement that are mainly derived from the growing penetration of renewable generated power into the power grid [5]. Due to distributed generation increasing, the renewable generation can be commonly placed near consumers or even being an integrant part of consumer's electric installations. Considering this power grid point of view, the life improvement is associated with de-bottlenecking of transmission lines, more reliable integration of renewable energies and consequent greenhouse gas emissions reduction. Moreover, the high-power capabilities can also be addressed to mobile applications regarding power electronics as in electric vehicles (EV) [4], where it performs as a coadjutant device working in parallel with vehicle's battery energy storage system. Supercapacitors not only are able to provide extra power in EV's demand peak situations, but also contributing for an autonomy extension and batteries lifespan increasing throughout the battery cycle's reduction. The methodology addressed in following sections show the theoretical development of a generic hybrid supercapacitor based on an increased performance electrode material that results in better parameters, such as higher capacitance, energy and power density, when compared to a commercial device.

## 3 Hybrid Supercapacitor Modeling

This paper presents a hybrid supercapacitor (HSC) modeling procedure based on cyclic voltammetry (CV) and galvanostatic charge and discharge curves (GCD) data obtained for both positive and negative electrodes materials [6, 7]. The approach takes into consideration the specific capacitance ($C_{sp}$), potential window ($\Delta V$), equivalent series resistance (ESR) and reminiscent relevant data, which were gathered from already published laboratorial experiments [6, 7], assumed as primary database for the procedure development. In addition, in order to obtain the theoretical HSC physical structure, a Maxwell 2.3 V 300 F [8] pseudocapacitor was selected as device's choice of design and dimensioning intent, which original size and mass have fit the intended purpose. Therefore, the data set acquired was implemented into the developed electrode-to-cell capacitance equations, from which the individual electrodes capacitances were obtained, thus developing a correlation between electrode and cell data so it could be properly converted.

## 3.1    From Electrodes to Cell Data

In order to transpose laboratorial data into approximate real values so a device can be modeled and simulated, a correct interpretation of basic equations is required [9]. Based on the general cell capacitance and specific capacitance Eqs. (3.1–3.2) the electrode-to-cell calculation procedure was developed.

$$C_{cell} = \frac{i\Delta t}{\Delta V} [F].$$
(3.1)

$$C_{sp,cell} = \frac{I\Delta t}{m_{total}\Delta V} \left[\frac{F}{g}\right].$$
(3.2)

Where $m$ states for the mass of active material, which correlation for asymmetric cells is defined as in (3.3), $I$ is the current, $\Delta t$ the time and $\Delta V$ the voltage.

$$m_{total} = m_+ + m_- [g].$$
(3.3)

In order to define the specific capacitances equations for asymmetric configurations, firstly, the correlation between cell and both electrodes capacitances must be defined. As described in [9], such correlation can be defined as a series equivalent circuit (3.4), consisting of two electrode-electrolyte interfaces represented as single capacitors $C^+$ and $C^-$ for the positive and negative electrodes, respectively [10, 11].

$$\frac{1}{C_{cell}} = \frac{1}{C_+} + \frac{1}{C_-} \left[\frac{1}{F}\right].$$
(3.4)

With regards to an asymmetric hybrid supercapacitor configuration, the electrode to cell capacitance is defined by the electrode with smaller capacitance (if $C1 >> C2$, $C_{cell} \approx C2$) [12]. Therefore, as the grater capacitance is not predefined as either positive or negative, $C1$ and $C2$ are hereafter defined as $C_{elec}^{c>}$ and $C_{elec}^{c<}$, respectively. Consequently, $C_{cell}$ is defined as (3.5).

$$C_{cell} = C_{elec}^{c<} [F].$$
(3.5)

Therefore, with regards to asymmetric cells, the specific capacitance can be obtained from (3.6), taking into consideration the total mass ($m_{total}$) of both active materials.

$$C_{sp,asymm.cell} = \frac{C_{cell}}{m_{total}} = \frac{C_{cell}}{m_+ + m_-} = \frac{C_{elec}^{c<}}{m_+ + m_-} \left[\frac{F}{g}\right].$$
(3.6)

Based on (3.5) and (3.6) it is possible to correlate the cell's specific capacitance to the specific capacitance of $C^{c<}$ by considering the cell's total mass as a sum of $m^{c>}$ and $m^{c<}$, defined by (3.7).

$$\frac{C_{cell}}{m_{total}} = \frac{C_{elec}^{c<}}{m^{c>} + m^{c<}} = \frac{C_{elec}^{c<}}{m^{c<}} = \frac{C_{cell}}{m^{c<}} = C_{sp.elec}^{c<} \left[\frac{F}{g}\right]. \tag{3.7}$$

From the equations above it is possible to stablish a relation between two ($C_{cell}$) and three-electrodes ($C_{elec}$) results for specific capacitance.

## 3.2 Electrodes Data

The nickel-copper (Ni-Cu) metallic foam developed in [6] was selected as positive electrode material for the developed HSC, whereas for negative electrode, activated carbon (AC) [7] was implemented. The data were extracted from CVs and GCDs results, as well as scanning electron microscopy (SEM) (as shown in Fig. 1) regarding Ni-Cu electrode-to-electrolyte porosity estimation (the representation shown Fig. 2). The Ni-Cu electrode laboratorial tests [6] have presented a specific capacitance of 105 $Fg^{-1}$ for a material deposition time of 180 s at 1.8 $Acm^{-2}$. From the CV results [6] a potential window of approximately 1.48 V (−0.5 V to 0.975 V) was obtained for a scan rate of 100 mV $s^{-1}$. With regards to the AC negative electrode, the considered specific capacitance was of 70 $Fg^{-1}$ [7], even though [26] has presented higher laboratorial results, while a negative potential of −1.0 V with a scan rate of 100 $mVs^{-1}$ [7, 30] was accounted.

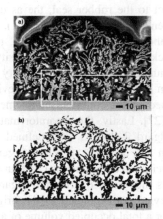

**Fig. 1.** (a) SEM 1.8 A.cm$^{-2}$ 180 s, electrode section, (b) image enhancing and cleanup [1].

**Fig. 2.** Electrolyte volume from electrode porosity modelling.

Based on the SEM result addressed in Fig. 1, an enhanced electrode image was obtained via various graphic software from Adobe Creative Suite 6. From the generated image, a generic section of 100 μm was extracted and 3D modeled with the aid of the modeling software Rhinoceros 5.0 [13], which resulted in a sample of $100.10^4$ μm$^3$ representing a proposed Ni-Cu electrode foam structure, from which the total electrode-to-electrolyte volume was obtained (and shown in Fig. 2). From the 3D model a porosity of over 89% was noticed. Despite the difference of foams manufacturing process, when comparing the obtained result with the information gathered from [14], which stated the material's porosity in the range of 75 to 95%, and based on the statement of [6] that metallic foams porosity values are above 50%, it has considered that the obtained value is acceptable. Therefore, by assuming the porosity values from the manufacturer, 95%, it was possible to calculate the respective electrolyte and electrode volumes shown in Sect. 3.4, Table 1.

### 3.3    Generic Supercapacitor Dimensioning

The hybrid supercapacitor dimensions were based on a Maxwell 2.3 V 300 F [8] pseudocapacitor. With this purpose, a three-dimensional generic model of such device was developed determining commonly implemented thickness for each of its composing layers as well as the device's general structure. In order to individually identify the volumetric proportion of each part of the base commercial device, a layer stack configuration was assumed based on [15–17].

For the volume distribution supercapacitors, commonly implemented materials were applied. With regards to the device structure it was separated in the following parts: metallic case, terminals, rubber seal, electrodes, current collectors, electrolyte and separator.

As device's metallic case material, an aluminum alloy described as Aluminum 1070, with density of 2.70 $gcm^{-3}$ and thickness of 100 µm, was assumed based on [18, 19]. Regarding the device's terminal, its material was assumed as brass (CuZn37), with density of 8.44 $gcm^{-3}$, based on [20]. With respect to the rubber seal, the assumed material for its composition was an Ethylene Propylene Diene Monomer (EPDM), with density of 1.40 $gcm^{-3}$ [21, 22]. With regards to the PC electrodes proposed, manganese dioxide ($MnO_2$) was assumed with a thickness of 0.5 µm and density of 5.02 $gcm^{-3}$ [23–25]. As current collectors an aluminum foil of 2.70 $gcm^{-3}$ density [26] was assumed, which thickness was defined as 30 µm [17]. With regards to the device's electrolyte, potassium hydroxide (KOH) was assumed as it is commonly implemented as such, which density was stated at 1.58 $gcm^{-3}$ [27]. Lastly, the separator material implemented for the developed HSC was the Celgard 2400 [28, 29], defined as a monolayer polypropylene, with thickness of 25 µm and density stated as 0.9 $gcm^{-3}$. Therefore, based on the presented procedure a generic pseudocapacitor configuration was defined, which resulted in a volume and mass individual distribution regarding each composing part. Furthermore, the generic device corresponded to the original mass stated in the datasheet [8], 24 g, accounting for a total occupied volume of about 7204 $mm^3$.

### 3.4    Ni-Cu//AC Hybrid Supercapacitor

Based on the acquired data presented in Sect. 3.2, the Ni-Cu//AC hybrid supercapacitor was developed by replacing the electrodes materials from the generic pseudocapacitor to Ni-Cu and AC parameters, where the total volume was divided equally between positive and negative electrodes.

With regards to the developed hybrid supercapacitor, the intent was to match its final mass to the base Maxwell device. Therefore, with the new materials implementation the total mass of 24 g was obtained by optimizing the internal case volume filling by its layers stacking, which resulted in a total volume of 14673.8 mm$^3$ (Table 1).

Therefore, the positive electrode capacitance ($C_{elec+}$) was obtained by (3.8).

$$C_{elec+} = C_{sp.elec} + m_{elec+} = 105 \times 6.36 \approx 668 \, [F]. \tag{3.8}$$

While the AC negative electrode, its capacitance is calculated by (3.9).

$$C_{elec-} = C_{sp.elec} - m_{elec-} = 70 \times 5.71 \approx 400 \, [F]. \tag{3.9}$$

**Table 1.** Ni-Cu//AC hybrid supercapacitor mass redistribution.

| Item | Volume (mm$^3$) | Mass (g) |
|---|---|---|
| Metallic case | 439.40 | 1.20 |
| Terminals | 49.80 | 0.42 |
| Rubber seal | 1421.00 | 2.00 |
| AC.Electrode | 960.09 | 0.63 |
| KOH.Electrolyte | 3214.19 | 5.08 |
| Current collector (Al) | 2408.24 | 6.50 |
| Ni-Cu.Electrode | 208.71 | 0.09 |
| KOH.Electrolyte | 3965.57 | 6.27 |
| Separator | 2006.79 | 1.81 |
| Total | 14673.8 | 24.00 |

Therefore, the cell capacitance ($C_{cell}$) was defined by assuming the smaller capacitance value ($C_{elec}{}^{c<}$) between both electrodes as described in Sect. 3.1 [12] (3.10).

$$C_{cell} = C_{elec}{}^{c<} = 400 \, [F]. \tag{3.10}$$

With regards to the cell voltage, it was proposed based on CV data from both electrodes materials and on [30, 31]. Therefore, based on the stated in [31] that the maximum charging voltage (MCV) for electrodes of different capacitances is obtained by the difference between the biggest potential value for the positive electrode (0.975 V) [6] and the smallest potential for the negative electrode (−1.0 V) [7, 30], (MCV − $E_{\Gamma2}$ − $F_{N1}$), the resulting proposed device's rated voltage ($V_R$) is 1.975 V ≈ 2 V.

The equivalent series resistance (ESR) was calculated according to [32, 33], which is defined by the voltage drop when the charge is interrupted, therefore, obtaining the discharge profile. In order to estimate the possible ESR value for the cell, both electrodes ESRs were obtained from the $IR$ drop (3.11–3.12) via GCD graphic interpretation, aided by Rhinoceros 5.0 [13], therefore, the respective data was extracted for the AC electrode from [7, 34, 36], while for the Ni-Cu foam, from [6, 35] 1.8 Acm$^{-2}$ at

180 s sample. The total ESR was considered as the summation of both electrode's internal resistances ($Ri_{AC}$, $Ri_{Ni\text{-}Cu}$) (3.13).

$$ESR_{AC} = \frac{V_{drop}}{2\Delta I} = \frac{0.07}{2*0.01} = 3.5\,[\Omega]. \tag{3.11}$$

$$ESR_{Ni-Cu} = \frac{V_{drop}}{2\Delta I} = \frac{0.019}{2*0.001} = 9.5\,[\Omega]. \tag{3.12}$$

$$ESR_{total} = Ri_{AC} + Ri_{Ni-Cu} = 3.5 + 9.5 = 13\,[\Omega]. \tag{3.13}$$

Therefore, the maximum energy storage (3.14) based on [6] and [30], gravimetric specific energy (3.15) [6] were calculated.

$$E_{max.hybrid} = \frac{C.V_R^2 1/2}{3600} \approx 0.23\,[Wh]. \tag{3.14}$$

$$E.sp_{hybrid} = \frac{E_{max.hybrid}}{m} \approx 9.6 \left[\frac{Wh}{kg}\right]. \tag{3.15}$$

## 4   Conclusions

The presented modeling procedure for a theoretical hybrid supercapacitor was developed in order to allow experimental promising electrode materials to be implemented in computational simulations, so their influence and interaction can be analyzed when applied to a wide range of situations, from UPSs to electric vehicle models. With regards to the procedure itself and obtained results, only publication-based analysis and verification where performed, thus experimental confirmation is defined as the next stage of this very study, characterized as future work. Therefore, when analyzing the developed Ni-Cu//AC hybrid supercapacitor results, despite the lack of experimental validation, one can propose that the obtained data has demonstrated promising values when compared to the Maxwell 2.3 V 300 F pseudocapacitor, presenting increased capacitance (400 F), energy (0.23 Wh) and specific energy (9.6 Wh $kg^{-1}$), which makes it an interesting candidate for further study and development.

## References

1. Grbovic, P.J.: Ultra-Capacitors in Power Conversion Systems. Wiley, IEE Press, Chichester (2014). 324 pp.
2. Zhu, C., Lu, R., Tian, L., Wang, Q.: The development of an electric bus with supercapacitors as unique energy storage. In: IEEE Vehicle Power and Propulsion Conference, Windsor, pp. 1–5 (2006)
3. Conway, B.E.: Electrochemical Supercapacitors: Scientific Fundamentals and Technological Applications. Kluwer Academic/Plenum Publishers, New York (1999). 698 pp.

4. Wang, G., Wang, H., Zhong, B., Zhang, L., Zhang, J.: Supercapacitors' Applications. 2016 Taylor & Francis Group, LLC, Electrochemical Energy Storage and Conversion, pp. 479–492 (2015)
5. Fthenakis, V.M., Nikolakakis, T.: Storage options for photovoltaics, Chapt. 11. In: Comprehensive Renewable Energy Encyclopedia, vol. 1, pp. 193–206. Elsevier (2012)
6. Eugénio, S., Silva, T.M., Carmezim, M.J., Duarte, R.G., Montemor, M.F.: Electrodeposition and characterization of nickel-copper metallic foams for application as electrodes for supercapacitors. J. Appl. Elec. **44**(4), 455–465 (2013)
7. Shabeeba, P., Thayyil, M.S., Pillai, M.P., Soufeena, P.P., Niveditha, C.V.: Electrochemical investigation of activated carbon electrode supercapacitors. Russ. J. Elec. **54**(3), 302–308 (2018)
8. Maxwell Technologies: Datasheet: 2.3 V 300F Pseudocapacitor Cell (2018)
9. Roldán, S., Barreda, D., Granada, M., Menéndez, R., Santamaría, R., Blanco, C.: An approach to classification and capacitance expressions in electrochemical capacitors technology. Phys. Chem. **17**, 1084–1092 (2015)
10. Elgrishi, N., Rountree, K.J., McCarthy, B.D., Rountree, E.S., Eisenhart, T.T., Dempsey, J.L.: A practical beginner's guide to cyclic voltammetry. J. Chem. Edu. **95**, 197–206 (2018)
11. Ratha, S., Samantara, A.K.: Supercapacitor: Instrumentation, Measurement and Performance Evaluation Techniques. Springer, Singapore (2018). https://doi.org/10.1007/978-981-13-3086-5
12. Eliaz, N., Gileadi, E.: Physical Electrochemistry: Fundamentals, Techniques, and Applications, vol. 2. Wiley, New York (2019). 480 pp.
13. Rhino 5.0 Product Release. https://www.rhino3d.com/download/Rhino/5.0
14. American Elements – The Materials Science Manufacturer: Datasheet: Ni-Cu Foam (2019)
15. Gualous, H., Louahlia, H., Gallay, R.: Supercapacitor characterization and thermal modelling with reversible and irreversible heat effect. IEEE Trans. Pwr. Elec. **26**, 3402–3409 (2011)
16. Béguin, F., Frackoviak, E.: Supercapacitors: Materials, Systems, and Applications. Wiley-VCH, Weinheim (2013)
17. Obreja, V., Obreja, A.C., Dinescu, A.: Activated carbon based electrodes in commercial supercapacitors and their performance. Int. Rev. Elec. Eng. **5**, 272–282 (2010)
18. Yassine, M., Fabris, D.: Performance of commercially available supercapacitors. Energies **10**, 1340 (2017). 12 pp.
19. Datasheet for Aluminum alloy 1070, manufacturer Indalco: http://www.indalco.com/. Datasheet link: http://www.indalco.com/wp-content/uploads/2013/10/1070.pdf. Accessed 21 Sept 2019
20. Datasheet for Copper alloy CuZn37, manufacturer Arubis: http://www.aurubis-stolberg.com/. Datasheet link: Datasheet CuZn37. Accessed 11 Nov 2019
21. Xu, R., Berduque, A.: Rubber sealing materials for high voltage and high temperature aluminum electrolytic capacitors. In: ECA, pp. 221–236 (2012)
22. Datasheet for Rubber material DRE80 EPDM Rubber, manufacturer Delta: https://shop.deltarubber.co.uk/. Datasheet link: https://shop.deltarubber.co.uk/media/blfa_files/DRE80_EPDM_Rubber_Sheet.pdf. Accessed 21 Sept 2019
23. Girard, H.-L.J.-P.: Modeling and Physical Interpretation of Cyclic Voltammetry for Pseudocapacitors. University of California, Msc. thesis (2015). 97 pp.

24. Safety datasheet for Manganese Dioxide, manufacturer Global Safety management Inc.: https://shop.deltarubber.co.uk/. Datasheet: https://beta-static.fishersci.com/content/dam/fishersci/en_US/documents/programs/education/regulatory-documents/sds/chemicals/chemicals-m/S25420.pdf. Accessed 21 Sept 2019

25. Viswanathan, B.: Fundamentals of chemical conversion processes and applications: Chapter 13 - Supercapacitors. In: Energy Sources, pp. 315–328. Elsevier (2017)

26. Datasheet for ALUMINIUM FOIL EXTRA PURE MSDS, manufacturer Loba Chemie: https://www.lobachemie.com. Datasheet link: https://www.lobachemie.com/lab-chemical-msds/MSDS-ALUMINIUM-FOIL-CASNO-7429-90-00889-EN.aspx. Accessed 21 Sept 2019

27. SAFETY DATA SHEET for Potassium Hydroxide (KOH), manufacturer Merck: https://www.merckgroup.com. Datasheet link: https://www.merckmillipore.com/PT/en/product/msds/MDA_CHEM-109918?ReferrerURL=https%3A%2F%2Fwww.google.com%2F. Accessed 22 Sept 2019

28. Tabatabaei, S.H., Carreau, P.J., Ajji, A.: Microporous membranes obtained from PP/HDPE multilayer films by stretching. J. Membrane Sci. 345, 148–159 (2009)

29. Datasheet for High Performance Battery Separators, manufacturer Celgard: https://www.celgard.com/. Datasheet link: http://www.jobike.it/Public/data/Daniele%20Consolini/2012517114032_Celgard_Product_Comparison_10002.pdf. Accessed 21 Sept 2019

30. Ye, B., et al.: A high-performance asymmetric supercapacitor based on $Ni_3S_2$-Coated NiSe arrays as positive electrode. New J. Chem. 43, 2389–2399 (2018)

31. Dai, Z., Peng, C., Chae, J. H., Chiang, K., Chen, G.Z.: Cell voltage versus electrode potential range in aqueous supercapacitors. Sci. Rep. 5 (2015). 8 pp.

32. Vicentini, R., Silva, L.M., Junior, E.P.C., Alves, T.A., Nunes, W.G., Zanin, H.: How to measure and calculate equivalent series resistance of electric double-layer capacitors. Molecules 24, 1452 (2019)

33. Keyvan, M., Reza, G.M., Francesca, S.: Toward low-cost and sustainable supercapacitor electrode processing: simultaneous carbon grafting and coating of mixed-valence metal oxides by fast annealing. Front. Chem. 7 (2019). 25 pp.

34. Ahmed, S., Ahmed, A., Rafat, M.: Supercapacitor performance of activated carbon derived from rotten carrot in aqueous, organic and ionic liquid based electrolytes. J. Saudi Chem. Soc. 22(8), 993–1002 (2018)

35. Mirzaee, M., Dehghanian, C.: Nanostructured Ni-Cu foam electrodeposited on a copper substrate applied as supercapacitor electrode. Acta Metall. Slovaca 24(4), 325–336 (2018)

36. Liu, R.-S., Zhang, L., Sun, X., Liu, H., Zhang, J.: Electrochemical Technologies for Energy Storage and Conversion, vol. 1. Wiley, New York (2012). 838 pp.

# Design of a SFCL with an Inductive Stage in Series with a Resistive Stage Which Transits by Magnetic Field

Belén Rivera$^{(\boxtimes)}$, Alfredo Álvarez$^{(\boxtimes)}$, and Belén Pérez$^{(\boxtimes)}$

Lab "B. Mahedero" of Electrical Applications of Superconductors (EAS),
Electrical Engineering School, University of Extremadura, Badajoz, Spain
{mbrivera, aalvarez, belenpc}@unex.es

**Abstract.** One of the most interesting applications of superconductors in power systems is the so called "Superconductor Fault Current Limiter (SFCL)". This is a device that makes the lines exhibit a variable short-circuit impedance: very low (almost null) under normal operation, and high when the current increases above the security limit of the line. There are two types of SFCL: resistive and inductive. The first one consists of a superconducting element in series with the line. The element is designed with a critical current equal the security limit of the line. When the current in the line is higher, the element transits and a high resistance arises, protecting the line. The second type is connected in series with the line too. It consists of an inductor with the magnetic core shielded by a superconducting screen. The screen is designed to transit by magnetic field when the current in the coil (line current) is higher than the security limit of the line. At this time, a high reactance arises protecting the line. The PhD thesis we are working on is a new concept of SFCL with two stages (resistive and inductive) in series designed to solve some problems of each type separately. In this case, the resistive stage is located in the gap of the inductive stage magnetic core. Firstly, the objective is to make the magnetic screen transit. When this happens, the magnetic field penetrates the core and surrounds the resistive stage provoking its transition. In this paper, we present the work philosophy of this novel device, which does not have equivalent in conventional (non-superconducting) technology.

**Keywords:** Superconductivity · Fault current limiter · Magnetic transition

## 1 Introduction

The superconducting fault current limiter (SFCL) is a device that detects the increase in the current above a certain value, (for which it is designed) and inserts in the network a high impedance that does not exist under normal conditions.

This variation of impedance in the network allows it to work in normal conditions with a low short-circuit impedance, with the consequent performance in terms of quality of supply and stability. In fault conditions this impedance increases, reducing the current and therefor the switchgear size and cost.

© IFIP International Federation for Information Processing 2020
Published by Springer Nature Switzerland AG 2020
L. M. Camarinha-Matos et al. (Eds.): DoCEIS 2020, IFIP AICT 577, pp. 299–308, 2020.
https://doi.org/10.1007/978-3-030-45124-0_28

SFCLs are reliable devices, with low environmental impact and easily adapt to power systems based on alternative energies, which makes them very attractive from a technological point of view and, under the right conditions, economically.

One of the most important challenges in electrical switchgear, is the fault current limiter, which has a clear application in two increasingly common situations: the demand for larger capacity in distribution networks and the inclusion in these of the distributed generation systems (DGS).

In the first case, increasing the capacity of the lines raises the value of the short-circuit currents above the capacity of the protection devices. Currently, there is no suitable solution to this problem.

The second case is the inclusion of distributed generation systems in the distribution networks, especially when it comes to renewable energy (wind turbines, photovoltaic panels, fuel cells, etc.) that needs connection systems to network based on power electronics.

For some years, especially since the appearance of high temperature superconductors (HTS) in 1987, research on the application of these materials to fault current limiters have been carried out.

A superconductor is a material that below a certain temperature (*critical* temperature, *Tc*) has zero electrical resistance and perfect diamagnetism, as long as the current it carries is not higher than a certain value (*critical current, Ic*) and is not held to a field magnetic higher than one given (*critical field, Bc*). That is, the superconducting material will retain its properties as long as the conditions of temperature, current density and magnetic field described are maintained below its critical values.

When the current exceeds this value, the material loses those properties, behaving as a resistive medium with permeability practically equal to that of air. This situation means that the material has moved from superconducting state to normal state.

For electrical application, the most interesting superconductors are the so called "high temperature superconductors". They work at temperatures higher than the liquefaction temperature of Nitrogen (77 K; −196 °C), its nature (usually ceramic), makes its Resistivity is high, which is a good feature for the purposes of current limitation.

Due to these characteristics and its design, a SFCL could lead to benefits not only in the protection, but in the quality of the output voltage in normal operation as no impedance is interposed at the protection point.

In summary, this system that gives the line characteristics of impedance adaptable to the current, so that when the current limit is exceeded, it presents an impedance that it did not have in normal operation, it is not necessary to size the rest of the protections to the impedance of normal regime.

## 2  Contribution to Life Improvement

The main issue in this research is relevant due to the impact that this type of device can have on DGS, to which sustainability seems to lead in Electrical Engineering. The initial hypotheses are:

(a) The SFCL increases the impedance of the short-circuit on the line that protects when its activation value is exceeded, this allows it to show very low impedance under normal operating conditions, improving the quality of the power supplied.
(b) SFCL allows to expand the capacity of the lines without changing the size of the protections. It is intended to quantify this possibility under different scenarios.
(c) SFCL operation is totally physical (a thermodynamic change of state) and therefore, environmentally free of impact.

# 3 State of the Art

The exhaustive study of the configurations of the SFCLs, their operating principles, characteristics, advantages and disadvantages have been carried out by several authors [1, 2] who have delved into some interesting structures in terms of operating principles, commercial possibilities and their integration in DGS.

Recent studies [3] offer a review and analysis of the different types of existing SFCLs. These studies are divided into three groups: Quench-type SFCLs, Non-quench-type SFCLs and Composite-type SFCLs. The typologies associated with the prototype presented here classified as Quench-type SFCLs and is constructed by combining two of them.

Regarding the present work, the main typologies of interest are the resistive and inductive type. Inductive SFCLs use the magnetic field of a low impedance coil, connected in series with the line to be protected. The core of the coil is shielded by a superconducting screen. The loss of superconducting properties on the screen results on a magnetization of the core and sudden increase of the impedance in the coil. The SFCL is designed to lose the screen superconducting properties when the magnetic field created by the line current exceeds the protection value [4, 5].

The resistive type uses the resistance of superconducting circuit connected in series with the line. When the circuit is in superconducting state no resistance is shown in the line. If the current in the line exceeds the protection value, the superconductor transits to normal state and inserts a high resistance in the line. The circuit is designed so that the maximum allowed current is the HTS critical current [6]. There are some applications of this SFCL typologies to real cases [7, 8].

Both types have advantages and disadvantages [9]. In the resistive typology, problems of non-uniform heating and hot spots may occur [2, 10]. The problems are controlled as several research activities, using different HTS materials, are carried out. In fact, several successful prototypes have been installed in medium-voltage distribution systems [11, 12]. The inductive typology has the disadvantage of weight gain due to the core and recovery times somewhat higher than the resistive type [3]. Both need cryogenic systems that are currently very reliable but increase the cost of these devices.

Nevertheless, other studies propose solutions by using technologies which combine both typologies, as in the case of the present work [13].

It is also interesting to mention the publications that analyze their optimal location in DGSs [14] and the benefits that imply their use in these networks [15].

Finally, in terms of basic design criteria, other documents, analyze topics such as the criteria for the selection of superconducting tapes [16], the analysis of their degradation [17, 18], studies for the improvement of the combined performance of impedances [19], thermal stress analysis [20], and loss analysis in HTS coils [5].

# 4 Proposed Model

## 4.1 Background of the Work Presented

The inductive-resistive SFCL is an original proposal of the "Benito Mahedero" Group of EAS designed to prevent the destruction of a resistive SFCL non-uniform heating conditions (hot-spots) [13]. In this proposal, a resistive SFCL is forced to transit by applying an external magnetic field greater than the critical magnetic field, just before the current transition. The magnetic field is created by a magnetic-shield iron-core-type inductive SFCL, sized to lose the magnetic shield just before the current reaches the critical current in the resistive SFCL. Connecting these elements in series, we take the advantage of an impedance reinforcement by including the inductance of the inductive SFCL after the transition. The prototype studied consisted of a ferromagnetic core with two air gaps, as shown in Fig. 1.

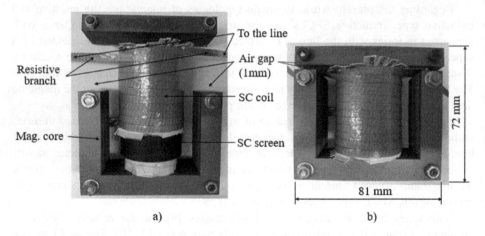

**Fig. 1.** SFCL prototype image developed by the "Benito Mahedero" group. (a) Prototype deployed. (b) Assembled prototype.

The inductive stage was made from HTS BSCO tape wound on a superconducting cylinder that shields a ferromagnetic core.

When the line current flowing through the coil exceeds the permitted limit, the magnetic field generated exceeds the cylinder critical magnetic field and the shielding disappears. Then the current in the coil establishes a high magnetic field in the core, affecting the HTS in the resistance stage.

The resistive stage consists of two sections of superconducting material in series with the line and the inductive element (in fact, they are extensions of the BSCO tape coil ends, avoiding joins). They are located in two 1 mm air gaps in the magnetic core of the inductive stage, as shown in Fig. 1. The transition to normal state of this section occurs after the transition of the inductive stage, by magnetic field and not by current as usual in conventional resistive SFCLs, avoiding the problems arising from current transitions. This is possible due to the correct sizing of the device, known the critical values of the screen and the tape so as the characteristics of the core.

## 4.2    Test and Results of the First Prototype

The prototype described above was tested in a simulated line consisting in a 15 A(rms) source feeding the rated load $Z_L$. Figure 2 shows the set-up of the line with no protection. A switch $S$ in parallel to the load permits to short-circuit the load. The current in the line was measured by a Hall probe connected to a DAQ where the waveform was recorded at a sample rate of 10 kS/s.

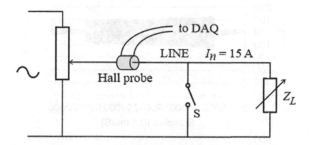

**Fig. 2.**  Test circuit with no protection in the line.

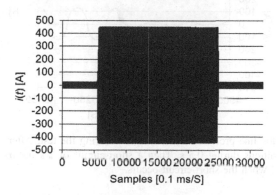

**Fig. 3.**  Current in the unprotected line during the test. After connection, the line works at rated conditions during 0.5 s. Then a short-circuit of 2 s is held.

The result of this test is shown in Fig. 3. The *rms* value of the short-circuit current was 318 A, corresponding to a short-circuit impedance of about 4.7%.

The measurements were repeated with the same source configuration and time sequence, but with the SFCL connected to the line as shown in Fig. 4.

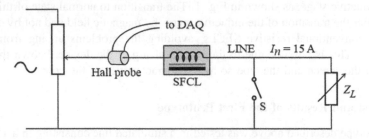

**Fig. 4.** Test circuit with the SFCL in the line.

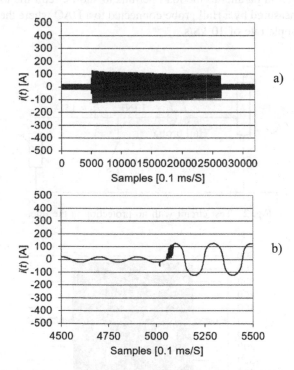

**Fig. 5.** Current in the line protected with the SFCL during the test. After connection, the line works at rated conditions during 0.5 s. Then a short-circuit of 2 s occurs. (a) Full sampling. (b) Waveform detail when the short-circuit occurs.

Figure 5 shows the results of this test. Before the short-circuit event, the rated current passes through the line just as in the previous test. That means that the SFCL is *transparent* to the current and the short-circuit impedance remains at 4.7%. However, the short-circuit, after 0.5 s, is initially reduced to 88 A(rms). That means that the short-circuit impedance (line + SFCL) has increased to a value of almost 17%, which is better for protection. And, what is much better, this increase of the short-circuit impedance only occurs when the fault occurs, remaining at a lower value (better for stability) in normal operation.

As the short-circuit is present, a slow reduction of the peak value can be observed. This effect is under study, but the high value of the time constant suggests that it is probably a thermal effect.

The results of the described prototype were uneven in both stages: The inductive stage (tested independently) showed a 70% reduction in the short-circuit current. On the other hand, the reduction of the current in the resistive stage was practically null due to the short length of the resistive branches.

### 4.3 New Prototype Description

The structure proposed in this new design represents a drastic change with respect to the models previously studied. The modifications mainly affect the structure of the magnetic circuit, and the resistive stage of the combined SFCL.

The aim is to increase the length of the tape in the SFCL's resistive stage, whereby, the available air-gap must be increased. Thus, we propose a new magnetic support (Fig. 6) consisting of a cross-shaped central body with four polar expansions, surrounded by an external ferromagnetic shell, forming a structure similar to that of a synchronous machine (e.g., 4-pole machine, as in figure).

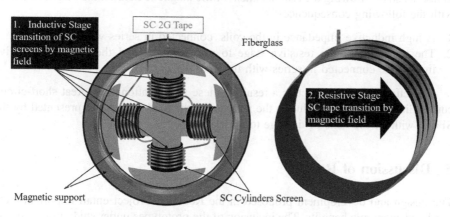

**Fig. 6.** Scheme of the SFCL prototype under study.

Surrounding the polar expansions (or poles), four superconducting cylinders will be inserted. Their mission is the same as in the previous prototype, i.e., to shield the pole from the magnetic field as soon as it is kept below the critical value.

The inductive stage coils are made by winding 2G HTS tape around the superconducting cylinders. The number of turns of the coils must be calculated again to ensure that the limit current (of the line to be protected), makes the superconducting cylinder to transit just before reaching the critical current in the belt.

When this happens, the poles and the air-gaps are magnetized, and the resistive stage tape is immersed in the magnetic field, which causes its transition to the normal state.

The winding direction of the coils must originate magnetic poles of opposite direction in contiguous poles.

These new modifications are expected to improve the operation of the inductive stage of the SFCL.

After finishing the winding of the SFCL's inductive stage, the arrangement continues to wind the resistive stage over a fiberglass support that surrounds the inner core and provides compactness to the application without modifying the magnetic properties or increasing its weight. As can be seen in Fig. 6, practically the entire cylindrical surface of the fiberglass support is under the influence of axial magnetic field, when it appears in the poles. This way, it is possible to increase the length of the tape in the resistive stage.

The final scheme of the prototype in Fig. 6, shows the terminals of the application that must be connected in series with the line to be protected.

Initially, while the intensity flowing through the line is kept below the limit value, the superconducting cylinders have a perfect diamagnetic behavior, and the ferromagnetic material does not detect the magnetic field. In this situation the impedance presented by the SFCL is negligible.

When the current in the line exceeds the limit, the superconducting screens transits to normal state, allowing the establishment of the magnetic field on the magnetic circuit with the following consequences:

1. A high inductive impedance in the coils, connected in series with the line.
2. The transition of the resistive stage to normal state, and the resulting resistive impedance connected in series with the line.

The effect that we expect as a result of these modifications is a great short-circuit current limitation capacity due to the increase in the total impedance presented by the SFCL, without the risks of damage to the HST tape.

## 5 Discussion of Results

The design and development proposed in the Research Project entail important technical and economic benefits. The inclusion of the prototypes under study in the current electric power system would reduce the rated value and the cost of the associated protection switchgear, since, for practical purposes, the short-circuit current of the lines that integrate them decreases considerably.

It would imply improvements in the efficiency of the network, an increase in the reliability of the supply for the users and a lower cost of the protection of the system as well as the improvement in the quality of the output voltage in normal operation, for the distribution companies.

From the point of view of the environmental impact, the cryogenic system needed for superconducting conditions, either by immersion in liquid nitrogen or by conduction in a vacuum chamber, is practically harmless with the medium in which it is installed, having no harmful effects of it.

In addition, other superconducting devices that take advantage of these cryogenic systems could be integrated, with possible consequences on the dimensions of the sections of lines, including the assigned voltages, which would affect the design of the transformation centers themselves.

The study that is proposed is, in that sense, bidirectional, that is, the inclusion of the limiters would lead to the optimization of the parameters of the electrical systems with DGS and the consequent resizing of them, and again, the situation would lead to the retrofitting of the SFCLs.

## 6    Conclusions and Further Work

The design of a new SFCL device is presented. The main objective is to solve some problems shown by the typologies presented before.

It is intended to define a reliable device with low environmental impact, easily adaptable within the distribution networks of distributed generation systems, especially when constituted from renewable energy.

The SFCL device not only aims to meet the protection requirements for which it is designed, but also focuses on improving the quality of service in normal operation, since it will not imply any impedance at the point of protection.

The current state of the investigation has already carried out an exhaustive review of the existing bibliography and a previous analysis of the losses in the different prototype elements. The possibility of replacing the Bulk-type cylindrical magnetic screens with others constructed with HTS tape is beginning to be studied. The first results obtained are promising.

**Acknowledgments.** The authors would like to thank Junta de Extremadura for supporting through the funding GR18092, IB18076 and Fondo Europeo de Desarrollo Regional *"Una Manera de Hacer Europa"*.

## References

1. Morandi, A.: State of the art of superconducting fault current limiters and their application to the electric power system. Phys. C. Supercond. **484**, 242–247 (2013). https://doi.org/10.1016/j.physc.2012.03.004
2. Noe, M., Steurer, M.: High-temperature superconductor fault current limiters: concepts, applications, and development status. Supercond. Sci. Technol. **20**(3), 15 29 (2007). https://doi.org/10.1088/0953-2048/20/3/R01
3. Barzegar-Bafrooei, M.R., Akbari Foroud, A., Dehghani Ashkezari, J., Niasati, M.: On the advance of SFCL: a comprehensive review. IET Gener. Trans. Distrib. **13**(17), 3745–3759 (2019). https://doi.org/10.1049/iet-gtd.2018.6842
4. Paul, W., Baumann, T., Rhyner, J.: Test of 100 kW high-TC superconducting fault current limiter. IEEE Trans. Appl. Supercond. **5**, 1059–1062 (1995). https://doi.org/10.1109/77.402734

5. Shen, B., Li, C., Geng, J., et al.: Investigation on power dissipation in the saturated iron-core superconducting fault current limiter. IEEE Trans. Appl. Supercond. **29**(2), 5600305 (2019). https://doi.org/10.1109/tasc.2018.2881706

6. Sharmal, D., Sahay, K.B.: Basic concepts of superconducting fault current limiter. In: IEEE (ICPEICES 2016) (2016). https://doi.org/10.1109/icpeices.2016.7853069

7. Bock, J., Hobl, A., Schramm, J., Krämer, S., Jänke, C.: Resistive superconducting fault current limiters are becoming a mature technology. IEEE Trans. Appl. Supercond. **25**, 5600604 (2015). https://doi.org/10.1109/TASC.2014.2364916

8. Liang, F., Yuan, W., Baldan, C.A., Zhang, M., Lamas, J.S.: Modeling and experiment of the current limiting performance of a resistive superconducting fault current limiter in the experimental system. J. Supercond. Novel Magn. **28**, 2669–2681 (2015). https://doi.org/10. 1007/s10948-015-3102-x

9. Didier, G., Bonnard, C.H., Lubin, T.: Comparison between inductive and resistive SFCL in terms of current limitation and power system transient stability. Electr. Power Syst. Res. **125**, 150–158 (2015). https://doi.org/10.1016/j.epsr.2015.04.002

10. Henning, A., Kurrat, M.: Thermal–electric simulations of coated conductors with a variable conductivity of the buffer layer. IEEE Trans. Appl. Supercond. **17**(2), 3443–3446 (2007). https://doi.org/10.1109/TASC.2007.898178

11. Nexans' supplies two superconducting fault current limiters for permanent use on Birmingham's distribution network' Nexans Superconductor. https://www.nexans.co.uk/eservice/UK-en_GB/navigatepub_149242_-33580/Nexans_supplies_two_superconducting_fault_current_.html. Accessed 5 Dec 2019

12. Superconducting fault current limiters, SuperOx. http://www.superox.ru/upload/FCL-full-information.pdf. Accessed 5 Dec 2019

13. University of Extremadura. Device of inductive-resistive modular superconductive short circuit current limiting with double transition by magnetic field. Patent No. P201031147 (2010)

14. Dubey, V.K., Jawale, G., Mangalvedhkar, H.A.: Impact of adding new generators in a loop network with optimally placed SFCL. In: 2016 IEEE PES 13th International Conference on Transmission & Distribution Construction, Operation & Live-Line Maintenance (ESMO). https://doi.org/10.1109/tdcllm.2016.8013234

15. Jain, A., Dubey, V.K., Jawale, G., Mangalvedhkar, H.A., Kanakgiri, K.: Feasibility analysis for optimal placement of SFCL in a loop network: a case study. In: 1st IEEE (ICPEICES 2016) (2016)

16. Majka, M., Kozak, J., Kozak, S.: HTS tapes selection for superconducting current limiters. IEEE Trans. Appl. Supercond. **27**(4), 5601405 (2017). https://doi.org/10.1109/TASC.2017. 2669191

17. Baldan, C.A., Weijia, Y., Shigue, C.Y., Ruppert, E.F.: Performance of modular SFCL using REBCO coated conductor tapes under repetitive overcurrent tests. IEEE Trans. Appl. Supercond. **26**(3), 5401905 (2016). https://doi.org/10.1109/TASC.2016.2528994

18. Suárez, P., Álvarez, A., Ceballos, J.M., Pérez, B.: Loss and transition studies of shunted free-stabilized YBCO tape for SFCL applications. IEEE Trans. Appl. Supercond. **21**(3), 1267–1270 (2011). https://doi.org/10.1109/TASC.2010.2102991

19. Alaraifi, S., El Moursi, M.S.: Design considerations of superconducting fault current limiters for power system stability enhancement. IET Gener. Transm. Distrib. **11**(9), 2155–2163 (2017). https://doi.org/10.1049/iet-gtd.2016.0549

20. Hayakawa, N., Matsuoka, T., Kojima, H., Isojima, S., Kuwata, M.: Breakdown characteristics and mechanisms of liquid nitrogen under transient thermal stress for superconducting fault current limiters. IEEE Trans. Appl. Supercond. **27**(4), 7700305 (2017). https://doi.org/10.1109/TASC.2017.2651115

# Power Transportation

# Study of Electrical Integrity of Low Voltage Nuclear Power Cables in Case of Plant Life Extension

Ehtasham Mustafa[1,2(✉)], Ramy S. A. Afia[2,3], Semih Bal[2],
and Zoltán Ádám Tamus[2]

[1] Department of Electrical Engineering, Faculty of Engineering and Technology,
Gomal University, Dera Ismail Khan 29050, Pakistan
[2] Department of Electric Power Engineering, Budapest University
of Technology and Economics, P.O.B. 91, Budapest 1521, Hungary
{mustafa.ethasham, bal.semih, tamus.adam}@vet.bme.hu
[3] Department of Electrical Power and Machines Engineering,
Helwan University, 1 Sherif Street, Helwan, Cairo 11792, Egypt
ramysaad@h-eng.helwan.edu.eg

**Abstract.** During the last couple of decades, many nuclear power plant operators are seeking the life extension of the operating nuclear power plants. This makes the condition assessment of major components in the plant an important topic. One such component is low voltage power and instrumentation and control cables, which are more than 1000 km in length and makes their replacement a severe cost burden. Since these cables during service are under high thermal and radiation stress, hence making the condition assessment of them inevitable. The thermal stress as compared to other stresses results in the structural change and hence effecting the electrical integrity of the cable insulation. In this work, the complex permittivity of the XLPE/CSPE based low voltage nuclear power cable will be studied under thermal stress. The potential electrical aging markers from the measurement will help in calculating the expected lifetime of the cable for the case of life extension of the nuclear power plants.

**Keywords:** Nuclear power plant · Life extension · Thermal aging · Low voltage power cables · Complex permittivity · Elongation at break

## 1 Introduction

Nuclear power plants (NPPs) are credited for supplying reliable, low carbon and affordable electrical energy. The worldwide production of electrical energy has a considerable share of nuclear energy which is expected to be 17% by the year 2050 [1]. Since the NPPs are initially designed for 40 years but in the last decade, many of the plant operators are seeking the life extension of the NPPs as it is more economical than building a new one and helps in avoiding supply shortages and support the country in reducing carbon emission. The safe and reliable operation of the NPP depends not only

L. M. Camarinha-Matos et al. (Eds.): DoCEIS 2020, IFIP AICT 577, pp. 311–318, 2020.
https://doi.org/10.1007/978-3-030-45124-0_29

on its structure but also on the systems and components [2]. One such component is low voltage (LV) cables, which are used to deliver power and control signals for the systems; safety and non-safety related. This makes the cables to be reliable not only for the normal operation but also during the design-based events (DBEs). The cables in the NPP are vulnerable to a number of stresses such as temperature, radiation, mechanical, electrical, chemical, moisture and humidity [3]. The temperature being more effective as compared to others as it creates physio-chemical changes inside the cable insulation. As a result, the cable degrades and may result in the exposure of the metallic parts of the cable, resulting in the short circuit, open circuit and even cable breakdown, which eventually leads to probable plant shutdown or transients.

The long term operation and safety issues have increased the importance of cable management in the NPPs. This has led to intensive research work in this regard. For the evaluation of the state of the cable, condition monitoring (CM) techniques can help in this context. In recent times, a number of CMs techniques have been presented and are listed by IAEA in its report [4]. The desirable features of the CM techniques are to be non-destructive and non-intrusive. Even though the presence of diversity in the CM techniques, there is no single CM technique which can access the condition of the cable during service, since each cable passes through different manufacturing processes and have its own composition [5]. Therefore, a number of techniques are combined to evaluate the state of the cable.

One such technique is dielectric spectroscopy which is based on the measurement of complex permittivity of the insulation material, which is a polymer in nature. The technique has recently been adopted for the insulation CM of a number of LV shielded cables [6–8]. But still, its application to LV unshielded cables has not been reported, as it is difficult to monitor the state of the cable without separating the jacket, insulation and conductor. So, in this work, thermal aging of the whole LV unshielded NPP power cables is studied without separating the cable components. The power cables are subjected to four thermal aging cycles in the oven at 120 °C. The morphological changes happening inside the cable are studied using the complex permittivity for a range of frequency 20 Hz–500 kHz. The electrical aging markers are evaluated, investigated and a correlation between the markers and the elongation at break (EaB) which is a time-dependent degradation evaluation technique has been established. The results show that the evaluated electrical aging markers have the potential to be used for the investigation of the level of cable degradation in the context of the field conditions.

## 2    Contribution to Life Improvement

Nowadays the economic development of any country is heavily dependent on a reliable and adequate supply of electrical energy. This also adds to the uplift of the social life of the country [9]. Although having high capital cost; the predictable, reliable and clean nature of nuclear energy has made it an attractive option, which is reflected by the increase in the number of NPPs in the last couple of years not only in developed countries but also in developing countries [10]. With more urbanization, nuclear energy can be used as a baseload provider, urban transport systems and non-electric applications such as district heating, industrial processes and water desalination, which are essential components of the life improvement of the people of a country. It is important that the NPP must work safely, efficiently and reliably during its service and life extension case, which is highly acknowledged for the socio-economic improvement of a country but also for the operators. This all depends on the safe operation of all the components of the power plant which are under multiple stresses during service. The CM of these components especially the LV cables is of utmost importance as it has to ensure the supply of power and signals to the equipment which have to operate during all sorts of conditions and operations. An effective CM technique can ensure the safe and efficient operation of the NPP which will have a profound impact on the socio-economy of the country.

## 3  Experimental Work

### 3.1  Low Voltage Cable

The cross-sectional view of LV NPP power cable under consideration is shown in Fig. 1. The outer jacket consisted of Choloro-sulfonated polyethylene (CSPE), a thickness of 0.762 mm, and the inner insulation was Cross-linked polyethylene (XLPE) with a thickness of 1.143 mm. A stranded tin-coated copper material was used as a conductor.

**Fig. 1.** The cross-sectional view of the cable sample under consideration.

### 3.2  Thermal Aging

The XLPE/CSPE based cable samples were exposed to thermal stress in an oxygen controlled oven at 120 °C. The accelerated aging period was calculated using the Arrhenius relationship and was 176, 342, 516 and 793 h.

### 3.3  Measurement of Dielectric Properties

The electrical properties, complex permittivity, of the cables were studied using the precision component analyzer. The technique is based on the phenomenon of conduction and polarization in the materials. Since there are a number of polarization phenomenon in operation in the material which have their own frequency response and can be separated on the basis of that. The atomic and ionic polarization operate at a very high frequency while the dipole orientation operates at a lower frequency. While the DC conduction and orientation polarization are significant at very low frequencies.

The range of frequency was chosen as 20 Hz to 500 kHz at 5 $V_{rms}$, where the dipolar orientation and interfacial polarization can be observed. The cable samples were kept in the Faraday cage to reduce any pickup noise during the measurement. The test temperature was kept at 25 °C ± 2%.

## 4   Experimental Results

The real part of permittivity ($\varepsilon'$) against the frequency range is shown in Fig. 2. The $\varepsilon'$ values decreased with the increase of frequency irrespective of the aging. After the first thermal cycle, a prominent increase in the values of the real part of permittivity was observed at all frequencies. But after the subsequent cycles, a very slight change was observed. The overall impact of aging was an increase in the values of $\varepsilon'$ irrespective of the frequencies.

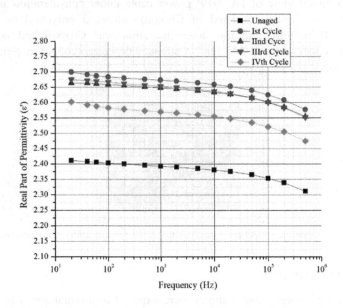

**Fig. 2.** The real part of permittivity ($\varepsilon'$) vs. frequency for different aging times.

The imaginary part of permittivity ($\varepsilon''$) profile is shown in Fig. 3(a). The $\varepsilon''$ started with high value at 500 kHz and then decreased with the decrease of frequency. It reached a minimum value and then started to increase. This profile of $\varepsilon''$ was the same for all the aging periods. With the thermal stress, it was observed that the $\varepsilon''$ increased at all frequencies. But the change in the values of $\varepsilon''$ was more prominent at the low frequencies than at the high frequencies. Figure 3 (b) shows the imaginary part of permittivity at four different frequencies; 100 Hz, 500 Hz, 10 kHz, and 20 kHz.

A sharp increase in the values was observed at 100 Hz after the end of the fourth thermal cycle, where the values have increased twofold.

## 5 Discussion

The primary insulation of the cable is composed of XLPE while the jacket material is based on CSPE. Through the modification of the backbone of polyethylene both the materials are produced and are classified as semi-crystalline [11, 12]. CSPE is formed through the process of chlorination and chlorosulfonation of polyethylene, on the other hand through the cross-linking the chains of polyethylene result in the formation of XLPE. Due to polar nature, any change in the material structure will affect the real and imaginary part of permittivity.

The increase in the values of $\varepsilon'$ and $\varepsilon''$ for all thermal cycles shows that the stress has strongly effected the morphological structure of the polymers. This phenomenon can be explained due to the polarization phenomenon and the losses; conduction and polarization, happening inside the material. The polarization has a strong relationship with $\varepsilon'$, while the $\varepsilon''$ correlates with the losses.

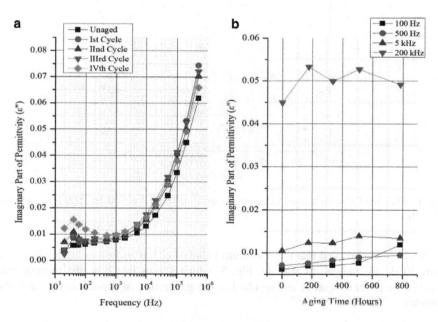

**Fig. 3.** (a) Imaginary part of permittivity ($\varepsilon''$) vs. frequency for different aging times. (b) $\varepsilon''$ vs. aging time at 100 Hz, 500 Hz, 5 kHz, and 200 kHz.

As it was observed that the $\varepsilon'$ showed no discrepancy in relation to the frequency either for unaged or aged cable samples, this made $\varepsilon'$ independent of the frequency. As an increase in the values of $\varepsilon'$ has been observed with each thermal stress cycle, this has resulted in the generation of dipolar species. These dipoles are adding to the polarization of the material and hence to the $\varepsilon'$.

In contrast to $\varepsilon'$, the variation of $\varepsilon''$ values with frequency and aging period show how the $\varepsilon''$ is dependent on both variables. Since the values of $\varepsilon''$ changed more at the low frequencies as compared to high frequencies, resulting in the generation of conduction particles. These particles are adding to the losses and hence an increase in the $\varepsilon''$ has been observed. Due to thermal stress in the case of XLPE and CSPE, there is a generation of alkyl radicals. These radicals add to the ionic leakage or conduction current and are reflected in the prominent change of $\varepsilon''$, which has also been reported in the literature [11] (Fig. 4).

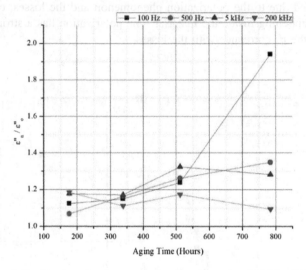

**Fig. 4.** Change of $\varepsilon''$ with unaged values vs. aging time (hours) at 100 Hz, 500 Hz, 5 kHz, and 200 kHz.

It was also observed that the minimum value of $\varepsilon''$ has shifted to higher frequency; from 20 Hz for unaged to 500 Hz, Fig. 5, which shows that how the thermal stress affected the polymer matrix and resulted in the generation of dipolar ionic conduction particles.

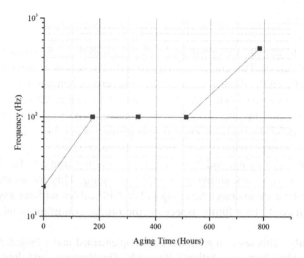

**Fig. 5.** Shifting of minimum value of $\varepsilon''$, corresponding frequency vs. aging time (hours).

The data of EaB as a function of aging time helps in validating the results of complex permittivity. The EaB values have been taken from the Laborelec Lab, Belgium, where the cable samples were thermally aged under the same conditions and EaB was measured. The EaB values decreased with aging time as reported in Fig. 6.

Since $\varepsilon''$ at 100 Hz has shown more variation with aging, hence it has been chosen as an electrical aging marker. A correlation between $\varepsilon''$ at 100 Hz and EaB has been established, Fig. 6. The decrease in the values of EaB and the increase in the values of $\varepsilon''$ shows that the thermal stress has effected the cable and has cause noteworthy embrittlement and also effected the dielectric property.

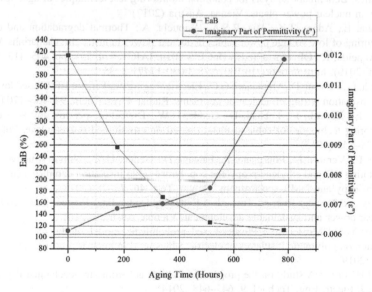

**Fig. 6.** Elongation at Break (EaB) and $\varepsilon''$ at 100 Hz vs. aging time (hours) correlation.

## 6    Conclusion

When it comes to the life extension of NPP, it is important to know the state of the insulation of LV cables. This could be achieved with the help of reliable CM techniques. In the lifetime of a cable, thermal stress is more severe as compared to other stresses in the power plants. Keeping in view the importance, in this research work LV NPP power cables are subjected to the thermal stress for four aging periods. The complex permittivity is measured for the aged samples. It was observed that both the real part $(\varepsilon')$ and imaginary part of permittivity $(\varepsilon'')$ increased with each aging cycle. The $\varepsilon''$ at 100 Hz showed more trend of aging, and was chosen as an aging marker. The $\varepsilon''$ developed a strong correlation with EaB, showing the effect of aging. This shows that the complex permittivity can be used to detect the aging in LV NPP cables without any destruction to the cable, which could be a future aspect for the online condition monitoring purpose.

**Acknowledgments.** This research work has been implemented under Project No. 123672 with the support provided from the National Research, Development and Innovation Fund of Hungary, financed under the KNN_16 funding scheme.

## References

1. Rising, A.: World Nuclear Performance Report 2019 (2019)
2. Chang, Y.S., Mosleh, A.: Probabilistic model of degradation of cable insulations in nuclear power plants. Proc. Inst. Mech. Eng. Part O J. Risk Reliab. **233**, 803–814 (2019)
3. Mustafa, E., Afia, R.S.A., Tamus, Z.Á.: Condition monitoring uncertainties and thermal - radiation multistress accelerated aging tests for nuclear power plant cables: a review. period. Polytech. Electr. Eng. Comput. Sci. **64**, 1–13 (2019)
4. IT Series: Benchmark analysis for condition monitoring test techniques of aged low voltage cables in nuclear power plants, Vienna, Austria (2017)
5. Mustafa, E., Ádám, T.Z., Afia, R.S.A., Asipuela, A.: Thermal degradation and condition monitoring of low voltage power cables in nuclear power industry. In: Camarinha-Matos, L. M., Almeida, R., Oliveira, J. (eds.) DoCEIS 2019. IAICT, vol. 553, pp. 405–413. Springer, Cham (2019). https://doi.org/10.1007/978-3-030-17771-3_35
6. Verardi, L., Fabiani, D., Montanari, G.C.: Electrical aging markers for EPR-based low-voltage cable insulation wiring of nuclear power plants. Radiat. Phys. Chem. **94**, 166–170 (2014)
7. Linde, E., Verardi, L., Fabiani, D., Gedde, U.W.: Dielectric spectroscopy as a condition monitoring technique for cable insulation based on crosslinked polyethylene. Polym. Test. **44**, 135–142 (2015)
8. Linde, E., Verardi, L., Pourmand, P., Fabiani, D., Gedde, U.W.: Non-destructive condition monitoring of aged ethylene-propylene copolymer cable insulation samples using dielectric spectroscopy and NMR spectroscopy. Polym. Test. **46**, 72–78 (2015)
9. Society and Nuclear Energy: Towards a Better Understanding. France, Paris (2003)
10. Nuclear power and sustainable development, Vienna, Austria (2016)
11. Chang, Y.-S., Mosleh, A.: Physics-based probabilistic model of the effects of ionizing radiation on polymeric insulators of electric cables used in nuclear power plants, California, USA (2019)
12. Lee, J.H., et al.: A study on the properties of CSPE according to accelerated thermal aging years. J. Electr. Eng. Technol. **9**, 643–648 (2014)

# Investigating the Complex Permittivity of Low Voltage Power Cables Under Different Stresses

Ramy S. A. Afia[1,2(✉)], Ehtasham Mustafa[2,3], Semih Bal[2], and Zoltán Ádám Tamus[2]

[1] Department of Electrical Power and Machines Engineering, Faculty of Engineering, Helwan University, Cairo, Egypt
ramysaad@h-eng.helwan.edu.eg

[2] Department of Electric Power Engineering, Faculty of Electrical Engineering and Informatics, Budapest University of Technology and Economics, Budapest, Hungary
{mustafa.ehtasham, bal.semih, tamus.adam}@vet.bme.hu

[3] Department of Electrical Engineering, Faculty of Engineering and Technology, Gomal University, Dera Ismail Khan, Pakistan

**Abstract.** This paper presents results of electrical tests carried out on nuclear power plant low voltage power cable samples based XLPE/CSPE polymer insulation. These cable samples have been subjected to accelerated thermal and mechanical stresses for 240, 480, 720 and 960 h. The effect of these aging stresses has been investigated through studying the real and imaginary parts of complex permittivity over frequency range from 20 Hz to 500 kHz. These two parameters are commonly used as aging markers to assess the insulation state of such kind of cables. The results show a non-uniform trend for the real and imaginary parts of permittivity. Also, it can be noticed that after the last two cycles, the imaginary part minimum values have been shifted to lower frequencies, 200 Hz.

**Keywords:** Nuclear power plant cables · Low voltage power cables · Aging stresses · Complex permittivity · Condition monitoring

## 1 Introduction

The continuous operation of Nuclear Power Plants (NPPs) relies on many components. One of these components is an enormous amount of cable systems. A typical nuclear power plant may compose of 1000 to 2000 km of cables. These cables are classified as Low Voltage (LV) & Medium Voltage (MV) Power cables, Instrumentation and Control (I&C) cables, special cables and general service cables [1–4]. These cables provide the communication between equipment, control and safety systems which monitor these plants. The insulation of these cables is mostly based on polymeric materials such as Cross-Linked Polyethylene (XLPE), Ethylene Propylene Rubber (EPR), Ethylene Vinyl Acetate (EVA), Polyether Ether Ketone (PEEK) and Cross-Linked Polyolefin (XLPO) [4, 5]. Different ageing mechanisms affect the polymeric insulation of such cables, multi-stress aging [6, 7]. As a results, the functionality of

© IFIP International Federation for Information Processing 2020
Published by Springer Nature Switzerland AG 2020
L. M. Camarinha-Matos et al. (Eds.): DoCEIS 2020, IFIP AICT 577, pp. 319–327, 2020.
https://doi.org/10.1007/978-3-030-45124-0_30

these cables is not ensured under the effect of these ageing mechanisms. However, the functionality of NPP cables should be guaranteed during the normal operation and during the Design Basis Event (DBE) [8, 9]. Multiple cable testing techniques have been widely developed for investigating the aging process of NPP cables [10]. The insulation state and role of low voltage power cables in nuclear power plants are frequently monitored through a destructive test technique. This testing technique named Elongation at Break (EaB) [11]. The advantage of this test is that, the aging can be effectively correlated but on the other hand, it requires sample scarification to be investigated and a proper laboratory is needed [3]. For lifetime extension, the cables must undergo a non-destructive test technique where some aging markers can be measured in-situ. Recently, measuring the electrical parameters of LV NPP cables became a trend of many researchers. For instance, measuring the capacitance, loss factor, impedance, insulation resistance and complex permittivity. A significant change in the electrical parameters of LV cables has been observed with aging. This paper presents a Frequency Domain Spectroscopy (FDS) of XLPE/CSPE insulation-based LV NPP power cable samples. The samples have been subjected to a sequential thermal and mechanical stresses. The study was based on the measurement of real ($\varepsilon'$) and imaginary ($\varepsilon''$) parts of permittivity. The real part represents the stored energy in the material when it is exposed to electric field while $\varepsilon''$ influence the energy absorption and attenuation. A high precision impedance analyser with frequency spanning from 20 Hz to 500 kHz has been used for the measurement of $\varepsilon'$ and $\varepsilon''$.

## 2    Relationship to Life Improvement

Energy makes marvelous things happen and its capacity to produce bright, radiant light makes an especially striking impression when it arrives. Electricity's introduction thus tends to be associated with progress and modernity. Electricity make big difference in many obvious places such as our homes, food, the commercial and manufacturing sectors, communication and transportation, entertainment, easier education and better health care. This makes the industry of electric power to have the large investments. Nuclear power plants are of the strategic ways to generate energy with many advantages like relatively low costs, providing a stable base load of energy and low pollution. In contrast, in case of accidents, radioactive waste possesses a threat to the environment and it is very dangerous for human beings. Because of the importance of the nuclear power plant cables, they must undergo a qualification process to ensure that these cables will do they intended functions. In addition, for lifetime extension, this qualification process has to be done in a non-destructive way since the replacement cost of these cables is not affordable. The harsh operating conditions in nuclear power plants accelerates the aging processes of cables causing failure. It is important to state the insulation state of these cables before insulation damage and this is a great challenge since there are many factors may cause this. Accelerated aging tests are required to examine the impact of different aging mechanism on insulation integrity of such kind of cables. So, in this paper, low voltage power cable samples used in nuclear power plants have been investigated to study the effect of thermal and mechanical stresses. The study based on frequency domain spectroscopy using impedance analyser over a wide frequency range. The two parts of complex permittivity, real and imaginary parts have been studied.

## 3  Experimental Work

### 3.1  Specimens

Low voltage (600 V) NPP power cable samples have been investigated. As shown in Fig. 1, the cable comprises three parts, tin-coated copper conductor, XLPE inner insulation and CSPE outer jacket. Table 1 lists the cable specifications.

**Fig. 1.**  Cable construction

### 3.2  Experimental Setup and Dielectric Measurements

Impedance analyzer has been used to measure the dielectric parameters over a range of frequency from 20 Hz to 500 kHz at 5 $V_{rms}$ output voltage. Based on the measured parameters, the real and imaginary parts of the complex permittivity have been calculated using Eqs. (1) and (2). As shown in Fig. 2b, the measurement was executed in Faraday cage to reduce the electromagnetic interferences. The test temperature was 25 °C ± 2%.

$$\varepsilon' = \frac{dC}{A\varepsilon_o} \tag{1}$$

$$\varepsilon'' = \frac{d}{AR\omega\varepsilon_o} \tag{2}$$

Where $A$ and $d$ are the electrode area and thickness of insulation respectively. The vacuum permittivity is given as $\varepsilon_o (\varepsilon_o = 8.85419 * 10^{-12}\,\text{F/m})$ and $\omega$ is the angular frequency ($\omega = 2\pi f$), f is the frequency expressed in Hz. $R$ is resistance measured in ohm ($\Omega$).

**Table 1.** Cable specifications.

| Parameter | Value |
|---|---|
| Nominal voltage | 0.6 kV |
| Inner insulation | XLPE |
| Insulation thickness | 1.143 mm |
| Jacket material | CSPE |
| Jacket thickness | 0.762 mm |
| Continuous bending radius | 38.1 mm |
| Overall diameter | 8.636 mm |

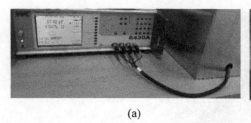
(a)

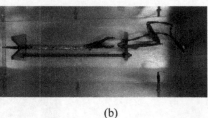
(b)

**Fig. 2.** Measurment setup (a) Impedance analyzer (b) Test sample connected to the measuring clamps in Faraday cage

### 3.3 Accelerated Aging Procedure

Two aging mechanisms have been applied to all samples. 4 aging cycles, the first and third are thermal aging cycles while the second and fourth are mechanical aging cycles. The thermal aging cycles are indexed as 1T, 2T while 1M, 2M for the mechanical aging cycles. The period of each cycle is 240 h. The thermal aging has been done by placing the samples in an oxygen-controlled oven at temperature 120 °C. After each thermal cycle and before starting the measurements, the samples left for one day at room temperature. For mechanical aging, the samples have been spiraled on a cylinder of 4.5 cm diameter.

## 4    Experimental Results

The behavior of the real part $(\varepsilon')$ of the complex permittivity is illustrated in Fig. 3. Regardless the aging type, the $\varepsilon'$ increased as the frequency stepped down. With the end of thermal cycle 1T, $\varepsilon'$ has increased over the whole frequency range. After the first mechanical cycle, 1M and the second thermal cycle, 2T, a reduction in $\varepsilon'$ has been observed for all frequencies. But after the second mechanical cycle, 2M, the $\varepsilon'$ has increased again over frequency range from 20 Hz to 250 kHz and slightly declined at frequencies 300 and 400 kHz.

Moving to the imaginary part $(\varepsilon'')$ of the complex permittivity, the plot of $\varepsilon''$ as a function of frequency is shown in Fig. 4. $\varepsilon''$ is plotted for frequencies from 200 Hz to

500 kHz as the resistance value at the frequencies below 200 Hz it greater than the maximum measuring range of the used device. As shown in Fig. 4, the $\varepsilon''$ increased as the frequency increased independent of the aging type. After thermal cycle 1T, the $\varepsilon''$ has increased over frequencies ranged from 20 Hz to 250 kHz while it decreased over frequencies 300, 400 and 500 kHz. At the end of the first mechanical cycle, 1M, the $\varepsilon''$ has increased from 200 Hz to 10 kHz while it decreased for the other frequencies up to 500 kHz. Also, the $\varepsilon''$ has decreased after the second thermal cycle, 2T over the entire frequency range. After the last cycle, 2M, the $\varepsilon''$ increased over all frequencies in comparison with the second thermal cycle, 2M.

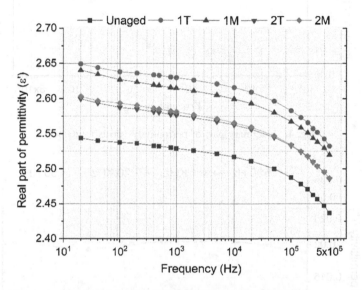

**Fig. 3.** Real part of permittivity versus frequency

To understand the changing behavior of $\varepsilon''$, frequencies 500 Hz, 1 kHz, 20 kHz and 50 kHz have been chosen as reference. As can be seen in Fig. 5, at frequencies 500 Hz and 1 kHz, an increment in $\varepsilon''$ has been observed after the first and second aging cycles then it declined after the third cycle and raised after the fourth cycle. While at frequencies 20 kHz and 50 kHz, $\varepsilon''$ went up after cycles 1T and 2M but dropped after 1M and 2T cycles (Fig. 5).

## 5   Discussion

Since the real part of permittivity, $\varepsilon'$ is related to the polarization phenomena and as the insulating materials are polar in nature. The considerable increment in $\varepsilon'$ after the first thermal cycle suggests an increase in the polarization process where chemical bonds were broken resulting in generation of dipoles and presenting micro voids between inner insulation and outer jacket which are source of space charges. The reduction in $\varepsilon'$

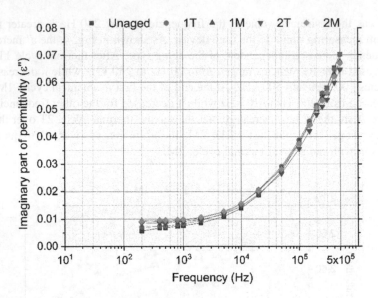

**Fig. 4.** Imaginary part of permittivity versus frequency

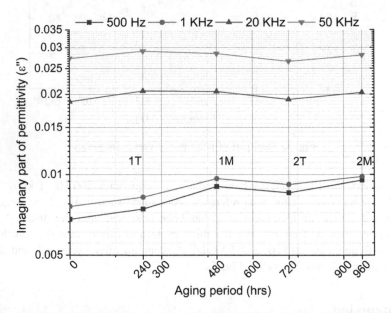

**Fig. 5.** Behaviour of imaginary part of permittivity at 500 Hz, 1 kHz, 20 kHz and 50 kHz

after the mechanical cycle, 1M, due to the mechanical stress, the micro voids which have been created after the first cycle have been reduced due to the compressive nature of the mechanical stress thus the polarization has decreased. With increasing the aging period, more structural changes happened to the insulation leading to reduction in the dipoles thus $\varepsilon'$ has decreased but after the second mechanical cycle, a noticeable increase in $\varepsilon'$ suggest the presence of micro cracks which associated with polymer materials under mechanical stress as reported in [12]. These micro cracks behave the same as the micro voids and hence add to the polarization.

The imaginary part of permittivity, $\varepsilon''$ is related to energy loss or insulation conductivity. The increment of $\varepsilon''$ after the first cycle, 1T is an indication for the presence of charge carriers produced due to structural changes also the presence of micro voids which contribute to the conduction process. The increase of $\varepsilon''$ after the first mechanical cycle shows the presence of chemical specious which are contributing to the conduction losses in spite of the reduction in micro voids. After cycle 2T, the chemical specious adding to the conduction losses have decreased due to re-creation of new bonds and hence resulted in reduction of $\varepsilon''$. As mention for $\varepsilon'$ after the second mechanical cycle, the space charges due to the presence of micro cracks are also added to the conduction losses.

Shifting the minimum values of $\varepsilon''$ to lower frequencies is plotted in Fig. 6. This shows that the polar or ionic particles have decreased while it contributes the conduction process.

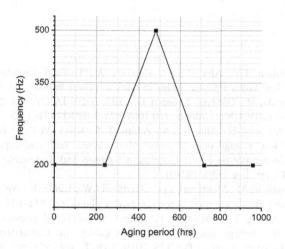

**Fig. 6.** Shifting the minimum values of $\varepsilon''$ versus the aging period

It should be noted that, during the manufacturing process of insulating materials, some additives are added to provide a special properties such as flame retardants, antioxidants. These additives affect the structural changes of insulating materials during aging processes. Chemical investigations such as OIT, DSC and TGA will provide a clear understanding for the effect of aging stresses [13].

# 6   Conclusion

The complex permittivity of low voltage insulation based XLPE/CSPE power cables has been studied in this research. The samples have been subjected to sequential thermal and mechanical stresses for four aging cycles each spanned to 10 days. The thermal stress carried out at temperature 120 °C and the mechanical stress carried out by spiraling the samples over a cylinder with a diameter of approx. 5% higher than the cable diameter. The results reported in this work shows that the polarization and conduction processes which are related to the real, $\varepsilon'$ and imaginary, $\varepsilon''$ parts of permittivity are affected with the thermal and mechanical aging mechanisms. Both, $\varepsilon'$ and $\varepsilon''$ have increased after the first thermal cycle and decreased after the second thermal cycle. For mechanical aging cycles, 1M and 2M, $\varepsilon'$ increased after 1M and decreased after 2M while $\varepsilon''$ has increased after both cycles. Only after 1M, $\varepsilon''$ has increased over frequency range 200 Hz to 10 kHz.

**Acknowledgments.** This research work has been implemented under Project No. 123672 with the support provided from the National Research, Development and Innovation Fund of Hungary, financed under the KNN_16 funding scheme.

# References

1. Mustafa, E., Ádám, T.Z., Afia, R.S.A., Asipuela, A.: Thermal degradation and condition monitoring of low voltage power cables in nuclear power industry. In: Camarinha-Matos, Luis M., Almeida, R., Oliveira, J. (eds.) DoCEIS 2019. IAICT, vol. 553, pp. 405–413. Springer, Cham (2019). https://doi.org/10.1007/978-3-030-17771-3_35
2. Asipuela, A., Mustafa, E., Afia, R.S.A., Ádám, T.Z., Khan, M.Y.A.: Electrical condition monitoring of low voltage nuclear power plant cables: tanδ and capacitance. In: 2018 International Conference on Power Generation Systems and Renewable Energy Technologies (PGSRET), pp. 1–4. IEEE (2019)
3. Verrardi, L., Fabiani, D., Montanari, G.C., Gedde, U.W., Linde, E.: Aging investigation of low-voltage cable insulation used in nuclear power plants, pp. 851–854 (2012)
4. Afia, R.S.A., Ádám, T.Z., Mustafa, E.: Effect of combined stresses on the electrical properties of low voltage nuclear power plant cables. In: Camarinha-Matos, Luis M., Almeida, R., Oliveira, J. (eds.) DoCEIS 2019. IAICT, vol. 553, pp. 395–404. Springer, Cham (2019). https://doi.org/10.1007/978-3-030-17771-3_34
5. Lee, S.H., Lee, J.D., Kim, M.Y., Jang, H.S., Jeong, C.H.: Evaluation of accelerated ageing cables used in nuclear power plant. In: Proceedings of 2012 IEEE International Conference on Condition Monitoring and Diagnosis, pp. 681–684 (2012)
6. Afia, R.S.A., Mustafa, E., Ádám, T.Z.: Mechanical stresses on polymer insulation materials. In: IEEE International Conference on Diagnostics in Electrical Engineering, pp. 2–5 (2018)
7. Mustafa, E., Afia, R.S.A., Tamus, Z.Á.: Condition monitoring uncertainties and thermal - radiation multistress accelerated aging tests for nuclear power plant cables: a review, 1–13 (2019)
8. Glass, S.W., et al.: Assessment of NDE for key indicators of aging cables in nuclear power plants - interim status. In: AIP Conference Proceedings, vol. 1706 (2016)

9. Anandakumaran, K., Seidl, W., Castaldo, P.V.: Condition assessment of cable insulation systems in operating nuclear power plants. IEEE Trans. Dielectr. Electr. Insul. **6**, 376–384 (1999)

10. Series, I.T.: Benchmark analysis for condition monitoring test techniques of aged low voltage cables in nuclear power plants. IAEA-TECDOC-1825, p. 179 (2017)

11. Banford, M., Fouracre, R.A.: Nuclear technology and ageing. IEEE Electr. Insul. Mag. **15**, 19–27 (1999)

12. Plaček, V., Kohout, T., Kábrt, J., Jiran, J.: The influence of mechanical stress on cable service life-time. Polym. Test. **30**, 709–715 (2011)

13. Mustafa, E., Afia, R.S.A., Tamus, Z.Á.: Investigation of complex permittivity of XLPO insulated photovoltaic DC cables due to thermal aging. In: Németh, B. (ed.) ISH 2019. LNEE, vol. 598, pp. 261–269. Springer, Cham (2020). https://doi.org/10.1007/978-3-030-31676-1_25

# Investigation of Power Line Sag Uncertainty in Day-Ahead DLR Forecast Models

Levente Rácz[✉], Dávid Szabó, Gábor Göcsei, and Bálint Németh

Budapest University of Technology and Economics, 18 Egry József Street,
Budapest 1111, Hungary
racz.levente@vet.bme.hu

**Abstract.** Dynamic line rating method (DLR) is a novel and cost-effective way to extend power overhead lines (OHLs) transfer capacity based on real-time monitoring of the weather parameters in the vicinity of the conductor. Via DLR models not only real-time, but also day-ahead transfer capacity calculation is possible which is more important from the aspect of TSOs. It is important to mention, that these DLR predictions are based on weather forecasts that usually has some uncertainty. The aim of the paper is to identify the potential risk of forecasted power line ampacity due to uncertain weather forecast. To investigate this rarely studied topic, several simulations were carried out applying real power line parameters and forecasted weather data. The results of the simulations showed that under unfavorable weather conditions the uncertainty of the weather prediction could significantly increase the sag of the OHLs if they fully utilized. To monitor the real-time state of the conductor's sag, a novel risk factor calculation method was also investigated that provides additional safety information for the system operators in real time.

**Keywords:** Dynamic line rating · DLR · Transmission system · Sag ·
Clearance · Weather forecast · Ampacity

## 1 Introduction

Today's rising demand for energy and the increasing pace of renewable energy production pose many challenges for engineers and electricity system operators. Although the emission of renewable energy sources is more favorable than conventional power plants, there are many problems with irregular, non-periodic energy production. This affects not only the producer and consumer side, but also the transmission and distribution network between them. The role of this existing power system is becoming more and more important as the close interrelation between the level of security of supply and safe operation is a central issue today. This was recognized by the transmission system operators (TSOs) responsible for the operation of the transmission network, which enabled the emergence of new technologies and methods. One of these methods is the dynamic line rating (DLR), which is used to calculate the transfer capacity of power lines in real time. While this can significantly increase transmission capacity, several other factors, such as sag and clearances need to be taken more carefully than previously due to potential physiological effects (possible carcinogenesis) of the

© IFIP International Federation for Information Processing 2020
Published by Springer Nature Switzerland AG 2020
L. M. Camarinha-Matos et al. (Eds.): DoCEIS 2020, IFIP AICT 577, pp. 328–336, 2020.
https://doi.org/10.1007/978-3-030-45124-0_31

operating OHLs [1–4]. The aim of this paper is to present the potential risk of sag-clearance deviation due to the uncertainty of weather forecast within the application of DLR.

## 2 Contribution to Life Improvement

With the advancement of technology, new approaches - such as DLR - become available for transfer capacity calculation of the power lines. The essence of DLR is to install special sensors and weather stations in the vicinity of the power lines to collect real-time data on load and environmental parameters. Sensors are mostly installed on the conductors as they measure mostly conductor temperature, while weather stations are usually installed on the structure of the towers. Using real-time data, it is possible to adjust transfer capacity to environmental changes at all time intervals without exceeding the maximum conductor temperature limit. Applying this method, trans-mission capacity could be extended by 5–30% in more than 95% of the time, which significantly contributes to increase network resilience (Fig. 1).

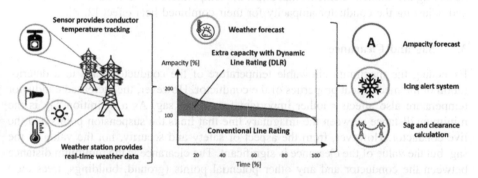

**Fig. 1.** Complex grid management system based on dynamic line rating

The application of DLR leads much further as it can serve as a basis for a complex transmission grid management system. The implementation of the DLR enables, inter alia, real-time conductor temperature tracking, real-time ampacity calculation, transfer capacity forecast, sag and clearance modeling and implementing an icing alert system for the conductor [5–7]. It is important to mention that this complex grid management increase the resilience of the existing grid and enables a higher level of energy supply. Another important issue is that while the quality of energy service increases the level of safety is not allowed to reduce. The aim of this paper is present the potential threats of potential sag problems due to weather forecast uncertainty and to present a novel risk calculation method to redound the exploitation of the DLR technology benefits.

## 3 Sag and Clearance of the OHLs

The design of power lines is a very complex task, as both electrical and mechanical aspects - which are interconnected on many fibers - need to be considered. It is important to mention, that for most power lines, the possibility of using DLR method has not yet been considered, so the thermal conditions, sag and clearance calculation are worth to be explored in more detail [2, 3].

### 3.1 Conductors' Thermal Behavior

One important factor that influences the OHLs ampacity is the temperature of the conductor, due to the transferred current heats up the conductor according to Joule-law. All OHLs has a maximum temperature that cannot be exceeded (in the range of 40 °C–95 °C) due to mechanical issues. Applying SLR it is extremely rare to exceed this temperature limit due to in most cases the environment is not worse than the designed case. However, applying DLR, the goal is to ensure the maximum transfer capacity while the maximum conductor temperature is not exceeded. This can be achieved by observing the ambient elements that affect the temperature of the conductor in real time and adjusting the conductor ampacity for their combined heat effect [2, 8].

### 3.2 Sag and Clearance

Exceeding the maximum allowable temperature of the conductor leads to a deterioration of the mechanical properties of the conductor. However, the increased conductor temperature also affects another important factor, the sag. As a definition sag is the minimum distance between the imaginary line that links the suspension points and the live conductor. However, from the aspect of safety and security, not the value of the sag, but the value of the clearance is significant. The clearance is the minimum distance between the conductor and any other potential points (ground, buildings, trees etc.) [2, 3] (Fig. 2).

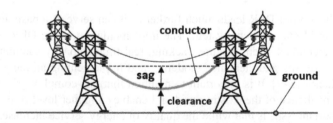

**Fig. 2.** Visualization of sag and clearance in case of a simplified OHL

The live parts of the power lines need to be separated and insulated from the other potential parts. Depending on whether the other potential object is part of the transmission line or not, there is a difference between internal and external clearance. Moreover, the design must also consider overvoltage cases in addition to the operating frequency range. Clearance values vary across voltage levels, the higher the operating voltage, the greater the required protection distance. Theoretically, the use of DLR does not violate the legally defined clearances, since the aim of this method is to always maintain the maximum allowable temperature. However, measurement and model errors or control inaccuracies may cause the temperature limits to be exceeded for a short time that need to be treated proper [2–4, 8].

## 4 Weather Forecasts

Although the great advantage of DLR is to calculate transfer capacity in real time based on the environmental parameter values, conductors' real-time ampacity is not sufficient for the system operator. From the aspect of TSOs, the emphasis is on scheduling the next day's network loads, which anticipates the need for the real ampacity of each OHL to be available day-ahead. However, applying DLR-based grid management system, this can be achieved, but for model inputs as solar radiation, ambient temperature, wind speed etc. forecasted values are necessary [5, 6].

### 4.1 Weather Forecast Systems

As it was mentioned, the input of DLR model needs to be forecasted weather data. It is important to mention that in case of DLR forecasts, there is no dedicated weather station, so meteorological data and models are in use. All over the world different meteorological forecasting models exist depends on the required forecasting issues. In Europe the most common models are the ALADIN and ECMWF models. For these models, the forecasting time and the temporal and spatial resolution of the data are different [6]. Table 1 summarizes their most important properties.

**Table 1.** Meteorological forecast models in Europe

|                      | ALADIN    | ECMWF     |
|----------------------|-----------|-----------|
| Forecasting period   | 1–3 days  | 2–10 days |
| Temporal resolution  | 1 h       | 1–3 h     |
| Spatial resolution   | 1 km      | 5–10 km   |

Based on Table 1, ALADIN model fits better for DLR as hourly resolution is a basic requirement for day-ahead load schedules and day-ahead electricity market.

### 4.2 The Effect of Weather Forecast Uncertainty

From the ALADIN model, the day-ahead forecast values for the weather parameters with hourly resolution are available. Applying these data as an input of the CIGRE DLR model, the transfer capacity limit for each hour can be determined considering the maximum allowable conductor temperature. This ampacity can be the basis for the TSOs' day-ahead load schedule. On the other hand, it is important to mention that all weather forecast has an uncertainty which need to be considered properly. If the combination of the real weather parameters results a worse case than the predicted one, applying the forecasted ampacity could lead to sag increment if the OHL is fully utilized. In these cases, it is important to take care of the reduced clearance whether it still meets the legal requirements of safety and security [9].

## 5   Risk Factor Analysis of OHL Sag

In order to find out the effect of weather forecast uncertainties a case study was carried out with the data of an existing power line within the framework of FLEXITRAN-STORE project.

For the simulations data of a 110 kV single-circuit OHL with 240/40 mm$^2$ AlFe conductor on each phase was applied. This OHL is equipped with conductor temperature sensors and weather stations on the tower which provides real-time data for every 15 min. The maximum allowable conductor temperature is 40 °C and the static line rating is 530 A for the summer period. Due to legal requirements, most of the spans need to fulfill 7 m as a clearance criterium, but there are some exceptions where 5.5 m is the safety distance [4–7].

### 5.1   The Applied Weather Forecast

The day-ahead weather forecasts applied in the simulations are from the ALADIN, which is a numerical weather prediction model applied for limited geographic areas. However, the spatial resolution of this model is still 1 km which is not proper for a long OHL. In order to get more precise forecast data, the national weather service interpolates these ALADIN data to the section of the OHL which is equipped with weather station equipped with solar radiation detector, anemometer etc. While these local weather station operates all day, the forecasted and real-time data for the forecasted are available for the same place which is the basis of the comparison (Table 2).

**Table 2.**   Forecasted parameters available from the meteorology

| Forecasted parameter | Dimension | Forecasted parameter | Dimension |
|---|---|---|---|
| Ambient temperature | °C | Wind speed | m/s |
| Precipitation | mm/h | Wind direction | ° |
| Solar radiation | W/m$^2$ | | |

### 5.2   Simulation Result

The simulation was carried out for the whole period of a summer months (July), due to the heating effect of the environment is the most dominant in this part of the year. For each hour of each day, a day-ahead transfer capacity limit was calculated for the OHL based on the thermal behavior of the conductor. All OHL has a maximum temperature value that cannot be exceeded due to legal and safety issues. If this temperature value and weather forecast is available, the transfer capacity – ampacity – of the OHL can be clearly calculated. Knowing the forecasted ampacity values, it was simulated how the conductor temperature varies on the next day if the real-time weather data are applied and the OHL is fully utilized. In these cases, the main problem is that the forecasted weather data and the real weather data for the forecasted period rarely matches. This could lead to sag-clearance problems that could be seen in Fig. 3.

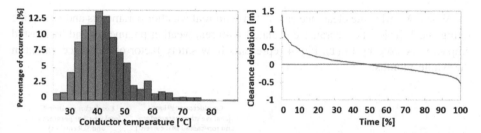

**Fig. 3.** Simulation results of conductor temperature and the duration curve for clearance in July

Figure 3 represents the deviation of sag due to weather forecast inaccuracy. It can be seen, that roughly in the half of the time the conductor temperature exceeds the 40 ° C limit value. According to this, sag increases which means lower clearance value shifting the risk factor to the higher region.

## 5.3 Risk Factor Calculation for the Sag and Clearance

When designing power lines, a safety margin in addition to legal distance is always insured for clearance, but its value varies in a great range, from a few centimeters to a few meters. It is therefore advisable to split the whole clearance value into a legal component and a safety margin component. This safety margin belongs to the worst-case condition and varies from span to span. For this OHL this safety margin value for the worst-case conditions is nearly 50 cm on the lowest conductor of the lowest span.

Thus, according to the Fig. 3, this safety margin is exceeded almost 8% of the time which results more frequent violation than the designed value and legally not permissible. However, this worst-case combination is very rare in reality, so it distorts the calculated risk. To eliminate this distortion, a dynamic clearance analysis was investigated that handles the risk according to the environmental conditions and not according to the worst-condition. This model defines a region between two boundaries and represents how the clearance calculated with the forecasted ampacity and the real-time weather fits into it. One of the two boundaries is the legal component, while the other one is the clearance simulated with real-time weather parameters and the static line rating.

In order to find out the real risk, which means that the conductor reaches the edge of the legal component, calculated clearances are reduced with the legally defined clearance components. The safety factor is calculated from the ratio of the reduced clearances obtained.

$$safety\,factor = \frac{X - legal\ component\ of\ clearance}{Y - legal\ component\ of\ clearance} \quad (1)$$

Where $X$ [m] is the clearance calculated with real weather parameters and static line rating and $Y$ [m] is the clearance calculated with real weather parameters and forecasted ampacity. According to (1), Fig. 4 represents how safety factor of clearance varies in the whole months.

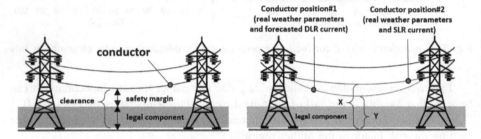

**Fig. 4.** Components of clearance and the visualization of dynamic clearance model

In Fig. 5 the region marked with blue means that safety factor is higher than 100%. This means that clearance calculated with the forecasted ampacity is less than the clearance calculated with the static line rating. In normal cases, these cases are extremely rare, and the area marked with green is more significant. However, for this OHL due to the sag and clearance limit the static line rating is also modified that makes weather forecast uncertainty less spectacular. One big advantage of dynamic clearance risk calculation is that the size of the range between the boundaries changes from hour to hour as the weather changes. In this model when safety factor reaches zero or turns into the negative range, it means that the sag increment of the conductor harms the legal component of the clearance which cannot be tolerated due to safety and security.

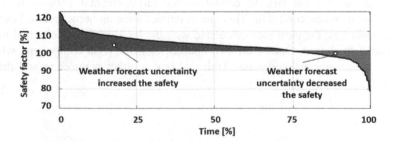

**Fig. 5.** Duration curve of safety factor for clearance in July (Color figure online)

# 6 Conclusion

From the aspect of TSOs the most relevant issue is to calculate the day-ahead transfer capacity of each power lines that requires proper weather forecast. The major aim of this paper is to present that sag/clearance problems that could appear due to weather forecast uncertainty. Investigating this phenomenon, conductor sag deviation was simulated for an existing, fully utilized OHL. Simulations showed that the ampacity of the line calculated with weather forecast data could be different that the ampacity calculated with the real time weather parameters present at the forecasted time. Due to this, in almost half of time higher ampacity is predicted than the real transfer capacity which reduces the safety factor of clearance. In those cases, when the forecasted weather is close to the worst-case design parameters this deviation could be significant and need to be handled. For other, so-called more general cases, a new dynamic clearance risk calculation method was implemented to represent the effect of the weather forecast uncertainty. According to the simulation, the risk increment for the clearance was not significant on the observed OHL. However, due to every OHL is different, further simulations are required to get a broader picture of how clearances could change in case of day-ahead DLR forecasts.

**Acknowledgments.** This work has been developed in the High Voltage Laboratory of Budapest University of Technology and Economics within the boundaries of FARCROSS GA No 864274 project funded by Horizon2020. The project aims to connect major stakeholders of the energy value chain and demonstrate integrated hardware and software solutions that will facilitate the "unlocking" of the resources for the cross-border electricity flows and regional cooperation.

# References

1. McCall, J.C., Servatius, B.: Enhanced economic and operational advantages of next generation dynamic line rating systems, Paris, France (2016)
2. Kiessling, E., Nefzger, P., Nolasco, J.E., Kaintzyk, U.: Overhead Power Lines. Springer, Berlin (2002). https://doi.org/10.1007/978-3-642-97879-1
3. Perneczky, G.: Szabadvezetékek feszítése (Tension of OHLs, in Hungarian), Műszaki Könyvkiadó, Budapest, Hungary (1968)
4. Rácz, L., Szabó, D., Göcsei, G.: Investigation of electric and magnetic field in the application of dynamic line rating. In: Németh, B. (ed.) ISH 2019. LNEE, vol. 598, pp. 145–153. Springer, Cham (2020). https://doi.org/10.1007/978-3-030-31676-1_15
5. Rácz, L., Szabó, D., Göcsei, G., Németh, B.: Grid management technology for the integration of renewable energy sources into the transmission system. In: 7th International Conference on Renewable Energy Research and Applications (ICRERA), Paris, France, pp. 612–617 (2018). https://doi.org/10.1109/icrera.2018.8566852

6. Szabó, D., Rácz, L., Göcsei, G., Németh, B.: DLR-based ice prevention method. In: 18th International Workshops on Atmospheric Icing of Structures, Reykjavík, Iceland (2019)
7. Rácz, L., Szabó, D., Göcsei, G., Németh, B.: Integration of Monte Carlo methods into ice prevention model. In: 18th International Workshops on Atmospheric Icing of Structures, Reykjavík, Iceland (2019)
8. Lovrenčić, V., Gabrovšek, M., Kovač, M., Gubeljak, N., Šojat, Z., Klobas, Z.: The contribution of conductor temperature and sag monitoring to increased ampacities of overhead lines (OHLs). Periodica Polytechnica, Budapest, Hungary (2015)
9. Szabó, D., Göcsei, G., Németh, B., Cselkó, R., Rácz, L.: Examination of clearances during high voltage live-line working. In: 37th Electrical Insulation Conference (EIC), Calgary, AB, Canada (2019)

# Biomedical Analysis and Diagnosis

# Combination of Medical Imaging and Demographic Data for Parkinson's Disease Diagnosis

Helena Rico Pereira[1,2]([⊠]), José Manuel Fonseca[1],
and Hugo Alexandre Ferreira[2]

[1] CTS – Center of Technology and Systems, Uninova,
NOVA University of Lisbon, 2829-518 Caparica, Portugal
hri.pereira@campus.fct.unl.pt, jmf@uninova.pt
[2] Instituto de Biofísica e Engenharia Biomédica da Faculdade de Ciências da,
Universidade de Lisboa, 1749-016 Lisbon, Portugal
hugoferreira@campus.ul.pt

**Abstract.** The identification of biomarkers to discriminate Parkinson's Disease from other motor diseases is crucial to provide suitable treatment to patients. This study proposes a novel approach for the classification of structural Magnetic Resonance Imaging (MRI), Dopamine Transporter scan data (DaTscan) and demographic information (age and gender) to differentiate PD patients, "Scans Without Evidence for Dopaminergic Deficit" (SWEDD) patients and healthy control subjects using Convolutional Neural Networks (CNN). In Control vs PD, the accuracy of the classifier increased by adding subject gender from 94.5% to 96.0%, while in PD vs SWEDD adding age lead to 88.7% accuracy using slices encompassing the basal ganglia. The CNN was not able to successfully discriminate SWEDD vs Control. Our results suggested that pattern changes in slices encompassing the basal ganglia and the mesencephalon are relevant biomarkers for PD suggesting that this approach may have the potential to aid in PD biomarkers detection.

**Keywords:** Parkinson's Disease · Convolutional Neural Networks · MRI · DaTscan SPECT · SWEDD

## 1 Introduction

Parkinson's Disease (PD) is a progressive neurodegenerative disease associated with the degeneration of the dopamine neurons located at the *Substantia Nigra* (SN). This neurodegeneration causes one of the main features of PD patients; the presence of motor symptoms [1]. However, these symptoms only begin to emerge when about 50% of the degeneration of the SN neurons has already occurred [2]. The incidence of PD is higher in the elderly [3] and men [4]. Nowadays, the diagnosis of PD is based on medical history, signs and symptoms, and positive response to PD medication [5]. However, misdiagnosis usually occurs mainly due to symptoms similarity between PD and other motor disorders [6]. Currently, medical imaging techniques, namely Magnetic Resonance Imaging (MRI) and Single Photon Emission Computed Tomography

© IFIP International Federation for Information Processing 2020
Published by Springer Nature Switzerland AG 2020
L. M. Camarinha-Matos et al. (Eds.): DoCEIS 2020, IFIP AICT 577, pp. 339–346, 2020.
https://doi.org/10.1007/978-3-030-45124-0_32

(SPECT), are not used for diagnosis but reveal useful insights regarding the disease progression [1, 7]. SPECT with Dopamine Transporter imaging (DaTscan) is used to detect presynaptic dopamine dysfunction, which is a biomarker of PD [7]. An interesting finding of DaTscan usage was the identification of a small group of patients (10–20%) [8] diagnosed as having PD but presenting "Scans Without Evidence of Dopaminergic Deficit" (SWEDD), that is, presenting a normal DaTscan. MRI is also of particular interest to differentiate PD from other motor diseases characterized by structural brain changes [1]. In the last few years, Artificial Intelligence (AI) algorithms have become a promising approach for the classification of medical imaging of PD patients [9]. Therefore, the following research question aroused: "Can MRI and SPECT imaging together with subject demographic data (age and gender) provide useful information to aid physicians in reducing diagnosis uncertainty?". In this paper, a model for PD and SWEDD prediction using MRI and SPECT imagens in combination with age and gender as additional information using Convolutional Neural Networks (CNN) is proposed.

## 2   Contribution to Life Improvement

It is possible to find in the literature numerous approaches using AI algorithms to detect diseases and relevant biomarkers [10, 11]. The model proposed in this study aims to address the need for accurate diagnosis, hence, contributing to the improvement of patients' quality-of life. Usually, these patients have difficulty doing their daily tasks due to the motor and non-motor symptoms such as sleep disturbances, mood disorders and smell impairment [12], which lead to poor quality-of-life. Therefore, early diagnosis at the disease onset may contribute to adjusting the therapeutics and relieve symptoms [13]. Besides, the identification of biomarkers allows PD monitorization and the understanding of the mechanism underlying the disease.

## 3   State of the Art

Several studies have used medical imaging techniques such as MRI and DaTscan to detect anatomical and physiopathological features of PD [1, 7]. For instance, a review study focused on MRI imagens and Voxel-Based Morphometry (VBM) reported volume differences in the grey matter of the frontal lobe, olfactory bulb, basal ganglia, and SN [1]. Regarding SPECT imagens, a study found that performing this exam during a two-year follow-up reduced the period of observation even in ambiguous cases [14] in 90% of the cases. In this regard, each imaging modality provides different biomarkers associated with PD [1]. More recently, some studies made use of AI, namely, machine learning algorithms to differentiate PD from other diseases [10, 11, 15–17]. Using Support Vector Machine (SVM), Singh et al. [18] classified previously extracted intensities from segmented T1-Weighted (T1-W) MRI images of PD, SWEDD and Controls subjects (accuracies above 95%), while Oliveira et al. [19] computed and classified striatal region ratios at voxel level from DaTscan images of PD patients and control subjects (97% accuracy). Adeli et al. [11] classified extracted features from MRI and SPECT images using a kernel-based SVM. However, studies using SVM have the disadvantage of using features that are known to be related to PD, which leads to lost information that may provide new insights regarding the disease. For instance, Oliveira et al. only considered binding ratio, a PD biomarker, which is expected to lead to higher accuracies. In single-modality classification, Choi et al. [15] used 3D CNN to classify PD and Control images (96% accuracy) and used the trained CNN to classify SWEDD patients, while Esmaeilzadeh et al. [10] used 3D T1-W images to discriminate PD patients from Control subjects and analyzed the heatmaps, highlighting the most relevant features for the classification (SN and basal ganglia). However, although presenting higher accuracy, the majority of these studies including those that used CNN have the disadvantage of using imbalanced data. Beyond medical imaging, demographic information, such as age [10, 20] and gender [10], have also been considered relevant to differentiate between PD patients from control subjects.

## 4 Model for Images and Demographic Data Classification

Data used in study were extracted from the Parkinson's Progression Markers Initiative (PPMI) database (www.ppmi-info.org/data). For up-to-date information on the study, visit www.ppmi-info.org. One MRI and one DaTscan image per subject were extracted from PD, SWEDD and Control cohorts. According to PPMI documentation [21], 3D T1-W images were acquired at 1.5T and 3T with MPRAGE GRAPPA or SAG FSPGR sequences, and DaTscan images were obtained 4 h after radiotracer Ioflupane I123 administration. The Mann-Whitney U and the Chi-Squared tests were performed to verify if the data sample used in this study were age and gender-matched using a 5% significance level. MRI pre-processing was performed using SPM12 [22] and included Anterior Commissure (AC) – Posterior Commissure (PC) alignment correction, bias regularization, spatial normalization to Montreal Neurological Institute (MNI) brain template, bias regularization and smoothing. According to PPMI documentation [23], DaTscan images were already pre-processed when extracted from the database. They were reconstructed using an iterative reconstruction algorithm based on hybrid ordered-subset expectation maximization in HERMES (Hermes Medical Solutions, Stockholm, Sweden). Then, a standard 3D Gaussian 6.0 mm filter was applied to the resultant image and normalized to the MNI template. In this work, DaTscan images were co-registered to the corresponding MRI image of each subject. Then, MRI and DaTscan data were divided into 2D axial slices to better adapt our approach and classification models to current clinical practice, and a Contrast Limited Adaptive Histogram Equalization was applied to each MRI slice to improve and uniformize image contrast without overamplify noisy regions [24]. For the classification, three slices of each subject encompassing SN and basal ganglia were averaged, since they are associated with PD. The architecture of CNN used in this work is illustrated in Fig. 1, and it was implemented using the Caffe framework [25]. The CNN, in contrast with other algorithms such as SVM, are able to directly extract features from images and classify their weights, which may result in higher classification accuracies and smaller classification times. The Monte Carlo Cross-Validation (MCCV) method was used to provide an unbiased classification performance estimation. Five batches were created using

MCCV with the proportion 2:1:1 for train, validation and test sets. Besides brain images, age and gender were also provided to the network. Two images were created for each feature to represent this additional information, as illustrated in Fig. 2.

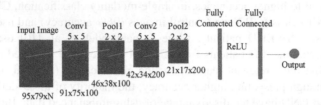

**Fig. 1.** CNN architecture

Males were defined with horizontal and vertical lines (similar to a chessboard), while vertical lines only represented females. Concerning the age of the subjects, each age value was divided by 100 to be in the range of 0 and 1. Then, for each age, an image with black squares and the background set with the value of the normalized age was created. The Gradient-weighted Class Activation Mapping (Grad-CAM) method proposed by Selvaraju et al. [26] was used to identify relevant regions in the classification. The proposed classification model was computed in a CentOS Linux7 and using the graphics card NVIDIA GeForce GTX TITAN X.

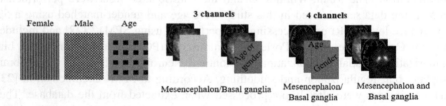

**Fig. 2.** The 3 channels comprised slices of the mesencephalon or the basal ganglia together with age or gender, while 4 channels comprise that data with both demographic information (age and gender) or alternatively slices of the basal ganglia and the mesencephalon simultaneously.

## 5   Results and Discussion

The developed model yielded relevant results for the discrimination of PD, SWEDD, and control subjects using a multimodal approach and demographic information. The number of subjects used was 168 control ($60 \pm 11$ years old, 59 females, 109 males), 378 PD ($62 \pm 10$ years old, 136 females, 242 males), 58 SWEDD ($62 \pm 10$ years old, 20 females, 38 males). The results of the Mann-Whitney U and Chi-Square tests suggest that those Control, PD and SWEDD groups do not show statistically significant age and gender differences ($p > 0.05$). The relevant features using by CNN to classify the images are illustrated in Fig. 3. The results of each classification are shown in

Table 1. Overall, the accuracy of the classifier was higher using slices encompassing the basal ganglia in comparison with slices, including the mesencephalon as in the study of Pereira [27]. As expected, the classification Control vs PD using slices encompassing the mesencephalon and the basal ganglia yielded higher accuracy (94.5%) corresponding to a Receiver's Operating Characteristic Area Under Curve (AUC) = 0.98 [0.95–1.00] and Cohen's kappa = 0.98 ± 0.05. These results are consistent with the study of Adeli et al. [20] in which SN, putamen and caudate were selected as the more relevant region of interest by the SVM model, and with Kollia et al. [28] which achieved 94% using also CNN (55 PD and 33 Control). Although with lower accuracy (79.3%) than SPECT slices, MRI slices encompassing the mesencephalon were able to discriminate Control from PD. Moreover, the analysis of the features extracted from de CNN, illustrated in Fig. 3, suggests the SN as a relevant region for the classification, corroborating other studies in which changes in the SN were found [1]. Concerning the classification of the Control vs SWEDD groups, the CNN was not able to discriminate these two groups, hence supporting the evidence that SWEDD patients present similar brain scans to Control subjects [8].

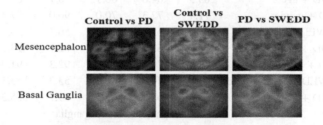

**Fig. 3.** The heatmaps obtained using the GRAD-Cam algorithm. Regions in red represent the most relevant features for the classification, while blue illustrate the regions less important. (Color figure online)

The classification of PD vs SWEDD using only MRI and DaTscan slices suggest that the performance of our model is better [29] when using slices encompassing the basal ganglia (AUC = 0.93 [0.83–1.00]) in contrast to slices encompassing the *mesencephalon* (AUC = 0.67 [0.82–0.86]), supporting the hypothesis that PD and SWEDD are two distinct groups, in which SWEDD shows no evidence of dopamine deficit [30]. Adding gender to the classification, only increased the accuracy in Control vs PD with slices encompassing the basal ganglia, while decreased in MRI slices encompassing the mesencephalon. These results support the study of Haaxma et al. [31] in which striatal dopamine levels differences were found between men and women. However, for both Control vs SWEDD and PD vs SWEDD, gender decreased the accuracy. It is important to note that in these two comparisons, the number of subjects used in train, validation and test (subjects = 116) was smaller than in Control vs PD (subjects = 336). In contrast to some studies in which age improved the classification of PD vs Control [10, 20], the results obtained in this study showed a decrease in the accuracy value. However, those studies used imbalanced data, which may lead to a biased classification towards the group with more subjects increasing misclassification of minority classes [32]. Interestingly, our classification of PD vs SWEDD improved when age was included. However, it is important to note that for this case, a small data set (test set = 30 subjects) was used which can potentiate biased estimations. Besides, this CNN model is only able to classify 2D imagens, loosing information that 3D imagens can provide, such as volume of brain structures [10].

**Table 1.** Results of the classification.

| Group | Mesencephalon | | | Basal ganglia | | |
|---|---|---|---|---|---|---|
| | Acc (%) | Sen (%) | Spe (%) | Acc (%) | Sen (%) | Spe (%) |
| Control vs PD | 79.3 | 82.9 | 75.7 | 93.1 | 93.8 | 92.7 |
| Control vs SWEDD | 52.7 | 56.0 | 49.3 | 57.0 | 48.0 | 57.3 |
| PD vs SWEDD | 63.3 | 66.7 | 60.0 | 87.3 | 90.1 | 84.0 |
| Control vs PD + age | 76.9 | 83.4 | 71.4 | 93.3 | 93.8 | 92.9 |
| Control vs SWEDD + age | 62.7 | 62.7 | 62.7 | 54.0 | 60.0 | 48.0 |
| PD vs SWEDD + age | 65.3 | 64.0 | 66.7 | 88.7 | 86.7 | 90.7 |
| Control vs PD + gender | 71.4 | 72.3 | 70.0 | 96.0 | 97.3 | 94.3 |
| Control vs SWEDD + gender | 52.0 | 65.3 | 39.7 | 56.7 | 56.0 | 57.3 |
| PD vs SWEDD + gender | 61.3 | 62.7 | 60.0 | 86.7 | 93.3 | 80.0 |
| Control vs PD + age + gender | 72.4 | 70.0 | 74.7 | 92.3 | 91.9 | 89.3 |
| Control vs SWEDD + age + gender | 53.3 | 46.7 | 60.0 | 53.3 | 53.3 | 57.3 |
| PD vs SWEDD + age + gender | 67.6 | 68.0 | 65.3 | 85.7 | 85.3 | 89.3 |
| | Mesencephalon + Basal ganglia | | | | | |
| | Acc (%) | | Sen (%) | | Spe (%) | |
| Control vs PD | 94.5 | | 92.9 | | 96.1 | |
| Control vs SWEDD | 53.3 | | 57.3 | | 49.3 | |
| PD vs SWEDD | 84.7 | | 84.0 | | 85.3 | |

Acc = Accuracy, Sen = Sensitivity, Spe = Specificity

## 6   Conclusion and Future Work

A multi-modality approach using CNN and additional demographic information is proposed to differentiate between PD, SWEDD and Control subjects. Notably, this work extends previous studies by adding age and gender as additional information for the CNN classifier, being the first study that combines MRI, SPECT, age and gender to distinguish between PD and SWEDD patients. The results support the relevance of biomarkers, such as the basal ganglia and the SN for the classification of images of PD and SWEDD patients. However, it is essential to note some limitations of this study. Although previous studies support the results, the model was only internally validated. Moreover, the images that represent age and gender were created arbitrarily. Therefore, future work should include an external validation of the proposed approach as well as optimization of network parameters or improve the CNN architecture to classify also 3D images. Additional techniques to translate and integrate the demographic information in the network should also be investigated.

**Acknowledgments.** The authors would like to thank the financial support from Fundação para a Ciência e Tecnologia (FCT) under the project UID/BIO/00645/2019 and UIDB/00066/2020 (CTS – Center of Technology and Systems), Programa Operacional Temático Competitividade e Internacionalização under the project POCI-01-0145-FEDER-016428, to the NVIDIA GPU Grant Program and to work by PPMI personnel that went into accumulating the data, as well as funding of the study. PPMI – a public-private partnership – is funded by the Michael J. Fox Foundation for Parkinson's Research and industry partners: https://www.ppmi-info.org/about-ppmi/who-we-are/study-sponsors/.

# References

1. Saeed, U., Compagnone, J., Aviv, R.I., et al.: Imaging biomarkers in Parkinson's disease and Parkinsonian syndromes: current and emerging concepts. Transl Neurodegener. **6**, 8 (2017)
2. Cheng, H.-C., Ulane, C.M., Burke, R.E.: Clinical progression in Parkinson disease and the neurobiology of axons. Ann. Neurol. **67**(6), 715–725 (2010)
3. Reeve, A., Simcox, E., Turnbull, D.: Ageing and Parkinson's disease: why is advancing age the biggest risk factor? Ageing Res. Rev. **14**(100), 19–30 (2014)
4. Wooten, G.F., Currie, L.J., Bovbjerg, V.E., et al.: Are men at greater risk for Parkinson's disease than women? J. Neurol. Neurosurg. Psychiatry **75**(4), 637–639 (2004)
5. Williams, D.R., Litvan, I.: Parkinsonian syndromes. Contin. Lifelong Learn. Neurol. **19**(5), 1189–1212 (2013)
6. Fearnley, J.M., Lees, A.J.: Striatonigral degeneration. A clinicopathological study. Brain **113**(6), 1823–1842 (1990)
7. Brooks, D.J.: Imaging approaches to Parkinson disease. J. Nuclear Med. **51**(4), 596–609 (2010)
8. Erro, R., Schneider, S.A., Stamelou, M., et al.: What do patients with scans without evidence of dopaminergic deficit (SWEDD) have? New evidence and continuing controversies. J. Neurol. Neurosurg. Psychiatry **87**(3), 319–323 (2016)
9. Xu, J., Zhang, M.: Use of magnetic resonance imaging and artificial intelligence in studies of diagnosis of Parkinson's disease. ACS Chem. Neurosci. **10**(6), 2658–2667 (2019)
10. Esmaeilzadeh, S., Yang, Y., Adeli, E.: End-to-end Parkinson disease diagnosis using brain MR-images by 3D-CNN. CoRR. abs/1806.05233 (2018)
11. Adeli, E., Wu, G., Saghafi, B., et al.: Kernel-based joint feature selection and max-margin classification for early diagnosis of Parkinson's disease. Sci. Rep. **7**(1), 41069 (2017)
12. Olanow, C.W., Schapira, A.H.V., Obeso, J.A.: Parkinson's disease and other movement disorders in Harrison's principles of internal medicine, 19th edn, pp. 2609–2626. McGraw-Hill Education, New York (2015)
13. Lang, A.E., Lozano, A.M.: Parkinson's disease. N. Engl. J. Med. **339**(16), 1130–1143 (1998)
14. Tolosa, E., Vander, B.T., Moreno, E.: Accuracy of DaTSCAN (123I-Ioflupane) SPECT in diagnosis of patients with clinically uncertain parkinsonism: 2-year follow-up of an open-label study. Mov. Disord. **22**(16), 2346–2351 (2007)

15. Choi, H., Ha, S., Im, H.J., et al.: Refining diagnosis of Parkinson's disease with deep learning-based interpretation of dopamine transporter imaging. NeuroImage Clin. **16** (September), 586–594 (2017)
16. Singh, G., Samavedham, L.: Algorithm for image-based biomarker detection for differential diagnosis of Parkinson's disease. IFAC-PapersOnLine **48**(8), 918–923 (2015)
17. Kollia, I., Stafylopatis, A.-G., Kollias, S.: Predicting Parkinson's disease using latent information extracted from deep neural networks. CoRR. abs/1901.07822 (2019)
18. Singh, G., Samavedham, L.: Unsupervised learning based feature extraction for differential diagnosis of neurodegenerative diseases: a case study on early-stage diagnosis of Parkinson disease. J. Neurosci. Methods **256**, 30–40 (2015)
19. Oliveira, F.P.M., Castelo-Branco, M.: Computer-aided diagnosis of Parkinson's disease based on [(123)I]FP-CIT SPECT binding potential images, using the voxels-as-features approach and support vector machines. J. Neural Eng. **12**(2), 026008 (2015)
20. Palumbo, B., Fravolini, M.L., Buresta, T., et al.: Diagnostic accuracy of Parkinson disease by support vector machine (SVM) analysis of 123I-FP-CIT brain SPECT data. Med. (Baltimore) **93**(27), e228 (2014)
21. Parkinson's Progression Markers Initiative. MRI - Technical Operations, PPMI (2015)
22. Friston, K.J.: Statistical Parametric Mapping: The Analysis of Functional Brain Images. Functional Neuroimaging: Technical, p. 656. Elsevier/Academic Press, Amsterdam (2006)
23. Marek, K., Chowdhury, S., Siderowf, A., et al.: The Parkinson's progression markers initiative (PPMI) – establishing a PD biomarker cohort. Ann. Clin. Transl. Neurol. **5**(12), 1460–1477 (2018)
24. Zuiderveld, K.: Contrast limited adaptive histogram equalization. In: Graphics Gems, pp. 474–485. Elsevier (1994)
25. Jia, Y., et al.: Caffe: convolutional architecture for fast feature embedding. In: Proceedings of ACM International Conference on Multimedia - MM14, pp. 675–678 (2014)
26. Selvaraju, R.R., Cogswell, M., Das, A., et al.: Grad-CAM: visual explanations from deep networks via gradient-based localization. In: IEEE Conference on Computer Vision, October 2017, pp. 618–626 (2017)
27. Pereira, H.R., Ferreira, H.A.: Classification of patients with Parkinson's disease using medical imaging and artificial intelligence algorithms. In: Henriques, J., Neves, N., de Carvalho, P. (eds.) MEDICON 2019. IP, vol. 76, pp. 2043–2056. Springer, Cham (2020). https://doi.org/10.1007/978-3-030-31635-8_241
28. Tagaris, A., Kollias, D., Stafylopatis, A., et al.: Machine learning for neurodegenerative disorder diagnosis—survey of practices and launch of benchmark dataset. Int. J. Artif. Intell. Tools **27**(03), 1850011 (2018)
29. Hajian-Tilaki, K.: Receiver Operating Characteristic (ROC) curve analysis for medical diagnostic test evaluation. Casp. J. Intern. Med. **4**(2), 627–635 (2013)
30. Bajaj, N.: SWEDD for the general neurologist. ACNRSO **10**(4), 30–31 (2010)
31. Haaxma, C.A., Bloem, B.R., Borm, G.F., et al.: Gender differences in Parkinson's disease. J. Neurol. Neurosurg. Psychiatry **78**(8), 819–824 (2007)
32. Longadge, R., Dongre, S.: Class imbalance problem in data mining review. Eur. J. Intern. Med. **24**(1), e256 (2013)

# Ventricular Assist Device in Health 4.0 Context

Marcelo Barboza[1]($\boxtimes$), Fabricio Junqueira[1], Eduardo Bock[2],
Tarcisio Leão[2], Jeferson Dias[1], Jonatas Dias[1], Marcosiris Pessoa[1],
José Ricardo Souza[1], and Diolino dos Santos[1]

[1] Department of Mechatronics and Mechanical Systems Engineering,
Escola Politécnica da USP, São Paulo, Brazil
Marcelo.barboza@usp.br
[2] Federal Institute of Technology in Sao Paulo, São Paulo, Brazil

**Abstract.** In the current digital era, the physical world has a cyber-representation. Both the real and virtual worlds are connected in areas, such as informatics and manufacturing. This phenomenon is currently emerging in health applications. Health 4.0 (H4.0) refers to a group of initiatives aiming to improve medical care for patients, change the business practices of hospitals and create new insight for researchers and medical device suppliers. Increasing collaboration in terms of physicians, medical equipment, artificial organs, and biosensors is a way to facilitate H4.0. In this work, a reference architecture model for Industry 4.0 (RAMI 4.0) is used to support such collaboration in medical devices control system projects. A methodology was applied to design a ventricular assist device. The results show that RAMI 4.0 is an adequate technique for modeling a device as a H4.0 component. Future works should implement the designed control system.

**Keywords:** Health 4.0 · Industry 4.0 · RAMI 4.0 · Control system · Ventricular Assist Device (VAD)

## 1 Introduction

A discussion regarding future trends in health equipment, artificial organs and biosensors is required for interoperability aiming to improve medical care for patients, change the business practices of hospitals and create new insight for researchers and medical device manufacturers [1].

In fact, in some industries, this practice, which is called digital and cyber convergence, has already been established, and the cyber-physical systems (CPS) or the Internet of Things (IoT) are the main technology used. Both are the basis of Industry 4.0 (I4.0) in manufacturing and digital convergence in informatics [2].

Based on the I4.0 concept, Health 4.0 (H4.0) has been derived according to the health domain. Connected sensors with cyber representations will be used more frequently and connected devices may be used to track patients or measure vital signs in the future with H4.0. For instance, an algorithm was developed to estimate arterial blood pressure with a noninvasive photoplethysmography sensor, and the estimated pressure is presented via a smartphone or smartwatch [1]; The Food and Drug Administration (FDA), which is the American department responsible for medical

L. M. Camarinha-Matos et al. (Eds.): DoCEIS 2020, IFIP AICT 577, pp. 347–354, 2020.
https://doi.org/10.1007/978-3-030-45124-0_33

equipment, has already approved some applications for iPhones and iPads with self-diagnostic and self-prognostic capabilities [3]; A telemedicine system structure oriented by service was proposed and implemented [4]. However, developing a standard for the use of this type of device is important for interoperability, the creation of more services and improving patients' quality of life.

Was not found in literature a Reference Architecture Model for Health 4.0. The IEC 62264-1:2013 standard (Enterprise-control system integration: Models and terminology) was used as an architecture model reference to develop control systems early in industry, and later in health [5]. However, the IEC 62264 standard alone is insufficient for modeling control systems in connected applications that requires that level of interoperability and collaboration.

## 1.1   RAMI 4.0

To develop an uniform architecture model as a reference, Plattform Industrie 4.0, which is a German organization responsible for developing and promoting I4.0, proposed the Reference Architecture Model Industrie 4.0 (RAMI 4.0) in 2015 [6].

RAMI 4.0 (as shown in Fig. 1) is a three-dimensional model used to represent the I4.0 components. RAMI 4.0 supports novel research in manufacturing as follows a study describes the machine controller as an I.40 component [7]. Pisching et al. proposed a method to create an architecture based in RAMI 4.0 and applied it to develop a system which a smart product discover an equipment to be manufactured [8]. RAMI 4.0 is based on the IEC 62264-1:2013 (Enterprise-control system integration: Models and terminology), IEC 61512-1:1997 (Batch Control: Models and terminology) and IEC 62890:2016 (Enterprise-control system integration: Models and terminology) standards [9] and was inspired in the smart grid architecture model (SGAM), a framework for design projects in smart grid domains [6].

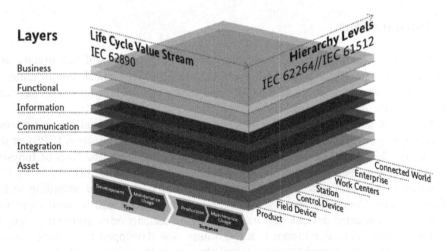

**Fig. 1.**  Reference architecture model for Industry 4.0 (RAMI 4.0) [6].

## 1.2   Ventricular Assist Device

Recently, ventricular assist device (VAD) therapy has emerged as an alternative for heart transplantation for heart failure patients. However, some adverse events, such as bleeding, stroke, and aortic insufficiency, still occur in VAD patients. Based on the hypothesis that a physiologically controlled VAD can prevent some of these events, various concepts of physiological controllers have been developed over the last decades [10–14].

VAD consist in pump with motor, controller, outflow, driveline cable and batteries as show in Fig. 2.

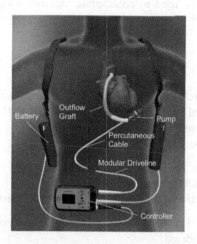

**Fig. 2.**   Ventricular Assist Device (VAD) [15].

The aim of the current study is design a VAD control system in H4.0 context. For reach interoperability, collaboration and connected requirements RAMI 4.0 was used.

## 2   Contribution to Life Improvement

According World Health Organization, 32,3 million people will die in 2060 in consequence of circulatory system decease [16]. Heart failure is a serious healthcare issue and affect about 23 million people worldwide [17]. With heart failure, the main organ cannot pump enough blood for body, Ventricular Assist Device (VAD) operates together with the natural heart, decreasing the mechanical work of the myocardia required to pump blood in patients with severe heart diseases. VADs are centrifugal pumps. VAD had already increased survival of more than 40,000 people [18, 19], but only 30% of VAD patients are free from any adverse events [20]. Physiological system control could solve adverse events, nevertheless is a big challenge [10–14].

Schlöglhofer et al. proposed a standard call every two weeks for a group of VAD patients during one year. Comparing with the control group without call, the group with call intervention increased survival from 59% to 89% after 2 years [20].

It believes that increase survival also if physicians analyze current and stored VAD data. A cloud connected control system for a VAD has been implemented. Based on hypothesis that physicians could improve the life of patients with remote management of VAD data, a connected VAD could send the telemetry data to a cloud platform.

IoT is used in other industries to bring device data to a cloud platform, nevertheless the device must to be describe as an IoT component. According Plattform Industrie 4.0, in manufacture, to connect an IoT device in a cloud service, is necessary to describe it as an I4.0 component using RAMI 4.0 [6].

RAMI 4.0 going to be used to describe and implement a cloud connected VAD control system. RAMI 4.0 could be used also to design other H4.0 components. That H4.0 components could be used to collaborate together with physicians and improve life of patients.

## 3   Methods

A VAD control system architecture that store data in cloud was designed. The proposed architecture was described as a H4.0 component using RAMI 4.0. Method proposed by Pisching et al. [8] was used to describe it.

That method consists:

(1)   Describe components function shared by layer;
(2)   Draw components as blocks in 3D model RAMI;
(3)   Conceptual and functional modeling of the processes using PFS/MFG technique.

For that study steps 1 and 2 was conducted. "Life cycle Value Stream" axe of RAMI 4.0 was not considered.

Technique proposed for Leão et al. [21] was used as basis for VAD local control system.

## 4   Results

A connected VAD can send data to a cloud platform to improve the patients' life quality.

Follow specifications, a standard VAD has a motor, integrated current sensor, pressure and flow estimators, speed control, flow control and automatic control [21]. To render VAD a H4.0 component, the VAD has also a historical data in cloud for storage VAD and patient data.

In this study, the life cycle axis was not considered in developing the VAD. The hierarchy levels control device, and connected environment were considered.

### 4.1   Control Device

The "Control Device Hierarchy" components are shown in Fig. 3(a). The "Control device hierarchy"/"Asset" layer was developed with two components:

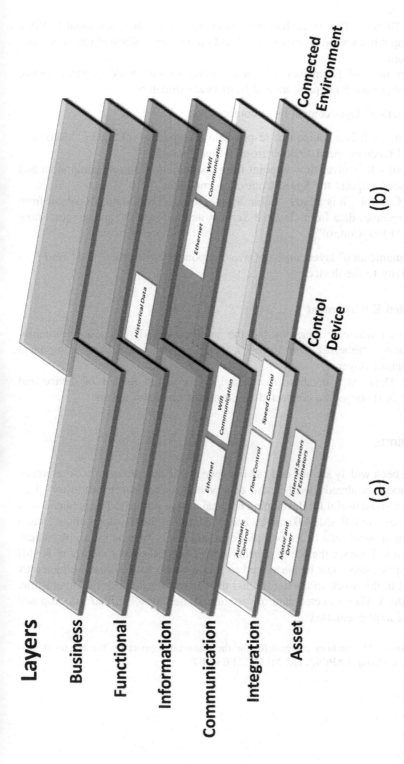

**Fig. 3.** VAD Control system proposed by Leão et al. [21] described as a H4.0 component. (a) Control device agents. (b) Connected environment agents.

- Motor and Driver – That is the hardware in charge to transfer movement to VAD pump. Its input is a voltage of motor speed and outputs are voltage of real speed and motor current.
- Internal Sensors and Estimators – That are other sensors build in local control system. In that case flow, pressure and heart beat estimators.

The "Integration" layer contain three components:

- Speed Control – It is a component responsible for updates voltage to "Motor and Driver" and receives speed setpoint from "Flow Control".
- Flow Control – It receives flow setpoint from "Automatic Control" component and provides speed setpoint to "Speed Control" component.
- Automatic Control – It is a Fuzzy Logic System that receives status of patient from physician, receives data from "Internal Sensors and Estimators" and suggests flow setpoint to "Flow Control".

The "Communication" layer consist of two components: "Ethernet" and "Wi-Fi" to bring connectivity to the device.

### 4.2   Connected Environment

The connected environment hierarchy has the same previously discussed communication components ("Ethernet" and "Wi-Fi"), including "Historical Data" component in the "Information" layer.

"Historical Data" is a database to maintain information related of device and patient. Figure 3(b) shows the connected environment hierarchy agents.

## 5   Conclusions

Health 4.0 has been widely studied and can improve the healthcare system. A reference architecture model is already used in the energy and manufacturing industry; thus, RAMI 4.0 can also be useful for developing medical device projects. The application in VAD design shows that RAMI 4.0 enables and standardizes the development of Health 4.0 components to send data to a cloud platform and bring information to physicians that could use it to improve the life of patients with VAD. Other case studies of RAMI 4.0 in H4.0 applications must be performed in future works to examine the hierarchy levels not used in this work and better discuss the life cycle patient-device interaction. Furthermore, the VAD connected control system and the physician platform proposed are in phase of implementation.

**Acknowledgments.** The authors are grateful for the financial support by the Brazilian government agencies, CNPq, FAPESP, and MEC/CAPES/PET.

# References

1. Sannino, G., De Falco, I., De Pietro, G.: A continuous non-invasive arterial pressure (CNAP) approach for Health 4.0 systems. IEEE Trans. Ind. Inform. 1–1 (2018). https://doi.org/10.1109/TII.2018.2832081

2. Lu, Y.: Industry 4.0: a survey on technologies, applications and open research issues. J. Ind. Inf. Integr. **6**, 1–10 (2017). https://doi.org/10.1016/J.JII.2017.04.005

3. Ferrer-Roca, O., Méndez, D.G.: Health 4.0 in the i2i Era. Int. J. Reliab. Qual. E-Healthcare. **1**, 43–57 (2012). https://doi.org/10.4018/ijrqeh.2012010105

4. Dubgorn, A., Kalinina, O., Lyovina, A., Rotar, O.: Foundation architecture of telemedicine system services based on Health 4.0 concept. SHS Web Conf. **44**, 00032 (2018). https://doi.org/10.1051/shsconf/20184400032

5. Yue, L., Li, X.: A smart manufacturing compliance architecture of electronic batch recording system (eBRS) for life sciences industry. In: Proceedings - 2018 3rd International Conference on Mechanical, Control and Computer Engineering, ICMCCE 2018, pp. 206–212. Institute of Electrical and Electronics Engineers Inc. (2018). https://doi.org/10.1109/ICMCCE.2018.00050

6. Adolphs, D.P., et al.: Reference Architecture Model Industrie 4.0 (RAMI4.0). ZVEI – German Electrical and Electronic, Frankfurt am Main, Alemanha (2015)

7. Langmann, R., Rojas-Pena, L.F.: A PLC as an Industry 4.0 component. In: 2016 13th International Conference on Remote Engineering and Virtual Instrumentation (REV), pp. 10–15. IEEE (2016). https://doi.org/10.1109/REV.2016.7444433

8. Pisching, M.A., Pessoa, M., Junqueira, F., dos Santos Filho, D.J., Miyagi, P.E.: An architecture based on RAMI 4.0 to discover equipment to process operations required by products. Comput. Ind. Eng. **125**, 574–591 (2018)

9. Lu, Y., Morris, K., Frechette, S.: Current Standards Landscape for Smart Manufacturing Systems. National Institute of Standards and Technology, EUA (2016). https://doi.org/10.6028/NIST.IR.8107

10. Uebelhart, B., et al.: Study of a centrifugal blood pump in a mock loop system. Artif. Organs **37**, 946–949 (2013). https://doi.org/10.1111/aor.12228

11. Petrou, A., Lee, J., Dual, S., Ochsner, G., Meboldt, M., Schmid Daners, M.: Standardized comparison of selected physiological controllers for rotary blood pumps. Vitro Study. Artif. Organs. **42**, E29–E42 (2018). https://doi.org/10.1111/aor.12999

12. Stevens, M.C., Stephens, A., AlOmari, A.-H.H., Moscato, F.: Physiological control. In: Mechanical Circulatory and Respiratory Support, pp. 627–657. Elsevier (2018). https://doi.org/10.1016/B978-0-12-810491-0.00020-5

13. Pauls, J.P., Stevens, M.C., Bartnikowski, N., Fraser, J.F., Gregory, S.D., Tansley, G.: Evaluation of physiological control systems for rotary left ventricular assist devices: an in-vitro study. Ann. Biomed. Eng. **44**, 2377–2387 (2016). https://doi.org/10.1007/s10439-016-1552-3

14. Daners, M.S., et al.: Left ventricular assist devices: challenges toward sustaining long-term patient care. Ann. Biomed. Eng. **45**, 1836–1851 (2017). https://doi.org/10.1007/s10439-017-1858-9

15. Heatley, G., et al.: Clinical trial design and rationale of the Multicenter Study of MagLev Technology in Patients Undergoing Mechanical Circulatory Support Therapy with HeartMate 3 (MOMENTUM 3) investigational device exemption clinical study protocol. J. Hear. Lung Transplant. **35**, 528–536 (2016). https://doi.org/10.1016/j.healun.2016.01.021

16. World Health Organization: WHO | Projections of mortality and causes of death, 2016 to 2060. WHO (2018)

17. Medvedev, A.L., Karimov, J.H., Kuban, B.D., Horvath, D.J., Moazami, N., Fukamachi, K.: Unlocking the box: basic requirements for an ideal ventricular assist device controller. Expert Rev. Med. Devices **14**, 393–400 (2017). https://doi.org/10.1080/17434440.2017. 1318059
18. Kormos, R.L., et al.: The society of thoracic surgeons intermacs database annual report: evolving indications, outcomes, and scientific partnerships. Ann. Thorac. Surg. **107**, 341– 353 (2019). https://doi.org/10.1016/j.athoracsur.2018.11.011
19. Kirklin, J.K., et al.: Second annual report from the ISHLT mechanically assisted circulatory support registry. J. Hear. Lung Transplant. **37**, 685–691 (2018). https://doi.org/10.1016/j. healun.2018.01.1294
20. Schlöglhofer, T., et al.: A standardized telephone intervention algorithm improves the survival of ventricular assist device outpatients. Artif. Organs (2018). https://doi.org/10. 1111/aor.13155
21. Leão, T., et al.: Development of rotational automatic control method to an implantable centrifugal blood pump. In: Abstracts ASAIO 61st Annual Conference, Chicago (2015)

# RehabVisual: Application on Subjects with Stroke

Ana Ferreira[1,2,3]([✉]), Patrícia Santos[1,3], Pedro Dias[1], Amélia Alves[3], Beatriz Carmo[3], Filipe Vilhena[3], Sofia Costa[3], Cláudia Quaresma[1,2], and Carla Quintão[1,2]

[1] Departamento de Física, Faculdade de Ciências e Tecnologia da Universidade Nova de Lisboa, Caparica, Portugal
aix.ferreira@campus.fct.unl.pt
[2] LIBPhys - UNL, Faculdade de Ciências e Tecnologia da Universidade Nova de Lisboa, Caparica, Portugal
[3] Departamento de Saúde, Escola Superior de Saúde do Instituto Politécnico de Beja, Beja, Portugal

**Abstract.** Strokes are a major cause of motor, perceptual and cognitive dysfunction. Thus, perceptual stimulation in individuals with stroke is a fundamental procedure in the rehabilitation process, since it contributes to improved performance in activities of daily living. Perceptive rehabilitation could be performed with conventional procedures or by applying technology. However, the methods used to evaluate and treat perceptual changes using visual stimuli are generic and not personalized. Therefore, an innovative platform called RehabVisual was developed and already used with little children. It has the objective of stimulating the visuomotor competence. The platform is now applied to 3 subjects with stroke. The purpose of this article is to describe the platform and present the results of the application in stroke patients.

**Keywords:** Visuomotor skills · Stroke · Rehabilitation

## 1 Introduction

Stroke is a leading cause of mortality and disability worldwide and the economic costs of treatment in poststroke care are substantial [1, 2]. The European countries, including Portugal, aren´t an exception. Strokes mainly affect individuals at the peak of their productive life [3]. They cause a greater range of disabilities than any other condition [4]. It is estimated that 60% of stroke survivors have visual problems immediately after their stroke [5].

A multitude of stroke presentations with various combinations of visual-perceptual impairments are seen in the post stroke population. The visual changes could be caused by deficits in movement of extraocular muscles or could be caused by lesions in cerebral areas related to visual processing.

In that area, neglect is the most common situation. This is a neurological disorder in which patients fail to detect or respond to contralesional stimuli and has long been considered a failure of attentional orienting mechanisms [6]. Unilateral body neglect

L. M. Camarinha-Matos et al. (Eds.): DoCEIS 2020, IFIP AICT 577, pp. 355–365, 2020.
https://doi.org/10.1007/978-3-030-45124-0_34

may occur independently of visual field cuts or visual inattention or may be compounded by these deficits [7]. Because of safety concerns related to this, neglect should be addressed early in the rehabilitation process [8]. Many patients with mild neglect have spontaneous improvement of their symptoms within weeks of onset. Those with profound neglect may improve over a period of many months [9]. The literature doesn't reveal a single intervention best suited for addressing neglect. A multifaceted approach can be helpful [5].

In a clinical setting, the therapist manages poststroke subjects with stroke sequelae due to motor disability in ocular muscles and due to damage to visual cortical areas. Human visual behaviour needs attention and visual demand. Visual attention is intentional visual feedback from the environment and visual search is a process of choosing objects and focusing their attention on the environment [10]. Visual attention is a method of meaningful information selection which enables human beings to act correctly in their daily lives [11].

Visuomotor skills are based on the coordination between the reception and processing of visual information with motor activity [12]. In people with stroke sequelae it is necessary to apply multidisciplinary rehabilitation in order to improve the outcomes. In recent years, technology brings an important contribution to the rehabilitation process and can be used with different disabilities.

Perceptive rehabilitation could be performed with conventional procedures or by applying technology. However, the methods used to evaluate and treat perceptual changes using visual stimuli are generic and not personalized. Therefore, our team developed an innovative platform called RehabVisual [13, 14]. The platform has the objective of stimulating the visuomotor competence [13].

New technologies have the potential to support clinical evaluation, precisely to control and measure therapy and implement novel forms of mechanical manipulation impossible for therapists to stimulate [15]. The creation and introduction of new tools require an evaluation by representative users of the target audience. Thus, there are several types of questionnaires that can be applied in order to obtain the usability of a new tool.

Usability is defined as the extent to which a product can be used by specific users to achieve specific goals effectively, efficiently and satisfactorily in a specific context of use [16]. There exist different methods to assess the usability of a tool and the system usability scale (SUS) is only one of them. The SUS was created by John Brooke with the aim of quickly obtaining a value relative to the subjective opinion of the individuals who used the tool [17]. This scale is widely used in health applications [18]. The questionnaire consists of ten statements, each of which has five response hypotheses ranging from "strongly disagree" to "strongly agree".

## 1.1   Motivation

Visual skills are fundamental to human performance in all areas of occupation. They are fundamental through the life span and can be compromised by a wide range of injuries. In that context it is extremely important to improve a patient's function when this is compromised due to acute neurological damage. Rehabilitation could be done in a more classic way, with conventional intervention. In recent years there has been an increase in technological tools, some of them with application in perceptive rehabilitation.

This work is developed under the intention to determine the utility of the Rehab-Visual platform. It is our goal to know the applicability for rehabilitation of stroke survivors that have sequelae of visuomotor skills. Another proposed element is to discover the users' opinion about platform usefulness.

For this investigation the research question is to explore the efficacy of the Rehabvisual platform in the stimulation of visuomotor skills in stroke patients.

## 2   Contribution to Life Improvement

The economic, social and individual problems due to stroke are already proven [1]. Particularly devastating are the visuomotor skills and the visual attentional problems [5]. They are respectively related to oculomotor problems and to cerebral visual lesions.

It is urgent to promote the full rehabilitation of these skills in order to contribute to stroke survivors' life improvement. The traditional ways of rehabilitation are predominantly static and based on "paper and pencil" tasks. They also privilege the therapeutic intervention in clinical settings and attribute less importance to home stimulation. With a different background and perspective, younger rehabilitation teams utilized classic strategies but integrated new ones with the use of technology in rehabilitation treatment. An example is the use of virtual reality for poststroke unilateral spatial neglect [19]. However, that systematic review also demonstrated that research is still limited and needs to improve.

Considering the results obtained by the application of the RehabVisual platform to babies with developmental problems [13, 14] it is intended to test the efficacy of RehabVisual in visuomotor skills rehabilitation of patients with stroke sequelae.

This technological solution allows the stimulation in clinical settings and in the home environment.

## 3   Materials and Methods

In this chapter, we describe the technological equipment applied during visual stimulation. We also present the protocol stimulation used and the characteristics of the group of participants.

### 3.1   RehabVisual Platform

This is a technological platform created in 2017 to promote the stimulation of visuomotor skills in children under 18 months and provide the systematic report [14]. It has already been presented [13, 14] but continues improving according to the findings obtained with the applications in different populations. RehabVisual was created using several programming languages included HTML, CSS, PHP, and JS. To create the database, the language chosen was SQL [13].

The platform should be delivered in a full screen version on a personal computer. It could be installed locally or hosted on a private website, depending on the preference of the rehabilitation team. The main characteristics of platform are:

– Could be used by different members of the team: occupational therapists, ophthalmologist and caregivers/patients. Each one has access to specific parts and some information (like an explanation about visuomotor skills) is accessible to all;
– Professionals have a specific part to record the evaluation of each patient;
– Therapists have access to all stimulation material and can select the specific frames that each patient can use. In that way, the stimulus provided is personalized according to the necessities of the patients;
– The patient/caregiver only has access to some stimuli selected by the therapists, not having access to any information that is in the domains of other users.

The RehabVisual platform has two sessions: database and protocol with the stimuli. In database, it records the clinical information (ophthalmological and behavioral evaluation) related to the patient. The protocol with stimuli is used according to the development of the participant and allows the selection of what is more appropriate for each patient [14]. In Fig. 1 we see the diagram with the platform structure (Fig. 1).

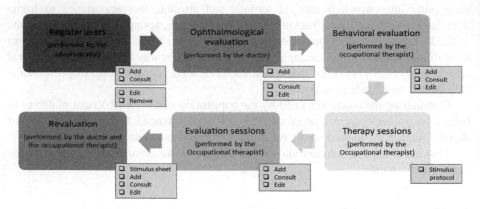

**Fig. 1.** Diagram with platform structure.

The ophthalmologist and the occupational therapists can record demographic information such as age, diagnosis and clinical issues. The occupational therapist can record all the information concerning the behavioral assessment, the functional evaluation and can choose the stimulus protocol during the procedure. The ophthalmologist can consult this information.

The stimulus protocol is developed based on the bibliography consulted and on the professional experience of collaborators in previous applications. So, the version used in this study is composed of geometrical figures which attributes that change in relation to the following parameters: geometric forms (squares, triangles, circles and mixed patterns); dimension (12 cm, 8 cm and 4 cm); color (red, yellow, blue, green, black and white); movement (static and moving figures – horizontal, vertical, circular and diagonal) and speed (slow, medium and fast).

The set of stimuli available allows the user to choose from a wide range of options with different levels of complexity to stimulate [14]. The information related to the diagnosis, Ophthalmological condition and behavioral performance was recorded in a database. Thus, it is divided in to patient chart; assessment of ophthalmological parameters; behavioral evaluation; functional evaluation of the vision; monitoring of intervention sessions [13] (Fig. 2).

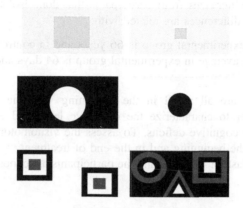

**Fig. 2.** Different characteristics of geometric figures

It is also important to note that the platform could be used online or offline, depending on the local conditions and goals of the team. When the tool is used by the rehabilitation team, members should register the information via the online platform to ensure that all staff have the most up to date information in real time. However, in another situation the platform could also be used offline. For that the platform is installed in the personal computer of therapist to be presented. In that case the data is recorded locally.

## 3.2 Participants in Clinical Investigation

This research is conducted on six post stroke subjects. The subjects are selected based on convenience, in two health units of Alentejo. The subjects have poststroke due to ischemia of middle cerebral artery (MCA) or posterior cerebral artery (PCA), and the distribution is the same in both groups. They are in acute phase and show deficits in visuomotor skills. The exclusion criteria are:

- have cognitive deficits which prevent them from following instructions accurately;
- have language deficits that interfere with the understating of protocol;
- have significant acuity changes, that aren´t compensated with glasses or contact lenses.

Is important to note that during the experiments there are 3 dropouts: two participants due to high clinic and one due to cognitive deficits. Three participants (n. 1, 2 and 3) included the experimental group, that have done the conventional occupational therapy treatment and the stimulation with Rehabvisual platform. The other three participants (n. 4, 5 and 6) had done the conventional occupational therapy treatment. In both groups, participants are all male. The injured arteries in both groups are the same: 2 participants have lesions in the MCA and 1 in the PCA in each of the groups. Related to schooling the averages are similar (6,6 years in experimental group comparing to 6,3 years in conventional group). The participants that use the RehabVisual platform had some differences from participants that done isolated the conventional treatment. The main differences are related with:

- Age: average in experimental group is 66 years and in control group is 58 years;
- Days post stroke: average in experimental group is 64 days and in control group is 57 days.

The participants are all assed in the beginning with the Montreal Cognitive Assessment, in order to characterize the cognitive level and exclude the possible participants that had cognitive deficits. To assess the visuomotor skills was used the trial making test in the beginning and in the end of treatment.

The experiment last for 4 weeks, and the participants are exposure to treatment two times per week.

### 3.3 Usability Test

The introduction of a new tool in the rehabilitation treatments follow a complex sequence of steps. Is important measure his usability and tests can be used to accomplish this. One of these is the SUS. The questionnaire score scale is from 1 to 100, with an average score of 68. The questionnaire score is affected by the complexity of the system and the tasks the user must perform [20].

Usability assessment was done in the final of protocol application. The questionnaire is delivery to the 4 students of Occupational Therapy Degree and his teacher. All the subjects experience the use of platform during 8 sessions, of protocol application.

## 4  Results

The results are presented in two sections. First shows the data obtained with the application of the platform on subjects with stroke sequelae. In Sect. 4.2 are presented the results about platform usability.

### 4.1  Results with the Platform Use

As described in Sect. 3.2, this pilot study refers to the platform used to stimulate the visuomotor skills of 3 people with ischemic stroke sequelae in conjunction with conventional occupational therapy treatment. Three other persons with ischemic stroke sequelae were treated at the same time and with the same frequency, with conventional occupational therapy treatment.

In our initial assessment, the people who benefitted from stimulation with the platform demonstrated inferior performance on the trail making test (TMT), but with stimulation all showed great improvement. The changes occurred in both sections A and B, (Table 1). If we do a more personalized analysis, it is noted that subjects with a worse initial time performance showed greater improvement.

**Table 1.** Performance in trail making test - experimental group

|    |           | Initial assessment | Final assessment | Evolution    |
|----|-----------|--------------------|------------------|--------------|
| P1 | Section A | 9M 10S             | 3M 12S           | 5M 58S faster |
|    | Section B | 11M 37S            | 8M 8S            | 2M 58S faster |
| P 2 | Section A | 3M 1S             | 1M 3S            | 1M 38S faster |
|    | Section B | 5M 11S             | 3M 49S           | 1M 22S faster |
| P3 | Section A | 50S               | 42S              | 8S faster    |
|    | Section B | 1M 20S             | 1M 1S            | 9S faster    |

The subject (case 3) that suffered the stroke in the PCA had (in both instances) a better performance compared with the other two subjects. When we look at the results of subjects receiving conventional treatment, it is evident there is better performance in the initial assessment compared to the results of the experimental group.

However, the subjects of the control group had a minor improvement in the final assessment. Additionally, it is noted that case 5 had a worse performance in final assessment. Participant no. 6 performed worse in the final assessment of section B (Table 2).

**Table 2.** Performance in trail making test - control group

|    |           | Initial assessment | Final assessment | Evolution    |
|----|-----------|--------------------|------------------|--------------|
| P 4 | Section A | 1M 10S            | 1M 5S            | 5S faster    |
|    | Section B | 5M 20S             | 4M 30S           | 50S faster   |
| P 5 | Section A | 3M 16S            | 3M 25S           | 9S slower    |
|    | Section B | 4M 10S             | 5M 5S            | 1M 22S slower |
| P 6 | Section A | 2M 19S            | 2MS 5S           | 14S faster   |
|    | Section B | 3M 40S             | 4M 45S           | 1M 5S slower |

## 4.2  Usability Test

When introducing a new rehabilitation tool, it is important to test its usability. In order to study that, the SUS questionnaire was administered. The questionnaire was completed by five persons that were using the platform during the study: four students in the last year of their bachelors and one occupational therapy degree teacher.

The results are quite satisfactory, with an average score of 88,5 which corresponds to an assessment of "Excellent" [21]. Only one participant rated the RehabVisual platform "Excellent". This user classified the platform with a score of 77,5 which corresponds to "Good".

In the qualitative domain the users highlight the RehabVisual positively, and point out these characteristics:

- It's easy to use;
- The platform allows offline access;
- Easy navigation within the platform;
- The customization and adaptability of the stimuli;
- The possibility of increasing the difficulty of stimuli during the sessions.

However, they also identify some aspects that could be improved:

- the stimuli always move in the same direction. In this way, the patient could memorize the movement of the stimuli and answer based on memory;
- The stimuli are all composed of geometric figures, which may not be the most appropriate for this age group. Of the available stimuli, those that best fit the age of the patients were the patterned stimuli;
- Slow-moving stimuli are too slow for this age range and the video of this stimulus is too long, causing patients to lose focus and interest.

## 5  Discussion of Results and Critical View

The analysis of the results reveals that there was an evolution in visuomotor skills in the three people who would benefit from the use of the platform. Contrarily, in the control group, only one of the subjects showed evolution with the conventional treatment. These data suggest that the evolution of the experimental group is due to the use of platform. These preliminary results are in line with research that has shown positive results for improving motor performance and engaging patients through technology [22]. In the experimental group it is important to note that the participant with the best performance in the initial assessment evolves less, and there seems to be a "ceiling effect".

It is important to note that the cases with the shortest time after stroke, namely case 1 (45 days) and case 5 (35 days), require the longest time to perform the initial assessment. The literature is not totally conclusive about the timeline of recovery from stroke. However, the recovery could be relatively rapid during the 4 weeks after treatment and then to a lesser extent decelerated between 3 and 6 months after stroke [23]. Although this is a recovery pattern, it is not deterministic.

TMT normative data are poorly specific (no disability vs. disability) [24]. This feature precludes a more detailed classification of the performance level of the subjects evaluated in the present investigation.

In all cases in which platform was applied, it was found that there was a better performance of TMT in the final assessment. This test requires skills such as attention span, mental flexibility, executive functions, processing speed, eye-motor coordination, searching, visual scanning and sequencing [24, 25]. The results of the test suggest that platform is effective in stimulating these skills.

Since the platform allows the stimulation of the visuomotor skills [13], the evolution of the participants in TMT performance could be related to the stimulation of these competences through the platform. It has been found that the time taken to perform the TMT varies depending on the injured territory. When this is the MCA, a longer time is needed compared to the cases where the injured territory is the PCA. In a global analysis these time differences could be surprising considering that the primary visual cortex is in occipital lobe. However, is also known that the territory irrigated by the MCA is more strongly related to spatial attention, difficulties in visuospatial function, and left and right discrimination, than the PCA [26]. Thus, the cases with MCA injury consequently presented a longer time to perform the TMT than the cases with PCA injury.

The usability test results are truly promising. They demonstrate that the platform is already at an advanced stage of development. Utilizing the qualitative results collected in this study, some improvements could be done. It will also be important to reinforce the possibility of using different tools offline, as this will be in line with the reality of various adult rehabilitation institutions.

# 6   Conclusion and Further Work

The current investigation has shown positive indications about the effectiveness of the RehabVisual platform to stimulate the visuomotor skills of adults with stroke sequelae.

The small size of group leads to the necessity of future work in order to understand if those indications are valid. In futures studies it is also important to clarify if this tool could be more useful for lesions in specific cortical areas. It is also important to characterize the performance of adults without pathology using the RehabVisual platform to understand if any changes occur in visuomotor skills.

It could also be important to apply this platform to adults with other neurological conditions to understand if this stimulation could be a helpful tool. Considering a framework of rehabilitation and quality of life improvement could be important in order to ascertain if the change in visuomotor skills brings any global performance impact to the subject.

The results of usability are very positive. Although future studies should consider users' suggestions regarding the platform, namely:

- alternate the direction of stimuli movement;
- adjust the stimuli to the adult population, not restricting them to geometrical figures;
- adapt the speeds used to adult skills, in particular, speeding up the slower ones.

The RehabVisual platform is an innovative tool to stimulate visuomotor skills. It allows the personalization of intervention methodology and can be applied in different populations and in distinct clinical settings.

# References

1. Johnson, C.O.: Global, regional, and national burden of stroke, 1990–2016: a systematic analysis for the global burden of disease study 2016. Lancet **18**(5), 439–458 (2019)
2. Khaku, A.S., Hegazy, M., Tadi, P.: Cerebrovascular Disease (Stroke). StatPearls Publishing (2019). https://www.ncbi.nlm.nih.gov/books/NBK430927/
3. World Health Organization: Stroke: a global response is needed, Geneva (2016)
4. Adamson, J., Beswick, A., Ebrahim, S.: Is stroke the most common cause of disability? J. Stroke Cerebrovascular Dis. **13**, 171–177 (2004)
5. Rowe, F.: Care provision and unmet need for post stroke visual impairment (2013). http://bit.ly/2iMfarz
6. Danckert, J., Feeber, S.: Revisiting unilateral neglect. Neuropsychologia **44**(6), 987–1006 (2006). https://doi.org/10.1016/j.neuropsychologia.2005.09.004
7. Duncan, P.: Management of adult stroke rehabilitation care (2005). https://doi.org/10.1161/01.STR.0000180861.54180.FF
8. Zoltan, B.: Vision, Perception and Cognition: A Manual for the Evaluation and Treatment of the Neurologically Impaired Adult. SLACK Incorporated, Thorofare (1996)
9. Rode, G., Pagliari, C., Huchon, L., Rossetti, Y., Pisella, L.: Semiology of neglect: an update. Ann. Phys. Rehabil. Med. **60**, 117–185 (2017). https://doi.org/10.1016/j.rehab.2016.03.003
10. Gentile, P.A.: Cerebrovascular accident. Mary Beth Early, Physical Dysfunction, pp. 468–490. Elsevier, Missouri (2013)
11. Frintrop, S.: VOCUS: A Visual Attention System for Object Detection and Goal-Directed Search. Springer, Heidelberg (2006). https://doi.org/10.1007/11682110
12. Bhat, R.B., Sanes, J.N.: Cognitive channels computing action distance and direction. J. Neurosci. **18**(18), 7566–7580 (2008). https://doi.org/10.1523/JNEUROSCI.18-18-07566.1998
13. Machado, R., Ferreira, A., Quintão, C., Quaresma, C.: RehabVisual: development of an application to stimulate visuomotor skills. In: Proceedings of the 11th International Joint Conference on Biomedical Engineering Systems and Technologies (BIOSTEC 2018) (2018). https://doi.org/10.5220/0006597001730178
14. Santos, C., Ferreira, A., Quaresma, C., Quintão, C.: RehabVisual: validation of an application to stimulate visuomotor skills in preterm babies with developmental alterations. In: Proceedings of the 12th International Joint Conference on Biomedical Engineering Systems and Technologies (BIOSTEC 2019) (2019). https://doi.org/10.5220/0007567102480255
15. Schenk, P., Colombo, G., Maier, I.: New technology in rehabilitation: possibilities and limitations. In: Pons, J.L., Torricelli, D., Pajaro, M. (eds.) Converging Clinical and Engineering Research on Neurorehabilitation. BB, vol. 1, pp. 963–967. Springer, Heidelberg (2013). https://doi.org/10.1007/978-3-642-34546-3_157
16. International Organization for Standardization: Ergonomics of human – system interaction – part II. Usability: definitions and concepts (9241-11) (2018). https://www.iso.org/obp/ui/#iso:std:iso:9241:-11:ed-2:v1:en
17. Barnum, C.: Usability Testing Essentials: Ready, Set… Test!. Elsevier, Amsterdam (2010)
18. Zhoul, L., Bao, J., Parmanto, B.: Systematic review protocol to assess the effectiveness of usability questionnaires in mhealth app studies. JMIR Res. Protoc. (2017). https://doi.org/10.2196/resprot.7826
19. Lohse, K., Hilderman, C., Cheung, K., Tatla, S., Van der Loos, M.: Virtual reality therapy for adults post-stroke: a systematic review and meta-analysis exploring virtual environments

and commercial games in therapy. PLoS One **9**(3), e93318 (2014). https://doi.org/10.1371/journal.pone.0093318

20. Klug, B.: An overview of the system usability scale in library website and system usability testing. Weave J. Libr. User Exp. (2017). http://dx.doi.org/10.3998/weave.12535642.0001.602

21. Lewis, J.: Can i leave this one out? The effect of dropping an item from the SUS. J. Usability Stud. **13**(1), 38–46 (2017)

22. Langan, J., Subryan, H., Nwogu, L., Cavuoto, L.: Reported use of technology in stroke rehabilitation by physical and occupational therapists. Disabil. Rehabil. Assist. Technol. (2018). https://doi.org/10.1080/17483107.2017.1362043

23. Le, K., et al.: Six month functional recovery of stroke patients: a multi-time-point study. Int. J. Rehabil. Res. (2015). https://doi.org/10.1097/MRR.0000000000000108

24. Cavaco, S., et al.: Trail making test: regression-based norms for the Portuguese population. Arch. Clin. Neuropsychol. (2013). https://doi.org/10.1093/arclin/acs115. Epub 7 Jan 2013

25. Strauss, E., Sherman, E.M.S., Spreen, O.: A Compendium of Neuropsychological Tests: Administration, Norms, and Commentary, 3rd edn. Oxford University Press, New York (2006)

26. Ponsford, J.: Cognitive and Behavioural Rehabilitation: from Neurobiology to Clinical Practice. The Guilford Press, New York (2004)

# Instrumentation in Health

# Algorithm for Automatic Peak Detection and Quantification for GC-IMS Spectra

Jorge M. Fernandes[1,2(✉)], Valentina Vassilenko[1,2], and Paulo H. Santos[1,2]

[1] Laboratory for Instrumentation, Biomedical Engineering and Radiation Physics (LibPhys-UNL), NOVA School of Science and Technology, NOVA University of Lisbon, Campus FCT-UNL, 2896-516 Caparica, Portugal
j.manuel@campus.fct.unl.pt
[2] NMT, S.A., Edifício Madan Parque, Rua dos Inventores, 2825-182 Caparica, Portugal

**Abstract.** Ion Mobility Spectrometry with a coupled Gas Chromatography (GC-IMS) pre-separation is an analytical technique suitable for detection of volatile organic compounds (VOCs) in complex sample matrices (indoor & outdoor air, breath samples, food, beverages, microbial cultures, etc.). Its outstanding sensitivity allows in-situ analysis of a very large range of organic compounds at low concentrations with detection limits typically in the low ppb or even ppt level. Automatic detection and quantification of VOCs through GC-IMS spectra is challenging and the lack of computational methodologies able to detect, quantify and deconvolute overlapped peaks are still scarce and diminished. In this work we present a preliminary algorithm and still in development for automatically identify and quantify VOC peaks directly from the spectra matrix with an established threshold, a noise filter, Reactive Ion Peak (RIP) measurements. Herein, proposed tools may be very useful for quick automatic detection and quantification of compounds in GC-IMS spectra.

**Keywords:** Ion Mobility Spectrometry (IMS) · Gas Chromatography (GC) · Volatile Organic Compounds (VOCs) · Peak detection · Quantification · Automation · Algorithm

## 1 Introduction

Ion mobility spectrometry (IMS) was developed in last the 50 years as a method for detecting and identifying trace levels (ppb$_v$ and ppt$_v$ ranges) of semi-volatile and volatile organic compounds (VOCs), mainly in security and military venues. IMS working principle is based on mobility determination in electric fields of gas phase ions in a sample from a large array of matrices [1].

Modern ion mobility analytical spectrometers were commercially available only in the late 1970s due to military and governmental control of the technology. Thus, the period afterwards saw a boom in intensive substance characterization by ion mobility spectrometry [2]. This analytical technique was initially known by other terms (*e.g.* plasma chromatography, gaseous electrophoresis or ion chromatography), however the

© IFIP International Federation for Information Processing 2020
Published by Springer Nature Switzerland AG 2020
L. M. Camarinha-Matos et al. (Eds.): DoCEIS 2020, IFIP AICT 577, pp. 369–377, 2020.
https://doi.org/10.1007/978-3-030-45124-0_35

working principle of current and modern instrumentation remained [1–5]. Nonetheless, engineering and technological improvements have opened numerous applications and uses of IMS such as the development of portable spectrometers for field use [1, 2, 4]. General IMS operational principles are summarized in Fig. 1 and include:

- Transference of sample as vapor into an ion source (radioactive sources: $^3$H, $^{63}$Ni; Non-radioactive sources: corona discharges, electrospray or lasers);
- Production of ions from neutral sample molecules at atmospheric pressure
- Injection of an ion swarm into the drift region;
- Determination of drift velocities of ions under the influence of an electric field in the drift region and in a supporting atmosphere, the drift gas;
- Detection of ions and electrical signal storage or display, with or without automated analysis of the result.

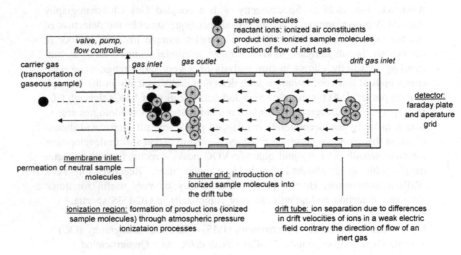

**Fig. 1.** Ion mobility spectrometry operation summary in a bidirectional flow system [1].

Ions movement speed, or the drift velocity ($v_d$) dissipated by collisions with neutral molecules of the supporting gas atmosphere, is proportional to the strength of the electric field (E) with the constant of proportionality being the ions mobility (K) [2, 5]. Thermalized ions typically travel with a speed of approximately 2 m s$^{-1}$ and traverses the drift region with lengths of 5 to 15 cm in a few milliseconds (2 to 15 ms). Ion drift time correlates with ions' mass, charge and collision cross section, which includes structural parameters (physical size and shape) and the electronic factors describing the ion-neutral interaction forces. Therefore, different drift velocities are attained for ions with different structure (shape) and mass, establishing the basis for ions separation in IMS [5].

Engineering advances provide to IMS-based methods a major advantage in analytical application due to the analyser's low size, weight and power consumption, making this instrumentation perfectly suitable for on-site or in-field monitoring, contrary to almost all analytical tools [1, 6, 7]. IMS analysers exhibit fast response and reliable performance (high sensitivity, recording of ion mobility spectra) and can be used in ambient pressure, with nitrogen, helium and air as drift gas.

Several IMS devices have been employed in airports worldwide for chemical-weapons monitoring and explosive detection in hand-held or bench analyser formats [8]. Applications in civilian fields are more diverse and include investigations with complex, humid gas-phase biological samples [6, 9], health and medical diagnostics [10], food quality and safety [11], as well as in the industrial process control [12], petrochemical, environmental analysis [13, 14] and air quality assessment [15–17]. However, in complex matrix analysis, a single IMS device has limitations, such as clustering forming in the ionisation region, thus making identification of the ions difficult or even impossible. Therefore, to solve this limitation and increase the selectivity, ion mobility spectrometry is usually coupled to a pre-separation method: Gas-Chromatographic column (GC), Multi-Capillary Column (MCC) or, not so frequently, Liquid-Chromatography (LC) [18].

## 2 Contributions to Life Improvement

Recent successful CG-IMS technology applications to environmental analysis, medical diagnostics, process control, air quality control, food quality control [19], biomolecules characterization and detection of biomarkers in bacteria [20] show a clear need for tools that allow quick and precise spectra processing.

Experimental research data derived from GC-IMS is represented by 3D graphs, also called heatmaps or spectra, where each analyte is given by retention and drift time for qualitative analysis, and intensity for quantitative analysis. Currently, software availability for automatically detect and process analyte peaks from 3D GC-IMS spectra is scarce, limited or functional for a single instrumentation type. Thus, a generalized automatic peak detection, identification and quantification algorithm will improve, accelerate and enrich IMS instrumentation when employed in the numerous life science fields previously mentioned.

## 3 Materials and Methods

### 3.1 Input Data Format

Ion mobility spectrometers produce data in 2D graphs format in which the $x$ and $y$ axis are respectively, drift time ($t_d$) and intensity (Fig. 2). Drift time is in milliseconds (ms) and it's usually expressed in relation to the Reactive Ion Peak (RIP) drift time (RIPrel). RIP refers to ionized ions of the drift gas and corresponds to the quantity of ions available to ionize analytes. RIP drift time varies with conditions such as drift gas type and humidity, and analytes' RIP relative drift times are employed to standardize drift times allowing their identification and peak comparison of analytes between measurements.

When IMS is coupled with pre-separation techniques, as CG or LC, experimental data obtained changes from 2D graphs to 3D plots, heatmaps, which often are called spectrum (singular) and spectra (plural), as it can be seen in the Fig. 2. Spectra in 3D format contains data with three variable: (a) retention time ($t_r$) of the gas or liquid chromatographic column, (b) drift time ($t_d$) for the separation of analytes in the drift tube and (c) intensity (I) detected in a faraday plate at the end of the drift tube. Retention time is expressed in seconds, drift time in relation to the RIP and intensity in volts. A more detailed description can be found elsewhere [21].

IMS devices typically have their proprietary software for signal processing, saving measurements files and processing them. The spectra selected for the development of the algorithm to automatically detect and quantify peaks derived from a GC-IMS device, commercially available from G.A.S. Dortmund (*Gesellschaft für analytische Sensorsysteme*) sold as BreahSpec®. The software Laboratory Analyser Viewer (LAV) was provided along the device and can load the output files of the GC-IMS that come in a *.mea* file format. The software represents the *mea* file data in a heatmap, allows the definition of peak areas for quantification and extraction of drift and retentions times, management of measurements projects (reading several *mea* files in simultaneous) among many other features. *Mea* files can be extracted into a CSV format file, containing three degrees of information.

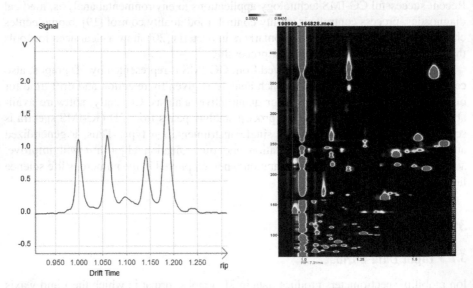

**Fig. 2.** Single IMS or 2D spectrum (right) and 3D spectrum or heatmap examples (left) (spectra processed and obtained from LAV of BreathSpec (GC-IMS) measurements).

Output data of a single IMS measurement, 2D spectrum, is a vector $S = (z_0, z_1, \ldots, z_n)$ of signal intensities $z_i$ measured in equidistant time point $dt_i$, $i \in \{1 \ldots N\}$. If a pre-separation technique is coupled to an IMS (GC or LC), an additional dimension is provided in the 3D spectrum, the retention time. Therefore GC-IMS data become a series of R one dimensional IMS spectra recorded at equidistant retention time point $rt_k$, $k \in \{1 \ldots R\}$. Such data is represented in the mathematical matrix by exporting a measurement file (*mea*) with LAV, which adds additional information in text ($i_{textual}$) into a CSV file as simplified below.

$$i_{textual} = \begin{bmatrix} machine & \ldots & gas_{drift} & \ldots & \ldots & Timestamp \\ units & \ldots & \ldots & kHz & {}^{\circ}C & \\ data & \ldots & Air & \ldots & serial & 2019\ldots \\ & \ldots & & blank\ line & & \ldots \\ \#specnum & RetTime[s]/Drift\ time[ms] & & \ldots & & \end{bmatrix} \quad (1)$$

$$M_{ims} = \begin{bmatrix} Z_{11} & \cdots & Z_{1n} \\ \vdots & \ddots & \vdots \\ Z_{1R} & \cdots & Z_{nR} \end{bmatrix} \quad (2)$$

Exported CSV files, employed in the developed algorithm, include all available information from *mea* files and are characterized by a 5-line header containing device's mechanical and analytical textual information followed by a mathematical matrix.

## 3.2   Coding Language and Library

The algorithm was developed in Python, an open-source coding language, version 3.7 and, additionally, the libraries and/or functions were imported and include: *scikit-image* algorithms collection for image processing, *scipy.ndimage*, multi-dimensional image processing, *pandas* 0.25.3, Python Data Analysis Library, *mathplotlib* 3.1.1, Python 2D plotting library, *NumPy*, fundamental package for scientific computing and *operator* a standard operators as functions.

# 4   Results and Discussion

Developed algorithm is divided into four phases, (i) reading textual data, (ii) IMS matrix (spectra) processing, (iii) automatic peak detection and (iv) peak filtering and quantification. The algorithm uses *pandas* to read the csv file where all the textual and numerical information is contained.

(i) *Reading textual data*: this phase comprehends reading and printing of data relevant contained in the 5-line header. Useful information extracted in this phase includes, name and date of the file, machine type used, its serial number and GC column information. Textual information is printed after adding a line for the file format and origin. An example is presented below:

```
FILE ORIGIN:                        LAV conversion
FILE FORMAT:                        CSV DATA
FILE NAME:                          190410_133432_1.csv
DATE:                               2019 04 10
TIME:                               13 34 32
SAMPLE:
Machine type :                      BreathSpec©
Machine serial :                    3G1-00074
GC Column :                         MXT-200. 30m X 0.53mm ID
```

Supplementary information can be included in this phase, *e.g.* retention flow variation chart showing carrier gas flow changes the analysed measurement. Additional textual information can easily be tailored to each user's preference. Herein is shown only the most important information as an example.

(ii) *IMS matrix (spectra) processing*: conducted after reading the csv file, and includes RIP automated detection, without showing RIP intensity or losing any peaks' information. Such processing is performed by detecting maximum intensity values in the mathematical matrix first line. Since recording is always started before any analyte is injected into the drift tube, the first line contains solely information about intensity from the drift and carrier gas without any sample. However, RIP is contained in a drift time interval and, to detect this interval or window, a simple idea is implemented in the algorithm. RIP is defined and identified as the number of columns in the first line that contain intensity above, 0.280 V and 0.100 V prior (left) and posteriorly (right) of the RIP maximum, respectively. Values before and after the RIP are not equal, due to the drift and carrier gas humidity influence. All matrix portions previously fragmented were correctly reconstructed by *matplotlib* functions (as done by LAV).

(iii) *Automatic peak detection* is achieved by applying a module from *skimage* know as measure, *skimage.measure.find_contours (array, level)*. By finding iso-valued level of the IMS matrix (or above a threshold), clusters concerning intensity peaks were found, contoured and marked. However, since IMS spectra regularly show low intensity regions with the same intensity value, "noise", *skimage* module outputs a high number of regions which are not to be considered as peaks (Fig. 3). Hence, the algorithm was able to detect and mark matrix regions with a threshold-value above 0.150 V, set for *skimage level*, and account the total number of contours, however this value did not have a direct correspondence with the effective total number of peaks.

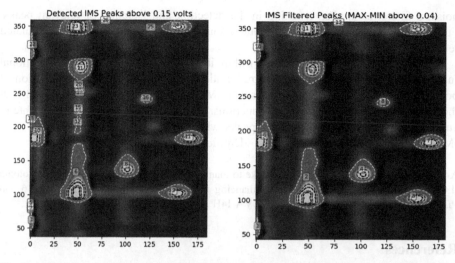

**Fig. 3.** Algorithm detected peaks before (left) and after using a filtering method (right) marked by dashed lines and labelled with number in a grey square. *Y*-axis represents the retention time in seconds and the *x*-axis the drift time with the RIP position as zero.

(iv) *Peak filtering and quantification*: a simple tactic was employed to filter "noise" regions (or ineffective peaks) from the peaks found by the *skimage.measure* module. Matrix maximum and minimum values were obtained for each region with the module *skimage.measure*, and if the difference between those values was lower or equal to, a defined threshold of 0.04 such region would not be classified as a peak. This threshold was defined based on observed values for general noise regions and peaks, nonetheless this value can be adjusted by the user in accordance to its study targets.

Once the noise filter was applied to the detection algorithm, results enabled the recognition of the effective (real) peaks of the spectra and allowed to estimate peak intensity. Such estimation was executed by summing all the matrix values inside the peak areas delimited previously. Furthermore, the matrix index for the maximum value of each detected peak was obtained with the intention of using it for peak identification based on a database of drift and retention times.

## 5   Conclusions and Future Work

The developed algorithm was able to read a csv file directly exported from the LAV software; a type of software used in ion mobility spectrometers. From csv files, the algorithm interpreted and separated text information and spectral matrix. A graphical representation was correctly performed from the reconstruction of the matrix values and peak detection was achieved by applying a *skimage* module. To reduce spectral noise, a filter was applied resulting in the detection and isolation of relevant peaks. Furthermore, specific maximum and total intensity of peaks were found and calculated respectively.

Aiming to apply the present algorithm in all kind of IMS spectra, additional functions or tools are planned for future iterations. For instance, the deconvolution of potential overlapping peaks, a major issue in IMS spectra, is intended to be solved with the application of adjusted Gaussian functions. With this, the algorithm will be able to automatically detect and quantify all peaks which could later be cross-checked with IMS drift time libraries for compound identification.

**Acknowledgments.** The authors would like to thank the Fundação para a Ciência e Tecnologia (FCT, Portugal) and NMT, S.A. for co-financing the PhD grants PD/BDE/114550/2016 and PD/BDE/130204/2017 of the Doctoral NOVA I4H Program.

# References

1. Borsdorf, H., Eiceman, G.A.: Ion mobility spectrometry: principles and applications. Appl. Spect. Rev. **41**(4), 323–375 (2006)
2. Cumeras, R., Figueras, E., Davis, C.E., Baumbach, J.I.: Review on ion mobility spectrometry. Part 1: current instrumentation. Analyst **140**(5), 1376–1390 (2015)
3. Kanu, A.B., Hill Jr., H.H.: Ion mobility spectrometry detection for gas chromatography. J. Chromatogr. A **1177**(1), 12–27 (2008)
4. St. Louis, R.H., Hill Jr., H.H., Eiceman, G.A.: Ion mobility spectrometry in analytical chemistry. Crit. Rev. Anal. Chem. **21**(5), 321–355 (1990)
5. Gabelica, V., Marklund, E.: Fundamentals of ion mobility spectrometry. Curr. Opin. Chem. Biol. **42**, 51–59 (2018)
6. Borsdorf, H., Mayer, T., Zarejoushe, M., Eiceman, G.A.: Recent developments in ion mobility spectrometry. Appl. Spect. Rev. **46**(6), 472–521 (2011)
7. Hopfgartner, G.: Current developments in ion mobility spectrometry. Anal. Bioanal. Chem. **411**(24), 6227 (2019). https://doi.org/10.1007/s00216-019-02028-1
8. Ewing, R.G., Atkinson, D.A., Eiceman, G.A., Ewing, G.J.: A critical review of ion mobility spectrometry for the detection of explosives and explosive related compounds. Talanta **54**(3), 515–529 (2001)
9. Kirk, A.T., Allers, M., Cochems, P., Langejuergen, J., Zimmermann, S.: A compact high resolution ion mobility spectrometer for fast trace gas analysis. Analyst **138**, 5200–5207 (2013)
10. Chouinard, C.D., Wei, M.S., Beekman, C.R., Kemperman, R.H., Yost, R.A.: Ion mobility in clinical analysis: current progress and future perspectives. Clin. Chem. **62**(1), 124–133 (2016)
11. Karpas, Z.: Applications of ion mobility spectrometry (IMS) in the field of foodomics. Food Res. Int. **54**(1), 1146–1151 (2013)
12. Baumbach, J.I.: Process analysis using ion mobility spectrometry. Anal. Bioanal. Chem. **384**(5), 1059–1070 (2006). https://doi.org/10.1007/s00216-005-3397-8
13. Salthammer, T.: Organic Indoor Air Pollutants: Occurence, Measurement, Evaluation, 1st edn. Wiley-VCH, Weinheim (1999)
14. Gallart-Mateu, D., Armenta, S., de la Guardia, M.: Indoor and outdoor determination of pesticides in air by ion mobility spectrometry. Talanta **161**, 632–639 (2016)

15. Śmiełowska, M., Marć, M., Zabiegala, B.: Indoor air quality in public utility environments - a review. Environ. Sci. Pollut. Res. **24**, 11166–11176 (2017). https://doi.org/10.1007/s11356-017-8567-7
16. Vautz, W., Ruszany, V., Sielemann, S., Baumbach, J.: Sensitive ion mobility spectrometry of humid ambient air using 10.6 eV UV-IMS. Int. J. Ion Mob. Spectrom. 3–8 (2004)
17. Fetter, V., Vassilenko, V., Fernandes, J., Moukhamedieva, L., Orlov, O.: Validation of analytical instrumentation for continuous online monitoring of large spectra of VOCs in closed habitat during simulation of space fligh. In: Proceedings of 69th International Astronautical Congress, Bremen, Germany (2018)
18. Vautz, W., Franzke, J., Zampolli, S., Elmi, I., Liedtke, S.: On the potential of ion mobility spectrometry coupled to GC pre-separation - a tutorial. Anal. Chim. Acta **1024**, 52–64 (2018)
19. Espalha, C., Fernandes, J., Diniz, M., Vassilenko, V.: Fast and direct detection of biogenic amines in fish by GC-IMS technology. In: 2019 IEEE 6th Portuguese Meeting on Bioengineering (ENBENG), Lisbon (2019)
20. Gonçalves, M., Fernandes, J., Fetter, V., Diniz, M., Vassilenko, V.: Novel methodology for quick detection of bacterial metabolites. In: 2019 IEEE 6th Portuguese Meeting on Bioengineering (ENBENG), Lisbon (2019)

# Algorithm for Automated Segmentation and Feature Extraction of Thermal Images

Anna A. Poplavska[1,2(✉)], Valentina B. Vassilenko[1,2],
Oleksandr A. Poplavskyi[3], and Sergei V. Pavlov[4]

[1] Laboratory of Instrumentation, Biomedical Engineering and Radiation Physics
(LIBPHYS), NOVA School of Science and Technology,
NOVA University Lisbon, Lisbon, Portugal
an.poplavska@campus.fct.unl.pt
[2] NMT, S.A., Parque Tecnológico de Cantanhede, Núcleo 04, Lote 3,
3060-197 Cantanhede, Portugal
[3] Kiev National University of Construction and Architecture, Kiev, Ukraine
[4] Vinnytsia National Technical University, Vinnytsia, Ukraine

**Abstract.** Medical infrared thermal imaging techniques can provide the high-quality images for monitoring and pre-clinical diagnostic of the diseases by showing the thermal abnormalities available in the body. Its biggest advantage is non-contact, non-invasive and very fast way of use. However, the incorrect interpretation of the thermal images via simple observation or manual analysis and detection approximate regions of interest lead to the numerous false positive results. The main objective of this research work is to develop an algorithm for automated image processing and analysis of the extracted features on thermal images for screening or pre-diagnosis of the diseases. This work presents the results of our previously developed Copyright algorithm applied to thermal images obtained from the patients with Axial Spondyloarthritis. This processing and analysis of the extracted features from thermal images can offer a novel quick and non-invasive tool for diagnosis and monitoring of rheumatoid diseases.

**Keywords:** Medical thermal images · Image processing · Automated segmentation · Rheumatic diseases

## 1 Introduction

Medical infrared thermal imaging (MITI) is currently a rapid developing technique that can provide the images for monitoring and pre-clinical diagnostic of thermal abnormalities present in the body in real time. MITI technique is a non-contact, noninvasive, imaging procedure which offers the two-dimensional temperature spatial distribution measurement.

With modern technology, a single image may contain several thousands of temperature points recorded in a fraction of a second. It has been used to study number of

L. M. Camarinha-Matos et al. (Eds.): DoCEIS 2020, IFIP AICT 577, pp. 378–386, 2020.
https://doi.org/10.1007/978-3-030-45124-0_36

diseases where the increased skin temperature can signal the presence of inflammation, or where blood flow is increased or decreased due to a clinical abnormality. MITI ware widely tested in the following areas of medical diagnostics, as: thermoregulation study [1], muscular pain [2], breast cancer [3], vascular disorder [4], rheumatoid diseases [5], osteoarthritis [6, 7], Raynaud's phenomenon [8] etc. Various thermography studies have been performed during the last decade for the assessment of thermal symmetry in hand regions [9]. Recently the thermographic technology was successfully applied in animal models as a tool for the quick evaluation of inflammation after invasive intervention in reconstructive plastic surgery [10].

In medical IRT, the abnormalities can be diagnosed by visual and subjective analysis, but the human based diagnoses are more likely to errors due to visual exhaustion, negligence, mental workload, etc. The segmentation by Regions of Interesse (ROI) is often an initial step in thermographic medical analysis, where the automatic approaches could lead to fast and highly reproducible outcomes [11]. Due to different geometrical shapes and proportions of body parts, it's not possible to capture the ROIs properly without background while data acquisition. Based on the procedure used to define these parameters, the segmentation process can be categorized as: (a) manual, where software is used to manually mark the ROI with pre-defined or user-defined shapes; (b) semiautomated, when the human intervention is required to reduce the search space for automatic segmentation or to inspect visually and modify the automatically obtained ROI; (c) fully-automated, where the different approaches, like thresholding, clustering, geometric and thermal features are used for automatic determination of parameters which define the ROI.

Thermography shows the exact location of thermal abnormalities related to physiological and metabolic processes; therefore, it has a great potential in medical use. However, MITI technology still has a limited use in diagnostic due to a lot of false negative and false positive rates. The problem is not connected to the equipment because the infrared (IR) cameras with a high thermal sensitivity, above the 0.06 °C, provide the high-quality images. One of the main problems is the wrong interpretation of the obtained results due to the lack of automated feature extraction on thermal images for specific diseases. Therefore, the main objective of this research work was to develop an algorithm for automated segmentation and extracted features on thermal images in order to support medical decision-making and help to specify feature that can be significant signs for disease classification.

## 2   Contribution to Life Improvement

The information extracted from the IR images after its proper analysis is the basis for identifying, monitoring or pre-diagnostic of different types of diseases. To automate this process, modern devices have enough capacity to provide superficial analysis using the special analytical tools. However, the huge amount of diseases and various individual anatomical thermal features of human body cause difficulties to implement one or few well-known algorithms for all cases.

The important contribution of the present work is development of a novel algorithm for the IR image segmentation and feature extraction for each cohort of patient with specific disease, related with the inflammation processes in the human body. Ankylosing spondylitis (AS), a common type of spondyloarthropathy, is a chronic inflammatory autoimmune disease that mainly affects spine joints, causing severe, chronic pain; additionally, in more advanced cases, it can cause spine fusion [12]. Early diagnosis is critical for establishing a proper therapy that halts the natural progression of the disease and clinical evaluation requires complementary radiological information through a combination of techniques (radiography, computed tomography and MRI) [13].

The algorithm suggested in this paper combined with IR thermal camera can offer a novel quick and non-invasive tool for diagnosing and monitoring some kinds of rheumatoid diseases. Another important task of this work is to improve protocol of thermal measurements and increase a database of thermal images of patients with specific diseases that may contribute to the use of medical thermography in hospitals in the future.

## 3  Materials and Methods

Present study was carried out in partnership with the Center for the Study of Chronic Diseases of the Faculty of Medical Sciences of the Nova University of Lisbon (CEDOC|FCM-UNL) in the research project: "MyoSpA: o papel do músculo nas espondiloartropatias, um novo paradigma".

The participant's cohort of 41 volunteers, 14 females and 27 males, between 18 to 50 years old, an average height $1.73 \pm 0.1$ (m) and weight $75.4 \pm 12.6$ (kg). The participants were divided into two groups: I group of 15 individuals with AS disease and II control group with 26 participants. The pain syndrome had more than 89.5% of participants with AS and 10.5% were without pain, thus signalizing that this disease has a big influence of daily lifestyle. On the other side, in the control group, without AS diagnosis, the 57.7% of participants had pain syndrome, which signalized that a lot of people are suffering from the back pain even without associated diagnosis.

The measurements were performed in the ambient temperature using a thermal camera FLIR® E6, with a thermal sensitivity of <0.06 °C. An IR resolution of 160 × 120 pixels was interpolated to 320 × 240 resolution within the camera electronics. The camera was switched on 15 min before acquisition. The emissivity parameter on the camera was set as that for the skin, $\varepsilon = 0.98$. The camera lens was placed in parallel to the frontal plane of the subject's body at the distance of 1.5 m. The measurements have been carried out in the laboratory room with no access of solar radiation and/or any heaters, the room temperature was about 21 °C and humidity was maintained at approximately 50%. The black matte curtain was used as background to prevent any infrared reflections and to make the background uniform.

All volunteers were completed a questionnaire regarding the general information and agreement to participate in the project. The volunteers were asked not to smoke, abstain from alcohol or coffee, not to perform physical activity, use skin creams or spray on the research area 6 h before the examination. Before measurement, each participant had to stay undressed for 10 min for the purpose of accommodation to the ambient temperature. During the measurements each participant was in the same standing position, facing the wall, the feet were together, the head was looking straight ahead and the arms were down to the sides.

## 4   Methodology

The medical images edge detection (MIED) is an important step toward understanding image features. With the increasing numbers of medical images techniques, the use of computers for processing and analysis of images has become critical necessary. The MIED is extensively used in image segmentation when images are divided into areas of interest. This information has greatly increased the knowledge of normal and pathological anatomy and are the critical components in diagnostic and treatment planning [11–14, 16].

Ankylosing spondylitis (AS) primarily affects the spine and the sacroiliac joints that connect the lower spine to the pelvis, resulting in pain in the lower back, hips, and buttocks. So, our work was concentrated on the posterior side of the back, the target region was specified in the thermal abnormalities in lumbar region, as one of the possible feature of AS disease. The principal steps that were taking into consideration during this study are shown in the Fig. 1:

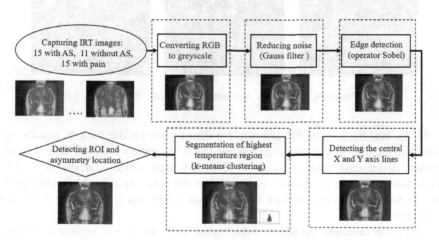

**Fig. 1.** Algorithm for automated segmentation and feature extraction of thermal image

Thermal images were obtained in pseudo colors and, as the first step, the infrared images were converted to a grayscale, using the formula:

$$Gray = 0.2126R + 0.17152G + 0.0722B \qquad (1)$$

The linear Gauss filter was applied to blur images and remove the noise:

$$g(x,y) = \frac{1}{2\pi\sigma^2} e^{-\frac{x^2+y^2}{2\sigma^2}}$$ (2)

where x is the distance from the origin in the horizontal axis, y is the distance from the origin in the vertical axis, and $\sigma$ is the standard deviation of the Gaussian distribution.

In our work the Sobel's operator [14] (Fig. 4, a) was used to detect edge of human body in each thermal image. The $I_m$ defined as the source image, and $G_x$ and $G_y$ were two images which at each point contain the vertical and horizontal derivative approximations respectively, the computations were as follows:

$$G_x = \begin{bmatrix} -1 & 0 & 1 \\ -2 & 0 & 2 \\ -1 & 0 & 1 \end{bmatrix} * I_m \quad \text{and} \quad G_y = \begin{bmatrix} 1 & 2 & 1 \\ 0 & 0 & 0 \\ -1 & -2 & -1 \end{bmatrix} * I_m$$ (3)

As example, in the Fig. 2 is shown a comparison between results from applying of different gradient operators into thermal image of patient with AS.

**Fig. 2.** Example of gradient operators: (a) Prewitt; (b) Canny; (c) Sobel

In the healthy persons the temperature distribution on the back is usually symmetrical relatively to the vertebral column (VC). Asymmetry on the region of temperature distribution relative to the VC is the main criteria on diagnosis of an inflammatory process or chronic disease. From the areas with an abnormally high or low temperature, the symptoms of many diseases can be recognized in the early stages of their occurrence.

Thus, after detecting the edges of the human body, the axes of vertical symmetry X and horizontal Y were found (Fig. 4, b) using the formulas:

$$X_S = \frac{\sum_{i=1}^{n-1} \frac{|L_i + R_i|}{2}}{n} \quad Y_S = \frac{\sum_{j=1}^{m-1} \frac{|Lw_j + A_j|}{2}}{m}$$ (4)

where n and m are the numbers of pixels in $L_i$ columns and rows, respectively; $R_i$ are the coordinates of left and right edge pixels of each row, $Lw_j$, $A_j$ – coordinates of lower and upper back edge pixels of each column.

Segmentation of medical images is an important challenging task in detecting the temperature abnormalities present in the body. Despite the huge effort in solving it, there is no single approach that can generally solve the problem of segmentation for the huge among of image varieties. In this study the K-means clustering algorithm was used for segmentation of infrared thermal images. This algorithm is based on minimization of the objective function using the formula:

$$J(V) = \sum_{i=1}^{C} \sum_{j=1}^{C_i} (\|x_i - v_j\|)^2 \qquad (5)$$

where $\|x_i - v_j\|$ is the Euclidean distance between $x_i$ and $v_j$, $c_i$ – the number of data points in $i^{th}$ cluster and $c$ – the number of cluster centers. The algorithm consists in choosing the number of cluster K, and then implying the K-means clustering to the image. In the Fig. 3 is shown an example of results obtained after applying the proposed k-mean clustering algorithm onto thermal images of the back of healthy person and one with AS disease. It could be clearly noticed from the cluster 5 that in healthy patient were not detected inflammatory zone, in opposite, as in patient that had AS disease. After ROI detection the targeted region was selected from vertical $Y_s$ axis of symmetry starting on the cervical part and ending on the sacral spine. This region was divided into two parts: left and right lower back. The areas of regions and horizontal $X_s$ coordinates were calculates by using the formula (5).

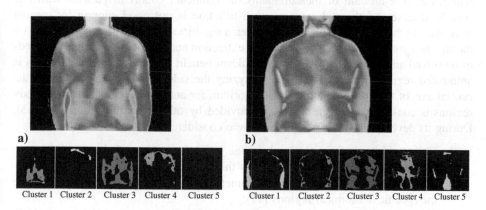

a)                                                    b)

Cluster 1   Cluster 2   Cluster 3   Cluster 4   Cluster 5        Cluster 1   Cluster 2   Cluster 3   Cluster 4   Cluster 5

**Fig. 3.** Results of k-mean clustering for IR images: (a) normal case; (b) patient with AS

In the Fig. 4 is shown results of automated segmentation and feature extraction of thermal image on one patient with AS disease.

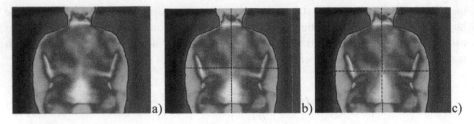

**Fig. 4.** Image processing: (a) edge detection, (b) Xs and Ys axis of symmetry, (c) ROI-segmentation

## 5  Discussion Results

The deep and objective diagnostic information, like severity and type of a disease can only be obtained by statistical analysis of the ROI. The segmentation of ROI is often an initial step in thermographic analysis, where the automatic approaches lead to fast and highly reproducible outcomes [14, 15]. Due to different geometrical shapes and proportions of body parts, it is not possible to capture the ROIs properly without the background during the process of data acquisition. The human back thermal picture varies individually, and it is difficult to state the exact features for some disease. This requires a large amount of measurements of significant cohort of patients with one specific disease. As thermal asymmetry distribution is not good enough for manual analysis, which can be appropriate only when a significant strong difference in color on thermal images are observed for the feature extraction and segmentation, the ROI needs to be solved automatically. The most significant benefit of the developed algorithm is automated segmentation of ROI with analyzing the side of asymmetry based on the central axis of the spine. The proposed algorithm for automatic segmentation of body regions is consistent with the solutions provided by other research groups [14, 15]. During its developing the main question were considered:

(i)   entire region segmentation, where the edge detection and thresholding techniques are commonly used to extract the body region from background [16];
(ii)  anatomical region segmentation, geometric and local thermal features to locate the specific anatomical regions [17];
(iii) diseased area segmentation, in order to locate the hottest or coldest regions [18].

The developed experimental protocol for IR thermal measurements turns to be appropriate for measurements in the hospitals, as well as it was well accepted by the participants. Analyzing features from the IR images of the patients with AS diseases we observe that for almost all patients with AS the significant feature was an abnormal temperature distribution among lumbar region or/and along all spine. The skin temperature distribution of those healthy as well as individuals with associate diagnosis represents the different pattern. Another important result observed in this study: the thermal images of the participants with the back pain complains clearly demonstrated the difference of temperature exactly in the places indicated by the participants. This allows to assume that thermography clearly shows the area of pain syndrome or thermal abnormalities. An additional information which can be obtained from thermal measurements: it was noticed that a lot of women has an area of higher temperature as a result of a bra strap that is too tight, that can cause poor posture, back and neck pain, shoulder grooves leading to numbness in the fingers and restrict circulation to muscle. It should be mentioned that the local temperature abnormalities and the asymmetry of the IR thermal image depends on the disease stage and severity, as well as the period of the disease treatment process.

# 6  Conclusions

The paper presents an algorithm for IR image segmentation as well as its features extraction. Its application to the cohort of patient with specific disease, ankylosing spondylitis (AS), shows that it can be used for automatic thermal image-processing, segmentation and feature. Proposed solution solves problem of ROI's detection by automatic segmentation and the location of thermal abnormalities in the patients' back.

The experimental protocol used in present for the IR thermal camera measurements shows a good correlation with a medical observation. However, the methodology needs to be validated in the further research study by increasing the database of IR images and statistical analysis. The developed algorithm and measurements protocol with combination of IR thermography can offer a novel quick and non-invasive tool for diagnosis and monitoring of rheumatoid diseases in real time for saving lives.

**Acknowledgment.** The authors would like to thank the Fundação para a Ciência e Tecnologia (FCT, Portugal) and NMT, S.A. for co-financing the PhD grant (PD/BDE/142791/2018) of the Doctoral NOVA 14H Program. Our acknowledgments to Fernando Pimentel Santos from NOVA Medical School|Faculdade de Ciências Médicas (NMS|FCM), Chronic Diseases Research Center (CEDOC), for the possibility to perform the measurements during the MyoSpA project. Special thanks to Diogo Casal from NOVA Medical School – NOVA University of Lisbon for assistance in some tasks that need to be solved from the medical point of view.

# References

1. Bouzida, N., Bendada, A., Maldague, X.P.: Visualization of body thermoregulation by infrared imaging. J. Therm. Biol. **34**, 120–126 (2009)
2. Park, J., Hyun, J.K., Seo, J.: The effectiveness of digital infrared thermographic imaging in patients with shoulder impingement syndrome. J. Shoulder Elbow Surg. **16**, 548–554 (2007)
3. Cherkas, L.F., Carter, L., Spector, T.D., et al.: Use of thermographic criteria to identify Raynaud's phenomenon in a populationsetting. J. Rheumatol. **30**, 720–722 (2003)
4. Holey, L.A., Dixon, J., Selfe, J.: An exploratory thermographic investigation of the effects of connective tissue massage on autonomic function. J. Manipulative Physiol. Ther. **34**, 457–462 (2011)
5. Denoble, A.E., Hall, N., Pieper, C.F., et al.: Patellar skin surface temperature by thermography reflects knee osteoarthritis severity Clin. Med. Insights: Arthritis Musculoskelet. Disord. **3**, 69–75 (2010)

6. Ammer, K.: Diagnosis of Raynaud's phenomenon by thermography. Skin Res. Tech. **2**, 182–185 (2006)
7. Vardasca, R.: Hand thermogram standardization with barycentric warp model. In: Proceedings of the 4th research student workshop, University of Glamorgan, South Wales, pp. 73–75 (2009)
8. Vardasca, R., Ring, E., Plassmann, P., et al.: Thermal symmetry of the upper and lower extremities in healthy subjects. Thermol Int. **22**(2), 53–60 (2012)
9. Casal, D., et al.: Optimization of an arterialized venous fasciocutaneous flap in the abdomen of the rat. Plastic and Reconstructive Surgery. Glob. Open **5**(8), e1436 (2017)
10. Casal, D., Mota-Silva, E., Iria, I., et al.: Reconstruction of a 10-mm-long median nerve gap in an ischemic environment using autologous conduits with different patterns of blood supply: a comparative study in the rat. PLoS One **13**(4), e0195692 (2018)
11. Singh, J., Arora, A.S.: A framework for enhancing the thermographic evaluation on characteristic areas for paranasal sinusitis detection. Infrared Phys. Technol. **85**, 457–464 (2017)
12. Zhu, W., He, X., Cheng, K. et al.: Ankylosing spondylitis: etiology, pathogenesis, and treatments. Bone Res. **7**(22) (2019)
13. Polidori, G., Kinne, M., Mereu, T., Beaumont, F., Kinne, M.: Medical infrared thermography in back pain osteopathic management. Complement. Ther. Med. **39**, 19–23 (2018)
14. Poplavskyi, A.A., Vassilenko, V.B., Poplavska, A.A.: Automatic threshold definition for dynamic images. Certificate of registration of computer program, no. 50151 (2013)
15. Duarte, A., Carrão, L., Espanha, M., et al.: Segmentation algorithms for thermal images. Proc. Technol. **16**, 1560–1569 (2014)
16. Fournet, D., Redortier, B., Havenith, G.: A method for whole-body skin temperature mapping in humans. Thermol. Int. **22**, 157–159 (2016)
17. Nandagopan, G.L., Haripriya, A.B.: Implementation and comparison of two image segmentation techniques on thermal foot images and detection of ulceration using asymmetry. In: International Conference on Communication Signal Processing, ICCSP 2016, pp. 356–360 (2016)
18. Mohiyuddin, N., Warhade, K.K.: Segmentation of thermal images for evaluation of rheumatoid arthritis disease. Int. J. Emerg. Eng. Res. Technol. **2**, 35–44 (2014)

# Development and Validation
# of an Experimental Protocol to Evaluate
# Posture Control

Daniel Noronha Osório[1]([⊠]), Emanuela Teixeira[2],
Fernando Pimentel-Santos[3], Hugo Silva[4], Hugo Gamboa[1,2],
and Cláudia Quaresma[1,2]

[1] Laboratório de Instrumentação, Engenharia Biomédica e Física da Radiação
(LIBPhys-UNL), Departamento de Física, Faculdade de Ciências e Tecnologias,
Universidade Nova de Lisboa, Monte da Caparica, 2829-516 Lisbon, Portugal
d.osorio@fct.unl.pt
[2] Departamento de Física, Faculdade de Ciências e Tecnologias,
Universidade Nova de Lisboa, Monte da Caparica, 2829-516 Lisbon, Portugal
[3] Department of Rheumatology, CEDOC-NOVA Medical School,
UNL, CHLO, Hospital Egas Moniz, Lisbon, Portugal
[4] IT - Instituto de Telecomunicações, Lisbon, Portugal

**Abstract.** Maintaining a stable upright position and body orientation are fundamental tasks to perform everyday activities and ensure the quality of life. The ability to maintain these can be damaged by various pathologies/disfunctions, such as stroke and aging. Therefore, it is important to quantify how the postural control reacts to different situation and how is affected by different pathologies, which could bring a big contribution in a clinical context, by helping to diagnose pathologies that can bring postural impairments. An experimental protocol was developed that combines both electromyography and posturography. To help validate this protocol, 53 patients (43 healthy and 10 stroke patients) performed it twice within a two-week period. By comparing the results from the two runs, it was possible to assess that these were not statistical different, and thus prove that the protocol is viable tool to build a normative database.

**Keywords:** Signal processing · Electromyography · Postural control · Balance

## 1 Introduction

Maintaining the upright standing position does not require much effort, however it is a task that involves the coordination of a few different systems. Out of all, the three most important systems for this task are the motor system, sensor system and the central nervous system [7, 30]. A correct posture is defined by the condition of balance between bones and muscles, and the relative alignments of the body elements, which enables the accomplishment of any action or just the sustenance of the body and it is a very important body ability [5, 15]. Maintaining a stable standing position and body orientation are fundamental tasks to perform daily activities and ensure the quality of life [5, 31].

© IFIP International Federation for Information Processing 2020
Published by Springer Nature Switzerland AG 2020
L. M. Camarinha-Matos et al. (Eds.): DoCEIS 2020, IFIP AICT 577, pp. 387–394, 2020.
https://doi.org/10.1007/978-3-030-45124-0_37

The combination of these systems has two important goals: ensuring that equilibrium is maintained, even if there is an outside stimulus destabilizing it, and help the body keep a relative position to the environment surrounding it [3, 15]. There are many factors that may cause problems in these systems, therefore it is important to study and comprehend its behavior [9, 23]. This can be achieved by simultaneously recording muscle activity (EMG) and the body center of pressure, while varying the posture of a person. With these recordings, a normative database can be built in order to study and compare the differences between healthy and patients suffering with different pathologies.

In this study, a protocol combining both EMG and posturography was developed and applied in two groups: individuals without pathology and stroke patients. In order to check the validity, the protocol was applied twice in a two-week period and the results have been compared to asses if the experimental conditions effected the results.

## 2    Contribution to Life Improvement

By defining a normative database, researchers and physicians/therapists are able to compare the results of different pathologies and postural influencing factors to what a normal muscle and center of pressure should be. The results from these studies can help physicians to make earlier diagnostics and objectively track the progression of diseases, such as in ankylosing spondylitis, a chronic inflammatory disease, very difficult to be diagnosed in its early stages [26], or the tracking the progress of patients that suffered a stroke. Furthermore, decrease postural stability is also a factor associated with new and recurrent lower extremity injuries in an active population [24, 25].

## 3    State of the Art

As previously mentioned, maintaining a stable standing position and body orientation are fundamental tasks to perform daily activities and ensure the quality of life [5, 31]. Therefore, it is important to study the subtle changes in center of pressure and muscle activity to achieve a good postural control.

A force platform can be used to provide an indirect and non-invasive measure about the body center of pressure (COP) [21], this technique being called posturography. By analyzing the COP trajectory in the platform, person's posture control can be studied [9, 29]. This technique is widely used, although there is a lack of standardization in experimental protocols. This lack leads to different tasks being performed, with different number of repetitions and different time acquisition periods, which contributes to a big variety of COP signal parameters, inducing the misinterpretation of the results [5, 16, 29, 32]. The first studies conducted can be traced to 1968, where tests were performed to assess the ability to maintain balance [18]. Benvenuti [1] created a protocol that uses the static upright standing position to quantify the nature and severity of the postural instability of each individual, but due to the lack of difficulty of the proposed approach, Nashner [6] developed the Sensory Organization Test (SOT), which is composed of six sensory conditions that evaluate the individual's balance.

The postural control system is highly controlled by the motor system and it is important to assess the muscle response when evaluating the postural control and equilibrium of a subject [12]. Trunk muscles have an important role in the preservation and stabilization of the upright standing position. Therefore, electromyography (EMG) analysis in these muscles can provide a more comprehensive evaluation of the muscular activity during balance perturbations [10, 14, 20, 28].

# 4   Research Contribution and Innovation

## 4.1   Developed Protocol

The protocol developed by this work combines both EMG and posturography data to provide a deeper and richer insight about the body postural control systems. As previously mentioned, this is very useful to clinicians in helping them to diagnose pathologies that can bring postural impairments at earlier stages.

The multichannel EMG recording were performed in four different muscles groups. These muscles and electrode placement are as follows: *rectus abdominis* (around 3 cm lateral to the midline above the umbilicus), *external obliques* (around 10 cm lateral to the midline above umbilicus and aligned with muscle fibers), *iliocostalis* (around 6 cm lateral to the midline at the L3[1]) and *multifidus* (around 2 cm lateral to the midline at the L5 (see footnote 1)) [18]. Figure 1 represents the placement of the electrodes during the realization of the protocol.

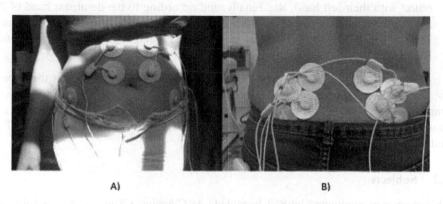

A)                                                    B)

**Fig. 1.** Illustration of the placement of the electrodes. (A) placement of the electrodes in the abdominal wall and (B) placement of the electrodes in the lower back.

The first step of the protocol is the recording of the basal muscle activity. To record that, subjects lay down on a marquise for 15 s in a supine position. Afterwards, the

---

[1] L3 and L5 – Third and Fifth Lumbar spine vertebra.

maximum voluntary contractions (MVC) for each muscle needs to be determined. There are three different tasks to obtain the MVC for each muscle.

For the *rectus abdominis*, the examiner asks the test subject to raise from a supine position using only the trunk, while at the same time counteracting the subject's efforts by placing his hand on the subject's chest [11]. For the *external obliques*, the examiner asks the subject to rotate one side of its body from a supine position, while at the sometime counteracting the subject's efforts by placing his hand on the shoulder being raised. This is done for both sides [11]. Finally, for the lower back muscles, the subject adopts a prone position and lifts their upper body, while the examiner places his hand between the subject's shoulders and counteracts this force [11]. Each of these MVCs procedures were repeated 3 times.

After obtaining the MVC for each muscle, the subjects were asked to perform nine different tasks, with duration of 30 s each (or as long as it could be managed), on top the force platform. The tasks were:

- Subjects stood on the force platform in a standing position, with, SEO, and without visual feedback, SEC [17, 19, 21, 27, 33].
- The subjects stood with only the right foot on the platform, with, REO, and without visual feedback, REC. These tasks were then repeated with the left foot (LEO and LEC) [19, 33].
- Finally, on top of a table an object is placed on the left side of the subject, at a distance of 15 cm from the extended left arm. The subject is then asked to pick up the object with their right hand, RR. This test is then performed on the right side of the subject, by placing the object on the right side asking the subjects to pick up the object with their left hand, RL. Finally, and according to the dominant hand of the subject, an object is placed in front of it at the previously mentioned distance. Then it was asked to the subjects to pick the object with their dominant hand, RC [2, 8, 13].

This protocol was performed twice within two weeks to ensure that the experimental conditions do not influence the results from the protocol. During the trails, it was observed that unipedal tasks caused great discomfort for the stroke patients, and thus the protocol applied to this group was reduced to remove the REO, REC, LEO, and LEC tasks.

## 4.2  Subjects

This study was conducted both at Faculdade de Ciências e Tecnologias da Universidade Nova de Lisboa and the Medical Center for Rehabilitation of Alcoitão (CMRA). The experimental protocol was approved by the CMRA ethical committee and all participants gave their written informed consent. The subject are divided into two different populations, one comprised of individuals without pathology and patients that suffered a stroke. Additionally, to be included in this study, the stroke patients had to meet two selection criteria: be able to maintain an upright standing position, and have cognitive ability with no total aphasia.

For the no pathologic group, a total of 43 individuals were recruited. There were 24 females and 19 males, with ages comprised from 18 to 55 years, heights from 150 to

190 cm, and weights from 47.5 to 110,0 kg. For the stroke patient group, 10 patients attending the CMRA were recruited, with ages comprised from 43 to 77, heights from 160 to 188 cm, and weights from 57.0 to 103.0 kg.

## 4.3 Data Recording and Analysis

COP displacements were recorded using a force platform provided by Plux (see footnote 1). This equipment is characterized by 4 steel load cells able to record a maximum force of 8000N (2000N per cell). The data is streamed over Bluetooth, being sampled with a sampling frequency up to 1000 Hz and a resolution of 16 bits.

For recording the EMG signals, a biosignalPlux (see footnote 1) acquisition module and 8 EMG sensors were used. The biosignalPlux (see footnote 1) is capable of recording 8 biosignals simultaneously with a resolution of 16 bits and sampling frequencies up to 1000 Hz. This bandwidth was chosen since EMG activity can go up to 500 Hz [4]. As with the force platform, the data is streamed via Bluetooth. The EMG sensors used were emgPLUX (see footnote 1) an EMG sensor from Plux (see footnote 1). To connect the sensors to the patient, 2 Ag/AgCL with solid adhesive pre gelled electrodes were used per sensor (TIGA-MED Gold 01-7500, TIGA-MED GMBH, Germany).

For recording the data streamed from the platform and the biosignalsPlux (see footnote 1), the software used was OpenSignals (see footnote 1).

EMG signals were averaged out and the signal envelope was extracted using the root mean square (RMS) algorithm, with a window of 100 samples. Each muscle RMS signal was then normalized using the maximum value of the respective MVC.

Platform signals underwent a pre-processing phase where the raw signal was converted to a COP displacement in the antero-posterior (AP) direction (Y direction) and medio-lateral (ML) direction (X direction). Then, and for each direction, the signal was averaged out. The velocity, standard deviation, and amplitude of the signal of each direction were calculated. The total area of COP displacement was also calculated, using the convex hull algorithm and the Green's theorem.

## 4.4 Statistical Analysis

To compare the two moments where the protocol was executed, the paired samples t-Test was used. This parametric test allows us to compare two means from two different and related conditions, by comparing the mean differences between the paired samples and if these significantly differ from zero [22]. The null hypothesis is then:

H0: $\mu1 - \mu2 = 0$, where $\mu1$ and $\mu2$ is the population mean of variable 1 and of the variable 2, respectively.

For this work, p-values bigger than 0.05 indicate than the null hypotheses cannot be rejected and the mean difference of the paired samples is 0.

# 5  Results

For the EMG data, the mean and median normalized activity (a percentage of the maximum voluntary contraction value) of each muscle for a certain task was compared with the corresponding value for the rerun, using the paired t-Test with the significance level set at $p > 0.05$. For all tasks, no significant differences were found between the trial and re-trial for both the mean and median values. As an example, the lowest p-value obtain when comparing the mean value for all task for all the muscles in the study was 0.07 for Right *Rectus Abdominis* muscle for reaching an object for an object on the right side of the body task.

For the COP data, the amplitude and standard deviations (in each frontal-distal and antero-lateral) were compared, as well as the velocity and total area. As with the EMG data, the paired t-Test p-values were all above the significance level, indicating no significant difference between both runs.

Finally, the same assessment was applied to the test subjects that suffered a stroke, and no significant differences were found between runs for the EMG and COP features, confirming the results found in the previous comparison. The protocol for these patients had to be simplified since only the first five tasks could be easily (without pain or too much effort from the patients) performed by the subjects.

# 6  Conclusion

The objective of this work was to assess the development and validation of an experimental protocol to evaluate posture control. In order to fulfill this objective, the developed protocol was applied twice within a two-week period to ensure that the results obtained were not affected by the experimental conditions or by any other external factor. This protocol was developed in order to build a normative database of both posturography and electromyographic features that can be useful in future studies to evaluate posture control.

Two different population were recruited for this study, one healthy and one composed of stroke patients, for a total of 53 test subjects (43 individuals without pathology and 10 stroke patients). The developed protocol was applied to this two groups and some features extracted from the raw data in order to compare the results of the two different moments when the protocol was applied.

To compare this two moments, the paired sample t-Test was used, and the result of this test revealed that for all the analyzed features, no statistical difference was detected.

Based on the results obtained, the proposed protocol can be considered as a viable tool to build a normative database, by providing a systematic and standard reference when developing further posturographic and electromyographic studies.

**Acknowledgments.** The authors acknowledge the Medical Center for Rehabilitation of Alcoitão (CMRA) for their support. This work was supported by the Portuguese Fundação para a Ciência e Tecnologia (FCT) with grants: I&D 2015–2020 "iNOVA4Health - Programme in Translational Medicine" (UID/Multi/04462/2013).

# References

1. Benvenuti, F., et al.: Kinematic characteristics of standing disequilibrium: reliability and validity of a posturographic protocol. Arch. Phys. Med. Rehabil. **80**(3), 278–287 (1999)
2. Bernhardt, J., Ellis, P., Denisenko, S., Hill, K.: Changes in balance and locomotionmeasures during rehabilitation following stroke. Physiother. Res. Int. **3**(2), 109–122 (1998)
3. Boukhenous, S., Attari, M.: A postural stability analysis by using plantar pressuremeasurements. In: Eighth International Multi-Conference on Systems, Signals & Devices, pp. 1–6. IEEE (2011)
4. Boxtel, A., Boelhouwer, A., Bos, A.: Optimal EMG signal bandwidth and interelectrode distance for the recording of acoustic, electrocutaneous, and photic blink reflexes. Psychophysiology **35**(6), 690–697 (1998)
5. Duarte, M., Freitas, S.M.: Revision of posturography based on force plate for balance evaluation. Braz. J. Phys. Ther. **14**(3), 183–192 (2010)
6. Ford-Smith, C.D., Wyman, J.F., Elswick Jr., R., Fernandez, T., Newton, R.A.: Test-retest reliability of the sensory organization test in noninstitutionalized older adults. Arch. Phys. Med. Rehabil. **76**(1), 77–81 (1995)
7. Forghieri, M., Monzani, D., Mackinnon, A., Ferrari, S., Gherpelli, C., Galeazzi, G.M.: Posturographic destabilization in eating disorders in female patients exposed to body image related phobic stimuli. Neurosci. Lett. **629**, 155–159 (2016)
8. Goldie, P.A., Matyas, T.A., Spencer, K.I., McGinley, R.B.: Postural control in standing following stroke: test-retest reliability of some quantitative clinical tests. Phys. Ther. **70**(4), 234–243 (1990)
9. Goto, F., Kushiro, K., Tsutsumi, T.: Effect of chewing gum on static posturography in patients with balance disorders. Acta Otolaryngol. **131**(11), 1187–1192 (2011)
10. Harel, N.Y., Asselin, P.K., Fineberg, D.B., Pisano, T.J., Bauman, W.A., Spungen, A.M.: Adaptation of computerized posturography to assess seated balance in persons with spinal cord injury. J. Spinal Cord Med. **36**(2), 127–133 (2013)
11. Hislop, H., Avers, D., Brown, M.: Daniels and Worthingham's Muscle Testing-E-Book: Techniques of Manual Examination and Performance Testing. Elsevier Health Sciences, Amsterdam (2013)
12. Horak, F.B.: Postural orientation and equilibrium: what do we need to know about neural control of balance to prevent falls? Age Ageing **35**(suppl. 2), ii7–ii11 (2006)
13. Huxham, F.E., Goldie, P.A., Patla, A.E.: Theoretical considerations in balance assessment. Aust. J. Physiother. **47**(2), 89–100 (2001)
14. Isho, T., Usuda, S.: Association of trunk control with mobility performance and accelerometry-based gait characteristics in hemiparetic patients with subacutestroke. Gait Posture **44**, 89–93 (2016)
15. Ivanenko, Y., Gurfinkel, V.S.: Human postural control. Front. Neurosci. **12**, 171 (2018)
16. Juras, G., Slomka, K., Fredyk, A., Sobota, G., Bacik, B.: Evaluation of the limits of stability (LOS) balance test. J. Hum. Kinet. **19**, 39–52 (2008)
17. Loughran, S., Gatehouse, S., Kishore, A., Swan, I.R.: Does patient perceived handicap correspond to the modified clinical test for the sensory interaction on balance? Otol. Neurotol. **27**(1), 86–91 (2006)
18. Mancini, M., Horak, F.B.: The relevance of clinical balance assessment tools to differentiate balance deficits. Eur. J. Phys. Rehabil. Med. **46**(2), 239 (2010)
19. Marioni, G., Fermo, S., Zanon, D., Broi, N., Staffieri, A.: Early rehabilitation for unilateral peripheral vestibular disorders: a prospective, randomized investigation using computerized posturography. Eur. Arch. Otorhinolaryngol. **270**(2), 425–435 (2013)

20. O'Sullivan, P.B., Grahamslaw, K.M., Kendell, M., Lapenskie, S.C., Moller, N.E., Richards, K.V.: The effect of different standing and sitting postures on trunk muscle activity in a pain-free population. Spine **27**(11), 1238–1244 (2002)

21. Palmieri, R.M., Ingersoll, C.D., Stone, M.B., Krause, B.A.: Center-of-pressure parameters used in the assessment of postural control. J. Sport Rehabil. **11**(1), 51–66 (2002)

22. Pestana, M.H., Gageiro, J.N.: Análise de dados para ciências sociais: a complementaridade do SPSS (2008)

23. Pivnickova, L., Dolinay, V., Vasek, V.: Evaluation of static posturography via the Wii Balance Board. In: Proceedings of the 2014 15th International Carpathian Control Conference (ICCC), pp. 437–441. IEEE (2014)

24. Pletcher, E., et al.: Normative data for the NeuroCom sensory organization test in United States military special operations forces (2017)

25. Romero-Franco, N., et al.: Postural stability and subsequent sports injuries during indoor season of athletes. J. Phys. Ther. Sci. **26**(5), 683–687 (2014)

26. Rudwaleit, M., Khan, M.A., Sieper, J.: The challenge of diagnosis and classification in early ankylosing spondylitis: do we need new criteria? Arthritis Rheum. **52**(4), 1000–1008 (2005)

27. Sadowska, D., Krzepota, J.: Influence of posturographic protocol on postural stability sways during bipedal stance after ankle muscle fatigue. Percept. Motor Skills **123**(1), 232–243 (2016)

28. Seo, H.R., Kim, T.H.: The effects of gyrotonic expansion system exercise and trunk stability exercise on muscle activity and lumbar stability for the subjects with chronic low back pain. J. Exerc. Rehabil. **15**(1), 129 (2019)

29. Taylor, M.R., Sutton, E.E., Diestelkamp, W.S., Bigelow, K.E.: Subtle differences during posturography testing can influence postural sway results: the effects of talking, time before data acquisition, and visual fixation. J. Appl. Biomech. **31**(5), 324–329 (2015)

30. Toth, A.J., Harris, L.R., Zettel, J., Bent, L.R.: Vision can recalibrate the vestibular reafference signal used to re-establish postural equilibrium following a platform perturbation. Exp. Brain Res. **235**(2), 407–414 (2017)

31. Vieira, T., Oliveira, L., Nadal, J.: Estimation procedures affect the center of pressure frequency analysis. Braz. J. Med. Biol. Res. **42**(7), 665–673 (2009)

32. Visser, J.E., Carpenter, M.G., van der Kooij, H., Bloem, B.R.: The clinical utility of posturography. Clin. Neurophysiol. **119**(11), 2424–2436 (2008)

33. Yarrow, K., Brown, P., Gresty, M.A., Bronstein, A.M.: Force platform recordings in the diagnosis of primary orthostatic tremor. Gait Posture **13**(1), 27–34 (2001)

# A Genetic Algorithm to Design Job Rotation Schedules with Low Risk Exposure

João Rodrigues[1(✉)], Hugo Gamboa[1], Nafiseh Mollaei[1],
Daniel Osório[1], Ana Assunção[2], Carlos Fujão[3],
and Filomena Carnide[2]

[1] Laboratory for Instrumentation, Biomedical Engineering and Radiation
Physics (Libphys-UNL), Costa de Caparica, Portugal
jmd.rodrigues@fct.unl.pt
[2] Faculdade de Motricidade Humana, CIPER, LBMF, Departamento
de Desporto e Saúde, Universidade de Lisboa, Lisbon, Portugal
[3] Volkswagen Autoeuropa Lda, Palmela, Portugal

**Abstract.** In automotive industries, the manufacturing processes are characterized by repetitive tasks and physically demanding work, with possible long-term implications on the musculoskeletal health of the workers. One key organizational strategy that provides an improvement in the prevention of musculoskeletal disorders are job rotation schedules. These are usually designed manually, being (1) time demanding and (2) a subjective evaluation of the schedule's risk. In this work, a genetic algorithm is presented, to generate automatically a daily job rotation schedule. The quality of the schedule is based on objective scores as- signed to workstations by the European Assembly Worksheet (EAWS) risk screening tool, guiding the algorithm in reaching a final solution that promotes schedules with lower exposure to the sequence of workstations assigned to each worker of the team. The schedules generated by the algorithm were compared to schedules designed by the team leaders and presented a better overall result.

**Keywords:** Genetic algorithm · Job rotation · Occupational exposure

## 1 Introduction

Job rotation schedules are usually the responsibility of team leaders, who must assign each worker to the set of workstations the worker has to perform over the working day. Considering this, (1) team leaders spend a considerable amount of time to design these plans correctly, and (2) do not have into consideration an objective measure of the occupational risk of each workstation.

In this work, a method based on a genetic algorithm for the automatic design of a job rotation schedule to support the task of team leaders is proposed. The algorithm considers the qualification of workers and the occupational exposure score of each workstation evaluated by the European assembly worksheet (EAWS) [10]. The proposed method will search for solutions that have low exposure scores for each worker and a balanced plan for the team.

© IFIP International Federation for Information Processing 2020
Published by Springer Nature Switzerland AG 2020
L. M. Camarinha-Matos et al. (Eds.): DoCEIS 2020, IFIP AICT 577, pp. 395–402, 2020.
https://doi.org/10.1007/978-3-030-45124-0_38

## 2   Contribution to Life Improvement

In this work we focus on the benefits of automatic generation of job rotation schedules, which have several advantages: (1) by generating solutions automatically, team leaders can focus more of their time on their main tasks; (2) as the algorithm is designed with the consideration of objective scores of each workstation, the result will promote a more balanced exposure over the working day of each worker. These factors contribute to maximize the mentioned advantages, improving the welfare of both workers and team leaders.

## 3   Literature Revision

The design of job rotation plans follows a specific purpose. Several strategies have been developed depending on the context and application of these tools. For instance, in Asensio-Cuesta et al., a model has been designed to prevent work related musculoskeletal disorders in environments with high repeatability of movements, considering mechanical (using the Occupational Repetitive Actions (OCRA)), environmental and organizational factors [1]. Another study presents a job rotation schedule that uses the workers' qualifications, the workstation's exposure (based on EAWS) and the most recent allocation of each worker applying a linear programming-based heuristic [7]. Finally, other works are found in which both reduction of exposure and increase of productivity are the focus [2, 9]. In these cases, the authors used a mixed integer programming model, considering organizational and mechanical variables.

Beyond reported studies, others were found in which the risk assessment was made to reduce the cumulative effect of sequential working tasks on the same body region by using the Rapid Entire Body Assessment (REBA) tool [11]. In [4] the proposed model adds posture diversity to reduce the accumulated risk of body postures. Additionally, a study (2014) with the purpose to reduce repetitive task sequences based on ergonomic, environmental, competence and skill factors was found [8].

Other works were found to include permanent and temporary disabilities of the workers as well as their preferences [6]. In Boenzi et al. (2013) an integer programming model was used to find not only the optimal job rotation schedule, but also the optimal break schedule, in order to minimize the workload on teams of the assembly lines of an automotive industry. Finally, literature has also been found where the age of workers is included in the model, given the importance of the associations between the ageing process and work-related musculoskeletal disorders [3]. Several of the reviewed approaches used genetic algorithms [2, 4, 6, 8], demonstrating to be reliable in reaching the desired solutions.

## 4   Research Contributions

This section outlines (1) the variables used to define the mathematical model used to design the function that guides the genetic algorithm in reaching a solution (2) the mathematical model, (3) the structure of the genetic algorithm and (4) the results.

## 4.1    Problem Definition, Variables and Mathematical Formulation

The problem in demand is combinatorial. For this case, a specific team (URQ) with 12 workers, of the assembly line of an automotive industry, was selected. The working shift considered was the early shift, divided in 4 working periods with the following distribution: (1) 22.6%; (2) 30.7%; (3) 27.0%; (4) 19.7%. The problem will be illustrated as a matrix (job rotation plan) that has the workstations assigned to each worker (rows) during each rotation period (columns) (e.g. Fig. 2a).

In this case, the generation of a job rotation schedule has to comply with several conditions and requirements, namely: (1) Each worker has to be assigned to 4 workstations during the working day; (2) On each rotation period, each workstation can only be performed once; (3) On each rotation period, one worker can perform the task of a single workstation; (4) Workers can repeat the same workstation during the working day, depending on their qualification; (5) Each workstation assigned to a worker has to be part of their qualification;

In order to design a job rotation plan and its quality assessment, the set of variables considered must be clearly exposed and described. Overall, there are two kinds of variables that were used to design a job rotation plan:

**Mechanical Exposure Variables (EAWS).** The main variable involved in defining the quality assessment of a job rotation schedule is the overall score that quantifies the physical workload of a workstation. This variable is extracted from the EAWS screening tool and is estimated by the scores as- signed to individual risk factors of the workstation. The score is presented by a traffic light scheme and is the variable that has the highest relevance on the fitness function.

**Organizational Variables.** The organizational variables contemplate (1) the qualification of workers in a specific URQ to guarantee valid sequences, as well as (2) the duration of each rotation period.

As aforementioned, the assessment involves calculating an averaged score of the occupational exposure associated with the sequence of workstations assigned over the rotation periods to a worker and how deviated are the exposure scores of the team.

The *occupational exposure* score given to a workstation on the rotation period rot is calculated by multiplying the workstation's mechanical risk score $(EAWS_{ws})$ with the percentage of time $\Delta t\%_{rot}$ of the rotation period in which the workstation is scheduled. The value of time is fixed depending on the rotation period in which the station has been allocated. Finally, the resulting score for a sequence of workstations $(OE_w)$ is given by the sum of the occupational exposure scores over the set of rotation periods $(n_{rot} = 4)$:

$$OE_w = \sum_{rot=1}^{n_{rot}} EAWS_{ws} \times \Delta t\%_{rot} \tag{1}$$

In order to have a value between 0 and 1 as an output, the $OE_w$ has to be normalized, such that if a worker has a score of 0, it means that he/she is ex- posed to the best possible sequence of workstations from the set of workstations the selected worker can do. On the other hand, a score of 1 means that he/she is exposed to the worst possible sequence of workstations. These scores are calculated for each worker based on the workstations they can do. The exposure score for the highest value ($max_w$) is associated to 1, while the lowest value ($min_w$) to 0. The calculation of the worst and best reference exposure sequences for each worker is not made in each step of the algorithm, but rather once before the algorithm is applied. The normalization is then made based on the reference scores ($max_w$ and $min_w$):

$$\overline{NOE} = \sum_{w=1}^{W} \frac{\frac{OE_w - min_w}{max_w - min_w}}{W} = \sum_{w=1}^{W} \frac{NOE_w}{W}, \tag{2}$$

being $NOE_w$ the normalized occupational exposure score for a worker's sequence, $W$ the number of workers on the team and w the iterator over the number of workers, $OE_w$ the occupational exposure score for a worker's ($w$) sequence, $min_w$ and $max_w$ the minimum and maximum occupational exposure scores of a valid worker's sequence, respectively.

The final variable that is used in the *fitness function* is the standard deviation of the occupational exposure scores of the team. This variable has the purpose to guide the algorithm finding solutions that balance the exposure scores of the team, not favoring one worker in regard to the other:

$$Dev = 1 - \sqrt{\frac{1}{W} \sum_{w=1}^{W} \left(NOE_w - \overline{NOE}\right)^2} = 1 - \sigma_{oe}, \tag{3}$$

being $\sigma_{oe}$ the standard deviation of the occupational exposure, $W$ the number of workers on the team, w the iterator over the number of workers, $NOE_w$ the occupational exposure score for a worker, $\overline{NOE}$ the mean occupational exposure score of the team and Dev the deviation score. The higher the value of $\sigma_{oe}$, the worst is the exposure balance of the rotation plan. In order to have a value that has a positive trend (*the higher the better*), the deviation score (*Dev*) is a result of an inverse sum of the standard deviation. The *fitness function* is now the combination of the previously explained variables. For a team there is the normalized occupational exposure score and the deviation score. The combination is made by adding these two variables with different weights:

$$MQ = M_{oe}\overline{NOE} + M_{dev}Dev, \tag{4}$$

being $MQ$ the matrix quality score, $M_{oe}$ the weight factor of the occupational exposure score and $M_{dev}$ the weight of the deviation score. In this work, $M_{oe} = 1$ and $M_{dev} = \frac{1}{3}$, The algorithm has the task of maximizing Eq. 4.

## 4.2   Genetic Algorithm and Results

Genetic algorithms are based on the theory of evolution, being structured with the following steps: (1) generation of the initial population; (2) evaluate the fitness of each chromosome of the population; (3) the selection of a set of chromosomes from the population pool; (4) apply crossover and mutation of the selected chromosomes to generate offspring for a new population and (5) evaluate final conditions to stop or continue to generate new populations. The proposed algorithm follows the same architecture. In this work, population means a set of job rotation plans; *chromosome* means a valid job rotation plan and gene means a workstation of a job rotation plan.

As presented in the Sect. 3, the methods used in genetic algorithms vary, depending on the type of problem itself and the restrictions that the problem implies. In the proposed algorithm: (1) the population has a size of 25 chromosomes; (2) the selection methods are elite selection (2%) and a method that merges the roulette-wheel and rank based selection (30%); (3) the crossover method is a permutation-based method called ordered crossover (OX) and generates 90% of the new population; (4) the mutation method is the bit-string mutation and generates 10% of the new population; (5) the closing conditions are met when the iteration number is higher than 500 and the best chromosome's score of the current population is higher than the mean value of scores for the weekly plan of the team leader, which is *0.78*.

Figure 1 shows how each variable of the Eq. 4 vary over the iterative process. The third subplot demonstrates that the algorithm is able to reach a solution that complies with the requirements of the mentioned equation, maximizing the overall matrix quality score. The first and second subplot show how the algorithm varied the variables over time to reach better solutions.

In Fig. 2a and b are presented a randomly selected job rotation plan from the first population, and the final outputted plan of the algorithm, respectively. The score of the initial and random job rotation plan is *0.76*, while the score of the final job rotation plan is *0.84*. In both cases, relevant sequences are highlighted. On the initial matrix, the sequences with higher and lower risk are showed with red and green circles, respectively. On the final matrix, sequences where red labelled workstations are outside the rotation with the longest period (*Rot 2*) are labelled blue, the sequences where red labelled workstations are located on the longest rotation period are labelled green and the sequence with the workstation with lowest risk is located on the longest rotation period is labelled orange. The result can also be compared with the job rotation plan designed by the team leader, which has a score of *0.78*. The table with the scores of the job rotation plans designed by the team leader for a week plan are presented in Table 1. The algorithm was able to give a solution in a mean value of 7.8 s.

## 5  Discussion

On Fig. 1 is seen that Dev score increases over each iteration, which means that the exposure score of each sequence of the matrix will be more similar between each other, balancing the occupational exposure of the team. It can also be noted that this balance is accomplished by no significant change from the mean exposure scores.

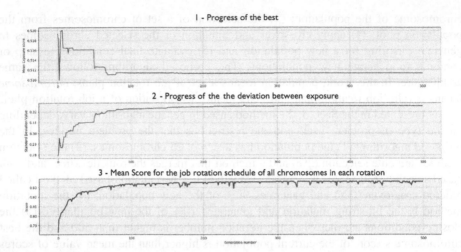

**Fig. 1.** Progress of the scores over the iterative process of the algorithm for the mean exposure (1), the deviation of the team's exposure (2), and the matrix quality score (3)

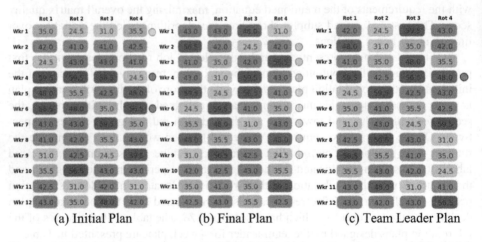

(a) Initial Plan          (b) Final Plan          (c) Team Leader Plan

**Fig. 2.** (a) Initial job rotation plan (score: 0.76). (b) Final job rotation plan (score: 0.84). (c) Job rotation plan designed by the team leader (score: 0.78).

In this case, there was a peak of the mean exposure score in the beginning, however this peak tends to decrease over the iterative process. The initial plan, from Fig. 2a showed flaws in the sequences, namely for workers (*Wkr*) 4 and 6, which have 3 red labelled workstations on their sequences, resulting in very high-risk exposure levels. Conversely, *Wkr* 1 had a very low risk exposure level, unbalancing the plan.

**Table 1.** Scores for the normalized occupational exposure (*NOE*), deviation (*Dev*) and the quality of the job rotation schedule (*MQ*) for the team leader's plans of the week and the algorithm's output.

| Plan | 1 | 2 | 3 | 4 | 5 | 6 | Initial | Final |
|------|------|------|------|------|------|------|---------|-------|
| *NOE* | 0.51 | 0.51 | 0.52 | 0.51 | 0.50 | 0.51 | 0.51 | 0.51 |
| *Dev* | 0.83 | 0.81 | 0.79 | 0.82 | 0.79 | 0.80 | 0.75 | 0.97 |
| *MQ* | 0.78 | 0.77 | 0.78 | 0.78 | 0.77 | 0.78 | 0.76 | 0.84 |

The job rotation plan that resulted from the algorithm, on Fig. 2b, shows that the main purpose of the algorithm in balancing the scores for all workers and keep the exposure as low as possible was achieved. The longest periods for the early shift are the second and third rotation periods (*Rot 2 and Rot 3*). These have an increased contribution on the exposure risk. In the final plan, when red labelled workstations are on the longest rotation period (*Rot 2*), such as on sequences of *Wkr* 6, 7 and 9, the risk is balanced with green and yellow labelled workstations. In the case of having red labelled workstations on the sequence, but not on the longest rotation period, such as in the sequences of *Wkr* 2, 3, 4, 5 and 8, lower risk exposure workstations balance the risk of the sequence with green and/or yellow on the longest rotation period. In the case of *Wkr* 5, having multiple red labelled workstations implies the need of the workstation with lower risk on the longest rotation period.

Comparing Fig. 2b and c and looking at Table 1, there are similarities in how the sequences are balanced. Nevertheless, the deviation between sequences scores is much higher in the case of the team leader's plan.

This model brings a new methodology in integrating EAWS variables as the main guiding factor to reach solutions for job rotation schedules. Compared to the work of Hochdörffer *et al.*, where partial scores were used, the information is less, but can be used to easily adapt the model in any environment that uses occupational scores and qualifications of workers in their protocols.

# 6   Conclusion and Future Work

The main purpose of this work was to guarantee that the results are reliable and realistic to support team leader's decisions and to reduce the burden imposed to them since it is a time-consuming process, and this was achieved.

In the industrial context, the implementation of such measures can have a great impact in reducing management and health related costs, by means of preventing work related injuries and complains. Additionally, such work is a tool for team supervisors and workers to evaluate the risk of the schedules and what can be improved on the team. For instance, simulations of schedules can be performed to identify problems such as the lack of versatility of workers, and how this versatility could be improved to ameliorate the quality of the schedule.

Improvements can be made on the current method. The use of the overall score only evaluates the workstation globally, while other aspects of the workstation, described on the EAWS tool are not used, namely posture, manual material handling and force scores. In a future approach, other organizational variables should also be considered, namely the skill level of workers and the diversity in the sequence.

**Acknowledgments.** This work was partly supported by Fundação para a Ciência e Tecnologia, under Grant UID/DTP/UI447/2019 to CIPER–Centro Interdisciplinar para o Estudo da Performance Humana (unit 447), Ph.D. grant SFRH/BDE/102750/2014, Ph.D. grant PD/BDE/142973/2018 and Ph.D. grant PD/BDE/142816/2018.

# References

1. Asensio-Cuesta, S., Diego-Mas, J., Cremades-Oliver, L., González-Cruz, M.: A method to design job rotation schedules to prevent work-related musculoskeletal disorders in repetitive work. Int. J. Prod. Res. **50**(24), 7467–7478 (2012)
2. Asensio-Cuesta, S., Diego-Mas, J.A., Canós-Darós, L., Andrés-Romano, C.: A genetic algorithm for the design of job rotation schedules considering ergonomic and competence criteria. Int. J. Adv. Manuf. Technol. **60**, 1161–1174 (2012). https://doi.org/10.1007/s00170-011-3672-0
3. Botti, L., Mora, C., Calzavara, M.: Design of job rotation schedules managing the exposure to age-related risk factors. IFAC-PapersOnLine **50**(1), 13993–13997 (2017). 20th IFAC World Congress
4. Cheshmehgaz, H.R., Haron, H., Kazemipour, F., Desa, M.I.: Accumulated risk of body postures in assembly line balancing problem and modeling through a multi- criteria fuzzy-genetic algorithm. Comput. Ind. Eng. **63**(2), 503–512 (2012)
5. David, R., et al.: Towards an operator 4.0 typology: a human-centric perspective on the fourth industrial revolution technologies (2016)
6. Diego-Mas, J., Asensio-Cuesta, S., Sanchez-Romero, M., Artacho-Ramirez, M.: A multi-criteria genetic algorithm for the generation of job rotation schedules. Int. J. Ind. Ergon. **39**(1), 23–33 (2009)
7. Hochdörffer, J., Hedler, M., Lanza, G.: Staff scheduling in job rotation environments considering ergonomic aspects and preservation of qualifications. J. Manuf. Syst. **46**, 103–114 (2018)
8. Mondal, P.K., Ahsan, A.N., Quayum, K.A.: An approach to develop an effective job rotation schedule by using genetic algorithm. In: 2013 International Conference on Electrical Information and Communication Technology (EICT), pp. 1–5. IEEE (2014)
9. Mossa, G., Boenzi, F., Digiesi, S., Mummolo, G., Romano, V.: Productivity and ergonomic risk in human based production systems: a job-rotation scheduling model. Int. J. Prod. Econ. **171**, 471–477 (2016)
10. Schaub, K., Caragnano, G., Britzke, B., Bruder, R.: The european assembly worksheet. Theor. Issues Ergon. Sci. **14**(6), 616–639 (2013)
11. Yoon, S.Y., Ko, J., Jung, M.C.: A model for developing job rotation schedules that eliminate sequential high workloads and minimize between-worker variability in cumulative daily workloads: Application to automotive assembly lines. Appl. Ergon. **55**, 8–15 (2016)

# Real Time Mental Stress Detection Through Breath Analysis

Paulo Santos[1,2(✉)], Peter Roth[3], Jorge M. Fernandes[1,2],
Viktor Fetter[3], and Valentina Vassilenko[1,2]

[1] Laboratory for Instrumentation, Biomedical Engineering and Radiation
Physics (LibPhys-UNL), NOVA School of Science and Technology,
Campus FCT UNL, Caparica, Portugal
ph.santos@campus.fct.unl.pt, vv@fct.unl.pt
[2] NMT, S.A., Edíficio Madan Parque, Rua dos Inventores, Caparica, Portugal
[3] Space Systems, Airbus Defence and Space GmbH, Immenstaad, Germany

**Abstract.** Modern work environment is changing from classic physiological to more psychological workloads. The capability to monitor biochemical processes within the human body positions breath analysis as a promising method to non-invasively and quickly detect mental stress. The present work aims to identify psychological stress biomarkers and breath profile changes after psychological interventions (PASAT or relaxing videos). In an exploratory study, 14 male participants followed a double cross-over randomized study which included two experimental sessions (stress and neutral/relax). GSR and HR were continuously measured to indicate physiological stress levels. NASA-TLX questionnaires were fulfilled to quantify individual stress. Breath samples were selectively collected by a recently developed advanced breath sampling prototype device and afterwards analyzed with a GC-IMS apparatus. Some promising results on mental stress detection were found and are presented and discussed in this paper.

**Keywords:** Mental stress · Volatile Organic Compounds (VOCs) · Breath analysis · Gas Chromatographic-Ion Mobility Spectrometer (GC-IMS) Paced Auditory Serial Addition Test (PASAT) · Galvanic Skin Response (GSR) · Heart Rate (HR) · NASA Task Load Index (NASA-TLX)

## 1 Introduction

In the psychobiology field, stress is an unpleasant emotional state and the physic and/or psychologic result to a threatening situation. The frightening experience is caused by an imbalance between environmental demand for performance and available personal resources, which triggers behavioral, emotional and cognitive reactions [1]. In response to an acute threat to survival, a stress pattern is prompted (*e.g.* as "fight-or-flight response") which is related to the release of stress hormones and, consequently, to the activation of specific muscles and other bodily functions [2]. Such process includes variations in cardiac activity, sweat gland activity, and skin temperature. A high number of physiological signals have been broadly used as reliable indicators of stress

© IFIP International Federation for Information Processing 2020
Published by Springer Nature Switzerland AG 2020
L. M. Camarinha-Matos et al. (Eds.): DoCEIS 2020, IFIP AICT 577, pp. 403–410, 2020.
https://doi.org/10.1007/978-3-030-45124-0_39

(*e.g.* GSR, HR, skin temperature, electrocardiogram, electromyography, blood volume pulse, electroencephalogram and respiration rate) [3].

Multiple wearable biosensors combine and process such type of physiological data with high temporal resolution [4] and can be used for basic research, clinical application, or during daily routines in real-life situations [5]. However, their use in real-world experiments poses several challenges in terms of reliable and useful measurements for emotion extraction [5]. Those challenges include: selection of a suitable sampling frequency (to depict the signal correctly), proper sensor placement (for signal ambiguities avoidance) and the data treatment regarding the small fluctuations of the raw signals, caused by the oscillations of the physiological status and inadaptation of sensors to daily human behavior through measurements.

Therefore, there is still a need for innovative approaches that can detect stress in real-world settings while overcoming the aforementioned challenges.

Exhaled air is a wealthy and complex matrix with hundreds of compounds. Recent health diagnosis and monitoring research points breath analysis and "breathomics" as one of the highest potential research fields for systemic metabolic processes assessment. Thus, a research need arose to investigate whether stress may be identified by breath analysis and whether any such putative VOC markers might have the potential to both detect and differentiate stress levels.

This study was sought to generate a stress response in human breath using PASAT interventions [6]. As proposition, breath composition is nearly constant and variations only occur with perturbations (*e.g.* disease, behavioral and environmental), which changes metabolism and volatalome. The underlying hypothesis was that induced stress cause a faster breathing rate, an increased pulse rate and blood pressure which would be related with changes in exhaled VOCs across the participant cohort.

## 2   Contribution to Life Improvement

Mental health disorders are among the most burdensome health concerns in developed countries. Nearly 792 million people (10.7%) worldwide reported any mental illness type in 2017. Additionally, 71% of adults reported at least one stress symptom, such as headaches, depression or anxiety. Human and financial costs of stress are enormous: around 120,000 people die each year from work-related stress, 5 to 8% of healthcare expenses only in the US are due to work-related stress (over $100 billion/year) [7].

In addition to the long-term effects of stress (*e.g.* increased stroke risk and negative influences on the cardiovascular system), work-related stress is also known to have a negative impact on work performance and concentration leading to burning out, confrontations and loss of productivity (with higher human error rates). Approximately 80% of aviation accidents are caused by pilot errors, a result of insufficient management of stress [8]. Therefore, the constant use of innovative and quick stress monitoring approaches in jobs with high responsibility and high stress levels (*e.g.* pilots or astronauts) remains crucial since it may prevent fatal accidents.

Breath profiling is innately attractive allowing noninvasive, quick and straightforward observations of multiple biochemical processes occurring in the human body. Recently the non-invasive detection of biomarkers in breath associated with tuberculosis (TB), chronic obstructive pulmonary disease (COPD), asthma and an array of cancers have been reported [9–11]. A link between psyche, emotions and the composition of exhaled breath has also been found in recent studies [12]. However, the observation and description of the effect of psychological stress on the VOC profile from breath is currently almost unreported.

Although breath analysis presents many advantages, the lack of standardized methods to both collect and analyze breath samples are still unresolved issues. The present paper reports the results of the application of a protocol for mental stress detection [13], combining: (a) a recently developed selective and adaptative system for breath sampling [14] and, (b) a fast, reagent-free and portable analyzer (GC-IMS) with high sensitivity and selectivity (ppb$_v$ - ppt$_v$ range) [15].

## 3 Study Design and Methodology Applied

The study was conducted in accordance with the ethical principles of good clinical practice of the Declaration of Helsinki. Fifteen healthy male non-smokers volunteers (excluding any lung diseases, heart conditions, schizophrenia), aged 20–35 years, gave written informed consent to participate in the study. Other pre-conditions were also required: (a) 2–5 h of fasting; (b) no consumption of caffeine or taurine containing products; (c) 2–5 h from the last mouth wash; (d) minimum of 5 h of sleep in the night before the measurements; (e) no use of hygiene products or perfume prior to the measurements and; (f) no heavy consumption of alcohol 24 h before sessions.

The presented study applied a previously described protocol for mental stress detection through breath analysis [13]. Such protocol includes the methodology specifications for stress inducement, the description of the equipment used for HR, GSR and breath acquisition and the data analysis performed [13]. Therefore, a randomized cross-over design study was implemented including two sessions (RS - neutral/relax and SS - stress), each comprising two stimuli (less and more intense, respectively).

Within SS, a standardized cognitive test (PASAT) was chosen to elicit stress [16], whereas RS included a relaxing video. Baseline measurements of breath (BS), heart rate (HR) and galvanic skin response (GSR) were collected before stimuli. Mid and long-term effects of stimuli were also assessed by measuring 5 min and 1 h after the last exposure, respectively. NASA TLX were also fulfilled in the end of each campaign to evaluate subjective workloads felt within sessions.

Fourteen complete sets of 5 end-tidal breath samples (with a 5.0 cm$^3$ volume) were collected: baseline (BS01), immediately after the first (BS02) and second stimuli (BS03), 5 min after BS03 (BS04) and 1 h after (BS05). All samples were obtained using an advanced prototype for selectively breath sampling (depending on the origin, *i.e.* oral cavity, esophageal or alveolar) developed by NMT, S.A [14].

# 4  Results and Discussion

## 4.1  Cohort Homogeneity

The homogeneity of the study population was evaluated according to the age, body-mass index (BMI), sleeping and fasting time of participants of both groups (A and B). Both age and BMI do not present any significant change (p-value > 0.05) between groups (26.6 ± 5.1 years and 24.4 ± 4.2, respectively). The fasting time of the participants from group A (3.6 ± 0.8 h) has only proven to be significantly different (p-value = 0.017) from group B (2.6 ± 0.2 h) within the neutral/relax session. Fasting time differences within the neutral session were not observed between sessions (p-value = 0.569). Sleeping time values present no significant differences on participants' cohorts within and between sessions. Since no significant or relevant differences between participants' cohorts were exhibited, onwards the population will be considered as a single group.

## 4.2  Heart Rate and Galvanic Skin Response

In order to verify the stress and relax condition of volunteers during the experimental procedure, traditional markers were used (HR and GSR). In Fig. 1, individual HR and GSR temporal responses through stress (SS) and the neutral/relax sessions (RS) are shown. As expected, for the RS, HR almost does not change from the baseline threshold. During both stimuli, HR and GSR values are undoubtfully different between sessions, with higher response during stress application. HR and GSR variation were higher for stimuli 1 and 2 of the SS.

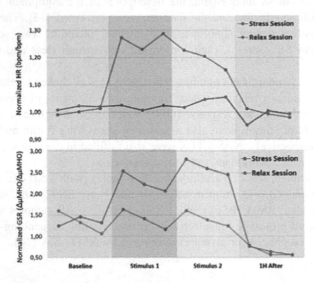

**Fig. 1.** HR (top) and GSR (bottom) mean responses of stress (red) and relax (blue) sessions (Color figure online)

Average HR observations (within each colored region) show significant differences between sessions for both Stimuli (p-value < 0.05). However, for GSR, no significant differences were observed between sessions.

High variations in HR and GSR presented under stressor application (versus baseline), validate PASAT suitability to cause physiological stress among volunteers.

### 4.3  NASA-TLX Response Score

NASA-TLX response scores range from 0 to 100. For RS and SS, NASA-TLX scores were statistically different (13.9 ± 8.5 and 70.4 ± 14.9, respectively). SS showed a greater range (42.3 to 94.0) when compared with RS (5.0 to 28.0). NASA-TLX response scores are consistent with the results of HR and GSR, thus confirming psychological stress from the PASAT interventions experienced among volunteers.

### 4.4  VOC Data and Multi-variate Analysis

GC-IMS data was also processed following previously described workflow [17]. For that purpose, Laboratory Analytical Viewer (LAV) software from GAS Dortmund GmbH, was used to export numerical information of relative intensities within each defined area set of spectra. Each area set included a single peak which represents a unique VOC found in breath A breath matrix was constructed with 68 (variables) intensity peaks (or breath compounds) against the participations (observations) to perform a multi-variate analysis (MVA) [18]. MVA was conducted using IBM SPSS Statistics for Windows, version 23 (IBM Corp., Armonk, N.Y., USA).

Partial least-squared discriminant analysis (PLS-DA) was initially performed on the post intervention samples (BS02, BS03, BS04 and BS05) from RS and SS. All variables were assigned to a single block and a weighting of $1/\sqrt{Block}$ was applied producing a total variance equal to 1. Pareto Variance was also selected for base scaling of the data set [18]. The S-plot indicated six possible VOC variables ($\alpha 1$ to $\alpha 6$) that changed in response to interventions. Principal component analysis (PCA) for these six VOC variables enabled the separation between the RS and SS observations. Observations were compared at the same measuring point (*e.g.* Stimulus 1 (RS) vs Stimulus 1 (SS)). The score plots obtained from Stimulus 1 and 2 (BS02 and BS03, respectively) are shown in Fig. 2. Responses from SS and RS are seen to cluster and a distinction between breath profiles obtained under the two experimental sessions can be observed.

Principal components (PC) exhibited 50.4% [PC1], 24.9% [PC2] and 16.7% [PC3] of the total explained variance of the data set for the observations after the first stimulus (BS02). Additionally, the results provided 61.5% of sensitivity and 71.4% of specificity for the stressed cases. The observations obtained from samples acquired immediately after the second stimulus (BS03) produced a stronger model and yielded a sensitivity of 78.5% and a selectivity of 71.5%. The total variance modelled by each component was 50.6%, 24.2% and 17.5% for [PC1], [PC2] and [PC3], respectively.

However, PCA for the observations related to the samples acquired 5 min (BS04) and 1 h (BS05) after the second stimulus showed no distinguishable specific patterns between observations from both sessions. Therefore, no mid and long-term effects of stress were evident in the collected breath samples. Results of multi-variate analysis of

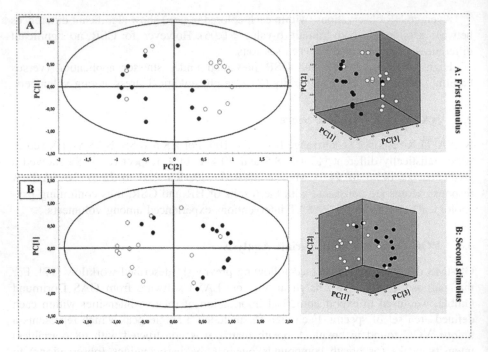

**Fig. 2.** Unsupervised PCA for the 6 stress sensitive breath compounds identified from PLS-DA. A – first stimulus (BS02): SS (black dots) and RS (white dots) observations. B – second stimulus (BS03): SS (black dots) and RS (white dots) observations. Observations are presented with the two (left) and three (right) most representative principal components.

chromatographic data show an immediate response of the breath composition to stress stimuli, which is consistent with HR and GSR responses (Fig. 1).

### 4.5   Identification of Discriminant VOCs

IMS spectra provides an increased intensity signal (intensity peak) with a drift time specific for each compound but, in some cases a single compound can produce two or even three peaks (dimers, trimers, etc.). Such effect is related to ionization phenomenon, sample humidity and proton transfer reaction that occurs in the ionization region. Combining IMS capabilities with GC, an additional dimension (retention time) increases the selectivity for VOC detection and quantification in complex biological mixtures.

Table 1 presents the retention and drift times for each of the six-discriminant stress sensitive breath compounds. Those values are specific to certain VOCs. $\alpha2$, $\alpha3$ and $\alpha4$ were identified by cross-checking retention times and drift times in database created from measurements of the corresponding pure compounds (ethanol, 2-propanol and 1-propanol respectively). Nevertheless, not all breath compounds could be identified with precision. For these cases a list of possible compounds was obtained by consulting a database provided by GAS Dortmund GmbH.

**Table 1.** Stress sensitive data (retention and drift time) with possible VOC identification.

| Peak ID | Drift time (RIP Rel.) | Retention time (s) | VOC (Molecular Weight) |
|---------|----------------------|---------------------|------------------------|
| α1 | 1.079 | 66.780 | Styrene (104,15 g/mol) |
| | | | 1 2-dimethylbenzene (106,17 g/mol) |
| α2 | 1.059 | 24.045 | Ethanol (46,07 g/mol) |
| α3 | 1.258 | 25.095 | 2-propanol (60,10 g/mol) |
| α4 | 1.215 | 28.245 | (dimer) 1-propanol (60,09 g/mol) |
| α5 | 1.216 | 28.820 | (dimer) 2-propanol (60.10 g/mol) |
| | | | 2, 3-pentanedione (100.12 g/mol) |
| | | | Benzaldehyde (106.12 g/mol) |
| α6 | 1.124 | 29.610 | (monomer) 1-propanol (60.09 g/mol) |
| | | | Ethyl acetate (88.11 g/mol) |

# 5  Conclusions and Future Work

Since stressing situations cause faster breathing (with increased pulse rates and blood-pressure), changes in the VOC profile of breath were expected. Inducing psychological stress (through PASAT interventions) confirmed our assumptions as preliminary results indicate three (of six) identified stress responsive VOCs in human breath. These VOCs were downregulated and may have been depleted through increased ventilation, HR, and respiratory rate during stress. Nevertheless, the combination of the six most discriminant stress responsive compounds was still able to classify stress states with higher sensitivity for breath samples acquired immediately after the most intense stimulus (second). Individuals who were not correctly classified by breath analysis exhibited stress during neutral sessions (induced by the unfamiliar surroundings) or might not have experienced a high stress load.

Demonstrations of the applications of breath analysis in providing next generation health assessment approaches continue to be reported [9]. Physical disease may not be the only contributing factor for breath profile changes and, people undergoing traumatic and emotionally challenging diagnoses related with serious diseases may need to consider such factor. This study shows that human VOC profile is also sensitive to non-physical stimuli. It is expected that the findings herein presented could lead to a quick and non-invasive test to detect mental stress states. However, is still soon to postulate the biological origins and the roles of the present VOCs as part of a stress-sensitive response. The study still needs to be scaled-up and include a higher sample size, with a wider age range and in conditions closer to real-world settings.

**Acknowledgments.** The authors thank all volunteers for participating in the study. The work benefitted from the continuous support from the combined effort of NOVA School of Science and Technology, NMT, S.A. and Airbus Defence and Space GmbH. Partial support comes from Fundação para a Ciência e Tecnologia (FCT, Portugal) through the PhD grant (PD/BDE/114550/2016).

# References

1. Heinrichs, M., Stächele, T., Domes, G.: Stress und Stressbewältigung. Hogrefe, Göttingen (2015)
2. Pacak, K., McCarty, R.: Acute stress response: experimental. In: Fink, I. (ed.) Encyclopedia of Stress, I edn., pp. 7–14. Elsevier (2007)
3. Jimenez-Molina, A., Retamal, C., Lira, H.: Using psychophysiological sensors to assess mental workload during web browsing. Sensors **18**, 458 (2018)
4. Healey, J.A., Picard, R.W.: Detecting stress during real-world during tasks using physiological sensors. IEE Trans. Intell. Transp. Syst. **6**, 156–166 (2005)
5. Birenboim, A., Dijst, M., Scheepers, F., Poelman, M., Helbich, M.: Wearables and location tracking technologies for mental-state sensing in outdoor environments. Prof. Geogr. **71**, 1–13 (2019)
6. Gronwall, D.: Paced auditory serial-addition task: a measure of recovery from concussion. Percept. Mot. Skills **44**, 67–373 (1977)
7. Goh, J., Pfeffer, J., Zenios, S.: The relationship between workplace stressors and mortality and health costs in the United States. Manag. Sci. **62**(2), 608–628 (2016). https://doi.org/10.1287/mnsc.2014.2115
8. Li, G.: Airline accidents. In: Fink, I. (ed.) Encyclopedia of Stress, pp. 114–118. Elsevier, San Diego (2007)
9. Phillips, M., et al.: Point-of-care breath test for biomarkers of active pulmonary tuberculosis. Tuberculosis **92**, 314–320 (2012)
10. Van Berkel, J.J., et al.: A profile of volatile organic compounds in breath discriminates COPD patients from controls. Res. Med. **104**, 557–563 (2010)
11. Dallinga, J., et al.: Volatile organic compounds in exhaled breath as a diagnostic tool for asthma in children. Clin. Exp. Allergy **40**, 68–76 (2010)
12. Turner, M.A., et al.: The effect of a paced auditory serial addition test (PASAT) intervention on the profile of volatile organic compounds in human breath: a pilot study. J. Breath Res. **7** (1), 11 (2013). https://doi.org/10.1088/1752-7155/7/1/017102
13. Santos, P., Roth, P., Fetter, V., Fernandes, J.M., Vassilenko, V.: Mental stress study (I): protocol for breath markers study in an academic healthy population over short periods of induced stress or relax conditions, manuscript in preparation (2019)
14. Santos, P., Vassilenko, V.: System for controlled and selective sampling of exhaled air and corresponding operating procedure, Patent No. PCT/IB2017/055322 (2017)
15. Borsdorf, H., Eiceman, A.G.: Ion mobility spectrometry principles and applications, pp. 323–375 (2016)
16. Gronwall, D.: Paced auditory serial-addition task: a measure of recovery from concussion. Percept. Mot. Skills **44**(2), 367–373 (1977)
17. Massart, D., Vandeginste, B., Deming, S.N., Michotte, Y., Kaufman, L.: Chemometrics: A Textbook (Data Handling in Science and Technology), vol. 2. Elsevier, Amsterdam (2003)
18. Weljie, A., Newton, J., Mercier, P., Carlson, E., Slupsky, C.: Targeted profiling: quantitative analysis of 1H NMR metabolomics data. Anal. Chem. **78**, 4430–4442 (2006)

# Multi-sensor Synchronization Model for Sensor Fusion Applied to Innovative Cardiovascular Markers

Paulo Bonifacio[1,2(✉)], Valentina Vasssilenko[1,2], Andreia Serrano[1,2], Filipa Cardoso[1,2], and Stanimir Valtchev[2,3]

[1] Laboratory for Instrumentation, Biomedical Engineering and Radiation Physics (LibPhys-UNL), NOVA School of Science and Technology, Campus FCT UNL, Caparica, Portugal
p.bonifacio@nmt.pt
[2] NMT, S.A., Edifício Madan Parque, Rua dos Inventores, Caparica, Portugal
[3] Department of Electrical and Computer Engineering (DEEC) & CTS-UNINOVA, NOVA School of Science and Technology, Campus FCT UNL, Caparica, Portugal

**Abstract.** Cardiovascular diseases remain the leading cause of morbidity, mortality, early disability and growing health costs worldwide. The difficulty for monitoring the evolution of cardiovascular related diseases can be, partially, attributed to the lack of appropriate indicators for arterial injury and cardiac disfunction during routine clinical practice. Non-invasive sensors, such as Photoplethysmography (PPG) devices, can be used for the measurement of several hemodynamic related parameters, albeit, most of current sensors require a skilled operator to interpret that sensory data. This paper presents a novel, method for an open architecture system where the simultaneous utilization of different types of devices is possible, PPG, Electrocardiogram (ECG) or other. Working, communicating and synchronizing through a wireless network, those can be placed on specific points of the patient's body and will allow to get better information of the cardiovascular marker of interest: hemodynamic or other, reducing the workload for the operator. The proposed open architecture is a simple cost-effective solution that can potentially achieve a widespread use in daily clinical practice.

**Keywords:** Wireless Sensors Networks (WSN) · Synchronization protocols · Photoplethysmography (PPG) · Health diagnosis · Cardiovascular markers

## 1 Introduction

Cardiovascular diseases (CVDs), remain the leading cause of morbidity, mortality, early disability and growing health costs worldwide. In response to this crisis the world health organization (WHO) proposed a global plan for prevention and control of Noncommunicable Diseases (NCDs) 2013–2020 [1]. Where, one of the key points states that, as a part of a global risk mitigation program for CVDs, prevention should come from a total cardiovascular risk assessment approach; this being achieved during

L. M. Camarinha-Matos et al. (Eds.): DoCEIS 2020, IFIP AICT 577, pp. 411–419, 2020.
https://doi.org/10.1007/978-3-030-45124-0_40

routine clinical practice. The difficulty for monitoring the evolution of cardiovascular related diseases during the routine clinical practice can be, to some extent, attributed to the lack of appropriate indicators for arterial injury and cardiac disfunction that can be readily, reliably and cheaply used. Non-invasive sensors, such as doppler ultrasound, magnetic resonance imaging (MRI), photoplethysmography (PPG) and cuff oscillometer devices, can be used for the detection and measurement of several hemodynamics and vascular stiffness related parameters, such as pulse wave velocity (PWV). The pulse wave velocity parameter can be calculated with a good degree of precision using the referred methods, albeit not all use the same working principles; ultrasound and magnetic resonance imaging use the pressure-and-volume and the pressure-and-diameter principle [2]. PPG and cuffs are typically used in pairs to simultaneously measure the travel time of the observed blood pressure wave in different body locations, thus deriving the value of the PWV velocity [3]. Figure 1 shows the points on the human body that are usually selected for those measurements.

Equation (1) describes the general principle for the calculation of the PWV measuring the difference of blood pulse wave travel time between two points, for PPG and cuff type devices, [2].

$$PWV = \frac{\Delta x}{\Delta t} \tag{1}$$

The complexity and costs of using anyone of these methods can vary significantly by type; MRI is the costliest of all the measurement methods, with steeper costs in equipment, training and maintenance. The next costly system is, doppler ultrasound, although being much cheaper than MRI; finally, PPG and cuff type devices are the least expensive, and usually do not require the same degree of specialized training for the operator as the previous ones. The utilization of more than one type of device or sensor, or even multiple devices of the same type, to obtain a better picture of a specific hemodynamic parameter, is an intricate issue. This is even more important if the devices to be used are of the wireless type, connected through a wireless network (WN); and so, becoming sensor nodes in a distributed network. This paper focuses on the particulars of using multiple, low-cost, non-invasive sensor type devices to monitor hemodynamic parameters from short-to-extended periods of time. Sensor nodal synchronization will be covered and an algorithm to improve the issues with these situations will be presented and discussed, specifically the algorithms' capacity of allowing for the automatic evaluation of cardiovascular markers from multiple sensors without the intervention of a human operator.

The rest of this paper is organized as follows; in Sect. 2 the contribution of this work to general life improvement is framed; in Sect. 3 a review of the relevant literature for synchronization problem is made. Afterwards, in Sect. 4, the proposed solutions are presented. Section 5 presents a discussion of the proposed method; a roadmap of the work being developed and some conclusions for this paper.

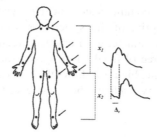

**Fig. 1.** Typical points of interest that can be used for PWV evaluation (left), and signal pulse wave difference at two monitoring locations (right). (Source: author, adapted from CCBY 3.0).

## 2  Contribution to Life Improvement

The methods referred in the previous section for cardiovascular assessment are commonly found in devices that can range from, bulky, with limited portability to simply non-portable (as MRI devices); those can take a variable amount of time to setup for operation and may require a significant degree of training and specialized maintenance. As such, their use in clinical daily practice is of limited use. PPG, oscillometer cuffs and doppler ultrasound devices on the other hand, have been made portable in the last few years and have seen increased utilization in the clinical practice. Currently, doppler ultrasound devices, even in their portable form, require a skilled operator with tens of hours of practice to use the device effectively each time a measurement is taken; PPG and cuffs can, to a significant extent, be set and operated remotely, after the device has been properly placed in the correct position on the patient; the health attendant can be free to perform other tasks. This type of hands-off remote monitoring allows for the patients to be followed over an extended time period and in a more relaxed environment, reducing the white coat effect[1] on the patient's taken measurements [4].

The almost exclusive utilization of any of these types of devices is in a single-channel, single-use form. Currently, in the daily clinical routine setting, only cuff oscillometer type devices are used for 24-h Ambulatory Monitoring Arterial Pressure (MAPA). Due to the nature of the device setup, the user discomfort can be significative, this being induced by the vascular constriction caused by the measurements at regular intervals – a situation that can become particularly unpleasant during sleep [5]. PPG devices, due to their low cost are now being offered by several vendors and system integrators in several forms. They can be found in smartwatches, as add-on accessories for smartphones or in sport monitoring devices. note that those are only single channel solutions that have, up to now, encountered only very limited clinical utilization.

An innovative device that can use more than one channel for hemodynamic parameter monitoring is a *multi-channel PPG hemodynamic monitoring system*, developed by Portuguese company NMT, S.A. The device can handle several,

---

[1] The white coat effect or white coat syndrome is a well-documented situation where some people tend to exhibit blood pressure above the normal range in the clinical environment, although this situation doesn't progress out of this setting (i.e. blood pressure readings are normal).

wearable, sensor nodes that communicate, and are synchronized in a secured distributed WN. The low footprint of the system's sensor nodes along with in-built
robustness aims to improve routine clinical practice, freeing doctors and medical staff
and allowing for a new degree of freedom of movement and comfort for monitored
patients, in and out of the clinic. Figure 2 shows the block diagram of NMT's prototype
system; currently at technology readiness between level 6 and $7^2$ (TRL 6/7).

## 3   State of the Art

Using multiple channels and sensors to record physiological markers in the patients the
sensor's physical footprint can become an issue. Usually, it's strongly defendant on the
type of sensors in use, however, any sensor setup can easily require several different
connectors becoming cumbersome, especially if it is hardwired and can't be used in a
more comfortable wearable form. With battery power, wireless operation and reduced
footprint, wireless sensor nodes (WSN), can be more user-friendly for the wearer
(patient) while maintain the same degree of measurements validity as their wired
counterparts; although they can present a series of drawbacks; multi-channel signal
analysis and aggregation in a WN can be affected by a number of issues, the most
significant ones being synchronization related, additionally, the vulnerability of the
sensor channel from outside manipulation should not be overlooked, as a corrupted
signal due to external manipulation could lead to a miss-diagnosis and be life-
threatening for the patient.

Synchronization of SN in a network has been an area of study for some years now,
with initial research being done since the early 2000's and focusing in time-
synchronization strategies for multi-nodal sensor networks with several degrees of
success and algorithm complexities [6, 7].

### 3.1   Time Synchronization

In a microcontroller, IC, computer or sensor node, the clock at time $t$, is given by
Eqs. (2) and (3):

$$C(t) = k \int_0^t \omega(\tau)d\tau + C(t_0) \tag{2}$$

Where, $\omega$ is the oscillator's frequency, $k$ is the oscillator related constant and $C(t_0)$
is the time of the tick (click) from the system's implemented hardware oscillator.
Where the approximation of the computer time with real time will be given by:

$$C(t) = q * t + b \tag{3}$$

Where, $q$ is the clock drift and $b$ is the clock offset; ideally $q = 1$ and $b = 0$.

---

[2] Technology readiness level (TRL) as defined in: *NASA Systems Engineering Handbook - NASA SP-
2016-6105 Rev2* and accepted as a *de facto* industry standard in system development.

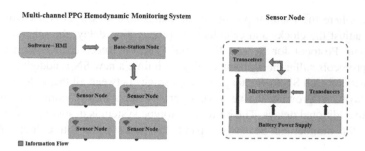

**Fig. 2.** Block diagram of *NMT, S.A.* multi-channel PPG hemodynamic parameter monitoring system. (Source: author).

The main reasons that different sensor nodes can present different time clocks can be summarized as follows: *(1)* nodes may have been started at different times; *(2)* the hardware quartz clocks of the nodes can be running at different frequencies; *(3)* the clock frequency can drift or skew due to several factors that can affect the crystal oscillator operation. Variations on the supply voltage, humidity, temperature, pressure and crystal ageing can result in a changing drift rate for the clock ($dC/dt-1$). More so if for SN implementation is chosen to use off-the-shelve, low cost component modules, (transceiver and such) as they can carry lower quality quartz clocks and other semi-conductor components, that can sum to the drift and skew of the system clock. Additionally, to those situations, events like waking-up, low-energy sleep modes or hardware interrupts can affect normal clock operation, as some clock ticks can be missed for transceiver message handling.

For networked computer-based systems, node protocol synchronization schemes are based on Network Time Protocol (NTP), as implemented in the internet. Where, time server nodes broadcast synchronization packets and each single node performs statistical analysis on the round-trip of the synchronization (sync), packets timestamps to adjust its internal clock's drift. When considering wireless networks and due to the nondeterministic nature of the transmission line (i.e. open air), this type of solution is not feasible; the Medium Access Control (MAC) of radio stack can lead to several milliseconds of delay in each hop exchange, a situation that can be reinforced if a multi-hop strategy is adopted for WSN [6]. Currently, there is no single standard protocol to solve or minimize these issues, but classification for the major topologies is generally accepted in the literature as follows: Unidirectional broadcast, receiver-to-receiver and sender-to-receiver; as shown in Fig. 3. The simplest time synchronization protocol type is the unidirectional broadcast type, as implemented by the flooding time synchronization protocol (FTSP); a beacon node with a precision clock broadcast sync signals with a time stamp. this is then used by each WSN to adjust their internal clock drift and jitter [8]. In receiver-to-receiver synchronization a beacon sync message is broadcasted, each SN then exchanges messages with each other to adjust their clock, this scheme type is used in the Reference Broadcast Synchronization (RBS) and adaptive clock synchronization (ACS) protocols [9]. A drawback common to these two types of synchronization methods comes from the limited physical wireless range of the beacon node. Finally, sender-to-receiver synchronization schemes rely on handshake protocols, where the round-trip time of the handshake messages is used by the controller to adjust the clocks and calculate the propagation delay; the scheme is used in Timing-sync Protocol for Sensor Networks (TPSN). Receiver-receiver and sender-receiver protocols suffer an additional delay each time a new SN is added; this is due to the necessity of each SN to exchange sync messages between all the nodes on the same network layer, so growing the network layer beyond a limited number of nodes can bring forth additional delays. The current prototype system is designed to support up to 4 SN, but this number can be easily expanded as necessary in future device iterations.

## 4   Research Contribution

The implementation of any sync protocol in a practical WSN presents several challenges. Firstly, sensor nodes IC's usually employ low-cost fast drifting clocks, additionally, in some applications, the nodes are battery powered, so an energy conservation strategy to prolong battery life must be adopted. Any single node will spend the maximum possible time in an "off" or "deep-sleep" state. Interrupt, wake-up, settle-time and synchronization times must be considered for operational, "real-world" synchronization schemes. Figure 4 presents the proposed network topology that's under development for this system. The network is divided in 4 depth levels with data communication and node discovery restricted by level and specific node function. Level 0 is the top level of the network and only communicates the HMI-CCV nodes (Human-Machine Interface, Command, Control and Visualization). Level 1 nodes can connect to one or more Level 2 nodes, their main purpose is configuration, setup and visualization of fused signals collected at Level 3 nodes. Level 2 nodes are patient dependent (i.e. 1 per patient is required, at this time) and connect and control the WSN placed on the patient. Per network level, data stream is expected to be done mostly as follows: from Level 1-Level 0, upstream, data with downstream communication mostly for diagnostics assistance results; Level 1-Level 2 communication downstream, done mainly for control and configuration purposes; Level 2-Level 3, here, there has been adopted a hybrid master-slave approach. Fusion nodes (FN), map, synchronize and command the WSN sync'd to them. Any SN can be classified as Level 0, tier 1 node at any given time. A node classified as tier 1 will be considered by the fusion node as the signal acquisition lead; this works in such a way that the sync beacon for all the other nodes will be offset to match the tier 1 clock timestamp. The proposed approach is such that the travel time of the PWV pulse between any node can be precisely synced to get accurate velocities between 2 or more relevant sample points. Sensor signal synchronization is critical at levels 2 and 3 of the network.

Due to the nature of the environment in which several FN and SN are placed, they can share the same physical space with nodes going online and offline at random intervals during routine clinical operation as systems are expected to be disconnected after the relevant patient data has been gathered, only to be reconnected in a new patient some minutes later; note that is expected that several patients can share the same space within the network's radio level coverage. Those nodes will typically be unknown to each other and as the radio signal bandwidth must be shared between wireless devices, the MAC layer can potentially be stressed to a point where the

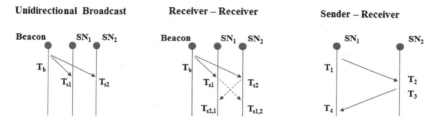

**Fig. 3.** Classification of the main types of time synchronization topologies.

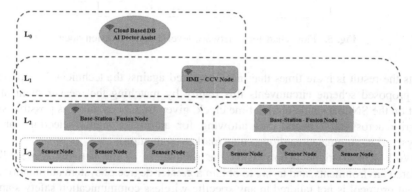

**Fig. 4.** Proposed network topology of hemodynamic parameter monitoring system with hierarchical levels (0–3).

number of collisions and message-time broadcast delays can further enhance the sync problem in the WSN, so disconnecting the SN and FN when not in use can be an important advantage under these conditions. As a reference, Fig. 5 shows the flow-chart for the fusion sensor at network level 2. Initially, as SN can be interchanged between networks and patients, the mapping of the network should be done at each FN reconnection. Wireless transceivers typically spend more transmission power in the mapping and discovery phase of the network. To minimize power consumption, connection should be done in the best possible conditions. Initial handshake messages can require close to 20ma of current against below 10ma for normal broadcast communication, this for the nRF24AP1 transceiver module (datasheet).

## 5   Discussion and Future Work

The proposed synchronization scheme for SN targets working at the lower levels of the network, Levels 3 and 2, is the stage where the data fusion is possible and critical. Most schemes applied to medical devices tend to use multi-channel data analyses as a tool that is used *posteriori*, by qualified personnel, to obtain some conclusions from the gathered data, for this, parts of the signal are selected by the technician for measurement. As it is difficult to guarantee a correct signal synchronization between sample

418    P. Bonifacio et al.

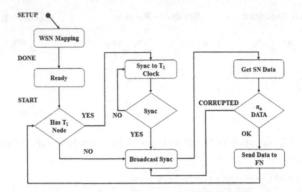

**Fig. 5.** Flow chart for a network level 2 node, a fusion node.

points the result is more times than not, weighted against the technician's experience. The proposed scheme circumvents this reality by matching the measurement at any point on the SN to a single unified time clock, given true, or as much as possible signal integrity across all sensors, thus allowing for automatic signal selection for data analysis, (i.e. automated cardiovascular marker evaluation).

Work will continue in increasing the robustness of the network, especially in cluttered environments, and trying to obtain a greater degree of system automation. The current protocol is not tailored to any specific wireless communication safety standard and so far, only the initial evaluation of embedded security protocols in wireless transceivers has been done. Future work will have to evaluate if those are enough for data safety or if watermarking techniques of messages are necessary for system security.

**Acknowledgments.** This work was funded and supported by the Fundação para a Ciência e Tecnologia (FCT) and NMT, S.A in the scope of the project PD/BDE/130083/2017 and UIDB/00066/2020 (CTS – Center of Technology and Systems).

# References

1. WHO: Global action plan for the prevention and control of noncommunicable diseases 2013–2020, p. 102. World Health Organization (2013)
2. Nichols, W.W., Vlachopoulos, C., O'Rourke, M.: McDonald's Blood Flow in Arteries: Theoretical, Experimental and Clinical Principles, 2006th edn. CRC Press, Boca Raton (2011)
3. Agrawal, D.P.: Embedded Sensor Systems. Springer, Singapore (2017). https://doi.org/10.1007/978-981-10-3038-3
4. Villalba Alcalá, F., Lapetra Peralta, J., Mayoral Sánchez, E., Espino Montoro, A., Cayuela Domínguez, A., López Chozas, J.M.: Ambulatory blood pressure monitoring to study white coat effect in patients with hypertension followed in primary care. Rev. Española Cardiol. (English Ed.) **57**(7), 652–660 (2004)
5. Carretero Ares, J.L., Martín Escudero, J.C., Bellido Casado, J., de Teresa Romero, G.: Algunas consideraciones sobre AMPA y MAPA. Atención Primaria **26**(9), 650–652 (2000)

6. Ranganathan, P., Nygard, K.: Time synchronization in wireless sensor networks: a survey. Int. J. UbiComp **1**(2), 92–102 (2010)
7. Djenouri, D., Bagaa, M.: Synchronization protocols and implementation issues in wireless sensor networks: a review. IEEE Syst. J. **10**(2), 617–627 (2016)
8. Maróti, M., Kusy, B., Simon, G., Lédeczi, Á.: The flooding time synchronization protocol. In: SenSys 2004 - Proceedings of the Second International Conference Embedded Networked Sensor Systems, pp. 39–49 (2004)
9. Cho, H., Kim, J., Baek, Y.: Enhanced precision time synchronization for wireless sensor networks. Sensors **11**(8), 7625–7643 (2011)

# Device Development for Evaluation of Gingiva Microcirculation

Hojat Lotfi[1,2(✉)], Valentina Vassilenko[1,2], Paulo Bonifacio[1,2], and Bibiana Falcao[1]

[1] Laboratory for Instrumentation, Biomedical Engineering and Radiation Physics (LibPhys-UNL), NOVA School of Science and Technology, Campus FCT UNL, Caparica, Portugal
[2] NMT, S.A., Edifício Madan Parque, Rua dos Inventores, Caparica, Portugal
h.lotfi@nmt.pt

**Abstract.** Since 1960 the technological evolution in dentistry have contributed to a greater demand for dental care. The success of dental implantology depends from several factors, one of which is the health of the gingiva microcirculation status. Due to the dental implant location, direct monitoring of the health of the gingiva is a complex task requiring specialized tools. In this paper we report an overview of the state of the art of implant health monitoring techniques and present our work on development of novel device for non-invasive direct gingiva health monitoring. Our technology is based on the pulse oximetry principle and allowing assessment into the microcirculation level of gums. This work is being supported by cooperation with the specialists as an advanced innovative device for routine clinical purposes.

**Keywords:** Pulse oximeter · Dental implant · Gingiva perfusion · Microcirculation

## 1 Introduction

Dental problems like cavities, gingiva diseases and periodontitis are prevalent and almost every person experiences it throughout life. In dentistry, diagnosis may be defined as the process of combining data obtained from several different sources to try to identify dental related deviations from normal, such as: patient history, observation, examination and exploratory testing [1]. The tooth is composed by several parts: enamel is the hardest tissue of the tooth, cementum also is a hard substance that covers the tooth roots, dentin is a softer tissue and then the pulp is the heart of the tooth full of blood vessels and nerves, is responsible to maintain the tooth alive, by receiving the nutrients through the complex network of micro vessels. The oral dental tissues are well vascularized and well innervated. The high vascularity explains the profuse bleeding that occurs with wounds/trauma to the mouth but also in part the remarkable potential for healing. The main arteries to the teeth and jaws are derived from the maxillary artery, a terminal branch of the external carotid. The alveolar arteries follow essentially the same course as the alveolar nerves. The blood supply for the mandibular teeth comes from the inferior alveolar artery, the buccal gingiva is supplied by buccal

L. M. Camarinha-Matos et al. (Eds.): DoCEIS 2020, IFIP AICT 577, pp. 420–428, 2020.
https://doi.org/10.1007/978-3-030-45124-0_41

artery, labial gingiva is supplied by mental artery and same branches of incisive artery, also the lingual gingiva is supplied by inferior alveolar artery and by lingual artery. The maxillary teeth and periodontium the blood supply is through the posterior superior alveolar artery that is a derived from buccal artery, that also gives branches to adjacent buccal gingiva, maxillary sinus and cheek. The palatal gingiva around the maxillary teeth is supplied primarily by branches of the greater palatine artery [2]. The pulp receives its blood supply through thin-walled arterioles entering through the apical and accessory foramina. These arterioles run longitudinally through the center of the pulp, branching out to its periphery where they form a capillary network in the sub odontoblastic area. These capillaries do not enter the dentin; they drain into the venules that run alongside the arterioles and pass out through the same apical foramen [3, 4]. For diagnosis of the dental pulp health status is should be use the results of several different tests and not the outcome of any specific one. The testing of the tooth vitality is an important marker for the diagnosis of pulp disease, if the result of these tests leads to the conclusion that the pulp is severely compromised endodontic treatment, or extraction may be necessary [5]. Ideally, any test should provide a simple, standardized, non-invasive, painless, reproducible, accurate and inexpensive way of testing [6]. The determination of the pulp's condition is determined by the vascular supply health and not the sensory fibers. Pulp sensibility tests are subjective and thus dependent on subjective factors such as the sensibility of both patient and dentist. As most of these methods are invasive (i.e. direct stimulation of the tooth), discomfort or pain for the patient might be possible. Therefore, work has been done in developing noninvasive methods that can provide measurements for dental pulp blood flow, such as spectrophotometry, laser doppler flowmetry and determination of the oxygen saturation (SpO$_2$) [1]. One of the most accurate method is laser doppler flowmetry but comparing to pulse oximetry, despite of its high accuracy, it has a higher cost and is also sensitive to radiation angle [6–8]. The modern endodontics is becoming influenced by novel biological, genetic and metabolic approaches toward new strategies for regeneration of dental pulp were the knowledge of perfusion status of tissue is very important. Keeping this in mind, the technology of pulse oximetry can be adapted for the objective evaluation of the progress of regeneration, which could be a leap into the future of endodontics [9, 10]. The potential of pulse oximetry as a tool in accessing the dental pulp condition comes from fact that is noninvasive method which evaluates a significative marker of the pulp's condition. This paper describes a prototype based on low cost, simple and accurate PPG technology as a potential device for assessment of gingiva microcirculation around the dental implant as well as teeth pulp. For this prototype we have modified the pulse oximeter technology to be used in dentistry according to the specific position of the mouth and the location of the teeth. It should be noted that, despite ongoing research in this field, there is not any similar device in the market yet.

## 2    Contribution to Life Improvement

Periodontitis is the most common oral disease worldwide, with an age-standardized prevalence of 11.2%. It is a multifactorial disease, with risk factors such as diabetes mellitus (DM), smoking and, most commonly, inadequate oral hygiene (OH). The accumulation of dental plaque and calculus is usually caused by improper tooth-brushing techniques, failure to carry out interdental cleaning and irregular dental visits. This accumulation predictably results in gingival inflammation. Persistent gingivitis is a key risk predictor for the breakdown of periodontal attachment. The device under development in this project can be used for both natural teeth and dental implants, since it can measure small amount of blood flow in natural dental pulp or microcirculation of gingiva around the dental implant. The most complicated problem with implants is peri-implant pathology that is defined as "the term for inflammatory reactions with loss of supporting bone tissue surrounding the implant in function". This, after osseointegration, represents the leading cause of late dental implant failure. Risk factors associated with this pathology can come from different sources namely, the patient's health condition, the morphology of the implant placement location, the implant itself, the restoration procedure, clinical parameters, and patient compliance with good oral care [11]. Currently clinical investigation of dental condition as well as dental implant status normally is by indirect methods like thermal (heat or cold) and electric stimuli testing and radiographic is the most commons. Usually the result of these tests has been considering determining the actual status of natural of implantable dental [12]. However, these tests can have false-negative or false positive results and is not usable for traumatic dental which lose their sensitivity temporary or permanently. According to importance of dental implants in human health improving, optimal maintenance and post-installation care will be important due to the high installation cost and long healing time process. Necessity of devices that can monitor dental implant status in gingiva seems to be essential, one of the best ways should be developing existing approaches to address the specific conditions that this project is intended to address. Pulse Oximeter as a simple, low-cost, non-invasive, non-radioactive and accurate device can be a good choice for dentists on periodic visits or in case happening problem for the patient with implant to test the implant in the gum with a simple and painless test. This technique has the potential to become a device for routine dentistry practice to help life improve living by reducing periodontal disease.

## 3    State of the Art

Pulse oximetry is based in measuring oxygen saturation ($SaO_2$) in the blood (i.e. measuring the amount of oxygen diluted in the blood). Typically, this is achieved by the combination of two light-emitting diodes (LED) working at different wavelengths, one of the LED works in the visible red spectrum, close to the 660 nm the other is set for the infrared (IR) spectrum, close to 940 nm. The tissue-reflected light form those LED is captured by a photodiode and its response is then used to calculate $SaO_2$ levels. In the arterial blood oxygenated hemoglobin (oxyhemoglobin, $HbO_2$) is found; its analogous, deoxygenated hemoglobin (Hb), circulates in the venous blood, both absorb different amounts of red and infrared light, with $HbO_2$ absorbing more infrared light than Hb [1, 13]. Figure 1 shows the spectral response of $HbO_2$, Hb and the skin-tissue model that is commonly used for pulse oximetry. The continuous component (DC), of the photodiode response represents the light absorbed by the tissue, the non-pulsatile arterial blood and the venous blood quantities. The variable component (AC) represents the pulsatile arterial blood component. The ratio of absorption at the two wavelengths is used as a basis for pulse oximetry and can be calculate by Eqs. (1) or (2).

$$R_{abs} = \frac{AC_{\lambda_1}/DC_{\lambda_1}}{AC_{\lambda_2}/DC_{\lambda_2}} \tag{1}$$

$$R_{abs} = \frac{\log_{10}\left(I_{AC_{\lambda_1}}\right)}{\log_{10}\left(I_{AC_{\lambda_2}}\right)} \tag{2}$$

If using Eq. (1) the $SpO_2$ rate is calculated trough the utilization of a stored conversion table with empirical formulas based on healthy patients' measurements, so it can vary with the implementation. As a reference, a ratio of $R_{abs} = 0.5$ would correspond to a $SpO_2$ of 100%; $R_{abs} = 1$ would correspond to $SpO_2$ of 82% and $R_{abs} = 2.5$ would correspond to a $SpO_2$ of 0%. Equation (2) uses only the AC component for $SpO_2$ calculations, here $I_{AC}$ is the intensity of the light measured at 660 nm and 940 nm, 1 and 2 respectively.

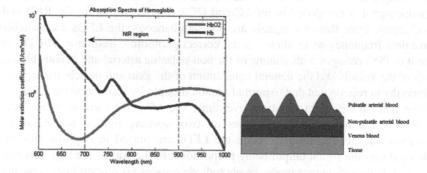

**Fig. 1.** The rate of absorption of HbO2 and Hb at different wavelengths, (CCBYSA 3.0), (right), skin tissue model for signal considerations, (not to scale).

The potential of pulse oximetry as a complementary resource tool for utilization in the evaluation of dental pulp condition has been the subject of research for some time. In normal conditions, a healthy dental pulp will have a measurably high percentage of oxygen in its contents, as the dental pulp progress from a healthy condition to an inflammatory condition the oxygen levels start to decrease, note that this decrease in oxygen levels has not been verified in all inflammatory conditions. Several studies have tackled the issue of determining the reference oxygen saturation levels for healthy dental pulps in different clinical scenarios. From those studies it was obtained that: for maxillary central incisors the oxygen saturation varied from 79.31% to 94%; for maxillary lateral incisors 78.51% to 87.47%; canine 79.85% to 91%; premolars 86.2%. Also, premolars and molars were evaluated as a single group whose mean oxygen saturation values was recorded as 92.2% [1].

The utilization of pulse oximetry as a noninvasive tool for human health monitoring is a relatively recent advance. The technology is basing its working principles in the modification of Beer's law and the reflectance, (absorption), response of hemoglobin when exposed light. In pulse oximeter, Red and IR wavelengths are used to trans-illuminate a tissue bed, the reflected portion of the signal is detected and processed. The processed signal is used to calculate pulse rate and oxygen saturation, as it varies with used wavelength and the characteristics of pulsatile blood circulation. Due to these characteristics, (detection of pulsatile blood absorbance), the technology appears to be suited for the detection of pulpal blood circulation, provided that is, that a sensor/sensor head that can be used in the tooth structure can be engineered [14, 15].

## 4 Research Contribution and Innovation

Pulse oximetry is an application of Photoplethysmography (PPG), an optical nonin-vasive measurement technique used for the assessment and measuring blood volume changes in the microvascular bed in tissues [16]. This technology is based on emitting light to tissues through LED and measure small variations in light intensity associated with changes in blood volume. As referred in the previous chapter, the photodiode response signal is composed of an AC and DC component, this for the RED and IR wavelengths. Note that, the signals are not simultaneous, the LEDs are switched at convenient frequency as to allow for the correct photodiode response. The DC com-ponent of PPG changes with volume of the non-pulsatile arterial and venous blood, the depth of the vessels and the general constitution of the skin and muscle tissue; also, its noteworthy to referee that due to normal motion brought by respiration the DC signal is not constant but has slight variations over time. The AC is the variable component and varies with the heart rate. PPG relies on two working modes: transmission and reflectance. In the transmission mode the LEDs are placed in opposite side to the photodiode, so the signal output being proportional to the part of the light that crosses the tissue. In the reflectance mode the photodiode response is proportional to the part of the light the is backscattered by the tissue with blood vessels. Figure 2 presents the differences with both, the transmission and reflectance techniques, where it uses on gum with dent or with an implant is exemplified. As tissue/bone diameter increases, or more dense materials are used (as prosthetics) this technique becomes more difficult to use. So, reflectance mode of operation becomes more adequate.

The utilization of reflectance mode pulse oximetry in the mouth cavity has advantages but also some drawbacks. As both, the LEDs and the photodiode can be packed close together, this configuration allows for a compact system, so the probe is easier to use in the dental environment, additionally one of the sources of interference with PPG signals, the ambient light is also diminished as the mouth skin attenuates some wavelengths of the ambient light that reaches the sensor. A drawback of this

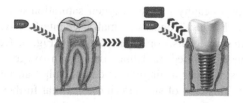

**Fig. 2.** Pulse Oximetry work modes across the dental tissue and tooth, transmission and mode reflectance modes, (right and left, resp.). Implant model used as a reference.

mode of operation comes from fact that, as the probe is typically difficult to stabilize for any significant amount of time in any location in the mouth cavity, the reflected signal can be affected by motion artifacts, so additional signal processing may be necessary to try and reduce these effects. Motion artifacts are mainly characterized by low-frequency random noise, induced by slight movements and probe pressure changes [17]. Their reduction can be done at firmware or software level by using filtering techniques; complementary to the filters, at controller level the utilization of accelerometer transducer coupled to the probes head, in the vicinity of the photodiode, can provide multi-axis signals which can be used to compensate for the motions. At this stage in the prototype development those have been considered but have not been implemented.

The prototype under development is composed of 3 main components, as shown in Fig. 3. A front detachable probe housing, where the LEDs, photodiode and signal condition circuit are placed; a middle connecting arm with a degree of flexibility for maneuvering the probe on the mouth cavity; and a final rear part where power signal acquisition, control and communications with the central software is located. The system is being built as an open architecture concept, thus allowing for modification on the probe's head sensors, or other hardware changes to be incorporated with minimal system redesign. Currently, the probe head sensor unit consists of red and infrared light sources and a photodiode which are mounted side by side, Fig. 3. The photodiode outputs the signal from the reflected Red/IR light from the gingiva during the cardiac cycle.

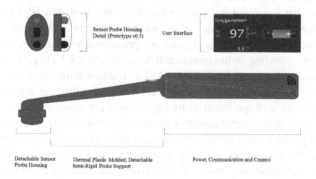

**Fig. 3.** Conceptual design of the probe prototype under development and the user interface.

The assessment of a healthy gingiva oxygen saturation is done in levels ranging between 90% to 99%. For test proposes a small user interface was used, this presents the measured oxygenation levels, top right corner of Fig. 3. Currently there are no international or other, established guidelines of median oxygen saturation levels that can be used to access whether a gingiva or dental pulp can be considered healthy, inflamed, or necrotic. This lack of standard indicates that further research in this area needed. The current prototype head is still quite cumbersome, so, miniaturization and ergonomics studies with dentists are being envisaged to be performed concurrently. Initial tests have shown acceptable signal quality for this stage of development, although it can already be foreseen that daily use of the system will require additional signal processing, even more if the PPG waveform is to be added to the interface. For user interface, the display unit will be expanded to include a PPG pulse-wave signal to complement the numerical information currently being shown, oxygen saturation $(SpO_2)$.

## 5  Discussion and Future Work

Preliminary results of the prototype head probe were satisfactory, showing a good potential to playing as an alternative device for daily routine procedures in dental clinics. One of the biggest problems in using the prototype other than the effective factors which cause deoxygenating of hemoglobin and changes in the blood oxygen saturation, should be movements of the probe which can complicate readings. For this it will be needed the utilization to some type of signal processing. According with the current development options for the prototypes' hardware, Fourier Analysis can be discarded as the signals are not truly periodic, so additional manipulation would be required to adapt the signals to allow for a cycle-by-cycle analysis, for quasi-periodic signals in PPG, as proposed in [18], this option would also require the adoption of advanced 16 or 32 bit microcontrollers with Digital Signal Processing capabilities (DSP), thus increasing the parts costs of the device. Moving Average Filter (MAV), have been used previously in PPG signals and with interesting results [19]. A third option being considered for the attenuation of motion artifacts on the signal is a Passive Motion Cancelation algorithm (PMC), where the motion interference on the photodiode is obtained by sampling its signal when both the Red and IR LEDs are disconnected, from here the step frequency of the motion artifacts is obtained. Later when the LEDs are connected the resulting signals are processed with a filter that extracts the frequencies corresponding to the motion artifacts, typical <0.3 Hz [20]. Any of the later 2 after-mentioned filters can be implemented at hardware/firmware level with similar degree of complexity. The propose model for the probe has the layout of an electric toothbrush, (Fig. 3), a shape select as its ergonomics are extensively tested by years of user's experience, their general dimensions can accommodate the new, in development models for the probe's head sensor and the motor/battery pack enclosure can provided enough space for the prototypes' electronics and power supply. Additionally, the materials that compose the shell of the probe are already approved for human utilization, so allergic skin contact reactions should be minimal. The next development steps will firstly go in testing the new head probe in a skeleton toothbrush shell, after the successful completion of those, the electronics will be adapted for custom printed circuit board (PCB), design to the specifications of the toothbrush shell. This PCB will accommodate the necessary IC's for signal acquisition and control, the power unit and a low-power wireless communication transceiver. According to a good acceptance of dental implants over the past few decades and the growing trend for their utilization worldwide, it is necessary to promote a simple, cost effective and non-invasive device that can help the dentists in the diagnosis, optimization and extending the life of the dental implants, which in turn will play an important role in global health improvement, decreasing costs of dental repairs due to late detection of problems. This project by using current techniques and technologies for developing a new, cost effective device to meet the specific limitations of the mouth cavity will contribute to this life improvement.

**Acknowledgments.** The authors would like to thank the Fundação para a Ciência e Tecnologia (FCT, Portugal) and NMT, S.A. for co-financing the PhD grant (PD/BDE/130083/2017) of the Doctoral NOVA I4H Program.

# References

1. Estrela, C., Oliveira, K.S., Alencar, A.H.G., Barletta, F.B., Estrela, C.R., Felippe, W.T.: Oxygen saturation in the dental pulp of maxillary and mandibular molars - part 2. Braz. Dent. J. **28**(6), 704–709 (2017)
2. Berkovitz, B.K.B., Holland, G.R., Moxham, B.J.: Oral Anatomy, Histology & Embryology, 5th edn. Elsevier Ltd., Amsterdam (2018)
3. Gopikrishna, V., Pradeep, G., Venkateshbabu, N.: Assessment of pulp vitality: a review. Int. J. Paediatr. Dent. **19**(1), 3–15 (2009)
4. Kakino, S., Kushibiki, S., Yamada, A., Miwa, Z., Takagi, Y., Matsuura, Y.: Optical measurement of blood oxygen saturation of dental pulp. ISRN Biomed. Eng. **2013**, 1–6 (2013)
5. Commander, L., Kenee, D.M., Mcclanahan, C.S.B., Johnson, C.J.D.: Clinical Update, vol. 22, no. 8, pp. 17–18 (2000)
6. A. S. Review: Methods of diagnosis and treatment in endodontics. Order A J. Theory Order. Sets Appl. **2012**(June), 49–113 (2012)
7. Todea, C., Canjau, S., Miron, M., Vitez, B., Noditi, G.: Laser doppler flowmetry evaluation of the microcirculation in dentistry
8. de Araujo Nobre, M., Mano Azul, M., Rocha, E., Malo, P.: Risk factors of peri-implant pathology. Eur. J. Oral Sci. **123**(3), 131–139 (2015)
9. Abd-Elmeguid, A., Yu, D.C.: Dental pulp neurophysiology: part 2. Current diagnostic tests to assess pulp vitality. J. Can. Dent. Assoc. **75**(2), 139–143 (2009)
10. Dutta, S.D., Maria, R.: Pulse oximetry: a new tool in pulpal vitality testing. People's J. Sci. Res. **6**(1), 2011–2014 (2013)
11. Radhakrishnan, S., Munshi, K., Hegde, A.M.: Pulse oximetry: a diagnostic instrument in pulpal vitality testing. J. Clin. Pediatr. Dent. **26**(2), 141–145 (2002)
12. Nivesh Krishna, R., Pradeep, S.: Recent diagnostic aids in endodontics - a review. Int. J. Pharm. Clin. Res. **8**(8), 1159–1162 (2016)

13. Shetty, K.P., Satish, S.V., Kilaru, K., Chakravarthi Ponangi, K., Luke, A.M., Neshangi, S.: An in vivo evaluation of the change in the pulpal oxygen saturation after administration of preoperative anxiolytics and local anesthesia. J. Dent. Res. Dent. Clin. Dent. Prospects 10(1), 31–35 (2016)
14. Abd-Elmeguid, A., Yu, D.C.: Dental pulp neurophysiology: part 1. Clinical and diagnostic implications. J. Can. Dent. Assoc. 75(1), 55–59 (2009)
15. Novaes, A.B., De Souza, S.L.S., Taba, M., Grisi, M.F.D.M., Suzigan, L.C., Tunes, R.S.: Control of gingival inflammation in a teenager population using ultrasonic prophylaxis. Braz. Dent. J. 15(1), 41–45 (2004)
16. Kakino, S., Takagi, Y., Takatani, S.: Absolute transmitted light plethysmography for assessment of dental pulp vitality through quantification of pulp chamber hematocrit by a three-layer model. J. Biomed. Opt. 13(5), 054023 (2011)
17. Matthewws, B., Vonhsaan, N.: Advantages and limitation of laser doppler flow meters. Department of Physiology, School of Medical Sciences, University of Bristol, Bristol, UK (1993)
18. Reddy, K.A., George, B., Kumar, V.J.: Use of Fourier series analyses for motion artifact reduction and data compression of photoplethysmographic signals. IEE Trans. Instrum. Meas. 58, 1706–1711 (2009)
19. Lee, J., Jung, W., Kang, I.T., Kim, Y., Lee, G.: Design of filter to reject motion artifact of pulse oximetry. Comput. Stand. Interf. 26, 241–249 (2004)
20. Wang, L., Lo, B., Yang, G.Z.: Multichannel reflective PPG earpiece sensor with passive motion cancellation. IEEE Trans. Biomed. Circuits Syst. I, 235–241 (2007)

# Arterial Stiffness and Central Hemodynamic Assessment by Novel Portable Device

Andreia Serrano[1,2(✉)], Valentina Vassilenko[1,2], Beatriz Ramalho[1], Paulo Bonifácio[1,2], and Anna Poplavska[1,2]

[1] Laboratory of Instrumentation, Biomedical Engineering and Radiation Physics (LIBPHYS), NOVA School of Science and Technology, NOVA University Lisbon, 2829-516 Caparica, Portugal
a.serrano@campus.fct.unl.pt
[2] NMT, S.A., Parque Tecnológico de Cantanhede, Núcleo 04, Lote 3, 3060-197 Cantanhede, Portugal

**Abstract.** Cardiovascular (CV) diseases are leading cause of mortality and arterial stiffness is a very important risk marker. It can be obtained by non-invasive measurements of carotid-femoral pulse wave velocity (cfPWV), recommended as a gold-standard marker of CV risk by European Society of Cardiology (ESC). Previous works proved that arterial stiffness's increase with ageing, sedentary lifestyle, smoking habits, etc. Central aortic pressure (CAP) is an important marker to evaluate blood pressure, in order to prevent cerebral vessels diseases, the most frequent causes of stroke and dementia. The present work reports a CAP and cfPWV data in order to characterize profile on different cohorts of Portuguese population: young adults with no associated diagnosis (NAD), adults with diagnosed axSpA and elderly with Sarcopenia. All measurements were performed using a novel, portable and low-cost device and developed protocol.

**Keywords:** Cardiovascular (CV) risk · Arterial stiffness · Pulse Wave Velocity (PWV) · Central Aortic Pressure (CAP) · Sarcopenia · Axial Spondyloarthritis (axSpA)

## 1 Introduction

### Arterial Stiffness

Mechanical properties of large arteries are complex and difficult to be measured [1]. This difficult is essentially caused by anisotropy and nonlinear viscoelastic properties, that are specific to each single arterial segment. Arterial stiffening is characterized by a reduced compliance and distensibility emerged as another distinctive feature of cardiovascular risk, which is related to endothelial dysfunction.

Increased aortic stiffness can be associated with decreased DBP (diastolic blood pressure); coronary ischemia and excessive DBP-lowering are therefore likely consequences, with cardiovascular accidents as a potential outcome [2]. Arterial stiffness is

© IFIP International Federation for Information Processing 2020
Published by Springer Nature Switzerland AG 2020
L. M. Camarinha-Matos et al. (Eds.): DoCEIS 2020, IFIP AICT 577, pp. 429–436, 2020.
https://doi.org/10.1007/978-3-030-45124-0_42

related to age, heart rate, and mean arterial pressure, and in hypertensive diabetic subjects, to diabetes mellitus duration and insulin treatment, a finding that is very important [3].

## Pulse Wave Velocity – PWV

Pulse waves travel faster in stiffer arteries so, arterial stiffness, could be characterized by Pulse Wave Velocity (PWV). Carotid-femoral PWV (cfPWV) is the gold standard for assessing aortic stiffness and one of the most valuable independent predictors of cardiovascular events.

Noninvasive assessment of cf-PWV has shown aortic stiffening to be consistently higher in patients with both hypertension and type 2 diabetes mellitus than in nondiabetic hypertensive subjects, for the same BP level [3].

Previous studies demonstrated also that exercise shows beneficial effects in physically active young individuals, appearing to perform as a protective factor against cardiovascular diseases, in keeping with an overall better preservation of arterial distensibility in youths [4].

## Central Hemodynamic

Nowadays, it is still very important to measure brachial BP in order to assess the cardiovascular risk associated with hypertension and assess the beneficial effect of treatment for lowering blood pressure [5]. In addition, there is also a big difference in the effects caused by vasoactive drugs on central and peripheral pressure, hence the need to evaluate both [6].

Currently, the interest of the medical community has been increasing in improving the estimates of cardiovascular risk through medical devices, using the more accurate measurement of central aortic blood pressure compared to those obtained by traditional methods, such as brachial cuff BP methods.

## Hypertension vs Arterial Stiffness

Intrinsic carotid arterial stiffness was only detected as elevated, independently of BP, in young hypertensives, which was not verified in older patients. Temporal relationship between carotid and aortic stiffness, and incident hypertension, suggests that arterial stiffening is precursor for future changes to the systolic hemodynamic load. However, in hypertension, arterial stiffness increases because of increases in distension pressure. Aortic stiffness may also be influenced by remodeling of small resistance arteries that are closely independent in sustained grade I hypertension, and likely during the early phases of prehypertension. The clinical combination of hypertension and arterial stiffness marks an important step toward the development of cardiovascular disease and the need for complete assessment of cardiovascular risk [7].

## Aging Effect on Arterial Stiffness

With ageing, the elastic arteries, like the aorta, undergo significant morphological changes, such as the stiffening and thickening of the arterial walls, which leads to changes in the arterial pulsatility [8] due to lower distensibility. As a result of these pathophysiological changes, inflammatory events can take place and induce endothelium dysfunction, which in turn can exacerbate the existent arterial stiffness and cause the establishment of chronic vascular inflammation [9].

Mean annual SBP (systolic blood pressure) levels increased significantly with age and were higher in men than in women [10].

In very old subjects ($\geq 75$ years), arterial stiffness remains a determinant of cognitive decline, morbidity and mortality [11]. The impact of SBP levels and arterial stiffness can be very different, possibly because low SBP levels mainly reflect age-related comorbidities and conditions of malnutrition or dehydration, whereas in relatively younger and more robust individuals, low SBP levels mainly reflect lower arterial stiffness and better arterial health [10].

Although hypertension and ageing are known factors contributing to arterial stiffness, the role of inflammation in arterial stiffness pathogenesis has been inciting interest within the scientific community, evidencing a strong tie between arterial stiffness and systemic inflammation.

**Sarcopenia**

Sarcopenia is characterized by muscle mass loose and skeletal musculature strength decreasing on older population, due to aging process. It affects about 29% of the elderly and 33% of patients using long-term care services [12].

Recently, it was found that increased arterial stiffness is associated with declining muscle mass, suggesting a relationship between arterial stiffening and the existence of sarcopenia [13], which may be explained by the loss of muscle mass that is often associated with chronic inflammation [14].

## 2 Contribution to Life Improvement

According to data provided by the World Health Organization (WHO), cardiovascular diseases (CV) are the main cause of death, causing 31% of deaths worldwide [15]. Because of this, there is a greater concern to develop more reliable methods of CV risk assessment. As arterial stiffness of the aorta is a well-known independent marker of CV morbidity and mortality [7], research and development of new methods for its measurement are very important for the general population.

Currently, there is a growing interest among clinicians towards improving CV risk estimates. Therefore, there is a need to develop or adapt current technologies that would provide accurate values for central aortic BP.

To answer this need, a new non-invasive, painless, portable, wireless and low-cost device is presented. Moreover, values of important CV markers were successfully measured with this novel device.

Obtained results showed that its implementation in clinical routine will help the health providers to get additional information, for instance, improved cardiovascular assessment and risk management.

## 3 Research Study and Innovation

Pulse Wave Velocity and Central Arterial Pressure were measured using an innovative low-cost, portable and wireless device – VasoCheck – developed by the Portuguese company NMT, S.A [16]. VasoCheck system is composed of main control unit and up to 4 signal acquisition units, allowing for up to 4 signal sampling points on one single object. VasoCheck device communicate with any computer by USB connection and a user interface VasoCheck Record Software. Signal acquisition is performed by sensors based on photoplethysmography technology, which is a big innovation on PWV and CAP measurements.

### 3.1 Age Effect on Cardiovascular Risk

Experimental measurements of cfPWV and Central Arterial Pressure (CAP) were performed at healthy people and a population diagnosed [1] with cardiovascular diseases (CVD) (dyslipidemia, hypertension, diabetes, and others) at FCT UNL, CEDOC, Santa Casa da Misericórdia de Almada (SCMA) and HSO Guimarães.

Pulse Wave Velocity was recorded in 110 subjects (50 male and 60 female) in different age ranges (see Table 1). Brachial SP was measured in all the subjects, in order to verify which marker better defines the population: BP or cfPWV. Figure 1 represents the linear regression model for age as the independent variable and cfPWV as the dependent one, being the p-value for age <0.001. In addition, the arterial stiffness was analyzed by measuring cfPWV, for subjects with hypertension, dyslipidemia and diabetes mellitus type II (Table 2). It was verified that cfPWV is higher in hypertensive subjects for both genders, but more severe in men. The same trend was seen for patients with dyslipidemia and diabetes.

**Table 1.** Measured values for cf-PWV for deferent age groups.

| Age range | | Height (m) | Weight (kg) | BMI (kg/m²) | SP (mmHg) | DP (mmHg) | HR (bpm) | cfPWV (m/s) |
|---|---|---|---|---|---|---|---|---|
| <30 | Mean | 1,7116 | 67,978 | 23,036 | 118,545 | 70,255 | 66,89 | 4,781 |
| | Min | 1,51 | 48,0 | 17,1 | 95,0 | 57,0 | 47 | 2,5 |
| | Max | 1,87 | 110,0 | 32,0 | 149,0 | 94,0 | 99 | 14,1 |
| | % of N | 50,5% | 50,9% | 52,4% | 50,0% | 50,0% | 50,0% | 50,0% |
| 30–60 | Mean | 1,6769 | 71,460 | 25,775 | 127,029 | 78,853 | 75,21 | 6,265 |
| | Min | 1,58 | 56,0 | 22,5 | 95,0 | 62,0 | 47 | 4,1 |
| | Max | 1,79 | 92,2 | 30,4 | 153,0 | 93,0 | 97 | 11,4 |
| | % of N | 14,7% | 13,9% | 11,4% | 15,5% | 15,5% | 15,5% | 15,5% |
| 60–90 | Mean | 1,5523 | 60,746 | 25,244 | 131,231 | 71,462 | 71,00 | 6,159 |
| | Min | 1,42 | 37,5 | 17,0 | 83,0 | 56,0 | 47 | 3,5 |
| | Max | 1,71 | 77,6 | 33,0 | 203,0 | 87,0 | 92 | 10,8 |
| | % of N | 23,9% | 24,1% | 24,8% | 23,6% | 23,6% | 23,6% | 23,6% |
| >90 | Mean | 1,4983 | 63,192 | 28,200 | 143,000 | 71,917 | 74,25 | 6,929 |
| | Min | 1,35 | 47,6 | 19,8 | 110,0 | 35,0 | 57 | 4,0 |
| | Max | 1,61 | 83,7 | 37,2 | 178,0 | 111,0 | 98 | 12,3 |
| | % of N | 11,0% | 11,1% | 11,4% | 10,9% | 10,9% | 10,9% | 10,9% |
| Total | Mean | 1,6450 | 66,189 | 24,486 | 125,523 | 72,050 | 69,95 | 5,570 |
| | Min | 1,36 | 37,5 | 17,0 | 83,0 | 35,0 | 47 | 2,5 |
| | Max | 1,87 | 110,0 | 37,2 | 203,0 | 111,0 | 99 | 14,1 |
| | % of N | 100,0% | 100,0% | 100,0% | 100,0% | 100,0% | 100,0% | 100,0% |

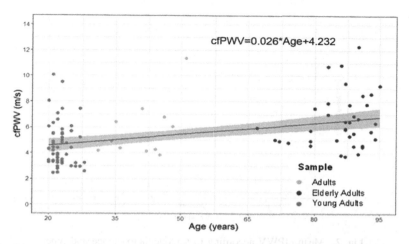

**Fig. 1.** Linear regression model for age and cfPWV. The shaded area represents the confidence interval for the regression line.

**Table 2.** Mean values of cfPWV, in m/s, for men and women with or without hypertension, dyslipidemia and diabetes mellitus type II diagnosed.

| Risk factor | | cfPWV (m/s) | |
|---|---|---|---|
| | | Male | Female |
| Hypertension | No | 4,9 | 5,1 |
| | Yes | 8,0 | 6,0 |
| Dyslipidemia | No | 5,1 | 5,4 |
| | Yes | 9,5 | 5,4 |
| Diabetes | No | 5,4 | 5,4 |
| | Yes | 6,9 | 5,7 |

Measurements for Sarcopenia and arterial stiffness evaluation were performed on 38 elderly (27 female and 11 male) over 67 years of age at SCMA. SCMA Measurement Protocol was established considering published studies for the sarcopenia suffering diagnosis. Among the most commonly techniques used in clinical practice, the following ones were selected for each sarcopenia diagnostic criteria: BIA for muscle mass, handgrip strength test for muscle strength, and gait speed test for muscular performance. In order to correlate sarcopenia with arterial stiffness, blood pressure and cfPWV was also acquired using VasoCheck. The differences observed in the mean cfPWV for the existence and type of sarcopenia in the elders is shown Fig. 2. Obtained data show a positive correlation for cfPWV with the sarcopenia severity degree, which represents an increasing arterial stiffness and might be explained by the fact that the loss of muscle mass is often associated with chronic inflammation [14].

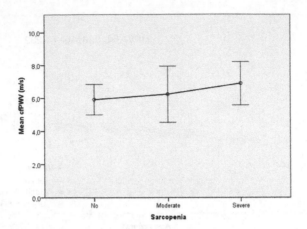

**Fig. 2.** Mean cfPWV according to sarcopenia existence and type.

Values of CAP were recorded in a sample of 220 subjects (116 male and 104 female) in different age ranges (see Table 3). Figure 3 represents the linear regression model for age as the independent variable and CAP as the dependent one, where it is possible to see that CAP increases with ageing.

**Table 3.** Sample description for CAP record and analysis.

| CAP analysis | | | | | | | | |
|---|---|---|---|---|---|---|---|---|
| Age range | | Height (cm) | Weight (kg) | BMI (kg/m$^2$) | SP (mmHg) | DP (mmHg) | HR (bpm) | CAP (mmHg) |
| <30 | Mean | 170,5168 | 68,419 | 23,382 | 119,35 | 73,21 | 71,06 | 95,085 |
| | Min | 151,00 | 48,0 | 17,1 | 94 | 57 | 47 | 76,0 |
| | Max | 191,00 | 133,0 | 42,9 | 153 | 94 | 157 | 132,3 |
| | % of N | 54,1% | 54,3% | 54,1% | 54,1% | 54,1% | 75,0% | 18,7% |
| 30–60 | Mean | 167,9597 | 70,710 | 24,570 | 121,48 | 81,02 | 65,57 | 105,898 |
| | Min | 150,00 | 44,0 | 0 | 63 | 62 | 45 | 76,1 |
| | Max | 186,00 | 108,0 | 35,2 | 172 | 115 | 89 | 153,0 |
| | % of N | 28,2% | 27,9% | 28,2% | 28,2% | 28,2% | 20,4% | 46,7% |
| >60 | Mean | 163,4872 | 72,718 | 27,118 | 131,90 | 80,24 | 68,29 | 112,970 |
| | Min | 147,00 | 54,0 | 22,3 | 98 | 68 | 50 | 76,0 |
| | Max | 179,00 | 101,0 | 35,4 | 174 | 97 | 92 | 142,7 |
| | % of N | 17,7% | 17,8% | 17,7% | 17,7% | 17,7% | 4,6% | 34,6% |
| Total | Mean | 168,5500 | 69,823 | 24,379 | 122,18 | 76,66 | 69,81 | 106,322 |
| | Min | 147,00 | 44,0 | 0 | 63 | 57 | 45 | 76,0 |
| | Max | 191,00 | 133,0 | 42,9 | 174 | 115 | 157 | 153,0 |
| | % of N | 100,0% | 100,0% | 100,0% | 100,0% | 100,0% | 100,0% | 100,0% |

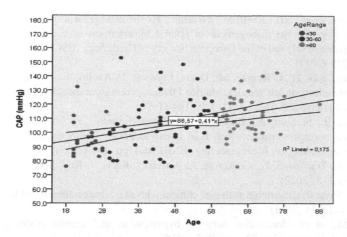

**Fig. 3.** Linear regression model for age and CAP. The lines over and above the regression line represent the area of the confidence interval.

## 4   Conclusions and Further Work

The age-related increase in aortic stiffness of the selected Portuguese cohort was confirmed. Our data shows a positive correlation for cfPWV with the sarcopenia severity degree, which represents an increasing arterial stiffness and might be explained by the fact that the loss of muscle mass is often associated with chronic inflammation [14].

Central Arteria Pressure was correctly and easily measured with VasoCheck in all age ranges population. It was possible to conclude that CAP increases with ageing, and in future work it is pretended to demonstrate that is a good marker of CV risk in this cohort.

**Acknowledgments.** The authors would like to thank the Fundação para a Ciência e Tecnologia (FCT, Portugal) and NMT, S.A. for co-financing the PhD grants PD/BDE/114551/2016, PD/BDE/130083/2017 and PD/BDE/150312/2019 of the Doctoral NOVA I4H Program. Special acknowledgments to the all volunteers participated in the study.

## References

1. Okamoto, R.J., Wagenseil, J.E., DeLong, W.R., Peterson, S.J., Kouchoukos, N.T., Sundt III, T.M.: Mechanical properties of dilated human ascending aorta. Ann. Biomed. Eng. **30**(5), 624–635 (2002). https://doi.org/10.1114/1.1484220
2. Protogetou, A., et al.: Diasltolic blood pressure and mortality in the elderly with cardiovascular disease. Hypertension **50**, 172–180 (2017)
3. Smulyan, H., Lieber, A., Safar, M.: Hypertension, diabetes type II, and their association: role of arterial stiffness. Am. J. Hypertens. **29**, 5–13 (2016)
4. Fernandes, F., et al.: Benefits of sports for arterial distensibility in youths. Am. Sci. Res. J. Eng. Technol. Sci. (ASRJETS) **27**(1), 1–11 (2017)

5. Mancia, G., et al.: 2013 ESH/ESC guidelines for the management of arterial hypertension: the task force for the management of arterial hypertension of the European Society of Hypertension (ESH) and of the European Society of Cardiology (ESC). J. Hypertens. **34**(28), 2159–2219 (2013)
6. Kelly, R., Gibbs, H., O'Rourke, M., Daley, J., Mang, J., Avolio, A.: Nitroglycerin has more favourable effects on left ventricle afterload than apparent from measurement of pressure in a peripheral artery. Eur. Heart J. **11**, 138–144 (1990)
7. Ramalho, B., Serrano, A., Bonifácio, P., Pimentel-Santos, F., Vassilenko, V.: Arterial stiffness in portuguese patients with axial spondyloarthritis: a pilot study. In: 2019 IEEE 6th Portuguese Meeting on Bioengineering (ENBENG), pp. 1–4 (2019)
8. Quinn, U., Tomlinson, L., Cockcroft, J.: Arterial stiffness. J. Roy. Soc. Med. Cardiovasc. Dis. **1**(6), 1–8 (2012)
9. Izzo, J., Shykoff, B.: Arterial stiffness: clinical relevance, measurement, and treatment. Clin. Sci. **2**(1), 29–34 (2001)
10. Safar, M., et al.: Interaction between hypertension and arterial stiffness. An expert reappraisal. Hypertension **72**, 796–805 (2018)
11. Watfa, G., et al.: PARTAGE study investigators. Do arterial hemodynamic parameters preditc cognitive decline over a period of 2 years in individuals older than 80 years living in nursing homes? J. Am. Med. Directors Assoc. **16**, 598–602 (2015)
12. Marty, E., Liu, Y., Samuel, A., Or, O., Lane, J.: A review of sarcopenia: enhancing awareness of an increasingly prevalent disease. Bone **105**, 276–286 (2017)
13. Abbatecola, A.: Pulse wave velocity is associated with muscle mass decline: Health ABC study. Age **34**(2), 469–478 (2012)
14. Rodríguez, A., Karim, M., Srikanth, V., Ebeling, P., Scott, D.: Lower muscle tissue is associated with higher pulse wave velocity: a systematic review and metaanalysis of observational study data. Clin. Exp. Pharmacol. Physiol. **44**(10), 980–992 (2017)
15. World Health Organization: Cardiovascular diseases (CVDs). https://www.who.int/. Accessed 17 May 2017
16. NMT, S.A.: Measurements protocol for VasoCheck device: Internal NMT, S.A. document. Protocol, NMT, S.A., Caparica, Portugal (2018)

# Indoor and Outdoor Air Profiling with GC-IMS

Pedro C. Moura[1](✉), Valentina Vassilenko[1,2], Jorge M. Fernandes[1,2], and Paulo H. Santos[1,2]

[1] Laboratory for Instrumentation, Biomedical Engineering and Radiation Physics (LibPhys-UNL), NOVA School of Science and Technology, NOVA University of Lisbon, Campus FCT-UNL, 2896-516 Caparica, Portugal
pr.moura@campus.fct.unl.pt
[2] NMT, S.A., Edifício Madan Parque, Rua dos Inventores, 2825-182 Caparica, Portugal

**Abstract.** Air Quality research is a trending topic that has received increasing attention from scientific community around the globe. Due to the high relevance of recent discoveries in areas like medicine or chemistry, analytical techniques with high sensitivity and selectivity play a crucial role in the characterization of the ambient air composition. This preliminary study intends to evaluate the air quality around a university campus by profiling VOCs from 14 locations with differentiated characteristics, intended for further industrial contextualization. Multiple air samples were collected from each defined location and further analysed with the GC-IMS technique. Totally, 33 compounds were detected, and their intensity peak values, and drift and retention times were used to identify 11 of them. The suitability of GC-IMS to quickly and easily assess air quality become evident. Further detailed studies should include a wider range of locations to identify new VOCs and their eventual consequences to human health.

**Keywords:** Gas chromatography · Ion mobility spectrometry · Air quality · Intensity profiling · Volatile Organic Compounds

## 1 Introduction

Volatile Organic Compounds as aromatic hydrocarbons, aliphatic, aldehydes, ketones, ethers, acids and alcohols, are inert compounds with the capability of passing through biological membranes and, according to its concentration, may be harmful to human health [1]. The increasing health problems related with the chemical composition of environmental air requires a careful and detailed study on the identification and quantification of these compounds in air samples and possible consequences to human health [1]. Being mainly released to the air from different sources, such as building materials, furniture, cleaning and preservation products, and activities-related materials, the study of Volatile Organic Compounds is crucial both for indoor and outdoor air quality assessment [2]. Although IMS spectra information of several VOCs is still unknown (e.g., Toluene, Xylenes and Ethylbenzene), [3, 4], there are some well-known VOCs that are characteristics of environmental air samples, like Ethanol, Acetone,

© IFIP International Federation for Information Processing 2020
Published by Springer Nature Switzerland AG 2020
L. M. Camarinha-Matos et al. (Eds.): DoCEIS 2020, IFIP AICT 577, pp. 437–444, 2020.
https://doi.org/10.1007/978-3-030-45124-0_43

Ethyl Acetate and 2-Propanol [5]. Common compounds such as Ammonia or Isoprene, for example, are characteristics of human breath [6]. The continuous exposure to possibly noxious and hazardous compounds, thus revealing the importance of air quality studies which should include VOCs monitoring and their quantification, at the workplace, home, schools and other public places [2, 7–9].

Nowadays, several techniques are used to assure the air quality of samples from several locations and matrixes [10].

GC-IMS is an analytical technique that was initially developed for use in military context, specially to detect explosive and chemical warfare agents [11, 12]. Recently, it gained a new role in several civil applications such as the detection of a wide range of analytes, for health, security or even food or air quality purposes [13, 14]. The wide range of applications is due to the technique advantages because it combines the best characteristics of both GC and IMS. GC is known for its good precision, wide dynamic concentration range and high selectivity and sensitivity [15, 16]. IMS, on its turn, is a highly sensible technique that allows good analytical flexibility and real time monitoring at a low cost [17]. Coupled in a single device, GC-IMS technique offers improved quality at differentiating organic compounds by its size, weight and shape when compared with other techniques [17, 18].

The functional principle of GC-IMS is easily and widely understood. A sample is injected into the apparatus and it will undergo pre-separation by Gas Chromatography in which the compounds are separated into individual components [19]. The time compounds take to elude from the GC column is called Retention Time (RT) [15, 17]. Compounds are, then, transported into the IMS, where they are ionized by a radiation source. After the ionization, the formed ions are exposed to a weak and homogeneous electric field that moves each molecule across a drift tube. The time that the ions take to go through the drift tube is called Drift Time (DT). The ions are, then, separated according with their specific ion mobilities thus arriving at different times at the detector, also known as Faraday Plate [20]. After the entire process, a three-dimensional spectrum is produced in which the drift time, the retention time and the intensity are represented. Intensity, normally, is represented by a colour scale and corresponds to the sample concentration of each compound [21].

## 2    Contributions to Life Improvement

As mentioned before, the characteristics and composition of the environmental air, the presence or absence of certain compounds and its concentrations/intensities have direct effects on population's health. The mapping, detection and quantification of these volatile organic compounds are very important parameters that should be studied. The study developed in this article intends to study the air quality around a university campus to prove the suitability of GC-IMS to identify and quantify distinct volatile organic compounds in different air samples. The obtained results are intended to demonstrate the eventual necessity of taking necessary measures about human exposure to possibly noxious compounds. Better knowledge about different locations profile will allow to protect human beings and prevent eventual health problems that may appear due to the presence of harmful compounds.

# 3 Materials and Methods

## 3.1 Chosen Locations to Collect Air Samples

To characterize the university campus air, fifteen locations were chosen based on its characteristics (i.e., specific smells, presence of different machines, use of distinct chemical products or big affluence of people). From these fifteen locations, one of them was used as reference air and the remaining fourteen were comparatively analysed against the reference. The ambient air present in the laboratory where the GC-IMS apparatus is located was selected as reference, and the other fourteen selected locations were mostly facilities where some specific VOCs are supposed to vary its production levels. Locations where air samples were collected are GC-IMS Laboratory (Reference Air), Electronics Laboratory, Chemistry Laboratory, Administration Building Entrance, Conservation and Restoration Laboratory, Atomic and Molecular Physics Laboratory, Biomechanics and Hemodynamic Laboratory, Electronic Engineering Building, Mechanical Engineering Building, FABLAB – Fabrication Laboratory, Canteen, Materials Engineering Laboratory, Bathroom, Parking Lot, Workshop.

## 3.2 Air Collection Method

A chemically inert manual Teflon pump with an accoupled stopcock valve was used to collect and isolate the air samples from the different locations. Such procedure allowed to obtain contamination-free gaseous-phase air samples, avoiding the interaction and influence of exogenous compounds. This way, location-characteristics samples were able to be transported for characterization with the GC-IMS.

## 3.3 GC-IMS

The GC column used was an MXT-200 with 30 m length and 0,53 mm internal diameter coated with stainless steel with a mid-polar stationary phase of trifluoropropylmethyl polysiloxane with a thickness of 1 μm. The IMS instrumentation used was a BreathSpec® device from GAS Dortmund equipped with a Tritium $H^3$ (ß-radiation) 300 MBq as an ionisation source. The drift tube has a 5-kV switchable polarity and a tube length of 98 mm with an electric field strength of 500 V/cm.

Air samples analysis was performed through its injection into the GC-IMS apparatus by compressing the plunger of the pump system for approximately 3 s. The above-mentioned procedure was repeated three times for each location to minimize the effects of potential contaminant compounds and losses of environmental airs'

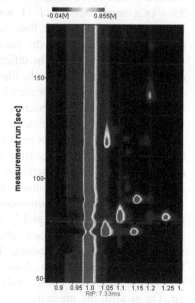

**Fig. 1.** Example of a spectrum produced by the GC-IMS technique.

specific compounds. Every single analysis performed in GC-IMS produced a three-dimensional spectrum (Fig. 1). All obtained spectra were analysed and compared with LAV software (G.A.S. Dortmund) and the values of intensity, drift time and retention time of all signals were collected.

The variation of each maximum relative intensity values (intensity peaks) among all spectra allowed to plot a characteristic graph of compounds for each studied location. Such graphs represent the relative intensity of each compounds in the labelled location. The presented intensity values are relative to the values in the reference air, i.e., a value of zero in the $y$-axis indicates a similarity in the concentration of that compound when comparing both locations. As relative intensity values, a bar that appears above the referential indicates a higher concentration of that compound relatively to the reference air. To provide a better understanding of the profiles, all the charts have the same $yy$ values (3.5), the bars that exceed this value are labelled with the corresponding value. A radar graph was also plotted coupled to the bars charts to ease the profile visualisation. Additionally, both drift and retention times allowed the identification of some of the found compounds using pre-developed libraries.

## 4   Results and Discussion

Overall, fourteen locations were studied and compared relatively to a fifteenth. The choice of GC-IMS apparatus laboratory as reference air is due to the deep knowledge authors already have about its composition. The choice of another air as reference would imply a change in the obtained profiles (further studies will have this topic in consideration). Three samples were done for all locations totalizing 45 spectra. In total, 33 VOCs were found and 11 were identified. Relative intensity values (bars) and intensity profile (line) for four locations are represented in Figs. 2(a)–(d). For the remaining locations, only the radar chart is represented (Fig. 3(a)–(i)), still allowing visual comparison among the different campus locations. Table 1 (appendix) lists all 11 drift and retention times for the identified compounds and their CAS numbers. Some of those identified compounds are dimers and trimers of a same compound. There are no new or extinguished compounds from place to place, however, their peak intensities vary considerably across locations.

Most of the compounds present in the air of Electronics Laboratory (Fig. 2(a)), of Chemistry Laboratory (Fig. 2(b)), and of Biomechanics and Hemodynamic Laboratory (Fig. 3(c)) have higher intensities relatively to the reference air. All three locations even contain two compounds which concentrations are much higher than the remaining, respectively, compound 8 (2-propanol) and 21 (unidentified) to the first location, 17 (unidentified) and 21 to the second, and 8 and 21 to the third. Compound 21 is also very intense in some other locations what proves its possible relation with the activities done in the location. There are other locations, such as the Electronic Engineering Building (Fig. 2(d)) and the Conservation and Restoration Laboratory (Fig. 2(c)), where the compounds intensity is lower when compared to the reference air. On its turn, the intensity profile for the Physics Laboratory (Fig. 3(b)) shows the VOCs concentration it is generally the same of the reference air. The compound Ethyl-acetate (bars 8 and 33) has similar concentrations across the different locations but in the Workshop (Fig. 3(i)) its intensity increases considerably which indicates that this location has some ethyl-acetate production source.

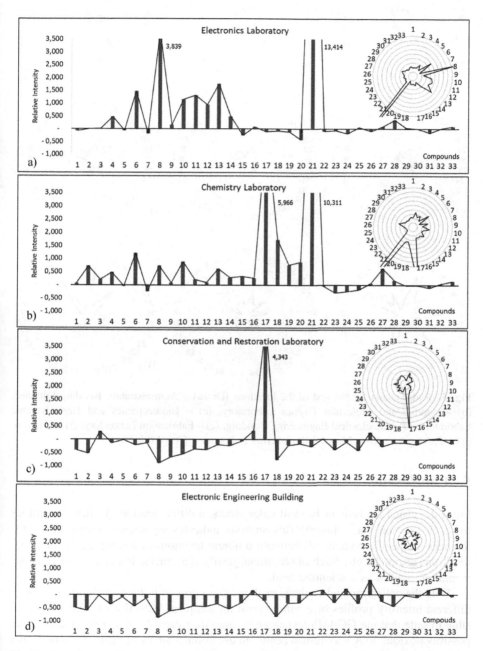

**Fig. 2.** Intensity profiles to some of the analysed locations across the campus (i.e. (a) – Electronics Laboratory, (b) – Chemistry Laboratory, (c) – Conservation and Restoration Laboratory, (d) – Electronics Engineering Building).

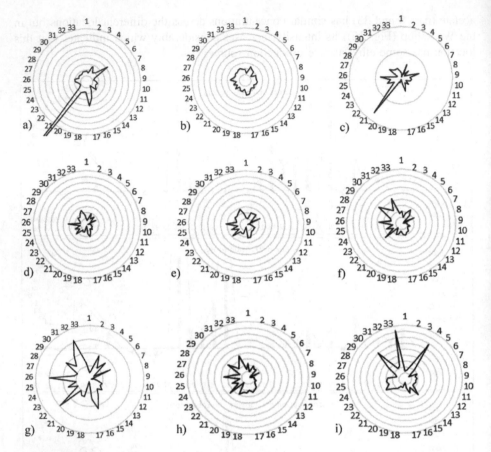

**Fig. 3.** Radar charts for the rest of the locations (i.e. (a) – Administration Building Entrance, (b) – Atomic and Molecular Physics Laboratory, (c) – Biomechanics and Hemodynamic Laboratory, (d) – Mechanical Engineering Building, (e) – Fabrication Laboratory, (f) – Canteen, (g) – Parking Lot, (h) – Material Engineering Laboratory, (i) - Workshop).

## 5  Conclusions

From the visual analysis of bar and radar charts, a differentiation of intensity profiles for each location was allowed. This analysis indicates significant concentration differences of specific compounds between different locations of a same area which may reach dangerous levels. Such observations justify the crucial importance of environmental air studies as a scientific field.

Both the collecting and analysis methods were proven to be suitable to distinguish different intensity profiles of environmental air samples. With that in mind, it is possible to state that the GC-IMS technique is more than capable of identify and quantify possibly noxious VOCs to human health, in environmental air of distinct locations and qualitatively evaluate indoor and outdoor air.

To have a more detailed study, a wider range of locations with distinct characteristics should be included and analysed, and the identification of relevant compounds for this study should be conducted, as well as, their consequences to human health.

**Acknowledgments.** The authors would like to thank the Fundação para a Ciência e Tecnologia (FCT, Portugal) and **NMT, S.A.** for co-financing the PhD grant (PD/BDE/130204/2017) of the Doctoral NOVA I4H Program.

# Appendix

**Table 1.** Drift time (sec.), relative retention time, CAS numbers and notes for the identified compounds in all samples.

| Peak number | Drift time (sec.) | Relative retention time | Identified compound | CAS number | Note |
|---|---|---|---|---|---|
| 1 | 1,055 | 72,823 | Ethanol | 64-17-5 | Monomer |
| 2 | 1,127 | 93,108 | 1-propanol | 71-23-8 | Monomer |
| 4 | 1,121 | 117,077 | Ethyl Acetate | 141-78-6 | Monomer |
| 7 | 1,284 | 246,377 | Hexanal | 66-25-1 | Monomer |
| 8 | 1,253 | 78,893 | 2-propanol | 67-63-0 | Trimer |
| 9 | 1,103 | 79,330 | 2-propanol | 67-63-0 | Monomer |
| 10 | 1,205 | 78,985 | 2-propanol | 67-63-0 | Dimer |
| 14 | 1,158 | 87,569 | Acetone | 67-64-1 | Dimer |
| 16 | 1,077 | 120,420 | 2-Butanone | 78-93-3 | Monomer |
| 18 | 1,149 | 71,803 | Ethanol | 64-17-5 | Dimer |
| 33 | 1,396 | 117,182 | Ethyl Acetate | 141-78-6 | Dimer |

# References

1. Montero-Montoya, R., López-Vargas, R., Arellano-Aguilar, O.: Volatile organic compounds in air: sources, distribution, exposure and associated illness in children. Ann. Glob. Health **84**, 225–238 (2018)
2. Wah, C., Yu, F., Kim, J.T.: Building pathology, investigation of sick building - VOC emissions. Indoor Built Environ. **19**, 30–39 (2010)
3. Bruno, P., Caselli, M., de Gennaro, G., Iacobellis, S., Tutino, M.: Monitoring of volatile organic compounds in non-residential indoor environments. Indoor Air **18**, 250–256 (2008)
4. Arnanthigo, Y., Anttalainen, O., Safaei, Z., Sillanpää, M.: Sniff-testing for indoor air contaminants from new buildings environment detecting by aspiration-type ion mobility spectrometry. Int. J. Ion Mobil. Spec. **19**(1), 15–30 (2016). https://doi.org/10.1007/s12127-016-0189-0

5. Hibbard, T., Killard, A.: Breath ammonia analysis: clinical application and measurement. Crit. Rev. Anal. Chem. **41**, 21–35 (2011)
6. Fenske, J., Paulson, S.: Human breath emissions of VOCs. J. Air Waste Manag. Assoc. **49**, 594–598 (1999)
7. Rösch, C., Kohajda, T., Röder, S., von Bergen, M., Schlink, U.: Relationship between sources and patterns of VOCs in indoor air. Atmos. Pollut. Res. **5**, 129–137 (2014)
8. Śmiełowska, M., Marć, M., Zabiegała, B.: Indoor air quality in public utility environments— a review. Environ. Sci. Pollut. Res. **24**(12), 11166–11176 (2017). https://doi.org/10.1007/s11356-017-8567-7
9. Chan, C., et al.: Characterisation of volatile organic compounds at hotels in Southern China. Indoor Built Environ. **20**, 420–429 (2011)
10. Marć, M., Zabiegała, B., Namieśnik, J.: Mobile systems (portable, handheld, transportable) for monitoring air pollution. Crit. Rev. Anal. Chem. **42**, 2–15 (2012)
11. Ruzsanyi, V., et al.: Ion mobility spectrometry for detection of skin volatiles. J. Chromatogr. B **911**, 84–92 (2012)
12. Vassilenko, V., Silva, M., Alves, R., O'Neill, J.: Instrumental tools for express analysis of lacrimal fluids. In: BIODEVICES 2013 - Proceedings of the International Conference on Biomedical Electronics and Devices, Barcelona, pp. 220–224 (2013)
13. Kanu, A., Dwivedi, P., Tam, M., Matz, L., Hill Jr., H.: Ion mobility - mass spectrometry. J. Mass Spectrom. **43**, 1–22 (2008)
14. Gallart-Mateu, D., Armenta, S., de la Guardia, M.: Indoor and outdoor determination of pesticides in air by ion mobility spectrometry. Talanta **161**, 632–639 (2016)
15. Santos, F.J., Galceran, M.T.: The application of gas chromatography to environmental analysis. TrAC Trends Anal. Chem. **21**(9–10), 672–685 (2002)
16. Vautz, W., Ruszany, V., Sielemann, S., Baumbach, J.I.: Sensitive ion mobility spectrometry of humid ambient air using 10.6 eV UV-IMS. Int. J. Ion Mobility Spectrom. **7**, 3–8 (2004)
17. Kirk, A., Allers, M., Cochems, P., Langejuergen, J., Zimmermann, S.: A compact high resolution ion mobility spectrometer for fast trace gas analysis. Analyst **138**, 5200–5207 (2013)
18. Louis, R., Hill Jr., H., Eiceman, G.: Ion mobility spectrometry in analytical chemistry. Crit. Rev. Anal. Chem. **21**, 321–355 (1990)
19. Kanu, A., Hill Jr., H.: Ion mobility spectrometry detection for gas chromatography. J. Chromatogr. A **1177**, 12–27 (2008)
20. Ewing, R.G., Atkinson, D.A., Eiceman, G.A., Ewing, G.J.: A critical review of ion mobility spectrometry for the detection of explosives and explosive related compounds. Talanta **54**, 515–529 (2001)
21. Gonçalves, M., Fernandes, J., Fetter, V., Diniz, M., Vassilenko, V.: Novel methodology for quick detection of bacterial metabolites. In: 2019 IEEE 6th Portuguese Meeting on Bioengineering (ENBENG), Lisbon (2019)

# Idle Tone Detection in Biomedical Signals Using Time-Frequency Techniques

Filipa E. Cardoso[1,3(✉)], Arnaldo Batista[1,2], Valentina Vassilenko[1,3], Andreia Serrano[1,3], and Manuel Ortigueira[1,2]

[1] Laboratory of Instrumentation, Biomedical Engineering and Radiation Physics (LIBPHYS), NOVA School of Science and Technology - NOVA University Lisbon, 2829-516 Caparica, Portugal
feo.cardoso@campus.fct.unl.pt

[2] UNINOVA CTS, NOVA School of Science and Technology - NOVA University Lisbon, 2829-516 Caparica, Portugal

[3] NMT, S.A., Parque Tecnológico de Cantanhede, Núcleo 04, Lote 3, 3060-197 Cantanhede, Portugal

**Abstract.** Sigma Delta based biomedical acquisition systems are popular amongst the possible hardware architectures developed for this purpose. It allows for the creation of high-resolution low power and cost-effective universal systems, where oversampling is used with the advantage of the associated simplified anti-alias filter design. However, spurious idle tone generation is commonly present, whose location in frequency and amplitude are not predictable. Despite their amplitude being typically low, in some applications it may tamper with the signal processing parameters. In the ECG, EMG and EEG processing, idle tones may degrade frequency energy content. Given the non-stationary nature of biomedical signals, time-frequency analysis is the adequate tool for idle tone detection due to its dual representation which includes time localization. The spectrogram along with other quadratic time-frequency representations (QTFR) are applied for idle tone analysis where QTFR's show to have appealing frequency resolution capabilities under low cross terms amplitude conditions.

**Keywords:** Time-frequency analysis · Wavelets · Idle tones

## 1 Introduction

Time-frequency representations (TFR) are widely used in the analysis of biomedical signals, since they are useful to understand the frequency content variations of non-stationary signals with time. The TFR concept was introduced by Ville [1], Blanc-Lapierre et al. [2], and Claasen et al. [3]. Nowadays several algorithms are available and are applied to the biomedical signals, such as the Continuous Wavelet Transform [4] and the Choi–Williams distribution [5]. Some biomedical signals are collected through acquisition systems based on Sigma Delta modulators, which are broadly used due to its high performance, low power consumption and design versatility [6]. However, idle tones are still a common phenomenon in Sigma Delta systems namely for modulators

© IFIP International Federation for Information Processing 2020
Published by Springer Nature Switzerland AG 2020
L. M. Camarinha-Matos et al. (Eds.): DoCEIS 2020, IFIP AICT 577, pp. 445–453, 2020.
https://doi.org/10.1007/978-3-030-45124-0_44

order below 3 [7], and their presence translates as a narrowband, low amplitude component, added to the original signal, that may vanish or increase during the acquisition session in a unpredictable way. The most common causes for idle tone presence are voltage-reference modulation, the DC signal level input and modulators orders below 3 [7]. To the best of the authors knowledge, no report was written describing idle tones detection and visualization in biomedical signals. The aim of this work is to show how the TFR can be a useful tool in the detection of idle tones in biomedical signals. The Choi-Williams distribution will be used as the best compromise involving the following factors: frequency resolution and computational cost [11, 12].

## 2    Contribution to Life Improvement

Diagnostic techniques in health care include a wide range of vital signals acquisition, such as the Electrocardiogram (ECG), Electroencephalogram (EEG) and the Electromyogram (EMG). Medical decision regarding diagnostic and treatment typically rely upon on the information obtained from these signals. Artifacts and interference should be kept at levels compatible with the ability for the downstream algorithms or the human expert evaluation reliability. Idle tones interference in sigma delta-based biomedical acquisition systems may introduce interference components not related do the electrophysiological processes under scrutiny. This may pose an array of signal interpretation problems, if the frequency band of interest overlaps with the tone's frequency. Unfortunately, this subject is often overlooked in biomedical signal processing. So, the adequate time-frequency analysis tool for idle tone detection in Sigma Delta based biomedical acquisition systems play an important role in medical decision and diagnosis.

## 3    Methods

Time-frequency representations (TFR) are the suitable tool for non-stationary signal analysis which include most of the bio-signals. Furthermore, for interference detection, whose frequency and time location have an unpredictable nature, this method outperforms the classic spectral analysis. However, one must take in account that a suitable time-frequency method should be selected. A key factor to have in consideration is the narrowband nature of the idle tones which prompts the use of TFR with an optimal time-frequency resolution such as the Wigner-Ville Transform (WVT). However, the WVT is also notorious by its high level of cross terms, which renders the tones identification a difficult task. Relatively to the WVT, the Choi-Williams transform (CWT) is a compromise between cross terms level reduction and frequency resolution. The CWT, which along the Spectrogram belongs to the Quadratic Time-Frequency Representations (QTFR), and uses a kernel function ($\Phi$) given by:

$$\Phi(\theta, \tau) = e^{-\theta^2 \tau^2 / \sigma}. \tag{1}$$

where $\theta$ and $\sigma$ are positive kernel parameters, being $\tau$ is the time lag. Substituting the kernel in the general Cohen [8] class expression, we obtain the QTFR:

$$P_{CW}(t,\omega) = \frac{1}{4\pi^{3/2}} \iint \frac{1}{\sqrt{\tau^2/\sigma}} exp\left[-\frac{(u-t)^2}{4\tau^2/\sigma} - j\tau\omega\right] s^*\left(u - \frac{1}{2}\tau\right) s\left(u + \frac{1}{2}\tau\right) dud\tau.$$

(2)

where $t$ is the time and $\omega$ is the angular frequency. For $\sigma \to \infty$ the CWT becomes the WVT, so that this parameter may be used as a control factor for cross-terms reduction, at expense of frequency resolution. The CWT is thus chosen for the idle tone detection task, upon on the selection of a suitable $\sigma$ parameter. For this application, the wavelet based scalogram non-uniform time-frequency plan tilling is an obstacle, since the idles tones may fall in a low-resolution frequency cell. This can be overcome by changing the mother wavelet length, but this would require a possible fastidious trial and error procedure. A test signal was implemented with a duration of 1800 s and a frequency sampling of 4 Hz, containing two linear chirps, and four sinusoidal segments, with different frequencies, two of them asymmetrical to test appropriate transform alignment. Signal overlap corners were also created to assess the transform resolution. A Dirac function was added at 400 s. There is a silence zone between 800 and 1000 s to test for transform compact support. Regarding real signals, idle tones were evaluated in the EMG, EEG and the ECG signals. All data was analyzed with MATLAB®.

# 4  Results

Figure 1 represents the effort in order to demonstrate that the CWT is the adequate tool for idle tone detection, for which, as mentioned, a reasonably good frequency resolution is required. The synthetic signal is plotted in the top plot. Considering that the spectrogram, represented in the second plot, is a widely used TFR with average computational cost, where the chirps and tones are clearly visible and cross terms are virtually nonexistent. Frequency resolution is around 0.05 Hz (Arrow A). The third plot shows the CWT using a $\sigma = 100$. The frequency resolution dropped to approximately 0.0175 Hz (Arrow A). However, an unacceptable level of cross terms is patent between tones and chirps (Arrow C). The fourth plot shows the same CWT with a $\sigma = 0.1$, where an acceptable cross terms level is present and with a frequency resolution of 0.025 Hz (Arrow A), approximately. It becomes also patent that signal overlap corners (Arrow B) are better defined in the CWT. In view of this results, the CWT with a $\sigma = 0.1$ is selected for idle tone detection in real signals. Figure 2 shows (top) an EEG signal [9] which includes a seizure occurring from 100 to 150 s. Idle tones are present at 16, 32 and 48 Hz. Compared to the higher power component, a reference 0 dB plateau, the idle tones amplitude is higher in the pos ictal area relatively to the pre-ictal area, as shown in Table 1. This could be explained by the shifting input conditions in the sigma delta modulator imposed by the ictal signal higher energy burst. Figure 3 is a comparison of the marginal power density of the EEG signal between the spectrogram and the CWT. In both methods peaks were found at 16, 32 and 48 Hz. Their amplitude does not stand out and could be easily taken as a bio-signal feature. However, in the TFR (Fig. 2) it is possible to determine that these peaks represent idle tones and not a physiological feature of the signal. Moreover, the 12 Hz peak is due to

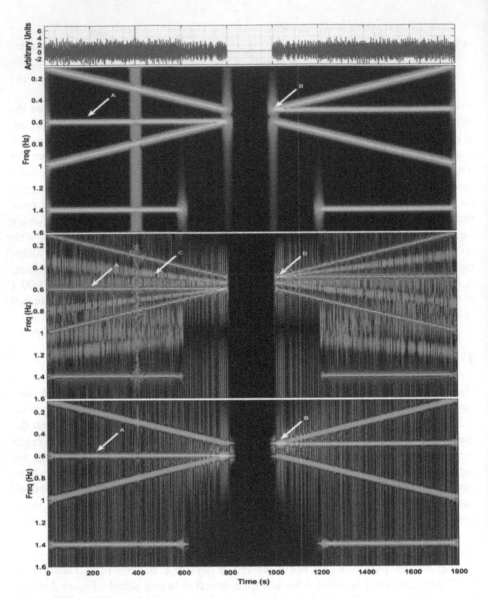

**Fig. 1.** From up to down: Test signal, Scalogram, Choi-Williams with $\sigma = 100$ and Choi-Williams with $\sigma = 0.1$. Refer to the text for explanations.

the EEG spindles as it can be observed in the TFR representation. As expected these frequency peaks are sharper in the CWT. Figure 4 shows the CWT for a hand movements EMG signal [10]. In order to enhance the idle tones, the selected analysis frequency band was between 55 and 145 Hz. Three idle tones are visible at frequencies 70, 100 and 140 Hz. There is a frequency feature at 80 Hz that could be a candidate to idle tone classification, but preventively is ruled out, since the frequency structure fades between 1.5 and 2.5 s. Table 2 shows the average relative amplitude of the idle tones compared to the peak plateau power reference. The acquisition systems used in both previous cases are not referred by the respective data holders. In the third case is presented an ECG (Fig. 5) where no idle tones are present, whose acquisition system is frequently used among the biomedical research and teaching community. The sigma delta modulator order is 3. No idle tones are identified using the CWT with the same $\sigma$ parameter as above.

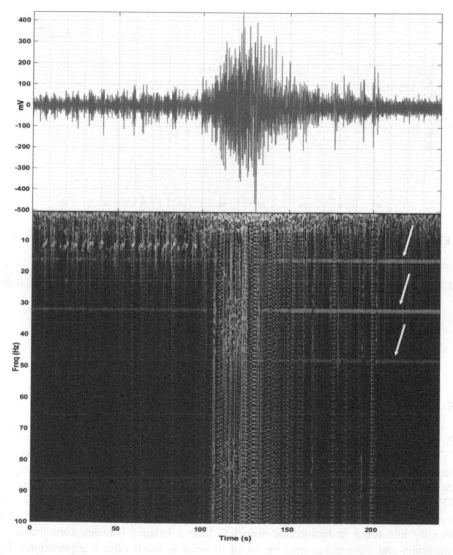

**Fig. 2.** Top: EEG seizure signal (onset at 100 s). Bottom: CWT with $\sigma = 0.1$ and time window = 1 s. Refer to the text for explanations.

**Table 1.** Idle tones compare table for the EEG epileptic seizure case. Power peak plateau reference of 0 dB is considered.

| Tone frequency (Hz) | Before seizure (dBW) | After seizure (dBW) |
|---|---|---|
| 16 | −33 | −26 |
| 32 | −36 | −28 |
| 48 | −42 | −39 |

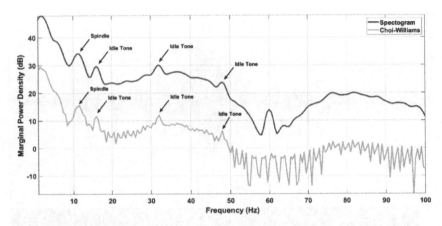

**Fig. 3.** Marginal Power Density of EEG signal in Fig. 2. Refer to the text for explanations.

**Table 2.** Idle tones compare table for EMG case for a power peak plateau reference of 0 db.

| Tone frequency (Hz) | (dBW) |
|---|---|
| 70 | −20 |
| 100 | −33 |
| 140 | −24 |

## 5    Discussion and Conclusion

A method of detection of idle tones in biomedical signals is herein presented, using TFR techniques. Figure 3, that has been mentioned earlier, is crucial to understand the importance of TFR, since it allows the identification of distinct peaks in the Marginal Power Density spectrum which might be idle tones or physiological signal features. TFR will allow to sort out the real nature of these frequency peaks through their time shape variation, thus conducting to its correct classification. TFR is an essential tool to identify idle tones in biomedical signals where a balance between time-frequency resolution and cross-terms must be found in order to reach valid interpretations. The Wigner-Ville TFR features the higher time-frequency resolution cells, however the high cross terms level restricts the use of this method in this application. The CWT with a $\sigma = 0.1$ was selected as a compromise. Other TFR kernels may be explored for optimal time-frequency resolution in idle tones detection and this would require exhaustive experimentation using the numerous available kernels. Some other kernels have been, for this work, tested with similar time-frequency resolutions, relatively to the CWT, however its computational cost and execution times hamper their application in mundane biomedical signal analysis platforms. Idle tones presence is systematically

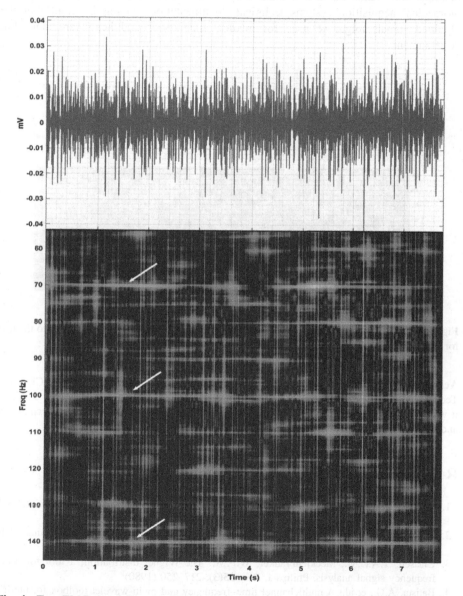

**Fig. 4.** Top: EMG signal. Bottom: CWT with $\sigma = 0.1$ and time window = 1 s. Refer to the text for explanations.

overlooked in biomedical signal processing with the associated analysis bias, namely if sigma delta modulators with an order below 3 are used. As shown in Tables 1 and 2, the idle tones power lies in an interval between −20 dB and −42 dB below the reference power plateau, which, despite being a low level interference, becomes a substantially higher if the bandwidth of the application happens to be restricted to the tones vicinity. This information is commonly not available in the systems technical specifications and stands out that a mandatory action should make this compulsory in biomedical acquisition systems technical documentation, having in mind that the obtained signals might be used for medical diagnostics and healthcare algorithm development.

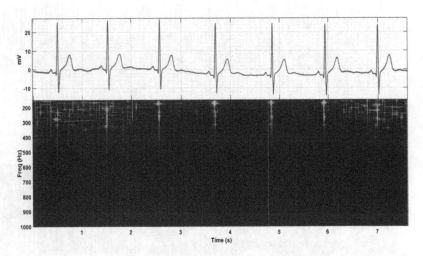

**Fig. 5.** Top: ECG signal. Bottom: CWT with σ = 0.1 and time window = 1 s. Refer to the text for explanations.

**Acknowledgments.** This work was funded and supported by the Fundação para a Ciência e Tecnologia (FCT) and NMT, S.A in the scope of the project PD/BDE/150312/2019. In addition, it was also funded by FCT under the project UIDB/00066/2020 (CTS – Center of Technology and Systems).

# References

1. Ville, J.: Théorie et applications de la notion de signal analytique. Cáble et Transmissions **2**(1), 61–74 (1948)
2. Blanc-Lapierre, A., Picinbono, B.: Remarques sur la notion de spectre instantane de puissance. Artech House (1955)
3. Claasen, T.A.C.M., Mecklenbrauker, W.F.M.: The Wigner distribution, a tool for time-frequency signal analysis. Philips J. Res. **35**(3), 217–250 (1980)
4. Batista, A.G., et al.: A multichannel time–frequency and multi-wavelet toolbox for uterine electromyography processing and visualisation. Comput. Biol. Med. **76**, 178–191 (2016)

5. Pereira, G.R., de Oliveira, L.F., Nadal, J.: Reducing cross terms effects in the Choi-Williams transform of mioelectric signals. Comput. Methods Programs Biomed. **111**(3), 685–692 (2013)
6. Jasutkar, R.W., Bajaj, P.R., Deshmukh, A.Y.: GA based low power sigma delta modulator for biomedical applications. In: IEEE Recent Advances in Intelligent Computational Systems Conferences (2011)
7. Buxton, J., Williams, D., Adams, B., Walt, J.: Analog dialogue. Analog Devices **28**(1), 27–28 (1994)
8. Cohen, L.: Time-Frequency Analysis. Prentice Hall, Upper Saddle River (1995)
9. Goldberger, A., et al.: CHB-MIT Scalp EEG Database (2010)
10. University New York - Department of Physical Therapy. https://www.nyu.edu/classes/mcdonough/downemg.htm
11. Elouaham, S., Latif, R., Dliou, A., Maoulainine, F., Laaboubi, M.: Biomedical signals analysis using time-frequency. In: IEEE International Conference on Complex Systems (2012)
12. Li, X., Li, D., Liang, Z., Voss, L.J., Sleigh, J.W.: Analysis of depth of anesthesia with Hilbert-Huang spectral entropy. Clin. Neurophysiol. **119**, 2465–2475 (2008)

# Correction to: Modeling of Asymmetric Supercapacitor Cells Based on Electrode's Laboratorial Tests Data

Leonardo Malburg and Rita Pereira

## Correction to:
### Chapter "Modeling of Asymmetric Supercapacitor Cells Based on Electrode's Laboratorial Tests Data" in: L. M. Camarinha-Matos et al. (Eds.): *Technological Innovation for Life Improvement*, IFIP AICT 577, https://doi.org/10.1007/978-3-030-45124-0_27

The original version of this chapter was revised. The numbers in Table 1 and subsequent errors were corrected.

**Table 1.** Ni-Cu//AC hybrid supercapacitor mass redistribution.

| Item | Volume ($mm^3$) | Mass (g) |
|---|---|---|
| Metallic case | 439.40 | 1.20 |
| Terminals | 49.80 | 0.42 |
| Rubber seal | 1421.00 | 2.00 |
| AC.Electrode | 960.09 | 0.63 |
| KOH.Electrolyte | 3214.19 | 5.08 |
| Current collector (Al) | 2408.24 | 6.50 |
| Ni-Cu.Electrode | 208.71 | 0.09 |
| KOH.Electrolyte | 3965.57 | 6.27 |
| Separator | 2006.79 | 1.81 |
| Total | 14673.8 | 24.00 |

The updated version of this chapter can be found at
https://doi.org/10.1007/978-3-030-45124-0_27

$$C_{elec+} = C_{sp.elec+} m_{elec+} = 105 \times 6.36 \approx 668 \,[F]. \tag{3.8}$$

$$C_{elec-} = C_{sp.elec-} m_{elec-} = 70 \times 5.71 \approx 400 \,[F]. \tag{3.9}$$

$$E_{max.hybrid} = \frac{C.V_R^2 1/2}{3600} \approx 0.23 \,[Wh]. \tag{3.14}$$

$$E.sp_{hybrid} = \frac{E_{max.hybrid}}{m} \approx 9.6 \left[\frac{Wh}{kg}\right]. \tag{3.15}$$

# Author Index

Printed in the United States
by Baker & Taylor Publisher Services